The Population of India and Pakistan

THIS book gives the most thoroughgoing analysis of Indian population data yet published. Demography is represented in the richest sense of the term—including not merely the rigorously scientific handling of population data, but also a thoughtful understanding and interpretation of the economic and social structure of the area under consideration.

Mr. Davis has made new computations and estimates based on data from the Indian censuses and vital statistics and from various field studies to draw new and striking conclusions regarding Indian population trends and their social and economic significance. Because of the broad view that is taken, the book is a contribution not only to population analysis but also to the sociology and social anthropology of India and Pakistan.

The book is profusely illustrated with maps and charts prepared by the Office of Population Research of Princeton University. The language is straightforward and, except for certain passages directed specifically to the experienced statistician, the entire volume is readily understandable to the general reader as well as the specialized student. In view of the great current importance of the problems of industrialization of densely settled agricultural areas, Mr. Davis's work has significance far beyond the confines of the Indian region. The book gives insight into the kinds of basic problems that are characteristic of large portions of the world today.

The author is director of the Bureau of Applied Social Research at Columbia University. He was formerly a research associate in the Office of Population Research at Princeton, and he has taught sociology at Princeton, Smith, Clark, Pennsylvania, Texas, and Harvard. He is author of *Youth in Depression* and *Human Society*, and, with collaborators, has written or edited *World Population in Transition, Urbanization in Latin America,* and *Modern American Society.*

THE POPULATION OF INDIA AND PAKISTAN

UNDER THE EDITORIAL SPONSORSHIP OF

OFFICE OF POPULATION RESEARCH

PRINCETON UNIVERSITY

THE POPULATION OF INDIA AND PAKISTAN

BY KINGSLEY DAVIS

PRINCETON, NEW JERSEY · 1951

PRINCETON UNIVERSITY PRESS

PRINTED IN THE UNITED STATES OF AMERICA
BY THE VAIL-BALLOU PRESS, INC., BINGHAMTON, N. Y.

++

FOREWORD

++

THIS book, the fifth of the studies of major populations to be undertaken by the Office of Population Research, is the first one to deal with Asiatic people. It will be followed in due course by a study of Japan now being prepared by Dr. Irene B. Taeuber.

The first four volumes dealt with Europe and were undertaken by the Office in cooperation with the Economic, Financial and Transit Department of the League of Nations and published by the League. They are: *The Future Population of Europe and the Soviet Union, Population Projections 1940–1970* by Frank W. Notestein, Irene B. Taeuber, Dudley Kirk, Ansley J. Coale, and Louise K. Kiser; *Economic Demography of Eastern and Southern Europe* by Wilbert E. Moore; *The Population of the Soviet Union: History and Prospects* by Frank Lorimer; and *Europe's Population in the Interwar Years* by Dudley Kirk.

When work on the League studies was under way, the Office was approached by the Geographer of the U.S. Department of State with the request that the studies be extended to include Asia, and a subsequent contract with the Department made the expansion possible. In this work considerable attention was given to India and Japan because they represented the two contrasting situations for which a considerable part of the data necessary for detailed analysis existed. With the end of the war, it seemed wise to ask Professor Davis to continue his work on India, which has resulted in the present volume.

The study has been made possible by the generosity of the Milbank Memorial Fund and the Rockefeller Foundation, whose grants to the Office of Population Research provided the principal source of its income during the years in which the book was in preparation. It goes without saying that neither of the foundations bears any responsibility for the substance of the work. To Professor Davis go both the responsibility and the credit, as well as the congratulations of his colleagues on what we believe to be an important contribution to demographic and sociological literature.

FRANK W. NOTESTEIN
Director, Office of Population Research

PREFACE

SOMETIMES it is said that no one can understand perfectly a foreign culture, and this is true. But it is also said that democratic world unity can arise only if different peoples learn to understand one another, and this too is true. Here is a case, then, in which the impossibility of perfection need not be a deterrent. A partial understanding is better than none at all. Such at least is the conviction behind the present book.

America and the Indian subcontinent are separated not only by many miles but also by many differences. Despite a surprising compatibility of outlook born of political circumstances, their mutual interest is an attraction more of opposites than of likes. They differ profoundly in geography, economy, social structure, and philosophy. Indeed it would be hard to find two other major regions that differ more. For an American to write on the people of India and Pakistan is therefore an unusually rash undertaking. Its only excuse is that the greater the difference, the greater the need of mutual comprehension.

Added to the foreigner's difficulty is the complexity of culture in the Indian region. The variety is such that no one can know it all, not even a native. The outsider cannot hope to equal the local scholar's intimate knowledge of the region. His contribution, if any, must lie in other directions. Consequently, Indians and Pakistanis will find in the pages that follow evidences of the foreigner's blindness, and for this their indulgence is begged. Although an attempt has been made to understand the region in the broadest sense, it is not in these terms that the book is justified. It is justified, if at all, by its persistently demographic focus and its attempt to bring comparative and sociological illumination to this focus.

The stock-in-trade of the foreign observer is always his fresh point of view, and that consideration is perhaps relevant here. When the author started he knew little about either India or its population. He did have an interest in comparative population studies, and the great value of India in this respect was that it had, among comparable areas, the best statistics. The region therefore afforded an opportunity to obtain a better understanding of demographic phenomena in the crowded agricultural regions of the world, and thus to contribute to our basic understanding of global trends. Also, since Indian society was itself of profound interest from a sociological standpoint, the project offered a chance to relate population trends to social factors in a manner that would broaden the frontier of both demographic and sociological theory.

These aims, of course, could not be realized unless at the same time a comparative approach were brought to the task. Accordingly, an attempt was made all along to look at the region against the background of population developments and economic conditions elsewhere, to find in what ways the region is unique and in what ways it is following patterns discernible in other societies. Whatever the success, it is hoped that this comparative approach will at least give Indian and Pakistani readers some compensation for any errors made respecting their own cultures.

During a period of eight years the author and his assistants, aided by the resources of a research office, have made a sustained effort to exploit the existing population data. The expenditure of the Indian government in securing the raw data in the first place has been enormous, as measured by the money and labor of taking censuses and registering vital statistics for hundreds of millions of people during seven decades. Yet this gigantic effort to get the raw data is worth little unless the material is adequately analyzed and interpreted. Until now, despite the full reports in the census volumes themselves and the publications of various governmental agencies, there has not been enough systematic analysis by social scientists, and as a consequence the full return on the original investment has not been realized. The original investment was a wise one, for it produced a substantial body of data that is not perfect but is nevertheless remarkable for a relatively underdeveloped region. Viewed in this light, our extended attempt to produce a reasonably full analysis, seemingly expensive but actually costing infinitely less than the original expenditure, seems justified.

The bulk of the statistical work on the volume and most of the writing were done while the author was on the staff of the Office of Population Research, Princeton University. However, it was still unfinished when he came to Columbia University, and so several of the chapters, together with some additional statistical work, were completed in the Division of Population Research, Bureau of Applied Social Research, at Columbia. The writer is grateful to his colleagues at both places for their interest and indulgence, and to his assistants—numerous by now—for their devotion to dry tasks and their respect for accuracy and thoroughness.

The charts and maps were drawn by Daphne Notestein. Her skill can be readily seen, but her pleasant and creative cooperation needs special mention. Among those who have read all or parts of the manuscript, always with profit to the author, are Dr. Louise K. Kiser and Professors Wilbert E. Moore and Frank W. Notestein of Princeton; Dr. Marshall C. Balfour of the Rockefeller Foundation; Dr. Mason Alcott, recently of the University of Pennsylvania; Elsa Jane Davis, the writer's wife; and a keen-eyed Indian critic unknown to the writer. In addition, the author has profited from his contacts with other members of the Joint Committee on Southern Asia, sponsored by the Social Science Research Council and the American Council of Learned Societies. Long contact with the chairman of this committee, Professor W. Norman

Brown of the University of Pennsylvania, has proved especially stimulating. Much has also been learned from the writer's students who studied India under him at the University of Pennsylvania and at Princeton, and from the students of population at Columbia who have perforce had to ponder the complexities of Indian demography whether they wished to or not. Finally, the author is grateful for the innumerable occasions on which Indians or Pakistanis have shown patience in answering his persistent questions. Among the most patient and long suffering has been Dr. C. Chandra Sekar of the All-India Institute of Hygiene and Public Health. There have been many others too numerous to mention.

It is with some trepidation that the writer parts with such an old friend as this book and entrusts it at last to the public. Knowing it so well, he has a lively sense of its deficiencies. He only hopes that, like any old friend, its better qualities, such as possible light on one of the world's major problems, will compensate for the inevitable defects growing out of a foreigner's interest in a strange but remarkable region.

KINGSLEY DAVIS

Columbia University
July 17, 1950

CONTENTS

MAPS

++

TABLES AND FIGURES

++

TABLES

FIGURES

PART I
THE OVERALL PICTURE

CHAPTER 1

The Task and the Tools

THE Indian subcontinent has long been known for the gravity of its problems. Until independence and partition came in 1947, the problem that most captured the world's attention was the political one; but, freedom having been won after a long uphill battle and the Hindu-Muslim [1] conflict partly solved by a painful partition, the focus of attention has shifted since 1947 from politics to economics. The most conspicuous evidence of economic trouble is the poverty of the Indian and Pakistani masses—a poverty roughly akin to that of the Chinese, Javanese, and Egyptians. Although so abject that an American has difficulty in comprehending it, this poverty would not be a world-disturbing problem if a clear road to improvement could be seen. But the truth is that the way of relief is not altogether clear and certainly not easy, and one of the reasons is the demographic situation. The subcontinent's proportion of the world's people (almost one-fifth) is far greater than its proportion of the world's area (only 3 per cent). The density of settlement is very high in view of the agricultural character of the economy; the population has been growing rapidly of late and shows every sign of growing rapidly in the future if conditions are favorable. The region apparently has, therefore, a population problem which is linked with but logically separable from its economic problems.

The task of the present volume is to explore and analyze the population problem in India and Pakistan. This does not mean, however, that the sole concern is with *over*population; for the scope and purpose of the work are much broader than that. As here construed the study of population covers not only the number of people and its relation to current and potential resources, but also the characteristics of the population and their relations to the society and economy of the region. In short the present work represents an approach to the analysis of social organization and social change in the area considered. It is meant to be a contribution to the sociology and economics, as well as to the demography, of India and Pakistan.

Briefly, our purpose is to be accomplished in four different ways: first, by describing the existing population and its past growth as accurately as possible; second, by studying causal relations between population and social organization; third, by exploring the general theory of population as applied to India-Pakistan and similar regions; and fourth, by using these three types of investigation to estimate, on the basis of certain assumptions, future population trends and their possible consequences. There can be no doubt that all four tasks are complex and incapable of perfect execution. Just how

[1] In the India-Pakistan region "Moslem" is ordinarily pronounced and spelled "Muslim," a usage followed throughout the present book.

complex they are can be seen by reflecting a bit on each task; and just how imperfect the execution must be can be seen by considering the tools we have to work with.

An exact description of the India-Pakistan population (Task I) involves treating its size, density, and regional distribution, and measuring its current and past rate of growth. Though not so easy as it sounds, this is one of the easiest of our undertakings. The density and rate of increase, however, do not tell us much—especially about future developments—unless we know what is causing them. Consequently, our description must include an accurate assessment of the three demographic variables through which alone the number of people can be determined—namely, fertility, mortality, and migration. What are, and what have been, the facts concerning these in India? Here, for various reasons, the difficulties begin to multiply; but assuming that the facts concerning the vital statistics can be ascertained, there still remains a further question. What are the social factors—economic, political, religious, familial—that account for trends in the vital rates? In other words, what changes have occurred in the social organization that explain the changes, if any, in births, deaths, and migration? Without such sociological analysis there could be no real understanding of population trends in the Indian region.

It happens, of course, that some of the fundamental features of the social structure are measured by facts from population censuses. These facts are the so-called characteristics of the population. Some of them, such as sex and age, are primarily biological, but through their variation from one group or region to another they reflect social realities. Others, such as literacy, religion, caste, birthplace, urbanism, and occupation are more directly social in nature, and consequently throw much light on Indian society. A description of the population is thus at the same time a description of the social order.

In a real sense, however, our aim is not merely descriptive. An attempt is also made to ascertain causal relations and to arrive at predictive conclusions. It is hoped, by the discovery and interpretation of relationships, to attain a dynamic view of India's population and to gain some insight into the future. Since demographic trends are determined mainly by social factors, a great deal must be said, accordingly, about the causal connections between Indian society and Indian population (Task II). This involves the application of social theory as well as the study of facts. Needless to say the theory must have the character of disciplined thought rather than idle speculation—i.e. it must be nailed down by evidence and tied together by logic. Such theory should help to answer questions like these: What aspects of Indian social institutions have primarily governed the birth and death rates? What future developments are likely to influence these rates, and consequently the growth of numbers? How will future demographic trends affect the society and living standards of the people? What social plans might avoid undesired consequences?

The Indian region is not completely unique. If it were, the application of social theory to its problems would be impossible. Instead the area is representative of a type case, and a study of its population should be not simply an application of, but also a contribution to the general theory of population (Task III). In science the particular is always a means to an end rather than an end in itself. We are concerned not only with India and Pakistan but with human society. This is not to minimize the importance of this region per se. Its troubles are real, and they require solution. But there are many other areas in much the same condition. A study of the Indian region, if it is capable of generalization, should promote an understanding of other areas. Also there are still other countries that have already been through conditions much like those of India and Pakistan today (e.g. Japan) or have not yet reached that stage but seem headed for it (e.g. Caribbean areas). Conclusions drawn from the Indian case help us understand these contrasting countries, and vice versa. It is only fitting that the study of this case, which must borrow heavily from the general science of population and society, should contribute something to that science as well.

The final task, that of projecting future population on the basis of certain assumptions (Task IV) is really an end product of the other three. It is a hazardous task in a region like that under consideration, but absolutely necessary for planning. It involves drawing fact and theory together, not only with reference to conditions in India-Pakistan but with reference to developments in the rest of the world as well.

In trying to attain an exact picture of population one is forced to undertake a certain amount of statistical analysis. Estimates, corrections, correlations, and short-hand summaries must be made, and the results presented in charts, tables, and maps. So far as possible the mechanics of this analysis, though fundamental, is kept from intruding itself in the following pages. The emphasis is on the results and conclusions rather than the techniques of the analysis. However, an attempt is made to keep the reader constantly informed of the sources and methods used. The aim is to enable any other investigator, if he so desires, to retrace the same steps and thus check the results. When an account of procedure is necessary but would impede the text, it is placed in an appendix.

It is hoped that new facts and relationships will be turned up by the analysis, and that the understanding of the Indian population will thereby be made fuller and clearer than it has been made in the past.

The Tools Available

When people hear of research on the Indian population, they are often incredulous. Though they admit the importance of the subject, they feel that it must be a blind alley, a dark unknown from which nothing definite can come. Believing that only the most advanced countries have good population statistics, they regard the numerical study of India's people as mainly an exercise of the imagination. Their major premise is correct; there are few countries with adequate demographic data, and India is not one of them. But their assumption that India has no data at all and that the effort is therefore quixotic, is quite wrong.

Compared with the world as a whole, India's past population statistics are above the average. Certainly she has had more usable data than any country of equal backwardness, and this fact constitutes one of the strongest reasons for making a special study of her population problems. She exemplifies some of the major difficulties besetting the heavily peopled rural economies of the world, particularly in the East; and yet her statistics have been for the most part better than those in these similar areas. Consequently, as mentioned before, she affords an invaluable insight into what is happening over a much wider but less understood area.

It is true that Indian statistics do not cover the whole history of India, nor even the fraction of that history represented by British rule. But what country exists whose history is so covered? In general, though scattered evidence exists for earlier periods, the Indian statistics began to be useful after 1870. They cover, then, a period of more than 70 years. For an Asiatic country this is an exceptional record.

The best demographic materials on India come from the censuses. The first systematic attempt to ascertain the whole population of India by actually counting heads was made between 1867 and 1872. Obviously it was not a synchronous census, nor was it complete even for the territory then embraced by India (and new territory was later added). But it was a good census for those times, an auspicious beginning. It set some precedents that have been followed throughout subsequent censuses, among them the habit of using regular government officials, receiving no extra pay, for the enumeration. This placed the census in the hands of the Indian Civil Service. This Service has sometimes been called unimaginative but seldom careless. In census work it has, considering the time and the conditions, been both imaginative and thorough.

The second census came in 1881. It was synchronous, and was more complete and more modern. Since then a new census has been taken every ten years—the last in 1941—comprising, all told, eight censuses. The results of each have been published in lavish detail and with exceptional scholarship. Usually there has been compiled by the Census Commissioner of the Central Government a summary for the whole country, the summary being divided into two or three separately bound volumes, called Parts. In addition there have been separate reports (always in two Parts—one for description, the other for tables) relating to each province and major state. The 1931 Census was published in 46 separately bound books of huge size (over a foot high), and most of the previous censuses were reported with equal extensiveness. Because of World War II, however, the publication of the 1941 Census, taken with as much thoroughness and detail as the others, was curtailed drastically. It is this fact that makes it necessary in the present volume to rely on the 1931 returns in many instances when reliance on 1941 figures would have been preferred. Yet in a surprising number of cases it has been possible to bring the population data up to 1941, and occasionally to make estimates for years after that date.

The Indian censuses are remarkable not only for the information they reveal but for the special obstacles they have had to overcome. Imagine a massive, diversified subcontinent with hundreds of millions of people nearly all of whom are illiterate, most of them rural and some isolated in jungles or mountains, some harboring superstitions inimical to census cooperation, some split by political and religious rifts, and some pure savages of the Stone Age—imagine all this and the difficulty of taking a census becomes apparent. No wonder the hospital rate for census officials has been high. The 1941 effort sent four provincial superintendents to the hospital and left three others in a weakened condition; the Commissioner himself was ill eleven months out of the year. The 1931 Census was confronted with a non-cooperative movement which designated January 11 of that year as Census Boycott Sunday. It also had to contend with religious propaganda advocating that people return themselves as of a certain religion regardless of the truth. In one province the Bhils, a primitive people, "would not have their houses numbered on superstitious grounds, while in Burma householders objected on artistic grounds. In the Shan States the thirteenth and last survivor of a pre-annexation raid happened to occupy the thirteenth house in a block. As the enumerator inconsiderately refused to rearrange the numbers, the man decided that his (number) was up indeed, went forth into the jungle and committed harakiri. In less law-abiding places the disposition was rather towards disemboweling the enumerator than the enumerated, . . . Here and there wild beasts interfered instead of wild men, and the Administrator of Bastar State, when inspecting census work on the night itself, was attacked by a tiger." The tiger, jumping on the hood of the car but finding the pace and the radiator too hot, "failed to make an end either of the inspector or his inspection." [2]

Fortunately for other investigators, the census officials in India have always in the past regarded their duties as transcending the mere gathering and reporting of statistics. Despite the special difficulties even on that level, they have gone ahead and made more work for themselves; for, unlike the census officials of many other countries, they have felt inclined to interpret their figures for the benefit of other scholars and of the public at large. First of all, they have discussed their methods frankly, exposed their difficulties, shared their misgivings, and expressed their plans and hopes. They have not hidden behind an official wall of infallibility. At the same time they have given to posterity elaborate and scholarly accounts of the variegated phenomena of Indian life—sometimes with no statistics attached, but usually with just enough statistics to give empirical underpinning to their conclusions. They have allowed their wide-ranging curiosity to lead them into many by-paths, and have gathered statistics on a fascinating multiplicity of topics. As a result they have enormously enriched our knowledge of India in nearly every branch of scholarship, from anthropology and sociology to geography and religion.

An imposing number of the greatest scholars in India have been connected with the Indian Census in one capacity or another. The list includes Sir William W. Hunter, historian, who directed the gigantic Statistical Survey of India made in 1869–1881 and published, among other books, the famous *Annals of Rural Bengal* (three volumes) and *A History of British India* (two volumes); Sir George Grierson, who wrote the chapter on Indian languages for the 1901 Census report and directed the famous Linguistic Survey of India; Sir Herbert Risley, who wrote *The People of India;* Sir Edward A. Gait, who wrote the noted article on "Caste" for the *Encyclopedia of Religion and Ethics;* L. S. S. O'Malley, who wrote several scholarly works on Indian social life and edited *Modern India and the West;* E. A. H. Blunt, who wrote the classic study, *The Caste System of Northern India;* and J. H. Hutton, who wrote two monographs on the Naga tribes of Northeastern India, a book on *Caste in India,* and now teaches anthropology at Cambridge University. These men have helped not only to make the Indian Census great, but also to make the entire world of Indian scholarship great. In their hands the Census has been a major vehicle for the intellectual understanding of the region.

If the census officials in India have had any defect at all, it is that they have been scholars and government men first and statisticians second. The Census Commissioner in 1931 (Hutton) was an anthropologist, and there were commissioners before him, notably Risley in 1901 and Gait in 1911, whose interest was heavily anthropological. Others, such as Yeatts in 1941, have been primarily civil servants. The selection of men trained chiefly in fields other than demography, however, was probably a wise policy. In an intricate, strange, and unknown country with a peculiar culture, the greatest need (from a Western point of view) was for broad understanding and preliminary data rather than for mathematical manipulation. Doubtless in the future a greater emphasis on statistical ingenuity will be in order. The groundwork for comprehending Indian civilization in general has now been well laid, and the time is ripe for more exacting techniques and finer detail. In the 1941 Census the transition was started. Mr. Yeatts, believing that the old style omnibus report was out of date, proposed to cut down the scope of the census volumes to such materials as were necessary to interpret and understand the tables.[3] Mr. Mukerjea, thrice Census Superintendent of Baroda, explained the change as follows:

"The great old Reports of the Indian Census—some of them classics for all time—were written with the view to lead and guide all thinking India in the matter of analysing and correlating the immense mass of figures which at every census was collected. . . . But now everywhere we find a group of scholars who are competent to deal with the measurement of social phenomena, as in western countries, and the role of the counter of peoples has to approximate itself to that of his opposite number in England or America,—the humbler role of just collecting the statistical data, doing as little as possible of writing and leaving the figures to speak for themselves." [4]

So modernization, with its advantages and disadvantages, has come even to the Indian Phoenix, the decennial Census. But the accomplishments under the old system have been outstanding, and the accumulated records for more than 70 years represent a rich treasure for demographic research. The startling fact is not that the Indian censuses have been used in so many different fields, but that so few people with an interest in India are acquainted with them. They represent the most fruitful single source of information about the country. They are an accomplishment of which India may be justly proud. The test of the new independent governments of India and Pakistan will be their ability to carry further the thoroughness, objectivity, and breadth of the census work accomplished under the British.

In addition to the Census there has long been an attempt in India to gather vital statistics. In the earlier days these attempts were usually for specific purposes and for limited areas. There were annual Provincial Reports on medical relief that covered vaccination (beginning 1861), hospitals (beginning 1852), and famines. There were numerous special

---

[2] *Census of India,* 1931, Vol. I, Part I, p. x. For an account of the difficulties encountered generally in tropical census taking, see P. Granville Edge, *Vital Statistics and Public Health Work in the Tropics* (London: Baillière, Tindall, & Cox, 1944).

[3] *Census of India,* 1941, Vol. I, p. 2.
[4] *ibid.,* Vol. 17 (Baroda), p. xi.

reports on epidemic diseases—e.g. for cholera, the reports of the Presidency Boards on the great epidemic of 1817, the report of the Commission of 1861, and the statistical records for certain areas from 1817 on. There were reports covering mortality in the army, in jails, and in particular cities going back to the first half of the 19th century. Since the initial concern was with mortality, the statistics on death were gathered first. But the attempt to register births did not come very far behind. In 1864 a uniform system was begun for registering both births and deaths, and about 1875 the system was supposedly representative of the whole of British India. Even today, however, not all areas of what once was British India and by no means all of the erstwhile States are covered.

In India, as in most countries, the attempt to register births and deaths has not been so successful as the effort to enumerate the population. The reasons will be examined later, but the trouble is not so much the failure to cover all areas as the failure to register all births and deaths in the areas covered. Also, for both births and deaths the amount of ancillary information obtained is wholly inadequate. In some areas, for example, it is merely the occurrence of the birth that is recorded, no information being given on such things as the religion, occupation, permanent residence, caste, or age of the parents or the birth order and name of the child. In other areas information along these lines is apparently gathered but not necessarily published. The death certificate usually contains only a statement as to the "cause" of death, and the possible causes (because of the scarcity of doctors and the understandable ignorance of the registering official) are in many jurisdictions limited to a relative few. In the publications of vital statistics for all of pre-partition India (confined mostly to "British India"), only eight causes were customarily given in the statistics, including of course "Other Causes." Some provincial statistics, however, give information on more causes than this.

India's morbidity statistics have been, to say the least, sporadic, although some excellent work has been done on the distribution and prevalence of hookworm, malaria, filariasis, ankylostomiasis, beriberi, and other chronic diseases.

There has been no attempt at all in India to register marriages and divorces. For information along this line the census returns on marital status are practically the sole source.

The figures on emigration from India, gathered either at the place of departure or the place of arrival, have been fair, but those on immigration, mainly across the land frontiers, have been practically nonexistent. Now that a great new land border has been created by partition, immigration data are even more lacking; because there has been little statistical control over the movement between Pakistan and the Indian Union. The greatest movement occurred immediately after partition, and for this we have only estimates.

With such incomplete and inadequate registration the assumption might be that Indian vital statistics are useless. This, however, is not true. In various ways, as we shall find, the registration figures can be used for estimates that must come somewhere near the truth, and for the discovery of trends that have some validity and great importance. When combined with census returns, they throw considerable light on basic features of Indian demography. This is especially true of mortality statistics. The pooling of death registration with census life-tables and special studies of epidemics, famines, and chronic diseases yields a considerable body of sound information.

Any inquiry into the social aspects of population requires not only census and vital statistics, but also economic and social data. It is fortunate, therefore, that India has had more complete economic and social statistics than most Asiatic areas. The materials are far from perfect, but they have been built up over a considerable period and are now impressive. Various survey schemes were contemplated under the East India Company between 1769 and 1855 and under the Crown between 1858 and 1869. The earlier efforts were fragmentary, unsystematic, and lacking in uniformity. In 1869 a plan was submitted to the Governor-General in Council for a Statistical Survey and an Imperial Gazetteer of India. This plan attempted to overcome the defects of previous survey schemes. It took twelve years to complete the new undertaking, but it succeeded where others had failed, and it furnished an elaborate account of each of the 240 districts then comprising the fifteen British provinces covered. The results were published in about 100 printed volumes aggregating 36,000 pages, and condensed in the *Imperial Gazetteer of India* which was published in 1881 in nine volumes. The Survey provided a rare and useful body of knowledge. Like the Census that accompanied it, it was a landmark in Indian statistics. The Gazetteer itself continued to grow. In 1881 it required nine volumes; in 1885–87, 14 volumes; in 1901, 26 volumes.

In addition India has had serial economic statistics, some running well back into the nineteenth century. These, dealing with such things as industry, labor, agriculture, prices, foreign trade, transportation, and communication, have been published in departmental and provincial bulletins and assembled in convenient form in the *Statistical Abstract Relating to British India,* which began at least as early as 1861–70. The *Abstract* has been published by the Department of Commercial Intelligence and Statistics, which has also issued the *Review of the Trade of India* and the *Indian Trade Journal.* Most of the data supplied related to British India, but some figures for the native states were also included. There were numerous other business, economic, and social science journals published in India which help to present necessary information.

When one recalls that India was the happy hunting ground of official investigating bodies, of voluminous official reports, one realizes the full extent of the materials available. The Sessional Papers of the House of Commons are strewn with reports of investigating bodies, simply because Parliament, being so far from India, had to govern that country mainly on the basis of paper information sent across the ocean. Whenever a scandal arose or a reform was proposed, over went a commission. The commission would gather such statistics as were available, would interview people on the scene, would make its own analysis; then it would publish everything in extenso for the benefit of posterity and the next investigating commission. The information thus gathered is invaluable and almost inexhaustible. Among the more noted Reports are the following: Royal (Montagu-Chelmsford) Commission on Indian Constitutional Reforms; Indian Statutory (Simon) Commission; Royal (Whitley) Commission on Labour in India; and Royal Commission on Agriculture in India. These reports, each issued in several large volumes, plus the official statistics and the wealth of books and periodicals, provide abundant material on India's social and economic history.

All told, the statistical and descriptive materials for India are far better than one might expect. They are useful not only for an understanding of India itself but for an indirect comprehension of similar areas which have much less information. In other words, the tools for studying India's population, while far from perfect, are sufficiently accurate and abundant to justify the effort. The greatest single lack at the present time is the absence of material bearing on Pakistan and the Union of India separately. Until each of these new countries takes a census in 1951 and publishes the data two or three years later, it will be impossible to deal elaborately with them as distinct countries. However, it is possible, by analyzing the data of 1931 and 1941 for regions that now constitute the two countries, to gain considerable demographic information about them. In so far as possible this has been done in the present study.

++

CHAPTER 2

The Subcontinent—Geographical Setting

++

THE notion of population always refers to a definite area. So, too, do geographical and political entities. Therefore the population of the subcontinent cannot be described until something is known of the physical and political geography of the region.

To a marked degree, in the past, the boundaries of geographical and political India have corresponded. There are points of discrepancy that must be kept in mind, but they are few and unimportant. A more complex question is what lay within the boundaries. To this we cannot give a complete answer, but only a general outline. Let us begin first with geographical India.

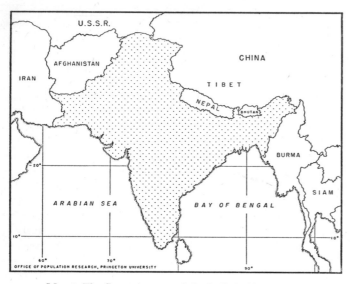

MAP 1. The Countries around the India-Pakistan Area.

THE LAND

If a man started at the extreme southern tip of India and walked in a straight line to the most northern border of Kashmir, he would cover 2,000 miles. In terms of latitude he would move from a point farther south than Panama City to one almost as far north as Washington, D.C. If he crossed the region the other way, starting at the western border of Baluchistan and going to the eastern boundary of Assam, he would cover nearly 2,200 miles, equivalent to a walk from San Francisco to Cleveland. The dimensions are thus huge. Pakistan and the Indian Union together embrace approximately 1,581,000 square miles, more than half the area of the United States (Map 2), or four-fifths that of Europe exclusive of Russia. This made pre-partition India the third most extensive unit in the British Empire, for she was exceeded only by

Canada and Australia. In fact she contained almost 15 per cent of the territory of the Empire. If she had been an independent nation India would have been the ninth world power in terms of area controlled.[1] This does not mean that

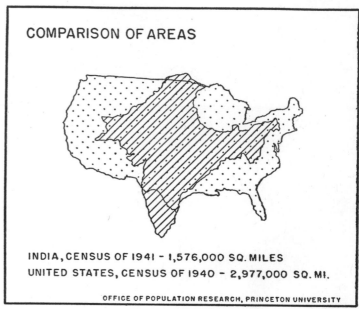

COMPARISON OF AREAS

INDIA, CENSUS OF 1941 - 1,576,000 SQ. MILES
UNITED STATES, CENSUS OF 1940 - 2,977,000 SQ. MI.

OFFICE OF POPULATION RESEARCH, PRINCETON UNIVERSITY

MAP 2. Area of the Indian Region Compared with That of the United States.

the land is ninth in value. On the contrary, it is one of the world's richest domains, far more valuable than either Canada or Australia. It is probably the third most gifted of the world's regions with respect to industrial capacity, and the second or third with reference to agricultural resources. But in sheer area alone it is big enough.

The geographical traits of the subcontinent are fabulous, and their description requires unblushing superlatives. The main features can be described in terms of topography on

[1] The list, taken from the League of Nations *Statistical Yearbook*, 1942–44, and giving the situation as of 1939, is as follows:

	Square Miles
U.S.S.R.	8,176,000
France and Empire	4,621,000
China and Dependencies	4,287,000
U.S.A. and Territories	3,739,000
Canada	3,695,000
Brazil	3,286,000
Australia and Possessions	3,065,000
United Kingdom and Colonies	2,243,000
INDIA	1,581,000

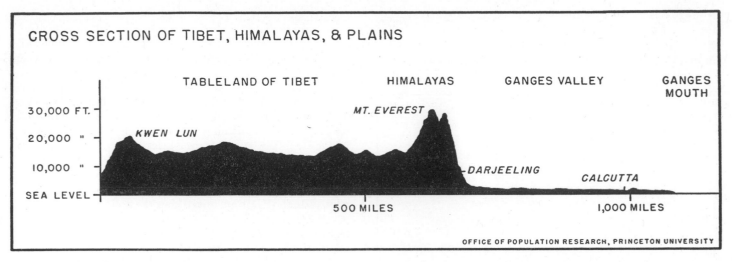

FIGURE 1. Cross-Section of Tibetan Tableland, Himalayan Mountains, and Indian Plain. From Cameron Morrison, *New Geography of The Indian Empire and Ceylon* (London: Nelson, 1926), p. 28.

the one hand (mountains, plains, and table-lands) and climate on the other (heat, wind, and rain). Since topography goes far toward explaining climate, it deserves first consideration.

The great key to the region's peculiar geography actually lies more outside than inside the boundaries, although it has its main effects inside. This is the Himalayan range, the loftiest mountain barrier in the world, which shuts off the subcontinent from the rest of Asia. From 150 to 250 miles wide, this Roof of the World stretches for 1,500 miles across the north of India. It boasts the three highest points on the earth's surface (Everest, 29,141 feet, and Kanchenjunga and K2, each about 28,150 feet), fifty summits of 25,000 feet or more, and an average elevation of 19,000 feet. The whole mighty barrier, with great subsidiary ranges curving southward at either end, looks on the relief map like a folded curtain pushed back and draped around northern India and Pakistan. (See Map 3.) The rest of the Indian region, though it contains some mountains in its central and southern parts, seems flat in comparison to the high Himalayan land mass (Fig. 1).

The Himalayas contribute greatly to the soil, climate, and

isolation of India. In addition to being the highest, they are also the newest mountain range in the world, having been formed by a gigantic upthrust from a former ocean floor. As a result they are eroding rapidly and sending out rich loam to the plains below. Because high plateau lands lie to the north and the snow and rainfall come mostly from the south, the drainage runs toward India. The three main rivers of the subcontinent—Indus, Ganges, and Brahmaputra—with most of their tributaries, all have their sources in the Himalayas and all bring down silt that has made the Indo-Gangetic plain, covering the whole of Northern India, the most fertile area of its size in the world. "Like two great arms the Indus and Brahmaputra completely clasp themselves round the Himalayan Ranges so that all the rain that falls and all the snow that melts whether on their northern or southern flanks, is bound to come into India. Geographically the Himalayas belong as much to Tibet as to India, but these river-systems bring all the *benefits* of these mountains to India alone."[2]

The other mountain ranges of peninsular India, much older and more beaten down, also influence the soil and climate of India, though not to such a great extent. First are the several ranges that run east-west across the waist of the subcontinent and cut off the Indo-Gangetic plain from the peninsular Deccan plateau. These, of which the Vindhyas and Satpuras are the most prominent, long prevented the Aryans from penetrating into lower India and have made the culture of the two regions to this day noticeably distinct. The next mountains are those running down the Malabar coast—the Western Ghats. Having an average altitude of nearly 4,000 feet, they really form a high coastal escarpment, the high edge of the Deccan plateau. The rivers that cross the Deccan have their origins in or near these mountains. On the other side they encounter India's third set of internal mountains, the Eastern Ghats. These are low and broken, so that the rivers can get through them easily and pass on to the sea. They are also farther from the shore than the Western Ghats, and tend to turn inland in the south until they meet the latter. The Deccan, which slopes downward from west to east, is enclosed like a large triangle by the three mountain chains discussed.

In addition to its mountains, the region has three low plains and one plateau, all of great significance. The most important

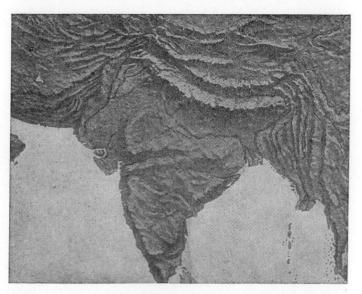

MAP 3. Relief Map of the Indian Peninsula and Neighboring Regions. From Cameron Morrison, *New Geography of The Indian Empire and Ceylon* (London: Nelson, 1926), p. 8.

[2] Cameron Morrison, *A New Geography of the Indian Empire and Ceylon* (London: Nelson, 1926), p. 67.

of the plains is the Indo-Gangetic, noted for its size, fertility, depth, antiquity, and flatness. It forms a great angular band across the northern portion of the region, from the Indus delta on the Arabian Sea to the Ganges delta on the Bay of Bengal. (See Map 4.) The entire plain, some 2,000 miles long and

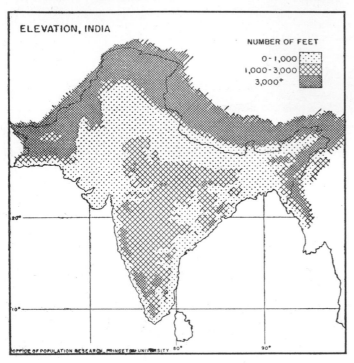

MAP 4. Elevation in the Indian Region. From L. Dudley Stamp, *Asia* (New York: Dutton, rev. ed., 1938), p. 173.

150 to 200 miles wide, is alluvial. A great part of its soil is renewed every year by floods, and the mud brought down from the hills is so fine that it is reputedly possible to traverse the entire length of the plain "without finding a pebble, however small." [3] The alluvium, in addition to being remarkably uniform over its entire extent of approximately 30,000 square miles, is extremely thick. The exact thickness has never been ascertained, but borings have penetrated it to a depth of 1,300 feet without reaching a rocky bottom. The plain is also exceptionally flat. It has "not a hill, not even a mound to break the monotony of the level surface." [4] Agra, half-way between the two deltas and 1,300 miles by river from the sea, is only 550 feet above sea level. "This flatness makes the rivers flow slowly, thus fertilizing the country thoroughly and affording easy waterways and irrigation channels." [5] This is one of the world's greatest expanses of rich, tillable soil, and thus one of the world's greatest agricultural regions.

The two other plains are the long coastal strips down each side of the peninsula. The one on the west, called Konkan in its upper and Malabar in its lower part, is the narrower of the two, being pressed close to the sea by the Western Ghats and averaging about 40 miles in width. The strip on the east, the Coromandel Coast, is broader because the land on that side has been gradually rising from the sea. Both coastal plains are alluvial, the eastern one, which receives the rivers flowing across the broad Deccan, being especially fortunate in the deltas it possesses.

In contrast to the low plains, the Deccan table-land, lying

[3] Morrison, *op. cit.*, p. 21.
[4] L. Dudley Stamp, *Asia* (2nd ed.; New York: Dutton, 1939), pp. 175–76, 181.
[5] Morrison, *op. cit.*, p. 21.

mostly from 1,000 to 2,000 feet above sea level, is broken up into many river valleys and hills. It is not alluvial, but is composed of ancient crystalline rock and has a thin soil. The black cotton soil of the northwestern part and a few river valleys are fertile, but on the whole the soil is not rich.

Although all of the subcontinent lies north of the Equator and approximately 60 per cent of it lies in the temperate zone, its climate is overwhelmingly tropical. The reasons are twofold: First, the Himalayan barrier effectively screens the region from the cold northern winds of the Asiatic continental shield and at the same time bottles up and concentrates the monsoon winds blowing up from the tropical seas. Second, most of India-Pakistan, apart from the northern barrier itself and the lower central and coastal mountains, has a negligible elevation. Over half the land lies below 1,000 feet and nearly all of it below 3,000 (Map 4). These two features, plus the very considerable land mass jutting into the ocean, give the area a hot monsoon climate more typical of the tropical than of the temperate zone. "We always think of India as essentially a tropical country. And rightly so, for the whole area within the mountain wall must be considered as a unit, with a common type of climate throughout, that of the tropical monsoon." [6]

The rainfall of India and Pakistan, and hence the capacity of their rich land to produce crops, depends on the monsoon. In March, April, and May when the sun has attained a vertical position, the land mass below the Himalayas becomes increasingly hot. As the air above becomes heated, it expands and rises. The air over the ocean south of the equator has at the same time become cooler and has increased in pressure. It rushes up toward India and Pakistan to fill the low-pressure area, coming in June and lasting four months. Blowing over thousands of miles of sea-water, this southwest or summer monsoon is full of moisture. As long as it strikes merely warm atmosphere it does not lose its moisture, because the hotter it is the more moisture it can hold. But as soon as it strikes high mountains and is cooled, it loses moisture in the form of heavy rain.

The peninsula of India divides the monsoon into two branches. The first and stronger branch comes in from the Arabian Sea and strikes the Western Ghats almost at a right angle. Against these cool mountains its moisture is condensed and precipitated in torrents of rain. It blows at an average speed of almost 20 miles per hour, depositing over 100 inches of rain on the Ghats and the coastal strip in front of them. The Ghats, however, are not high enough to block the monsoon completely. Some of the moist air slips past and gives the Deccan enough rainfall to prevent its becoming a desert. Farther up the western coast the Ghats become insignificant and disappear. Toward the middle (north of Bombay) the monsoon rushes past the coast and up through the east-west valleys made by the Satpura and Vindhya mountains, taking more rain farther inland. Still farther north, between the Gulf of Cambay and Karachi, there are no mountains at all to catch the monsoon. Instead there is only a hot, flat plain—the Indus plain—stretching clear up to the foot of the Himalayas. The monsoon, its direction being more northward at this point, therefore gives no rain until it reaches the Himalayas. This is why the Indus plain, including Sind and parts of Baluchistan, Rajputana, the Punjab, and the North-West Frontier Province, is arid and barren. This is why the Great Indian Desert is found there.

[6] Stamp, *op. cit.*, p. 170.

The other branch of the monsoon comes up the Bay of Bengal, strikes the Ganges delta, and spends its force on the hills and mountains north and west of the delta. Here, in the Garo, Khasi, and Jaintia Hills of Assam, the rainfall is reputed to be the heaviest in the world. "The average is 480 inches, and in 1861 no less than 805 inches, or 67 feet, were registered." A part of the wind turns to the right and rushes up the Brahmaputra valley, making this one of the wetter sections of India. Another part turns left and moves up the broader and longer Ganges valley. Here it runs almost parallel with the mountains for a great distance and loses its moisture only gradually. It thus distributes its rainfall more evenly than do the monsoon winds over other parts of the subcontinent. The rainfall is greatest, of course, at the eastern end, or delta, of the Ganges, and it gets less and less as the monsoon moves up the plain until in the Punjab, where the Indus and Ganges plains merge, it virtually disappears.

The southern part of India's eastern coast gets relatively little rain from either monsoon. The wind through the Bay of Bengal passes it by, and that from the Arabian Sea crosses the peninsula and has no moisture left. However, in the period of the retreating monsoon, stormy winds blow westward across the Bay of Bengal which bring considerable rain in November and December to the southeastern part of the peninsula.[7]

All accounts of Indian geography stress the summer monsoon, because it furnishes in four months 90 per cent of the annual rainfall. A map of rainfall for the whole year (Map 5)

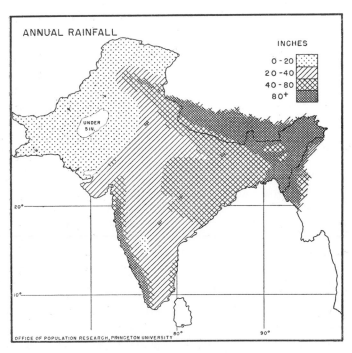

MAP 5. Annual Rainfall in the Indian Region. From L. Dudley Stamp, *Asia* (New York: Dutton, rev. ed., 1938), p. 196.

is little different from one for the rainy season alone. Only the extreme northwest and the extreme southeast get much moisture during other seasons. Without the summer monsoon the whole region would be a barren place like Afghanistan. The importance of the monsoon to agricultural India and Pakistan is therefore obvious. It is only this precious rain that enables the rich soil to produce the crops on which some 420 million people depend.

[7] This account of the monsoons owes much to Morrison, *op. cit.,* pp. 36–44.

A vital question, then, is whether or not the monsoon is regular. The melancholy answer is that it is not. Sometimes the rain fails to come, or again it comes with greater than its accustomed violence. In either case tragedy is likely to follow. It is the irregularity of the monsoon that has made India a land of famine.

It happens that the greatest irregularity, amounting to more than 20 per cent variation in rainfall from year to year, occurs in those areas that are dry anyway (Map 6). The great-

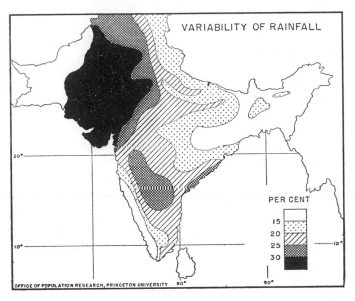

MAP 6. Variability of Rainfall from Year to Year. From A. V. Williamson and K. G. T. Clark, *The Geographical Review,* Vol. XXI, No. 4 (October, 1931), p. 676.

est variation is found in the Indus plain in West Pakistan. Here the ordinary rainfall is so scant (about five inches per year) that it makes little difference if rain fails to come. Life is not built on the expectation of rain. But farther east, in Rajputana, Kathiawar, Central India, and the Deccan, where some rain usually comes but the variation is great, famine descends frequently. In certain areas, notably Punjab and Madras, irrigation has made the settlers somewhat independent of rainfall changes; but a prolonged failure of the monsoon causes rivers and wells, the sources for irrigation, to have less water than usual and thus to be less adequate for irrigation.

It becomes clear that the subcontinent can be divided roughly into several geographical regions. In the north certain parts, such as Kashmir and the northern part of the United Provinces, are in the Himalayas, and are consequently rugged with cold winters, rain through the year, and a generally temperate climate. The strip of land lying just at the foot of the Himalayas, usually called the Terai, is quite different, being very wet, low, swampy, and malarial. It runs along the border of Nepal and Bhutan. In the far west we find, in Baluchistan, a section of the dry Iranian plateau, which is hot in the summer and cold in the winter. To the east of it is the Indus basin, which is extremely hot in summer, cool in winter, with marked variations of temperature. Though the soil of the Indus valley is alluvial and rich, the climate is so dry that desert conditions are avoided only by irrigation. In fact, in the eastern part of the basin a great desert, the Thar Desert, is encountered. The dryness keeps this part of the Indo-Gangetic plain from being as rich an agricultural area as the Ganges part. In the Punjab extensive irrigation from the five tributaries of the Indus, plus some winter rainfall, have made possible a good agricultural development. This is, of course, extended on down the Ganges plain. In the upper part of the Ganges plain temperatures are less extreme than in the Punjab, but still it is very hot in summer and cool in winter; there is also light to moderate rainfall, with frequent floods and occasional drought. In the lower Ganges and in the Brahmaputra delta region the rainfall becomes very heavy, rice displaces other cereal cultivation, the temperature is constantly warm, the humidity high. The Assam valley to the northeast, a long and narrow alluvial area, continues the same conditions, except that the rainfall, particularly in the middle portion, is less. Here rice and tea are grown. In what might be called the Indian Union's central highlands, forming the southern limit of the Ganges basin, a rugged topography gives rise to some of the wildest country in the subcontinent. This area has light rainfall in the west, getting heavier as one moves east. It includes parts of Rajputana, Central Provinces, and Central India. South of it lies the Deccan, the moderately high and rough table-land characterized by extreme temperatures, slight to moderate but irregular rainfall. It has black cotton soil in the northwest, reddish soil in the south. On the former a great amount of cotton is raised, while on the latter millet and tea are grown. Finally, there are the two coastal strips. The western strip is characterized by warm even temperature, heavy seasonal rains, numerous alluvial streams. It can be divided into three parallel strands—a heavily forested belt on the slopes of the Ghats, an intermediate alluvial plain, and sand dunes next to the shore. Rice and other tropical crops, including coconuts and rubber, are grown. The eastern strip is wider, especially in the south. It is usually flat near the coast, with some alluvial soil, but gets hilly farther inland. Rainfall is light and irregular in the central portion, but greater at either end. Rice is heavily cultivated where rainfall allows, millet in the drier portions. If these regions are kept in mind, they will facilitate an understanding of India's population distribution, as discussed in the next chapter.[8]

Isolation

Island nations such as Australia and Japan enjoy a certain natural isolation not ordinarily shared by continental countries. Pre-partition India, with a longer land than sea border (some 5,000 as against 4,000-odd miles), was no island, but it nevertheless enjoyed a remarkable isolation. It owed this isolation to two geographical features, first the mountainous character of its land frontier and second the unnavigable nature of its seacoasts. The land frontier was blocked not only by steep mountains but also by the vegetation and climate that go with them. In the northeast, between Burma and India, an extremely heavy rainfall produces on the sharp mountain slopes and in the deep valleys a dense forest, with impassable streams flowing southward. In the north the Himalayan range is covered with snow and ice. Only in the northwest, where the elevation is still high but the rainfall is too scant to produce much vegetation, could entrance to India be gained. Here, however, barren conditions, such as those that make the Karst desert, created a sparse population and difficult travel conditions. The northwestern border was there-

fore comparatively easy to defend, and the fact that it was not always successfully defended is due more to the weakness of the Indians (possibly a result of their normal isolation) than to the ease of passage. To this day there are no railways that cross the mountain barriers. There are a few short lines that cross the border, such as two into the foothills of Nepal and one into Iran, but none that links Pakistan or the Union of India with the rest of the world. The real traffic across the frontier comes by mule and camel, in seasons when the passes are open. As a result the trade across pre-partition India's 5,000 miles of border amounted to only about 5 per cent of her total foreign trade; it is doubtful if the proportion is now any different for the region.

In early days the isolation by sea was due as much to great ocean distances as to anything else. The Indian coasts were far from any other land, and the nearest foreign coasts in Burma and Persia were peculiarly unpromising. Once long-range sailing was inaugurated, the inappropriateness of the coasts for navigation had its effect. These coasts, lying mostly in the torrid zone, are practically devoid of natural harbors. For much of their distance they are blocked by coastal islands and mangrove swamps. "The whole is storm-swept and scourged by fierce currents; there are hundreds of miles of bare rock-wall in the western half and of mangrove-swamp in the eastern; the river harbours are amongst the most dangerous and expensive in the world; and the only seaport that was naturally and always first-class, Bombay . . . , was rented by Charles II to the East India Company for as little as £10 a year!"[9] Today contact of both Pakistan and the Indian Union with the outer world is almost wholly by sea, but with few ships of their own and a Hindu tradition against ocean voyages, neither is as yet a maritime nation.

India's long geographical isolation explains the uniqueness of Indian culture. Indian ideas and institutions, taken as a whole, resemble those of no other people. They have a peculiar shape and flavor of their own. They have tended to transform and absorb any foreign elements that trickled into the region; for India, though politically conquered by outsiders, was never (except possibly by the original Aryans) culturally conquered.

This peculiar culture has to some degree penetrated and pervaded nearly every part of what is geographically India. It has everywhere been affected by local, indigenous variations that often make the common elements seem a very thin veneer. It has everywhere been affected by class and caste cleavages. But neither the geographical nor the social barriers inside the subcontinent have been sufficient to prevent the widespread diffusion of a common, basic culture, which, despite great variation, is peculiarly Indian.

The presence of a general cultural homogeneity underlying great local variations does not, however, mean anything with reference to political unity. The only time when geographical India has been together as one single aggregate was under the British. It has been India's fate that whenever a substantial portion of her territory has been politically united, it has been by virtue of a foreign ruler. As one writer said, "there is only one obvious unity in India today, and that is a unity of British control; and, as that is being relaxed, the great disunities are being intensified in the urgent scramble for place and power, for prizes and patronage."[10] The truth of this statement is seen in the partition of India into two independent commonwealths when the British left.

It has been claimed that the degree of unity in pre-partition

---

[8] A more detailed classification and fuller description of the natural regions will be found in Stamp, *op. cit.*, pp. 258–341, and in Lionel W. Lyde, *The Continent of Asia* (London: Macmillan, 1938), pp. 352–55, 367–472.

[9] Lyde, *op. cit.*, pp. 356–64.
[10] *ibid.*, p. 356.

India lay somewhere between that of Europe and that of the United States. Like Europe, India manifested linguistic, religious, racial, and economic differences from one section to another, yet had a basic common culture cutting across these differences. Like Europe it had not been able, by its own efforts, to unify itself politically. But unlike Europe it had a greater possibility of achieving such independent unity, and in that sense approached the sort of federation that the United States once exemplified. It had the chance to subordinate, as in America, the cultural, class, religious, and regional differences to an over-all national unity, although it could not fully realize this potentiality. The partition of India need not have happened, because the geographical and cultural basis for a single united India was present. This basis had been provided by centuries of geographical isolation—isolation not sufficient to keep out the foreigner entirely, but adequate to make the term "India" meaningful.

PAKISTAN AND THE UNION OF INDIA

The separation of India into two dominions in 1947 greatly changed the political map of the region. Map 22 in Chapter 20, which depicts the two countries in relation to each other and in relation to their neighbors, shows that Pakistan is a bifurcate nation. One part of it, Western Pakistan, embraces what were the provinces of Baluchistan, Sind, the North-West Frontier, and most of the Punjab, together with minor States that were in this area. The other part, Eastern Pakistan, embraces the greater part of Bengal (the boundary being east of Calcutta and running almost directly north through the province) together with nearly all of Sylhet district in Assam. Western Pakistan is by far the larger of the two parts, having approximately 307,000 square miles, which is somewhat larger than Texas. Eastern Pakistan, with 54,000 square miles, is only a sixth as large as Western Pakistan, or about the size of Illinois. The total area of Pakistan is approximately 360,000 square miles, which is about twice the size of pre-war Germany. Thus, although Pakistan is less than a third the size of the Indian Union, it is still a large country.

The most curious feature of Pakistan, geographically speaking, is the fact that its two parts are separated by more than 1,000 miles of alien territory. This presents formidable problems of communication between the two areas, especially since the capital, Karachi, is located on the coast of the Arabian Sea near the boundary between Baluchistan and Sind. Communication by water between the two areas must go around the peninsula of India, a distance of almost 3,000 miles. The problems of military defense created by this separation are obvious. In addition, the two areas are extremely different geographically. Whereas West Pakistan is extremely arid, East Pakistan is extremely wet. The former grows wheat and cotton primarily, the latter rice and jute. As a consequence of the difference in climate and economy, the population density is quite different. West Pakistan has almost six times the territory but only two-thirds the people that East Pakistan has.

The disputed territory of Kashmir is almost exactly the size of Kansas, although with over 4 million inhabitants it has more than twice as many people.

The Union of India, including Kashmir, has 77 per cent of the territory that pre-partition India contained. Without Kashmir it would still contain 72 per cent of its former area, although this would mean, if Kashmir went to Pakistan, an increase of 23 per cent in the latter's territory. Because the Union of India is more densely settled than the territory that went to Pakistan, it retains approximately 82 per cent of its former population, or 319 million in 1941. Both territorially and demographically, therefore, the Union of India remains one of the largest of the world's nations.[11]

NEIGHBORS—INDIAN AND NON-INDIAN

To a remarkable degree geographical India coincides with cultural and political India. The British in certain cases pushed the political border into remote fastnesses that were not Indian—e.g., Baluchistan and the North-West Frontier Province. Such areas, however, are not many or important. In other cases, through historical accident, certain areas that are geographically and culturally Indian have come to be excluded from India and Pakistan—e.g., Portuguese and French India. These must perforce be excluded in our population statistics, although they may soon join the Indian Union. Finally there are other cases, such as Nepal and Ceylon, that have some cultural and regional affinity with India and are thus often confused with it, but which are really distinct in every sense. All of these various cases taken together are not numerous, but it is necessary to be clear about them. Above all it must be realized that when the population of historical India is spoken of in these pages, it does not include Burma, Bhutan, Nepal, Portuguese India, French India, or Ceylon. Since, however, for one reason or another they are often confused with India, a brief account of them is now given.

Burma, with an area of 192,000 square miles and a population in 1941 of 16,824,000, is geographically a northern part of the Indo-China bulb of Asia, and extends far down the Malay peninsula. It is separated from India by rugged mountain chains curving southward from the eastern end of the Himalayas. These are characterized by such dense vegetation that they are still inhabited by wild tribes, and have always operated as an effective barrier keeping the two countries racially and culturally distinct. As early as 1612, however, the East India Company had agents and "factories" there, and a Resident at Rangoon from 1796. Thereafter successive wars with Burma gave the British an increasing amount of Burmese territory, and eventually in 1862 the various acquisitions were amalgamated and formed into the Province of Burma as a part of British India. Upper Burma was conquered and added to the province in 1886. Despite its long identification with India, Burma never fitted well into the Indian picture. Its people were Mongols, not Aryans; Buddhists, not Hindus; extroverts, not introverts. They had no caste system, child marriage, or widow celibacy. They did have a hearty dislike of the Indians. Under these circumstances the affiliation with India was always artificial, and Burma felt that she was the Cinderella Province. A constant source of friction was the migration of Indians into Burma and the formation there of a substantial Indian minority. Eventually, under the Government of India Act of 1935, Burma was separated from India. In the meantime, however, it had been included in every Indian census from 1872 through 1931. For this reason most of the figures on Indian population that one sees include Burma. In the present work one of the trying but constant tasks has been to take Burma out of the figures, because our concern is with pre-partition India proper. Unless otherwise stated, therefore, Burma is always assumed to be omitted.

[11] The comparative demography of Pakistan and the Union of India is more fully dealt with in Chapter 20.

Some attention is given the country, however, in connection with Indian emigration.

Bhutan, a small state with an estimated 300,000 inhabitants on approximately 18,000 square miles (about the size of New Hampshire and Vermont together), is located on the northern border of Assam and Bengal in the eastern Himalayas. It is one of the least-known portions of the inhabited world, but has had contact with Britain. Because of "outrages" by Bhutan hillmen on defenseless British subjects, various submontane tracts in the original Bhutan territory were annexed and added to India. In 1865 the British granted the Bhutan Government a subsidy of Rs. 50,000 per year on condition of good behavior. This subsidy was raised to Rs. 100,000 (and to 200,000 still later) when, by a 1910 treaty, the Bhutan Government gave control of its external affairs to the British in return for protection and non-interference in its internal affairs. The Indian Union has continued this arrangement, raising the subsidy somewhat. The British kept a Bhutan Agent at Kalimpong, in northern Bengal, who was also Assistant to the Political Officer in Sikkim for Bhutanese affairs. Bhutan thus had, and still has, somewhat the position of an Indian State, but actually it has been left far more to itself. Its governing class is apparently of Tibetan origin, its religion Buddhistic, and its trade mainly with Tibet. It has never been a part of India and has never been included in Indian statistics.

Nepal, the Hermit Kingdom of the Himalayas, stretches for 500 miles along the northern border of India. With a maximum width of about 150 miles it has an area of some 55,000 square miles (nearly equal to Wisconsin) and a population said to be 6,282,000 in 1941. Its southern border runs along the wet tropical jungles of the malarial Terai, its northern border along the eternal snows of the main Himalayas. The interior is exceptionally rugged, but there are four valleys nestled among the peaks. There is some trade with both Tibet and India. In 1814 British India declared war on Nepal, the hostilities ending in 1815 with the Sagauli treaty which called for the exchange of ministers. A British Envoy Extraordinary and Minister Plenipotentiary then resided at the Nepalese capital but did not interfere with the country's affairs. The country is proudly independent, but has been since 1815 on friendly terms with Britain. In 1924 the Survey of India undertook, by request, a survey of the country. Telephone communication has been established with the capital, Katmandu, and two Indian railway lines have been extended 25 and 33 miles respectively into the southern region. Nepal's chief connection with India, however, has been neither economic nor political, but military. The nation's ruling ethnic group, the Gurkhas, not only make up the backbone of the Nepalese army but also supply the Indian army with its most intrepid and most famous fighters. In addition, Nepal has furnished a large and steady migration into India, particularly into Sikkim and the northern districts of the United Provinces. It is this movement of Nepalese into India that will again attract our attention to Nepal.

Portuguese India consists of Goa (a mainland section and several small islands on the Malabar Coast), Damão (with the territories of Dadara and Nagar-Aveli) on the Gulf of Cambay, and Diu (with Gocola and Simbor) on the coast of Gujerat. It covers all told an area of 1,537 square miles (slightly larger than Rhode Island), most of which is in Goa and all of which is on India's west coast. The colony produces salt and manganese, and grows coconuts, spices, and nuts. It engages in shipping, and the port of Goa, Mormagão,

is connected with the Indian Union by a 51-mile railway. The population of over 600,000, about half of whom are Christians, furnishes a considerable number of migrants into India, principally into Bombay. Though a fascinating place, this Portuguese colony must be excluded from our discussion, except with reference to migration.

French India, smaller than Goa, has included five separate but tiny colonies, the chief of which is Pondicherry on the Coromandel Coast below Madras, the rest being scattered over India. The total area in 1941 was only 196 square miles, and the estimated population 325,000.

Ceylon, an island of 25,332 square miles and some 6,200,000 people, is separated from India by narrow Palk Strait. A string of islands practically crosses the strait, and the water is so shallow that a railroad to be built on a filled bank has been proposed to cover the twenty miles now separating the railroads of the two countries. Formerly administered as a part of India, Ceylon was separated and formed into a Crown Colony in 1802. Its prosperity has come from estate agriculture in coffee, tea, rubber, cacao, coconuts, and cinnamon. A large part of the labor for these estates has been obtained from India, so that today approximately 15 per cent of the population represents recent immigrant stock from southern India. In addition, there is an older Tamil stock of about the same size representing an earlier migration. Although Buddhism was introduced from India in the third century B.C. and, as in Burma and Bhutan, still persists among the majority, the island is less of a Buddhist stronghold than formerly because of these Hindu immigrants. Ceylon's importance to the study of India's population lies primarily in its role as a large-scale receiver of Indian migrants. In this connection it will be encountered again in a later chapter.

BRITISH AND NON-BRITISH INDIA

Obviously, as distinct from the territories just described, all of historical India proper may be designated as a political unit which owed allegiance to Britain. Within this unit, however, there was a further division of great importance. It was between the British Provinces—confusingly called British India—on the one hand, and the Indian or Native States on the other. (See Map 7.) The first were those areas whose previous Indian rulers had been set aside and their people subjected to direct British rule. They were governed by provincial officials, both elected and appointed, according to constitutions approved by Parliament. Their allegiance and subordination were to the Viceroy, and their laws were integrated with those of the Central Government according to the all-India constitution. The States, on the other hand, were territories not thus annexed. Some of them represented kingdoms in existence before the coming of the British, their hereditary rulers being allowed to stay in power under treaty. Others represented new principalities set up or recognized by the British during the period of final consolidation under the Company.

The States varied greatly in size and importance, but in all cases they were granted, by treaty or agreement, the control of their own internal affairs in exchange for protection and the handling of foreign affairs by the British. Their citizens were not British subjects but "British protected persons." Their governments had no foreign relations with other countries or diplomatic relations among themselves, for these were handled through the Government of British India. In 1921 a Chamber of Princes was formed, but merely as a consultative and ad-

MAP 7. Native States and British Provinces, 1941.

visory rather than a legislative or executive body. Only in extreme cases of misrule did the Government of India interfere with a State's internal affairs, but it generally sought to elicit cooperation on matters of concern to India at large.

The States were territorially as well as politically separated, being scattered all over India and thus interspersed in British territory. In all they embraced nearly half the land of India (45 per cent) and nearly a fourth (24 per cent) of the population. The total number of States, large and small, was 562, and their population in 1947 was estimated as about 100 million. They were thus no small part of the pre-partition Indian Empire. Today some of the smaller states have been consolidated into larger ones or combined with provinces, though some of the larger ones, such as Hyderabad and Mysore, remain as entities within the Indian Union.

Fortunately, the States cooperated with the Government of India in census work. They took censuses at the same time and by the same methods as British India, and did some of the best work. Our historical population data therefore refer to all of political India, whether British or Native. Unhappily, however, the same is not true of the registration statistics nor of the economic and social statistics. These occur only sporadically for the States and hence must often be limited to British India alone. Nevertheless, unless specification is made to the contrary, the term "India" as used in the present volume always refers to the whole of historical India under British paramountcy—i.e. to both British India and Native India. When figures refer to British India alone, the fact will be so stated. To designate the Union of India the term "India" is not used, except occasionally as a shorthand description when combined with Pakistan. On the whole the term is reserved either for historical India or for the entire region.

What Is India?

Geographically, India is a subcontinent cut off and isolated by the cold Roof of the World and an inhospitable shore. It is a tropical region, fertile of soil but perilously dependent on the caprice of the fickle monsoon. It is no longer a political entity whose borders are almost but not quite coterminous with its natural geographical limits, but rather a partitioned region, one of whose countries is itself divided into two widely separated parts. It is a cultural region of a sort, made unique by its long isolation but showing great variation from one locale to another, between one group and another. It is a split personality, divided and yet somehow not divided between states and provinces, races and castes, religions and localities. It is a sick region, poor and conflictful and ready to fly apart. During several decades it was kept together by the British Raj, and the information assembled during this regime enables us to feel its historical pulse, take its temperature, examine its anatomy, and make a prognosis concerning it. The data also allow us to say something about the two new countries of India and Pakistan into which the region is now politically divided.

CHAPTER 3

++

People: How Many and Where?

++

WHAT has most distinguished India's population is its size. Returns from the 1941 census gave a massive total of 389 million, and estimates for 1947 push this figure up to around 420 million at the time of partition. Today Pakistan and the Union of India together have about 18 per cent, or almost a fifth, of the world's population. They have, in fact, more people than all of Europe exclusive of Russia, and almost as many as the continents of Africa, North America, and South America combined. Their number exceeds that of Australia by 57 times, and that of Great Britain by nine times. At least three out of every four persons in the British Empire before partition were Indians.

Looking at a dot map of the population of the entire world, we find that there are on the globe three major clusters of people compared to which all the other areas of settlement seem sparse and insubstantial. One of these clusters occurs in Europe in the region roughly demarcated by England, Italy, and European Russia. Another occurs in Eastern Asia in an area embraced by China, Korea, and Japan. The third, which is now the second in size, occurs in the Indian subcontinent.

Yet the figure of 420 million in 1947, perhaps 430 by 1950, is an estimate for only the territory embraced by Pakistan and the Indian Union. It does not, as mentioned before, include Burma, Bhutan, Nepal, Ceylon, or Portuguese or French India. All of these, if included, would add about 33 million. But our concern is only with the Indian Union (whose territory had 319 million inhabitants in 1941 and perhaps 355 million in 1950) and Pakistan (whose territory had 70 million in 1941 and perhaps 79 million in 1950).

Doubtless the very size of the population in the two countries, and especially in the Indian Union, creates administrative and political difficulties. It has often been remarked that a small citizenry, such as is found in Australia, Sweden, or Switzerland, is more manageable than a large one, such as that found in the United States, Russia, or China. Common agreement is somehow reached more easily and plans are carried out more efficiently. If difficulties of size are present in countries like the United States, how much truer must this be of historical India and of the Indian Union today. To find uniformity of culture, opinion, language, or religion in such a large mass of mankind would be strange indeed, and to create such unity extremely difficult. Any administrative measure, for whatever purpose, must reckon with the tremendous task of merely communicating with, not to mention controlling, this huge number of people. On the other hand there are certain advantages to sheer size. One of these is military power. Another is a vast and ready market for trade, unimpeded by political barriers. In the past in India the disadvantages of size were more evident than the advantages, because poverty, cultural diversity, and political strife prevented the potential advantages from being realized. The same may be true of the Indian Union today and perhaps of bifurcated Pakistan. Sheer size alone is certainly not the most important variable in national efficiency, but taken in conjunction with other conditions, it is apparently a significant one. It is one of the things that must always be kept in mind with reference to the Indian region.

OVER-ALL DENSITY

When confronted with the massiveness of the Indian population, many observers automatically jump to two questionable conclusions: first, that the *average* density of population for the whole region is abnormally great, and second, that the population growth has been unusually rapid. Both views are half-truths and require examination. The first will be examined now and the second in the next chapter.

The first conclusion stems from a failure to realize the dimensions of the Indian subcontinent. The area of India and Pakistan together, as described in the last chapter, embraces over a million and a half square miles, a very big expanse. When this is divided into the population, the average density turns out to be 246 per square mile, as of 1941.[1] This is certainly a high average density, but it is by no means the highest. It falls considerably under that of England, Germany, Puerto Rico, Japan, Java, and several other countries, as Table 1 shows. Thus the region as a whole is not more thickly settled than any Western country, as is sometimes thought. For the sake of correctness, however—and this is the truth in the assumption that the density is high—the region should not have its over-all density compared with that of much smaller areas. It should be compared with that of regions more similar in size, such as Brazil, the United States, and China. When this is done, as in Table 1, it is found that the Indian subcontinent does have an unusually high density. It has an over-all density greater than that of any other political entity of equal or greater size in the world. Its figure of 246 per square mile exceeds that of the United States by five and a half times, and that of Greater China by about two and a half times. Since the region's population is growing faster than that of most other countries at the present time, its average density is bound to become not only absolutely but relatively greater.

Taking the Union of India and Pakistan separately, we find that there is considerable disparity in density. The Union has the greatest average density of any country in its size class, with 261 per square mile. Pakistan, being smaller,

[1] The figure had grown to approximately 268 by 1947.

TABLE 1

Average Densities of Selected Countries [1]

Country	Date	Area (sq. mi. in thousands)	Population (in thousands)	Density
Large Countries				
Indian Union [2]	1941	1,220.5	318,863	261
Pre-partition India [3]	1941	1,581.0	388,998	246
Greater China [a]	1939	4,287.0	450,000	105
United Kingdom & Colonies	1939–43	1,967.0	106,413	54
U.S.A. & Territories [a]	1939–40	3,685.0	150,147	41
U.S.S.R.	1939	8,351.0	192,667	23
France & Empire	1939–40	4,623.0	106,011	23
Brazil	1940	3,286.0	41,565	13
Canada	1941	3,466.0	11,507	3
Australia & Possessions	1943	3,065.0	7,332	2
Intermediate Countries				
Japan [a]	1940	147.5	73,114	496
Germany	1939	226.3	79,530	352
Pakistan	1941	361.0	70,135	194
France	1939	212.7	41,200	194
Turkey	1940	296.1	17,620	59
Mexico	1940	760.2	19,654	26
Chile	1940	286.5	5,024	18
Small Countries				
Java & Madura	1941	51.0	49,144	964
England & Wales	1940	58.3	41,862	718
Holland	1943	12.7	9,130	717
Puerto Rico	1940	3.4	1,869	544
Korea	1940	85.3	24,326	285
Switzerland	1941	15.8	4,266	269
Ceylon	1943	25.5	5,922	232
Hungary	1941	66.3	14,683	221

[a] The density for China proper is approximately 130; that for the U.S.A., 44; and that for the former Japanese Empire, 401.

[1] Except for India, figures are compiled from the League of Nations, *Statistical Year-Book*, 1942–44.

[2] Calculated on basis of territory awarded to Indian Union and Pakistan, according to 1941 district figures given in 1941 provincial census volumes. Indian Union includes Kashmir.

[3] *Census of India*, 1941, Vol. 1, pp. 56–57.

has a density (194 per square mile) that is exceeded by several countries in its size class.

REGIONAL CONCENTRATION

The truth is, however, that average density means very little. The larger and more diversified the country, the less it means. In the case of the Indian subcontinent, with almost a fifth of the world's people but only about a thirtieth of the inhabitable surface, it signifies simply that the land must support more than its proportion of humanity. The sheer density says nothing about the adequacy of this land for such support, or the capacity of the region to draw sustenance from other parts of the world. To talk more realistically, then, one must speak of the land and its regions, of the richness of the land, and of the distribution of population in relation to regional capacities.

The economy of Pakistan and the Indian Union, as every-

one knows, is primarily agricultural. About 70 per cent of the people are directly dependent on farming for a livelihood. The region raises nearly all of its own food, about 82 per cent of its crops being food crops. Its place in the world economy is based mainly on the export of agricultural products—e.g. oil-seeds, cotton, tea, and jute—for which it gets, in return, manufactured goods. Its cities are disproportionately few and small in comparison to its total population; its people remain overwhelmingly rural. All this being true the location and concentration of the population is easy to deduce. The people will not be found in huge industrial and metropolitan aglomerations, as in an industrial country. They will be found rather in good farming areas—i.e. where the terrain is level, the soil rich, the rainfall (or irrigation) adequate, and the climate livable. In other areas, where these optimum agricultural conditions are absent, there will be correspondingly fewer people. Map 8 shows the highly variable degree of density throughout the subcontinent.

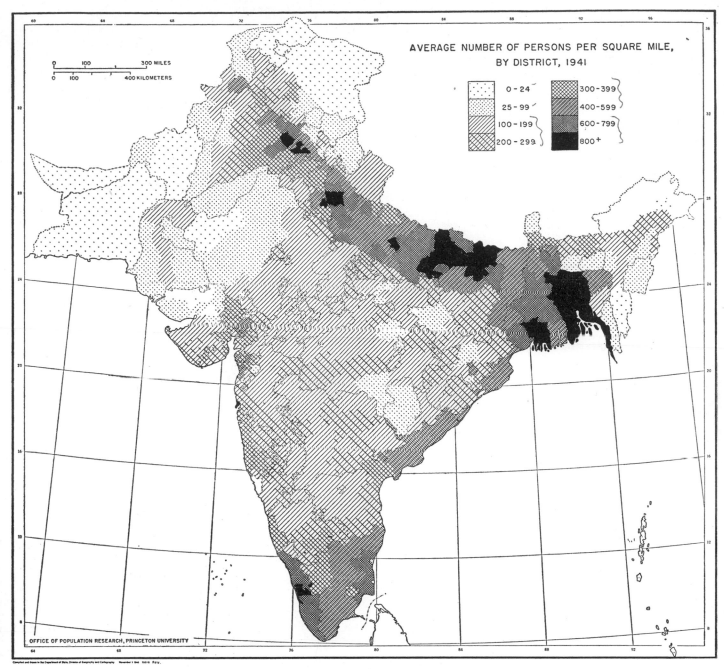

MAP 8. Density of Population in Pre-Partition India, 1941.

The degree of concentration of the region's population in certain limited areas is startling. When the districts having more than the average density are shown in black on the map (Map 9), they virtually all fall in one belt. This belt begins on the irrigated plains of the Punjab, descends the Ganges valley, comes down the Eastern Coast, goes around the tip of India, and ascends the Western Coast to the Gulf of Cambay. Here, in an area that is only 32 per cent of that of all India, are found 69 per cent of the people. In other words, the region's population is heavily concentrated on the well watered river and coastal plains. The greatest of these plains, that of the Ganges, achieves an average density of 686 per square mile, according to the 1941 census. In the Bengal portion it reaches an average of 829. If we recall that the areas involved are huge—the Ganges plain alone has over 200,000 square miles and is thus as large as Germany and four times as large as Java and Madura—these high densities mean that the sub-

continent has concentrations of population rivaling those of any other region in the world.

If the districts having a density of 500 or more are grouped together, we find that they contain nearly half the population but less than a seventh of the area (Table 2). The districts with a density of 700 or more contain nearly a quarter of the population but only one-eighteenth of the area. Such concentration is not due primarily to cities. The results are much the same when the cities are eliminated. The high densities represent mainly the piling up of agriculturalists on the land. In some almost purely agricultural districts the general density rises above 1,000 per square mile, and in many others, above 550. Thus the region is definitely in a class with Java, Egypt, Japan, and China in having areas of heavy rural concentration.

Some of the provinces are the equals of major nations in population. When they are compared with specific nations (compare Tables 1 and 3) we find that they rival even the industrial nations in density of settlement. Pre-partition Bengal, for example, had about the same population as Germany, but her area and resources were much less. The fact that she had roughly two and a half times the density of Germany meant that her poverty was many times as great, though she was commonly reputed to be the most prosperous province in India. Bengal had a greater area than Java and Madura, but her density nevertheless approaches theirs. Other parts of India were not far behind Bengal.

It now becomes plain why the average density for all of pre-partition India and a comparison of it with the density of smaller industrial countries mean very little. There are vast regions that have a scant population, the outstanding case being Baluchistan. There are others that have an extremely dense population, the outstanding one being the lower Ganges. It is possible to maintain that the first are just as crowded in terms of their agricultural resources as are the second, but

the latter are the more spectacular and therefore capture the attention. It is the inordinate compactness of particular Indian regions (such as the low wet plains), the prevailingly low standard of living, and the unusual massiveness of the total population that give the popular impression that the subcontinent, as a whole, is more densely settled than it is. But though this impression is not wholly true, the fact remains that huge sections are phenomenally crowded. The region represents simply another case, on a gigantic scale, of Oriental pressure on agricultural land. The nearest parallels are to be found in Egypt, China, Formosa, Korea, Java, Japan, and to our dismay, Puerto Rico.

Pakistan contains greater disparities of density than does the Union of India. East Pakistan, with 777 per square mile, is 8½ times as dense as West Pakistan, with 92 per square mile. The difference, however, tells us nothing about living levels in the two areas. East Pakistan, located in a low-lying, alluvial, and humid delta area, has greater agricultural re-

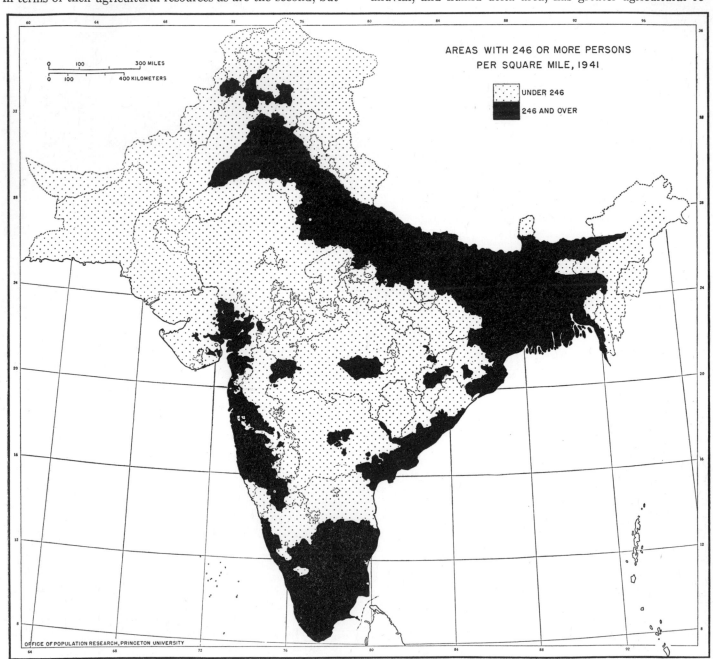

MAP 9. Districts with Greater than Average Density, 1941.

TABLE 2

Concentration of Population in Areas of High Density 1941 [1]

All Districts	Per Cent of India's Total Area	Per Cent of India's Population	Average Density (sq. mi.)
With density above Indian average of 246	31.9	69.0	533
With density above 500	14.5	44.7	755
With density above 700	5.5	22.9	1,021
Lying in the Ganges Plain [a]	13.4	37.2	686
Lying in the Western Coastal Plain [a]	1.7	3.7	540
Lying in the Eastern Coastal Plain [a]	4.1	8.5	510

[a] In general only those districts were taken which seemed to lie almost wholly on the plain. Parts of districts were not taken. Consequently, in each case the figures do not cover the entire plain.
[1] Compiled from *Census of India,* 1941, Vol. 1, pp. 56–57, 76–83, 86–94, 116–37.

sources than does West Pakistan; with an average density equal only to that of the latter area, it would have a much higher level of living, but its population is so great that it has, if anything, a poorer population.

AGRICULTURAL CROWDING

Crude density is not the best measure of crowding. A better one, at least in agricultural countries, is the number of persons dependent on agriculture per square mile of cultivated land. In 1931 this figure for British India stood at 432, and in 1941 it can be estimated as 535. Even in 1931, as Table 4 and Figure 2 show, India's agricultural density was higher than that for European countries having a comparable percentage of their population dependent on agriculture. India's figure

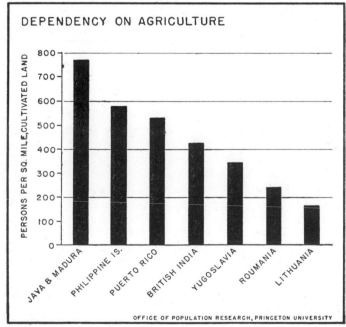

FIGURE 2. Persons Dependent on Agriculture per Square Mile of Cultivated Land, Selected Countries, 1931.

TABLE 3

Area, Population, and Density of Major Political Divisions in India, 1941 [1]

	Area in sq. mi.	Population	Persons per sq. mi.
Provinces	*865,446*	*295,808,722*	*342*
Delhi	574	917,939	1,599
Bengal	77,442	60,306,525	779
Bihar	69,745	36,340,151	521
United Provinces	106,247	55,020,617	518
Madras	126,166	49,341,810	391
Punjab	99,089	28,418,819	287
Bombay	76,443	20,849,840	273
Orissa	32,198	8,728,544	271
Ajmer-Merwara	2,400	583,693	243
North-West Frontier	14,263	3,038,067	213
Panth Piploda	25	5,267	211
Assam	54,951	10,204,733	186
Central Prov. & Berar	98,575	16,813,584	171
Coorg	1,593	168,726	106
Sind	48,136	4,535,008	94
Andamans & Nichobars	3,143	33,768	11
Baluchistan	54,456	501,631	9
States	*715,964*	*93,189,233*	*130*
Cochin	1,493	1,422,875	953
Travancore	7,662	6,070,018	792
United Provinces	1,760	928,470	528
Baroda	8,236	2,855,010	347
Madras	1,602	498,754	311
Deccan & Kolhapur	10,870	2,785,428	256
Mysore	29,458	7,329,140	249
Bengal	9,408	2,144,829	228
Hyderabad	82,313	16,338,534	198
Gujarat	7,352	1,458,702	198
Orissa	18,151	3,023,731	167
Gwalior	26,008	4,006,159	154
Central India	52,047	7,506,427	144
Punjab	38,146	5,503,554	144
Western India	37,894	4,904,156	129
Chattisgarh	37,687	4,050,000	107
Rajputana	132,559	13,670,208	103
Punjab Hill	11,375	1,090,644	96
North-West Frontier	24,986	2,377,599	95
Assam	12,408	725,655	58
Kashmir & feudatories	82,258	4,021,616	49
Sikkim	2,745	121,520	44
Baluchistan	79,546	356,204	4
Total India	*1,581,410*	*388,997,955*	*246*

[1] *Census of India,* 1941, Vol. 1, Tables, pp. 56–57.

was lower, however, than that for some other Asiatic countries. This seems to indicate that India was in better shape than some of her Asiatic neighbors, but allowance should be made for the fact that crop yields in India are poorer than in most other countries, including those of Asia.

Table 5 gives the agricultural densities for the Provinces and States in 1931. These show quite a range. The pattern is much the same as that found with reference to general density. The least rural crowding is found in dry or hilly areas and consequently does not necessarily represent a favorable situation. The heaviest agricultural densities are found in good agricultural areas. The figures for 1941 are not available, but there is reason to believe that the density increased about as fast as the population, because neither the occupational structure nor the amount of land under cultivation changed much during the intervening ten years.

The effect of agricultural pressure on the land can be seen in certain indices. The average agricultural holding is quite

TABLE 4

Persons Dependent on Agriculture per Square Mile of Cultivated Land, Selected Countries, for Dates Available

	Date [a]	Per Cent of Population Dependent on Agriculture [b]	Persons Dependent on Agriculture per Square Mile of Cultivated Land [c]
Korea [1]	1930	79	981
Java & Madura [2]	1930	63	826
Philippine Islands [3]	1939	70	573
Puerto Rico [4]	1930	66	533
BRITISH INDIA [5]	1931	68	422
Yugoslavia [6]	1931	76	344
Rumania [7]	1930	72	240
Lithuania [8]	1930	70	162
Chile [9]	1940	38	147
Mexico [10]	1930	74	88
United States [11]	1930	25	48
Argentina [12]	1930	30	32

[a] In most cases the date for the per cent of population dependent on agriculture is the same as that for the population used in computing the actual number so engaged. In cases where the two dates differ slightly, the date given is that for the actual population.

[b] It is hard to standardize figures on occupational distribution. Many of these figures involve an estimate of one sort or another, and some are consequently only roughly accurate. In many instances the per cent of all occupied males who are engaged in agriculture has been taken, and the population dependent on agriculture has then been estimated by means of a regression line showing the relation between the per cent of occupied males engaged in agriculture and the per cent of the population dependent on agriculture in numerous countries.

[c] "Cultivated land" is defined as that actually sown or lying fallow. It does not include pasture, forest, or land that is potentially cultivable. Again, however, standardization is difficult.

[1] *Statesman's Year-Book*, 1933, p. 1074. *Résumé statistique de l'Empire du Japon*, 45 année, 1931, p. 4.

[2] *Indisch Verslag*, 1937, Parts 1–2. Netherlands Indian Report 1937, II, Statistical Abstract for the Year 1936, pp. 221–23, 229.

[3] *Census of the Philippines*, 1939, Vol. 2, pp. 53, 496, 906.

[4] *15th Census of the United States*, 1930, *Outlying Territories and Possessions*, pp. 183, 207.

[5] *Census of India*, 1931, Vol. 1, Part 2, pp. 3, 206. India, Department of Commercial Intelligence, *Statistical Abstract for British India*, 15th No. of New Series, 1927–37, p. 458.

[6] Yugoslavia, *Statistique Générale d'Etat, Annuaire Statistique*, 1934–35, pp. 74–75. *Statisticki Godisnjah*, 1937, pp. 18ff.

[7] *Census of Roumania*, 1930, Vol. 10, pp. xcvi–ciii. Estimated from number of persons *not* engaged in agriculture. Institut de Statistica Generala, *Buletinul Statistic al Romaniei*, 1931–32, pp. 60–63.

[8] *International Yearbook of Agricultural Statistics*, 1933–34, p. 78. *Census of 1923. Annuaire Statistique de la Lithuanie*, Vol. 3, p. 12.

[9] Chile, Ministerio de Agricultura, *Almanaque* 1940, pp. 17, 310, and Anexo No. 1.

[10] International Institute of Agriculture, *The First World Agricultural Census*, 1930, Vol. 4, p. 391. Mexico, Direccion General de Estadistica, *Quinto Censo de Poblacion*, 1930, Parts 1–9, 11, 14–19, 21–22, 24–27, 29–32, Cuadro 1 in each part.

[11] International Institute of Agriculture, *op. cit.*, p. 136. United States, *Census of 1930, Population*, Vol. 5, *General Report on Occupations*, p. 39.

[12] Argentina, Ministerio de Agricultura, *Almanaque*, 1940, p. 310. Per cent dependent on agriculture estimated by us. Total population to which percentage applied is an official estimate.

TABLE 5

Persons per Square Mile of Cultivated Land in India by Provinces and States, for Area Available, 1931

	Per Cent Population Dependent on Agriculture [1]	Cultivated Area (sq. mi.) [2]	Number Dependent per Sq. Mi. of Cultivated Land
British India	68	401,418	432
Bengal	70	45,366	769
Bihar & Orissa	79	48,164	615
United Provinces	73	59,591	594
Assam	84	12,389	588
Madras	60	69,608	405
Ajmer-Merwara	45	780	325
North-West Frontier	57	4,506	308
Delhi	15	352	277
Punjab	53	47,929	260
Central Prov. & Berar	71	44,864	245
Coorg	70	483	236
Bombay	58	67,387	186

[1] Males dependent on agriculture were first obtained from *Census of India*, 1931, Vol. I, Part 2, pp. 218, 222, 227. The percentage that these constituted of all males engaged was then calculated, and the population dependent on agriculture read from a regression line involving these two variables, prepared in the Office of Population Research using European data primarily.

[2] *Statistical Abstract for British India*, 1921–31, p. 432.

small. Pasture land is overgrazed. Few forests are left. Rural housing is extremely inadequate. Excess labor is backed up and wasted. Rural indebtedness is burdensome. And most lamentable of all, the competition for bare sustenance is very grim even in the richest food-growing areas. There should be a surplus of the means of subsistence, but there is none. Everywhere in this fertile land of abundance the people who live on the soil and grow the food have less than enough to eat, not because the land is poor, not solely because the techniques are antiquated (though they are bad enough), but because the numbers are too great.

The agricultural situation will be discussed more fully in Chapter 21. For the present it is sufficient to note that the general picture of the Indian region's population is that of an oriental agricultural people, long settled in its territory and exploiting that territory intensively. The areas most suited to agriculture are generally filled to capacity with people who, despite the richness of the soil, barely eke out a livelihood. Like other hot alluvial plains of great fertility and adequate water, such as the Nile valley or the Yellow River, the Ganges plain has an extremely concentrated population. Similarly, like other alluvial and rainy coastal plains in the tropics, India's monsoon coasts are excessively crowded. There are a few parts of the region that are not yet fully exploited, the most promising being Assam. There are still some areas where irrigation may be extended. But on the whole the territory is very fully occupied today. Pakistan and the Indian Union are thus much like some of their crowded Asiatic neighbors. The only difference is that, with the exception of China, their combined problem is more gigantic. Even Kashmir, an area that seems almost like a mountain frontier from the vantage point of the crowded Ganges plain, has a density (49 per square mile in 1941) that exceeds that of the United States.

CHAPTER 4

A History of Accelerating Growth

AT PRESENT the subcontinent's population is growing at a rate of about 1.2 per cent per year. To those lucky individuals who receive 5 per cent compound interest on their money, this may seem a low rate; but money and population are two different things. When it is realized that the region's current rate of increase, if continued, will double her already swollen population in 58 years, the rate seems altogether too high. There is little reason to believe that the rate is any different as between Pakistan and the Indian Union.

One should not, however, jump to the conclusion that this rate of increase is higher in Pakistan and the Indian Union than that of any other modern country. It has been eclipsed by many nations in recent times. Nor should one assume that the current rate has persisted in India for an extended length of time. It is, in fact, so exceptional that it has never before to our knowledge been equalled in India's history. Only since the end of the influenza epidemic in 1919 has the total number shown such a rapid or such a sustained increase. Up until that time the growth had been sporadic—sometimes negative, sometimes positive, but never so fast as recently.

ANCIENT HISTORY

A moment's reflection will show that the region's population could not have increased long at the present pace or even at a tenth of it. Being near the center of origin of Neolithic culture traits, India received these traits earlier, apparently, than did most of Europe. As a consequence India had, thousands of years ago, the basis for a thickly settled population. During the succeeding centuries, until say the 17th century, the growth in numbers must have been extremely slow, being surely imperceptible within a lifetime.

India's Neolithic technology—including agriculture, domesticated animals, polished stone tools, and pottery—apparently dates from perhaps 7,000 years ago. But sometime later two different civilized peoples were in India, each possessing not only the Neolithic arts but also metal implements. These two peoples were, on the one hand, the city-building settlers in the Indus valley, represented by finds at Harappa and Mohen-jo-daro, and on the other hand, the Aryan settlers in the Punjab and Ganges plain.

The Harappa and Mohen-jo-daro excavations reveal that "as far back as the 3rd or 4th millennium B.C. and probably much earlier still, India was in possession of a highly developed civilization with large and populous cities, well built houses, temples and public buildings of brick and many other amenities enjoyed at that period by the peoples of Mesopotamia and Egypt." Both sites contain the ruins of five or six cities superimposed one on top of another. The lower strata have hardly been investigated, but the upper levels disclose public and private buildings, mostly two stories high, built of well-burnt brick, and containing "gold and silver jewellery, some remarkable statuary in stone and copper, engraved seals of stone, ivory and paste, some of them exquisite specimens of glyptic art, copper implements and vessels, terracotta figurines and toys, shell ornaments, potteries, both painted and plain, and polished stone weights progressively ascending in a regular scale all denoting a well-developed artistic sense and business-like habits." These finds "establish the existence in Sind and the Punjab during the 4th and 3rd millennia B.C. of a highly developed city life; and the presence, in many of the houses, of wells and bathrooms as well as an elaborate drainage system betoken a social condition of the citizens at least equal to that found in Sumer and superior to that prevailing in contemporary Babylonia and Egypt. The inhabitants of these cities lived largely no doubt by agriculture . . . the specimens of wheat found at Mohen-jo-daro and Harappa resemble the common variety grown in the Punjab today." They had numerous types of domesticated animals, including sheep, pigs, humped bulls, and elephants. "Besides gold and silver they used copper, tin, bronze and lead; they were familiar with the arts of spinning and weaving and with cultivation of cotton. . . . That they possessed a well-developed system of writing is evidenced by the discovery of over a thousand tablets engraved with well-executed animal devices and pictographic legends in an unknown script." [1]

The other source of advanced culture was the Aryans, who came into India from the northwest around 2000 B.C. They were an agricultural and pastoral people who understood the principles of irrigation and manuring and used the animal-drawn plow. They knew the use of the wheel, employing chariots for fighting and racing and carts for hauling. They used metal, probably copper, and understood spinning and weaving. They exhibited a marked division of labor, differentiating wood workers, metal workers, leather workers, weavers, soldiers, priests, and slaves. After arriving in India they made additional acquisitions, the most important of which was alphabetic writing borrowed from Semitic sources about 800 B.C. and iron, acquired even earlier. [2]

So in India some three to seven thousand years ago there were peoples possessing a technology sufficiently advanced to support a dense population; and they encountered in the soil

---

[1] *The Indian Year Book*, 1944–45 (Bombay and Calcutta: Bennett, Coleman), pp. 19–20. See also Sri Ramakrishna Centenary Committee, *The Cultural Heritage of India*, Vol. 3 (Calcutta: Swami Avinashananda), pp. 1–86.

[2] *The Cambridge History of India* (Cambridge: Cambridge University Press, 1922), Vol. 1, *Ancient India*, pp. 56, 67–68, 99–104, 140–41.

and climate of India favorable conditions for the application of this technology.

Contemporary accounts of the later but still ancient historical periods bear out the belief that the country was well peopled in a remote age. Whereas the earliest literature, the Rigveda, makes it "clear that population was scanty and spread over wide areas" in small villages,[3] the Brahmana literature, around 800–600 B.C., reveals that some of the villages had grown into towns and capitals with an urban mode of life. The caste system was crystallizing and the division of labor growing more complex. Rice as well as other new plants were being cultivated. "The plough was large and heavy: we hear of as many as twenty-four oxen being harnessed to one: it had a sharp point and a smoothed handle." [4]

The Buddhistic literature indicates that between the 7th and 4th centuries B.C. the economy of northern India was comparable to that of the later middle ages in Europe. Crafts and commerce were flourishing, and were highly organized. Money and credit were everyday instruments. The ordinary town seemed to embrace anywhere from 30 to 1,000 families, and approximately 20 cities existed in northern India alone. One tribal area, that of the Sakiyans is supposed to have contained half a million people. Sea commerce extended to places as far away as Babylon.[5]

This impression of a numerous population was confirmed by Alexander's army which invaded India in 327–26 B.C. One small kingdom was said to have 37 towns of over 5,000 inhabitants.[6] Later, India's first real empire under the sway of Chandragupta (c. 321–297 B.C.) left records indicating a standing army of approximately 700,000 men, the maintenance of which must have required a substantial population.[7] Under Açoka (c. 274–236 B.C.) this empire achieved one of the highest points of Indian civilization, based on efficient administration, the use of written commands, abundant commerce, intensive agriculture, and the use of metals.

These were the conditions in northern India. There were still parts of India, as there are even today, that were in the hands of wild tribes. But contemporaneous with or only a little later than the Aryan culture of the Ganges and the Mohen-jo-daro culture of the Indus there were almost equally advanced civilizations in the south. So putting the evidence from archeology, literature, and history together, we reach the conclusion that before the Christian era India had a substantial population, first because of its advanced technology and second because of the fertile environment for the application of this technology. Though great sections remained sparsely settled, some of the plains must have had a dense population. This view is confirmed by Pran Nath, who after careful examination of the evidence believes that the population of ancient India, say around 300 B.C., was between 100 and 140 million.[8]

During the two thousand years that intervened between the ancient and the modern period India's population could not have grown rapidly. It must have remained virtually stationary. The usual course was surely a gradual growth for a short period followed by an abrupt decline. The population would tend to grow slightly in "normal" times, because the customs governing fertility would provide a birth rate slightly higher than the usual death rate. This would build up a population surplus as a sort of demographic insurance against catastrophe. Inevitably, however, the catastrophe would come in the form of warfare, famine, or epidemic, and the increase of population would suddenly be wiped out. Thus while there would be short-run periods of population growth and decline, the long-run trend would be one of virtual fixity of numbers. No real change could have occurred in this condition until the coming of European control, and then only slowly.

One indication of how slowly the population grew is the fact that the careful estimate of the total number in 1600 made by the historian Moreland, gave India only 100 million.[9] If Moreland and Nath are both right, the population declined rather than increased during the two thousand years in question. In any case, independently of the precise accuracy of the estimates, it seems clear that the number of people was virtually stationary. Dr. Nath, who has examined later as well as earlier documents, believes "that the population of the country as a whole did not greatly vary between the early Hindu period and the first advent of the Muhammadans, and it may be supposed to have lain roughly between the above limits [100 to 140 million]." [10]

1600 to 1870

In making his estimate for 1600, Moreland cites contemporary accounts to show that in the 15th and 16th centuries Europeans were impressed, both on the plains and in the Deccan, by the density of settlement in India. In fact, some of the visitors definitely considered the country overpopulated at the time. Their accounts indicate that India had cities of a quarter to half a million in size. For a numerical basis of calculation Moreland relies, in the south, on the strength of the armed forces and in the north, on the land under cultivation, on both of which subjects contemporary figures are available. Assuming a ratio of 30 people to one fighting man (a ratio like that of France and Germany in 1914), he estimates that the southern part of India had about 30 million people. From Akbar's records of land under cultivation, together with contemporary accounts of densely and sparsely settled areas, he concludes that the middle Ganges and the Punjab had close to 40 million. Adding other thickly settled areas, such as Bengal and Gujarat, and the thinly occupied areas not included in the contemporary empires, he concludes that the total population was around 100 million.

If this estimate errs at all, it probably errs on the low side. In the first place, the ratio of population to armed men in Europe in 1914 is not a safe gauge for India in 1600; the Indian ratio was probably greater. In the second place, the population attributed to other parts of India than those for which direct information was obtainable seems too small. Gujarat, Assam, and Bengal, for example, contained well over a fifth of the whole population of India in 1911 (after the partition of Bengal). If they had represented this proportion in 1600, and if the total population had then been only 100 million, they would have had 20 million, and this with the 70 million estimated for the two empires would have left only 10 million for the more thinly settled parts not yet mentioned; and this seems too small a number. A better estimate for India at this time would perhaps be 125 million.

[3] ibid., p. 90.

[4] ibid., pp. 118, 130, 135–37.

[5] ibid., pp. 175–76, 200–01, 212, 219.

[6] ibid., p. 369. See also Chapter 15.

[7] ibid., p. 223.

[8] A Study in the Economic Condition of Ancient India (London: Royal Asiatic Society, 1929), Chapter 5.

[9] W. H. Moreland, India at the Death of Akbar (London: Macmillan, 1920), pp. 9–22.

[10] Nath, op. cit., p. 122.

Europe including Russia is estimated to have had 100 million inhabitants in 1650.[11] Since the area of Europe is larger than that of India, which had at least this many people in 1600, India's density in that century was evidently greater than in Europe. Such a conclusion would fit what has been said about the long history of thick settlement in India. Not until after 1800, apparently, did Europe including European Russia pull ahead of India (Fig. 3); and for many centuries

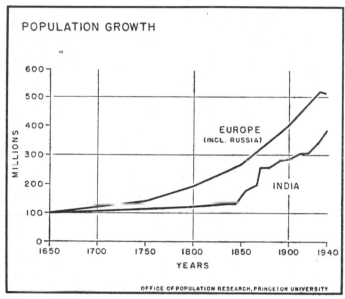

POPULATION GROWTH

FIGURE 3. Growth of Indian Population According to Estimates and Adjusted Census Figures, and Growth of European Population, 1650–1940.

before this date India had probably been the more densely inhabited of the two.

But since 1600 Europe has had a more rapid growth than India, mainly because of the industrial revolution that it initiated. If the early estimates were right, the difference of growth is not so great as we might expect. Europe's 1947 population (with European Russia) was approximately 560 million, that of India 420 million. Assuming each had 100 million in 1600, this would mean that during the intervening 350 years India's population grew about three-fourths as fast as Europe's. This, however, seems hard to believe. The centuries in question saw Europe move through the industrial revolution and complete the transition from a wasteful demographic balance based on high birth and death rates to a modern one based on low birth and death rates. Such a transition was accompanied by an enormous growth of population. India, on the contrary, went through no such cycle. She is today merely in the initial stages of it, and her population has not yet reached its peak of potential growth. How then has she managed to keep so near Europe in her population increase? One answer is that she has lost less by emigration. Another is that her apparent growth is partly illusory, because the estimate of her 1600 population is too low, that for Europe perhaps too high. If we give India 125 million and Europe 95 million in 1600 (not improbable figures), Europe then has, from 1600 to 1940, an over-all increase nearly double that of India. This two-to-one ratio seems far more plausible than the four-to-three possibility.

[11] A. M. Carr-Saunders, *World Population* (Oxford: Clarendon, 1936), pp. 29–32.

The first effect of European control in India was to lessen warfare and banditry, and later to reduce famine and disease. Without this outside stimulus it is doubtful if India's condition would have changed for several centuries. Her rigid social system was not conducive to change. Like most other parts of the world she was not apt to start an industrial revolution by herself. The Europeans, in bringing parts of an advanced industrial and political regime to India, laid the basis for demographic effects at least partially similar to those that have occurred in the West.

Even so, it took awhile for European influence to make itself apparent in the population trend. The increase in numbers continued to be slow, though gradually accelerating. Unfortunately, our knowledge of the trend comes mainly from the Indian censuses, and these cover only the latter part of the British regime. For a full century of British rule (from 1767 when Clive departed to 1871 when the first general census occurred) there is nothing to go on except estimates. These estimates, alas, have the double disadvantage of being not only deficient but also unequally deficient. The earlier they are the poorer they are.

Table 6 gives a list of estimates made during the first two-thirds of the 19th century. It also gives, for comparison, the two earlier estimates and the corrected 1871 census figure.

TABLE 6

Estimates of India's Population, 300 B.C. to 1871 A.D.

Date	Millions	Average Annual Per Cent Growth During Preceding Period
300 B.C.	100–140 [1]	- - -
1600 A.D.	100 [2]	- - -
1800	120 [3]	0.09
1834	130 [4]	0.24
1845	130 [5]	- - -
1855	175 [6]	2.97
1867	194 [7]	0.86
1871	255 [8]	6.84

[1] Pran Nath, *A Study in the Economic Condition of Ancient India* (London: Royal Asiatic Society, 1929), Chapter 5.

[2] W. H. Moreland, *India at the Death of Akbar* (London: Macmillan, 1920), pp. 9–22.

[3] Wm. Playfair, *The Statistical Breviary* (London: J. Wallis et al., 1801), p. 58. The figure of 120 million is not the one given by Playfair. He gives 41 million for what he calls the total British Interests in India. The area he gives for this territory, however, is less than a third the area of India today, so for our purposes his estimate has been roughly tripled. This is not entirely justified, because the British held the more populous areas, but since Playfair's population figure is obviously too low there is some reason to raise it in the manner followed.

[4] J. R. M'Culloch, *A Dictionary, Practical, Theoretical and Historical of Commerce and Commercial Navigation,* Vol. 1 (2nd ed., London: Longman, Rees, et al., 1834), pp. 546–47.

[5] *ibid.,* American Edition, 1835, Vol 1, pp. 1108–09.

[6] Great Britain, *Statistical Abstract for the Several Colonial and Other Possessions of the United Kingdom,* 1854–1868, Sessional Papers, Cmd. 146, Sixth Number (London: Her Majesty's Stationery Office, 1870), p. 5. Only an estimate—124 million—for British India is given, but by assuming that non-British India then constituted 29 per cent of the all-India population (somewhat above the present 24 per cent), we arrive at the figure given.

[7] Great Britain, Parliamentary Papers, *Statistical Tables Relating to the Colonial and Other Possessions of the United Kingdom,* Part 13, 1867 (London: Her Majesty's Stationery Office, 1869), p. 1.

[8] This is the 1871-72 census figure corrected for territory omitted and for defective methods. See Table 7 and Appendix A.

Two things stand out in the table: first, the sharp fluctuation of the growth rates indicates that the estimates vary unpredictably; second, the growth from 1845 to 1871 was incredibly rapid. If, for example, the estimate for 1845 is accepted, the increase by 1871 amounted to almost 100 per cent, or about 35 per cent per decade, a rate of growth never even half reached during the subsequent period of more accurate knowledge. If such rapid growth had occurred from 1845 to 1871, we should be at a loss to explain the extremely slow growth before that date. Even more questionable is the great jump between 1867 and 1871, when in only four years, if the estimate is to be believed, the population grew 31 per cent, or 61 million!

The conclusion inevitably emerges that, prior to the censuses, people guessed the population of India to be much less than it really was. There is an almost universal tendency on the part of Europeans, who are highly urbanized, to underestimate the population of peasant regions. The less they know about the region the greater the error. India affords a clear illustration.[12] As time went by and the Europeans became better acquainted with the territory they were administering, the estimates improved. As the time of the census approached they were increasingly based on detailed district reports. Such improvement, commendable in itself, conveys a false impression of rapid growth. Yet despite the steady improvement, we find that even as late as 1867, when a few provinces had already taken censuses, the all-India estimate was apparently far too low; for if the corrected census figure for 1871 is roughly correct, the 1867 estimate was too small by about 55 million!

Obviously there is little use trying to puzzle out India's growth rate prior to the census period. The estimates will lead us to a false notion of stagnation between 1600 and 1845, and to an equally false notion of rapid growth between 1845 and 1871. The best policy seems to be to revise Moreland's figure for 1600 upward to 125 million, and to assume that the population remained at this point for one and a half centuries more, after which a gradual enhancement of growth began, accelerating as 1870 approached. This trend would seem to fit the history of the period, and consequently, though frankly speculative, it has been incorporated in Fig. 3, which also includes the corrected census figures to be discussed in the next section.

1871 to 1941

After 1870, because of the censuses, our knowledge of India's population growth rests on surer ground. Yet the actual census figures cannot be taken at face value. They exaggerate the increase for two reasons: first, additional territory was covered by each new census; second, improvements in enumeration were made each time up through 1901.

For example, the census of 1871–72, which gave a total of 203 million, omitted territories which, in 1881, totaled some 33 million.[13] It omitted the native states entirely, and it omitted the provinces of Oude, Berar, and the Punjab because these had taken censuses only a few years before.[14] In addition, because of poor methods and adverse conditions, it failed to count an estimated 12 million even in the area covered.[15] Nevertheless on the basis of this census and those taken in particular provinces in the 1860's, together with estimates, the population of India proper in 1871–72 was announced as 236 million, considerably more than the 203 million actually enumerated.[16] The total figure (236 million) was obviously below reality, because for Oude, Berar, and the Punjab the census figures of earlier dates were utilized without change, and because for some of the native states the pure estimates were far too low. Yet, just because the bulk of the country had for the first time been actually enumerated, this all-India total based on the census plus estimates for uncovered territory was far above the guesses made only a few years previously, and it presumably came somewhere near the truth.[17]

If we are to get a truer picture of the population in 1871–72, the first census must be corrected on the basis of the 1881 census, which is more reliable than the estimates for uncovered territory made at the earlier date. The problem does not end there, however, for in 1891 the territory covered was still greater and the techniques used were still better than in 1881. On the basis of the 1891 census, then, the 1881 census must be corrected, and if it is corrected, the original census (1871–72) must be corrected a second time. In this way one must add corrections to each census on the basis of all subsequent censuses up through 1931.

This process of correction we have carried through, and the results are given in Table 7, the method described in Appendix A.[18] Although the figures are not to be taken as literal fact, they must come near to describing the actual population of India since 1870.

On the basis of these corrected figures it can be stated with some confidence that from 1871 to 1941 the average rate of increase of India's population was approximately 0.60 per cent per year. This was slightly less than the estimated rate

---

[12] A recent example of the confusion to which these estimates lead is found in S. Chandrasekhar, *India's Population* (New York: John Day, 1946), p. 14. At first glance his list of population figures at successive dates looks reasonable, but a closer examination shows that it is misleading. The author claims, for instance, that he himself made an estimate of 164 million for 1861. He does not tell us how he made it, but the figure is 42 million less than his amount for all of India just eleven years later. This would mean a 26 per cent increase in India's population in one decade, an improbable jump. Yet his estimate seems plausible when related to previous guesses, and this is doubtless what confused him.

[13] *Census of India,* 1931, Vol. 1, Part 1, p. 5.

[14] Oude in 1869, Berar in 1867, the Punjab in 1855 and 1868. In presenting the data on the population for 1871–72, the authorities incorporated these provincial censuses. This fact means that the census period really extends over five or six years, from 1867 to 1872, instead of over two years. In general we shall refer to the results as applying to 1871, this being what would appear to be the modal year.

[15] Great Britain, *Memorandum on the Census of British India of 1871–72,* Sessional Papers, Cmd. 1349 (London: Her Majesty's Stationery Office, 1875), pp. 5, 45, 47; *General Report of the Census of India,* 1901, Sessional Papers, Cmd. 2047 (London: His Majesty's Stationery Office, 1904), p. 45.

[16] Great Britain, *Memorandum on the Census of British India of 1871–72, op. cit.,* p. 5.

[17] To illustrate the superiority of a census we may take the case of Bengal. Prior to the census "no one knew exactly the population of a single . . . District of Bengal. . . . The Census of 1872 suddenly disclosed the presence of 22 millions of British subjects whose existence had never previously been suspected. The population of Bengal and Assam, up to that time reckoned at 40 millions, was ascertained to number 67¾ millions of souls." Sir W. W. Hunter (ed.), *The Imperial Gazetteer of India,* Vol. 1 (London: Trübner, 1881), p. xx.

[18] The report of the census of 1901 states that the 1871–72 count actually yielded a total of 206 million in those parts of India and British Burma that were covered. *Loc. cit.* (Cmd. 2047), p. 45. This figure is repeated in the report for 1921 (Vol. 1, Part 1, p. 7) and is used in all official calculations of population growth in India. Without Burma it comes to 203 million. It is the figure we use as a base for our calculation of population growth.

TABLE 7

Census Returns and Estimated Populations, 1872–1941 [a]

Year	Census Population [1] (000's)	Estimated Population [2] (000's)
1871 [b]	203,415	255,166
1881	250,160	257,380
1891	279,593	282,134
1901	283,870	285,288
1911	303,041	302,985
1921	305,730	305,679
1931	338,171	c
1941	388,998	c

[a] Burma is of course omitted throughout.

[b] The first census of India was not synchronous, but was gathered between 1867 and 1872. We have chosen to treat it as if it represented 1871. Since the growth rate during these years was very slight, the error is small no matter which date is adopted as the date of the census.

[c] The censuses of 1931 and 1941 were accepted as representing the population of India. Hence no estimates for these years were required. Doubtless there is underenumeration in India, so that all figures are lower than they should be; but further correction would be hazardous and would not significantly change the trend.

[1] *Census of India*, 1931, Vol. 1, Part 1, p. 5; Vol. 11 (Burma), Part 2, p. 6; 1921, Vol. 1, Part 2, p. 6.

[2] Made by adjusting the territory of all censuses to that of 1931 and 1941, and by allowing for underenumeration officially said to have occurred in the first three censuses.

for the whole world (0.69) from 1850 to 1940.[19] India's modern growth, therefore, is not exceptional either way, but close to average. It is, however, less than that found in Europe, in North America, and in a good many particular countries. Figure 4 compares the absolute and relative increase with that in the United States, demonstrating the much faster growth in America. Figure 5 compares various countries with India. The total Indian increase during 1871–1941 was 52 per cent. The British Isles during the same period increased 57 per cent, and during the 70-year period from 1821 to 1891 (more comparable to India's recent history) they increased 79 per cent. Similarly Japan, during the 70 years from 1870 to 1940, experienced a growth of approximately 120 per cent, and the United States a growth of 230 per cent.

Clearly, India's past increase has not been rapid when compared with that of countries farther along in the industrial revolution. The popular notion that it has been faster than in most modern countries—a notion derived from the massiveness, density, and poverty of the population—is obviously unwarranted.[20] Nevertheless, the 52 per cent increase in 70 years is abnormal when compared with the growth in India or in any other country prior to the 18th century. During the last three centuries the population of the whole world has been growing at a phenomenally fast rate, the fastest ever known. India's increase is simply part of this world movement. The social explosion that started the global wave of growth

[19] Kingsley Davis, "The World Demographic Transition," *Annals of the American Academy of Political and Social Science*, Vol. 237 (January, 1945), p. 3.

[20] The same popular notion on the part of Westerners seems to attach to every dense Oriental population. "With few exceptions, recent writers have asserted that the rate of increase of the Japanese population has been and is exceptionally high. . . . None the less, it is an illusion, and there is nothing in vital statistics to support it." E. F. Penrose, *Population Theories and Their Application* (Stanford University: Food Research Institute, 1934), p. 98.

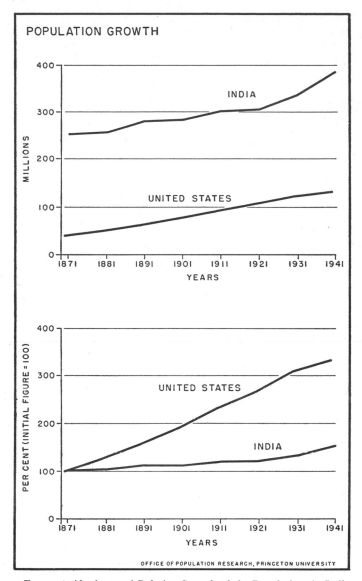

FIGURE 4. Absolute and Relative Growth of the Populations in India and the United States, 1870–1941. (In the lower chart the population is expressed as an index. 1870–1871 = 100)

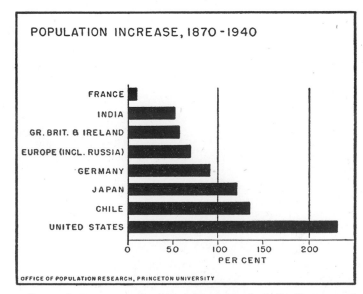

FIGURE 5. Percentage Growth of Population in India, Europe, and Selected Countries, 1870–1940.

was surely the industrial revolution, as shown by the fact that the growth spread around the earth as industry and commerce spread. Some countries, such as those of Northwestern Europe or of new areas settled by Northwestern Europeans, have virtually completed the cycle. Their populations are approaching a stationary state again. Other areas, such as parts of Africa, have hardly yet entered the cycle. India appears to be in the early stages, with plenty of potential growth ahead.[21]

Another feature of India's population growth since 1870 has been its extremely sporadic nature. This can be seen by examining the increase in each decade, as follows (see also Fig. 6):

	Per Cent Increase During Previous Decade [22]
1881	.9
1891	9.4
1901	1.0
1911	6.1
1921	.9
1931	10.6
1941	15.0

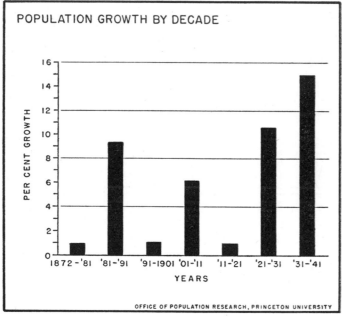

FIGURE 6. Percentage Growth of Indian Population in Each Decade, 1871–1941.

These figures show that for a long time, decades of marked increase have regularly alternated with decades of slight increase. The greater part of the census period thus conforms to the pattern of sporadic growth believed to have existed in earlier times—with one difference, namely that in place of

[21] Davis, "The World Demographic Transition," *op. cit.*, pp. 1–11. Frank W. Notestein, "Population—The Long View," *Food for the World*, edited by Theodore W. Schultz (Chicago: University of Chicago Press, 1945), pp. 36–57.

[22] These percentages are obtained after the census at the end of the decade has been adjusted to that at the beginning of the decade by correcting for changes of territory or method. The correction factors are taken from *Census of India,* 1921, Vol. 1, Part 1, p. 7; and 1931, Vol. 1, Part 1, p. 5. The calculation is less open to error than the estimate of the actual all-India population at each census date, as described above.

periods that now show a slight increase, there were periods showing actual declines, so that the net effect was previously one of long-range fixity rather than growth of numbers. Also, war as a deterrent factor has dropped out of the picture, leaving only famine and disease. In the decades of negligible growth, the trouble lay in one or the other of these catastrophes. During the 1871–81 period there occurred the great Indian famine of 1876–78; during the 1891–1901 decade, another famine; and during the 1911–21 decennium, the great influenza epidemic of 1918. We know that these calamities were largely responsible for the lack of growth in the decades when they occur, because the provinces and states most affected by them were precisely those that showed the lowest growth rates. During the other decades, called "normal" by the Indians, no widespread catastrophes occurred and the population grew rapidly.

Something appears to have happened after 1920, however, for the alternating process stopped. From 1921 to 1931 the increase, almost 11 per cent, was the highest on record for India, and during the following decade, 1931–41, the record was broken again by a 15 per cent growth.[23] The twenty-year period from 1921 to 1941 was thus "extremely normal." It was the first time in India's known history that she experienced rapid growth during two successive decades. At a time when the Western nations were approaching demographic stability, India with its much larger population was just starting what appears to be a period of rapid and gigantic expansion.

To be sure, the *rate* of growth since 1921 (1.2 per cent per year) has not been phenomenal for modern times. The United States population increased 16 per cent during the decade 1920–30, a rate never yet equalled in India. But because of the massiveness of India's existing population, even a moderate percentage increase means a huge absolute increment. The modest 1.2 per cent annual increase during the two decades from 1921 to 1941 added no less than 83 million inhabitants to India's teeming masses—more people than all of Germany contains and nearly two-thirds the population of the United States. Even if Great Britain, Germany, and the United States resumed regularly higher rates of growth than India (which none is likely to do again), it would take them centuries to overtake her population. What is important about India's recently accelerated growth is not simply the rate, but the huge absolute increments to which it gives rise and the promise of even greater increments in the future.

How long can the region keep up this demographic pace? Can it actually double its 1947 population in 58 years, thus harboring in the year 2005 something like 840 million human beings, more than a third of the world's present population? If so, how will she support them? If not, what is going to stop the present trend?

These and other questions call for an answer. They cannot be answered, however, without further analysis of the factors responsible for India's population growth up to now. Our discussion in the present chapter has described rather than explained the growth; now the causes must be analyzed in detail. Demographically speaking the increase of population in India, as in any other country, has been determined by only

[23] The political and economic disturbances of 1931 may have led to more underenumeration than usual in the census of that year. If so, the growth rate during 1921–31 would be greater, that during 1931–41 lesser than stated; but the increase from 1921 to 1941 would remain the same. It is therefore better, in speaking of recent growth, to use the whole twenty-year period than either of the component decades.

three factors—fertility, mortality, and migration. Since migration has not been numerically important as a factor affecting growth in India (although important in other ways), the problem really comes down to fertility and mortality. All other factors, whether biological or sociological, must take effect through these. In attempting to explain India's past growth, therefore, the first step is to ascertain the relative responsibility of these two variables and to analyze the conditions affecting them. This is the task to which we now turn.

PART II

THE FIGHT AGAINST DEATH

+++

Evidence of the Declining Death Rate

+++

THROUGHOUT its history the lulls and spurts in India's population growth have been governed not by fluctuations in the birth rate but by wide variations in the death rate. In those years when the population remained fixed or even declined, the reason lay in some great catastrophe—a famine, an epidemic, a war, or a combination of these—which took millions of lives. In the so-called normal years when numbers increased, the reason lay in the relative absence of such catastrophes. In such ordinary years the death rate was still high, as a result of poor diet and endemic disease, but since it was surpassed by an even higher birth rate, the population grew moderately. Coming every few years, however, a calamity of one sort or another would suddenly increase the death rate and wipe out the population increment that had been accumulating. During the period for which we have statistics there have been, as we have seen, three decades during which the population hardly grew at all. The first two of these are explained by two great famines, the first occurring in 1876–78 and the second in 1898–1900. The third such decade is explained by the influenza epidemic of 1918, which according to our estimate killed more than 15 million people. In this disastrous year the official returns showed a death rate of 63 per thousand, whereas the rate was only 33 the year before and 36 the year after this date. Since the birth rate shows no sharp fluctuations, and since emigration is a negligible quantity, it seems plain that the factor chiefly responsible for population changes in the region has been mortality. An analysis of forces affecting mortality is therefore valuable not only for understanding the health and longevity of the people but also for understanding the past and future population trends.

Unhappily, despite its central importance, the actual death rate is unknown, because the system of registration is grossly deficient. There are, however, five lines of statistical evidence that throw some light on trends in mortality. These are (1) the registered deaths which, though defective, may nevertheless reveal trends; (2) the registered infant mortality; (3) the expectation of life in successive life tables; (4) the proportion of widows among females aged 40 and over; and (5) the estimated deaths on the basis of births less population growth. Each of these lines of evidence is open to criticism, and each one, if it stood alone or disagreed with the others, would be of little value. But the interesting thing is that they are based on different kinds of data [1] and yet all roughly agree and point unanimously to one conclusion, namely, that mortality in the Indian area has been declining, especially since 1920—a reduction that has been responsible for the greatest

[1] The life tables are made by differencing the censuses, not by using vital statistics. Infant mortality relates deaths to births rather than to population.

spurt of growth ever experienced by the population. Let us examine each kind of evidence in turn.

OFFICIAL RETURNS

A glance at Table 8 and Fig. 7 will show that after 1918, the year of India's last great epidemic, the rate of reported

TABLE 8

Death Rates in British India, 1911–1948,
Based on Official Returns

Year	Annual Rate [1]	5-Year Average	10-Year Average
1911	32.3		
1912	29.8		
1913	28.8	30.2	
1914	30.2		
1915	29.9		
			34.3
1916	29.2		
1917	32.9		
1918	63.1	38.2	
1919	35.8		
1920	30.8		
1921	31.0		
1922	23.9		
1923	24.7	26.3	
1924	28.0		
1925	24.1		
			25.4
1926	25.8		
1927	23.7		
1928	24.1	24.6	
1929	24.2		
1930	24.9		
1931	25.3		
1932	21.8		
1933	22.5	23.6	
1934	25.0		
1935	23.6		
			23.0
1936	22.5		
1937	22.1		
1938	23.9	22.3	
1939	21.7		
1940	21.3		

TABLE 8 (*continued*)

Death Rates in British India, 1911–1948,
Based on Official Returns

Year	Annual Rate	5-Year Average	10-Year Average
1941	21.8		
1942	21.3		
1943	23.6	22.5	
1944	24.1		
1945	21.5		
1946	18.7		
1947	19.7		
1948	17.1		

[1] Except for years after 1940, the deaths are taken from *Statistical Abstract for British India*. The annual populations for the registration area were estimated by us, by the method described in Appendix D. The rates for years after 1940 were taken from the United Nations *Demographic Yearbook* (1948) for 1946 and 1947 and *Monthly Statistical Bulletin* for 1948. The rates for 1947–48 refer to the registration area of the Indian Union only (excl. states).

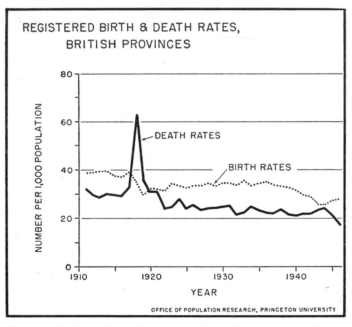

FIGURE 7. Birth and Death Rates in the British Provinces According to Registration Returns, 1911–1946.

deaths in the British provinces declined steadily. In 1921 it stood at 31 per thousand inhabitants, but after that time it was never above 30. The average rate during the 1911–20 decade was 34 per thousand (or 31 if the deaths for 1918 are removed), as contrasted to 25 during the next decade and 23 during the 1931–40 decade.

These rates are not nearly so high as they should be. The amount of underregistration certainly exceeds 30 per cent at all times, and is probably nearer 50 per cent.[2] Nevertheless, with this defect admitted, the rates are still much higher than

[2] The Population Committee for the Government of India recently found that the underregistration of deaths ranged from 35 per cent in some places to 55 per cent in others. It expressed the view that the average underregistration is probably near 50 per cent. When the ages of those dying are taken into account, the range of underregistration seems to run from 25 to 65 per cent. Department of Education, Health and Lands, *Report of the Population Data Committee* (Simla: Government of India Press, 1945), p. 6.

those of the West. They are, for example, more than twice the rates of England and Wales during the same decades. If all the Indian deaths were registered, the rates would doubtless be three or four times as high as the British rates.

In spite of their deficiency and their regrettable magnitude, the rates based on reported deaths reveal an unmistakable downward trend. The reality of this trend is vouchsafed by the fact that if any change in the accuracy of death registration has occurred in India, it has probably been in the direction of improvement. Certainly the earliest figures were more deficient than the later ones, and this doubtless explains why the reported deaths between 1911 and 1916 were comparatively low; the farther back of 1911 one goes, the poorer are the statistics, yet even so the death rate is surprisingly high. After 1918 the tendency to decline is clear to see, although one would expect, on the possibility that registration may have improved, a slight increase. The decline that appears is probably, therefore, a minimum quantity. The actual decrease in mortality has probably been greater.

INFANT MORTALITY

The officially reported infant mortality rates, as exhibited in Table 9, also reveal a high point in 1918 and a gradual

TABLE 9

Infant Mortality Rates: 1911–1945 [1]

Year	Annual Rate	5-Year Average
1911	205	
1912	208	
1913	195	204.2
1914	212	
1915	202	
1916	202	
1917	205	
1918	267	218.8
1919	224	
1920	195	
1921	198	
1922	175	
1923	176	174.3
1924	189	
1925	174	
1926	189	
1927	167	
1928	173	177.6
1929	178	
1930	181	
1931	179	
1932	169	
1933	171	174.0
1934	187	
1935	164	
1936	162	
1937	162	
1938	167	161.4
1939	156	
1940	160	

TABLE 9 (*continued*)

Infant Mortality Rates: 1911–1945 [1]

Year	Annual Rate	5-Year Average
1941	158	
1942	163	
1943	165	161
1944	169	
1945	151	

[1] Figures from 1911 to 1928 taken from *Census of India,* 1931, Vol. 1, Part 1, p. 92. Those from 1929 to 1945 were taken from the *Annual Reports* of the Public Health Commissioner.

decline thereafter. A comparison of these figures with those for general mortality reveals one surprising fact—namely, that the percentage decline in infant mortality has not been so great as that in general mortality. The fall in the infant rate has of course contributed a major share to the reduction in general mortality, simply because there are so many more infants and infant deaths in the population as compared to any other age, but the percentage decline has not been so great as for the rest of the population. If we take the years 1916, 1917, and 1920 as our base, we find that the average general mortality decreased 27.6 per cent by 1936–40, whereas infant mortality declined only 19.6 per cent. But despite its failure to drop quite as fast as general mortality, infant mortality has nevertheless been reduced substantially since 1918, according to the official returns.

Of course, the infant mortality rate is subject to peculiar sources of error even in countries having good statistics. It depends on the accuracy of both birth and death registration, each of which is known to be very defective in India. Any conclusions drawn from the official figures on this subject must be recognized as tentative and subject to wide margins of error. If postneonatal infant mortality were studied, it would doubtless show a greater percentage decline than that for all infant mortality, because neonatal mortality is known to be relatively unresponsive to changes in social conditions.

SUCCESSIVE LIFE TABLES

The construction of Indian life tables has been a hazardous undertaking. In the absence of accurate vital statistics, reliance has been placed on the method of differencing successive censuses. This method is quite shaky in a country where age reporting is extremely defective and underenumeration quite evident; but for our present purpose it has the advantage of furnishing independent evidence—independent, that is, of the vital statistics—with reference to the trend of mortality.

Altogether five official life tables have been made for India as a whole, beginning with the decade 1872–81 and ending with 1921–31. During the 70 years of census taking in India the officials have failed to make life tables for only two decades —1911–21 and 1931–41. We have, by methods described in the next chapter, constructed life tables for the two omitted decades. These two tables, together with the five official ones, give us seven life tables all told, covering the span from 1871 to 1941.

Unluckily, however, these life tables are not the guileless witnesses they at first appear to be, because some of the earlier actuaries who made them had in the back of their heads a

metaphysical concept called the "normal decade." They reasoned that if the decade had suffered a widespread famine or epidemic that decimated the population, the life table for that decade should be so adjusted as to ignore, or at least modify, the statistical effect of this catastrophe—on the assumption that widespread famines and epidemics were not "normal." But a life table is not obligated to show the "normal" mortality; it is merely supposed to show the actual mortality during the period in question, whatever the causes; and if adjustments are made with reference to cause—i.e. if deaths due to some causes are excluded—then this fact must be stated as an integral part of the life table, not covered by a term such as "normal." Furthermore, if we must think in terms of normality, there is every reason for regarding recurrent famines and epidemics as normal in India. A life table that ignores the effects of these catastrophes necessarily distorts the truth and gives us an idealized picture of Indian mortality.

In 1881 Sir George Hardy, who made the first three Indian life tables, did not simply difference the two censuses, because a severe famine occurred in 1876–78. Instead, he combined the 1871 and 1881 age distributions to get an average distribution, and deduced the mortality rates from this.[3] In 1891, finding that the decade had been relatively free from famine or epidemic, he was satisfied with simply comparing the 1881 and 1891 censuses. But in 1901, because of both starvation and plague, he combined the census figures of 1881, 1891, and 1901, giving double weight to the 1891 figures, and thus got an average age distribution from which the mortality rates could be deduced. In 1911, conditions having been good, Sir Hardy's successor merely differenced the 1901 and 1911 censuses; but in 1921 the recent influenza epidemic led to the abandonment of any idea of making a life table for the 1911–21 decade.[4] It appears, therefore, that *the life tables do not give a true picture of India's mortality trend, because some of them overlap in time and minimize by varying degrees the actual mortality.*[5] It does not follow, however, that absolutely no historical information can be gained from the tables. The knowledge that the earlier life tables understate the chance of death merely makes their results all the more extraordinary, because the mortality they reveal is exceedingly high—higher than in nearly any other country. They give Indians an expectancy of life at birth of between 23 and 25 years. How much shorter could the lives of the people actually have been? A table made by the writer for the decade 1911–21 shows a life expectancy of only 20 years. Probably this decade was no worse than some of the earlier ones. Since 1920 the life tables show a decline in the force of mortality, the expectancy rising to 27 in 1921–31 and to 32 in 1931–41. The following are the figures for all seven life tables, together with the average annual death rate that they imply: [6]

[3] G. F. Hardy, *Memorandum on the Age Tables and Rates of Mortality of the Indian Census of 1901* (Calcutta: Superintendent of Government Printing, 1905), p. 1.

[4] *Census of India,* 1931, Vol. 1, Part 1, p. 110.

[5] This conclusion will be further substantiated and explained in the next chapter on Indian life tables.

[6] The fifth and seventh tables were made by the writer. Possibly the 1911–21 table exaggerates the mortality during that decade, but there seems to be no reason why it should. The influenza epidemic had a powerful influence, and one may fairly say that the 1911–21 life table is the first one that tries to include *all* the mortality of a bad decade in India. The 1931–41 table is made on the basis of a sample only. Since there was perhaps some underenumeration in 1931 as compared with 1941, it may be that the last life table exaggerates the improvement in mortality. Chapter 8 discusses both of these tables in considerable detail.

	Life Expectancy at Birth	Implied Average Annual Death Rate
1871–1881	24.6	40.7
1881–1891	25.0	40.0
1891–1901	23.8	42.0
1901–1911	22.9	43.7
1911–1921	20.1	49.8
1921–1931	26.8	37.3
1931–1941	31.8	31.5

The average expectation of life in the first five tables is 23.3, and in the last two tables 29.3. This means that during the two decades after 1921 the expectation of life was 25 per cent higher than in the five decades prior to that date. The average annual death rate implied by these tables, which is simply the reciprocal of the life expectancy at birth, multiplied by 1,000, necessarily shows the same trend.[7] Thus the life tables, imperfect as they are, confirm what the death registration figures indicate, a noticeable decline in mortality in recent times.

THE PROPORTION OF WIDOWS

Still another indication of the declining mortality is the proportion of women aged 40 and over who are widowed. If the Indian custom of non-marriage of widows were strictly observed, this would be a good measure of long-run trends in mortality. Actually, however, there is considerable remarriage of widows, and the possibility that it may be increasing vitiates this datum as a reliable evidence of the mortality trend. Yet authorities agree that the taboo on widow marriage is not being broken down in India very fast. It is still the practice of lower castes, when they raise their standard of living, to attempt to enforce the rule as a mark of enhanced social prestige. For this reason the slight but steady decline in the proportion of women widowed over age 40, as follows, probably represents, at least in part, a real decline in mortality:

	Per Cent of Women 40 and Over Who Are Widowed
1891	61.1
1901	59.3
1911	59.6
1921	58.6
1931	58.3
1941	55.2

ESTIMATED DEATH RATES

There are various ways of estimating India's crude death rate. One of these is simply to take from the life tables the reciprocal of the life-expectancy at birth, as was done above. These figures show that India's death rate prior to 1921 was above 40 per thousand, or in other words some four times the recent rate in the United States. A second technique of estima-

[7] It may be objected that the life table death rate does not represent the actual crude death rate in India, because the former is based on a life table population which has a different age distribution from that of the actual population. Actually, for the 1921–31 life table, the death rate of each specific age group was computed, and the resulting rate was then applied to the age groups in the actual population of 1931. The resulting crude death rate was almost identical with the life table death rate—37.4 as against 37.3.

tion depends upon a knowledge of births. If the births occurring between two censuses are known, their number minus the increase of the population (assuming no migration) should equal the number of deaths during the period. Of course we do not know the number of births in India, but we can estimate it with reasonable accuracy by moving back from the children aged 0–9 in the census to the births that must have occurred during the previous ten years to give rise to these survivors at the census.[8] With the estimated births in hand, we find it possible to estimate the number of deaths. Here are the results in terms of average rates per decade:

	Average Annual Death Rate
1881–1891	41.3
1891–1901	44.4
1901–1911	42.6
1911–1921	48.6
1921–1931	36.3
1931–1941	31.2

This is the best method of estimating deaths that we have, but it is far from perfect.[9] The earlier figures probably fall short of reality by a greater amount than the later ones, and consequently no significance should be attached to changes during the first four decades. What stands out as beyond question is the fact that before 1920 India had a death rate somewhere between 40 and 50 per 1,000, and that after that it underwent a remarkable decline. The average death rate apparently fell 25 per cent between 1911–20 and 1921–30, and 14 per cent between 1921–30 and 1931–40.

The decade averages of course exaggerate the steadiness of the decline. The fall in mortality has not been steady, as the previously mentioned registration figures show. The fact remains, however, that there has apparently been a sharper and steadier decline since 1920 than at any previous time, although there is ground for believing that a slight secular decline had been going on long before that.

It is possible to estimate the death rate not only for the decade, but also for each year, and thus to observe the short run fluctuations. One simply takes the decade average rates given above, compares these in each case with the decennial average obtained from the registered deaths, and gets a correction factor that can be applied throughout to the yearly rates derived from official returns. In other words, one assumes that each year during the decade the official statistics were deficient to the same degree as they were for the decade taken as a whole. The resulting annual estimates are depicted in Fig. 8. The estimated birth rates are also given in this chart, so that the reader can see the relationship between birth and death rates and understand its effect on population growth

[8] The technique of estimating births is more fully described in Appendix E.

[9] The procedure is defective for various reasons. To begin with, it requires, as mentioned, a means of estimating births. The latter, described and evaluated in Chapter 9 and Appendices E and F, underestimates rather than exaggerates the number of births. In addition, the intercensal increase is probably higher in most decades than is actually the case, because later censuses tend to be more complete than earlier ones. When, therefore, an exaggerated intercensal increase is subtracted from an underestimated number of births, the resulting estimate of deaths is too small. Such defects are especially great in the earlier decades, and this is why an upward trend occurs in the death rate between 1881 and 1921. If anything the course of mortality was either level or downward.

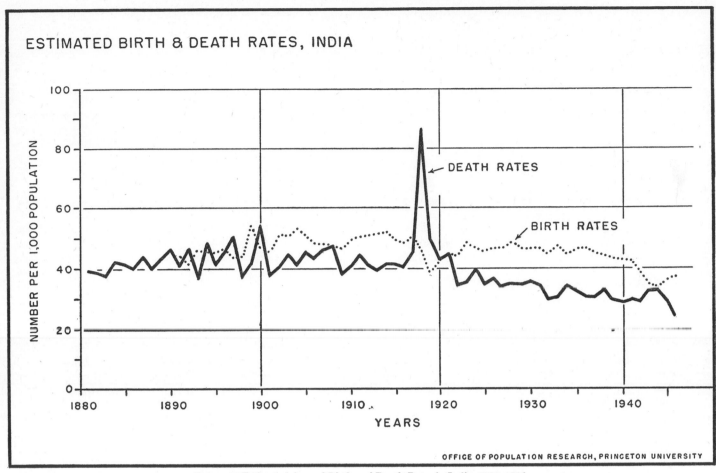

FIGURE 8. Estimated Annual Birth and Death Rates in India, 1881–1946.

in India. One can see that it is the marked decline in mortality, plus the maintenance of a high birth rate, that has caused the gigantic upswing in population since 1920. In view of this evidence it is surprising that some writers profess to see no decline in mortality during the period of British control. The fact would seem to be that the acceleration of population growth in modern times has been due almost solely to improvements in mortality.

++

CHAPTER 6

Causes of the Declining Death Rate

++

THE causes of the decline in Indian mortality are harder to establish than the fact itself. One reason is that an adequate explanation embraces not one but several levels of analysis—medical, economic, political, sociological. Another reason is that the causal factors are even more poorly measured than mortality itself, so that we are forced to explain the obscure by the still more obscure. Nevertheless, it is possible to discern the major outlines of at least three great gains in the fight against death. The first of these was the reduction of war and banditry under British rule. The second was the control of famines. And the third was the control of epidemic disease. These gains were all slow, hard, and lengthy, and they are not yet complete. Also, they did not come in a neat 1-2-3 series, but were being achieved simultaneously; the order in which we have enumerated them is merely the order in which their major results began to be apparent. There is, of course, an inherent reason why they should occur in the order named, since the later victories presuppose the earlier ones.

ELIMINATION OF WAR AND BANDITRY

In a way the effect of the lessening of war and banditry on improved mortality is purely hypothetical. The poor state of the early population estimates makes it impossible to prove any effect. Yet every form of indirect evidence points to the conclusion that the death rate must inevitably have improved when political peace and public security finally came to this land of internecine war, governmental inefficiency, rapacious taxation, and hereditary banditry under the later Mogul rulers. We know that chronic warfare and popular brigandage in other countries is a cause of high mortality. Thus in a penetrating work on China, Walter H. Mallory devotes a chapter to what he calls "Political Causes of Famine." [1] His observations, based on firsthand experience, indicate that warlordism, chronic warfare, and widespread robbery make it impossible to store surplus foodstuffs against times of need, to use public funds for medical relief, to rely on transportation for stricken areas, to save a surplus against the demands of a numerous soldiery, to evade the exaction of confiscatory taxes, or to achieve security of life and property. His description of China in the present century sounds much like the description of India in the eighteenth century.

The eighteenth century in India was a period of bloody rivalry between competing warlords, each having a corrupt and autocratic administration that had, of necessity, to milk the people of their sustenance. "The economic life of the country was dominated by the prevailing insecurity, for war might break out almost anywhere, while bands of robbers made the roads unsafe, and harried the villages at their pleasure." The standard assessment on peasants was near one-half of the produce, "but in practice the amount claimed was decided by no standard other than ability to pay under the severest pressure; and when one collector had done his worst, the officers of some rival claimant might come to glean whatever had been overlooked. To possess visible or tangible wealth was merely to invite stronger men to take it by force." [2] The fierce Marathas, revolting against alien domination, raided and fought from the west to the east coast. All told, this was not a condition of life in which natural disasters could be provided against and in which crises could be successfully met. It was not a condition in which mortality was likely to be low. The gradual emergence of a new order must have been the first step in lowering mortality and thus providing a new phase of population growth. During the nineteenth century when the effects of peace and order were being felt, there was a general impression that India's population was growing fairly rapidly—a fact which was apparently not true in previous centuries. The new regime must have won a slight victory, an initial skirmish, over the extraordinarily strong mortality, and thus inaugurated a new phase of population growth in India.

THE CONTROL OF FAMINE

Writers on India have customarily pointed out that the famines of this region are rooted in its geography. Because of the natural features described in Chapter 2, the rainfall of the subcontinent is highly seasonal and is scanty over large areas. Worst of all, however, it is also quite variable from year to year, and this irregularity, striking large areas that normally lack surplus rainfall, brings severe droughts. Sometimes an extra large rainfall brings floods that are as damaging to crops as a drought. The uncertainty of the monsoon has therefore been characterized as "the biggest single factor influencing life in India." [3] In some years, over either a small or a great portion of India, the rains almost completely fail to appear. Sometimes they are late in beginning; sometimes they stop abruptly; and sometimes they come in such concentrated outpourings that mighty floods result. Not only agriculture but also trade and commerce are affected by the monsoons. "The framing of the Annual Budget of the Government of India has been described by several Finance members

[1] *China: Land of Famine* (New York: American Geographical Society, 1928), Chap. 3.

[2] W. H. Moreland and Atul Chandra Chatterjee, *A Short History of India* (New York: Longmans, 1936), pp. 280–82. See also pp. 336–37.

[3] L. Dudley Stamp, *Asia, an Economic and Regional Geography* (2nd ed.; New York: Dutton, 1938), p. 199.

as a 'gamble in rain.' " [4] It is easy to see, therefore, that from a geographical point of view the stage is set for frequent famine, resulting from unexpected droughts and floods.

But the tangibility of geographic facts should not mislead us into exaggerating their importance. The irregularity of rainfall is a factor in the occurrence of famines in Pakistan and the Indian Union, but it is not "the cause." Certain other conditions must also prevail if a famine is to occur. What are some of these other conditions?

First, the region has always been predominantly agricultural, which means that rainfall is directly connected with the main source of wealth. Second, the population has always been poor and densely settled in relation to developed resources, which means that the people have had no great surplus to tide them over an agricultural disaster. Third, the subcontinent has been characterized by poor transportation and local isolation, which means that an afflicted region could not get succor from other regions. Fourth, the area has had a feudal type of commercial capitalism, which means that famine conditions were exacerbated rather than helped by the operation of the price system. Fifth, though India had irrigation projects from prehistoric times, she did not have enough to protect her from irregularities of rainfall. Finally, the Indian region has suffered from political disorder, caste barriers, and cultural diversity, so that the large-scale planning necessary for the prevention of famine was usually impossible. [5]

These conditions are just as important as geographic factors in explaining Indian famines. From a strategic standpoint they are even more important, because they are the factors subject to control and hence the objects of attack in any attempt to eliminate famines. They are conditions of long standing, and coupled with the irregularity of rainfall, they have made India one of the world's most famine-ridden areas. Historical records of the Muslim empires provide accounts of famines which apparently decimated the population as tragically as those of modern times. [6]

It is impossible to gauge the exact amount of mortality caused by famines. Many famines occurred before vital statistics were even attempted, and those occurring since that date still fall in a period when vital statistics are deficient. The registration system, furthermore, tends to break down under famine conditions, so that an even lesser proportion of deaths are recorded than is ordinarily the case. One very crude measure of the effect of famines is to study the population growth during decades when famines occurred and during those when famines did not occur. The decade of 1891–1901, for example, was distinguished by the occurrence of terrible famines in its closing years. Despite the initial outbreak of plague in this decade, deaths from epidemic disease seem to have been, if anything, fewer than usual, and no other causes of death stand out as of peculiar importance. The fact that the population grew only 1 per cent during this decade is therefore attributable mainly to the occurrence of famines. [7]

How much might the population have grown otherwise? Well, in the previous decade it grew 9.4 per cent, and in the following decade 6.1 per cent. If the 1891–1901 decade had experienced the average rate of growth shown by these two decades, it would have grown by 7.8 per cent instead of 1 per cent. The difference is a matter of some 19 million persons, which may be taken as a rough estimate of loss due to famines. [8]

It should be borne in mind, however, that relief measures were functioning at this time and that this saved the lives of millions of persons who otherwise would have died. "In ancient times the occurrence of a severe famine was marked by the disappearance of a third or a fourth of the population of the area afflicted." [9] By the decade under consideration the relief measures had reached the point, not of nullifying the effects of famine, but of greatly reducing the mortality resulting from it. After the turn of the century both relief and preventive measures became more effective.

The decrease in the number and intensity of famines, most noticeable after 1900, could not have been due to changed geographical conditions. The climate of India remained the same, the rainfall being as irregular as ever. What was changing was the set of social conditions that had formerly been implicated in famine phenomena. India still remained predominantly agricultural and extremely poor, but certain mitigating changes, both planned and unplanned, had taken place.

In the first place, the characteristic local isolation had diminished; and since famines are usually local affairs, this meant amelioration. The production of food crops ceased to have an overwhelmingly subsistence character, but became increasingly commercial, the exports operating as a local reserve of food against seasons of drought. "More food was now grown in ordinary years than India could eat because there was a market for the surplus abroad; in a bad season the rise in Indian prices put a stop to export for the time, and the entire produce of the country was available for its needs." [10] In times of scarcity the same channels which ordinarily took food out of the country could bring food into it, and the breakdown of isolation inside India enabled areas of surplus to succor areas of deprivation.

What was responsible for this breakdown of internal and external isolation? On the technological side it was improved transportation and communication. Some of the railways and hard-surfaced roads in India were undertaken precisely for the purpose of preventing famines. When private companies hesitated to build new railroads, the government itself (after 1869) undertook construction. The famine havoc of the seventies re-emphasized the need for railways, and the Famine Commission of 1880 successfully advocated a program of railway construction as a specific protection against the recurrence of famines. [11] "Railway communication did not really become widespread till the last decade of the nineteenth century. In 1891 there was still only one mile of railway to every 90 square miles of area"; in 1940 there was 1 to every 25 square miles. [12] The construction of hard-surfaced roads began slightly before the building of railroads, but received its real impetus about the same time as the latter—that is, in

---

[4] Pramathanath Banerjea, *A Study of Indian Economics* (5th ed.; London: Macmillan, 1940), p. 17.

[5] Nearly all these conditions, plus the geographic, were paralleled in the great northeastern section of Brazil, which was long subject to terrible famines. Accounts of the famines occurring here bear a remarkable similarity to accounts of Indian famines. See, e.g., T. Lynn Smith, *Brazil: People and Institutions* (Baton Rouge: University of Louisiana Press, 1946), pp. 310–17.

[6] Charles Blair, *Indian Famines* (London: Blackwood, 1874), Chaps. 1 and 2.

[7] *General Report of the Census of India,* 1901, Sessional Papers, Cmd. 2047 (London: His Majesty's Stationery Office, 1904), pp. 83–85.

[8] The official estimates place the famine mortality at around 5 million, but these estimates seem to rest on the faulty vital statistics. See *ibid.,* p. 84.

[9] *ibid.*

[10] Moreland and Chatterjee, *op. cit.,* p. 377.

[11] Banerjea, *op. cit.,* pp. 302–03.

[12] L. S. S. O'Malley, "Mechanism and Transport" in O'Malley (ed.), *Modern India and the West* (London: Oxford University Press, 1941), pp. 238–39.

Dalhousie's energetic regime. The Mogul Empire had built roads, but they lacked a hard surface, became infested with robbers, and were too limited in scope. The creation of great trunk routes between principal cities, and later of networks penetrating into outlying areas, was the contribution of the modern period. As for water transport, the coastal routes had always served India, and their use, especially after the coming of steam, tended to grow, although it was not given particular attention by the British and suffered in competition with the railways. Telegraph communication was started and an efficient postal system was achieved in Dalhousie's regime. The latter half of the nineteenth century therefore saw the full development of a technology of transport and communication.

Another technological advance, made (like the railways) with famine relief partly in mind, was the development of irrigation. Since the geographical cause of famine is always an irregularity—a drought, cyclone, flood, or scourge—which suddenly lowers the food supply below that necessary for a population built up under a different expectation, any countermeasure giving security offers a solution. Irrigation, by overcoming the effects of irregular rainfall, eliminated drought-produced famine in areas where it was practiced.

Though Indians had employed irrigation for thousands of years before the British came, most of the projects had fallen into decay. The East India Company, stimulated by both the desire to increase agricultural production and the need to avoid famines, began its work by restoring some of the old systems. It commenced as early as 1819, and after the famine of 1832–33 it increased its effort—enlarging, for example, the Western Jumna Canal project.[13] So successful were the remodeling projects in Northern India and Madras, and so appalling were the famines which continued to ravage the country, that the Company soon launched great new schemes financed from surplus revenue. The Ganges Canal was begun in 1842 and finished in 1854. Adjoining the Eastern Jumna Canal, it irrigates the northern portion of the Ganges-Jumna Doab, and now consists of 3,888 miles of main and subordinate lines, irrigating about 1.25 million acres annually. "It has converted a famine-ridden tract into one of the richest in Northern India."[14] The Upper Bari Doab Canal was opened in 1859, converting a wild jungle into one of the most fertile tracts in the Punjab, and today comprising 1,845 miles of main lines irrigating about 1.25 million acres. During the same period the Godavari projects in Madras were completed, now irrigating about a million acres; and several smaller projects were undertaken.

By 1858 India already had one of the greatest irrigation systems in the world, directed by an experienced staff of officers and engineers who were teaching other nations what they had learned in India. But there was no stopping at this point. The new Government of India took over the work, and after the great Orissa Famine of 1865–66, which allegedly killed a million people (one-quarter of the population of the affected area), it decided to finance its huge irrigation projects by loans raised in the open market.[15] It undertook five major schemes and numerous minor ones. As an example of the success it attained, the Sirhind Canal may be mentioned. Drawn from the Sutlej River, it "commands an area of 8,500

square miles, of which 47 per cent is British, 35 per cent in Patiala State," and the rest in other states. "With a total mileage of 3,733 miles it irrigates an area of about 1,800,000 acres annually and pays a return of 11½ per cent on the capital invested."[16]

The government had stipulated that only projects likely to yield a profit were to be undertaken. The great famine of 1877–78 showed the inhumanity of this limitation, and led the government to set aside each year £1,500,000 as a Famine Relief and Insurance Fund. Part of this was earmarked for district famine relief when necessary, but half was allotted to the construction of protective railways and canals. The railways ultimately ceased to receive support from this source, so that the whole amount became available for irrigation works. The latter were to be undertaken where needed, regardless of their prospects for profit. Under this provision, millions of dollars were spent on irrigation systems for the prevention of famine, mainly in the Bombay Deccan, the Bundelkhand region of the United Provinces, and the Central Provinces.[17]

The relentless recurrence of famines did not cease, however. The years 1895–1900 saw acute famines in various parts of India, and stimulated the government to even greater effort. An Irrigation Commission was appointed and, reporting in 1903, summarized the work up to that time. It found that in an area having a population of 270 million and an average cultivated acreage of 297 million, there were 53 million acres annually irrigated. Of this, 19 million acres were irrigated from canals, 16 million from wells, 10 million from tanks, and 8 million from other sources. The percentage of cultivated area under irrigation was 19.5 for British India and 10.9 for the Indian states.[18] As a result of the Commission's recommendations, many new projects—some big, some small, many extremely difficult—were undertaken. By World War I the waters of virtually all the northern rivers had been utilized for irrigation. Approximately 360 million dollars had been spent.[19] Yet during the period of prosperity in the 1920's new projects of huge size but often of doubtful value were launched. Today the total irrigated area is close to 60 million acres, about 20 per cent of the total cultivated area and (because of double cropping on irrigated land) an even greater percentage of the crops. The area irrigated is three times the irrigated surface of the United States, and ten times that of Egypt.[20]

Irrigation has probably done more than any other technological factor to eliminate famines from the Indian subcontinent. Not only has it assured regular crops in regions of irregular rainfall, but it has increased the total productivity of these areas, so as to give them more of a surplus against periods of drought. It has also increased the total productivity of all India. Finally, by bringing prosperity and people to regions formerly barren, it has drawn off excess population from denser areas. It has thus reduced famine enormously.

The tangibility of roads, railways, and irrigation canals should not blind us to the fact that such technological developments are dependent upon parallel changes in social organization. For railroads and canals to be built and maintained, there must be some elements of a commercial and

[13] Sir Bernard Darley, "Irrigation and Its Possibilities" in Radhakamal Mukerjee (ed.), *Economic Problems of Modern India*, Vol. 1 (London: Macmillan, 1939), p. 150.

[14] *ibid.*, pp. 151–52.

[15] Sir Thomas R. J. Ward, "Irrigation" in Sir John Cumming (ed.), *Modern India* (London: Oxford University Press, 1931), p. 194.

[16] Darley, *op. cit.*, p. 155.

[17] *ibid.*, pp. 158–61. Ward, *op. cit.*, p. 195.

[18] Ward, *op. cit.*, pp. 192–93.

[19] *ibid.*, pp. 200–01.

[20] Vera Anstey, "Economic Development" in L. S. S. O'Malley (ed.), *op. cit.*, p. 270.

industrial economy, some reliability of government, and some technological and scientific proficiency. These features, like the railroads themselves, were in part importations from the West when they first arrived in India. In so far, then, as the control of famine rests on modern technology, it also rests on modern social organization. Both the Indian Union and Pakistan may be expected to continue modernization on all fronts (perhaps faster than before independence), and so famines should be increasingly controlled. Yet, because the present population density has been built up on the expectation of famine control, a breakdown of the technology and social framework supporting that control might cost more lives than even the great famines of the past.

In India a system of advanced famine warnings and famine relief was gradually developed. By keeping a check on rainfall, prices, and other conditions, it became possible to know ahead of time where famines were likely to arise. Relief could then be brought to these areas in time to prevent, or at least reduce, mass starvation and panic. As an illustration, the following paragraph is taken from the Health Commissioner's report for 1939:

"*Punjab.*—Owing to the failure of the monsoon during 1938 and 1939 famine conditions in the Hissar and Rohtak districts were considerably intensified. Consequently relief had to be afforded on a large scale. With the onset of the cold weather following a period of inadequate nutrition, the general health of the people in some parts of the Hissar district showed signs of deterioration. Special measures were carried out for meeting the situation and these included the provision of medical relief and the supply of germinated grain and *amla* to the people for improving the quality of their diet." [21]

The preventive and relief measures have never been adequate to prevent starvation and undernourishment, but they have greatly reduced famine mortality. The measures are constantly in operation, for famine control is a continuing thing, requiring constant vigilance. They have enabled India to avoid really great famines since 1900. The failure of the monsoon has repeatedly laid the basis for such famines, but human planning has markedly diminished this tragic result.

The famine of 1943 in Bengal, which (with the extra mortality from diseases that accompanied it) is estimated to have taken between 1.5 and 3 million lives, was a small thing compared to the great famines that once ravaged India. It apparently arose not from a natural catastrophe but from a temporary breakdown in the ordinary economic machinery owing to the war situation. The actual food deficit, resulting from poor crops in Bengal in 1942 and from the loss of imports from Burma, Siam, and Indo-China, was not sufficient to explain the famine, because equal or greater deficits had been experienced in prior years without famine resulting. The trouble lay much more in the breakdown of transport because of military demands, the inflation of prices because of wartime conditions, and the hoarding of grain because of profiteering and insecurity.[22] Nevertheless, even though it was not so severe as the great famines prior to the twentieth century, the Bengal disaster serves as a sharp warning. It shows how precarious is the food supply, and how easily even a slight economic and political dislocation can lead to mass starvation. The people of Pakistan and the Indian Union are perpetually engaged in a fight with hunger. As long as they live so close to the brink of defeat, occasions are bound to come when the scales are tipped and they must experience a famine.

THE CONTROL OF EPIDEMIC DISEASE

Rivaling famine as a widespread killer in the Indian subcontinent is epidemic disease. Like famine, its frightfulness should not be considered solely in terms of the deaths it causes from year to year, but also in terms of its unexpectedness, its virulence, and its aftermath. Without overpopulation, a death rate that is fairly regular from year to year is perhaps better, socially and economically speaking, than one that jumps suddenly to extremes, even though the *average rate* is the same. The influenza epidemic of 1918 more than doubled the regular mortality rate in India. This means, by a conservative estimate, that it took 16 million lives and killed 5 per cent of the population. It more probably took 20 million lives.[23] In any case, when to this swollen mortality we add the cost and inconvenience of widespread sickness, we see that an epidemic of this size is profoundly disturbing. It perhaps falls short of being as disruptive as a famine of equal deadliness, because it does not affect livestock to such an extent; but it does interfere with the regular course of economic production and leave many people in a physically weakened condition.

The remarkable thing about both epidemics and famines, however, is the quickness with which a dense population seems to recover from the effects of the disaster. During an epidemic, it is said, "Life goes on as usual in the neighborhood and funeral processions wending their way almost unnoticed to the burial ground and the burning ghat may be the only indication of the tragedies of the epidemic. During severe epidemics some measure of hardship results from the temporary failure of the food supply, the disruption of trade, the interference with agriculture and the interruption of traffic; but even the most virulent pestilence is short lived and these ill effects disappear with astonishing rapidity and with them all memory of the epidemic." [24] In an overpopulated country such as India, a highly irregular death rate (caused by famines, epidemics, etc.) has two effects that may possibly give it an advantage over a steady mortality of the same long-run intensity: (1) The sudden catastrophe wipes away excess population and thereby temporarily relieves the population pressure. If such pressure has been a hindrance to economic advance, as it must have been if there has been "overpopulation," then the relief afforded by the epidemic proves beneficial until the pressure is built up once more. With a steady but high mortality, on the other hand, the pressure is continual; it gets no relief, and stagnation is therefore unvarying. (2) "Since the brunt of epidemics is usually borne by children and old people, the survivors of an epidemic, who are mainly breadwinners, have in consequence of the epidemic fewer dependents to support. Epidemics are therefore sometimes fol-

[21] Public Health Commissioner with the Government of India, *Annual Report,* 1939 (Delhi: Manager of Publications, 1941), pp. 10–11.

[22] The literature on the Bengal famine is voluminous, and some of it is misinformed and propagandistic. The best references that have come to the writer's attention are as follows: Famine Inquiry Commission, *Report on Bengal* (Madras: Government Press, 1943); Andrew J. Grajdanzev, "Food Crisis in India," *Far Eastern Survey,* Vol. 13 (January 12, 1944), pp. 2–7; Sir Norman Angell, "The Indian Famine," *ibid.,* pp. 7–10; J. C. French, "Man-Made Famine," *National Review,* Vol. 121 (December, 1943), pp. 428–31; Wm. Ernest Hocking, "Famine Over Bengal," *Asia and the Americas,* Vol. 44 (February, 1944), pp.

74–75. A number of publications have appeared in India, but the writer has not seen them.

[23] See Appendix B for our method of estimating the mortality from the influenza epidemic.

[24] C. A. Gill, "Epidemics," *Encyclopaedia of the Social Sciences,* Vol. 5 (New York: Macmillan, 1931), p. 571.

lowed by a temporary rise in the standard of living." [25] In so far as the epidemic or famine affects children and old people more than young adults, the birth rate tends to rise again immediately after the disaster, and it is not long until the regular course of population growth is resumed. The period of relief is therefore not long, but it is worth noting that, through humanitarian sentiment, we have perhaps exaggerated the harmful effects which famines and epidemics have in themselves. We have perhaps attributed some effects to them which, more properly, belong to the kind of social and economic order that permits famines and epidemics to occur. Given such a social and economic order, catastrophic mortality may be better than steady mortality (assuming the same average rate over long periods).

There is one important reason why India was, during the last two centuries, the home of great epidemics: She was being exposed to *foreign contact* for the first time on such a great scale. The nature of bacterial parasitism is apparently such that, at least in many cases, a natural immunity is built up after a number of generations of exposure. Hence isolated and stable communities do not suffer much, because they have developed a natural immunity to old infections and are not exposed to new ones. The great epidemics in Europe did not come during the period of greatest medieval stagnation. They came, instead, at the time of the Crusades and after, when trade and migration were once again bringing communities into frequent contact and creating cities with populations drawn from diverse places. Later in Europe, the same diseases that caused these epidemics (plague, cholera, typhus, tuberculosis, smallpox, scarlet fever, and diphtheria), though they remained endemic in many areas, lost a great deal of their virulence and their power to spread. India's medieval stagnation was broken down later than that of Europe, so that her period of virulent epidemic disease occurred much later. There is considerable evidence to support the comparison with Europe at an earlier time. It seems clear, for example, that the invasion of India by tuberculosis began in the cities, and that at the present time, with the breakdown of the isolation of rural villages, it is spreading rapidly and alarmingly to the countryside.[26] Also, it is believed that India was not exposed to plague prior to 1896.[27] The disease raged in a spectacular manner for a while, but at the present time, without the public health measures being mainly responsible, the disease is declining steadily, perhaps due to the acquisition of immunity by the rat rather than the human. In 1898–1918 there were approximately 500,000 annual deaths from it; in 1931–34 there were only 50,000 annual deaths and in 1935 only 32,000.[28]

Seemingly, even without medical aid, India's full participation in world contact would have brought her the worst of the epidemics and then, within one or two more centuries, a gradual immunity reducing their virulence. The process of natural immunization, according to this theory, may be taking place even today, although many of the diseases are in such different stages of evolution that it is difficult to say what the total trend is. We do know that there are some epidemic diseases not yet experienced in India, which may sometime ravage the population. Yellow fever, for instance, despite its presence in Africa and other parts of the world, has never visited the Indian subcontinent; yet the conditions for its spread are ideal if the virus should ever be brought there, the mosquito which carries the virus being indigenous and widespread in the region.[29]

Fortunately, however, the people of Pakistan and the Indian Union will not have to wait until natural immunity develops. The same scientific medicine which finally stopped most epidemics in Europe is coming to the aid of Asia. Already public health work has brought a sharp decline in Indian epidemics, especially during the last two decades. This is especially true of those diseases whose control does not require fundamental changes in the living habits or in the general economic level.

To demonstrate the increasing control of mortality in India, we shall discuss some particular diseases in detail. First, however, it is necessary to say a word concerning the deficiencies in the Indian statistics on causes of death.

THE "CAUSE OF DEATH" IN INDIAN STATISTICS

Most people in Pakistan and the Indian Union die without ever having been seen by a doctor. The man who first reports the death (if it is registered at all) and who usually makes the diagnosis, is the village headman, or Chaukidar. This ill-paid person is, in most villages, the sole representative of the government and has a multitude of duties to perform besides the gathering of vital statistics. He must tend to the personal needs of officers on tour, report crimes, keep watch over bad characters, and supply information on a bewildering variety of subjects. His low wage is sometimes paid by land grant, sometimes by salary; a system of rewards for meritorious aid to the regular police augments his income. His greatest defect as a reporter of vital statistics is that he is often illiterate; his greatest obstacle, in addition to his numerous other duties, is that he must collect his information from people who, throughout most of India, are under no obligation to give it to him and who do not and cannot appreciate the necessity of it.[30] Bad as he is, his reporting of births and deaths is often more accurate than that of urban registrars.

The village headman is certainly not learned in medical affairs, yet in most instances of death it is he who must state the "cause." There is usually no qualified practitioner to give him any aid. The Chaukidar's slogan is, "when in doubt, call it 'fever.'" In the published reports 60 per cent of the total deaths are ascribed to "fever," and over 25 per cent to the catch-all category, "other causes." These proportions have remained virtually unchanged ever since death records began to be kept in India (Fig. 9). They show, of course, that the cause of death is unknown in at least 85 per cent of the reported cases.[31]

In practice, most provinces have only a limited number of certifiable causes of death. Table 10 gives those that were certifiable in the various provinces and certain cities in 1932.

---

[25] *ibid.*

[26] Sir John Megaw, "Public Health. The Great Diseases of India," in Sir E. A. H. Blunt (ed.), *Social Service in India* (London: His Majesty's Stationery Office, 1938), p. 228. Also Gyan Chand, *India's Teeming Millions* (London: Allen & Unwin, 1939), pp. 120–21.

[27] O'Malley, *Modern India and the West*, p. 639.

[28] Megaw, *op. cit.*, pp. 226–27.

[29] Megaw, *op. cit.*, p. 224.

[30] By 1932 only one province, Bengal, had instituted compulsory registration in all rural and urban areas. Bihar and Orissa had instituted it for all 58 municipalities, but not for the rural areas. Commissioner of Health, *Annual Report*, 1932, p. 26. A fuller account of the defects of registration is contained in Health Survey and Development Committee, *Report* (Delhi: Manager of Publications, 1946), Vol. 1, Chap. 12.

[31] This characterization of the Chaukidar and his influence on the statistics is taken mainly from Cumming (ed.), *op. cit.*, p. 111, and from Chand, *op. cit.*, pp. 95, 118–19.

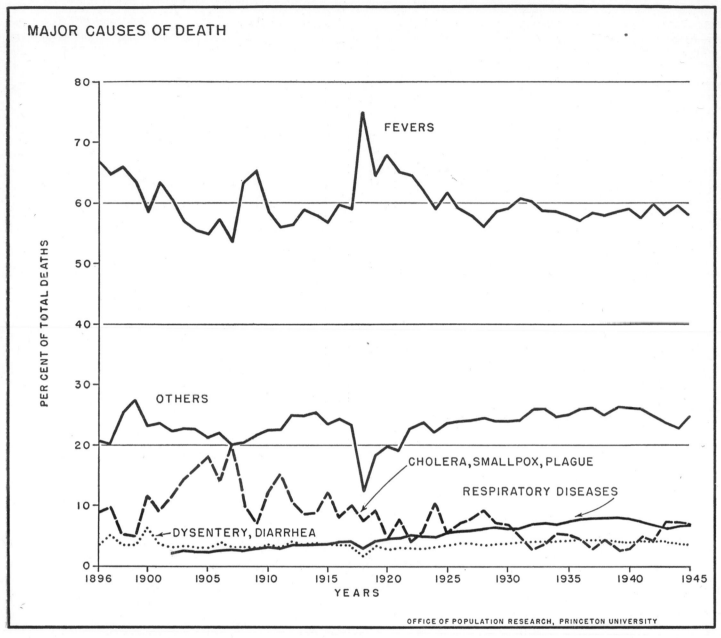

FIGURE 9. Percentage of Total Registered Deaths Attributed to each Major Group of Causes, British India, 1896–1945.

Since that time there has been improvement, especially in municipalities. As reported in the statistics for British India as a whole, the categories are eight in number, as follows:

1. Cholera
2. Smallpox
3. Plague
4. Fevers
5. Dysentery and diarrhea
6. Respiratory diseases
7. Injuries
8. Other causes

Of these, the most specific are the first three, and it is generally believed that our information on these is better than on other diseases. "The only diseases for which registration can be said to have reached a fair standard of accuracy are cholera, smallpox, and plague, these being the most common and most fatal of the epidemic diseases which periodically devastate India." [32] For most other diseases, such as tuberculosis, malaria, pneumonia, syphilis, etc., there is no way of knowing what the incidence and prevalence are. It is true that hospital statistics are kept, and that field investigations are frequently made. From these we can learn something, but because of sampling difficulties, they seldom give us an accurate notion of the situation in the general population.

Because of such poor vital statistics, comparisons must be made with great caution. Above all, it is not safe to compare different regions, or to compare the city with the country. Not only are different diseases notifiable in different provinces and towns, but there are varying degrees of completeness and accuracy as between one region and another. The fact that after 1919 public health was a "transferred subject," for which the provincial governments were primarily responsible,

[32] Public Health Commissioner with the Government of India, *Annual Report,* 1932 (Delhi: Manager of Publications, 1934), p. 28.

TABLE 10

Diseases Notifiable in Various Provinces and Cities, 1932 [1]

DISEASES	PROVINCES												CITIES								
	Cent. Prov.	Punjab	Baluchistan	Madras	United Provinces	Assam	Bengal	Delhi	Bihar & O.	Bombay	N.W. Frontier Prov	Coorg	Nagpur	Lahore	Bombay	Vizagapatam	Delhi	Madras	Lucknow	Karachi	Calcutta
Cholera	X	X	X	X	X	X	X	X	X	X	X	X	X	X	X	X	X	X	X	X	X
Plague	X	X	X	X	X	X	X	X	X	X	X	X	X	X	X	X	X	X	X	X	X
Smallpox	X	X	X	X	X	X	X	X	X	X	X	X	X	X	X	X	X	X	X	X	X
Diphtheria	X	X	X	X	X	X							X	X	X	X	X	X	X	X	X
Influenza	X	X					X	X	X	X			X	X	X	X	X				X[a]
Tuberculosis	X	X	X	X	X[b]	X[b]							X	X	X	X	X		X	X	
Enteric fever	X	X	X	X	X[c]	X[c]								X	X			X	X		
Cerebrospinal f.	X	X					X						X	X	X				X	X	X
Measles	X	X			X								X	X			X	X	X		
Relapsing fever	X	X				X	X						X	X		X		X			
Chicken pox	X	X		X									X	X		X	X				
Scarlet fever	X	X			X								X	X	X			X		X	
Typhus	X	X	X				X						X	X	X		X				
Leprosy		X	X	X										X	X	X					
Puerperal fever	X	X											X	X	X			X			
Mumps	X	X	X										X	X							
Pneumonia	X												X			X		X			
Whooping cough	X	X											X	X							
Beriberi																	X	X			
Dysentery	X	X												X							
Erysipelas		X															X	X			
Kala-azar					X[c]											X		X			
Paratyphoid													X	X							
Typhoid													X			X					
Anthrax	X									X			X								
Encephalitis l.	X												X								
Glanders				X												X					
Sprue		X														X					
Acute Polio	X												X								

a Notifiable under Bengal Port Sanitary Regulations.
b Notifiable in municipalities by medical practitioners only.
c In municipal towns only.

[1] Public Health Commissioner with the Government of India, *Annual Report,* 1932 (Delhi: Manager of Publications, 1934), p. 31.

has tended to increase the regional differences of definition, fullness, and exactitude in reporting deaths. One of the best uses that can be made of the official statistics is the determination of trends for given regions. But even so, the lack of refinement in delineating the causes of death makes such determination of only limited value.

To illustrate the capricious character of the reporting of causes of death, Table 11 is reproduced from the Health Report of 1938. It relates to an investigation in Delhi, where a

TABLE 11

Comparison of the Causes of Registered and of Verified Deaths in Delhi 1938 [1]

Cause	Registered Deaths	Verified Deaths
Malaria	4	266
Measles	222	222
Smallpox	81	81
Typhoid	410	410
Pneumonia	1,184	2,470
Phthisis	850	850
Puerperal fever	—	83
Infantile diarrhea	72	492
Premature birth	9	245

[1] Public Health Commissioner with the Government of India, *Annual Report*, 1938, p. 9. The source does not state why the two columns do not add up to the same total. Presumably the investigation was made by going into the histories of nearly all deaths registered during the course of the year. Perhaps the extra "verified deaths" come from an "others" category, not given.

committee of medical men verified the cause in every death that occurred, and compared this with what was given in the registration files. For some causes there was good recording, for others there was valueless reporting.

In short, because of under-reporting, inaccurate diagnosis, and regional variations in notifiability and efficiency, the vital statistics on causes of death are almost hopeless. Only when handled with extreme caution can trends with respect to two or three diseases be determined. When taken in conjunction with hospital statistics and sample studies, however, they are worth something. Taking all sources of information into account, the surprising thing is not how little, but how much we know about disease in the Indian region.

PARTICULAR DISEASES

Now that we have seen how shaky is our evidence, let us return to the main theme, the trend of particular kinds of mortality. The subcontinent enjoys the dubious distinction of being the world center for at least three highly epidemic maladies—plague, smallpox, and cholera—all of which have been brought under control in most other countries. As Figure 10 illustrates, the mortality from these three has been reduced considerably, but by no means eliminated. In addition, the population pays a heavy toll to countless other diseases about which we have less accurate information. Among the outstanding are tuberculosis, malaria, and dysentery. A discussion of each of these diseases will reveal how far the region has progressed on the road to control, and how far it still has to go.

Plague. The most spectacular decline of the three universally notifiable epidemic diseases has been registered by plague. This malady, which in general shows the greatest fluctuation, probably caused close to two million deaths in 1907. After that, despite wide ups and downs, it rapidly subsided, and since 1929 has been a more negligible factor in mortality than smallpox. Its virulence has not only declined faster, but has been of shorter historical duration. In the 1911 Census Report,[33] it is stated that India had been practically free from plague "in recent times" until it broke out in Bombay in 1896. "Spreading from that city it had already by March of 1901 caused a recorded mortality of about half a million. . . . This moreover is only the recorded mortality. As is well known, when epidemics are raging, the reporting agency breaks down and a large number of deaths escape registration." In 1904 the number of plague deaths in India was nearly 1,150,000. It has even been said that prior to 1896 the disease did not exist in India, and that it was brought there at that time in ships. Though this theory may be questioned, there can be no doubt that plague suddenly broke out and rose to tremendous proportions at the date mentioned, and that it subsequently died down with considerable rapidity. Concerning the decline, medical opinion appears to be divided. On the one hand Megaw asserts that we do not know why the decrease occurred, or whether the disease will flare up again in future years; nor do we know why it has never invaded some areas—especially Orissa and Assam.[34] On the other hand, Chand maintains that the most important reason for the decrease has been the evolution of a new race of rats immune to the malady.[35] In support of this view, one can point out that the places of greatest decline are precisely those which were formerly the worst affected.[36] Furthermore, the theory fits well with what we know about the temporary character of disease as a manifestation of bacterial parasitism.[37] In any case, no authority seems inclined to attribute the drop in plague mortality mainly to public health work. Research in India has, however, made notable contributions to the understanding of the disease and potential measures of control. Haffkine developed an anti-plague vaccine that has become increasingly popular in recent years. Sulfa drugs have also been found useful in treatment, and lately streptomycin. Preventive measures have taken the direction of eliminating or controlling infected fleas and rats. The Indian Plague Commission was responsible for discovering the more important facts about the spread of plague and for working out preventive tactics. In more recent years extensive research has been carried out in Cumbum Valley of Madura District in Madras. It was ascertained that the use of cynogas fumigation for rat-holes was effective in reducing plague incidence, and also that a rat-proof hut costing less than Rs. 100 could be built. Rat-proofing of grain storage bins and use of DDT have also been tried. In Bombay alone in 1945 there were 662,300 anti-plague innoculations, and almost an equal number in Madras. Although there are endemic areas in India, although the public is still somewhat resistant to inoculation, and although rat control has not gone far yet, it looks as

[33] Vol. 1, Part 1, p. 58.

[34] *op. cit.*, p. 227.

[35] *op. cit.*, p. 126.

[36] Commissioner of Health with the Government of India, *Annual Report*, 1929, p. 66.

[37] Hans Zinsser, *Rats, Lice and History* (Boston: Atlantic Monthly Press, 1935), pp. 224–26. In this case the immunity developed in a primary host, making it unnecessary to develop immunity in the secondary (human) host.

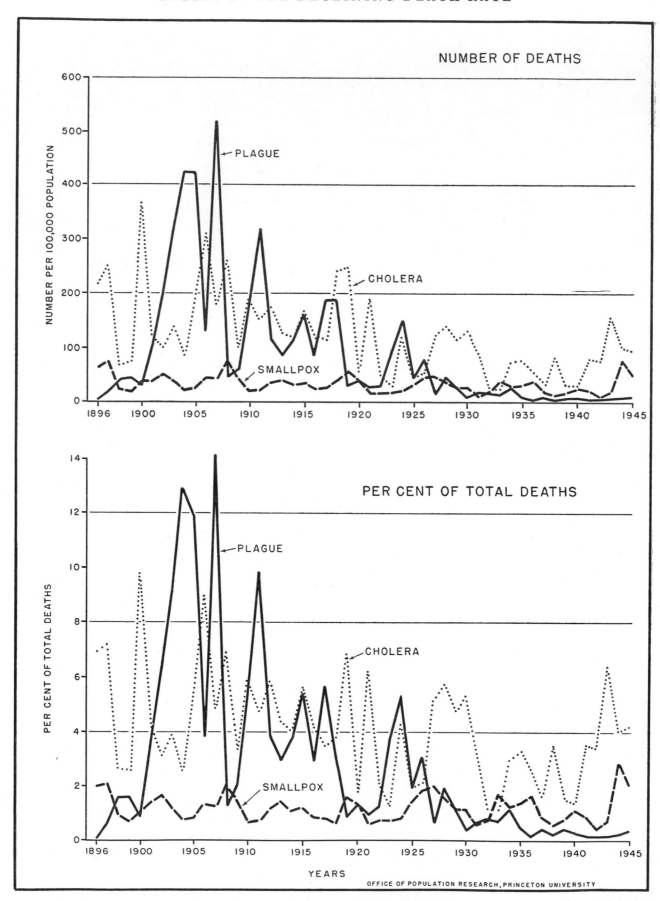

FIGURE 10. Registered Deaths from Plague, Smallpox, and Cholera per 100,000 Population, and per 100 Deaths: British India, 1896–1945.

though India and Pakistan have a good chance of virtually eliminating this disease.[38]

Smallpox. The surprising thing about smallpox is that, since the turn of the century, it has diminished no faster than the general death rate. One reason for this is the fact that the main progress in controlling the disease was made prior to 1900, as shown by the following annual smallpox and vaccination rates: [39]

SMALLPOX MORTALITY AND VACCINATION RATES

	Vaccinations per 1000	Deaths per 1000
1878–1887	27	0.772
1888–1897	34	0.466
1898–1907	38	0.374
1908–1917	36	0.363
1918–1927	33	0.347
1928–1937	** [40]	0.360 [43]
1937–1943	83 [41]	0.174
1944–1945	158 [42]	0.580

In nineteenth century India this disease must have carried away huge numbers. The Sanitary Commissioner for the Government of India wrote in the 1870 report: "The mortality which is due to small-pox is year by year so heavy that the prevention of no one disease is of so great importance to the people of India." [44] The disease was an old one in India; it was more evenly distributed over the country than either cholera or plague; and it was of the most virulent type, the fatality being higher than in most other countries. Since nearly half the registered deaths are among children under ten, it may be assumed that smallpox pretty well saturated the population, sparing almost solely those who had acquired immunity by previous exposure.

The interesting thing about smallpox, however, is that it is one of the easiest diseases to control, and since the means for controlling it was discovered in 1798, it was inevitable that measures should be applied in India. It was not until late in the last century that full control in some parts of Europe was beginning to be achieved, and control is still not complete in such countries as Spain. India, therefore, has lagged behind in this matter, but, considering its size and poverty, it has lagged no more than one might expect.

A disease such as smallpox is easier to control in a country like India than most other diseases. The act of vaccination is quite simple, it costs little per person, it can be accomplished on a mass basis with an exceedingly small medical staff, and it lasts for about ten years and is partially effective throughout life. This means, then, that no slow campaign of popular education, no costly governmental action, no systematic campaign of community sanitation, and no thoroughgoing reorientation of outlook or change of habits is necessary. In other words, smallpox control is agreeably easy in colonial and non-industrial areas where the control of many other diseases is difficult if not impossible. As proof of this, the great progress made in smallpox elimination in several Far Eastern countries may be cited.

"In the Netherlands East Indies, for instance, the annual number of vaccinations and revaccinations rose from 58,500 during 1890–1899 to 1,690,000 in 1899–1909, then to 7,270,000 during 1909–1919 and to the remarkable figure of 10,280,000 for the years 1920–27. As a result of this continuous vaccination campaign, smallpox is now practically non-existent in these islands; during 1932, only 39 cases with 2 deaths were recorded as compared with 3,500 cases and 800 deaths in 1913. . . . In a tropical country like India, the difficulties are great but these are gradually being overcome by patient research and by active organisation. The maintenance of potency in the seed lymph has already been placed on a satisfactory basis; the problem of the distribution of potent lymph to the remotest villages has also reached a satisfactory solution; and other problems are receiving constant attention. It only remains for legislatures and Governments to lend support to Public Health Departments by making vaccination and revaccination compulsory in order to obtain a progressive diminution in the incidence of this easily preventable disease." [45]

As late as 1945, primary vaccination was compulsory in only 83 per cent of the towns and 47 per cent of the rural circles of British India; and revaccination was compulsory in only 26.5 per cent of the towns and 30.3 per cent of the rural circles.[46] In 1944 there were 12.4 million primary vaccinations and 47.6 million revaccinations, these being far higher (especially as concerns revaccination) than in any previous year. Yet these efforts have not been adequate. A resurgence of smallpox mortality occurred in 1944 and 1945, with 216,500 and 137,100 recorded deaths respectively from this cause in British India. During 1932–41 the average annual deaths from smallpox were 69,500. It has been noticed that a large share of smallpox deaths occur to children under 10 in India. During 1937–41, deaths from smallpox among infants under one year, when expressed as percentages of the total mortality from this cause, ranged from 12.1 to 19.7, and for children aged 1–9 the figures varied from 19.2 to 30.5.[47] Actually the latter percentages represent roughly the same proportion as children 1–9 constitute of the total population, but their smallpox mortality is somewhat high when we realize that the children under 1 have far greater than their share. It looks as though the death rate from this disease could be greatly reduced, and perhaps eliminated, by more widespread primary vaccination among very young children. As it is, smallpox control has not been a significant factor in the reduction of the Indian death rate since around 1900, although in the last century it must have been a significant factor in improving mortality.

Cholera. Like smallpox, cholera is apparently an old disease

[38] Health Survey and Development Committee, *op. cit.*, Vol. 1, pp. 114–17; Megaw, *op. cit.*, p. 227; Public Health Commissioner with the Government of India, *Annual Report*, 1945, pp. 9–11.

[39] Compiled from Public Health Commissioner with the Government of India, *Annual Reports,* especially those for 1932 (p. 55), and those for 1940–44 and 1945.

[40] Not available to the author.

[41] For years 1940–43 only.

[42] Does not include Bengal for 1945.

[43] In part based on rates published in *Statistical Abstract for British India,* 1937–38, p. 91. Since these rates are carried to only one decimal, the average for 1928–37 is not so accurate as the others. All figures in the table are official figures.

[44] Sanitary Commissioner with the Government of India, *Annual Report,* 1870 (Calcutta: Office of the Superintendent of Government Printing), p. 105.

[45] Public Health Commissioner with the Government of India, *Annual Report,* 1932, p. 57.

[46] Public Health Commissioner with the Government of India, *Annual Report,* 1945, Statistical Appendices, pp. 67–68.

[47] Health Survey and Development Committee, *op. cit.,* Vol. 1, p. 109.

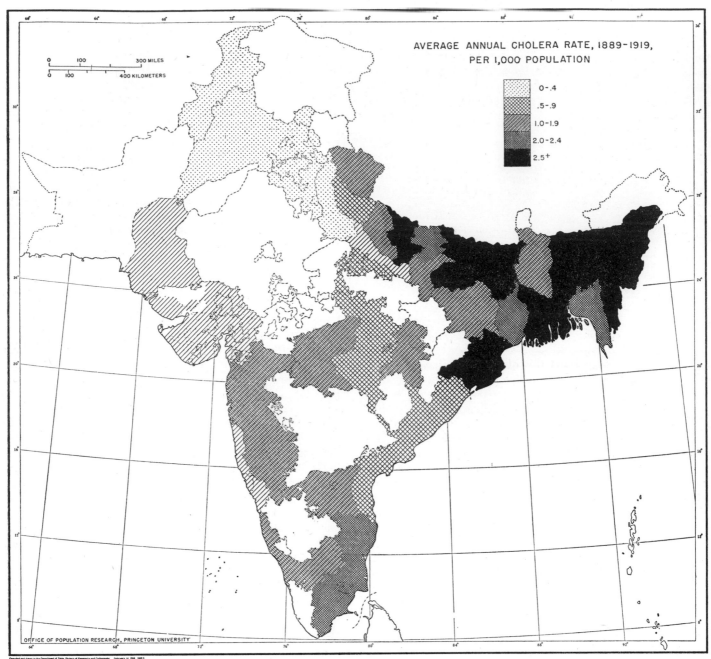

MAP 10. Distribution of Cholera in 1889–1919. From Leonard Rogers, "The Conditions Influencing the Incidence and Spread of Cholera in India as a Whole," *Indian Journal of Medical Research,* No. 9 (Calcutta: Thacker, Spink & Co., March, 1928), p. 21.

in India. Yet "the first great outbreak" did not occur until 1817–19.[48] This epidemic, probably the most terrible of all Indian cholera epidemics, started in Bengal, where the disease had long been endemic, and spread to nearly all parts of India. Great epidemics subsequently occurred in 1863–65, 1875–77, 1891–92, 1894–97, 1900, 1905–08, 1918–19, and 1921 (see Figure 10 for the later dates). The theory prevailing for more than a century was that all cholera epidemics originated in Bengal. Rogers was able to discredit this view by the use of ingenious statistical techniques. His analysis of seasonal mortality, differentiation of areas where cholera had always been present, and study of the correlated incidence in neighboring

districts all showed that India had several endemic areas from which the disease often spread in epidemic form. (Map 10) The disease was long studied in India before a correct knowledge of its causation was achieved. During an extended period prior to 1890 the health commissioners of the provinces and of British India published exceedingly lengthy and careful reports, as did other medical agencies. Indeed, research in India contributed greatly to an understanding of the disease, and it was on a trip to Egypt and India that Koch and the German Cholera Commission discovered the cholera vibrio. Before that time Pettenkofer, the German epidemiologist, used Jameson's report on Indian cholera in his first great work on the spread of this disease.[49] He was greatly influenced in his views by Indian research generally, including the work of

[48] Sir Leonard Rogers, "The Incidence and Spread of Cholera in India; Forecasting and Control of Epidemics," *Indian Medical Research Memoirs,* No. 9 (Calcutta: Indian Research Fund Association, March, 1928), p. 6.

[49] C.-E. A. Winslow, *The Conquest of Epidemic Disease* (Princeton: Princeton University Press, 1943), p. 312.

James Cunningham, a Sanitary Commissioner with the Government of India.[50] The Pettenkofer theory was of course largely erroneous; it was responsible, as late as 1893, for the Indian Army medical regulations ordering troops, when attacked by cholera, to march at right angles to the wind (on the basis of the wind-extension idea). Noteworthy, however, is the fact that cholera was not a disease suddenly approached by advanced medical techniques developed exclusively in Europe. Rather, its control depended on slowly evolving techniques, many of which were contributed by India itself.

The decline in cholera mortality came later than that of smallpox. The latter was reduced sharply before 1900, remaining practically stable since then, but cholera was rampant both before and after that date, showing however a gradual though irregular tendency to decline (Fig. 10). Only in one year, 1933, was the registered mortality from cholera less than that from smallpox. In general during the last four decades the rate for cholera has been two or three times the rate for smallpox, although during 1900–20 it was considerably more than this.

The slowness of progress in cholera control resulted from two factors: First, the knowledge of how to control the disease was late in coming. Second, the knowledge, when it did come, was difficult to apply. Long after the bacterial agent had been discovered, debate still went on as to how the agent was transmitted. In the case of smallpox the problem of transmission was not crucial, because, even without a positive identification of the virus agent, vaccination offered a convenient means of prevention. After 1900 enough was known about cholera transmission to control it. As John Megaw says, there is "no serious disease which is easier to eradicate. . . . If all cases of cholera were notified *immediately* and placed under proper control, the disease would soon disappear."[51] But the social and economic conditions necessary for control were more far-reaching than in the case of smallpox—despite the fact that cholera is actually less easy to transmit than smallpox and hence has a greater tendency to remain in one limited area.[52] Cholera would be easy to control if only physiological or medical conditions were involved. Unfortunately, economic and sociological factors are also important. Effective control of the disease requires fundamental changes in the sanitary habits of the people, extensive community effort in the purification of food and water supplies. The difficulties can be best understood when specific control techniques are examined. These are six in number, as follows:

(1) *Inoculation.* By far the simplest and most widely used method of controlling cholera in the India-Pakistan region has been that of inoculation with dead cholera vibrios. Statistical evidence for the effectiveness of inoculation was adduced by Rogers in 1928 [53] and more recently and accurately by Adiseshan, Pandit, Venkatraman, and Chandra Sekar.[54]

But cholera inoculation is a more complicated weapon than is vaccination in the case of smallpox. There are two apparently different strains of V. *cholerae* in India, and there is some dispute as to the effectiveness of the same serum (usually mixed) against both of them.[55] This matter, however, is not at all serious as compared to another feature, namely that cholera vaccination is effective for only a short range of time. It is seemingly not effective within the first three days after inoculation, and not highly effective until after eight or ten days. When it is realized that the usual cholera epidemic is extremely rapid in its attack (the mean duration per village being 19 days in a Madras wave), and that "the people are willing or can be persuaded to accept inoculation only when cholera actually occurs in a village," [56] one realizes that the early lack of immunity is something of a handicap. Also, the case fatality rate is not greatly lowered (about 25 per cent in one study) by inoculation.[57] A greater disadvantage of cholera inoculation is that the immunity, once established, lasts for only a short length of time. Ahuja and Singh find experimental evidence that it does not last beyond six months,[58] while Adiseshan et al. give statistical indications that it retains some effectiveness until 12 months.[59] In any case the period is much shorter than in the case of smallpox; and Ahuja and Singh find that a second inoculation six months after the first does not produce much immunity.[60] By reason of these limitations, inoculation has not freed the people of the subcontinent from cholera. Without considerable improvement in the technique, the cooperation of the public, and the economic support, it is hard to see how inoculation alone can do the job. It is true, however, that Adiseshan and coworkers adduce interesting data to show that the chance of an epidemic coming to a village varies inversely with the proportion of the population inoculated. Inoculating even 10 to 30 per cent of the population helps to prevent an outbreak.[61]

(2) *Bacteriophage and Chemotherapy.* Cholera bacteriophage was widely distributed in certain parts of India for a number of years. Some authorities claimed that it played a part in preventing epidemics, but the weight of opinion seems negative.[62] Recently, on the other hand, attempts at chemical treatment have been tried with some sign of success. Curiously, the cholera vibrio is one of the few organisms that have escaped the chemotherapeutic net. It seems quite possible that it will not escape this net forever.[63]

---

[50] *ibid.*, p. 320.

[51] Megaw, "Public Health. The Great Diseases of India," *op. cit.*, p. 231.

[52] See Map 10. More than 75 per cent of the total deaths from cholera occur in only four provinces—Bengal, Bihar, Orissa, and the United Provinces—which together have approximately 50 per cent of the population under registration. Taking districts rather than provinces, one finds an even greater concentration.

[53] *op. cit.*, pp. 42, 172–73.

[54] R. Adiseshan, C. G. Pandit, and K. V. Venkatraman, "Statistical Evaluation of Anti-Cholera Inoculation as a Personal Prophylactic against Cholera and Its Efficacy in the Prevention and Control of Cholera Epidemics," *Indian Journal of Medical Research*, Vol. 35 (July, 1947), pp. 131–52. C. Chandra Sekar, "Statistical Assessment of

the Efficacy of Anti-Cholera Inoculation from the Data of 63 *Cheris* in South Arcot District," *ibid.*, pp. 153–76.

[55] See M. L. Ahuja and Gurkirpal Singh, "Observations on Cholera Vaccine," *Indian Journal of Medical Research*, Vol. 36 (January, 1948), pp. 3–14.

[56] Adiseshan et al., *op. cit.*, pp. 133, 143–47. The reluctance of the Indian population to be vaccinated is mentioned by many authors. In the case of cholera immunization, the reluctance may be due in part to the unusually severe reaction that occurs in a noticeable portion of cases. See C. G. Pandit, "Composition and Efficacy of Cholera Vaccines" in *Proceedings of the Fourth International Congresses on Tropical Medicine and Malaria*, 1948 (Washington, D.C.: Department of State, 1948), Vol. 1, p. 304.

[57] Adiseshan et al., *op. cit.*, p. 143.

[58] *op. cit.*, p. 8.

[59] *op. cit.*, pp. 147–48.

[60] *op. cit.*, p. 9.

[61] Adiseshan et al., pp. 148–49.

[62] Chand, *op. cit.*, p. 124. Health Commissioner for Government of India, *Annual Report*, 1932, p. 35.

[63] S. S. Bhatnagar, F. Fernandes, and P. V. Divekar, "The Chemotherapy of Cholera," *British Medical Journal*, No. 4554 (April 17, 1948), pp. 719–23. A. Castellani, "The Fuchsin Treatment of Cholera," *ibid.* (Feb. 21, 1948), p. 364. These articles are both summarized in *Indian Physician*, Vol. 7 (June, 1948), pp. 214–16.

(3) *Environmental Sanitation*. The annual reports of the Health Commissioner have commented year after year on the lack of municipal and district funds for three essentials of public health—conservancy, water supply, and drainage. In 1935, of 163 towns of over 30,000 population, only 112 had a proper water supply; of 1,131 towns of less than 30,000 inhabitants, only 149 had it.[64] The Bhore committee reported as follows: [65] "The percentage of population, urban and rural, served by protected water supplies is 6.6 in Madras, 7.3 in Bengal, 4.1 in the United Provinces and 9.0 in the North-West Frontier Province. In Orissa there are only two towns in which protected water supplies have been provided, while, in Sind, there are five. In the Punjab the percentage of the population served with protected water supplies is 57.5 in urban areas but, in the rural areas . . . , the proportion is only 0.8 per cent."

The rural areas, containing the great majority of the people, are worse off than the cities. Their drinking water comes from rivers and canals (which often carry wastes), from tanks (in which people often bathe and launder), from open wells (subject to several kinds of contamination), or from tube wells (which also can be contaminated and which readily get out of repair). One public health observer says, in a private communication, that the Indian is less particular about his drinking water than other peoples of the Far East, that he tends to take water from any source. But the rural areas are better off than the towns in one respect. The multiplicity of small sources of supply offers some protection from widespread water-borne epidemics. "The consequences of contamination of a particular source of water in the rural areas may, therefore, not be so spectacular as in an urban community served by a piped supply from a single large source." [66]

The usual method of sewage disposal in the cities is collection by sweepers and removal in carts, but in the rural areas the open fields are generally the latrines. Where there is collection, the refuse may be piled in public "dalaos" or enclosures, from which it is later carted away to be dumped in trenches, in the sea, or some other place. In the absence of adequate supervision, the "dalaos" often become breeding grounds for flies and other insects, the carts are often leaky, and the eventual dumping is not such as to prevent contamination. Composting has been recently tried in some towns, particularly in Madras. Even in towns provided with sewers (e.g. Madras, Calcutta, Dacca, Lucknow, Hyderabad), the system is not adequate for the population. The total population in areas normally served by sewers is probably only 7 million. In Dacca, a sewerage system designed for 45,000 people had not been remodelled by the time the population reached 250,000. In rural areas attempts at improvement have been made. In Madras septic-tank latrines have been built for individual houses in some areas. Here and in other parts of India bore-hole latrines have been introduced to some extent.[67]

Despite some progress, the general picture of environmental sanitation is bleak. The conditions are ideal for the spread of cholera. Poverty, apathy, and ignorance are still so great that there seems no immediate prospect of large-scale improvement. If village sanitation were the only means of controlling cholera, the disease would remain virtually unchecked.

(4) *Sanitation of Pilgrim Centers*. The spread of cholera epidemics in India has been shown repeatedly to be correlated with pilgrimages to religious festivals. Every year millions of Indians go on these pilgrimages (Table 12). For example, extremely large gatherings have taken place every twelfth year in late March or early April at Hardwar, where one to two million people collect in a few days. Every one of these gatherings from 1867 to 1928 was said to have been followed in the neighboring Punjab by an epidemic of cholera more severe than any occurring in the intermediate eleven years. Similar consequences have been found to follow most other large festivals (Table 13).[68]

TABLE 12

Annual Attendance at Pilgrimages and Fairs with over 10,000, in Certain Provinces [1]

Province	Numbers of Fairs with over 10,000 Attending	Numbers of Fairs with over 100,000 Attending	Total Yearly Attendance
Bengal	85	4	1,971,000
Bihar & Orissa	107	10	4,437,000
Central Provinces	52	1	1,305,000
United Provinces	30	9	4,339,000
Punjab	89	6	2,538,000
Bombay	22	4	1,583,000
Madras	135	3	2,495,000
Burma	14	0	280,000

[1] Sir Leonard Rogers, "The Incidence and Spread of Cholera in India; Forecasting and Control of Epidemics," *Indian Medical Research Memoirs*, No. 9 (March, 1928), p. 168. The compiler did not succeed in getting the figures for the United Provinces with its extremely important pilgrimages to Benares, Allahabad, Fyzabad-Ajodhya, Muttra-Brindaban, Hardwar, and other sacred places, the total attendance at which probably exceeds the figure of Bihar and Orissa even in ordinary years. At the twelve-yearly Kumbh Fairs in the United Provinces one million commonly assemble at Hardwar and two million or more at Allahabad within a few weeks.

TABLE 13

Percentage of Cholera Cases in Certain Bengal Districts Attributable to Puri Pilgrims, 1902 [1]

Districts	Total Cholera Cases	Cases Traced to Puri Pilgrims	Percentage
Puri	349	286	72
Cuttack	14	7	50
Balasore	20	10	50
Midnapore	27	9	33
Calcutta	160	40	25
Others	184	32	17
TOTAL	754	384	51

[1] Sir Leonard Rogers, "The Incidence and Spread of Cholera in India; Forecasting and Control of Epidemics," *Indian Medical Research Memoirs*, No. 9 (March, 1928), p. 142. Originally taken from the returns from the Civil Surgeons of the Bengal Districts compiled by Major S. Anderson. The period runs from July 5 to August 2. The Puri festival occurred in July. Of interest is the fact that this was not an unusual cholera year for the districts observed.

[64] Megaw, "Medicine and Public Health," *op. cit.*, p. 197.

[65] Health Survey and Development Committee, *Report*, Vol. 1, p. 141.

[66] K. Subrahmanyan, T. R. Bhaskaran, C. Chandra Sekar, "Studies on Rural Water-Supplies," *Indian Journal of Medical Research*, Vol. 36 (July, 1948), pp. 211–12.

[67] Health Survey and Development Committee, *Report*, Vol. 1, pp. 143–46.

[68] Rogers, *op. cit.*, pp. 41, 102, 142, 167–68.

The reason these religious festivals provoke outbreaks of cholera is clear. People from widely scattered places, including endemic areas, congregate suddenly in one place. They frequently practice communal and ceremonial bathing in stagnant and polluted river waters. They live in crowded and makeshift shelters and enjoy inadequate sanitation facilities. A religious rule may forbid the changing or washing of clothes before reaching home again.

The importance of pilgrimages in the spread of cholera has provided the health authorities with a significant avenue of control. Although it has not been possible to make all of India sanitary, or to inoculate all the people, it has proved possible to introduce more sanitation into the religious centers and travel stations, and to inoculate prospective or returning pilgrims when necessary. By thus getting hold of a strategic factor, the authorities have achieved a large result with a minimum effort and cost. This illustrates how, in countries such as India and Pakistan, it is possible to reduce the death rate with a minimum degree of social change, a minimum degree of popular cooperation, and a minimum degree of contact between physician and public.

(5) *Famine Control.* Because famines bring poverty, dietary deficiency, mass travel, use of bad water, disrupted sanitation, and refugee camps, they are commonly thought to encourage cholera epidemics. To the extent that famine is controlled, then, we may expect that some advantage will accrue to cholera control.

(6) *Forecasting Epidemics.* As in the case of famine, the control of an epidemic is greatly facilitated if it can be known in advance when and where the disease is likely to strike. The inoculation of religious pilgrims in advance of their journey rests on a well-founded prediction of what is likely to happen. But there are also other bases for prediction. One of these is the appearance of cholera in a contiguous territory. The paths by which cholera usually spreads have been mapped, so that appropriate measures to prevent spread can be taken in threatened villages. Increasingly, the cyclical character of cholera is becoming understood. Finally, the variation of cholera incidence with climate aids prediction. When the absolute humidity falls below 0.400, cholera tends to disappear. On the other hand, cholera tends to break out after a period of deficient rainfall. Taking account of all these factors enables the authorities to take measures at the most crucial time and place, thus economizing the region's slender medical resources.

Kala azar. Another infectious disease of the subcontinent, less widespread then cholera but more fatal when untreated, is kala azar. Sometimes called Black Fever, it is caused by a parasitic flagellate that infests the spleen, liver, and bone marrow. The fatality in untreated cases is about 90 per cent; and since it is easily transmitted through the common sandfly (*Phlebotomus argentipes*), it is capable of almost wiping out the population of whole areas. Fortunately, the epidemics are confined to low-lying regions.

Between 1854 and 1873 Burdwan in Western Bengal was devastated by an epidemic, now thought to have been kala azar, that caused a considerable decrease in the population as shown by subsequent census returns. The disease apparently spread eastward into Assam, reaching Nowgong district and being firmly established in the intervening territory by 1891. From that year until 1901 there raged, especially in the Nowgong area, a terrible epidemic. In the stricken area of Nowgong at least one-fourth of the arable land went out of cultiva-

tion within five years. Whole villages were wiped out or deserted, their land reverting to jungle.[69] The disease continued to spread up the Brahmaputra valley, and it has also been noticed in Bihar, Orissa, Madras, and the United Provinces.

From a demographic point of view, kala azar is interesting primarily as showing how a great potential source of death in the Indian region has been largely avoided by modern medicine. As early as 1915 antimony was successfully used, and in 1923 greater success was attained with organic compounds of antimony. The treatment at first required 2–5 months but was later shortened to 2–5 weeks. Treatment quickly caused the disappearance of parasites from the peripheral blood and thus rendered the patient non-infectious. Consequently, the first public health measure consisted of rapid mass treatments at tremendous cost. Had it not been for this mass attack on the disease, the epidemic of 1917–27 would perhaps have been as deadly as that of 1891–1901. In the three years 1924–26 no less than 156,000 cases were treated in Assam; left untreated, they would probably have spread their infection to others and the epidemic would have reached gigantic proportions.[70]

In recent years improvements in both diagnosis and treatment, as well as knowledge of the vector, have aided the fight against kala azar. New drugs have proved more effective than the old ones, one of them (sodium antimony v gluconate) affecting an immediate cure in 96 per cent of the cases.[71] Such effective treatment led to the belief at one time that mass treatment of all cases would virtually eliminate the disease, because in India the infected human being seems to be the only reservoir of infection. Although the incidence in an area can be brought to a very low level by such treatment alone, it cannot be reduced to zero because infection is maintained during inter-epidemic periods by post-recovery skin infection (dermal leishmaniasis) and non-response to treatment in a few cases. Consequently, attention has recently turned to the vector. Modern insecticides are effective against the sandfly and its larva, and research is now under way to assess the value of spraying as a public health measure against kala azar in villages.[72]

THE LESSON OF THE EPIDEMIC DISEASES

Our discussion of some epidemic maladies has been lengthy in order to illustrate several fundamental points. The recent salutary stress in public health circles upon social and economic factors in medicine has perhaps led to a false conclusion—namely, that basic social changes among the masses are always necessary for marked improvement in public health. Over a very long period this may be true, but certainly not in a few decades. The case of cholera shows that even with reference to diseases at first seeming to require radical changes in popular habits, standards of living, and philosophy of life, techniques of control may be worked out by the authorities that greatly reduce mortality without such changes. The history of smallpox and kala azar show that control is possible by relatively simple means, with virtually no disturbance of private folkways at all.

[69] H. E. Shortt, "Reports of the *Kala-Azar* Commission, India, No. II, 1926–1930," *Indian Medical Research Memoirs,* Supplementary Series, No. 25 (August, 1932), p. 37.

[70] *ibid.,* pp. 48–49.

[71] P. C. Sen Gupta, "Researches on Kala-Azar in India, 1938–48," *Proceedings of the Fourth International Congresses on Tropical Medicine and Malaria,* Vol. 2, pp. 1138–41.

[72] *ibid.,* p. 1141.

The danger in such ingenious control of mortality without basic social change is that the gains are insecure. Reduced mortality itself is a social development which ultimately will either force social changes to occur or will prove self-defeating. If, for example, no changes are induced which lower fertility, a situation is created wherein the population density is steadily increased. Without major economic changes, this growing density tends to worsen both the capacity for economic development and the capacity to support the public health measures that have gained some control over mortality. Furthermore, a population that remains ignorant of the rationale behind modern medicine, which does not comprehend personal and community sanitation, can hardly be counted on always to approve the science, the education, and the expenditures which maintain its rather remote medical authorities. Ultimately, then, the imposition of ingenious mortality control from the top down, without basic social changes among the masses, runs a strong risk of failure.

Perhaps this is what Mr. Chand had in mind when he said that nature always balances her account, and that if social conditions do not change, the disappearance of one disease will be balanced by the appearance of another.[73] It may take a considerable time for the tragic balancing to take place, but this should not obscure the possibility. Fortunately, in India and Pakistan there are signs that social changes are occurring on a massive scale, as subsequent chapters will show. Furthermore, the control of disease itself, though achieved through a science that was largely Western in origin, has been remarkably enriched by the research of Indians themselves. Their modern medical tradition, their schools and research institutes, are well established and capable of new triumphs

[73] op. cit., pp. 129–30.

in the future. Strenuous attempts are being made to educate the public in health matters, to change popular habits and institutions. Up to now not enough change has taken place, particularly on the fertility side. The danger we speak of is therefore real, although by no means inevitable.

The Precarious Hold on the Death Rate

Not only is the tenuousness of mortality control seen in the history of the major infectious diseases, but it is also suggested by other ways in which mortality in India has seemingly been reduced—the control of internecine war and the control of famines. Today the Indian subcontinent is subject to a new international tension (between Pakistan and the Indian Union) which has already resulted in warfare. Within each country a stable government is by no means assured. Similarly, the economic situation does not look altogether favorable. It is not certain, then, that some of the major conditions for the reduction in mortality will continue on the subcontinent. In a sense these major conditions were first established by foreign influence. They were maintained for a time both by this foreign influence and by indigenous alacrity to learn and develop. But if the gain has not depended on a great change in the texture of Indian life, it does not have now any such change to rely on in the future. The local village still remains unsanitary, the public apathetic to health measures, and the poverty almost as abject. It follows that the reduction of the death rate in recent decades is a tenuous thing. It will remain so until basic changes are incorporated into the warp and woof of Hindu and Muslim society. Viewed in this light, the growth in the region's population during recent times represents a potentially disturbing factor.

‡‡

CHAPTER 7

The Risks Ahead

‡‡

THE death rate in India and Pakistan still remains high, although it has been reduced. In trying to assess the future trend in this death rate, one must begin by studying the factors that make it high at present. The first thing to note is that the controls described in the last chapter—the control of warfare, of famine, and of epidemic disease—are not only tenuous but also incomplete. The improvements in mortality have been effected with a minimum change in Hindu and Muslim social organization; but not all causes of death are yet shown to be amenable to such "remote control." Some of these, such as tuberculosis and dietary deficiency, are discussed below. Malaria, with which we begin, may be a disease more amenable than some of the others to this kind of control.

MALARIA

Plague, smallpox, and cholera are, as previously mentioned, the only diseases universally notifiable in British India. The rest are notifiable only in certain areas, and in all other areas they are reported only in catch-all categories that make statistical treatment virtually impossible. Malaria deaths, for example, are usually registered under "fevers," along with deaths from many other causes. The exact proportion of "fever" deaths due to malaria is unknown, but it is estimated to be as high as one-third, which would mean that roughly 20 per cent of all deaths in India are traceable to this one disease alone.[1] This estimate of the proportion of deaths due to malaria is surely too high, but let us compensate for that a bit by other assumptions. In 1939 there were over six million deaths *registered* in India, and 20 per cent of these would yield over a million deaths due to malaria. If the registration of deaths is about 25 per cent deficient, which is certainly a low estimate, this means that in 1939 approximately 1.4 million malaria deaths occurred in the registration area of British India.[2] It seems unwise, in view of our high initial assumption, to correct this figure to apply to India as a whole, in which case there would have been 1.9 million malaria deaths. In any case, the annual death rate from this disease is almost 5 per

thousand inhabitants, nearly three times the rate for plague, smallpox, and cholera combined.

In a disease that is usually not fatal, such a high mortality rate indicates an astonishingly high prevalence of infection. The malaria morbidity rate in India remains unknown, but it must be extremely great. Most authorities agree that malaria "causes more sickness and loss of working-power than any other disease in India."[3] It has been estimated that each year about 100 million suffer from it. In 1936 the number of malaria cases treated in hospitals came to 12 million, which was 17 per cent of the total hospital cases.[4] In some areas a majority of the people lose several weeks of working time out of each year because of the disease. "It is therefore certain that malaria constitutes the major public health problem in India, from the point of view both of morbidity and of mortality."[5]

The disease is widespread, affecting especially the riverine plains, the Himalayan foothills, and the rainy slopes of the coastal ghats. In certain parts of the country, it has been imported or made more severe by the works of man himself— for example, by the building of irrigation canals, rice terraces, road and railway embankments, and dams.[6] Map 11 shows the wide distribution of malaria in India, as revealed by spleen tests and other data. The malaria problem in the India-Pakistan region is so enormous that no dent has yet been made on it by preventive or curative methods. In the past the main weapon used in the region has been the distribution of medicines such as quinine and cinchona febrifuge. Such medicines have been administered in considerable quantities, as Table 14 indicates. Even if plentiful, however, they would hardly have been adequate to control the disease, and the truth is that they have never been anything like plentiful in India. The Bhore committee stated that, during the years it observed, the supply of quinine was only about one-eighth of the minimum requirement. Furthermore, it said that even if the larger quantity became available, the existing health organization would not be adequate to distribute it.[7] The Central Government has maintained an all-India organization, now known as the Malaria Institute of India, for research and teaching. It has done excellent work in both regards and has greatly assisted public health programs. The

---

[1] Gyan Chand, *India's Teeming Millions* (London: Allen & Unwin, 1939), p. 119.

[2] The Health Commissioner's Annual Report for 1935 suggested that the total for the registration area was 1.25 million. The Report for 1936 says that "the recorded figures for 1936 amount to 1,567,084, but there is reason to think that may be . . . exaggerated" (p. 49). The 1939 Report gave 1.5 million as the number of malaria deaths (p. 219). Colonel Sinton, director of the Malaria Survey of India, claimed that over a million deaths from malaria occur each year, and that if its debilitating effects in causing other deaths from other factors are taken into account, it is responsible for more than two million deaths (Chand, *op. cit.,* p. 119).

[3] Sir John Megaw, "Public Health, The Great Diseases of India" in E. A. H. Blunt (ed.), *Social Service in India* (London: His Majesty's Stationery Office, 1938), p. 219.

[4] Health Commissioner with the Government of India, *Annual Report*, 1936, p. 49.

[5] *ibid.*

[6] Health Survey and Development Committee, *Report*, Vol. 1, pp. 90–91.

[7] *ibid.,* p. 92.

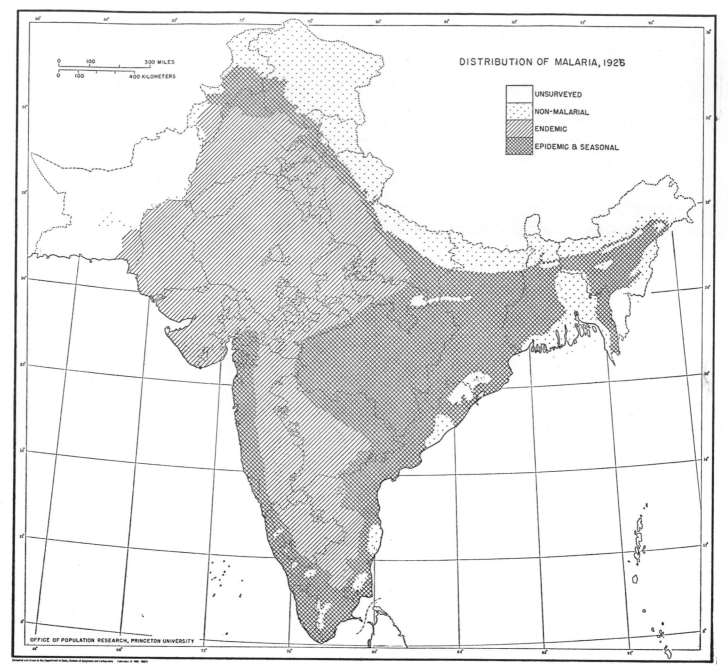

MAP 11. Distribution of Malaria in 1926. From S. R. Christophers and J. A. Sinton, *Indian Journal of Medical Research 1926–1927* (Calcutta: Thacker, Spink & Co.), p. 178.

provincial efforts at malaria control have on the whole been spasmodic in character. Local successes have been followed by over-optimism and subsequent loss of control. Yet, in particular provinces, anti-malarial organizations have been built up which could serve as a nucleus for expanded developments.[8]

Although not much progress has been made in the past in solving the malaria problem of the subcontinent, the battle is beginning to be waged now with new weapons. On the side of chemotherapy, experiments made in 1946 indicate that paludrine can cure a primary attack with a single administration of 300 milligrams, "which revolutionizes treatment of malaria in rural areas." [9] One or two 100-milligram tablets per

[8] *ibid.*, pp. 92–97.

[9] D. K. Viswanathan, "Activities of the Bombay Provincial Malaria Organization, 1942–47" in *Proceedings of the Fourth International Congresses on Tropical Medicine and Malaria*, Vol. 1, pp. 878–79.

week will give protection against infection. Chloroquin, "Camaqi," and plasmoquin also promise results far more powerful than quinine.[10] On the side of vector control, the work recently reported from Bombay is extremely interesting. The Bombay Provincial Malaria Organization was created by the provincial government in 1942. It conducted intensive studies of the vector species (A. *fluviatilis*) in Kanara district. When DDT became available in 1945 and 1946, an area comprising 6,000 square miles in Dharwar and Kanara districts, with about 1200 malaria-stricken villages and a population of over a million, was subjected to experiment.

"The results showed that a dose of about 60 milligrams per square foot DDT indoor residual spray once in 2 months in the case of *fluviatilis*, and once in 6 weeks in the case of

[10] M. Y. Ansari, "Anti-Malarial Drugs Old and New," *The Indian Physician*, Vol. 7 (July, 1948), pp. 177–84.

TABLE 14

Quinine and Cinchona Febrifuge Issued by Various Government Departments in British India, 1938 [1]

	GRAMS PER CAPITA	
	Quinine	Cinchona Febrifuge
British India	2.1	0.6
N. W. Frontier Prov.	3.8	2.1
Punjab	0.6	0.1
Delhi	2.1	1.1
United Provinces	0.7	0.5
Bihar	0.7	—
Orissa	1.4	0.5
Bengal	6.2	1.9
Central Provinces	1.6	0.4
Bombay	2.2	0.2
Sind	1.1	0.3
Madras	0.8	0.1
Coorg	35.9	16.6
Assam	3.4	1.1
Ajmer-Merwara	1.1	0.9

[1] Health Commissioner with the Government of India, *Annual Report*, 1938, p. 222.

culicifacies, is efficacious in keeping them down below the critical density for transmission. For the first time in the history of malaria epidemiology, parasite rates and infant parasite rates exhibited signs of approximation to zero point in hyperendemic areas in the tropics. . . .

"Spleen and parasite rates have dropped considerably. In several villages they are now less than 10 percent as against 50 to 100 percent in the past. More than all, infant parasite rates are almost nil, about 0.8 percent in the sprayed villages as against 15 percent in unsprayed villages.

". . . The approximate cost of the scheme is about 6 to 8 annas (12–15 cents) per capita per annum . . ." [11]

Although such results by indoor spraying would be possible only with mosquito species that transmit infection mainly inside the house, this remarkable experiment nevertheless shows that startling malaria control is possible by the use of new insecticides, and at low cost. It seems within reason, therefore, to think that by a combination of cheap and powerful insecticides and drugs, India and Pakistan will eventually solve their malaria problem. Complete elimination by wholesale spraying of outdoor breeding grounds, as has been done in Ceylon and Cyprus, does not at present look feasible for a whole subcontinent; but even without this it appears that rigid control is possible.

TUBERCULOSIS

With the exception of malaria, tuberculosis probably kills more people in Pakistan and the Union of India than any other single disease. Nobody knows exactly how many it does kill, because it is difficult to diagnose and register properly. "The value of the recorded figures is greatly vitiated by the

[11] Viswanathan, *op. cit.*, pp. 876–77.

fact that correct diagnosis of the cause of death is rarely obtained and numerous deaths from tuberculosis are without doubt registered both in towns and in villages as due to fevers or respiratory disease. Indeed, it may safely be assumed that the majority of the deaths from tuberculosis are registered under one or other of these groups. There exists also the general tendency to conceal the cause of death in tubercular cases for fear of social disabilities or of quarantine and other disinfection measures." [12] Because of inaccurate registration the estimates of the deaths due to tuberculosis ranged from 450,000 to 820,000 per year in British India during the period 1932–41, or from roughly 7 to 13 per cent of all deaths.[13]

What is most alarming about tuberculosis in the Indian region is that, in contrast to most of the diseases already discussed, it seems to be increasing. The percentage of all deaths listed as due to respiratory causes has shown a marked increase since 1902, as Fig. 9 in the previous chapter shows. In fact, "respiratory ailments" is the only class of causes that has shown a long-range increase—from 2.2 per cent of all deaths in 1902 to 8.1 per cent in 1939. This increase is perhaps due in part to changes in registration habits, but probably also to a real trend. Since tuberculosis in India-Pakistan is predominantly of the pulmonary type, representing 93.5 per cent of the cases in one set of dispensary records, a rise in respiratory deaths may well represent in large part an increase in tuberculosis. In areas where tuberculosis is notifiable, the mortality from this cause has apparently increased. During ten years in Calcutta, for example, the recorded tuberculosis mortality rose 77 per cent.[14] The first survey of tuberculosis in India, made by Dr. Arthur Lankester during 1914–16, concluded that the incidence of the disease was steadily increasing. He said:

"The impression left upon the mind after careful inquiry . . . is that many large areas in India, which 40 years ago were practically 'virgin soil' to tuberculosis, have now become to a considerable extent infected; that phthisis has been for generations, probably centuries, a common disease of the larger cities, yet even in these there has been considerable actual increase during the last 40 years; that while in smaller towns and in the village districts it was formerly comparatively rare or even absent, yet in these during a similar period the disease has made its appearance and spread widely. The increase has been most marked in connection with those centres which have shown the greatest commercial and educational development, and in the village districts which have been linked up with them by direct lines of communications." [15]

This conclusion seems to be universally accepted today. Sir John Megaw, for instance, believes that tuberculosis is still increasing at a rapid and alarming rate.[16]

An increase of the disease on the Indian subcontinent is

[12] Commissioner of Health with the Government of India, *Annual Report*, 1932, p. 87.

[13] Health Survey and Development Committee, *Report*, p. 97. For the Indian Union as a whole the total deaths in recent years are estimated by one authority as between 600,000 and 1,000,000. A. C. Ukil, "Tuberculosis in India" in *Proceedings of the Fourth International Congresses on Tropical Medicine and Malaria*, Vol. 2, p. 1509. Assuming a population of 350 million, these figures would yield an estimated rate of between 171 and 286 per 100,000 population.

[14] A. C. Ukil, "The Epidemiology and Pathology of Tuberculosis in India," *Indian Journal of Medical Research*, Vol. 17 (January, 1930), p. 822. The ten years evidently run from 1919 to 1929.

[15] Quoted by Health Survey and Development Committee, *Report*, Vol. 1, p. 99.

[16] *op. cit.*, p. 228.

what one would expect according to prevailing theory. It is well known that isolated rural peoples, when brought into contact with the outside world through the growth of cities, industry, and rapid transport, show an extreme susceptibility to tuberculosis. Opinions differ as to how much of this susceptibility is due to the lack of acquired immunity and how much to the low standard of living. It is now doubted that there are marked racial differences.[17] Upon contact with urban-industrial peoples, the most susceptible of all appear to be purely primitive groups. A peasant agricultural people, such as one finds in most of the Indian region, has more resistance than primitive tribes but less than Europeans. Consequently, the disease is increasing in the expanding cities with their hordes of rural migrants and spreading rapidly to the countryside. The diffusion is hastened by the tendency of Indian industrial workers to return to their rural villages after a short period of work in the city.

The "lack of immunity" theory seems to receive confirmation in India on the basis of tuberculin reaction tests. Between 1927 and 1929 the Pirquet cutireaction was found for 6,500 people in four eastern provinces. The percentages of positive reaction were:

Rural areas	33.4
Semirural areas	47.9
Urban areas	55.1
Industrial areas	70.3

In well isolated rural areas away from rail routes the proportion of positive reactors fell as low as 21 per cent.[18] Such results have been confirmed by other studies. A later tuberculin survey (Mantoux reaction) in a jute-mill population 23 miles from Calcutta showed that, for 4,816 mill operatives, 81.2 per cent showed positive reactions. Among relatives and friends of the mill hands, the percentage was 65 and 67 respectively. In villages 10 miles from the industrial environment, the proportion was only 42.5 per cent.[19]

The thesis that the rural people represent virgin territory because they have not built up immunity by being exposed to small and harmless tuberculosis infections early in life, receives confirmation also from the course of the disease once it is contracted. It is more virulent than in European populations. The infection is usually massive in type, and is characterized by soft exudative lesions rather than by the formation of connective or fibrous tissue. The lesions advance rapidly and consequently lead to death more often and more quickly.[20]

Actually, the theory that the low standard of living is responsible for the susceptibility of peasant and primitive populations to T.B. once they are exposed, seems almost as convincing as the non-immunity theory. Dormer claims that among the Bantu in South Africa the type of lesion and the general course of the disease depend on how well nourished and rested the people are, not on how much exposure they have had. Under good tribal conditions "the type disease is that seen in the average white citizen of any well-fed state today." But when the Bantu go to the city to live, they encounter new conditions of life for which they are ill-prepared; they suffer fatigue, undernourishment, and social disorganization. Their incidence of tuberculosis is correspondingly high, and "the type disease is a soft, exudative, rapidly advancing, lethal type of tuberculosis." But good care can change this picture. The urban Bantu child with massive primary infection progresses rapidly toward death unless he has rest and adequate food, but he recovers with good care. In one study of such children, "80 percent of those whose parents refused hospitalization for them were dead in 3 months, whereas over 80 percent of those admitted to hospitals were calcified and healed in 18 months." [21]

The two explanations of high tuberculosis rates in newly exposed peasant populations suggest somewhat different policies. However, it is possible that the two views are not mutually exclusive. In the Indian region there is evidence that the standard of living is a factor in susceptibility. For instance, in contrast to most advanced industrial countries, the tuberculosis rate is greater among women than among men. "Up to 10 years the mortality is greater among boys, but between 10 and 30 years the female death rate is markedly higher." For ages 15 to 20 years, the female rate in Calcutta is "five times" the male rate. After age 30 the male rate is greater than the female in urban and industrial communities, but not in rural areas.[22] The reasons for the higher female mortality are apparently the heavy burden of rapid childbearing, prolonged lactation, extremely early marriage, and the purdah system. The influence of purdah is seemingly shown by a greatly enhanced incidence of infection immediately after the age when girls begin to be confined to the home.[23]

For both sexes general conditions favor a high tuberculosis mortality. Ukil lists such practices as "the habit of spitting inside habitations, eating and drinking from common vessels, and sleeping together in the same room," along with the poorly balanced and inadequate diet.[24] Fortunately, the cattle of the region are remarkably free from tuberculosis, and the people universally boil their milk before using. Consequently, the bovine type of tuberculosis is rarely encountered in the human population. As commercial dairies become more numerous, with the tendency to keep the cattle in sheds, bovine tuberculosis may spread.[25]

Whether one stresses lack of immunity or disadvantageous living conditions as responsible for susceptibility, it appears that the urbanization and industrialization of India and Pakistan will tend to enhance tuberculosis mortality unless heroic measures are undertaken. Already some of the cities

[17] B. A. Dormer, "Tuberculosis in South Africa" in *Proceedings of the Fourth International Congresses on Tropical Medicine and Malaria*, Vol. 2, pp. 1493–1502. This author tends to stress the standard of living rather than acquired immunity as explaining susceptibility. Ukil, on the other hand, in the works cited, emphasizes the degree of acquired immunity as the main factor.

[18] Ukil, "Tuberculosis in India," *loc. cit.*, p. 1504.

[19] *ibid.*, pp. 1505–06.

[20] "In Europe and America, the average duration of life in the case of lung tuberculosis is from 3 to 10 years, but in India the following ratios hold good in average cases if modern treatment is not undertaken or is not successful—"

Age	Duration till Death—Years
16–25	0.5–2
26–40	1.0–3+
40+	3.0–10

Ukil, "Epidemiology and Pathology," *loc. cit.*, p. 839.

[21] Dormer, *op. cit.*, pp. 1493–99.

[22] Ukil, "Tuberculosis in India," *loc. cit.*, p. 1509.

[23] Ukil, "Epidemiology and Pathology," *loc. cit.*, p. 833. Also, Commissioner of Health with the Government of India, *Annual Report*, 1932, p. 87.

[24] *ibid.*, p. 822.

[25] R. G. Dhayagude and B. R. Shah, "Variation in the Virulence of *M. Tuberculosis* and its Correlation with the Clinical Type of Tubercular Disease," *Indian Journal of Medical Research*, Vol. 36 (April, 1948), p. 89. Health Survey and Development Committee, *Report*, Vol. 1, pp. 98–99, 102.

are manifesting extremely high rates, as the following tabulation shows: [26]

T.B. Deaths per 100,000

Paris	117	Cawnpore	432
Mexico	170	Lucknow	419
New York	128	Madras	290
Berlin	120	Calcutta	230
London	96	Bombay	140

The measures suggested fall into three types—improving living standards, improving medical care, and utilizing vaccination. Of these the first promises very little for a long time, because a rise in the general level of living will come only with further urbanization and industrialization and hence will increase the chances of infection. The improvement of medical care itself depends greatly on economic progress. Ukil estimates that in India the cases respond well to institutional treatment, but that for each 3 million population there are 10,000 cases requiring to be institutionalized, and that "no country can provide for tuberculosis care on this scale," although the expenditure can be minimized "in the warm tropical regions by constructing simple and efficient types of hospitals in dust-free localities outside town limits." [27] It must also be remembered that a low wet tropical climate (where most of the subcontinent's population live) is itself probably bad for tuberculosis, and that the expense of moving patients to cooler altitudes above 5,000 feet should doubtless be incurred.[28] Furthermore, in India there is "hardly 1 X-ray unit per 2 million population; and where there is 1 qualified doctor per 10,000 population, it can be easily understood why 54 percent of the persons, when they first attend the tuberculosis clinics, are far-advanced cases, and why only 14 percent of cases are in minimal and 32 percent in moderately advanced stages." [29] Attempts are now being made to establish more clinics, dispensaries, and sanitoria, to work out systems of home care, and to improve diagnosis and reporting; but one gets the impression that as yet the cost of adequate medical care cannot be met in India and Pakistan in the face of the mounting tuberculosis problem.

Accordingly, the possibility of vaccination becomes extremely important. BCG vaccine is now widely used in several European countries, and its usefulness has been experimentally proven in India and North America as well.[30] There is, however, still some controversy over its degree of effectiveness and over the manner in which it should be used. "In Denmark a person must have been free from exposure to tuberculosis six weeks before the vaccination is performed. Children from tuberculous families who have been vaccinated are not permitted to associate with the source of infection at home until after they show a positive reaction." [31] Such precautions would be difficult to observe in India or Pakistan. Nevertheless, Ukil has the following to say: "I hold the view that it deserves a sustained trial in economically and industrially backward tropical countries. The vaccinated population should, however, be controlled by periodical inquiries, examination, and statistical analysis. For India, I can think of the following groups at the present moment: (1) newborn infants in tubercular environment, (2) tuberculin-negative school children and students and nurses who migrate from villages to towns, (3) all tuberculin-negative entrants to the police, army, industry, and tea-garden labor. Miniature mass radiography will be a valuable adjunct to the examination and follow-up of these groups of controlled population. With the consolidation and expansion of the administrative machinery, further groups and even the general population may be included." [32] It seems quite possible that eventually, before the development of natural immunity or a large rise in the general standard of living, the population of the Indian subcontinent may be immunized against tuberculosis by use of BCG or some other vaccine.

DIARRHEA AND DYSENTERY

In the Indian registration statistics, "diarrhea and dysentery" constitute a catch-all category embracing a large number and variety of intestinal disorders. There is no doubt that these disorders kill on a gigantic scale. Since they are particularly prone to attack infants, whose deaths are most likely to go unregistered, their relative role in the total mortality is perhaps understated by the official returns. Deaths in this category, as Fig. 9 of the previous chapter shows, have not declined more rapidly than total mortality. Their percentage of all registered deaths has remained almost constant, with a slight tendency to increase since 1918. Less attention seems to have been given to this general class of disorders in India than to some other classes. It is known that hygienic living conditions—purified drinking water, sanitary food, and cleanly personal habits—can greatly lower the incidence of such diseases. Since these conditions are difficult to secure in a poor country, the next question is whether short-cut methods may become available. The use of DDT for the control of insect carriers (above all the housefly) promises some relief. The development of new chemotherapeutic agents, such as the sulfa drugs, has been advancing rapidly and may be expected seriously to reduce the mortality from intestinal disorders. There seems every reason to think that the medical authorities, working gradually on all fronts, will be able greatly to reduce this cause of death in India and Pakistan in the next two or three decades. If so, it will contribute substantially to the lowering of the total death rate.

TYPHOID

Typhoid, it has been maintained, is so widespread in the Indian subcontinent "that most Indian infants suffer from the disease, and so acquire an immunity which often lasts throughout life. Numbers of adult Indians do get typhoid fever, but not nearly so many as might be expected considering the unhygienic conditions in which they live." [33] If true, this statement means that the disease must be one of the factors in the high infant mortality, and that control measures would

[26] Health Commissioner with the Government of India, *Report*, p. 101. Quoted from *Indian Medical Gazette* (October, 1941). No dates for the data given.

[27] "Tuberculosis in India," *loc. cit.*, p. 1513.

[28] K. Eisenstaedt, "On Tuberculosis: Some Outmoded Concepts and Practices in Phthisiology," *Indian Physician*, Vol. 7 (May, 1948), pp. 111–12.

[29] Ukil, "Tuberculosis in India," *loc. cit.*, p. 1512.

[30] Armand Frappier, "Some Experimental and Clinical Observations on the Stability of BCG Vaccine," *Proceedings of the Fourth International Congresses on Tropical Medicine and Malaria*, Vol. 1, pp. 187–202; Joseph D. Aronson, "The Use of BCG Vaccine in the Control of Tuberculosis," *ibid.*, Vol. 2, pp. 1517–27.

[31] Sally Preas, "BCG Vaccination against Tuberculosis," Milbank Memorial Fund *Quarterly*, Vol. 25 (April, 1947), p. 221.

[32] "Tuberculosis in India," *loc. cit.*, p. 1514.

[33] Megaw, "Public Health. The Great Diseases of India," *loc. cit.*, p. 235.

have an important effect on the death rate. It is known that the typhoid rate tends to rise in India in seasons when the water supply is bad. The following sentence sums up the conditions responsible for the widespread occurrence of the disease: "Enteric fever continues to be endemic in Ajmer City owing to defective water supply, bad drainage, flies and absence of legislation to control carriers." [34]

Since the means for controlling typhoid are already available—the chlorination and protection of water supplies, the hygienic disposal of excreta, the control of flies through insecticides, the understanding and diagnosis of different typhoid strains, the indentification of typhoid carriers through the Viagglutination test, and the use of T.A.B. vaccine—it seems only a matter of time before enough measures are taken in India and Pakistan to reduce mortality from this source. To a certain extent virtually all of the measures are being used in various parts of the region now, although sporadically and disconnectedly.

DIETARY DISEASES

The Indian subcontinent shares with most other tropical regions the handicap of an insufficient and ill-balanced diet. The reasons lie not only in the peculiar conditions of tropical existence but also in the heavy population density, the inadequacy of the transport system, the retardation of economic development, the lack of education, and the food habits which custom and religion have fixed in the populace. The poor diet is one of the principal factors in the high mortality of the region. Recent surveys and experimental research have given us a good knowledge of the dietary inadequacies, and medical investigations have revealed many of the deleterious physical consequences.

From the purely quantitative standpoint, the total number of calories available for actual consumption is estimated to be about 22 per cent below minimal requirements for good health.[35] Diet surveys in different parts of the region, including both urban and rural areas, have shown that the food consumed is insufficient to provide necessary energy for some 30 per cent of the families.[36] The shortage is greater in bad years and less in good years, but seems to be always present. The region simply does not produce enough food for its growing population; it is claimed that in recent decades the per capita production of cereals has declined.[37] By no means all of the production is available for human consumption. Some of it must be used for seed and for cattle. There is considerable waste caused by wild animals, insects, rats, and roaming cattle while the crops are still in the fields, and yet more waste from deterioration and insect and rodent pests during the process of shipping and storage, because the facilities are poor. In the past some food has been exported. Except in periods of rationing the distribution of food has been extremely unequal as between rich and poor. In times of real or supposed scarcity the well-to-do classes tend to purchase and store food for "security" purposes, thus aggravating the shortage for the masses.[38] There are thus many factors involved in the lack of calories.

[34] Public Health Commissioner with the Government of India, *Annual Report,* 1945, p. 21.

[35] Baljit Singh, *Population and Food Planning in India* (Bombay: Hind Kitabs, 1947), p. 101. The standard taken is 2,800 calories per average man daily.

[36] Health Survey and Development Committee, *Report,* Vol. 1, p. 57.

[37] Singh, *op. cit.,* p. 64.

[38] *ibid.,* Ch. 6. See also Ch. 3.

In addition to the shortage of food from an energy standpoint, the diet of Indians and Pakistanis suffers from serious qualitative deficiencies. Comparing an "average" Indian diet with the daily requirements for a balanced diet, Dr. Singh gives figures that show the following percentages of adequacy.

	Average Consumption as Percentage of Requirement [39]
Cereals	105.7
Fruits	90.0
Sugar	78.5
Pulses	57.7
Milk	38.2
Oil and Ghee	34.5
Vegetables	33.5
Fish, meat, eggs	14.4
Buttermilk	—— [40]

The list suggests grave deficiencies in calcium, fats, and protein, and various studies have shown this to be the case in large groups of Indians. In addition, it has been shown that essential vitamins—notably vitamins A, B_1, C, and D—are deficient in many of the diets, particularly in the rice-eating areas. The people therefore do not get the most out of the scanty amount of food they do have to eat. If their diet were better balanced, the shortage of calories would not be so serious as it is.

The precise effect of the dietary situation on mortality in the region is hard to estimate. Certainly the influence is not to be measured solely by the number of deaths from specific deficiency diseases such as beriberi, pellagra, dropsy, etc., but also by the deaths from other diseases in which dietary deficiency is a contributing cause. Perhaps, for example, poor diets contribute more deaths through increasing the susceptibility to tuberculosis than they do directly by causing deficiency diseases. Yet it is difficult to measure this indirect effect, and so we fall back upon specific deficiency diseases as our best index of the fatal effects of diet. Such afflictions represent an extreme degree of food inadequacy. Their presence therefore implies that many others in the same population, though less afflicted, still are made susceptible to other diseases that thrive on lowered resistance.

Recent research, much of it in India, is uncovering more and more deficiency disorders hitherto not identified. These, taken together, may "affect public health to a greater degree than the classical deficiency diseases at their height and may be more difficult to attack." [41] It is not possible to discuss all of the dietary afflictions here. In what follows only certain ones of them are selected as illustrations.

BERIBERI

Although beriberi has long been known and is easily prevented, it still occurs in India as well as other regions. The true incidence, however, is not known. In 1930–32 there were 63,460 cases treated in the hospitals and dispensaries of British India, and 636 deaths.[42] These figures do not measure

[39] Computed from Singh, *op. cit.,* p. 108.

[40] Apparently buttermilk does not occur in the Indian diet.

[41] W. R. Aykroyd, "Malnutrition and the Rice Problem" in *Proceedings of the Fourth International Congresses on Tropical Medicine and Malaria,* Vol. 2, p. 1174.

[42] Public Health Commissioner with the Government of India, *Annual Report,* 1932, p. 93.

the problem, because the number of hospitals and dispensaries is tiny in comparison to the total population, and because beriberi is a poor man's disease which usually runs its course without benefit of treatment. Furthermore, the fatality rate is probably higher outside of hospitals than in them. The figures by provinces do suggest, however, that the northwestern provinces (now mostly in West Pakistan but also including Delhi and the United Provinces) suffer less from the disease than the eastern and southern areas, because the northwestern parts are wheat-eating areas. In Madras the endemic home of beriberi "is the flat, inundated area which includes the deltas of the Kistna and Godivari rivers. . . . Whole families and often whole villages suffer from minor degrees of beriberi. . . ."[43] It is now recognized that beriberi in infants, a disease often unrecognized, needs special emphasis. "Investigations in the Madras Presidency during the years 1939–45 showed that beriberi was much more common than had formerly been supposed and was responsible for much mortality among infants. The disease in its acute form often leads to the sudden death of breast-fed infants during the second to the fourth month of life. If recognized, it can be effectively treated by the timely injection of thiamine."[44] The methods of preventing beriberi are those designed either to retain the nutrient values of rice or to supplement it more adequately with other foods. The specific remedy, once the disease is present, is the administration of thiamine in one form or another. There seems no reason why it cannot be banished from India.

NUTRITIONAL DIARRHEA

"Cases of chronic diarrhea of obscure etiology which do not respond to any kind of present treatment and slowly waste away and die are seen in hospitals in south India."[45] A 3-year experiment in India showed that the disorder could be produced in monkeys by a poor rice diet. Improvement of the diet could cure the animals in the early stages of the disease, but in the later stages such improvement had no effect. Postmortem examination showed degeneration of the small intestine. From this it was deduced that "the health of the small intestine is dependent on good nutrition, and deficient diet may produce irreversible changes in the gut."[46]

CIRRHOSIS OF THE LIVER

Investigations in south India seem to show that dietetic deficiencies are important in the causation of cirrhosis of the liver. The evidence is not all in yet, but some forms of the disease appear to occur among people with dietary deficiencies, to attack children as well as adults, and to respond well in the early stages to nutritional therapy.[47] Hepatic cirrhosis "may perhaps prove to be the most common of all deficiency states among ill-nourished populations in the tropics and the East."[48]

BLINDNESS

The number of blind persons in pre-partition India was estimated at anything from one to two million, although the 1931 census disclosed only 601,000. Most authorities regard the chief cause of the high incidence of blindness as vitamin deficiency. In the rice-eating areas of southern India and the eastern Ganges valley, for example, keratomalacia, an eye condition due to vitamin A deficiency and producing blindness, is quite common, although "it is practically unknown in the wheat and milk consuming Punjab."[49] In addition, "blindness from cataract associated with advanced years is also widespread and can be traced to a deficiency of vitamin C in the diet, . . ." Glaucoma, which heads the Public Health Commissioner's list (1929) of causes of blindness, is said to have vitamin B deficiency as its main contributing factor. "The incidence of partial blindness and defective eye-sight is not yet fully known and it is possible that a considerable number of the. . . . illiterates in India might find reading and writing, when they are taught, too strenuous for their eyes. At present illiteracy conceals blindness and consequently. . . . vitamin deficiency."[50]

THE COST OF DIETARY DEFICIENCY

The list of diseases of dietary etiology is much longer than those already mentioned. It includes epidemic dropsy, stomatitis, glossitis, cheilosis, and oedema, all of which occur more frequently among the rice-eating than among the wheat-eating population; pellagra in a few limited areas; scurvy occasionally; burning feet; sprue; and tropical sore. Yet, as mentioned, the mortality from all of these disorders, great as it undoubtedly is, does not represent the main contribution that food deficiency makes to the total mortality of India and Pakistan. The indirect cost, chiefly in the form of lowered resistance to diseases of infectious origin (such as tuberculosis, leprosy, influenza, and pneumonia) and also in the form of inefficiency in food production and food distribution (which produces a vicious circle), is much greater.

It has been shown experimentally in the United States and Canada that even slight deficiencies in essential nutrients in an apparently well-fed population can markedly lower resistance to disease, complicate pregnancy and childbirth and the production of healthy children, and significantly lessen intelligence.[51] If these consequences of slight deficiency show up in groups with an extremely high standard of living, how much greater must be the consequences in populations with major deficiencies. It seems hardly an exaggeration to say that lack of calories, vitamins, and essential nutrients is the greatest single source of death in the Indian subcontinent. It produces specific dietary diseases that are fatal, it lowers resistance to most other diseases, and it lessens the strength, incentive, and effective intelligence which are necessary if the people are to remedy their situation. Unfortunately, it is a source of death that stems from major economic and cultural conditions which are not easy to change.

RICE, TROPICS, AND FOOD DEFICIENCY

In the Indian region, as in most other areas of Asia, rice is a principal culprit in the dietary situation. The level of health in rice-eating areas seems generally lower than in wheat-eating areas. This is shown not only by higher mortality

[43] Lieut. Colonel R. McCarrison, "Beriberi Columbarum," *Indian Medical Research Memoirs,* No. 10 (Calcutta: Indian Research Fund Association, March, 1928), p. 52.

[44] Aykroyd, *op. cit.,* p. 1173.

[45] M. V. Radhakrishna Rao, "Some Common Deficiency Diseases in India" in *Proceedings of the Fourth International Congresses on Tropical Medicine and Malaria,* Vol. 2, p. 1204.

[46] *ibid.,* p. 1205.

[47] *ibid.,* pp. 1206–07.

[48] Aykroyd, *op. cit.,* p. 1173.

[49] Singh, *op. cit.,* p. 122. See also Sir John Megaw, "Public Health. The Great Diseases of India," *loc. cit.,* p. 244.

[50] Singh, *op. cit.,* p. 123.

[51] F. F. Tisdall, "The Role of Nutrition in Preventive Medicine" in Milbank Memorial Fund, *New Steps in Public Health* (New York: Milbank Fund, 1945) pp. 79–93; Joseph Warkany, "The Importance of Prenatal Diet," *ibid.,* pp. 106–17.

but also by the clinical evidences of malnutrition and the marked change when supplementary foods are added to the rice diet.

The trouble with rice as a staple is twofold: first, it loses more of its natural elements between field and table than do other staple cereals; second, it tends to become too large a proportion of the total diet, especially in the tropics.[52] Research on beriberi first revealed the harm done by the milling and polishing of rice. As early as 1921 the Far Eastern Association of Tropical Medicine proposed that the government prohibit the milling of rice. But milling is only part of the story. Rice varies greatly in its original elements according to the conditions under which it is grown. "Rice grown under 'dry conditions' (natural rainfall or light watering) has a higher vitamin B-value than the same rice when grown on the same soil under 'wet conditions' (in standing water). Manurial conditions may also cause variation in its vitamin-value. . . . At the very best the whole rice grown in endemic areas of beriberi in the Madras Presidency has no vitamin B to spare for removal by refined milling processes." [53]

Furthermore, "rice is the only cereal which is usually washed and cooked in water before consumption, and these processes lead to serious depletion of nutrients." An investigation in Coonoor showed the following losses from washing and cooking methods practiced in south India:

	Per Cent Loss
Iron	75
Calcium and Phosphorus	56
Protein	10
Calories	15

"The loss of thiamin may be as high as 85 per cent." Milled parboiled rice, used in some parts of India, retains more nutrients than raw milled rice; but since people accustomed to raw milled rice usually do not like it, improvements to make it look and taste better are required. "So-called converted rice is essentially similar to parboiled rice in its nutritive properties; conversion is, in fact, parboiling technically perfected, modernized, and protected by patents." [54] As yet no improvements are being practiced in India and Pakistan which will retain most of the nutrients lost in the growing, milling, storing, washing, and cooking of rice.

As compared with those who eat other staple cereals, rice eaters are most faithful to their staff of life. "There is a great preponderance of rice in typical rice diets: More than 70 percent of total calories may be obtained from rice, while other foods, e.g., food of animal origin, are present in small and often negligible amounts. Diets containing so high a proportion of cereal do not comply with current standards of nutrient requirements. . . . The wheat eater, on the other hand, is, in general, less dependent on wheat for the nutrients he needs." [55] The reasons for this heavy reliance on rice are complex. It is not to be explained solely as due to preference, although this may be a by-product of long concentration on rice. Because rice swells in cooking to about 5 times its dried bulk, the consumer is forced to eat large quantities of it. "Such

large quantities cause the digestibility and protein absorption to fall, sometimes by as much as 50%," and they may diminish the absorption of elements from other foods not themselves bulky.[56] In addition, the preponderance of rice in the diet is to be explained by the unavailability of other foods. It seems often to be assumed that Hindus do not eat eggs, poultry, and meat because of their religious taboos. Actually, these foods are not plentiful for reasons other than religion, and it may be that the taboos exist because of non-consumption, not vice versa. When such foods are obtainable, they are eaten by rather large sections of the Hindu public, although some classes adhere strictly to the dietary restrictions.

In an experiment with south Indian army recruits, it was found that the regular army diet liberally supplemented with fresh meat was superior both to army diet and to the army diet supplemented with fresh milk. The group placed on the "meat" diet gained weight and recovered from nutritional deficiencies more rapidly than the other two groups. This result, combined with other studies showing the superiority of meat in blood regeneration, suggests that a lacto-vegetarian or semi-vegetarian diet "may be intrinsically inferior to a meat dietary. The implications in respect of a predominantly vegetarian population like that of India do not require stressing." Furthermore, the investigators found no difficulty in persuading the recruits to eat 12 ounces of meat daily. They add: "This is stressed, since it is often stated that the majority of Indians would not eat meat even if it were provided." [57]

But regardless of attitudes or requirements, meat is scarce in most tropical areas. In hot climates animal foodstuffs are highly perishable, difficult to keep in a palatable and nutritious condition until consumed. Also, livestock raising is hazardous. The continuous high temperature affects adversely the development and performance of most present breeds of cattle and, to some extent, other livestock as well. Too often in tropical areas cattle are expected to obtain all their feed from pasturage. Especially in densely populated areas, they are not given enough other kinds of feed; and the pastures themselves are not sufficiently improved. In addition, cattle diseases and parasites abound in tropical countries. These conditions not only cut down the supply and quality of meat, but do the same for milk; and milking practices are seldom efficient in tropical areas.[58]

REMEDIES FOR THE FOOD PROBLEM

Of the two food problems in the Indian subcontinent—the deficiency in calories and the deficiency in particular food elements—the first seems more difficult to remedy. A great increase in the total production of food is an economic task of major magnitude. (For this reason it is discussed in Chapter 21.) But it should prove possible to improve the nutrient quality of the food available with less economic cost. To be sure, for reasons just given, the protein and other deficiencies cannot be easily overcome by creating overnight a thriving beef cattle and dairy industry. But they can perhaps be overcome by improved processing, distribution, and preparation of the foods available, together with the addition of strategic

[52] Aykroyd, op. cit., pp. 1172–73. Most of the present discussion of rice except as other sources are given, is taken from this excellent paper.

[53] McCarrison, op. cit., pp. 13–15. Aykroyd, op. cit., p. 1172, believes that in general the whole rice grain is as nutritious as that of other cereals.

[54] Aykroyd, op. cit., pp. 1175–76.

[55] ibid., p. 1174.

[56] McCarrison, op. cit., pp. 17–22.

[57] O. P. Verma, C. K. Dilwali, and A. M. Thomson, "A Feeding Experiment on Indian Army Pioneer Recruits, with Special Reference to the Relative Value of Meat and Milk in Rations," Indian Journal of Medical Research, Vol. 35 (April, 1947), pp. 41–57.

[58] R. E. Hodgson, "General Problems of Human Nutrition in the Tropics in Relation to Animal Husbandry" in Proceedings of the Fourth International Congresses on Tropical Medicine and Malaria, Vol. 2, pp. 1181–86.

food elements of small bulk but major dietary importance, some of them possibly synthetic. Systematic planning, rigorous control, and vigorous public education, together with an effort to push total production as fast as possible, should reduce greatly the dietary factor in Indian mortality.

CONCLUSION

No matter which major cause of death in India and Pakistan we consider, the picture is dark but with a potential silver lining. The present toll is high, but medical research is going forward, improvements are being made here and there, and almost miraculous remedies are already known. One has the feeling that mortality in the region can be reduced much more than it has been—*if* certain things can be done. The real question is whether or not the "if" will come true. In view of the economic and demographic conditions, the search must be always for quick and inexpensive means—some way to prevent malaria at a few annas per head per year, some simple vaccination for tuberculosis, some ready chemical specifics for the diarrheas and dysenteries, and some cheap synthetic foods capable of manufacture in huge quantities and food elements capable of wide distribution. The process of improving economic conditions, changing the social institutions, improving general hygienic conditions, and altering popular habits seems too slow. There is no inherent necessity why India and Pakistan should recapitulate all the gradual stages that Western peoples went through in lowering their mortality to the present revolutionary level. It should be possible to find a shortcut, to take the very latest scientific inventions—DDT, BCG vaccine, anti-biotic drugs, converted rice, deep-freeze storage, hundreds of others—and apply them directly to the Indian population. Such wholesale application of the latest scientific achievements would produce the sharpest decline in mortality the world has ever known.

Nevertheless, the *if* is still persistently present. All the scientific shortcuts known to man cannot divorce the death rate from economic and demographic realities. The reason is that a reduction in mortality itself has repercussions on the entire bio-social situation. A drastic decline in deaths would mean a drastic increase in population, which in turn means, in an already densely settled region, that the once cheap shortcuts would become more expensive. An old cause of death is not banished forever simply because it is banished temporarily. Unless changes were soon made in the economic organization and the social institutions, in the Hindu-Muslim pattern of life and the world position of the Indian subcontinent, there would be the danger that no change would be made in the fertility of the people. There would then be the possibility that famine, war, epidemic disease, and malnutrition would once again stalk the land and undo what a temporary miracle had done. In fact, these dangers are already present even without a quick and drastic reduction in mortality. Our argument is not that further declines in the death rate are impossible or improbable, but rather that a continued low death rate without a modern economy and a civilized fertility is inconceivable.

┿┿

CHAPTER 8

Indian Life Tables

┿┿

WITH two exceptions life tables have been constructed in India for every decade since 1871–81. The two exceptions were the decades 1911–21 and 1931–41, when the actuary dismissed the task because of defective age data. All of the life tables were constructed solely with censuses, because India's defective or insufficient death registration precluded the more usual method of using the vital statistics. It appears, in fact, that India was the first place to use the differencing technique, which has little to recommend it other than sheer necessity.

In order to have a continuous series of life tables and thus to form a better judgment of the mortality trend, we have made two additional tables, one for the decade 1911–21 and the other for the decade 1931–41. Though using the differencing technique, we have made these tables by abridged methods. They are not so accurate as they might have been if more complete actuarial methods had been used, but the loss of accuracy is probably not great enough to influence the results seriously for our purposes. Appendix C describes the mechanics of construction in some detail, while the present chapter discusses the significance of the entire series of life tables.

EXPECTATION OF LIFE

Perhaps the most vivid measure of a people's mortality is the average length of life at birth. Historically in India, according to the official life tables, the lowest figure occurred in 1901–11, when the average length of life for males was 22.6 years and for females, 23.3. That the lowest figure should occur in this particular decade is astonishing, because this was a decade when there were few calamities and when the population grew rather rapidly. The previous decade had been a decade of famine, and yet the average length of life for that period was a little higher, being 23.6 for males and 24.0 for females. This points to the fundamental defect in the official life tables. As mentioned previously, the actuaries who made them were searching for a "normal" experience. If the decade in question had experienced a severe famine or epidemic, they did not simply base their findings on the censuses that began and ended the decade, but adopted some other device that would *decrease* the ultimate rate of mortality used. The idea that there is somehow a "normal" mortality is a mystical notion hardly applicable to life-table work. If we must think in terms of "normality," there is every reason for regarding recurrent famines and epidemics as normal in the history of India. A series of life tables ignoring the effects of these famines and epidemics greatly distorts the actual survival rates and gives us an idealized picture rather than the truth.

For this reason it is interesting to notice (Table 15) that the lowest expectation of life yet found for India comes not from an official life table but from the 1911–21 table constructed by ourselves. Here the expectancy for males at birth

TABLE 15

Mean Expectation of Life at Birth in Life Tables for India, 1872–1941, and in Those for Comparable Areas

Country	Period	Male Expectation	Female Expectation
India [1]	1872–1881	23.67	25.58
	1881–1891	24.59	25.54
	1891–1901	23.63	23.96
	1901–1911	22.59	23.31
	1911–1921	19.42	20.91
	1921–1931	26.91	26.56
	1931–1941	32.09	31.37
Egypt [2]	1927–1937	30.26	31.59
Korea [3]	1930–1931	30.21	37.27
Mexico [4]	1930	32.44	34.07
Chile [5]	1930–1931	38.36	40.28
Brazil [6] Distrito Federal [9]	1890–1920 1939–1940	38.84 42.37	40.01 43.71
U.S.S.R. [7] (Siberia)	1926–1927	39.18	43.20
Puerto Rico [8]	1939–1941	43.60	45.47
Japan [7]	1935–1936	46.92	49.63
U. S. Negro [10]	1929–1931	47.55	49.51

[1] *Census of India*, 1931, Vol. 1, Part 1, pp. 165–66.
[2] From Clyde Kiser, unpublished material.
[3] From Irene Taeuber, unpublished material.
[4] *Revista del Instituto de Salubridad y Enfermedades Tropicales*, Vol. 1 (May 1940), pp. 140–43.
[5] From Kingsley Davis and E. Jane Davis, unpublished material.
[6] U. S. Department of State, Eighth American Scientific Congress, *Proceedings*, Vol. 8, p. 331. (This table, however, does not give males and females separately. In order to estimate them, the expectation for the total population was doubled, then the percentage of this for males and females according to the average for the remainder of the countries appearing in this table, was taken.)
[7] *Population Index*, Vol. 9 (July, 1943), pp. 222–23.
[8] From Kingsley Davis and E. Jane Davis, unpublished material.
[9] Giorgio Mortara, "Estudos de demografia interamericana," *Estadística*, No. 3 (September, 1943), p. 74. See note under (6) above.
[10] U. S. Bureau of the Census, Vital Statistics—Special Reports, Vol. 1, No. 20 (July 27, 1936), pp. 396, 398.

is 19.4 years, and for females, 20.9 years. Even if the figure is in error by as much as two years, it is nonetheless a record low mark for any modern nation. Table 15 gives figures for nine other countries, all of which have rather low life expectancy. The most comparable are Egypt and Korea, both of which, at the dates mentioned, have an expectancy over ten years higher than India's for 1911–21.

The highest life expectancy for India—32.1 years for males and 31.4 for females—is also found in a table constructed by ourselves, this time for the 1931–41 decade. The age data for this table were not complete, because the 1941 census did not tabulate age for all of India, and so there is more chance for error, but still the result shows to what extent mortality conditions fluctuate in this region. It shows too that in this period India was probably better off than some other countries.

The expectation of life at various ages in India tells an interesting story. It will be noticed from Table 16 that for all the tables the expectation at age 10 is much higher than

tion exists: in nearly all of the life tables the expectancy at age 20 exceeds that at birth. This means that a man of 20, on the average can expect a longer life than a child just born. Indeed, in some of the Indian life tables the expectation of life even at age 30 is as great as that of a newborn infant. In this Asiatic region the hazards of life come heavily in the early years.

It will be observed from Fig. 11 that the life expectation of Indians becomes more like that of white Americans as age advances. According to 1921–31 tables, an average male child in India can at the moment of birth expect to live 26.9 years, whereas an American white boy, according to United States life tables for 1929–31, can expect to live 59.1 years, or more than twice as long. But at age 70, the two expectations are 6.4 and 9.2. In other words, the unhealthiness of India manifests

TABLE 16

Male Life Expectation at Various Ages in Seven Indian Life Tables [1]

Age	1872–1881	1881–1891	1891–1901	1901–1911	1911–1921 [2]	1921–1931	1931–1941 [2]
0	23.7	24.6	23.6	22.6	19.4	26.9	32.1
10	34.0	35.5	34.7	33.4	26.7	36.4	41.2
20	28.6	24.2	28.6	27.5	25.5	29.6	35.0
30	23.8	23.7	22.9	22.5	21.6	23.6	29.0
40	18.9	18.8	17.9	18.0	17.9	18.6	23.3
50	13.9	14.3	13.6	14.0	14.3	14.3	17.8
60	9.3	10.1	9.5	10.0	10.7	10.3	12.6

[1] All figures except those otherwise designated come from *Census of India,* 1931, Vol. 1, Part 1, p. 165.
[2] From life tables constructed by the writer. See Appendix C for a description of the methods used.

that at age 0. This is not unusual in countries with high infant mortality; for example, in Puerto Rico, for 1931, the expectation was four years greater at age 10 than at age 0. In countries with low death rates, however, the expectation is considerably lower at age 10 than at birth; in the United States, for instance, the 1929–31 expectancy at age 10 is five years less than that at birth. But in India an unusual condi-

itself at all ages, but it is greater in the younger ages. Those few Indians who survive to advanced ages perhaps have a natural vitality that helps to counterbalance but does not fully outweigh the health hazards which have affected and will continue to affect them.

THE NUMBER WHO DIE

In addition to the expectation of life, one should pay attention to the number who die and the number who survive. Table 17 gives, for six Indian life tables and one from the United States, the age at which only half of the males born still survive, and also the proportion surviving at age 20. It

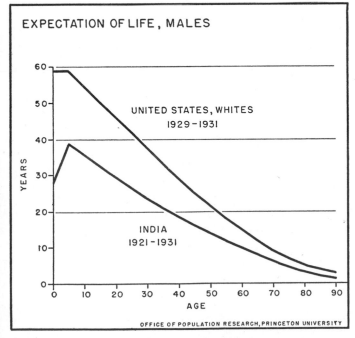

FIGURE 11. Expectation of Life for Males at Five-Year Intervals, India, 1921–1931, and United States, 1929–1931.

TABLE 17

Survivorship in India and United States: Males [1]

Life Table	Per Cent Surviving to Age 20	Age to which Half Survive
India		
1881–91	46.6	14
1890–1901	45.2	12
1901–11	43.8	10
1911–21	37.9	7
1921–31	51.2	22
1931–41	55.6	28
United States		
1929–31 (whites)	88.9	66

[1] Computed from various life tables previously described.

will be noticed how much fluctuation there is in the various Indian life tables. According to the 1911–21 rates, half of the Indians born are dead by age 7; whereas according to the 1931–41 rates, half of them are dead by age 28. But even the higher figure still falls far short of the United States, for the whites in this country still had 50 per cent of their number alive by age 66. The proportion surviving to age 20 also varies greatly in the Indian life tables. The highest proportion is that for 1931–41—namely, 55.6 per cent. But the figure for the United States—88.9 per cent—greatly exceeds this. Fig. 12 shows, for India and the United States, the number who still survive at selected ages out of 100,000 born.

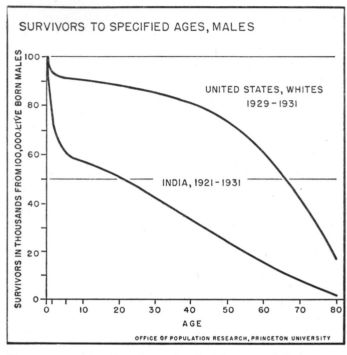

FIGURE 12. Number Surviving to Specified Ages out of Each 100,000 Live-Born Males, India, 1921–1931, and United States, 1929–1931.

Just what such great nearness of death does to the outlook of a people is hard to say. Presumably it is connected with an emphasis on religion, because it keeps the other world constantly before the minds of those lucky enough to be alive. Certainly it is connected with an emphasis on kinship and the joint household, because these protect the individual who loses his immediate relatives through death. Certainly, also, it is connected with high fertility, for if half of those born are dead before they reach adulthood, then the only guarantee of having grown children to protect one's old age and one's afterlife is to have as many babies as possible. It may be, too, that some of the prematurity in Indian life—the habit of child marriage, the employment of children, the beginning of reproductive life at puberty—is due to the imminence of death. The quickest way to guarantee having a few grand-children is to get one's children married and start them re-producing as soon as possible. The effect of high mortality would seem to be, then, to strengthen the tendency toward high fertility. Indeed, this would have to be the case, or else the Indian people, bearing their burden of frequent death, could not have survived.

PROVINCIAL LIFE TABLES

Life tables have been constructed for parts as well as for the whole of India. Prior to 1921, they were constructed for most of the British provinces but not for the States. For the 1921–31 decade the actuary included the adjoining Feudatory States along with each British province. On the surface, there-fore, it looks as though the life tables should afford us a basis for comparing mortality in different parts of India. Actually great caution must be exercised in such comparison, because the role of internal migration, the differences in accuracy of age reporting, the adjustments for changes in territory—all make the construction of a life table for a province of India a more hazardous undertaking than the construction of one for the whole territory. This is why no attempt was made by the writer to make life tables of the Indian provinces and states.

The following are the 1921–31 life expectancies at birth for the major areas of India, taking males and females to-gether.[1]

Burma	30.8
Madras	29.4
Central Provinces, Berar, & Hyderabad	28.1
Bihar & Orissa	27.9
Punjab	27.3
Bombay	27.1
Bengal, Assam, & Sikkim	24.9
United Provinces	24.8
Rajputana	24.8
N. W. Frontier Prov., Sind, & Baluchistan	24.4

Burma is included for the sake of comparison. It has a better record than any part of India, and this has always been the case. The difference seemingly represents a real fact about Burma in comparison to the Indian area. As for the other parts of historical India, there seems no particular reason to expect the differences that are found. It may well be that the differences are smaller than the probable errors of the pro-vincial life tables.

CONCLUSION

Certain of the Indian life tables more accurately represent Indian reality than others. These are the ones—such as those for 1881–91, 1901–1911, and 1921–31—that refer to one decade only. These, however, happen to be the best decades from the point of view of mortality. To understand the full range of Indian mortality possibilities, one needs a life table for a bad decade. Consequently, an unofficial table was made by the writer for the decade (1911–21) in which the influenza epidemic occurred. This table reveals a phenomenally high mortality, and its structure is interesting for that reason. In addition, a table was made for nearly half of India covering the 1931–41 decade. This was the decade of India's most rapid population growth, and if the two censuses were equally complete, the life table reflects a correspondingly good mor-tality situation—the best so far seen in life tables for the country. Appendix C describes the methods by which the two unofficial life tables were constructed.

[1] *Census of India,* 1931, Vol. 1, Part 1, pp. 175–94. The male and female expectancies have been simply averaged in each case, with no attempt to correct for the sex ratio.

PART III

HUMAN FERTILITY IN INDIA

CHAPTER 9

The Trend of the Birth Rate

IF DEATH in Pakistan and India is still tragically prevalent, if its reduction to date is dangerously tenuous and possibly temporary, a fundamental reason lies in the continuing high fertility. It is this high fertility, moreover, which, along with the decline in mortality, explains the rapid growth of the population during the last thirty years. Since migration offers no possible solution to the population problem of this large region, and since economic development cannot indefinitely provide for increasing numbers, the alternative to a calamitous rise in the death rate is a decline in fertility. Consequently, an understanding of the demographic situation requires, especially on its remedial side, an understanding of fertility. What, for example, has been the actual trend in the birth rate? What are the factors responsible for the trend and for the absolute magnitude of the rate? What are the rural-urban, class, and religious differentials? And above all, what are the prospects for an early decline?

THE OFFICIAL RECORD

As in the case of deaths, the student of the history of the birth rate in India is handicapped by the inadequacy of the official statistics. Yet, since these statistics can be used for certain purposes, it does not pay to dismiss them entirely. Instead, their strengths and weaknesses must be clearly understood. To this end the four major defects of the reported birth rates are given below. Some of these defects are more serious than others, but they are all worth bearing in mind.

(1) *Registration covers only three-fourths of the population.* In the past, although a few returns were incidentally published for certain Native States, the regular birth statistics related only to British India. Actually the figures did not include quite all of British India, but related only to the "population under registration." [1] The population under registration, however, included nearly 99 per cent of the inhabitants of British India, and almost exactly 75 per cent of the population of all of India. Since the parts of India not under registration (i.e. the States) were scattered over the whole of India and did not therefore differ profoundly from British India, the registration area of India was roughly typical of the whole.[2] Certainly the sampling error produced by this cir-

cumstance is much less than that produced by other defects presently to be mentioned.[3]

(2) *Published rates, until 1932, were calculated on the wrong population.* Until 1932, in order to evade the problem of post-censal population estimates, the government simply calculated birth and death rates on the basis of the population under registration *at the last census.* In other words, it kept the same population base throughout the ten years until the next census. This had the effect of artificially inflating the rates toward the end of each decade, especially in those decades when the population grew rapidly. Fortunately, not all the provinces followed this practice in their own reports, and the central government abandoned it after the 1931 census. It began at that date to estimate midyear populations on the basis of natural increase, though another method was substituted about 1935. For earlier times it is possible, by a technique described in Appendix D, to estimate for each year the intercensal population under registration. The results will be found in Table 18.

(3) *No age-specific rates were published.* Since birth statistics have ordinarily not been published in India according to age of mother, substitute methods must be used if refined rates are to be calculated.

(4) *Birth reporting is incomplete.* Even though an area may be "under registration," this does not mean that its reporting of births is complete. On the contrary, we know that in British India the number of births reported was, on the average, between 25 and 50 per cent below the actual number.[4] To understand why this deficiency existed and still exists, we have simply to recall the illiterate, rural character of the populace and the man, the village watchman, who usually serves as registrar. But whatever its cause, the huge underregistration of births throws a heavy obstacle in the way of using the official returns. The figures for one region cannot be compared with those of another, because the adequacy of birth registration varies significantly from district to district and city to city. Nowhere can the official figures be accepted as representative of the total number of births, though this error is frequently made in published works on India. To get

---

[1] Birth statistics were published in the *Annual Report* of the Commissioner of Public Health with the Government of India (Delhi: Manager of Publications). From this source they were taken for the *Statistical Abstract for British India,* so often referred to here. Prior to 1937 the vital statistics of British India included Burma, but the reader will recall that in the present study Burma has been excluded from all figures for India unless otherwise specified. The percentage of the population under registration in various provinces is given in Appendix D.

[2] The case is therefore different from the situation formerly existing in the United States. The areas that once lay outside the Birth Registra-

tion Area were quite dissimilar to the Area itself, and therefore the official birth statistics were hardly applicable to the whole country.

[3] Birth reporting in the States has gained ground, and in the publications of the Public Health Commissioner for British India the rates are often given in an incidental table. In 1930–31, for example, the births in seven States—Baroda, Gwalior, Hyderabad, Jammu and Kashmir, Cochin, Travancore, and Mysore) were reported. It is worth noting that the rates, with only one exception, were all lower than any rate for the British provinces. The birth reports for the States are as yet too defective, therefore, to be of much value.

[4] A discussion of the completeness of birth registration will be found in Appendix E, where various tests are considered.

a total number that is somewhere near the truth, one must make systematic estimates on the basis of other information than that furnished by birth registration. This we shall presently try to do, but first it is wise to recognize that the registered statistics prove useful in one way. They help to reveal the trend, or lack of trend, in Indian fertility. Since the adequacy of registration has apparently changed very

little in India during several decades, any pronounced increase or decrease in the registered birth rate should indicate a similar trend in the actual rate.

The officially reported births and the calculated rates for British India since 1911 are given in Table 18. The table, deficient as its figures may be, does suggest three conclusions: First, Indian fertility is high; the rate, even with very defective registration has only since 1941 dropped below 30 and has generally remained above 33 per thousand. Second, the range of variation is not so great or so rapid as that exhibited by urban-industrial nations; the lowest annual rate was 25.8, the highest 39.6. Third, and most important, there is a slight suggestion of a long-run downward trend, although it rests so heavily on the beginning and ending periods that due caution should be exercised in giving it emphasis. Between 1918 and 1941, a period embracing five-sevenths of the entire series, there was almost a dead level of fertility. It is possible that there has been a real drop since 1941, but it is also possible that registration declined during the war years. The official data are therefore not conclusive, but they do suggest a slight tendency toward decline in the extremely high birth rate.

ESTIMATED BIRTH RATES

The deficiency of registration statistics being what it is, recourse must be had to estimates. From time to time qualified statisticians have prepared estimates of the Indian birth rate. These have generally been made on the basis of census returns and life table values—independently of the registration statistics—and they have had some claim to validity. For instance, Mr. G. F. Hardy, the actuarian employed by the Indian Census to make life tables for the period 1891–1911, also made estimates of the average annual birth rate for the three decades in question. His findings are given below. The fourth column, showing the *reported* rates for 1901–11, is inserted for purpose of comparison.

TABLE 18

British India: Birth Rates Based on Officially Reported Births and Estimated Yearly Populations: 1911–1945

Year	Population under Registration [a] (000's)	Reported Births [1] (000's)	Birth Rates	5-Year Average Rates
1911	228,810	8,887	38.8	
1912	229,169	8,979	39.2	
1913	229,195	9,062	39.5	39.0
1914	229,760	9,098	39.6	
1915	230,130	8,676	37.7	
1916	230,496	8,524	37.0	
1917	230,862	9,023	39.1	
1918	231,230	8,106	35.1	34.7
1919	231,583	6,919	30.0	
1920	231,951	7,532	32.8	
1921	323,406	7,453	32.1	
1922	232,838	7,369	31.6	
1923	235,046	8,147	34.7	33.0
1924	237,278	8,021	33.8	
1925	239,530	7,851	32.8	
1926	241,806	8,097	33.5	
1927	244,102	8,245	33.8	
1928	246,419	8,603	34.9	33.8
1929	248,758	8,279	33.3	
1930	251,120	8,378	34.8	
1931	253,614	8,815	34.8	
1932	257,184	8,719	33.9	
1933	260,804	9,318	35.7	34.6
1934	264,475	8,923	33.7	
1935	268,197	9,299	34.7	
1936	271,972	9,566	35.2	
1937	275,801	9,388	34.0	
1938	279,683	9,398	33.6	33.5
1939	283,619	9,346	33.0	
1940 [2]	289,978 [b]	9,284	32.0	
1941	293,219	9,426	32.2	
1942	295,853	8,715	29.5	
1943	297,680	7,776	26.1	28.3
1944	298,321	7,708	25.8	
1945	299,621	8,374	27.9	

[a] Our estimates. For the technique by which they were calculated, see Appendix D.

[b] For years 1940–1945, figure represents the estimated population of the former registration area of the British provinces, representing approximately 75 per cent of the total of former India, excluding Burma.

[1] Dept. of Commercial Intelligence and Statistics, *Statistical Abstract for British India* 1911–12 to 1920–21, pp. 376–77; 1914–15 to 1923–24, pp. 868–69; 1922–23 to 1931–32, pp. 498–99. Public Health Commissioner, *Annual Report*, 1937, p. 8.

[2] For years 1940–1945, United Nations, *Demographic Yearbook*, 1948, pp. 100–01.

	ESTIMATED [5]			REPORTED
	1881– [6] 1891	1891– 1901	1901– 1911	1901– 1911
Bengal	52.9	43.9	56.0	37.6
Bombay	50.3	43.9	50.8	33.4
Madras	51.3	44.8	47.2	30.8
Punjab	46.8	47.1	52.9	41.2
United Provinces	45.1	44.7	47.7	41.4

Although these estimates are very rough and are not made by a uniform method, they are correct enough to show the magnitude of India's birth rate at the turn of the century and the inadequacy of the official returns on it.

Using, like Hardy, life tables for India, but following a different method, we have prepared our own estimates of India's birth rate. These are made by taking the children at each age from 0 to 9 in the census and, with the survival rates in the life table, working back to the births that must have occurred to give rise to each cohort. Adding up the births

[5] Gyan Chand, *India's Teeming Millions* (London: Allen & Unwin, 1939), pp. 97–98. Taken from the Actuarial Report for 1911 prepared by G. F. Hardy.

[6] One version of the figures in this column appeared in *The Imperial Gazetteer of India*, Vol. 1 (Oxford: Clarendon, 1907), p. 506. The figures, while not the same, agree rather closely with those given by Chand.

estimated for the ten cohorts, we can calculate an average annual birth rate for the decade in question.[7] Since the census authorities, as shown earlier, have made life tables for four decades (1872–81, 1881–91, 1891–1901, and 1921–31), and since in addition we have made tables for the two missing decades (1911–21 and 1931–41), we possess a complete series covering six decades. The fact that these life tables were all constructed by using census data rather than by relying on death registration, gives them more validity than the vital statistics would have.

On the basis of this technique the average crude birth rates, as contrasted with the reported rates, were as follows:

	Estimated	Reported
1881–91	49	—
1891–1901	46	34
1901–11	48	37
1911–21	49	37
1921–31	46	33
1931–41	45	34

There is some evidence here that after 1921 the birth rate started to decline slightly. This evidence is more impressive when we realize that an important source of error—the underenumeration of children below 10—is likely to be less significant in later than in earlier censuses.[8] This error would tend to diminish with progressive censuses in India, thereby pushing up the estimated birth rate in the later decades. That the rate has instead gone down a bit suggests that there has been a real, though perhaps small, drop in fertility since 1921. In this matter the estimated birth rates tend to agree with the official ones, although the two sets of figures are derived independently. We may take it as a fair conclusion, therefore, that the level of the Indian crude birth rate has been slightly lower since 1921.

It is also possible to estimate the birth rate for each year. This can be done by assuming that the average underregistration for the decade applies to every year within the decade, thus raising the registered births for each year by the required percentage. Furthermore, by assuming that after 1941 the underregistration of the previous decade still applies, one can estimate the births for those years for which reported births are obtainable. The results have been previously shown in Figure 8 of Chapter 5, where the trend of the

[7] The method is described more fully in the second section of Appendix E.

[8] In 1931 the proportion of children 0–9 to the total population was 3 per cent greater than it was in 1911. This increased proportion was perhaps due partly to a decline in child mortality and partly to the smoothing of the 1931 published age distribution. But in 1941, according to the sample for which age is recorded, the percentage was still a bit higher, and no smoothing entered into it. Consequently, assuming the life tables to be accurate, the decline in fertility may be slightly greater than appears from the estimates as they stand.

annual birth rate from 1881 to 1943 is compared with that of the annual death rate. The chart, it will be recalled, indicates that since 1921 mortality has declined noticeably while fertility has fallen only slightly if at all. The increasing gap between birth and death rates has given rise to a sizable natural increase and hence to the huge population growth during the last 26 years.

Our estimated birth rates are probably lower than is actually the case, mainly because in preparing them we made no attempt to correct the census for underenumeration of children, preferring to be conservative rather than radical in our estimates. The figures may therefore be taken as minimum, not maximum, approximations. Nevertheless, they show that India's birth rate has been, and still is, exceedingly high. India undoubtedly ranks among the countries having the highest fertility. Yet, on the other hand, they are not incredibly high. They are rather what one might expect in a backward country having a semi-colonial economy under the dominance of a Western power. Egypt, by way of comparison, has for 1939 an estimated rate of 47, Palestine for 1931–35 an estimated rate of 49, Puerto Rico for 1945 an estimated rate of 42.3, and Mexico for the same year a recorded rate of 43.7.[9] In comparison with these countries, India's crude birth rate does not seem uniquely high.

Despite the currently high birth rate, there is some evidence of a slight decline having occurred. In other words, the rate was even a little higher in the past. But the decline is far less noticeable than the decline in the death rate. The picture is one of prevailingly high fertility, somewhat lowered mortality, and a growing rate of natural increase which is adding huge increments to India's population.

FUTURE OF THE BIRTH RATE

What we should like to know is the *future* of fertility in the Indian area. What is the trend going to be for the next few decades, and how will this affect population growth?

It would not do to extrapolate the past trend, partly because of possible errors in the figures and partly because there is hardly any "trend" observable. Some other kind of prognostication must be found, but such a task is anything but easy. The best way of proceeding, it would seem, is to investigate as thoroughly as possible the nature and causes of India's high fertility. From this investigation perhaps something can be deduced concerning future possibilities. We shall therefore postpone further discussion of India's future birth rate until we have examined such topics as differential fertility, family attitudes, and reproductive practices.

[9] For comparative rates see P. K. Whelpton and Clyde V. Kiser, "Trends, Determinants, and Control in Human Fertility," *Annals of the American Academy of Political and Social Science*, Vol. 237 (January, 1945), pp. 114–15. For official rates see tables carried in *Population Index*.

++

Differential Fertility

++

Not all women, not all classes, not all places in the Indian region manifest the same fertility. There are differences, and these differences are important in understanding the region's human reproduction. Unfortunately, however, the amount that one can learn about these differences is strictly limited. Birth registration, as previously mentioned, does not even give us the total births occurring, much less data on the *parents* of each child born. In fact, for the study of differential fertility, the registered statistics seem to be of almost no help, though they are occasionally worth something. One is forced to rely heavily upon census data, and above all upon the child-woman ratio—the ratio of children to women in the reproductive ages—as an indirect and somewhat erratic measure of fertility. When this is used, along with whatever other data exist, certain information concerning intercaste, rural-urban, religious, educational, and occupational differences can be obtained. The following sections give the main findings.

RURAL-URBAN DIFFERENTIALS

In India and Pakistan, as in other places, the cities manifest a lower fertility than the country. Furthermore, the larger the city the lower its fertility becomes, so that there is an intercity as well as a rural-urban differential. The differentials, though significant, are not so large, however, as those found in West European and American countries. Because of this, and because such a small part of the Indian masses are as yet urbanized, the lower fertility of the cities does not at present have much effect in reducing the general birth rate or depressing population growth. Nevertheless, an analysis of rural-urban differentials throws some light on the nature of Indian fertility and thus helps us to judge what the future may bring.

THE BIG THREE—CALCUTTA, BOMBAY, AND MADRAS

Each of the three largest cities has a lower fertility than its surrounding region. During 1921–31, for instance, the reported births per 1,000 women aged 15–39 averaged 119 for the three cities in question, whereas the provinces of Bengal, Bombay, and Madras (without these cities) averaged 154. (Table 19)

Because comparisons based on recorded births are not reliable, it is necessary to check this finding by other, independent measures of fertility. One such measure is the ratio of children 0–4 to women 15–39—a child-woman ratio.[1] When

[1] This measure will occur frequently in the following pages. The reason age 39 was taken instead of 44 or 49 as the upper limit was as follows: age 44 is impossible because some of the age distributions merely give 40–49 as a single category; age 49 was not taken because

this measure is employed, it appears that in 1931 the three largest cities averaged only 506 children per 1,000 women in the specified ages, whereas the three provinces, without these cities, averaged 735. In 1941 the data indicate an analogous situation, as Table 19 shows. The difference is not strictly a rural-urban difference, because in each case the rest of the province includes a considerable urban population, but it closely approximates a rural-urban differential.

TABLE 19

Fertility in the Three Major Cities, Contrasted with Rest of Their Provinces, 1921–1941

	Average Annual Reported Births per 1000 Women 15–39	Average Children 0–4 per 1000 Women 15–39	
	1921–1930 [a]	1931	1941
Bombay City	95	447	468
Calcutta [b]	94	565	531
Madras City	167	504	—— [c]
Average for Cities	*119*	*506*	*500*
Rest of Bombay [d]	173	766	640
Rest of Bengal [e]	134	754	685
Rest of Madras [d]	155	685	—— [c]
Average for Provs.	*154*	*735*	*663*

[a] Populations used are those for *registration area*. With exception of populations under registration, which were calculated from the data on vital statistics in the *Statistical Abstract for British India*, the data were taken from the appropriate provincial census volumes.
[b] Excludes Howrah and 24 Parganas.
[c] No data for 1941.
[d] British Districts only.
[e] British Districts and States.

Perhaps infant mortality is worse in the city, so that the child-woman ratio exaggerates the rural-urban difference. Perhaps, also, many urban women return to their home villages when they become pregnant. On the other hand, the enumeration of children under 5 may be better in the city—a circumstance that would minimize the differential. Since the biases appear to run in opposite directions, one may assume, until further evidence comes to light, that the child-woman ratio is a fair index of relative fertility. This being accepted,

many Indian women have ceased reproduction long before that time and because the proportion of celibate widowhood is very high in ages 40–49. Tests have been run using the higher age bracket; these show that the results are much the same regardless of whether age 39 or age 49 is taken as the upper limit. In some cases, when the situation warranted it, we have used the ages 15–49 in our ratios.

the data with respect to the three largest cities and their environs indicate a substantial difference between rural and urban birth rates. The difference approximates, but does not equal, that found in most European and American countries. In the United States in 1941 the three largest cities had an average ratio of 271, whereas the states in which they were found, outside these cities, had an average ratio of 355, but this is hardly a fair comparison, because these states, outside the main city, were heavily urbanized. A fairer comparison is shown in Fig. 13, where it seems clear that the Indian region has a lower rural-urban differential than either Chile or the United States.

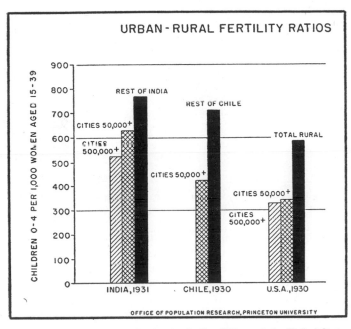

FIGURE 13. Child-Woman Ratios for India, Chile, and the United States for Two Classes of Cities and the Rural Area, about 1930.

CITIES BY SIZE

A fertility differential exists not only between rural and urban areas but also between larger and smaller cities. In general, as measured by the child-woman ratio, reproduction varies inversely with size of city. In the census of 1931, for example, age distributions were reported for 99 cities and in 1941 for 26 cities. When the child-woman ratio is computed for these cities, the results shown in Table 20 appear.[2] The inverse correlation between city size and child-woman ratio is not perfect, but it is consistent enough to be entirely convincing; indeed, there are in the table only two exceptions to the general rule: the larger the city the lower the fertility.[3]

It seems evident from Table 20 that the main differentials are two: first, between the giant cities and the lesser ones; second, between the lesser cities and the rest of the area. Be-

[2] Since the data for 1931 and 1941 are not comparable, Table 20 should not be construed as showing any time trends; it should be read vertically rather than horizontally.

[3] A sampling error is probably involved in the grouping of cities by size class in Table 20, but the error would tend to minimize rather than exaggerate the negative correlation. It happens that only certain cities have age distributions reported in the census. The smaller the city, the less likely it is to have a published age distribution. Consequently, the smaller the class category in Table 20, the smaller is the representation of that class in the table. It may well be that the more "urban" of the smaller cities get into the table, so that the differential between the smaller and larger cities is less than what it would be if all cities in every class were included.

TABLE 20

Child-Woman Ratios by Size of City, 1931–1941

Size of Cities	1931		1941	
	Number of Cities	Average Child-Woman Ratio [a]	Number of Cities	Average Child-Woman Ratio [a]
500,000 plus	3 [b]	523	4 [c]	545
100,000 to 500,000	33 [d]	666	11	621
50,000 to 100,000	45	649	3	665
Below 50,000	18 [e]	701	8	621
Rest of India [f]		770		714

[a] Obtained by adding all the children within the class of cities, totaling all the women 15–39, and dividing the latter into the former, multiplying by 1000.

[b] Calcutta includes only Calcutta proper, not Howrah and 24 Parganas. The latter are included as separate units among the smaller cities.

[c] Includes two new cities for this class (Delhi and Ahmedabad), but not Madras, for which data were lacking.

[d] There are a few other cities with over 100,000 population, but no complete age distribution for them could be found.

[e] These by no means comprise all the cities and towns below 50,000, but only those for which age distributions could be found. Only two of them are below 25,000.

[f] The "rest of India" necessarily includes, as well as rural areas, all those cities and towns not specifically treated in the urban sections. Figures for it are obtained by subtraction. That is one reason why the fertility ratio for the "rest of India" in 1941 is so much lower than in 1931.

tween cities of intermediate sizes (i.e. from 25,000 to 500,000) the differences are not very pronounced. The relationships can be most easily grasped if each ratio is expressed as a percentage of the ratio for the total population excluding the cities, as follows:

	1931	*1941*
500,000 plus	67.9	76.3
100,000–500,000	86.5	87.0
50,000–100,000	84.3	93.1
Below 50,000	91.0	87.0
Rest of India	100.0	100.0

The greatest difference, of course, lies between the giant cities on the one hand and India excluding all cities on the other.

THE EXPLANATION OF RURAL-URBAN DIFFERENCES

With existing evidence it seems impossible to explain satisfactorily the inverse correlation between reproductivity and urbanism in the India-Pakistan region. It is quite possible that, because the laboring classes in the cities are attached to their village homes, pregnant women, or women with one or more small children, are often sent back to the country. On the other hand, it is probable that women in the larger cities use contraception to a greater degree than their more rural compatriots. Some proof of this comes from a study of women in Calcutta and in a country region outside of Calcutta.[4] It was found that 38 per cent of the women in a wealthy section of the city, 13 per cent in a lower-middle-class Hindu section, and 3 per cent in a lower-middle-class Muslim section practice

[4] C. Chandra Sekar and Mukta Sen, "Enquiry into the Reproductive Patterns of Bengali Women," Conducted under the auspices of the Indian Research Fund Association, not yet published. The results cited here and elsewhere in this chapter and Chapter 23 are tentative; they were lent to the writer through the kindness of the authors, both of whom are on the staff of the All India Institute of Hygiene and Public Health at Calcutta.

contraception. In the rural area, however, only 0.3 per cent (or 4 out of 1,459 women) do so. The same study indicates that the urban use of contraception affects fertility, because, with age held constant, the women in the upper-class section have only two-thirds the number of live-births that the women in the lower-middle-class sections have, and the latter in turn have only four-fifths the fertility of the rural women.

Another recent study of urban fertility found only 3 women out of 1,661 married women, who practice contraception.[5] However, this study was made in Kolhapur City, a town of 96,000 inhabitants in 1941. It is thus not so much contrary to the Calcutta study as illustrative of the point that, at least in so far as contraception causes the rural-urban differential, it is in all probability confined mainly to the great cities. This helps to explain why it is the great cities that have the lowest fertility.

One aspect that can be examined on the basis of census data is whether widowhood and nonmarriage have anything to do with the rural-urban differential. Later it will appear that the taboo on widow remarriage is one of the main explanations of caste and religious differentials. Is the same true of the rural-urban pattern?

The figures presented in Table 21 and depicted in Fig. 14 show that the differentials between the classes of cities are just as great when the ratio of children to *married* women is taken as when the ratio of children to *all* women aged 15–39 is used. Also, the ratio of widows to married women in the specified ages does not vary consistently with size of community. Finally, although the proportion of single women tends to be somewhat larger in the cities than in the country, the size of this group is so small in any case that it can have no marked effect on fertility. Presumably, therefore, the apparently lesser fertility of the cities cannot be explained in terms of nonmarriage.

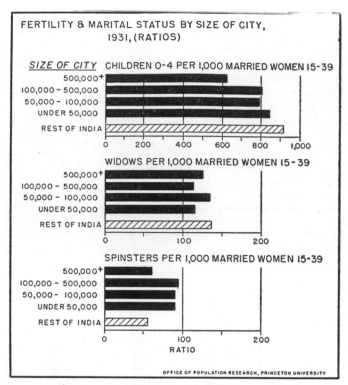

FIGURE 14. Child-Woman Ratios and Marital Status for Women Aged 15–39 for Cities of Various Size Classes and the Rest of India, 1931.

was carried back as far as the data would allow—to 1891. Surprisingly enough, as Figure 15 shows, the data reveal no trend at all. The differences between city and country and between cities of different size remained about the same over the whole period from 1891 to 1941.

The data used are not all they should be,[6] but the conclusion

TABLE 21

Child-Woman and Other Ratios by Size of City, 1931 [1]

Size Class of Cities	Children 0–4 per 1000 Women 15–39		Children 0–4 per 1000 *Married* Women 15–39		Widows per 1000 Married Women	Spinsters per 1000 Married Women
	Ratio	Per cent of "Rest of India"	Ratio	Per cent of "Rest of India"		
500,000 plus	523	68	620	68	125	61
100,000–500,000	666	87	806	88	114	95
50,000–100,000	649	84	795	87	135	90
Below 50,000	701	91	845	92	115	90
Rest of India	770	100	918	100	136	56

[1] Computed from Imperial Table 7, "Age, Sex, and Civil Condition," in the Provincial volumes of the *Census of India*, 1931. This table is usually divided into two parts, the first dealing with districts and states, the second with cities.

THE TREND OF THE RURAL-URBAN DIFFERENTIAL

In Western nations a decline in fertility has generally begun in the cities and then spread to the country. Does the presence in the Indian region of a rural-urban differential suggest that the same process is occurring there? Will the Indians and Pakistanis as a whole soon enjoy the same lowered fertility that the cities now enjoy?

In order to test this hypothesis, an effort was made to ascertain the time trend in rural-urban differences. The analysis

[5] N. V. Sovani, *The Social Survey of Kolhapur City*, Part I—*Population and Fertility* (Poona: Gokhale Institute of Politics and Economics, Publication No. 18, 1948), p. 40.

seems correct that the cities have *not* inaugurated a sharp decline in the birth rate. They have not had an accelerating effect. To be sure, the proportion of people living in cities has

[6] In the 1931 census the age data were "smoothed" before publication, whereas in 1941 they were not. Also, the 1941 age reports are for samples only and do not cover the entire country. These facts make it impossible to compare ratios between different age groups in the two censuses. The ratios for 1931 and 1941, in short, are comparable neither with each other nor with those of previous censuses. For example, Fig. 15 suggests that the ratio of children to women rose slightly in all classes of community in 1931, but no such conclusion is warranted.

It should be noted also that in Fig. 15 "Rural India" is really all of India exclusive of the cities used in our calculations. Since India is 89

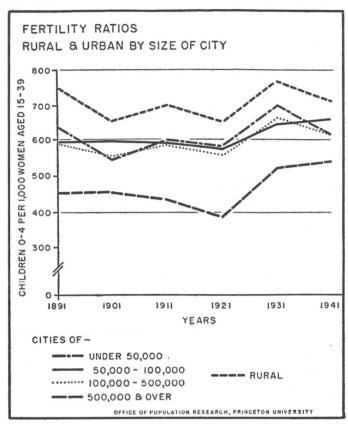

FIGURE 15. Child-Woman Ratios for Women Aged 15–39 for Rural Area and Cities by Size Class, India, 1891–1941.

grown. In 1891 the percentage in places over 5,000 was 9.4, whereas in 1941 it was 12.8. In so far, then, as urbanization continues it will have some slight effect in decreasing total fertility; but there is apparently no extra diffusion, no multiplier effect, that intensifies the influence of cities beyond their natural growth as time goes by. In short, the rural-urban and intra-urban differentials do not indicate an imminent decline of general fertility in India.[7]

CLASS AND CASTE DIFFERENTIALS

Differences of fertility as between one caste, or class of castes, and another would be expected on *a priori* grounds. The Brahmans, for example, have long been regarded as less fertile than the rest of the population; indeed they have steadily diminished as a proportion of the total Hindu popula-

per cent rural anyway (1931), India outside the major cities is virtually synonymous with rural India. Since in 1941, however, fewer cities are included in the sample, "Rural India" is not quite the same as in 1931, and this explains the apparently sharp dip in the ratio for this category in 1941.

The statistics are valuable merely for showing that the pattern of rural-urban and inter-city differentials has remained approximately the same during the half century.

[7] Using a slightly more sensitive measure, a "census reproductivity coefficient," A. J. Jaffe found a substantial rural-urban differential in Bengal in 1881. He did not follow this up with an attempt to determine a trend in this area. He did present historical data on four countries. In two of them, Sweden and the United States, he found a noticeable increase in the rural-urban differential over several decades. In England and Mexico the evidence was not conclusive. His data suggest that our finding in India is different from that characterizing the history of most modernized nations, and thus helps to confirm the point being made in the present case. See "Urbanization and Fertility," *American Journal of Sociology*, Vol. 48 (July, 1942), pp. 48–60.

tion despite an infiltration from other castes of persons who manage to pass as Brahmans.[8] But such differences in fertility are hard to prove empirically, because births are not registered by caste of parent. Reliance must therefore be placed again on indirect measures, primarily on age returns.

In 1931, as in previous censuses, a general table was published giving major castes by age and civil status. The age breaks are peculiar, but they do allow the number of children aged 0–6 and the number of women 14–43 to be obtained. Thus a child-woman ratio can be computed, and though it differs from the ratio used above with reference to cities, it is equally satisfactory. Since the census also gives occupation and literacy by caste, it becomes possible to study differential fertility by social status, occupation, and literacy, using castes as the units in each case.

SOCIAL STATUS

Computing the child-woman ratios for major castes and grouping them according to social status,[9] one gets the figures shown in the third and fourth columns of Table 22 and depicted graphically in Fig. 16. The trend is not perfect, for the "Common" castes have a higher fertility ratio in each case

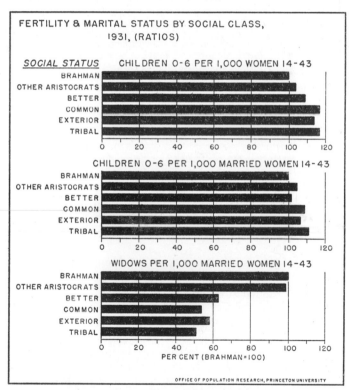

FIGURE 16. Child-Woman Ratios and Proportion of Widows for Women Aged 14–43 for Castes Grouped by Social Status, India, 1931.

[8] *Census of India*, 1931, Vol. 28 (Travancore), Part 1, p. 369.

[9] It is not always easy to group castes by social status. Certain categories, such as Brahman, Scheduled Castes, and Tribals are fairly clear; but within the large group designated as "caste Hindus" (aside from the Brahmans) the distinctions must be made on the basis of judgment. Our procedure was to go through the literature and pick up impressionistic accounts of the social rating assigned to different castes. Thus we grouped certain castes in categories called "Other Aristocrats" and "Common." In the footnotes to Table 22 the actual castes placed in each group are named, so that the reader, especially if he is familiar with India, can form his own judgment with reference to the accuracy of our classification. Needless to say, we did not use criteria such as literacy and occupation in making the classification, because we were anxious to treat social status as a factor in and of itself, regardless of its cause.

than the "Exterior." (Perhaps both the Exterior and Tribal groups report children less completely than do the other groups.) But among the caste Hindus themselves the inverse relation between social position and fertility seems to hold. It must be kept in mind that the castes were the units of calculation, and that it was the castes, not individuals, that were grouped according to social status, and the same is true of the groupings according to occupation and literacy presently to be mentioned.

a preliminary step was necessary—namely, the computation of the percentage in each caste who were engaged in given occupations. The usual procedure is to group castes according to the "traditional" occupation of the caste, but since many castes have largely abandoned their historical calling, this would not be satisfactory in the present case. Instead we took as the occupation of the caste that pursuit in which a majority of the members were engaged. Calculating the fertility ratios for all women 14–43 and for married women 14–43, the re-

TABLE 22

Child-Woman Ratios of Hindu Castes Classified by Social Status, 1931 [1]

	Number of Castes	Combined Population	Children 0–6 per 1000 Women 14–43 [a]	Children 0–6 per 1000 Married Women 14–43 [a]	Widows per 1000 Married Women [a]
Brahmans	1	13,628,000	746	967	235
Other Aristocrats [b]	4	4,244,000	779	1,021	233
Better [c]	7	19,154,000	815	982	149
Common [d]	10	21,862,000	876	1,052	127
Exterior [e]	17	25,968,000	849	1,033	137
Tribal [2]	6	5,522,000	872	1,075	119
Total	*45*	*90,378,000*			

[a] These are weighted averages obtained by adding the women of all castes in each class falling in the specified ages and dividing by the total number of children in these castes.

[b] The standing of caste Hindus other than Brahmans was determined by consulting the impressionistic accounts in the literature on castes. A few mistakes may have been made. The castes classified as "Other Aristocrats" are the following: Baidya, Banya, Kayastha, and Komati.

[c] The seven castes classified as "Better" are Bhat, Brahmbhat, Chetti, Darzi, Khatri, Kumbi, and Yadava.

[d] Includes Bhil, Gadaria, Gujar, Halwai, Kachhi, Kahar, Kumhar, Shaha, Teli, and Viswabrahman.

[e] Includes Arayan, Bhangi, Bhar, Chamar, Chuhra, Dhobi, Dom, Dosadh, Ghasi, Ilwan, Kaniyan, Khatik, Mahar, Megh, Namasudra, Panika, Paraiyan.

[1] Computed from *Census of India,* 1931, Vol. 1, Part 2, pp. 158–87.

[2] *ibid.,* Part 1, p. 494.

The fourth column of Table 22 brings out a striking fact— namely, that the differentials are greater between the general ratios (column 3) than the marital ratios (column 4). In fact, the whole tendency toward an inverse ratio between social status and fertility seems to be sharply curtailed when only married women are taken into account in computing the child-woman ratio.

The clue to this fact lies in the last column in the table (or the last set of bars in Fig. 16), which gives the ratio of widows to married women. The higher the widow ratio, the lower the general ratio of children to women. When the widows are excluded, the resulting ratios of children to *married* women exhibit much smaller differences. It appears, then, that the primary, though not the sole, cause of the lower fertility of the upper castes is the fact that a greater proportion of their women of reproductive age are withdrawn from motherhood by the taboo on widow remarriage.

OCCUPATION

An attempt was also made to discover fertility differentials by grouping castes according to occupation.[10] For this purpose

[10] One could expect that, in addition to the caste tables, there might be other sources of information concerning occupational differentials. Actually, however, there seems to be no other source. If the sample study of fertility in the 1931 census had been done well, it would have cross-tabulated occupation with duration of marriage, as well as with number of children born. This would have made the study of some use in computing occupational differences. Unfortunately, however, the published table gives number of children by father's occupation without any reference to the ages of the parents or the duration of the marriage. (*Census of India,* 1931, Vol. 1, Part 1, pp. 207–08.) It is therefore worthless for our present purpose.

sults shown in Table 23 and Fig. 17 were obtained. The differentials are not so striking as those found for social status, but they are nevertheless observable. The trading and professional castes, along with owners and tenants on farms, had the lowest general ratios, while artisans and the group embracing field laborers, woodcutters, raisers of livestock, fishermen, and hunters had the highest general ratios.

When the married women alone were used in getting the ratio, the differences between the various occupational groups virtually disappeared. Again the explanation seems to lie in the widow ratio. The latter is high for those occupational groups having a low general fertility; so that, as in the case of social status, it appears that occupational groups having a low fertility accomplish this result, at least in part, by refusing to let their widows remarry. In fact, the widow ratio seems to have more of an effect on the differentials between occupational groups than on those between status groups.

Though not so sharp as one might anticipate, the occupational differentials run along the lines that could be expected. The agricultural peoples apparently have a higher fertility than the trading and professional classes, and within the agricultural category there is a sharp distinction between the owners and tenants, who have a low fertility, and the field

S. P. Jain, *Relationship between Fertility and Economic and Social Status in the Punjab* (Lahore: Punjab Board of Economic Inquiry, Publication No. 64, 1939) gives some data on occupational differences in fertility.

D. Ghosh and Rama Varma, in an article entitled "A Study in Indian Fertility," *The Eugenics Review,* Vol. 31 (July, 1939), pp. 115–19, say that they included questions on both income and occupation, but (at least in the article referred to) no results by occupation were given.

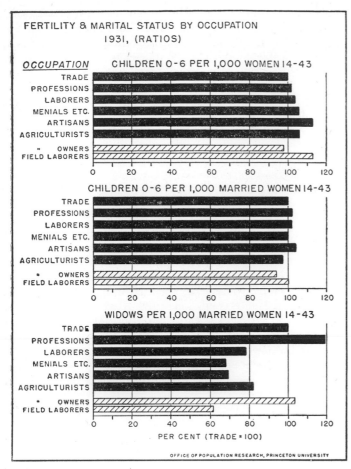

FERTILITY & MARITAL STATUS BY OCCUPATION
1931, (RATIOS)

OFFICE OF POPULATION RESEARCH, PRINCETON UNIVERSITY

FIGURE 17. Child-Woman Ratios and Proportion of Widows for Women Aged 14–43 for Castes Grouped by Occupational Classes, India, 1931.

laborers, etc., who have a high fertility. The high figure for artisans, as compared with laborers and servants and scavengers, is not easy to understand. However, in view of the unsatisfactory character of Indian occupational statistics and the consequent vagaries of the sample, it is surprising that the table exhibits as much consistency as it does. As in the case of social status, the occupational differentials run counter to the distortion that might result from census deficiencies. This fact strengthens the inference that in India there really are occupational differentials along expected lines. If more precise returns were available, the picture would probably be clearer but substantially the same in general outline. An analysis of detailed figures from the United Provinces for 1931 shows essentially the same kind of differentials.

LITERACY

In addition to social status and occupation, literacy was also used as a basis for grouping the castes and computing average child-woman ratios for each group. Fifty-seven castes, with a total population of nearly 107 million, were included in the tabulation. The results, as shown in Table 24 and Fig. 18, indicate that the general child-woman ratio is inversely correlated with literacy. The highest ratio, that for castes with less than 1 per cent literate, is more than a tenth greater than the lowest ratio, that for castes with 15 or more per cent literate.

The ratio of children to *married* women, however, shows no correlation with literacy whatsoever; and as in the other cases, the explanation seems to lie mainly in the differential prevalence of widowhood. In general the proportion of widows is greater when literacy is greater. In fact, the highest widow ratio (for castes over 15 per cent literate) is nearly double the lowest ratio (for castes less than 2 per cent literate). Since very few women aged 14–43 are single—only 6.2 per cent

TABLE 23

Child-Woman Ratios of Castes Classified by Occupation, 1931 [1]

Occupation of Majority of Caste Members	Number of Castes	Combined Population	Children 0–6 per 1000 Women 14–43	Children 0–6 per 1000 Married Women 14–43	Widows per 1000 Married Women
Trade [a]	5	5,607,000	771	1,016	191
Professions [b]	2	2,586,000	789	1,032	227
Laborers [c]	2	1,608,000	802	1,038	149
Agriculturalists [d]	13	50,164,000	817	990	157
Owners & Tenants [e]	5	22,103,000	754	951	197
Field Laborers, etc. [f]	4	17,021,000	873	1,020	118
Servants, Scavengers, etc. [g]	6	8,966,000	818	1,012	129
Artisans [h]	4	7,601,000	869	1,052	132
Total	32	76,531,000			

[a] Includes Baniya, Khatri, Komati, Lingayat, and Lohana.
[b] Includes Baidya and Kayastha.
[c] Includes Paraiyan and Od.
[d] Includes the Brahmans but not the Rajputs, who are partly Muslim. The Brahmans, of course, are a very special agricultural group. If they are omitted, the three ratios for the Agriculturalists, reading horizontally, become 843, 998, 131. The other castes included are Bhat, Bhil, Chamar, Chodhra, Kachhi, Kunbi, Lodha, Mali, Maratha, Panka, Taga, and Yadava.
[e] Includes Bhat, Brahman, Kunbi, Maratha, and Taga. If the Brahmans are omitted, the three ratios for Owners and Tenants, reading horizontally, become 767, 926, and 142.
[f] Includes Banjara, Chamar, Gadaria, and Mahar. Embraces wood cutters, raisers of livestock, fishermen, and hunters.
[g] Includes Bhangi, Chuhra, Dhobi, Naibrahman, Megh, and Kahar. Embraces menials, washermen, and barbers.
[h] Includes Dom, Viswabrahman, Kumhar, and Darzi, and embraces such occupations as bamboo workers, tailors, potters, carpenters, wood workers, blacksmiths, goldsmiths, etc.
[1] Ratios computed from *Census of India*, 1931, Vol. 1, Part 2, pp. 158–87. Occupational groupings are derived from the summary and provincial volumes of the census. The occupation of a caste was judged to be that actually (not traditionally) practiced by a majority of the caste members.

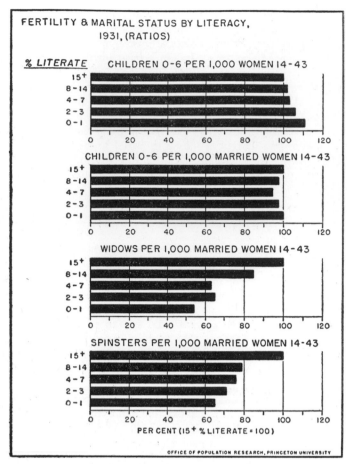

FERTILITY & MARITAL STATUS BY LITERACY,
1931, (RATIOS)

FIGURE 18. Child-Woman Ratios and Proportion of Widows and Spinsters for Women Aged 14–43 for Castes Grouped According to Literacy, India, 1931.

according to female literacy only. The necessary data could be found for 86 castes in Bombay, Bengal, and Mysore. Instead of confirming our hypothesis, however, the results, as shown in Table 25 and Fig. 19, refuted it. The ratios showed a curious U curve, with the lowest ones in the middle of the range. This may mean that a high female literacy, implying good general education, provides a sufficiently better infant survival rate to compensate for lowered fertility, whereas a low female illiteracy yields such a high fertility that a lower survival rate is overcome. Regardless of the interpretation, however, the curious fact remains that the expected differential of castes when grouped by literacy shows itself only when the literacy of males is included in the calculation.

RURAL CLASS DIFFERENTIALS IN THE PUNJAB

The preceding differentials cover a sample of castes from the whole of India. Quite possibly some of them reflect rural-urban differences; but a study has been made of 275 villages in 25 districts of the Punjab, giving us an exclusively rural sample, thereby eliminating the rural-urban factor.[11] This study covered only couples married 10 years or more, and consequently does not tell us the fertility of all women in a given class. It therefore does not tell us the role of non-marriage and widowhood in class fertility. Furthermore, even for married couples, it neglected to get the age of the woman. But it does convey some information about class differences in marital fertility.

Relating income to the number of children ever born, the study finds a very low order of correlation. For 24 villages having enough cases, the coefficient of correlation for couples married 20 years or more is not above 0.19 in a single village. In seven villages, the correlation was 0.10 to 0.19; in another seven, it was 0.05 to 0.09; and in the remaining ten it was 0.00 to 0.04. Such low correlations indicate virtually no con-

TABLE 24

Child-Woman Ratios of Castes Classified by Literacy, 1931 [1]

Per Cent Literate by Caste	Number of Castes	Combined Population	Children 0–6 per 1000 Women 14–43	Children 0–6 per 1000 Married Women 14–43	Widows per 1000 Married Women	Spinsters per 1000 Married Women
15 plus	15	22,662,000	782	1,030	220	99
8–14	7	17,239,000	800	1,012	187	78
4–7	8	17,435,000	808	980	138	75
2–3	7	21,726,000	831	1,007	143	70
0–1	20	27,812,000	869	1,029	120	64
Total	57	*106,873,000*				

[1] Computed from *Census of India*, 1931, Vol. 1, Part 2, pp. 158–87, 449–70, 521, 535. In some cases it was necessary to refer to provincial volumes in order to secure the required data. Only castes predominantly Hindu are included.

for Hindu women in comparison with 12.8 per cent widowed —the differential fertility ratios must be attributed mainly to the varying proportions of widows in the literacy categories. The proportion of single women, like the proportion of widows, is greater in the upper grades of literacy, but the differences are not so sharp as those with respect to widows. Non-marriage and non-*re*marriage therefore seem to offer a complete explanation of the differentials in the general child-woman ratios.

On the assumption that the female literacy of castes might have a more direct effect on fertility than the total per cent literate, child-woman ratios were computed for castes grouped

nection between fertility and income. To be sure, all but two of the correlations are positive, and the contingency coefficients (more valid for such a skewed distribution as the income data have) are of a slightly higher order, but nevertheless the surprising thing is the virtual absence of a relationship.[12] It should be borne in mind too—a point not mentioned by the author—that in India, people's memory of the number of children ever born is quite deficient; [13] and since the upper

[11] S. P. Jain, *op. cit.*
[12] *ibid.*, pp. 5–6, 8–9, 21.
[13] In a study done in Bengal villages by the All India Institute of Hygiene and Public Health of Calcutta, only 67 per cent of the total

TABLE 25

*Child-Woman Ratios of Castes Classified by Literacy of Females,
Bombay, Bengal, and Mysore, 1931*

Per Cent Females Literate [1]	Number of Castes [a]	Population Included	Children 0–6 per 1000 Women 14–43 [2]	Children 0–6 per 1000 Married Women 14–43 [2]	Widows per 1000 Married Women [2]
25 plus	5	468,716	847	1,116	214
10–24.9	7	3,371,004	787	1,031	245
5–9.9	8	1,212,655	722	919	180
3–4.9 [b]	6	2,977,249	693	941	328
2–2.9	8	1,502,736	776	1,036	256
1–1.9	9	3,222,247	806	1,066	275
0–0.9	43	7,538,284	820	1,038	167
Total	*86*	*20,292,891*			

[a] Chakma and Lepcha in Bengal are omitted because of the small populations involved. Fifteen other castes in Bengal are omitted due to lack of information on marital status and/or age.

[b] Excluding Maratha.

[1] Computed from Imperial Table 14 in Part 2 of 1931 census volumes for Bombay Pres., Bengal & Sikkim, and Mysore.

[2] Computed from Imperial Table 17 in Part 2 of 1931 census volumes for Bombay Pres., Bengal & Sikkim, and Mysore.

income groups may have slightly better memories in this regard, such positive correlation as exists may be more fictitious than real.

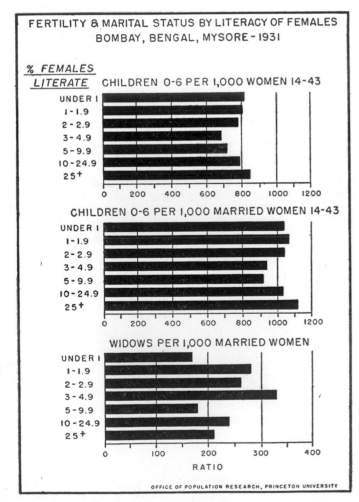

FIGURE 19. Child-Woman Ratios for Women Aged 14–43 and Proportion of Widows for Castes Grouped According to Literacy of Female Members: Bombay, Bengal, Mysore, 1931.

In addition to income, the study also obtained data on fertility according to occupational class. It found that, for all couples married longer than 10 years, the agriculturalists [14] had an average of 5.07 children, the menials [15] an average of 5.01, and non-agriculturalists [16] an average of 4.99.[17] Again the striking thing about this is the virtual absence of differences. The slight variation can be as easily attributed to possible errors of procedure as to real differences of reproduction.[18]

These occupational classes were further subdivided into eight subclasses. The average number of children ever born to couples married 10 years or more came out as shown in the first column of Table 26. Here the differences are somewhat greater. In general it looks as if the higher the occupational status, the higher the fertility. The menials constitute one exception, because (assuming a positive correlation) their fertility is not so small as their position at the bottom of the social scale would imply. The professionals are an even greater exception. Theirs is "the only group in a village which, as a class, is educated and is comparatively more refined in habits and culture. It is high up in the social scale, whatever be its economic position." [19] The low fertility of the professional class therefore suggests a negative correlation between education and fertility. This interpretation gains strength when

births for the previous year and 53 per cent of those for the year before that were discovered by field investigators. C. Chandra Sekar, "Sample Surveys for the Estimation of Birth and Death Rates," digest of a paper given at the International Statistical Congress, Washington, D.C., September, 1947.

[14] Persons who own land above 10 acres or whose income is predominantly from agricultural sources.

[15] Laborers whose pay is in kind rather than cash, including artisans, provided the income is less than Rs. 200 per annum.

[16] Persons who are not agriculturalists and not menials—shopkeepers, money-lenders, and those following other vocations.

[17] Jain, *op. cit.*, pp. 6, 23.

[18] Evidently, for example, these averages are for all couples married 10 years or longer. The method of equating the couples (see Jain, *op. cit.*, p. 5) is one that could go astray if the concentration of reproduction within the marital span were different for different classes. Also, mobility between classes might distort the results.

[19] *ibid.*, p. 18.

TABLE 26

Children Born and Surviving per Couple, by Occupational Status, Punjab, 1939 [1]

Occupational Class	Average Number of Children Ever Born	Average Number of Children Surviving	Percentage Surviving
Agriculturalists	*5.07*	*3.48*	*68.6*
Upper [a]	5.29	3.70	69.9
Middle [b]	5.04	3.48	69.0
Lower [c]	4.87	3.24	66.5
Non-Agriculturalists	*4.99*	*3.30*	*66.1*
Upper [d]	5.27	3.72	70.6
Middle [e]	5.12	3.37	66.2
Lower [c]	4.82	3.08	63.9
Professionals [f]	*4.82*	*3.16*	*65.6*
Menials	*5.01* [g]	*3.18* [h]	*63.5*

[a] Owning 30 or more acres of land or having income of Rs. 400 or more per annum.
[b] Owning between 10 and 20 acres of land or having income of Rs. 200–400 per annum.
[c] Having income below Rs. 200 per annum.
[d] Having income of Rs. 400 or more per annum.
[e] Having income between Rs. 200 and 400 per annum.
[f] School teachers, priests, clerks, etc.
[g] Listed as 5.00 on p. 24.
[h] Listed as 3.17 on p. 24.
[1] Compiled from S. P. Jain, *Relationship between Fertility and Economic and Social Status in the Punjab* (Lahore: The Board of Economic Inquiry, Publication No. 64, 1939), pp. 23–24.

possible memory errors are considered. Some of the other class differences, whereby low status is associated with low fertility, may be in part due to class variations in ability to remember. Since doubtless the professional group has the best remembrance of children ever born, its low fertility cannot be due to poor recall. All told, the occupational data show, for the relatively uneducated portion of the rural community, a very small but positive correlation between occupational status and fertility, though the reverse is true for the educated class. The differences are not great: the highest number of children born per couple is only 10 per cent higher than the lowest.

Not only were the villagers asked to give the number of children ever born, but also the number surviving. The results (column 3 of Table 26) indicate that in general the higher the status, the greater the proportion of children surviving. But again the professionals are an exception. Next to the menials and the lower non-agriculturalists they have the lowest percentage of live births surviving. This may possibly be due to their greater recall of children now dead. In any case, the differences in percentage surviving ("effective fertility") are quite small, and may be due to error rather than fact.

URBAN CLASS DIFFERENCES

Already mentioned are the two urban fertility studies, one in Kolhapur and the other in Calcutta. The Kolhapur study found no statistically significant difference in the fertility of married women when grouped by occupation, caste, and income.[20] Several considerations are in order, however. First, the sample was small for the amount of subdivision necessary.

[20] N. V. Sovani, *op. cit.*, pp. 55–62.

Second, it consisted exclusively of *married women*, whereas there is reason to believe that a substantial part of the class differentials are due to nonmarriage and widowhood. Third, even though the results are claimed to be not statistically significant, their direction favors the hypothesis of differential fertility. For instance, Jains and Brahmans both have fewer births than the calculated expectancy, whereas Marathas and Harijans both have more births than expected. The results can be put in fourfold form, as follows: [21]

	Observed	*Expected*
High Status	286	311
Low Status	960	933

Furthermore, the study revealed a difference in average age at marriage according to status:

Brahmans	14.4
Jains	13.8
Marathas	12.5
Harijans	12.0

These differences could have an effect on class fertility in the direction suggested by the figures above. The data from this study, however, reveal no positive relationship between family income and fertility.

If the survey of the small city of Kolhapur shows virtually no differential fertility according to socio-economic status, this is not true of the Calcutta data of Chandra Sekar and Mukta Sen. This investigation, as previously mentioned, found the women in an upper-class neighborhood to be only two-thirds as fertile as the women in two lower-middle-class neighborhoods. Also, it appears that use of contraception may be in part responsible for this differential. We should expect the large city to show a greater amount of class-caste differential fertility than either the rural areas or the small city.

SUMMARY OF CLASS DIFFERENCES

The rural Punjab study confirms our findings from the census data on caste. The latter show, it will be recalled, that in so far as the child-woman ratio measures fertility, a high socio-economic status—whether measured by social standing, occupation, or literacy—is associated with somewhat diminished reproduction. Indeed the inverse correlation is perhaps greater and more regular than that shown in the tables, because the bias attributable to poor enumeration of children and to childhood mortality would in all probability be against this type of differential. The exact degree of differential fertility along class lines remains unknown; it looks smaller than the western differential, though the direction is the same.

At first it may appear that the Punjab study, which finds a very slight association between high status and high fertility, refutes our caste results. But the contrary is true, because the Punjab study deals only with the fertility of *married* women, not with that of *all* women. It will be recalled that when the child-woman ratios for castes are computed for married women instead of all women, the differentials become greatly reduced (as with social status) or disappear entirely (as with occupation and literacy). In each case the differential fertility is mainly attributable to the factor of non-marriage. The Punjab study does not tell us anything about non-mar-

[21] Expected births were defined as those that would have occurred if age of mother were the only factor affecting fertility. See pp. 48, 57.

riage, but does agree that among married couples in the village there is no inverse differential (except possibly for the small professional class) such as would arise from contraception.

Perhaps some of the caste differentials arise from the rural-urban differences mentioned earlier; but this factor appears negligible, because the castes in our sample are nearly all predominantly rural. Of the class factors discussed (status, occupation, and literacy), it is hard to say which is the most important. The number of castes in the sample is too small to permit a tabular analysis that will hold two factors constant. Since the Indian social system is so hierarchic in principle, the three factors should be heavily intercorrelated.

Whatever the background cause, the main mechanism through which differential fertility occurs in India is not the deliberate control of reproduction by contraception, but the indirect control of it through such institutional practices as the non-marriage of widows. This means that the existing differentials do not in themselves point to an early decline of Indian fertility; for if the controls are indirect and institutional, a long time will be required for them to be abandoned and deliberate controls adopted. Indeed, while the institutional controls are gradually dying out and the deliberate controls are hardly yet started, fertility may actually increase.

RELIGIOUS DIFFERENTIALS

As is well known, the Muslim population of the subcontinent has been steadily gaining in proportion to the total population, whereas the Hindu population has been steadily losing. Also, the proportion of so-called Tribal people has remained fairly constant. In Table 27 the percentage of the Indian population represented by each of these three groups from 1881 to 1941 is given.[22] Part of the Muslim gain is possibly

TABLE 27

Per Cent of Total Indian Population in Each of Three Religions, 1881–1941 [a]

	1881	1891	1901	1911	1921	1931	1941 [b]
Hindu	75.1	74.2	72.9	71.7	70.7	70.7	69.8
Muslim	20.0	20.4	21.9	22.4	23.2	23.5	24.3
Tribal	2.6	3.3	2.9	3.2	3.0	2.3	2.3

[a] Computed from the Imperial Tables on religion in each of the censuses.
[b] Because of a change of classification in the 1941 census, many persons who would formerly have been enumerated as Hindu were classified as Tribal. This resulted in only 65.5 per cent of the population being reported as Hindu on that date, and as many as 6.5 per cent being reported as Tribal. Consequently, it was necessary to estimate the number who would have been classified as Hindu and as Tribal in 1941 according to the old definition.

due to conversion, but since relatively little conversion has apparently occurred in modern times, this could hardly be the sole explanation. Indeed, any conversion of Hindus to Mohammedanism is probably more than balanced by the conversion, or infiltration, of Tribals into the ranks of Hinduism. The Tribals have steadily lost great numbers to the Hindus, Christians, Muslims, and Sikhs, probably in the order named. Therefore, it is remarkable that the Tribals have so well retained their percentage of the total population. Mortality, too, is probably greater among the Tribals; as between the Muslims and the Hindus there is no evidence (scanty in any case)

[22] Fig. 43 in Chapter 19 gives the rate of growth of all religious groups.

that there is any significant difference in this respect. It seems necessary to assume, then, that the more rapid growth of the Muslims as compared with the Hindus and the relative constancy of the Tribal proportion are due to superior fertility.

This hypothesis can be tested statistically. Unfortunately, the reports of the Health Commissioner for all of what was British India do not give births by religion of parent, although in some areas the data are available. Also, it is not safe to compare the reported birth rates of Muslim districts with those of Hindu districts, because differences of registration, as well as other factors, would bias the results to an unknown extent. So, as in the case of rural-urban and class divisions, reliance must once more be placed on child-woman ratios—in this case the relation of children 0–4 to women 15–39 again —with some help from the rural Punjab study.

For each of the main religious groups in India an average child-woman ratio was computed from the three censuses, 1911, 1921, and 1931. The results, as Table 28 and Fig. 20

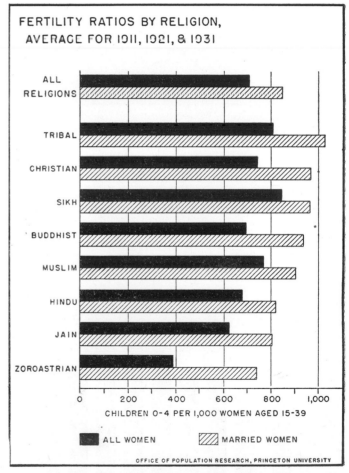

FIGURE 20. Child-Woman Ratios for Women Aged 15–39 by Main Religious Groups in India: 1911, 1921, 1931, Averaged.

show, disclose the kind of differential that one might expect. At the top of the social ladder, the rich, urban, and better educated sects, the Parsis (or Zoroastrians) and the Jains have the lowest proportion of children. At the other end the Christians and Sikhs, who have recruited large numbers of new members from the lower ranks of Hindu society, and presumably also from the younger age groups, have higher ratios —roughly twice as large as the Parsis. The highest of all, however, are the Tribals and Sikhs. The Tribals are primitives, with presumably the reproductive behavior of most aboriginal groups.) Both Muslims and Hindus fall in an intermediate position, with the Muslims having a substantially higher ratio than the Hindus.

TABLE 28

Child-Woman Ratios by Religion, Average for 1911, 1921, and 1931 [1]

	Children 0–4 per 1000 Women 15–39	Children 0–4 per 1000 Married Women 15–39
Parsis	388	735
Jains	624	804
Hindus	678	817
Buddhists	698	932
Christians	741	966
Muslims	770	900
Tribals	808	1,023
Sikhs	841	960
All religions	*705*	*844*

[1] Computed from *Census of India*, Vol. 1, Part 2, 1911, pp. 44–46, 51; 1921, pp. 46–48, 56; 1931, pp. 121–23.

What is the explanation of these religious differentials? Certainly it must be related to the socio-economic status of the groups in question, but we must also ask how the socio-economic status translates itself into demographic results. We must try to trace the causal nexus between social position and lower fertility. A good part of the answer, as in the case of the caste differentials, is to be found in nonmarriage, especially of widows. Those religious groups that permit a great amount of widow remarriage have, apparently, a higher general fertility than those that permit a small amount. Fig. 21 makes clear that the religious groups differ sharply in marital status.

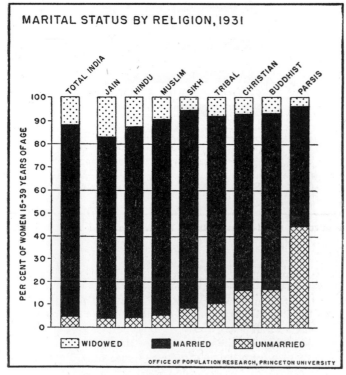

FIGURE 21. Marital Status of Women Aged 15–39 by Religious Groups, India, 1931.

In other words, as Fig. 20 reveals, the ratio of children to *married* women shows smaller differences between religions than does the ratio of children to *all* women of the specified ages. This, however, is not the sole factor, because there is a definite differential even when the nonmarried are excluded from the calculation.

In the study of Punjab villages the four main religious groups came out as follows: [23]

	Average Children Ever Born per Couple	Average Survivors	Percentage of Survivors
Hindus	4.84	3.17	65.5
Sikhs	4.98	3.48	69.9
Muslims	5.12	3.39	66.2
Christians	5.58	3.93	70.4

These results strikingly confirm our findings based on the census. To see this, compare the "Average Survivors" with column 2 of Table 28. The order of increasing effective fertility is the same in both cases: Hindu, Muslim, Sikh, Christian. Furthermore, the distance between the extremes is very similar. In Table 28 the Hindu figure is 85 per cent of the Christian, whereas in the Punjab returns it is 81 per cent.

But the Punjab study goes further than one can go with census statistics. It separates children ever born from survivors. On the basis of the first, the Muslims turn out to have a higher fertility than the Sikhs; but the Sikhs have a greater proportion of survivors, so that their effective fertility is greater. In general, however, the percentage of survivors varies positively with fertility, at least so far as religion is concerned. Hindu couples have fewer living children, not only because of low fertility but also because of high infant mortality. When we add to this, the fact that there are fewer Hindu couples in proportion to the female population (because of widow nonmarriage), we can see why the Hindus are steadily diminishing as a proportion of the total population.)

THE MUSLIM-HINDU DIFFERENTIAL

In any discussion of religion and fertility in the history of India, primary interest centers on the Muslim-Hindu differential, not only because these groups have been the focus of religious controversy but also because together they make up 94 per cent of the Indian population. Figures taken from censuses dating from 1891 to 1941 show that the Muslims have consistently had a higher child-woman ratio than the Hindus. (Fig. 22). They have been substantially above the all-India average, whereas the Hindus have been slightly below it.

(Here again the rate of widow remarriage is important in explaining the fertility differential. As is well known, the Mohammedan religion does not forbid the remarriage of widows, whereas the Hindu religion does.) Although the Indian Muslims have to some extent, in the writer's opinion, acquired the Hindu prejudice in this matter, they have not fully incorporated it into their way of life, as proved by their lesser proportion of widows.[24]

[23] Jain, *op. cit.*, p. 28.
[24] Some of the difference in proportion widowed may conceivably be due to greater Hindu mortality, but there is no reason to think that any but a small fraction of it might be thus explained. Some Muslims maintain that their group has no prejudice whatsoever against widow remarriage, but this sounds like an exaggeration for the ethnocentric purpose of drawing as sharp a contrast as possible between them and the Hindus.

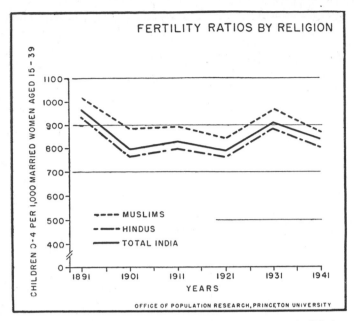

FIGURE 22. Child-Woman Ratios per 1,000 Married Women for Hindus, Muslims, and Total India, 1891–1941.

One way to measure the influence of widow marriage on Hindu-Muslim fertility is this: Suppose that in both religious communities the proportion of widows in each age group were the same as that in the United States at the most comparable census year. Suppose, further, that all of the Indian widows eliminated by this supposition were remarried and had the same fertility as other married women in India at the time. By using an indirect schedule of age-specific fertility,[25] we can calculate the number of births that would be added on the basis of our assumption. This will enable us to estimate the percentage by which fertility would be raised in each religious group by eliminating the taboo on widow remarriage. From 1901 to 1941 the percentage increase would be as follows: [26]

	Hindus	Muslims
1901	17.0	11.1
1911	14.9	11.1
1921	17.0	11.0
1931	14.4	9.6
1941 [27]	13.4	7.0

In this calculation the initial birth rate is assumed to be the same for the two religions. Actually, as the evidence previously cited shows, the Muslim birth rate is higher than the Hindu. Hence an important question is this: Is widow remarriage the sole factor in the difference with respect to the two birth rates? The answer is no, because the birth rate difference is too large to be thus explained. If, for example, Hindu and

[25] The age schedule of Chile in 1930 was used. All that this does is serve as a basis for distributing the births in India as between different age groups.

[26] It may be objected that the American percentage of widows is too severe a basis of calculation to take, because of the difference in mortality between the two countries. There is some truth in this, but it should be recalled that the sex ratio in India is more masculine than in the United States (105 as against 99 in 1930 for the age group 15–39). Also, polygyny is still practiced to some extent in India. Finally, to take some other country for comparison—say Bulgaria—would simply decrease the percentage for both religions; it would not eliminate the proportional difference between the two.

[27] The figures for 1941 relate to a sample which includes some 41 per cent of the Hindu women and 71 per cent of the Muslim women.

Muslim fertility are measured in terms of the ratio of children to married women only, thus ignoring widows altogether, the Muslim figure still remains higher. Table 29, which gives for 1891–1941 the Muslim ratio as a percentage of the Hindu ratio, shows that the Muslim child-*married*-woman ratio has long been at least 108 per cent of the Hindu, as compared with the Muslim child-*all*-woman ratio which has long been at least 112 per cent of the Hindu. The difference between these two figures (i.e. the difference between the two columns of Table 29) represents the margin contributed by the greater rate of

TABLE 29

Muslim Child-Woman Ratio as Percentage of Hindu Ratio, 1891–1941 [1]

	Based on Ratio of Children to *All* Women 15–43	Based on Ratio of Children to *Married* Women 15–43
1891	114.3	108.6
1901	119.6	115.1
1911	114.8	111.8
1921	114.1	110.0
1931	111.9	109.0
1941	112.2	108.6

[1] Compiled from census volumes.

widow remarriage among Muslims. This margin, however, accounts for only a third of the difference between the two religious groups. A good part of the other two-thirds is contributed by the difference in marital fertility, as revealed not only by the census statistics but also by the Punjab study. The rest of the difference, since a child-woman ratio has been used, is probably contributed by a slightly lesser infant mortality on the part of Muslims, although, according to the Punjab study, the difference in the rate of survivorship is not great.

CONCLUSION

One reason for analyzing differential fertility is to find whatever clues it may yield concerning future trends in the general birth rate. In the previous chapter it was pointed out that the Indian birth rate has remained at a high figure, despite a substantial decline in the death rate. The increasing difference between the two has been responsible for the rapid growth of population. The crucial question is therefore this: Will fertility be brought down in time to avoid either a disastrous growth of population or a calamitous rise in the death rate? The study of differential fertility in the present chapter leads us reluctantly to a negative conclusion, based on the following facts:

(1) A consideration of rural-urban differentials during half a century indicates that the cities have not yet, as in some other countries, inaugurated a general decline in the birth rate. The rural-urban differentials are certainly present, and are correlated with size of city, but they have not increased in fifty years.

(2) An analysis of caste fertility on the basis of social status, occupation, and literacy shows that in the Indian region, as in most other areas, fertility is inversely correlated with social position. But the explanation does not apparently lie primarily in the use of contraception by the higher castes, as a Westerner might expect, but rather in the fact that non-

marriage, especially in the form of widow celibacy, is much higher in the upper classes. This result is confirmed by a study in Punjab villages, which found the differences in married fertility to be very slight according to income and occupation. In other words the causes of the inverse differential do not occur within marriage, but rather in non-marriage.

(3) The religious differentials also demonstrate the role of non-marriage in controlling the Indian birth rate. The superiority of Muslim and Tribal fertility over the Hindu is due in part to their greater toleration of widow remarriage. Here there are also some important differences in the fertility of married couples, but the exact causes are not clear.

It follows from these considerations, together with material given in the previous chapter, that Indian fertility, though very high, is not the highest in the world. Nor does it approach the theoretical maximum allowed by biology. It is controlled to a considerable degree by indirect, institutional, non-deliberate customs, such as the taboo on widow remarriage. The presence of such institutional controls does not suggest that fertility will decline soon in India and Pakistan. On the contrary, there is a possibility that under Western influence the effect of such controls will be lessened, because some of them seem objectionable to modern opinion. Some compensation may arise from the tendency, under Western influence, to postpone marriage, but this may not equal the effect of greater liberality with reference to widows. At any rate, no sharp decline in the birth rate can be expected until deliberate control by means of contraception, sterilization, abortion, etc. is inaugurated. Today there is no real evidence that such methods are being adopted by any wide sector of the population. It may take a considerable while for such controls to displace the indirect kind now being unconsciously practiced. All told, the observer inevitably reaches the melancholy conclusion that an early and substantial decline of fertility in India seems unlikely unless rapid changes not now known or envisaged are made in Indian life.

PART IV

THE NET BALANCE: NATURAL INCREASE

CHAPTER 11

Natural Increase: Past and Future

Up to this point births and deaths have been treated separately. Now they must be considered together, and in doing so, one must remember, first, that they are not independent of each other and, second, that the difference between them (the natural increase) is capable of refined measurement.

The crude rate of natural increase, obtained by subtracting the death rate from the birth rate, has fluctuated sharply in India because of fluctuations in the death rate. This is made clear by Fig. 8 in Chapter 5. It is also clear from the decade rates, as follows:

AVERAGE ANNUAL RATES

Decade	Births	Deaths	Natural Increase
1881–1891	48.9	41.3	7.6
1891–1901	45.8	44.4	1.4
1901–1911	49.2	42.6	6.6
1911–1921	48.1	47.2	0.9
1921–1931	46.4	36.3	10.1
1931–1941	45.2	31.2	14.0

With migration playing little part, population growth in the Indian region has been determined primarily by natural increase; it is the fluctuations in the latter that explain the unsteadiness of the growth rate.

For the purpose of understanding future trends, however, it is not enough to know the crude rate of natural increase. It is necessary also to know the age structure of the population, because the age structure, capable of considerable variation, influences the number of births and deaths "per 1,000 population." Knowing the age structure in addition to the vital statistics, one can determine better the effect of birth and death rates on each other and the effect of present demographic conditions on future population growth.

THE AGE STRUCTURE

As a result of high mortality and high fertility, Pakistan and the Union of India have extremely young populations. Their combined age pyramid reveals a very broad base and a quickly attenuated top. It stands in marked contrast to the kind of pyramid found in countries with a low fertility and mortality. Figure 23 compares the Indian age pyramid of 1941 with that of the United States for 1940, both in percentage and in absolute terms. It demonstrates an astonishing fact: although the total Indian population is three times that of the United States, it has only the same number of people aged 65 and over, and approximately six times as many chil-

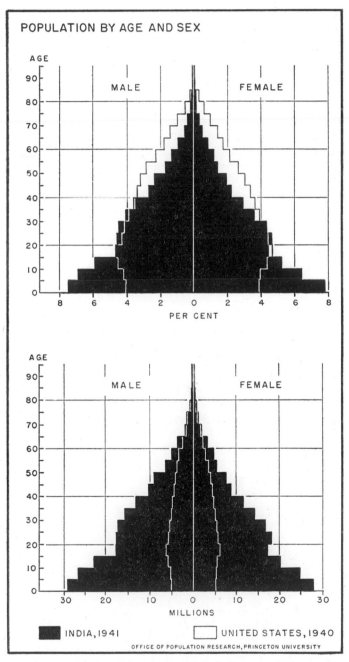

FIGURE 23. Superimposed Age Pyramids for India, 1941, and the United States, 1940.

dren aged 0–4. Fig. 24 shows in detail the comparison of the two countries for the advanced ages.

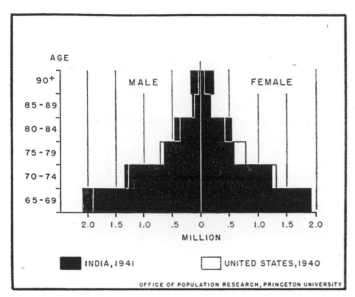

FIGURE 24. Similarity of the Indian and United States Populations in the Upper Age Brackets.

The difference between the two kinds of age structure is profound. It affects, among other things, the kind and degree of dependency. In India and Pakistan most of the dependents are children, there being almost seven times as many children under 5 as adults over 65. In the United States, on the other hand, an increasing proportion of the dependents are oldsters rather than youngsters; in 1940 the persons over 65 almost equalled the children under 5. The Western nations, because of sharply curtailed fertility and mortality, have enjoyed during the last few decades a type of age structure that yields few dependents. Time, however, is rapidly catching up with these nations. They are, as is well known, faced with the prospect of having an increasing proportion of their population in the advanced ages.[1] It is believed by many experts that this kind of old-age dependency is more expensive and disadvantageous than the other kind. In any case, it is a less hopeful kind. Before Pakistan and the India Union ever reach this stage they will pass through a period similar to that through which the advanced Western nations have gone, a period in which the bulk of the inhabitants are in the middle years of life and only a minimum are at the two extremes. In other words, the Indian countries may look forward at some time to a period of minimum dependency in terms of age. But for the present they have a great deal of dependency because of their young age structure.

The extent to which countries like England and the United States still have a greater proportion of their population in the productive ages (20–60) than do countries like India, Pakistan, and Colombia can be seen from Fig. 25. The United States had over 55 per cent of its population in these productive ages in 1940, whereas India had less than 47 per cent in 1941. For the present, therefore, the Indian region suffers from a substantially larger burden of dependency, most of which is in the young ages. Of course, on top of this is the extra dependency contributed, at all ages, by bad health conditions, associated with a high mortality.

The age structure affects not only the amount of dependency but also the future population growth. A glance at the age pyramids shows at once that the Indian subcontinent has a greater potential growth during the next few decades than does the United States. In America the diminutive groups at the bottom of the pyramid will eventually occupy the middle position and the present bulge in the middle will move to the top, at which time the crude birth rate and rate of population growth will both decline, given the same intrinsic fertility.[2] In India, on the other hand, if mortality continues to decline, the growth of population will be enormous. Huge numbers now in the lower age brackets will grow into adults, giving birth in turn to still larger cohorts. In the past a high mortality has flattened the sides of the age pyramid; a lessened mortality will make them more perpendicular. As a result the total population within the pyramid will be greater than now.

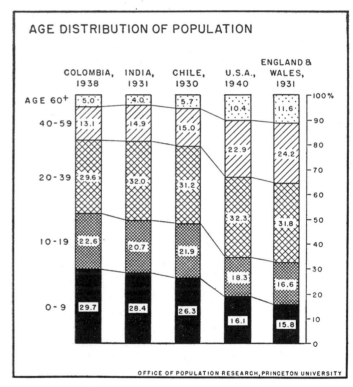

FIGURE 25. Percentage of Population in Major Age Groups, Five Countries.

It is on this basis that we can predict, if present trends in fertility and mortality continue, a rapid growth of the Indian and Pakistani populations—a growth which, in absolute numbers, seems fantastic to contemplate.

If, while mortality continued to decline, fertility were also lowered in the Indian region, the potentially huge population of the future would be somewhat more supportable, because there would be a larger proportion in the economically produc-

[1] The consequences of an aging population are ably discussed in Frank W. Notestein et al., *The Future Population of Europe and the Soviet Union* (Geneva: League of Nations, 1944), pp. 108–63. See also John D. Durand, "The Trend Toward an Older Population," *Annals of the American Academy of Political and Social Science,* Vol. 237 (January, 1945), pp. 142–51; and Jean Daric, *Vieillissement de la Population et Prolongation de la Vie Active,* Institut National d'Etudes Démographiques, Travaux et Documents, Cahier No. 7 (Paris: Presses Universitaires de France, 1948).

[2] The writer realizes that a general rise in the birth rate of advanced nations has taken place in connection with World War II, but he believes this to be a temporary phenomenon. If temporary, it will not greatly altar the general character of the age structure. See "World-wide Resurgence in Birth Rate," *Statistical Bulletin* of Metropolitan Life Insurance Company, Vol. 28 (September, 1947), pp. 1–3; also P. K. Whelpton and Clyde V. Kiser, "Trends, Determinants, and Control in Human Fertility," *Annals of the American Academy of Political and Social Science,* Vol. 237 (January, 1945), pp. 112–22.

tive ages. But there is little evidence that fertility will soon be substantially lowered.

REPRODUCTION RATES

One measure of the future effect of present demographic behavior is the net reproduction rate, which tells us to what extent each generation is replacing itself in the next generation. This measure eliminates the influence of the age structure, because it shows, in effect, the likelihood that one woman, if she had the fertility exhibited by the present population at each age, would, as she passed through the reproductive period, replace herself with another woman. It follows that the net reproduction rate can vary independently of the crude birth rate, depending on the age structure. In a population such as India's, where a large portion of the population is below the reproductive ages, the crude birth rate tends slightly to mask an essentially higher fertility. In other words, as high as the crude birth rate is in the Indian countries, it may well go higher without any change in the reproductive behavior of each woman, simply because of the changing age structure (although the age structure, as we shall see, is not much younger than the stable population). The net reproduction rate enables us to separate two variables (fertility and the age structure) which the crude birth rate confuses, and thus enables us to predict more accurately the hypothetical consequences of present behavior.[3]

When the net reproduction rate is unity, it means that according to current fertility and mortality the population is just replacing itself. When it is below unity, it means that it is failing to replace itself by the amount of the difference. The latest figure for the Indian population, as we might guess, is quite high, but Table 30 shows that the rate fluctuated in the past between 1.0 and 1.3. The fluctuation is in accord with what we know about India's relatively slow increase of population. Recently, however, the net reproduction rate has risen until it gives the region a rather high replacement tendency.

Whereas the net reproduction rate takes account of mortality, the gross reproduction rate does not. The latter is therefore a measure of fertility rather than of replacement. As Table 30 shows, India's gross rate, staying close to 3.0 during the last five decades, is higher than that for most other countries for which the computation has been made. Egypt, which has already been seen to have much the same demographic situation as Pakistan-India, appears to be one of the few exceptions. The gross rate of course fluctuates much less than does the net rate, simply because in the Indian region the thing that remains steady is fertility rather than mortality.

An interesting feature of Table 30 is the size of the difference between the gross and the net reproduction rates. In the case of India the net rate has been (in 1921) as low as 36 per cent of the gross rate, although in 1941 it was 47 per cent. In the United States, on the other hand, it has been between 88

[3] The net reproduction rate is not a perfect instrument for gauging population change, because it does not take account of the influence of past fertility and age at marriage upon current fertility. The total number of offspring that any one cohort of married women is likely to have remains much more stable than the net reproduction rate at any one moment. However, the inadequacy of the net reproduction rate applies much more to countries in which fertility varies greatly from year to year because of economic and social fluctuations than it does in a country such as India, where planned fertility is conspicuous by its absence. For a critical appraisal of reproduction rates, see J. Hajnal, "The Analysis of Birth Statistics in the Light of the Recent International Recovery of the Birth-Rate," *Population Studies,* Vol. 1 (September, 1947), pp. 137–64.

TABLE 30

Reproduction Rates for India and Other Countries in Years Around 1931 and 1941

	Date	Gross Rate	Net Rate
India [a]	1901	2.99	1.09
	1911	3.14	1.06
	1921	2.83	1.03
	1931	2.99	1.25
	1941	2.76	1.30
Egypt [1]	1937	3.11	1.44
U.S.S.R. [2]	1924, 26–27	2.64	1.72
Puerto Rico [3]	1920–30	2.50	1.50
	1930–40	2.46	1.62
Japan [4]	1930	2.37	1.57
	1937	2.14	1.44
Chile [4]	1930–32	2.26	1.30
Rumania [1]	1930–31	2.16	1.40
Canada [1]	1930–32	1.55	1.30
	1938	1.28	1.09
	1940–42	1.42	1.29
U.S.A. (white) [4]	1930	1.22	1.08
	1942	1.27	1.19
England & Wales [4]	1930–32	0.93	0.81
	1940	0.85	0.75

[a] For methods of computing India reproduction rates, see Appendix F.
[1] P. K. Whelpton and Clyde V. Kiser, "Trends, Determinants, and Control in Human Fertility," *Annals of American Academy of Political and Social Science,* Vol. 237 (January, 1945), pp. 114–15.
[2] Frank Lorimer, *The Population of the Soviet Union* (Geneva: League of Nations, 1946), p. 90.
[3] Christopher Tietze, "Human Fertility in Puerto Rico," *American Journal of Sociology,* Vol. 53 (July, 1947), p. 35.
[4] *Population Index,* Vol. 12 (April, 1946), pp. 150–55.

and 94 per cent. The contrast between the Indian and Pakistani populations and the advanced countries in this regard shows the wastefulness of Asiatic reproductive behavior. A great many children are born, but most of them die. The people of Pakistan and the Indian Union therefore expend a tremendous amount of biological and social energy in obtaining a fairly modest rate of population growth. In this respect their reproduction is like their agriculture, for there, too, they spend much labor in producing only mediocre results.

Reproduction rates were computed for all the provinces and states of India, but it is difficult to tell to what extent they reflect true variations. The figures below show what are perhaps reliable figures for some major provinces in 1931:

	Gross Rate	*Net Rate*
Punjab	3.57	1.63
United Provinces	3.13	1.36
Delhi	3.08	1.34
Bombay	2.94	1.35
Bengal	2.89	1.26
Madras	2.61	1.40

The results agree with what one would expect. The Punjab is generally regarded as one of the most fertile provinces, demographically speaking, whereas Bengal is believed to have a somewhat depressed fertility. The position of Madras is questionable.

THE INTRINSIC RATE OF INCREASE

The net reproduction rate tells us to what extent, under given conditions of fertility and mortality, the women of one generation are replacing themselves with women in the next, but it does not tell us the annual rate of increase that would ultimately take place. We know that a continuance of a given age-specific rate of mortality and fertility will, after two or more generations, lead to a stable age structure, and that then the crude birth and death rates will be fixed and can be determined by calculation. Then also the rate of increase will be constant, and since it was implicit in the conditions of fertility and mortality in the first place, it is called the "intrinsic" or "true" rate of natural increase.

In 1931 India had an intrinsic rate of increase of approximately .0099, which means that, given the fertility of 1930–31 and the average mortality conditions of 1921–41, her population would eventually grow steadily at a rate of almost 1 per cent per year. This would lead, if continued, to a doubling of the population every 70 years. An intrinsic rate for 1941 is more difficult to compute on an accurate basis, but it should be rather close to that for 1930–31.

During 1930–31 India's average estimated crude rate of natural increase was 11.26 per thousand, or .0113 per person. It was thus rather close to the intrinsic rate for that time. This correspondence between the crude rate and the intrinsic rate means that India's age structure is fairly close to the stable age structure, as Fig. 26 demonstrates. The actual age structure has a slight excess of people in the younger age groups, and a slight deficiency of people in the upper age groups, especially above age 50. This is the result of a recent decline in mortality, which has affected children and young

persons more than older persons. A continued decline in mortality without a corresponding decline in fertility will further distort the age distribution, as compared with the stable; but if mortality and fertility were both to remain fixed, the actual population would be virtually identical with the stable age distribution from the present time on. This close similarity between the actual and the stable age distribution is worth noting in connection with population projections, a subject to which we now turn.

PROJECTIONS OF FUTURE POPULATION

The term "projections," as used in demography, means those statements of future trends which follow mathematically from certain explicitly stated quantitative assumptions. Whether or not the statements will prove true in practice is another matter; they will do so only if the assumptions turn out to accord with reality, which may or may not be the case. It is possible, and often instructive, to make projections on the basis of entirely unrealistic assumptions, simply in order to demonstrate the demographic consequences of these assumptions. Naturally, in estimating the actual course of future populations one is obligated to use assumptions most likely to accord with reality, and this necessitates the employment of judgment and intuition (resting on vague assumptions that go beyond the explicit quantitative assumptions of the projections).[4] But for the present we are not so much concerned with estimates as with projections. The actual course of India's future population, in so far as it can be foreseen, will be discussed in a subsequent chapter. One must obviously have the projections in mind before such a topic is considered, and since the projections rely heavily upon a knowledge of births, deaths, and the age structure, they are given at this point.

There are two general methods of making population projections. One of these—the synthetic or logistic method—involves fitting a curve to the actual population growth, and using the formula as a means of extrapolation into the future. This method, originating with Verhulst and independently developed by Pearl and Reed, has achieved some remarkable successes as well as some notable failures from the point of view of prediction. The type of curve used, called the logistic, expresses the mathematical assumptions and has the following form,

$$P = \frac{K}{1 + e^{2 + bt}}$$

which, when plotted, shows a characteristic S-shape.[5] In order to use this projection for purposes of estimating the actual future growth of a population, one must make the intuitional assumption that the social factors determining population growth in the area in question will remain constant in their effects. If the technological and economic situation should be radically changed, then obviously a change in population growth will result which will not fit the curve as extrapolated.

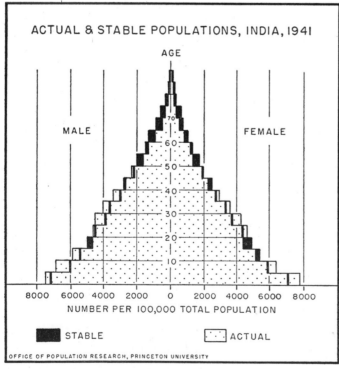

ACTUAL & STABLE POPULATIONS, INDIA, 1941

AGE

MALE   FEMALE

70

60

50

40

30

20

10

8000 6000 4000 2000 0 2000 4000 6000 8000
NUMBER PER 100,000 TOTAL POPULATION

■ STABLE   ⠒ ACTUAL

OFFICE OF POPULATION RESEARCH, PRINCETON UNIVERSITY

FIGURE 26. Comparison of Stable and Actual Age Distributions, India, 1941.

[4] cf. Notestein et al., *op. cit.*, pp. 19ff.

[5] For a discussion of various methods of long-range projection see Lowell J. Reed, "Population Growth and Forecasts," *Annals of the American Academy of Political and Social Science,* Vol. 188 (November, 1936), pp. 159–66, and also Irene B. Taeuber, "The Development of Population Predictions in Europe and the Americas," *Estadistica,* No. 7 (September, 1944), pp. 323–46. The method of fitting the logistic is given in Raymond Pearl, *Medical Biometry and Statistics* (3rd ed.; Philadelphia: W. B. Saunders, 1940), Ch. 18.

Thus in Puerto Rico it has been noted that one logistic curve cannot fit the total history of the island's population growth. Instead, two different curves must be fitted, the point of intersection being around 1890–1900.[6] Any prediction of the Puerto Rican population after 1900 made on the basis of the curve prior to that date is consequently erroneous. The assumption of stability in social trends is of course an important but very dubious proposition in the case of Pakistan and the Union of India. Consequently, the logistic method must be thought of as furnishing a projection, not a prediction.

The other projection method—the analytical or component method—attempts to fit curves to the biological components of population growth (births and deaths) and, bearing in mind the age distribution, to use the extrapolations of these to obtain an estimate of the overall population. In this way Notestein and his colleagues have prepared population projections for European countries and the Soviet Union.[7] The method has the advantage that, given projections of age-specific birth and death rates, the future population can be calculated by simply adding births and subtracting deaths. But it has the disadvantage that birth and death rates fluctuate more than the natural increase which is a function of the two, and our knowledge of components is often less than our knowledge of the population growth as a whole. It would seem that for short-run estimates the component method is preferable, while for long-run estimates the logistic is better. This can be seen in the tendency to revise component projections frequently, as Thompson and Whelpton have done for the United States.

In the case of India-Pakistan it is difficult to use the component method, for three reasons. First, age-specific birth rates are lacking; second, the trends in both birth and death rates are not clearly known; and third, comparable experience with other countries in a similar position is not available. How is one to know, for example, the likely rate of future decline in a birth rate as high as India's? In virtually no European country can we get a series of statistics going back to such a high birth rate; and so we cannot formulate a general height-slope pattern that will be applicable. Consequently, we have relied on simpler and generally less systematic techniques than the component method.

Our first projection rests on the assumption that the relatively high rate of natural increase observed between 1921 and 1941 will continue. This gives a maximum projection (in the sense that we believe the most favorable social condition conceivable for India and Pakistan would not yield a greater growth). It gives us a population of approximately 550 million in 1970 and 790 million in the year 2000 for the two countries combined. In other words, if the population of the Indian region grew during the six decades following 1941 as it grew during the two decades preceding that date, it would almost double its size. But in view of the past history of India's population growth (which has been quite sporadic), and in view of the fact that population growth never proceeds for very long at a uniform rate, this projection cannot be regarded as an estimate of actual future trends. It is merely a top limit which the actual growth might conceivably approximate.

Our second projection rests on the assumption that during the next six decades the region's population will grow at the average speed it exhibited during the last seven decades. India's growth, as we saw in Chapter 4, has had its ups and downs, and it can be expected in the future to have ups and downs. This assumption yields a total of 465 million in 1970 and 560 million in the year 2000. The trouble with such a projection, however, is that the assumption of a constant rate of growth is entirely unrealistic. The figure for the year 2000 might be roughly accurate, without the population at intervening points being so.

Our third projection, made by fitting a simple logistic curve, gets rid of the constant-rate difficulty. The curve was fitted to the population of all of India at eight census dates—1871 to 1941. These populations, it will be recalled, are estimated by us from 1871 to 1921, while the 1931 and 1941 census figures are taken as they stand. The estimates may be inaccurate, and in any case eight points do not make a large number for fitting a logistic curve. The projection cannot be taken, therefore, as giving us anything like a prediction; in fact, the past history of logistic projections in India has not been impressive from a predictive point of view. Swaroop and Lal, for example, using a projection that included the 1931 population, missed the population of 1941 by some 47 million, or 12 per cent.[8] Furthermore, one should bear in mind that, as stated earlier, the use of logistic curves for purposes of prediction rests on the general assumption that social trends will remain as they have been, and that no great innovation or novel calamity will suddenly make itself felt. Since this is a long assumption for the modern world, and especially for the Indian countries, the fact that our curve hits 525 million in 1970 and 635 million in the year 2000 should not be taken as an estimate of future occurrences. The 635 million is close to the asymptote for the curve, which is 700 million. The projection assumes that after the year 2000 the rate of growth will begin to taper off rapidly.

The three projections are charted in Fig. 27. It will be seen that the logistic falls between the first one, which is high, and the second, which is low. By way of summary, we give below the populations of all India which these projections yield at 1970 and 2000:

	1970	2000
First Projection	550	790
Third Projection (Logistic)	525	635
Second Projection	465	560

We feel that in actual practice the highest projection will not be exceeded, but we cannot say with equal confidence that the lowest estimate represents a minimum possibility. Any estimate for the subcontinent is bound to be hazardous. It is quite possible that the use of atomic energy, either in peace or war, or some other great technological transformation, will make possible an increase or a decrease of population so great that it now seems inconceivable. We assume that India's spurt of growth during the last century and a half has been due to the importation of European industrialism and commercialism, and that as this new regime becomes firmly established, the rate of population growth will level off again. But industrial society is inherently unstable, and so we must be prepared to see new technological systems emerging, some of which may

---

[6] José L. Janer, "Population Growth in Puerto Rico and Its Relation to Time Changes in Vital Statistics," *Human Biology*, Vol. 17 (December, 1945), pp. 267–82.

[7] Notestein et al., *op. cit.*, especially pp. 183–98. To get a realistic projection, one must make assumptions about the rate of migration. This can seldom be done by an extrapolative procedure.

[8] Satya Swaroop and R. B. Lal, "Logistic Law of Growth and Structure of Indian Population," *Population*, Vol. 2 (August, 1938), pp. 100–21. See Appendix G for a brief discussion of logistic projections in India, including our own.

well affect population growth. Their effect may be particularly great in Pakistan and the Indian Union if, when these effects emerge, the erstwhile industrial revolution has not run its course, so that there is a telescoping of social change. Should atomic energy come into use for peaceful production while the region still had customs that produce high fertility, the resulting population growth, before the establishment of

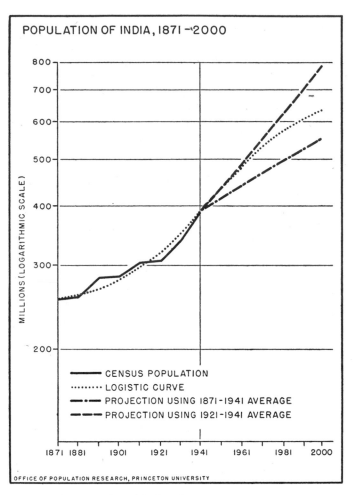

FIGURE 27. Population of India, 1871–1941, and Three Projections of India's Future Population to the Year 2000: (1) Assuming the same rate of growth as in the period 1921–1941, (2) assuming the same rate of growth as in the period 1871–1941, (3) extrapolating a logistic curve fitted to corrected all-India populations, 1871–1941.

a new equilibrium, would probably be enormous. On the other hand, it is possible that the next war may kill far more people, proportionately, than the last several wars put together. Some people even speak of the extinction of the human race and of human civilization. Without accepting such superficial conclusions, however, one can still envision possibilities of population change that would make any prediction based on past demographic trends seem foolish.

CONCLUSION

India's natural increase has not been exceptionally high, because her high birth rate has been almost matched by her high death rate. But the rate of natural increase has been climbing of late, so that a continuance of the average 1921–41 rate would give India-Pakistan an enormous population of nearly 800 million by the year 2000. If the rate of natural increase should start to diminish gradually according to the logistic law, the growth of population would also be great, reaching almost 650 million by the year 2000. Even if the same sporadic rate of increase as was observed between 1871 and 1941 were continued, the rise in population would be heavy. The chance of such projections representing the real future growth, however, is rather small, because the Indian countries are unstable entities in an unstable world. The value of such projections is that they show what the region is potentially capable of under fairly normal conditions. Under ordinary conditions the industrial revolution will bring about an extremely rapid rate of population growth followed by a declining rate until stability is reached. The astounding thing about this view of the future is that the Indian region, starting with such a huge population, can hardly be expected to go through the usual process. The enormous population itself shows signs of becoming a dampening factor on industrial progress. The past growth of population during the industrialization of England and Japan is hardly comparable to the present Indian situation, because Indian development comes later in history. England and Japan had the advantage of trading with a world that was not generally industrialized. Now practically the whole world threatens to pass through the industrial revolution as rapidly as India and Pakistan. What this will do to population growth in the subcontinent is hard to say. It may possibly enhance it. But if it gives this area a billion inhabitants by the year 2000, then the whole world, and India-Pakistan too, will be a vastly different place from what we think of it as being now.

The projections in this chapter have ignored the factor of migration. Up to now this factor has not been important in the rapidity or slowness of India's population growth. By an orderly process of development in the world it will probably not be an important factor in the future. Yet it is conceivable that a huge loss of population in other areas, such as North America or Europe, will leave a vacuum that Indians can fill; or, if Pakistan or especially the Indian Union could gain military power commensurate with her manpower, she might force her way into certain parts of the world now thinly settled but barred to her. The division of India into Pakistan and the Union of India does not suggest, however, that this subcontinent will consolidate itself soon into a major military power, or that either country will do so. Consequently, in turning to the subject of migration in the next two chapters, we shall not deal primarily with these speculations but with the facts of migration as they have shown themselves in the past and as they may show themselves under normal development.

PART V

MIGRATION: ITS DIRECTION AND EXTENT

CHAPTER 12

Immigration: The Foreign Trickle

THOUGH India has been mainly a place where the natives stay at home and foreigners stay away, both the departure of Indians to other areas and the entrance of foreigners into India have been important enough to create international problems. The demographic importance of these movements, however, has been far less than their political importance. As previously noted, the numbers crossing India's boundaries prior to partition, though seemingly large in absolute terms, have been relatively small in comparison to the total population. This has been particularly true of immigration into India. In 1931 there were only 678,000 persons living in India who were born outside—a mere 0.2 per cent of the population. At the same time the United States had 11.6 per cent of its population born outside, France had 6.6 per cent, Yugoslavia 2.2 per cent, and England and Wales had 0.8 per cent. In short, from a comparative point of view, India has not been a country of immigration.

In certain respects and certain areas, however, immigration has been of great significance to India. The British were always extremely few there, but their influence was immeasurable—certainly greater than the influence of the Nepalese, who have always outnumbered them. In certain parts of India —e.g. in border districts—the number of immigrants was sizable in relation to the local population.

Unfortunately, the statistics on past immigration into India are extremely scanty. Except for Indian laborers returning from abroad, most of the immigrants came across the Northern and Western land frontiers. Here no check whatsoever seems to have been kept on the number crossing the boundary, on the length of stay, or on the characteristics of the persons. The only information comes from census statistics on birthplace, tribe, language, and religion. These cannot give an accurate knowledge of the current of immigration, but they can give some notion of its general trend and direction. In 1931, for reasons of economy, the statistics on birthplace were not published in their usual detail, although enough were published to provide rough information; in 1941, except for certain provinces and states, nothing was published on this topic. Even when birthplace statistics were published for most of India, certain frontier districts, such as the trans-border territory of North-West Frontier Province, were not enumerated on the regular schedule; consequently, our data often disappear precisely where we would most like to have them.[1] It becomes plain, then, that any conclusions we reach about immigration into pre-partition India must be meager and tentative.

[1] *Census of India,* 1931, Vol. 15 (N.W. Frontier Prov.), Part 1, p. 52; Vol. 4 (Baluchistan), Part 1, pp. 4–7.

THE GENERAL TREND

From 1891 to 1931 the proportion of foreign-born persons in the population remained virtually fixed, varying between 0.23 and 0.19 per cent and showing no consistent trend (Table 31). Although no 1941 figure is available for the whole country, an examination of such provincial figures as are published suggests that the proportion did not increase in that year. Whereas World War I took foreigners out of India, World War II brought them in, but not permanently.

TABLE 31

Foreign-Born as Percentage of Total Population, 1891–1931

	Census Population [a]	Born Outside [b]	Per Cent of Census Population
1891	279,592,618	643,364	0.23
1901	283,870,432	661,455	0.23
1911	303,041,179	652,555	0.22
1921	305,730,288	567,180	0.19
1931	338,170,632	677,679	0.20

[a] These populations exclude Burma.
[b] These figures include persons born in Burma, French India, and Portuguese India but enumerated in India proper.

It is easy to understand why there was relatively little movement into India. The peculiar Indian way of life was not attractive to most foreigners. The standard of living was comparatively low, the population already dense. The countries from which immigrants might come, by land at least, were sparsely populated. Industry was not developed on a scale that would require much outside labor, whether skilled or unskilled. The areas accessible by water—Burma, Malaya, Ceylon—were importers rather than exporters of labor. The political security of India under the British prevented immigration by conquest, and the British ruled with remarkably few people of their own nationality in the country.

Those who did migrate to India came from a diversity of motives. Some found new advantages (Chinese carpenters and shoemakers in Calcutta); some traded their foreign wares (Afghans); some became highly prized soldiers (Gurkhas); some came to rule (English), others to return to the ancestral home (descendants of Indians abroad), others to worship (Tibetan Buddhists), and others to marry (Nepalese). But the total number who were impelled by these diverse motives was quite small.

World War II undoubtedly led to the permanent repatriation of many Indians settled or born in Burma. How many returned from Malaya is hard to say. Probably the census of 1951 will show a larger proportion of foreign-born in the Indian Union than ever before (even apart from those born in Pakistan), even if the Europeans themselves are fewer; but the percentage, as always, will be extremely small.

The males born abroad have tended consistently to outnumber the females by two to one. The number of males per 100 females among the foreign-born in four different censuses was as follows:

1891	196
1911	222
1921	204
1931	203

In general the British Provinces have received far more than their share of the foreign-born in India. In 1931 they had 614,193 foreign-born residents (or 0.24 per cent of their total population) as against only 63,480 in the Indian States (or 0.08 per cent of the total population of these States). Also, the cities have received a disproportionate share. Twenty-eight of the leading cities in 1931 had 18.2 per cent of the foreign-born population, as compared to 2.5 per cent of the total Indian population.

The Main Countries of Origin

The great majority of immigrants into India prior to partition came from other Asiatic countries (Table 32). These countries accounted for 81 per cent of the foreign-born persons in 1931, and this percentage was approximately the same in all censuses. Of the Asiatic countries those that contributed most were Nepal (45 per cent of foreign-born), French and Portuguese India (12 per cent), Afghanistan (12 per cent), Burma (3.6 per cent), and Arabia (3.5 per cent).

TABLE 32

Per Cent of Foreign-Born Persons by Place of Origin, 1891–1931 [1]

	Total	From Asia %	From Europe %	From Other Places %
1891	643,364	82.34	15.46	2.19
1901	661,455	83.52	14.86	1.62
1911	652,555	78.95	18.96	2.09
1921	567,180	78.22	20.19	1.59
1931	677,679	81.24	16.31	2.45

[1] Compiled from table on Foreign Born by Place of Birth in Part 2 of each summary volume, *Census of India,* 1891, 1901, 1911, 1921, and 1931.

Europe was the second largest contributor. Its share in 1931 was 15 per cent of the foreign-born, almost all of which was British. Africa came third with 1.7 per cent, the Americas fourth with 0.6 per cent, and Australasia last with 0.2 per cent.

For all practical purposes, migration into India came from six sources: Nepal, United Kingdom, French and Portuguese India, Afghanistan, Burma, and Arabia. These together have supplied nine-tenths of all immigrants, as the 1931 figures show:

	Per Cent of Foreign-Born
Nepal	44.7
United Kingdom	14.7
French & Portuguese India	12.0
Afghanistan	11.9
Burma	3.6
Arabia	3.5

With the exception of the United Kingdom, all of these sources were Asiatic.

NEPAL

By 1931 there were 303,000 Nepalese (by birth) living in India, more than three times the number of British. The changes in number have been small, as the following figures show:

	Nepal-Born	Per Cent of All Foreign Born
1891	234,260	36.4
1901	239,127	36.2
1911	274,251	42.0
1921	260,220	45.9
1931	303,139	44.7

The number of Nepalese males per 100 females was 152 in 1931, a lower ratio than foreign-born groups in India usually had. Since Nepal is a long thin country having contact with India along an extended border, and since female migration is generally short-run migration, the high proportion of females is to be expected. However, the sex ratio has gradually risen since 1891, when it stood at 123; and the rise suggests that labor and military recruitment have played an increasing role in Nepalese immigration.

In 1931 over 91 per cent of the Indian residents born in Nepal were concentrated in only five political divisions, as follows:

Bengal	97,631
Assam	86,897
United Provinces	43,387
Bihar & Orissa	36,410
Sikkim	12,571
Total	276,896

Since these divisions embraced all the Indian territory fronting on Nepal, it appears that the Nepalese did not go far into India when they settled there.

Examining the districts within each of these provinces, one finds that a considerable portion of Nepalese migration is marriage migration, similar to that found for internal migration within India. It is the districts bordering on Nepal that have the greatest percentage of Nepalese in their population; in Bihar and the United Provinces, for example, these districts average ten times the percentage found in other districts. The border districts also have an excess of Nepalese females. In the border districts of Bihar, for instance, there were only 37 males to every 100 females of Nepalese birth, while in the non-border districts the ratio was 303 per 100. Such statistics strongly suggest that Indian villagers along the border take Nepalese brides, in conformity with the usual practice of village exogamy in India. Doubtless Nepalese villagers also take Indian brides.

The majority of the Nepalese in India "are merely settlers from the other side of the common boundary, who have married or taken up land in the contiguous districts in British territory, and who have been replaced in Nepal by an equal or greater number of emigrants from [the Indian] side of the frontier." Identical in physical type with the Indians along the border, they are quite distinct from the warlike races of the Nepal hills (Khas, Mangar, Gurung, and other tribes—collectively known as Gurkhas). The Nepalese in the army are not so numerous as one might suppose. In 1921 only 8 per cent of the Nepalese in India were in the army. The influence of the army on immigration is greater than this suggests, however, because many of the recruits bring their families with them and, on the expiry of their term of service, settle permanently in the country, especially in Assam.[2]

Even in most border districts the Nepal-born constitute only a small part of the population. In Bihar there is only one district (Champara) where the proportion rises as high as a half of one per cent. In the United Provinces the districts with the greatest proportion are Naini Tal, 3 per cent; Dehra Dun, 2 per cent; and Garhwal, 0.5 per cent. In the east, however, we find Sikkim and certain Bengal districts with larger proportions. Darjeeling District had, according to the 1931 census, 18.5 per cent of its population born in Nepal, Jalpaiguri District had 3 per cent, and Sikkim State 11.4 per cent.

Birthplace figures of course do not accurately measure the total influence of the Nepalese. The persons of Nepalese descent are considerably more numerous. In Sikkim, for instance, whereas the number born in Nepal was only 12,571 in 1931, the number who spoke a Nepalese language as the mother tongue was 84,101, or 76.5 per cent of the total population.[3]

Although the total Nepalese migration to India has tended slightly to increase, that part of it which went to these particular districts of concentration declined. In 1881 nearly two-fifths of the Darjeeling population was Nepal-born, whereas in 1931 the proportion was less than one-fifth. In Sikkim in 1901, when the first enumeration of that state was made, the proportion of Nepal-born was also about two-fifths, whereas it was down to slightly more than one-tenth in 1931.[4] Such changes, together with data on the frontier provinces as compared with the rest of India, suggest that the Nepalese immigrants are tending to spread out rather than to concentrate in border areas.

This conclusion is not wholly borne out in Assam, where the number and proportion of Nepal-born persons have continued to rise, albeit with increasing slowness.

	Nepal-Born in Assam	Per Cent of Total Population
1901	21,347	0.35
1911	47,654	0.67
1921	70,344	0.94
1931	88,306	1.02

It can be assumed that the preference of the Assamese for local labor or for aboriginal labor from Central India and Bihar, together with restrictions by the Nepalese government, will eventually reduce migration from Nepal into Assam. In the meantime Assam has a sizable Nepalese population. In 1931 the census found 120,287 persons of Nepalese castes and 140,000 speaking Nepalese languages. This group has experienced some friction with the native population over the use of land, and Assam is not likely to encourage future immigration of this type.

No one knows how many Indians cross the border into Nepal, but census authorities think that the number is nearly equal to the number of Nepalese who move a short way into India. The territory is much the same on either side of the border, and the pressure of population has been, if anything, less on the Nepal side than on the Indian side.[5]

AFGHANISTAN

The number of Indian residents born in Afghanistan has been reported as follows in the censuses:

1891	84,871
1901	112,249
1911	91,531
1921	47,758
1931	80,921

These figures, however, are grossly deficient, because the border districts of the North-West Frontier Province, which lie closest to Afghanistan, and which make up nearly half the provincial population, have never been enumerated with respect to birthplace.[6] Thus the very section of India that contains the greatest number of Afghans is the one from which none are reported. In our judgment, the census returned between 30,000 and 200,000 too few Afghan-born persons. Such a margin of error affects greatly our conception of the total number of foreigners living in India. We know that the number was always higher than that reported, but we do not know how much higher.

Up until the division of India into Pakistan and the Union of India, it was felt that Afghan immigration was either declining or ready to decline. Most of the movement was seasonal, in connection with trade, labor, or grazing, and the opportunities along these lines were shrinking. The areas in British India available for grazing appeared to be contracting, partly because of the extension of irrigation; the migratory tribes were tending to settle down; and the Afghan government was placing greater restrictions on movement across the border. The Afghans had caused considerable friction in British India, and at times there had been some intriguing with the Afghan government. What the situation will be under the Pakistan regime it is too early to say, but relations have not been entirely cordial in spite of the common religion.

EUROPE

More is known about the Europeans than about any other foreign group. Since most of them were born in Europe, they are found together in the birthplace tables; since they form a separate caste, they appear in the caste data; and since they speak languages different from those of India, they appear again in the linguistic tables. Having been the governing

___

[2] Census of India, 1901, Vol. 1, Part 1, pp. 93–94.

[3] ibid., 1931, Vol. 5 (Bengal & Sikkim), Part 1, p. 103.

[4] ibid., 1921, Vol. 1, Part 1, p. 95; 1931, Vol. 5 (Bengal & Sikkim), Part 2, p. 26.

[5] ibid., 1931, Vol. 18 (United Provinces), Part 1, pp. 639–40; General Report of the Census of India, 1911, Sessional Papers, Cmd. 7377 (London: His Majesty's Stationery Office, 1914), p. 97.

[6] Census of India, 1931, Vol. 15 (N.W. Frontier Prov.), Part 1, p. 4; 1941, Vol. 10 (N.W. Frontier Prov.), Tables, pp. 1–3.

group, they have naturally been given full treatment in official statistics.

The number of people reported in five censuses as being born in Europe is as follows:

1891	99,263
1901	98,306
1911	123,237
1921	114,146
1931	110,330

Among these, of course, persons from the United Kingdom predominate. The British have constituted 90 to 96 per cent of the total all along. In 1931, for instance, 99,187 persons reported themselves as born in the British Isles, which was 90 per cent of the total European-born.

Naturally there have been in India many people of European ancestry who were not born in Europe. Although these do not figure as migrants, they do belong to the European group and are in many respects alien to the country. In 1931 a total of 145,000 reported themselves as British Europeans.[7] If true, this means that nearly 46,000 British Europeans were born in India. But the census authorities believe that the figure is too high, because the Anglo-Indians who have light pigmentation often return themselves erroneously as Europeans. It can be estimated that the number of British-born and India-born Britons in India was about 115,000, instead of 145,000, in 1931.[8] Their number seems to have decreased after 1911.

Britain's long domination of India with but a handful of people was a political miracle. In 1931, for every 100,000 Indians, there were only 34 Englishmen in the country. Some 338 million people were being ruled by a group of foreigners that could be put into a single American football stadium. Nowhere is there a clearer illustration that political dominance does not depend on numbers alone.

A great proportion of the British have been army personnel. In 1921 there were 72,151 in this category, and in 1931 there were 70,034. Over half of the ruling elite were thus military men.

The sex ratio of the British-born is naturally quite different from that of the British-descended, as Table 33 shows.

TABLE 33

Sex Ratio and Place of Birth of the British in India,
1901–1931

Census Date	Total British[1]		Born in Britain[2]		Born in India[2]	
	Population	Sex Ratio	Population	Sex Ratio	Population	Sex Ratio
1901	146,082	266	90,960	548	55,122	113
1911	173,606	265	115,565	527	58,041	99
1921	157,657	256	109,509	406	48,148	113
1931	144,928	245	99,187	362	45,741	123

[1] *Census of India,* 1931, Vol. 1, Part 1, p. 425. The sex ratio is the number of men per 100 women.
[2] Calculated from tables on Birth Place and on European Population, *ibid.,* 1901, 1911, 1921, and 1931.

Although the latter ratio is far less masculine than that of the British-born, it is still more masculine than normal. This

[7] *Census of India,* 1931, Vol. 1, Part 1, p. 425.
[8] cf. *ibid.,* p. 426.

suggests either that more Anglo-Indian males than females pass as British at the census, or that British females born in India go to Britain in larger proportions than do the males.

The Anglo-Indians, who constitute a special group in Indian society, numbered 119,195 in the 1931 census. This figure is probably too small, because many (possibly as many as 27,000) recorded themselves as British rather than Anglo-Indian. On the other hand, it is also likely that a considerable number of Indian Christians registered improperly as Anglo-Indians. Making allowance for these sources of error, the Census Commissioner estimated the total number of Anglo-Indians in 1931 as 143,000.[9] The group has been growing faster than the general population, but now that the British have left India, it will probably begin to merge into the general population.

The number of persons who gave English as their mother tongue (292,000) was somewhat greater than the total reported number of European British and Anglo-Indians combined (264,000). The discrepancy may have been due to confusion between the "mother language" and the "subsidiary language" columns on the census schedule. In some provinces—e.g. the United Provinces—the two kinds of data check quite closely.

The Europeans, in proportion to the population, were twice as numerous in the Provinces as in the Indian States. Yet in 1931 there were 35,500 British subjects in the States, a surprisingly high figure.

As might be expected, the Europeans are concentrated in the cities. In 1931 more than a fourth of the European-born lived in the three cities of Bombay, Madras, and Greater Calcutta. The rest were scattered primarily through the smaller cities. In the United Provinces, for example, no less than 82 per cent of the 18,000 Europeans lived in the province's 23 cities.[10] The concentration of Europeans in the cities was growing during recent decades. In the United Provinces, for example, there was, between 1911 and 1931, a withdrawal of Europeans from outlying districts. During the 1911–21 decade this was due to World War I, and during the 1921–31 decade, to the progressive Indianization of the services. The same tendency toward greater urban concentration is observable among the Anglo-Indians.[11] These are, in fact, more concentrated than the Europeans, "the bulk of the community being found in the large cities and railway centers and industrial and mining areas."[12]

PORTUGUESE AND FRENCH INDIA

The Portuguese and French colonies in India have always furnished a stream of migrants into the rest of India. In 1931, for example, there were some 81,000 persons born in these colonies who were enumerated in the Indian census. This was 10 per cent of the population of the two sets of colonies, and therefore represents a substantial proportion. The following figures give the number of persons born in these colonies enumerated in Indian censuses:

1891	77,324
1901	69,617
1911	86,790
1921	78,219
1931	81,378

[9] *ibid.,* pp. 429–30.
[10] *Census of India,* 1931, Vol. 18 (United Provinces), Part 1, p. 195.
[11] *ibid.,* pp. 539–40.
[12] *ibid.,* 1921, Vol. 1, Part 1, p. 231.

Most of these immigrants are from the Portuguese rather than the French areas, the Portuguese proportion being estimated in 1931 as 83 per cent.[13] Most of the immigrants from both areas went to British territory rather than the States, and by far the major portion, especially of the Portuguese subjects, went to the Bombay Presidency. In 1931 the number in the latter area was 58,856, or 72 per cent of the total in India. Of these, no less than 38,702 were found in Bombay City, where the Portuguese Indians are especially popular as domestics. The close proximity of these colonies, plus their fragmented geographical distribution, doubtless explains their tendency to furnish immigrants to India. They apparently give more migrants to India than they receive, and for this political disturbances and lack of economic opportunity in the areas themselves probably offer the main explanation.

INDIANS BORN ABROAD

An increasing proportion of immigrants to India have been from Indian settlements abroad. They were either former Indians or descendants of Indians, and some have returned involuntarily. South Africa has long had a policy of encouraging the repatriation of Indians. In other places, notably Burma, public antagonism and economic problems have caused a return to India. Thus in 1931 there were nearly 40,000 such persons enumerated. During World War II, when Indian settlements in Southeast Asia fell into enemy hands, there was a considerable evacuation of Indians to the home country. There seems no way of estimating how many came back at this time, nor how many have since returned to their erstwhile foreign homes. The permanent residue of immigrants to India from this cause in World War II is not likely to be great.

CONCLUSION

Lack of information precludes a thorough treatment of migration into pre-partition India. Enough knowledge exists to show that the amount of immigration was extremely slight in comparison to the total population. Even in absolute numbers, one finds that France had four times the number of persons born abroad that India had despite the fact that its total population was less than one-eighth that of India. There are numerous reasons why India should have attracted few foreigners—notably the density and poverty of the populace and the peculiarity of the social organization. Conditions discouraging immigration are likely to continue in the future; hence there is little prospect that either Pakistan or the Indian Union will become an area of net in-migration, but every likelihood that they will continue to be areas of net out-migration.

There was little trend in immigration, the flow tending neither to increase nor decrease noticeably. The upheaval caused by World War II, which brought in many temporary Europeans and many Indian evacuees, will undoubtedly be short-lived in its effects on migration.

The chief sources of immigrants to what was India were Nepal, Europe, French and Portuguese India, and Afghanistan. The last, because of unenumerated populations in frontier areas, is more uncertain than the others as to its volume. A substantial number of immigrants has in recent decades consisted of persons from Indian communities overseas.

The partition of India seems unlikely to increase immigration into the whole subcontinent. One might expect Pakistan to favor immigration from the Muslim countries immediately to the west, but the truth is that the Afghan tribesmen are as much a threat to stable government now as they ever were, and the religious bond with Iran is weak because of sectarian differences.

The only effect of partition, from the standpoint of geographical movement, has been to increase such movement *within* the subcontinent, at least temporarily. But at the same time, by creating long international borders where none had been before, the partition also changed the definition of movement between certain areas. What had been "internal" migration now became "external" (i.e. international) migration. Nevertheless, since most of our discussion of migration relates to the pre-partition period (when all movement between Indian areas was internal), we shall defer consideration of the partition-induced movement until Chapter 14 on Internal Migration. In this way we shall be geographically, if not politically, consistent.

[13] *ibid.*, 1931, Vol. 1, Part 1, p. 68.

++

Emigration: The Overseas Movement

++

THE movement of Indians to other countries has acquired an economic and political importance far beyond its actual volume. It began, so far as significant numbers are concerned, in 1834, when slavery was abolished in the British Empire and the notorious indenture system was inaugurated. Since that time it has continued in fluctuating fashion. The exact numbers who left and who returned are impossible to determine, because the records are defective, but we know that the total volume never reached anything like the flood of migrants who left Europe during the same period. An estimate of those who left would place the figure at roughly 28 million between 1846 and 1932. This exceeds the overseas emigration of any single country of which we have record (Table 34), but does not

TABLE 34

Overseas Emigrants from Various Countries: 1846–1932

Country of Emigration	Number (millions) [1]	Per Cent of Population in 1900
British Isles	18.0	43.3
Portugal	1.8	33.3
Italy	10.1	31.1
Spain	4.7	25.3
Sweden	1.2	23.5
Austria-Hungary	5.2	19.8
Germany	4.9	9.7
INDIA	27.7	9.4
Russia [a]	2.3	1.8

[a] The Russian figure goes only to 1924.
[1] Except for India, these figures are taken from A. M. Carr-Saunders, *World Population* (Oxford: Clarendon, 1936), p. 49. The Indian figure is derived from our own estimates.

nearly equal that of all the European countries combined. Since the European countries have smaller populations than India does, the *proportional* volume of their emigration has been much greater than India's. For example, the British Isles, which sent out approximately two-thirds as many people as India did between the dates mentioned, actually sent four times as many in proportional terms. Furthermore, these figures cover solely those who left, not those who returned. An unusually large proportion of those who left India have eventually returned, so that the net emigration from both an absolute and a relative point of view, has been rather small, amounting only to a little over six million since 1834.

Today the number of persons living abroad who were born in India or descended from Indians slightly exceeds four million, or almost exactly 1 per cent of India's total population

at the time of partition. There are, by contrast, something like 85 million people living outside the British Isles who derive from those Isles [1]—a figure that is approximately 167 per cent of the present population of Great Britain and Ireland. The persons of European origin now living in other parts of the world approximate something more than 200 million, or more than 40 per cent of Europe's total population. The total number of Chinese living abroad, estimated at between 8 and 10 million,[2] is at least twice the number of Indians. India has not, therefore, contributed its share to permanent world migration. One reason for this is that India started late. Europe had been sending out millions by the time India got under way, and many of the virgin territories were already preempted. As a consequence, when they did come, the Indians met discrimination on racial and cultural grounds. In fact, Indian emigration has been of greater importance politically than geographically, because of the treatment of Indians overseas.

THE STATISTICAL RECORD

In Table 35 the statistics of Indian overseas emigration, return migration, and net migration are given. They begin with 1834 when the movement first began in a modern and sizable form. The figures for the early years are less reliable than those for later ones, being based more on estimates. The entries for return migration are less reliable than those for out-migration. Since a small error in either out-migration or return migration, or in both, leads to a large error in net migration, the figures for the latter must be taken with great scepticism.

For given areas in certain periods, estimates have had to be prepared, because the official figures were not complete or uniform.[3] All possible use has been made of the available

[1] Computed from data given in A. M. Carr-Saunders, *World Population* (Oxford: Clarendon, 1936), pp. 165–69.
[2] Radhakamal Mukerjee, *Migrant Asia* (Rome: Tipografia Failli, 1936), p. 23.
[3] The chief sources of error: (1) Most official figures cover only British Indian ports, not ports in the Indian States. (2) Most official figures are only for persons going "to various colonies under the Indian Emigration Acts," and therefore do not apparently include certain categories of persons not embraced by those Acts. (3) The statistical definition of an emigrant has varied with the legislation, the same type of person being described as an emigrant under one act but not as an emigrant under an earlier one. (4) The official figures do not include any data on movements across land frontiers. (5) Until Burma's separation from India in 1937, no statistics on the movement of Indians into that area, either by land or sea, were kept. (6) The official statistics for certain areas are incomplete in particular years, especially during the earlier period. Some of the deficiencies can be remedied by comparing the Indian figures with those of the areas to which Indians migrated, and by various modes of estimation from indirect evidence

TABLE 35

Estimated Total Migration to and from India, 1834 to 1937 [a]
(000's)

Year	Emigrants	Returned Migrants	Net [b]
1834–35	62	52	10
1836–40	188	142	46
1841–45	240	167	72
1846–50	247	189	58
1851–55	357	249	108
1856–60	618	431	187
1861–65	793	594	199
1866–70	976	778	197
1871–75	1,235	958	277
1876–80	1,505	1,233	272
1881–85	1,545	1,208	337
1886–90	1,461	1,204	256
1891–95	2,326	1,536	790
1896–1900	1,962	1,268	694
1901–05	1,428	957	471
1906–10	1,864	1,482	383
1911–15	2,483	1,868	615
1916–20	2,087	1,867	220
1921–25	2,762	2,216	547
1926–30	3,298	2,857	441
1931–35	1,940	2,093	—162
1936–37	815	755	59
Total	30,191	23,941	6,250

[a] These estimates, prepared by the writer on the basis of migration data and census statistics in India and in the countries of destination, are extremely rough and should not be taken literally, particularly for the early years.

[b] Net migration refers to *net emigration*. The figures do not always correspond to the exact difference between the first two columns because of rounding.

official figures, taken mainly from Ferenczi,[4] the Sanderson Report,[5] the Statistical Abstract for British India, and the official publications of the areas to which Indians have migrated. The figures are as complete as could be expected in view of the somewhat fragmentary sources.

The total net emigration from 1834 to 1937 comes to more than 6 million, a figure considerably higher than the 3½ or 4 million usually given. It may well be too high, but the important thing to note is that the great bulk of Indian emigration has been of an ephemeral character, with approximately 30 million leaving and 24 million returning.

The trend of migration, depicted in Fig. 28, manifests several major fluctuations, with four periods being prominent. The first, running from 1834 to 1908, is the period of relatively uncurtailed indentured emigration, representing a rather steady rise in emigration until the turn of the century. The second period, from 1908 to 1923, saw increasing regula-

tion and final abolition of the indenture system but a rise in the individual contract method, and, during World War I, a slight drop in total emigration. The third period, from 1923 to 1929, represents the spurt of emigration under the Act of 1922 and under conditions of general prosperity. The fourth, from 1929 to the present, shows the dampening effect of the great depression and of World War II.[6] During this last period the return migration was greater than the out-migration.

Analysis of these periods shows two factors controlling emigration: (1) economic conditions abroad, (2) legislative enactments in India. It is doubtful if economic conditions in India have had any effect at all; we may assume, indeed, that the pressure to migrate, in an economic sense, has always been great enough to provide a stream of emigrants much larger than the actual stream, given the opportunity.[7] In other words, the demand has been less than the supply.

The total current of emigration is a summation of many lesser currents reaching into all major areas of the world (Table 37). The trends in these lesser currents are by no means uniform, because of dissimilar economic and legal conditions in the different areas to which Indians have gone. The Indian government's sensitivity to the treatment of Indians abroad has meant sudden stoppages and releases of the flow of migration with respect to particular areas.

The countries receiving the most Indians have been those accessible by water routes—Burma, Ceylon, British Malaya, Mauritius, Fiji, the Caribbean, and East Africa. Some of these countries have been far from India, e.g. the West Indies and Fiji; distance, however, has not been the primary factor, but rather the availability of water transport and type of economy. India's mountain barriers, plus the inhospitable nature of the plateaus on the other side, have prevented much emigration across the land borders. Approximately 99.6 per cent of Indian emigration has gone to ports in the British Empire, partly because the Empire embraces enormous areas enjoying a plantation economy adapted to coolie labor, and partly because the Indian government naturally favored the Empire in its direction of Indian labor. An equally high percentage of Indian emigration has gone to tropical areas, because it was there that the European-controlled plantation economy flourished. (This tropical distribution will be discussed more fully in a moment.) We see, then, that the areas that have drawn migrants from India have not necessarily been those that were close to India, but those that were (a) British colonies, (b) in tropical regions, and (c) accessible by water.

As time went by, Indian migration became increasingly confined to the Asiatic area—Burma, Ceylon, and British Malaya. This tendency resulted from four related facts: (1) The Asiatic area remained more profitable for commercial agriculture. (2) The use of seasonal labor became more imperative with the decline of the indenture system. (3) The Asiatic areas, being nearer, could more easily use Indian labor on a seasonal basis. (4) The hostility to Indian labor in Asiatic colonies was less than in other areas such as Africa and the Caribbean.

Indian migration has also increased its already exceptionally high percentage of return movement. Whereas experts believe that only 30 per cent of the Europeans migrating to

---

such as birthplace statistics. Wherever possible we have made necessary corrections, but the resulting figures cannot be assumed to be complete, although the amount of error should not be great.

[4] Imre Ferenczi, *International Migrations,* Vol. 1, *Statistics* (New York: National Bureau of Economic Research, 1929).

[5] Committee on Emigration from India to the Crown Colonies and Protectorates, *Report,* Sessional Papers, Cmd. 5192 (London: His Majesty's Stationery Office, 1910).

[6] cf. G. Findlay Shirras in Walter F. Willcox (ed.), *International Migrations,* Vol. 2, *Interpretations* (New York: National Bureau of Economic Research, 1931), p. 595.

[7] Étienne Dennery, *Foules d'Asie* (Paris: Armand Colin, 1930), p. 202.

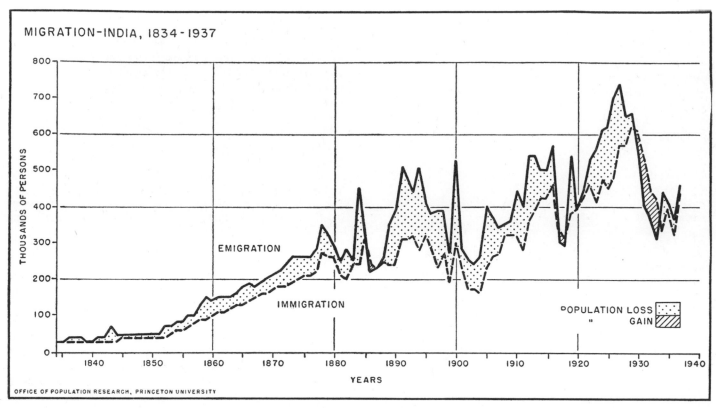

FIGURE 28. Emigration, Return Migration and Net Migration for India, 1834–1937.

the United States between 1821 and 1924, and 47 per cent of those going to Argentina between 1857 and 1924, returned home,[8] the percentage for Indians, by conservative estimate, was 80 per cent. The disparity is due to different conditions. The Indians went primarily as laborers, either under indenture or in a labor gang. They went to places where, because of their racial and cultural contrast to the native population, they were not particularly welcome as settlers. Above all, many of them went under short-term contracts virtually as seasonal laborers, and were not emigrants at all in any permanent sense. As the overseas use of Indian labor became increasingly seasonal, the percentage of returnees of course grew accordingly; and World War II dislodged a good many otherwise permanent Indian settlers from areas occupied by the enemy.

Despite the shrinkage in the distance and area of migration

[8] A. M. Carr-Saunders, op. cit., p. 49.

and in the proportion of permanent emigrants, the total volume of movement increased after the turn of the century. During the 1900–37 period the average number of emigrants per year was 451,000, whereas from 1834 to 1900 it was 202,000 (Table 36). The greatest increase occurred, of course, in the Asiatic area, since the volume going both to Africa and to the Americas decreased sharply after the turn of the century. But so far as the total volume of emigration is concerned, the pendulum has, with World War II and its aftermath, swung violently in the direction of decrease. In the near future there is little likelihood that Indian emigration will regain even the volume it had prior to 1900. Furthermore, as mentioned above and as Table 36 shows, the average volume of *net* emigration was considerably less after 1900 than before. Viewed in terms of sending permanent settlers abroad, Indian emigration has been on the downgrade for the last five decades.

TABLE 36

Average Annual Emigration and Net Emigration for Two Periods (1834–1900 and 1901–1937) and as Per Cent of Total, by Major Regions

	EMIGRATION				NET EMIGRATION			
	1834–1900		1901–1937		1834–1900		1901–1937	
REGION	Average Annual [a]	% of Total	Average Annual [a]	% of Total	Average Annual [a]	% of Total	Average Annual [a]	% of Total
Asiatic	186,000	92.2	443,700	98.4	41,000	78.4	67,400	96.9
African	8,600	4.3	3,200	0.7	5,800	11.1	200	0.3
American	6,900	3.4	2,600	0.6	5,300	10.1	1,300	1.8
Oceanic	200	0.1	1,200	0.3	200	0.4	600	.9
Total	*201,700*	*100.0*	*450,700*	*100.0*	*52,300*	*100.0*	*69,500*	*100.0*

[a] Computed from estimates made by the writer.

The Distribution of Indians Abroad

The migration figures can be checked by reference to the statistics on Indians living abroad, drawn mainly from censuses in the countries where Indians have settled. Unfortunately, however, the censuses do not always distinguish the themselves widely over the world. Considering the relatively small volume of Indian migration and its recency, this wide distribution is remarkable. But the distribution is wider in longitude than in latitude. Though Indians have gone all the way around the world, they have done so between the latitudes of 20° N. and 20° S. The only important exception is sub-

TABLE 37

Rank of Countries of Indian Immigration in Terms of Immigrants and Descendants of Indians [1]

| | INDIAN IMMIGRATION | | | INDIANS NOW SETTLED | | |
| | | Net Immigration | | | Indians Now Settled | |
COUNTRY	Date	in 1000's	Rank	Date	in 1000's	Rank [c]
Burma	1852–1937	2,595	1	1941	1,018 [a]	2
Ceylon	1834–1938	1,529	2	1940 est.	1,963	1
British Malaya	1860–1938	1,189	3	6/1/41	766	3
Mauritius	1834–1920	285	4	1940	272	4
British Guiana	1845–1924	160	5	12/31/38	143	7
Trinidad & Tobago	1845–1924	116	6	12/31/38	158	6
Natal, Union of South Africa	1860–1937	76	7	1936	220	5
French West Indies	1856–1884	51	8			8
Fiji Islands	1881–1938	35	9	12/31/41	102	9
British West Indies	1856–1877	28	10	(1921–31)	6 [d]	14
Dutch Guiana	1873–1937	22	11	12/31/37	44	11
La Réunion	1861–1877	19	12	1936	10 [b]	13
Jamaica	1845–1916	19	13	12/31/37	19	12
Mombasa, Kenya	1895–1921	17	14	12/31/39	45	10
U.S.A.	1834–1924	6	15	1940	5	15
New Zealand	1912–1927	1	16	12/31/41 est.	1	16

[a] Same number of Indians as was there in or about 1931 was used.
[b] Estimated on the basis of net migration to La Réunion.
[c] Rank for French West Indies taken as same as immigration rank.
[d] Including East Indians and Chinese in Granada (1921), East Indians in St. Vincent (1931) and St. Lucia (1921).
[1] Based primarily on census statistics in the various countries concerned.

three classes of Indians abroad—namely, those who are still Indian citizens, those who were born in India but are now naturalized, and those who were born in the new country but are descended from Indians. Consequently there is no sure way of relating the number of "East Indians" in a country to the migration from India. In general the more net immigration of Indians a given country has had, the more Indians should be settled there, assuming that roughly the same birth rates prevail from one place to another among the Indian immigrants and that no movement of Indians between countries of immigration has taken place.[9] Table 37 gives the rank of each major area in terms of net immigration and of Indians now settled. The correlation is rather close, for the ratio between the two figures is fairly constant.[10]

It is evident, as Map 12 shows, that Indians have spread tropical Natal in South Africa. A few thousand Indians have found their way into such northern places as British Columbia and the United States, but for the most part they have settled in tropical areas.[11] In fact, most of the emigrants have settled in climates more tropical than the one they left behind. This has not been due to any racial preference for warm climates, but to economic selection. The Indian emigrants were obtained for the purpose of replacing the emancipated slaves on estate plantations, and these plantations, for various reasons, were located in tropical areas. The advantage of Indians for this kind of work was that they were already adjusted, culturally and physically, to tropical conditions and to a low plane of living; and their economic conditions at home were so bad that it took relatively little inducement to get them to leave.

From Table 38 it can be seen that Mauritius is the only place in which Indian migrants and their descendants have come to constitute the majority of the population. In a few other places, notably Fiji, British and Dutch Guiana, Trinidad, and Ceylon, they make up a substantial portion of the total, and may eventually constitute a majority.

---

[9] The first assumption is untrue if the sex ratios have been markedly different, and the second is untrue at least in the case of Mauritius and Zanzibar, which were way stations for many Indians bound for other areas.

[10] The correlation is not to be taken as proof of our estimates of net emigration, for in some case (e.g., for Burma and British Malaya) the estimates were made with the help of census materials. The total number of persons of Indian descent living abroad, 4,117 million, is less than the total estimated net emigration, 6,077 million. In spite of a rather high fertility, this result could be expected because of the high death rates and distorted age and sex distribution of the Indian emigrants.

[11] cf. Mukerjee, *Migrant Asia*, pp. 70–72.

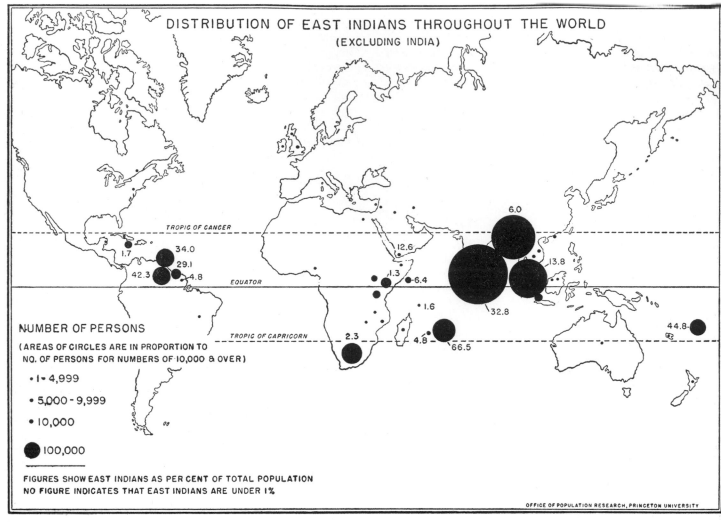

MAP 12. World Distribution of Emigrants from India, about 1940.

TABLE 38

Persons of Indian Descent Settled Abroad and Their
Percentage of Total Population Around 1940

(Countries or Colonies with 2 Per Cent or More) [1]

Place	Date	Number (000's)	Per Cent
Mauritius	1940	272	67
Fiji Islands	1941	102	45
British Guiana	1938	143	44
Trinidad & Tobago	1938	158	40
Ceylon	1941	1,963	33
Dutch Guiana	1938	44	29
British Malaya	1941	766	14
Aden & Perim	1939	8	13
Burma	1941	1,018	6
Zanzibar & Pemba	1939	16	6
French Guiana	1936	2	5
Union of South Africa [a]	1946	285	3

[a] Natal, with 232,000, has by far the major portion of South Africa's Indians, which constitute 11 per cent of the population of the state.
[1] Nearly all of these figures are estimates, either made by the writer or taken from statistical sources on the areas concerned. Some places— e.g. Kenya—have sizeable Indian populations, especially in proportion to the European population, though not in proportion to the total population.

LEGAL AND SOCIAL ASPECTS OF INDIAN EMIGRATION

Why did Indian emigration begin when it did? The abolition of slavery in the British colonies left the plantation owners with no safe and cheap labor supply, for the emancipated slaves and the natives alike were reluctant to do plantation labor. The Indians, on the other hand, had a disciplined culture adapted to tropical agriculture, and they were willing to work. The huge Indian population was an inexhaustible reservoir of manpower, sufficiently advanced to be ready to migrate but sufficiently backward to accept cheap terms. India was under the British, whose Empire controlled most of the tropical lands where plantation agriculture was practiced. Under these circumstances it was only natural that an exodus from India should arise at the time it did.

The miracle is that there was not an even greater exodus. In practice several factors limited the outflow. Indian opinion was sufficiently vocal to condemn the adverse treatment of Indian nationals abroad. This feeling was heightened by the consciousness of being a part, the largest part, of the British Empire, and of having a claim to equality of treatment within its territories. Also, the tropical plantation economy fell upon evil days and proved less absorptive of migrants than the temperate industrial economy. Even so, the movement from India made up the major share of migration to the British colonies. It eclipsed in magnitude, if not in its permanent effects, the slave migration that preceded it.

From the standpoint of drama, ethics, and international relations the most fascinating aspect of Indian migration is the treatment of Indians abroad. In every country to which they went they found themselves a minority differing both culturally and racially from the native population, and under European masters. The only comparable situation was that of Africans crossing the Atlantic, but this had been under the aegis of slavery whereas the Indian migration was a substitute for that condition. The Indians, in contrast to the Negroes, had a nation that could plead their case. Yet their own government was European in ultimate control, and hence had divided sympathies as between the migrants and their European masters.

In these four elements—racial difference, cultural difference, European domination, and governmental ambivalence—are to be found the main ingredients giving rise to "the Indian problem abroad." In different areas the particular conditions produced divergent outcomes, but everywhere the same four ingredients were involved, and everywhere the same three characters—the Indian, the Native, and the European—played their complex and interrelated roles.

TYPES OF MIGRANTS

Several distinctions must be made between different kinds of emigration. For example, there is the distinction between assisted and unassisted emigration. The first comprises all those forms in which the laborer is financially aided by another party to get to a foreign country; the second, those cases in which no such assistance is given. The great bulk of Indian emigrants were of the assisted type, especially from 1834 to 1900, and this is what the statistics and laws mainly refer to.

Within the assisted category, however, there are two different types—one composed of those assisted on the basis of an indenture contract; the other, those assisted on the basis of a short-term, or *kangani*, contract. It is hard to say which of these was numerically more significant, but probably the latter because it was preeminently the kind used for nearby areas (especially Ceylon). In the course of time indenture declined in importance relative to the kangani system, partly because of criticism of indenture and partly because of increasing confinement of emigration to the Asiatic area.

Finally, there is the distinction between labor emigration, of whatever type, and professional and commercial emigration. The latter can be called "trader migration," because it consisted of money-lenders, merchants, and professional men who followed the initial wave of Indian laborers. These were far less important numerically than the laborers, but they raised different problems and acquired a political significance far beyond their numbers.

THE INDENTURE SYSTEM

As a half-way stage between slavery and free labor, indenture was different from peonage or serfdom. It was peculiarly adapted, like slavery, to the recruitment of labor through migration. It enabled business enterprise to transfer labor to newly developing areas, and yet restrained that labor from immediately taking holdings of its own where unexploited land was abundant. Less satisfactory than slavery because less permanent, it nevertheless could attract people too proud to become slaves. It did imply a social gulf between employer and laborer, but it held the possibility of eventual freedom for the latter.

An interesting aspect of Indian emigration into areas where slavery had prevailed was the social rank assumed by the indentured arrivals. Here there was a conflict of two sociological principles, one to the effect that the stigma of the slave status still clings to the emancipated slave, and the other to the effect that in ecological succession, as regards labor, it is the latest arrival who assumes the lowest social status. Obviously the stage was set for competition between the two classes, each claiming superiority but on a different basis. Why such competition never resulted in sharp conflict is a story in itself, but the gist of it is that in most areas one or the other group had such a clear predominance that challenge by the other was fruitless, while at the same time both of them felt more heavily the hand of the whites than their own mutual competition.

Indenture supposedly originated with a contract, usually written and voluntarily assumed. But it was an unusual contract, because it bargained away the laborer's personal freedom for an extended period. Hence exceedingly strong motives were required before anyone would agree to it. One motive was the desire to escape dire want and heavy indebtedness. Often, in addition, it was the result of ignorance on the part of the laborer and coercion or fraud on the part of the employer. It was therefore often not a true contract at all, but merely a fictional one.

Presumably the contract led to the status of free laborer at the end of the period (usually five years), but it could also lead to reindenture or to a return to India. Naturally the employer undertook to maintain the workers at as small a cost as possible, to work them as hard as possible, and to keep them on the job as regularly as possible. At the end of the indenture he tried to renew the agreement for another stretch if the worker was still productive, or to get rid of him if he was not. One prominent Indian leader, Gopal Krishna Gokhale, in an address to the Imperial Legislative Council, summed up the leading characteristics of the system from the laborer's point of view:

"Under this system, those who are recruited bind themselves, first to go to a distant and unknown land, the language, usage and customs of which they do not know, and where they have no friends or relatives. Secondly, they bind themselves to work there for any employer to whom they may be alloted, whom they do not know and who does not know them, and in whose choice they have no voice. Thirdly, they bind themselves to live there on the estate of the employer, must not go anywhere without a special permit, and must do whatever tasks are assigned to them, no matter however irksome those tasks may be. Fourthly, the binding is for a certain fixed period, usually five years, during which time they cannot voluntarily withdraw from the contract and have no means of escaping from its hardships, however intolerable. Fifthly, they bind themselves to work during the period for a fixed wage, which invariably is lower, and in some cases very much lower, than the wage paid to free labour around them. And sixthly, and lastly, and this to my mind is the worst feature of the system, they are placed under a special law, never explained to them before they left the country, which is in a language which they do not understand and which imposes on them a criminal liability for the most trivial breaches of the contracts, in place of the civil liability which usually attaches to such breaches. Thus they are liable under this law to imprisonment with hard labor, which may extend to two and in some cases to three months, not only for fraud, not only for deception, but for negligence, for carelessness and—will the Council believe it?—for even an impertinent word or gesture to the manager or his overseers."[12]

As a device for recruiting labor from a distance for the exploitation of "new" lands by European techniques, indenture was bound to be a temporary system, as was recognized all along.[13] The system became increasingly unpopular in India after 1900. In view of twentieth-century ideals and the rising position of the Indian nation, it was felt to be an insult to India. In the British Empire it was creating more problems than it was solving; and in certain areas the labor need was beginning to be met by other methods—notably the use of native labor or seasonal migratory labor. There was such depression in tropical agriculture that planters could no longer pay for the importation of labor. The abuses of the system had led to increasing legal restriction which destroyed many of the advantages of indenture for the employer. Finally, there was unmistakable evidence of a rising prejudice against Indians in such areas as South and East Africa, Burma, and Fiji. The eventual and inevitable result was the abolition of the system. In 1917, after numerous investigations, all new indenture was suspended for the duration of World War I. In 1920 the system was completely abolished, and the event was hailed as a red-letter day throughout India, where it was regarded as an event paralleling the abolition of slavery nearly a century before.[14] It was natural that it should be followed by a system that had already developed, a system freer but not quite free, the kangani system.

THE KANGANI SYSTEM

The so-called kangani system involved a short-term (usually 30-day) contract, generally verbal rather than written. It received its name because of the peculiarly important role of the kangani, or head man, who was both recruiter and field foreman. Sent by an employer or association of estate owners to bring back his friends, neighbors, and relatives in his home district, the kangani undertook to provide food, clothing and transit for the recruits in connection with the overseas trip. Frequently he was empowered to discharge their local debts or to leave money with their relatives. Considerable responsibility rested on him to choose the right sort of recruits and, as compared with indenture, there was a better chance that whole families or neighborhood groups would come together.[15]

Started in Ceylon, where it had entirely replaced indenture by 1910, the system was patriarchal, since the kangani was usually the senior member of a family group to which were added other families drawn from the same vicinity. The labor force thus formed was subdivided into smaller groups, each under its own sub-kangani (*silara kangani*), each holding its earnings in common, and each assuming joint liability for advances made to it by the head kangani. It was often through the head kangani that all advances were made, and in all financial transactions except the payment of wages he was frequently the sole intermediary between the coolie and the employer. The coolies might, indeed, owe more to him than he owed to the estate, so that in a sense he actually assisted the estate in financing its laborers.

In return for his services the head kangani generally received payments for recruits and also "head money"—a cent or two per day for each laborer who showed up for work. In addition he was occasionally paid a fixed salary for special services, and he might get additional money by sharp practices. The sub-kangani usually worked in the field, either as a laborer or an overseer. For this he received a "name," which entitled him to a day's pay, in addition to "pence money," a sum of 3 or 4 cents daily for each laborer in his gang.

The laborer was conceived as obligated to pay back within two years the sum advanced to bring him to the place of work. He could not be compelled to pay, since the law clearly allowed him to leave his job with 30-days' notice and did not hold him liable for any debt to the kangani; but in fact he would find it difficult to get work at another plantation if he failed to pay, and he took the debt as a point of honor.

In British Malaya the system was imported about 1890 from Ceylon. By 1902 the proportion of unindentured plantation laborers in the Straits Settlements had risen to $2/5$, and by 1907 it was up to $5/6$. Within twenty years after its inception, the kangani system virtually replaced indenture in British Malaya.[16]

One effect of this method of securing Indian labor was to encourage the transplantation of Indian culture to a new region. In Ceylon and Malaya the South India coolie acquired a paternalistic security that he did not have in India. It enabled him to live within his own community, among neighbors and relatives from his homeland, without greatly disturbing his native customs. This was particularly true of Ceylon, where the proportion of women among the migrants was high, where each plantation usually had a Hindu temple, where the Indian diet was maintained, the same costume worn, the native language spoken. They had little relation with the natives, whether Cinghalese or Malayan, and scarcely ever intermarried with them. Their exodus therefore led to the building of little Indias in new lands. They showed little ambition beyond the daily task. Unlike the Chinese, they migrated to survive rather than to climb socially. The celestial emigrant left his country in order to enrich himself, to rise to the position of a business man or land owner; but the Tamil emigrant under the kangani system left his country in order to survive.[17]

FREE LABOR

The kangani emigration reached its peak later than indentured emigration, and in turn it gradually gave way to individual (unrecruited) migration. In Malaya, for example, kangani recruiting slowly declined after 1920, partly because of increased legal regulation and partly because of greater knowledge and sophistication on the part of the Indians. Whereas in 1920 about 88 per cent of the Indian laborers entering Malaya were recruited, in the middle 1930's less than 9 per cent were. The demand for Indian labor itself was declining because of restrictions on rubber production, because

---

[12] Quoted by Dharam Yash Dev, *Our Countrymen Abroad* (Allahabad: J. B. Kripalani, All Indian Congress Committee, 1940), p. 14.

[13] Committee on Emigration from India to the Crown Colonies and Protectorates, *Report*, Sessional Papers, Cmd. 5192 (London: His Majesty's Stationery Office, 1910), p. 22. This was the famous Sanderson Report.

[14] C. F. Andrews, "India's Emigration Problem," *Foreign Affairs*, Vol. 8 (April, 1930), p. 434. For a full account of the legal and social history of Indian indenture, see Lanka Sundaram, "The International Aspects of Indian Emigration," *Asiatic Review*, Vol. 26 (October, 1930), pp. 741–48; Vol. 27 (January, 1931), pp. 113–21, (April, 1931), pp. 287–96, (July, 1931), pp. 588–98. These articles were published in book form under the same title (London: East & West Ltd., 1930); Sundaram also has a long treatment of the same subject in *India in World Politics* (Delhi: Sultan Chand, 1944), Ch. 4.

[15] Sanderson Report, pp. 15–16.

[16] Sanderson Report, pp. 27–28, Minutes (Cmd. 5193), pp. 167, 349, 378–79, 402–05, 430. Mukerjee, *Migrant Asia*, p. 93. Sundaram, "International Aspects of Indian Emigration," *Asiatic Review*, Vol. 27 (January, 1931), pp. 120–21.

[17] Dennery, *op. cit.*, pp. 215–24.

of the large number of Indians and Chinese already in Malaya, and because of the availability of local labor. "The Sastri report of 1936 brought about the formal abolition of kangani plantation recruiting. Thereafter it retained its usefulness only for the recently established palm-oil industry and for estates which had not yet built up their own recruiting grounds in India." After 1934–35 the Government of India imposed quotas on emigration to Malaya. In 1938 Malaya retaliated by enforcing a wage cut for Indian laborers. The result was a ban on all assisted emigration of Indian labor to Malaya.[18]

The free labor migration to Asiatic regions was essentially seasonal labor, resembling in many respects the later Italian migration to Argentina. It was marked by a short stay in the new country and by a high rate of return to India. For this reason it had less effect than the other types on Indian population growth.

TRADER MIGRATION

In the wake of the indentured and assisted laborers there "followed an army of petty contractors, merchants, bankers, shopkeepers and pedlars." These knew how to cater to the special needs and to exploit the peculiar weaknesses of the Indian laborers. They also knew how to undercut the European in the trade with the natives. They were free emigrants in every sense of the word. Generally of higher caste than those who had gone as contract laborers, they came on their own resources, usually with a small capital and a wide experience in the kind of trade they sought to practice. They were Chettiars from Madras, Marwaris from Rajputana, Banyias from the United Provinces, Pathans from the Northwest. They included more Muslims than was usual among Indian emigrants; and they were more accustomed to travel and more resourceful, ambitious, and aggressive. They lent money at usurious rates to the small Indian agriculturalist, took mortgages on his land, sold him trinkets, imported Indian sweets and jewelry, acted as intermediaries, organized commercial transportation, and in general played the role of a petite bourgeoisie in the Indian community.[19] At the same time, holding a racial status and maintaining a living standard intermediate between the European and the native, they outbid the latter in many types of business enterprise. Though they probably cheated the native as heartlessly as did the European, they did it with less hauteur and more skill. In Africa, for example, "the simple Negro would like to enter the shop and handle and examine the goods he wanted to purchase," and the Indian shopkeeper would permit this. "Moreover, the Negro never feared the Indian traders."[20]

The success of these middlemen was phenomenal. Many of them became rich and, after the habit of Orientals everywhere, attempted to invest their savings in land. They also pushed on into new territories, thus giving a wider spread to the already widely dispersed Indian migration. It was this class of Indian that came nearest to threatening the position of the European and who consequently incurred the greatest European prejudice. This was particularly true in South and East Africa, where major conflicts arose.

[18] Virginia Thompson, *Postmortem on Malaya* (New York: Macmillan, 1943), pp. 122–23.
[19] Dennery, *op. cit.*, pp. 190–92.
[20] M. K. Gandhi, *Satyagraha in South Africa* (Triplicane, Madras: S. Ganesan, 1928), p. 43. cf. Lord Olivier, *The Anatomy of African Misery* (London: Wolf, 1927), pp. 27–28.

EMIGRATION LAW IN INDIA

Indian legislation paralleled the changes in the character of emigration. At first there was little government control, but indenture soon raised such problems that control became necessary. The earliest laws were aimed at protecting the prospective emigrant from force and fraud and at securing his health during the passage and upon arrival. As the kangani system began to replace indenture in some areas, its regulation fitted readily with the regulation of indenture that had gone before. As for free migration, the government had long insisted that it had nothing to do with this. Individuals could leave or not as they saw fit.

Gradually, however, as the number of Indians in various colonies increased in numbers, problems arose that had never been foreseen in the early days of emigration. These problems were concerned with the rights and duties of Indians as inhabitants and citizens of the colonies in question; and they did not fall easily within the scope of emigration control, because many of the Indians concerned had not been in India for decades and many others were not even born there. Yet the Indian government could not fail to take cognizance of the problems raised, and its reaction was bound to affect the future emigration policy. Criminal prosecutions by employers, the compulsion to re-indenture, the disproportion of the sexes, and the development of race prejudice all created a situation at once harmful to Indians abroad and discreditable to India as a nation.

In trying to control the conditions of Indian nationals abroad, the government had several weapons. First, it could appeal directly to Whitehall, which had jurisdiction over the colonies, and which, being remote from the colonies in question, was not so swayed by local white opinion as were the colonial governments themselves. Second, it could stop Indian emigration to any particular colony until conditions there were improved. Third, it could give publicity to the conditions and call upon world opinion to bring pressure to bear. Fourth, it could apply economic sanctions.

Under a policy of laissez-faire only the first two expedients were regarded as properly governmental, especially in view of the ambivalent position of the Indian government within the Empire. But in applying these the government was handicapped in the early stages by lack of information. The distances were too great and communications too slow to allow the mother country to be adequately conversant with the conditions as they took shape. The Indian government felt it could not afford to maintain its own agents in the colonies, and it had to rely upon the reports of occasional officials sent out for the purpose of a temporary investigation.

In case a colony became a commonwealth, as happened with Natal, the Indian government was helpless except in so far as it chose to use the last two expedients. The prohibition of further emigration to the region in question was no threat, because the commonwealths, one and all, maintained exclusionist policies with reference to Indians and were anxious to be rid of the Indians they had.

Clearly, when Indian populations had become settled abroad the problem was no longer one simply of regulating migration but of protecting an affiliated ethnic group—a type of problem that has always been one of the most delicate in international relations. The natural conflict between master and laborer, the deeply embedded notions of race superiority among Europeans, and the conflict of widely divergent cultures all created an ethnic problem of major proportions.

These were the things the Indian government could not control by its laissez-faire techniques, but which, in the name of India, it was bound sooner or later to take into account.

Its first step away from traditional policy was the abolition of indenture. It is a matter of speculation as to whether this step came after the demand for indentured labor had already subsided anyway, but the government's action was strongly supported by Indian opinion.

Though indenture was abolished, there still remained the migration of Indian laborers by short-term agreement with the agents of colonial governments. The Act of 1922, which attempted to consolidate and renovate previous regulations, was a partial transition from laissez-faire to a much stricter form of legal control.

The Act drew a distinction between skilled and unskilled labor, and subjected the latter to much more rigid regulation than the former. It provided that emigration for the purpose of unskilled work was unlawful except to such countries and on such terms as the Governor-General in Council should specify, with approval by both chambers of the Indian Legislature. The age below which persons of either sex might leave was declared subject to decree, and in the Rules (1923) it was laid down that individuals of less than 18 years might not be assisted to migrate unless accompanied by a parent or guardian. Women could not be assisted to emigrate unless accompanied by a relative over 18 years of age. On the other hand, the total number of unmarried men, or men unaccompanied by their wives, who might be assisted to emigrate to any one country in any one year should not exceed one to every five persons (over eighteen) so emigrating. The Governor-General in Council could suspend emigration to specific countries if he deemed it necessary. Any person emigrating or attempting to emigrate except in conformity with the provisions of the Act was punishable with a maximum fine of 50 rupees, and any person inducing another to emigrate under such conditions was subject to a maximum penalty of 500 rupees. In every case recruiting was to be placed in the hands of a responsible official appointed by the government of the recruiting country. The Emigration Commissioner of each country to which emigrants were to go was solely responsible for all the recruiting transactions carried out in the name of his government. His remuneration could not depend upon the number of workers whom he recruited but should be in the form of a fixed salary. He was responsible for information about his country, for all recruitment by his staff, and for the appointment of emigration agents and inspectors. And any person desiring to recruit was required to apply for the permission of the local government of the port from which the emigrant was to depart. A copy of the permit, if granted, was to be forwarded to the Protector of Emigrants at the port of embarkation, who issued a recruiting certificate after ascertaining that each emigrant had received in writing a full explanation of the period of his engagement and the general conditions in the country of destination. The expenses of the emigrants, as well as their food and lodging, had to be provided by the country of destination.

Each recruiter of *skilled* labor was required to state in his application the number of persons whom he proposed to engage, the place to which they were to emigrate, the accommodation to be provided before and during the voyage, the provision to be made for their health and well-being during the period of engagement, the provision for repatriation at the end of the work-period, the terms of the employment, and the security furnished for the due observance of the agreement.[21]

Under these conditions, in the late '20's, as we have seen, probably the peak of Indian emigration was reached. But it was nearly all short-term migration, with an extremely high proportion of returns. Increasingly it was directed to Ceylon, Burma, and Malaya, rather than to more distant ports. Indeed, it must be recalled that in the total amount of Indian emigration from 1834 to 1930, those going under indenture were far fewer than those going under kangani arrangements. Also, the amount of free emigration, unassisted in any way, tended to increase its proportion of the total. The result was that the new emigration was not emigration in the full sense of the word, but was to a great extent seasonal migration of a temporary character. This tended to reduce the problems raised by emigration, but unfortunately the basis for acute problems already lay in the populations settled abroad. With these the Indian government was forced to become increasingly occupied. The Act of 1922, then, had the effect of taking care of the question of further emigration of Indian labor abroad, so far as the wishes of India were concerned; but it left open the broader questions of the treatment of Indian descendants abroad.

CONCLUSION

It should now be clear why emigration from the Indian subcontinent in the future is not likely to be large, and why it certainly is not likely to have much effect in lessening the pressure of population in the homeland itself. In the first place, the total volume of migration has never been large in proportion to the total population. It has been sufficient to place Indians in various tropical parts of the world, but not sufficient to lessen seriously the rate of population growth in India. In the second place, the current of migration has lessened in the last two decades. It has decreased in total volume and in the proportion of those who stay. It has tended to become seasonal migration, which is not true emigration at all. In the third place, the factors that have led to this decline—the treatment of the Indians abroad, the growth of a supply of native labor, the increasing nationalism of colonial areas—show no real sign of slackening in the future. Latin America now has a policy of Asiatic exclusion. Burma is now independent and is not likely to welcome Indians in addition to those that are left there. South and East Africa are continually embroiled with their Indian communities. Australia maintains its White-Australian policy. All over the world there is little sign that Indians would be welcomed, and there is little evidence that the division of India into Pakistan and the Union of India is likely to alter this situation; in fact, in so far as it weakens the Indian subcontinent as an international power, it will lessen the chance of forcing an outlet for the citizens of either Pakistan or the new India. Only a major world catastrophe would seem to alter the situation. Short of such a catastrophe, it seems unlikely that Indian emigration will again regain the volume it had prior to the great depression of the 1930's. Certainly it seems unlikely that emigration will constitute a release, a solution, for the population problem of the teeming millions below the Himalayas.

[21] International Labour Office, *Migration Laws and Treaties*, Vol. 1, *Emigration Laws and Regulations* (Geneva, 1928), *passim*.

CHAPTER 14

Internal Migration

OUR information on internal migration in the Indian region is scanty and indirect. There was, before the creation of Pakistan, no check whatsoever on the movement of persons across provincial and state borders. The only information available concerns the place-of-birth data gathered by the census, plus some descriptive material and linguistic data.

In general the place-of-birth returns are roughly accurate. Sometimes the birthplace of children is arbitrarily assigned to the place of residence of the parent, and sometimes the birthplace question is not answered in an intelligible fashion, but on the whole the data are susceptible to correction and have seemingly improved as time has gone on.[1]

The main difficulty does not lie in the accuracy of birthplace material but in its use as an index of migration. A person's place of birth may be accidental. Hindu wives, for example, usually return to their parents' home for their first confinement; if this happens to be a few miles across a provincial or district boundary, the child then becomes an "immigrant" at the next census. Again the child may be born while its mother is traveling. Similarly, the place of enumeration may be fortuitous, having nothing to do with the individual's regular place of residence. The Indian *de facto* census did not, except partially in 1941, attempt to ascertain the normal residence; consequently, casual visitors, religious pilgrims, railway passengers, etc. are counted in the population of the district or province where found. Finally, the difference between place of birth and place of enumeration gives no indication of the number of moves the individual may have made during his lifetime. At best the analysis of birthplace data at different censuses can give but a sketchy picture of the actual movement of people. Even though many of the fortuitous factors cancel out, the full details of internal migration cannot be known.

THE AMOUNT OF INTERNAL MIGRATION

In an area as large, diverse, and transitional as the Indian subcontinent, the movements of people are necessarily large in numbers but, in this case at least, small in proportion to the total population. The people of the Indian region have long been famous for their attachment to their native locale, and the statistics confirm this reputation. In 1911 only 8.7 per cent, and in 1921 only 9.8 per cent, of the population lived in districts where they were not born. In 1931, though district figures were not published, only 3.59 per cent of the population lived in provinces or states where they were not born.[2]

The degree of Indian immobility can be seen clearly upon comparison with other countries. Such comparison, however, is hard to make, because the number and size of the units are never comparable. Yet there is a rough similarity between the states in the United States and the provinces and states in India. In 1940 no less than 22.5 per cent of the native population of the United States lived outside the state in which born.[3] Contrast this with the 3.6 per cent living outside the province or state of birth in India in 1931. Indeed, as already mentioned, the percentage living outside the *district* of birth was only 9.8 in India. So the movement between the Indian districts is not half so great as the movement between the American states, measured in the same terms, despite the fact that the latter are on the average more than 17 times as large as the Indian districts. In Australia in 1934 the persons living outside the province of birth formed 24 per cent of the total population; in Bulgaria in 1934 those living outside the arrondissement of birth were 16.2 per cent; in Yugoslavia those living outside the banovine of birth were 7 per cent. The population of the Indian region is low in the scale of mobility.

The evidence of stability is even more impressive when one realizes that the birthplace statistics exaggerate rather than minimize the amount of movement. Bearing in mind the custom of taking a wife from a neighboring village (which accounts for over half the persons outside the district of birth), the custom of returning to the parental home for the first birth, and the *de facto* character of the Indian censuses, we can see that the birthplace data do not underestimate the movement of people—as compared, say, with similar data in the United States. Much of the past so-called migration in India has involved an extremely short distance. In 1921 it is estimated that about two-thirds of the persons living outside the district of birth were living in a contiguous district.[4] They had not moved far, and even much of this short-distance movement was probably a statistical artifact.

Yet, even though the proportional movement is small, the absolute numbers, due to the sheer size of the Indian population, are impressive. In 1921 there were some 30 million

[1] *Census of India*, 1931, Vol. 19 (Baroda), Part 1, p. 86. In certain areas the returns may be poor. In the Bombay Presidency for example, Bombay City, the Suburban District, and the Gujurat districts returned a good many blanks in 1931 because of non-cooperation, and the village rather than the district of birth was often given. *ibid.*, Vol. 8 (Bombay Pres.), Part 1, p. 61.

[2] *General Report of the Census of India*, 1911, Sessional Papers, Cmd. 7377 (London: His Majesty's Stationery Office, 1914), p. 91; *Census of India*, 1921, Vol. 1, Part 1, p. 83; *ibid.*, Vol. 1, Part 2, p. 114.

[3] U.S. Bureau of the Census, "State of Birth of the Native Population: 1940," *Population—Special Reports*, Series P-44, No. 13 (June 24, 1944), pp. 1–2.

[4] *Census of India*, 1921, Vol. 1, Part 1, p. 83.

people enumerated outside the district of birth, in 1931 some 12 million outside the province or state of birth. The population is not wholly static.

WHY THE IMMOBILITY?

Among the reasons commonly advanced prior to partition for the comparative immobility of the population are the following:

(1) *The predominance of agriculture.* Since farming requires no travel but rather constant attention, journeys are discouraged. Moreover, a frequent change of residence, such as occurs among tenant farmers in Texas and Argentina, is discouraged in India because the agrarian laws generally favor the old settler as against the new. Also, the predominance of agriculture means that as yet city growth, and hence rural-urban migration, has not reached its peak. Most of the farming is done at a subsistence level that allows little surplus to be accumulated to meet the cost of travel or of change of residence.

Nevertheless, as will appear presently, two chief types of migration in the Indian area are agricultural in character.

(2) *The caste system.* Because castes have geographical as well as social boundaries, travel removes a man from the local caste group and, by virtue of the ubiquity of caste restrictions, makes life uncomfortable for him.

"Not only is he unable to marry beyond [the caste] limits; he may not even eat or drink with members of other groups, nor may he smoke from their huqqa. He often finds it difficult to get any one to cook his food; and if he dies, there will be no one to perform his obsequies, and his body may have to be removed by scavengers. . . . A man who is long away from home is often looked at askance on his return; he is suspected of having broken the rules of his caste, and he may find it hard to regain his old position. . . . On the west coast of India the crossing of certain rivers is [forbidden] in some cases, especially where women are concerned." [5]

Rigid stratification gives the stranger a position of disadvantage. He cannot very well "make a new start." When Indians migrate, therefore, they tend to go in groups, as persons whose status is already fixed. Seldom do they "strike out for themselves." Thus does the suppression of social mobility lead to the suppression of geographical mobility. [6]

(3) *Early marriage and joint family.* So early does a Hindu or Muslim marry, so soon does he have children, so close are his family bonds, that there is no period, as among Westerners, when adolescent wanderlust can express itself. Adult status and responsibility in the village tend to be assumed just after puberty. The discouragement this offers to migration is great, especially since the inheritance laws call for equal division of property. There is no group of sons forced to leave by an inferior right to inherit.

(4) *Diversity of language and culture.* With some 225 languages, the Indian subcontinent suffers a linguistic barrier to spatial movement. The diversity of tongues, however, is only a striking instance of the general diversity of custom. An individual moving from one locale to another encounters numerous customs different from his own, and consequently encounters prejudice.

(5) *Lack of education.* Migration is the result of an idea—an idea of what lies somewhere else. "The ryot's ignorance of what is beyond the confines of [his] very limited horizon" [7] tends to burden him with superstitious fear of what lies beyond rather than fire him with pictures of golden opportunities.

These factors in the immobility of the population of this region do not exhaust the topic, but they serve to point up some of the main features and to show that the lack of migration is not due to the vague "innate love of home" with which some census officials have endowed the Indian people.

ABSENCE OF TREND IN INTERNAL MIGRATION

Some conditions in India have favored migration. Religious festivals, commercial fairs, dire famines, general wars, and ruthless taxation have in the past stimulated movement. Some of these were overcome by British rule, but the British brought other changes that favored migration—e.g. the development of better transportation and communication, more education, a decline of caste and family solidarity, the growth of large-scale industry, the development of cities, the expansion of irrigation, and the increase in security.

Looking at these changes, one might conclude that an increase in internal migration must have occurred. But the statistics fail to prove such an increase. Table 39 shows how uniform at various censuses has been the percentage of per-

TABLE 39

Persons Enumerated in a State or Province Different from the One in Which They Were Born, 1891–1931

	Total Population [a]	Enumerated Outside State or Province of Birth	Per Cent of Total Population
1891 [1]	279,245,118	10,652,359 [b]	3.8
1901 [2]	283,367,932	9,360,026 [c]	3.3
1911 [3]	301,319,182	10,811,678	3.6
1921 [4]	312,787,491	11,197,376	3.7
1931 [5]	336,632,184	12,079,576	3.6

[a] These populations exclude Burma, which is treated throughout as a foreign country, and also those persons for whom birthplace was not returned, or who were born outside of India.

[b] The number of those born outside India, 661,637, is excluded from this figure, as it is from all the subsequent figures in this column.

[c] This is an estimate. Every figure that could be found for 1901 seemed to include a lesser number of units than were included for any other year. However, comparisons were found with both 1891 and 1911 on the basis of the smaller number of years. It was assumed that the ratio to the larger figures for these years was the same as the ratio to the smaller figures.

[1] *Census of India,* 1891, Vol. 1, Part 2, p. x.
[2] *General Report of the Census of India,* 1901, Sessional Papers, Cmd. 2047 (London: His Majesty's Stationery Office, 1904), p. 579.
[3] *Census of India,* 1911, Vol. 1, Part 2, p. 141.
[4] *ibid.,* 1921, Vol. 1, Part 2, p. 134.
[5] *ibid.,* 1931, Vol. 1, Part 2, p. 114.

sons living in a province different from the province of birth. [8] Apparently the number of "migrants" has not increased any faster than the population.

[7] *Census of India,* 1931, Vol. 8 (Bombay Pres.), Part 1, p. 63.

[8] The figures are only roughly comparable from one census to another, because the number and character of the political units changed

---

[5] *General Report of the Census of India,* 1911, *loc. cit.*

[6] Of course, given new areas where frontier conditions and Western influence are present, caste may operate as a stimulant to migration. It is, for example, a spur to cityward and to foreign migration. The untouchables are not blind to the fact that in the city or across the sea they lose their untouchability. The movement to the Assam tea gardens has been a movement of low caste laborers. See *Census of India,* 1931, Vol. 14 (Madras), Part 1, pp. 86, 88–89, 93; *ibid.,* Vol. 9 (Bombay Cities), Part 1, pp. 20–24, 38–44; *ibid.,* Vol. 23 (Hyderabad), Part 1, p. 62.

This result may not mean that genuine internal migration has remained stationary. It is possible that casual movement across state and provincial boundaries for purposes of marriage and childbirth has declined, while migration for economic purposes has increased, though this seems unlikely.

that the dominant movement of people prior to partition was from West to East and from South to North. The evidence lies in the figures for net movement across boundaries between contiguous provinces; and it is best to use males alone, because this eliminates the marriage migration of females.

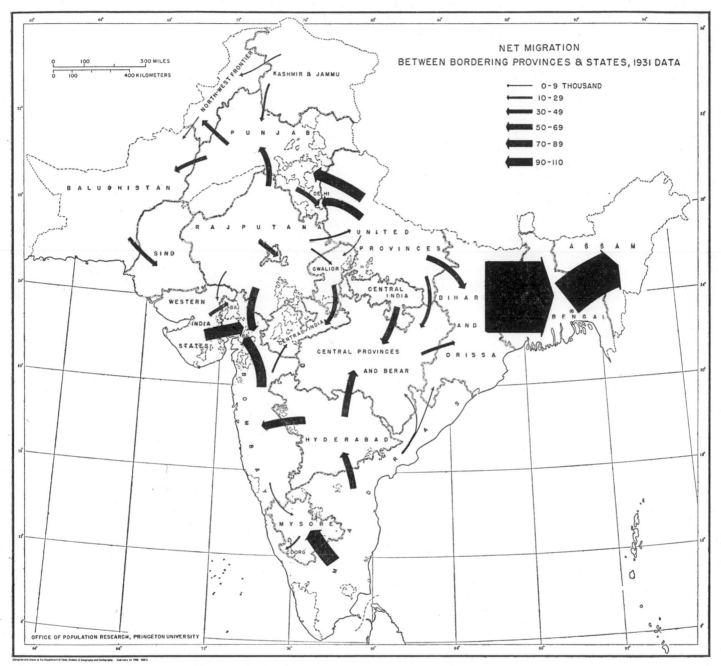

MAP 13. Net Migration Across State and Provincial Boundaries, According to Birthplace Data of 1931.

THE DIRECTION OF INTERNAL MIGRATION

One way of judging the migration is to study the directional orientation of boundaries and analyze the movement across them. When this is done a startling fact emerges—namely,

from time to time. Thus in 1911 Bengal and Bihar-Orissa were two separate provinces, and movement between them was counted as migration. In 1901, however, they had been one province, and such movement was *not* counted as migration. This single change in the political map meant that, in 1911, about 1,500,000 more persons were listed as born outside the province of their birth than would otherwise have been the case. See *General Report of the Census of India,* 1911, pp. 104–05.

The results, presented in Table 40 and Map 13, show that, in Northern India, the net pairings give over a million men enumerated East of where they were born, while only one-seventh of a million were enumerated West of where they were born. In Southern India, however, this West-East movement is reversed, all Western provinces showing a gain of males as against their Eastern neighbors. In neither part of India does the northward or southward movement enjoy such a preponderance.[9]

[9] These results are confirmed by taking *all* males residing outside the province (not merely those residing in a contiguous province) and

TABLE 40

Net Migration of Males between Border States and Provinces, as Judged by Birthplace Figures, 1931 [1]

Place of Birth	Place of Enumeration	East	West	North	South
NORTHERN PORTION OF INDIA		*1,058,681*	*136,164*	*307,139*	*264,095*
United Provs.	Bihar & Orissa [a]	22,851			22,850
United Provs.	Cent. India Ag.				18,940
United Provs.	Gwalior		2,829		2,830
Rajputana	United Provs.	10,302			
United Provs.	Delhi		66,203		
United Provs.	Punjab		32,852	32,852	
Bihar & Orissa	Bengal	727,916			
Cent. Prov. & B.	Bihar & Orissa	14,753		4,918	
Bengal	Assam	145,680		145,681	
Madras	Cent. Provs. & Ber.	2,875		2,875	
Bombay	Cent. India	7,049		7,048	
Bombay	Baroda			47,537	
Western India	Bombay	43,653			43,653
Rajputana	Bombay				60,754
Baluchistan	Bombay	8,645			8,645
Hyderabad	Cent. Provs., B & O	8,259		35,481	
Cent. India Ag.	Cent. Provs. & Ber.	22,654			22,653
Western India	Baroda	18,325			
Gwalior	Central India	7,658			7,658
Rajputana	Gwalior	9,966			9,966
Rajputana	Punjab			14,778	
Rajputana	Western India				3,824
Punjab	Baluchistan		12,372		12,372
Punjab	N.W. Frontier Province		15,969	15,969	
Jammu & Kash.	Punjab				23,408
N. W. Frontier Prov.	Baluchistan		2,258		
Punjab	Delhi	8,095			24,284
Jammu & Kash.	N. W. Frontier Prov.		3,681		
SOUTHERN PORTION OF INDIA			*141,312*	*37,551*	*71,270*
Madras	Hyderabad		37,551	37,551	
Madras	Mysore		60,776		60,776
Bombay	Mysore				7,544
Mysore	Coorg		2,950		2,950
Hyderabad	Bombay		40,035		
TOTAL FOR ALL OF INDIA		1,058,681	277,476	344,690	335,365

[a] In those cases where the boundary does not run predominantly in one direction, or where it runs at an angle with reference to the four directions, the migrants have been split up into halves or quarters and distributed accordingly. This procedure is somewhat rough, but in the aggregate it should not introduce much of an error.

[1] Data taken from Part 2, Imperial Table 6, "Birthplace," of each of the volumes on the provinces or states concerned, *Census of India*, 1931.

The eastward movement of males in the North is attributable mainly to the industrial and urban development of Bengal and the growth of tea estates in Assam. The counter determining whether they are north or south of where they were born. The figures are as follows, in thousands:

	East	West	North	South
Northern India	2,434	793	762	1,744
Southern India	146	493	483	146

It can be seen that here there is a pronounced movement in Northern India toward the South and in Southern India toward the North, but otherwise the results are similar. (Some individuals in this tabulation were counted twice, depending on their direction from place of birth.)

attraction of new irrigation areas in the Punjab has not been strong enough to overcome this pull. In the Southern portion of the country the westward drift of males is due to the attraction of the Bombay urban centers and the estate agriculture of the Western Ghats.

In a very rough way one can see a movement toward the outer edges of the subcontinent, whether these are on the seacoast or near the frontier. The large magnets are Assam, Bombay, Bengal, Mysore, and the Punjab States. The pattern just described is not entirely consistent, but the trend seems noticeable.

MIGRATION BETWEEN BRITISH INDIA AND THE NATIVE STATES

As between what was British India and the erstwhile Indian States, migration has been rather even, as Table 41 shows. For five censuses the balance of migration was apparently in favor of the States and Agencies, although there was considerable fluctuation.

but not great gainers. On the negative side, Rajputana, Hyderabad, and Jammu and Kashmir have been invariable losers, the first two by large amounts. It is safe to say that the amount and direction of the movement has depended little on whether the area was a State or not, but rather upon other factors.

TABLE 41

Net Gain or Loss Between Major States and the Whole of British India, According to Birthplace Figures, 1891 to 1931 (000's omitted)

	1891 [1]	1901 [2]	1911 [3]	1921 [4]	1931 [5]	Total
ALL STATES	918	—220	—107	—118	495	968
Mysore	49	168	174	205	211	807
Punjab States & Ag.	8	xx	34	84	187	313
Bengal States	441	xx	98	126	155	820
Cent. Prov. States	550	xx	75	54	135	814
Bihar & Orissa	xx	xx	232	153	105	490
Baroda	16	—23	—5	—7	77	58
Bombay States	78	xx	—157	—207	69	217
Travancore			39	50	87	176
Cochin	67	xx	21	16	37	141
Other Madras States			25	27	23	75
Unit. Prov. States	xx	xx	—7	19	10	22
Gwalior	xx	xx	xx	15	7	22
N.W. Frontier Tribal	6	xx	—49	—3	1	—45
Central India	42	91	—95	—28	—8	2
Jammu & Kashmir	—19	——	—8	—20	—27	—74
Hyderabad	—49	—11	—59	—160	—88	—367
West. India States	xx	xx	xx	xx	—148	—148
Rajputana	—271	—445	—425	—442	—326	—1909
Others	xx	xx	xx	xx	—12	—12

[1] *Census of India*, 1891, Vol. 1, Part 2, pp. 415–21.
[2] *General Report of the Census of India*, 1901, Sessional Papers, Cmd. 2047 (London: His Majesty's Stationery Office, 1904).
[3] *Census of India*, 1911, Vol. 1, Part 1, p. 96; Vol. 1, Part 2, pp. 134–40, 146–49.
[4] *ibid.*, 1921, Vol. 1, Part 1, p. 93; Vol. 1, Part 2, pp. 120–23, 128–29.
[5] *ibid.*, 1931, Vol. 1, Part 1, p. 68.

This is the opposite of what one might suppose on the assumption of better economic and political conditions in British territory. The net figure, however, is only a small part of the total movement. In 1931, for example, the total number of persons found in one of these two parts of India and born in the other was slightly over 6 million. The net balance of half a million in favor of the States was therefore only 8 per cent of the total "migrants," and only 0.61 per cent of the total population of the States.

The currents of movement between particular States and Agencies on the one hand and the British Provinces on the other have tended to remain fairly constant, few of them reversing their direction between one census and another. Table 41, which gives the available figures, indicates that in general if a State lost population to British territory in one decade, it did so in other decades, and vice versa. Mysore, the Punjab States and Agencies, the Bengal States, the Central Provinces States, and the Bihar and Orissa States have invariably shown a net gain when data were obtainable, and they have piled up huge net gains over the total span of years. Travancore, Cochin, and Other Madras States have also been consistent

SHORT-RUN MIGRATION

As noted, a good portion of the discrepancy between place of birth and place of enumeration has been constituted by short-range movement across provincial and district boundaries. Some of this movement was not migration at all, because either the place of birth or the place of enumeration was accidental; but some of it was genuine migration and has a pattern of its own. In order to separate the accidental from the true migration, one must deal with the lesser movements in detail. The most important type is "marriage migration," which has some peculiarities worth noting. A second type, which falls in the accidental category, is "birth migration." Also, there is "festival migration." The first is the most important.

MARRIAGE MIGRATION

The so-called marriage migration arises from two facts of Indian family behavior in the Indian region, the one concerned with matrimonial selection, the other with matrimonial residence. The selection arises from the widespread Hindu custom of taking the bride from another village. One basis for this practice lies perhaps in the close-knit character of the rural village, which causes a slight feeling of incest to be attached to marriages within the community.[10] But more important is the rigid rule of caste endogamy, which specifies that the mate must be chosen from within the caste. Since as a rule each caste, if represented at all, is represented in the village by only one or at most a few families,[11] its members in that place are apt to be related within the prohibited degrees. Marriage outside the village therefore becomes a necessity.

The rule of matrimonial residence is simply the patrilocal principle, which is rooted deep in the whole Hindu family organization. Descent is through males. The children are regarded as belonging to the father's line and to his household, and they inherit exclusively through him. The young wife, often while she is still a child, has a definite though lowly status in the husband's household, and her relationship to his older female relatives is close and minutely institutionalized.

So, putting these two facts together—informal village exogamy and patrilocal residence—one can see that there must be many women who are born in one village but living in another. When the villages in question happen to be in different districts or different provinces, the census, through its birthplace data, has recorded them as "migrants."

Of course, marriage migration also implies some subsidiary movement which may happen to get into the census returns. Guests from another village may come to the wedding. If the bride is wealthy, she may bring to her new residence a retinue of servants; if poor, she may bring her needy aunts and grandmothers.[12] The Madras Census Commissioner for 1931 maintained that the census date fell in the middle of the period, February 22 to March 2, which was auspicious for Hindu marriages, and that consequently the cross-border movement was probably brisker than usual.[13]

Statistical Evidence of Marriage Migration. The data on place of birth show conclusively that marriage migration takes place on a sizable scale. For instance, the sex ratios of those born in districts contiguous to the district of enumeration usually show a feminine sex ratio, whereas all other kinds of migration, especially those over a greater distance, show a predominantly masculine ratio. Furthermore, the migration of females across the boundaries of contiguous districts tends to be reciprocal, each district receiving a substantial contingent from the other.

The situation is neatly illustrated in Delhi for 1931. Here a separation was made, according to place of birth, between those living in the urban and those living in the rural part of the Province. The sex ratios were as follows:

MALES PER 100 FEMALES
ENUMERATED IN

Birthplace	Rural Area	Urban Area
Within the Province	153	127
Contiguous Provinces	46	185
Other Parts of India	129	157
Foreign Countries	2327	257

The only feminine sex ratio is that for persons born in contiguous provinces but living in the rural area. The Census Commissioner, by way of explanation, says: "The wives taken from the neighbouring districts in the Punjab and the United Provinces swell the number of female immigrants" to the rural area. But the migration to the City of Delhi is primarily for other purposes—trade or employment—and tends to draw males, who leave their wives at home.[14] The sex ratio of those born in the province and enumerated there is predominantly masculine, because Delhi Province has sent many women as wives to men in contiguous districts of the Punjab and the United Provinces. Thus the marriage exchange is roughly reciprocal.

In this Delhi case the statistics were given only for those born in a contiguous *province,* but the evidence of marriage migration can be brought out more clearly if figures are taken for those born in contiguous *districts.* An approximation to this was accomplished in the Baroda report for 1931, in which migration was divided into five categories according to distance. The nearest one, embracing persons born in contiguous areas, was for the most part confined to districts that bordered on the scattered Baroda areas. The results were as follows: [15]

	Males per 100 Females
Contiguous Area	61
Fairly Near	138
Remote	331
Very Remote	228
Outside India	145

Tabulations published in the census volumes do not show, for each given district, the sex ratio of persons born in all districts immediately contiguous. Since the basic data existed in five states and provinces,[16] such a tabulation was made. It yielded these results:

	Males per 100 Females
Born in district of enumeration	102
Born in contiguous districts	71
Born elsewhere	121

Numerous other data indicate the same thing. All in all, it seems beyond doubt that, other things being equal, the smaller the size of the unit and the shorter the distance of migration, the greater the part played by the marriage factor. This affords specific documentation of the more general rule that feminine migration is short-range, masculine migration long-range.

What Proportion of Migration Is Marriage Migration? In the absence of sample studies it is impossible to know exactly what proportion of the short-range movement is caused by the marriage factor. A rough idea, however, can be obtained by assuming that all the "extra" females—i.e. those above the number of males born outside the district—came by marriage. This is not an entirely unrealistic assumption, because there is reason to believe that the accidental factors tend to cancel out. It is probably a minimum assumption, because many of the out-born males have doubtless come without female attachments, so that subtracting from the total out-born females a number equal to the number of out-born males, leaves a minimum number of females who probably came by marriage.

---

[10] Blunt says that "the exogamous unit of the primitive Dravidian was the village," and "that the villager still looks on a fellow casteman, residing in the same village, as in some sense his relative—a *ganw ka bhai* (village brother) as he calls him." E. A. H. Blunt, *The Caste System of Northern India* (London: Oxford University Press, 1931), p. 46.

[11] S. S. Nehru, *Caste and Credit in the Rural Area* (London: Longmans, 1932), Chapter 2.

[12] *Census of India,* 1931, Vol. 23 (Hyderabad), Part 1, p. 63.

[13] *ibid.,* 1931, Vol. 14 (Madras), Part 1, p. 81.

[14] *ibid.,* Vol. 16 (Delhi), Part 1, p. 43.

[15] *ibid.,* Vol. 19 (Baroda), Part 1, p. 88.

[16] Travancore, Gwalior, Mysore, Hyderabad, Bihar and Orissa.

In any case, employing the data obtained for the five provinces and states mentioned above as allowing calculation of the number born in contiguous districts within each area, this assumption leads to the conclusion that 17.1 per cent of the short-range (contiguous district) and 8.5 per cent of the total movement into the district is by marriage. On an impressionistic basis, these percentages seem low. They should not be taken seriously as anything more than vague guesses as to the minimum influence of the marriage factor.

Is Marriage Migration More Characteristic of Hindus than of Muslims? The usual assumption is that, though both are patrilocal, the Hindus practice village exogamy more than the Muslims. Among the Muslims the same factors are not present which, among the Hindus, give rise to village exogamy. For instance, their religion presumably does not have a Dravidian element in it, their village life is not so close-knit as that of the Hindus, and they are not so caste-ridden. Nevertheless, the Muslims follow a Hindu way of life to such an extent that one might expect a considerable amount of marriage migration among them too.

Fortunately, statistical evidence exists which can throw light on this problem. In the Punjab, the North-West Frontier Province, and Jammu and Kashmir it was possible to take nineteen heavily Muslim districts, and to secure data on persons living in these districts who were born *in contiguous districts having more than 70 per cent of their population Muslim.* Thus the situation was very similar to the study, mentioned above, of movement from contiguous districts made in five predominantly Hindu provinces and states. But the results were far different. The sex ratio of those born in the contiguous Muslim districts, instead of being heavily feminine as was the case with the Hindus, was chiefly masculine, there being 133 males per 100 females in the group. Table 42 gives the results. It appears that there is far less marriage migration between Muslim districts than between Hindu districts.

Obviously, as the table shows, there are special circumstances governing the sex ratio of migrants between contiguous districts. In Travancore there has been a heavy influx of laborers to the new tea, rubber, and cardamom plantations opening up in the Highland Division.[17] Since such labor migration tends to be predominantly masculine, this accounts for the exceptionally high sex ratio (118) found among those born in contiguous administrative divisions in that State. If the data could be secured for taluks rather than administrative divisions in Travancore, it seems certain, in view of the data cited above on migration from contiguous districts in Cochin and Madras, that the State would conform to the general rule.

In the North-West Frontier Province the exceptionally high sex ratio of persons from contiguous districts is due, in part at least, to the number of cantonments, especially in Peshawar District. The ratio of 226 should therefore be discounted somewhat. Nevertheless, a masculine sex ratio for short-range migrants to Muslim districts is consistent throughout this province, the Punjab, and Jammu and Kashmir. In fact, the data were secured for 19 districts all told. In all of these, with only one exception (Mirpur District in Jammu, with a ratio of 71), the sex ratio was more than 100.

Possibly Muslims living as small groups in large Hindu communities would follow the Hindu practice of village exogamy more frequently. But until contrary evidence is produced, it seems true that marriage migration is primarily a Hindu rather than a Muslim phenomenon.

[17] *Census of India,* 1931, Vol. 28 (Travancore), Part 1, pp. 79–80.

TABLE 42

Sex Ratios of Those Born in Districts Contiguous to Those in Which Enumerated, Hindu and Muslim Areas, 1931

| | MALES PER 100 FEMALES | |
	Home Born	Born in Contiguous Districts
HINDU DISTRICTS, Total [a]	102	71
Travancore [1]	101	118
Gwalior [2]	117	81
Mysore [3]	105	80
Hyderabad [4]	104	83
Bihar & Orissa [5]	100	62
MUSLIM DISTRICTS, Total	119 [b]	133
Punjab [6]	121	129
North-West Frontier Prov.[7]	119	226
Jammu & Kashmir [8]	113	107

[a] These ratios for all the districts combined are unweighted averages. The populations involved in the various units are so uneven that a weighted average gives undue importance to some areas, *o.g.* to Bihar & Orissa, which has more people involved in this tabulation than the four other areas combined.

[b] The figures in this column for Muslim districts are those for the total population, not merely for the home-born. The latter were not calculated, but they should not be greatly different from those for the total population.

[1] *Census of India,* 1931, Vol. 28 (Travancore), Part 1, p. 18; Part 2, p. 2.
[2] *ibid.,* Vol. 22 (Gwalior), Part 1, p. 44; Part 2, p. 2.
[3] *ibid.,* Vol. 25 (Mysore), Part 1, p. 91; Part 2, p. 2.
[4] *ibid.,* Vol. 23 (Hyderabad), Part 1, p. 70; Part 2, p. 2.
[5] *ibid.,* Vol. 7 (Bihar & Orissa), Part 1, p. 114; Part 2, p. 2.
[6] *ibid.,* Vol. 17 (Punjab), Part 2, pp. 62–63.
[7] *ibid.,* Vol. 15 (North-West Frontier Province), Part 2, pp. xx–xxi.
[8] *ibid.,* Vol. 24 (Jammu & Kashmir), Part 2, pp. 23–25.

Hypergamy and the Westward Drift. Theoretically the choice of mates outside the village should lead to a generally equal exchange of women between villages, but actually this is not quite the case. The reason is that a hypergamous tendency is operative throughout Hindu society. Marriage is compulsory, and parents are bound to marry off their daughters as early as possible, and to secure for them grooms of as high a status as possible. Although the rule of caste endogamy precludes, in most cases, the marriage of a daughter into a higher caste, it does not so frequently preclude her marriage into a higher subcaste or a higher section of a subcaste. Since subcastes and branches are distributed on a geographical basis, since the more prosperous ones generally lie to the northwest, and since the sex ratio in the northwest is higher (more masculine) than in any other region, there is a general drift of females in a westward direction.

E. A. H. Blunt, Supervisor of the census of 1911 in the United Provinces, was one of the first to call attention to this phenomenon. In his classic treatise on the caste system, he says: "Amongst all Hindus there is probably a tendency towards hypergamy. A curious proof of this fact is provided by the statistics of birthplace in the United Provinces. In two successive census reports (1901 and 1911), it is shown clearly, firstly, that the bulk of persons living in districts other than that in which they were born are women; secondly, that the migration is from east to west. As the lower branches of a widespread caste, generally speaking, live in the east of the Provinces, and the higher in the west, the conclusion that hypergamy has something to do with the nature of this 'marrlage' migration appears sound."[10] The same fact, previously pointed out in the 1901 census report for the United Provinces, was again documented in 1931. The 1931 report added that a lesser current of marriage migration goes from south to north.[19]

OTHER FORMS OF SHORT-RANGE MIGRATION

Another custom contributing to short-range "migration" is the female's practice of returning to her family homestead to bear the first child. The extent of this behavior seems impossible to determine, but it doubtless has some effect on birthplace statistics for contiguous areas.

A good part of rural-urban migration is short-range in character. As shown in the chapter on cities, the sex ratio of urban migrants from nearby districts is less masculine than that of migrants from remote areas. This suggests that a certain amount of marriage migration is involved, but also that such female employment as exists in the cities draws women from the surrounding area rather than from remote places. The same is of course true of male employment, but to a lesser degree.

migration? Second, what is the extent of daily movement—i.e. commuting—to the city? Our data permit only tentative answers.

THE STRENGTH OF THE URBAN MAGNETS

For three large provinces the birthplace of the city population is substantially known.[20] Analysis shows that the cities have a far greater share of the persons born outside than do the rural sections (Table 43). They account for between 13 and 32 per cent of all the persons born outside the district, which is far above their 5 to 7 per cent proportion of the total population. Furthermore, as the distance increases, the percentage of migrants going to the city also increases. As Table 43 shows, between 42 and 60 per cent of those from beyond adjacent provinces are found in the cities analyzed.

Assuming that our data cover half the attractive power of the urban population in each of the three provinces, and that the provinces are typical, one can say that rural-urban migration constitutes something like 45 per cent of all migration between districts and an even greater share of all migration between provinces. This makes rural-urban migration the most important kind of internal migration in the Indian region.

TABLE 43

Percentage of Out-Born in Three Provinces Found in Cities, by Distance of Birthplace, 1931

| | | | BORN OUTSIDE DISTRICT | | |
	Population	Total	Outside District But in Province	Adjacent Provinces	Elsewhere
United Provinces [1]	49,614,833	4,665,435	4,105,830	439,724	119,881
Cities [2]	2,486,152	594,774	454,322	86,797	53,655
Per Cent City	5.01	12.75	11.06	19.74	44.76
Bombay [3]	26,271,784	3,620,222	2,394,739	914,946	310,537
Cities [4]	1,816,525	1,148,365	734,805	227,814	185,746
Per Cent City	6.91	31.72	30.68	24.89	59.81
Madras [5]	47,193,602	2,144,558	1,924,158	177,104	43,296
Cities [6]	2,242,403	447,462	404,471	24,884	18,107
Per Cent City	4.75	19.95	21.02	14.05	41.82

[1] *Census of India,* 1931, Vol. 18 (United Provinces), Part 2, pp. 74–75.
[2] *ibid.,* pp. 101–107. (23 cities are included, all having a population of more than 35,500.)
[3] *Census of India,* 1931, Vol. 8 (Bombay Pres.), Part 2, pp. 52, 72.
[4] *ibid.,* Vol. 9 (Bombay Cities), Part 2, pp. 178–80, 249–50, 270–71, 283. (4 cities are included, all large ones.)
[5] *ibid.,* Vol. 14 (Madras), Part 2, p. 26.
[6] *ibid.,* pp. 36–41. (22 cities are included, all over 50,000.)

Nearly every migratory situation in India has a heavy short-range element in it. Long-distance migration can be regarded as a residual, representing the number of persons who, for one reason or another, could not be supplied from the immediately surrounding districts. In view of this fact, we shall not discuss long-range migration as such, but will consider only the types of migration in terms of their social and economic causes.

RURAL-URBAN MIGRATION

Rural-urban migration is discussed in the chapters on cities, but there are two questions that can appropriately be raised now: First, how much of the internal migration is cityward

COMMUTING TO THE CITY

The 1931 census pointed out that 26,000 persons come daily into Calcutta by train alone, to say nothing of those who use buses, trams, or cars. "In some industrial areas it is already becoming common practice for persons to live outside the place of employment. . . . This is apparent in Nagpur, for instance, where in some cases clerks live even 25 to 30 miles away at Ramtek and come in by train to their work every morning," the morning and evening trains being timed to suit the need. Other villages outside Nagpur provide workmen who come in daily to work, and there is a tendency toward suburban development around the city, with well-to-do people building houses outside the municipal limits along the main

[18] *The Caste System of Northern India* (London: Oxford University Press, 1931), pp. 46–47.
[19] *Census of India,* 1901, Vol. 18 (United Provinces), Part 1, pp. 38, 192.

[20] Only the larger cities, mostly those over 50,000, are available. The provinces, together with the percentage of the total urban population embraced by the data, are as follows: United Provinces, 45 per cent; Bombay, 33 per cent; Madras, 35 per cent.

highways. This tendency is expected to grow as municipal taxes increase and transportation improves.[21] The Travancore census reports that "daily migration is now a common feature of important towns like Trivandrum, Nagercoil, Quilon and Alleppey. A number of people live outside the towns, go there for work in the morning and return home in the evening. Owing to the convenience afforded for traveling by motor buses and cars, persons living in places within a radius of about 50 miles find it possible to visit the capital and the division and taluk headquarters, transact their business and get back home on the same day. Hundreds of persons are thus visiting Trivandrum and other towns daily." [22]

On the other hand, the United Provinces reports that daily commuting is "as yet negligible" in that province.[23] With reference to industrial labor, the Bhore Committee reported that transport facilities are very poor. "Workers who live at a distance have to walk as many as four or five miles to and from work. When it is remembered that the Indian labourer has to work in perennial factories 54 hours a week and in seasonal factories 60 hours, it will be seen that the question of transport assumes considerable importance. . . . While in some of the smaller places it may be possible to provide working class quarters in areas not too far from the factories, such provision has to be ruled out in the case of large cities like Bombay, Calcutta, Ahmedabad and Cawnpore. In these towns new housing schemes can obviously be undertaken only in suburban areas situated at considerable distances from the factories." [24]

Suburbanization and commuting represent a certain maturity of urban growth. In India and Pakistan they have not developed very far, but have definitely begun. Commuters' ticket sales in Calcutta show, furthermore, that the commuting habit is growing.[25]

The Movement of Estate Labor

One of the greatest magnets drawing Pakistanis and particularly Indians away from home is the development of commercial agriculture of the estate type. Many of these new enterprises, which grow industrial and export food crops, have been started in sparsely settled areas—e.g. forested hill ranges —where the demand for labor must consequently be satisfied from outside. The estates have generally undertaken a regular policy of recruitment resembling in many respects the tactics pursued by foreign plantation owners. Thus both indenture and the kangani system have been utilized.

There are two main areas of great importance for drawing estate labor. One, distinctly less important, is a strip in the upland part of the Western Ghats embraced by the Kadur and Hassan districts of Mysore, the Highland Division of Travancore, the Province of Coorg, and the Nilgiri, Coimbatore, and Malabar districts of Madras. These seven small areas contained, in 1931, 14 per cent of all the laborers in India engaged primarily in the cultivation of the three main estate crops—tea, coffee, and rubber. The other main area is a broad strip extending on either side of the Brahmaputra River, beginning with the districts of Darjeeling and Jalpaiguri in Bengal and extending through Sylhet, Cachar, Goalpara,

Kamrup, Darrang, Nowgong, Sibsagar, and Lakhimpur in Assam. These ten districts contained, in 1931, 82 per cent of all persons gainfully occupied in the three principal estate products. Putting the two areas together (both relatively small), one can see that they contain 96 per cent of all India's estate laborers in the crops mentioned.

MIGRATION TO THE SOUTHWESTERN ESTATE BELT

Although the Madras districts falling in the southwestern estate belt do not draw many laborers in proportion to their total population, this is not true of Travancore and Mysore, where the proportion of outborn persons is higher in the estate districts than in the other districts. The Highland Division of Travancore, for example, had in 1931, 41.4 per cent of its total population born outside the district of enumeration, whereas the Midland and Lowland divisions had only 3.7 per cent so born. In Mysore, Kadur district had 19 per cent of its population born outside, and Hassan had 8 per cent, these two districts standing to each other in this regard about as they stood with reference to the number of estate laborers. Both districts slightly exceeded the proportion of outborn found in other districts of Mysore, and exceeded them in about the same ratio regardless of the distance of the migration. In fact, it is worth noting that in this belt as a whole, the estate districts tend to draw as heavily upon local areas right around the district as upon more distant sources of labor.

The Travancore census authorities of 1931 gathered special information with regard to estates. They found that Travancore had 224 tea and rubber plantations, comprising an area of about 75,000 acres under tea, 62,000 under rubber, and 30,000 under cardamom. The three crops together supported a population of 105,224 persons, of whom 79,433 were immigrants from outside Travancore. Of the 79,433 immigrants, 3,314 were workers in cardamom gardens, the rest in tea and rubber. The immigrants on estates constituted 59 per cent of all immigrants to Travancore State.

In answer to a circular letter, the estate managers gave information on the length of time the immigrant laborers had been on the estates. Forty-eight per cent of them had been on the estates for only one year or less; 29 per cent had been on the estate between one and three years; and 23 per cent had been there for three years or more. This indicates that a large majority of the immigrants are only temporary or semipermanent sojourners, although there is a small contingent who bring their families and settle permanently. They all come mostly from the depressed classes.[26]

MIGRATION INTO THE NORTHEASTERN ESTATE REGION

The plantations of Assam and Eastern Bengal are much more important than those of the region just discussed. Employing, as we have seen, no less than 82 per cent of all workers in the estate crops (of which tea alone is important in Assam), they have been a factor causing Assam to be the fastest growing province in India.

Period	Per Cent Growth [27]
1872–1881	9.1
1881–1891	9.2
1891–1901	5.9

[21] Census of India, 1931, Vol. 1, Part 1, p. 67; Vol. 12 (Central Provinces & Berar), Part 1, pp. 103–04; Vol. 16 (Delhi), Part 1, p. 42.

[22] ibid., Vol. 28 (Travancore), Part 1, p. 86.

[23] ibid., Vol. 18 (United Provinces), Part 1, p. 186.

[24] Health Survey and Development Committee, Report Vol. 1 (Delhi: Manager of Publications), p. 83.

[25] Census of India, 1931, Vol. 5 (Bengal & Sikkim), Part 1, pp. 97–98.

[26] Census of India, 1931, Vol. 28 (Travancore), Part 1, pp. 83–84.

[27] These figures make allowance for changes of boundaries. They are therefore not derived from the raw census data. The percentages have been computed by the census authorities. See Census of India, 1931, Vol. 3 (Assam), Part 1, p. 5; and 1941, Vol. 1, p. 63, for the final decade.

Period	Per Cent Growth
1901–1911	14.6
1911–1921	12.8
1921–1931	15.6
1931–1941	15.5

Tea cultivation began in 1840, and thirteen years later, in 1853, the importation of laborers commenced. Curiously, this was about the time that recruitment for estates in foreign countries also got under way, and from then on the history of labor recruitment in Assam closely resembled the recruitment of Indians for overseas areas. Assam had to obtain laborers from outside its borders for the same reason that foreign tropical estates did. "The indigenous Assamese could not be persuaded to leave their farms and villages to work on the gardens, and there were few landless labourers to be found in the province." [28] In short, the development of estate agriculture in this out-of-the-way corner of India was absolutely dependent on the recruitment of labor from those sections where the population was denser, less secure, and more accustomed to working for wages. In this respect Assam differed from the Southwestern region discussed above. It was like a foreign country.

The labor system was that of indenture. In the early days, about 1860, the coolies were recruited from depots in Calcutta, being selected much like animals or slaves. They were placed under five-year indenture by "contracts" containing penal provisions for breach of the agreement. Since the tea plantations were located in a remote wilderness, with very little communication between them and the rest of India, the workers were virtual prisoners for the duration of their contract.

After 1870 legislation was introduced to protect the coolies. As was the case with indentured emigrants going overseas, the initial legislation aimed primarily at preventing fraud and force in the process of recruitment. There was no more legislation concerning Assam recruitment, however, than there was concerning recruitment for foreign areas. The treatment of the coolies was as bad, if not worse, than the treatment accorded them in overseas British colonies.

In 1921, after serious rioting which led to a wholesale exodus from some tea gardens, the Indian government appointed an Assam Labor Inquiry Committee. The Committee found scandalous conditions, more appropriate to the nineteenth than the twentieth century. Its report led the tea growers to put their house in order. The Royal Commission on Labor in India, which dealt with plantation as well as industrial labor, reported in 1931 that conditions were considerably better, although there was still much room for improvement. [29]

The indenture system, as everywhere else, was finally abolished. The kangani or sardari system was substituted. Under this system the sardars were sent to home districts in the recruiting season. They there described the advantages of Assam as a place to work, emphasizing the regularity of wages, the possibility of ultimately acquiring a farm, and the security of a region where the monsoon never fails. In recent times movies of life on the tea estates have been exhibited. The sardar, as well as the Labor Supply Association, received a commission for each coolie brought to a tea garden. [30]

An effort was made to secure families rather than single men, because the latter tended to run away from the estates more often than did men with families. This explains why women are almost as numerous in tea garden work as men— a different situation from that found among Indian laborers overseas. In 1931, for example, the sex ratio of persons born in some other part of India but living in the province was 135, and of all persons employed in tea garden labor, 113. Not only women, but also children, were employed on the estates. "There was evidence that in some gardens children began work at 4, 5 and 6 years of age, and that special baskets were made for them to carry the tea. The general starting age, however, was 8 or 9 years and in the best gardens children did not begin work till 10 or 11 years of age. There was no legal limit, however, and it depended entirely on the manager, or as one of them told the Commission, 'on circumstances.' " [31] The wages were calculated on a family basis. The earnings of the children were essential, because of the generally low wage scale.

The peak decade in labor recruitment seems to have been that of 1911–21, when, according to the Immigrant Labor Reports, 769,000 new immigrant coolies entered Assam. [32] In only two years, 1918–19, of this decade no less than 234,000 came in. [33] Immediately after these two years, however, the tea industry found itself depressed, because of the closure of the Russian market and the general trade dislocation. The number of laborers was reduced, large areas went out of cultivation, and riots and other disturbances occurred among the coolies in several districts. In 1921, with restricted output and a rise in the tea market, the industry began to recover; but it was caught again when the world depression curtailed business, so that the total number of coolie recruits (422,000) during the 1921–31 decade was only a little more than half the number during the previous decade.

The continuance of large-scale recruitment over many decades is due to the heavy loss of workers from three causes: a high death rate, a tendency to return to the original home, and the acquisition of small farms in Assam. At least up until 1925 Assam had a notoriously high mortality, her people suffering severely from kala azar, cholera, and malaria. The coolies, often in bad condition upon arrival, being unadjusted to the climate and having a low standard of living, were especially susceptible.

How many coolies have returned to their homes is hard to say, but the proportion is apparently high. There has been an increasing use of short-run contracts stipulating work for a period of three years or less, and it is thought that many workers return home when the period is over. Workers are also "repatriated" on account of ill health or unsuitability. And the labor market fluctuates greatly. In June 1923 the labor force on tea estates was 40,000 less than in June 1921 and 140,000 less than in June 1920. The birthplace statistics confirm the large homeward movement. In 1921, for example, 571,000 persons from Bihar and Orissa were enumerated in Assam. During the subsequent decade 169,000 new coolies arrived from Bihar and Orissa. Yet, in 1931, only 472,000 persons were found in Assam who were born in Bihar and Orissa. Taking account of death rates, there was a loss during the decade of at least 100,000 persons through departures for home. [34]

The tendency of laborers to leave the estates and settle on

[28] Margaret Read, *The Indian Peasant Uprooted* (London: Longmans, 1931), pp. 131–32.

[29] *ibid.*, pp. 132, 136–37.

[30] *Census of India,* 1921, Vol. 3 (Assam), Part 1, p. 37, 49.

[31] Read, *op. cit.*, p. 139.

[32] *Census of India,* 1931, Vol. 3 (Assam), Part 1, p. 45.

[33] *ibid.*, 1921, Vol. 3 (Assam), Part 1, p. 37.

[34] *ibid.*, 1931, Vol. 3 (Assam), Part 1, pp. 46–47.

farms in Assam is also unmistakable. A number of the estates have made it a practice to grant rice plots to their workers at nominal rent. No boon is greater than this in the eyes of the worker. The chief goal of the laborer is to save money, buy land, and thus be his own master. The provision of garden plots partly meets this aim. "Unfortunately when the tea gardens were being laid out the importance of providing rice land was not recognized as a factor in keeping a contented labour force. Hence some gardens have no rice land, others have a very limited amount and others again possess extensive tracts of jungle which can be cleared and planted. The Inquiry Committee of 1921–2 found that a garden possessing extensive rice land usually had a more stable labour force. They found also that the allotment and distribution of the land was on no fixed system and that the irregularity was a grievance among the workers." [35] Many workers have moved off the estates altogether to take up rice land elsewhere. Since Assam, especially in the upper Brahmaputra valley, has been a pioneer land where new soil was available, this was easily possible. In 1921 it was estimated that half a million persons were living outside the gardens whose presence was initially due to the gardens. These, added to the 840,000 immigrants and their descendants still on the estates, made approximately 1.3 million, or one-sixth of Assam's total population, who were there on account of the tea industry.

In the future less recruitment will be necessary. Already some estates have gone for decades without additional recruits from outside the Province. The trend of recruitment is downward. The natural increase of the estate population and of the population of Assam as a whole, make it increasingly possible to secure local labor. Various observers have called attention to the increasing fluidity of labor within the province, and the increasing tendency of estate managers to look to local sources. Some of the estates have adopted the practice of sending out motor buses to bring in labor from the villages. Outside recruitment will continue, especially in unusually good years when a big labor force is needed quickly. Short-term enlistment was instituted around 1926–27, during a period of great demand. After two more decades the migration of estate labor to Assam should, however, virtually cease.

To the Assamese the immigrant workers on the estates are "foreigners," and their great influx has created a problem of accommodation and assimilation in the Province. Some of the recruits belong to clean castes, others to unclean castes, and some to aboriginal tribes, such as Mundas and Santals. But in Assam they are all of one class, and that the lowest of all. "In Assam a 'cooly' is always a 'cooly' and whether he works on a garden or whether he has left the garden and settled down as an ordinary agriculturist, his social position is nil. From the point of view of Assamese society a person belonging to any cooly caste or tribe is a complete outsider and is as 'exterior' as any of the indigenous castes I have classed as exterior. Indeed from many points of view the social position of coolies and ex-coolies is worse than any class in the province; they are educationally terribly backward; they have no recognized leaders or associations to press their claims or to work for their social advancement, they are foreigners to the country and, as a class, they are much addicted to liquor." [36] In 1931 there were about 1.4 million persons falling into the coolie class in Assam. Of these approximately 900,000 were employed in the gardens, and 500,000 were living outside the gardens and earning their livelihood in some other way.

The districts in which the greatest number of tea garden workers are found, according to the 1931 census, are Lakhimpur (250,000), Sibsagar (234,000), Sylhet (178,000), Cachar (148,000), Darrang (133,000), and Nowgong (24,000). These district figures are too high, because they include management and clerical personnel as well as laborers; but they show the relative magnitude and hence the relative drawing power so far as migration is concerned. [37]

So far the estate agriculture of the Northeastern region has been treated as if it were an exclusively Assam affair. Actually this is not the case, for no less than 257,000 tea estate workers, or roughly a fourth of the total for the entire region, were found in Bengal, according to 1931 figures. Practically all of the Bengal tea workers are concentrated in two districts, Jalpaiguri (186,953) and Darjeeling (60,288). These districts contain the same type of territory as Assam. Bounded by Assam, Bhutan, Sikkim, and Nepal, they draw many non-Indian workers, especially from Nepal. [38] But they also draw Indians as well. For instance, in 1931 Darjeeling had 24,540, or 7.7 per cent, of its people born in Bihar and Orissa, and Jalpaiguri had 29,191, or 3 per cent, born there. [39]

It is now possible to summarize our findings concerning the movement of estate labor. To begin with, there are only two regions (the southwestern and northeastern) where the demand for this type of labor exercises a significant influence on internal migration. The estates are so concentrated within these regions that 96 per cent of all workers principally occupied in tea, rubber, and coffee cultivation are found in only 17 districts (out of a total of several hundred districts in India). As between the two regions, the northeastern has by far the preponderance of estate labor. Ten districts, two in Bengal and eight in Assam, have 82 per cent of all those principally occupied in estate cultivation, whereas seven districts in the southwestern region have only 14 per cent of such workers. The southwestern region is able to draw labor from local sources to about the same extent as any other region, since the area around the estates is already densely populated. In the Assam-Bengal area, however, the demand is greater and the local population much sparser, with the result that long-range migration is stimulated. The province furnishing most of this estate labor is apparently Bihar and Orissa, with Bengal, Central Provinces and Berar, United Provinces, and Madras coming next in the order named. The Assam-Bengal estates therefore draw labor liberally from half way across India. So remote is this northeastern estate area, so different its people, that it has seemed like a foreign country to the migrants. Indeed, the system of recruitment, the abuses, the complaints, the legal revisions—all are reminiscent of Indian emigration to overseas colonies. The effect of the migration upon the estate territory has been to create a numerous coolie class at the bottom of the social scale and to promote a very rapid growth of population. In the nature of the case the migration is bound to be a temporary phenomenon. Whereas it was for a long time the second strongest current of internal migration—second only to the movement to the cities—it is bound to diminish and come to a halt during the next two or three decades.

MOVEMENT TO NEW FARM AREAS

It happens that Assam is the center not only of one type of migration but also of another. Being one of the few places

---

[35] Read, op. cit., pp. 148, 151–52.
[36] Census of India, 1931, Vol. 3 (Assam), Part 1, p. 222.
[37] ibid., pp. 222–24.
[38] See Chapter 12, supra.
[39] Census of India, 1931, Vol. 5 (Bengal & Sikkim), Part 1, p. 89.

left in the subcontinent where extensive tracts of rich agricultural land awaited the plow, this province became the destination of a swarm of indigenous farmers seeking new land to cultivate. The movement, as distinguished from the recruitment of estate labor, may be called "farmer migration." It involves short-distance movement and is not facilitated by systematic recruitment.

Elsewhere in the subcontinent—notably the Punjab—there are other cases of "farmer migration," but usually such movements, presently to be discussed, have been set in motion by the development of new irrigation projects. In Assam, however, no irrigation was necessary. The rich lands simply needed clearing to be ready for cultivation.

THE MOVEMENT TO NEW ASSAM FARM LANDS

Curiously, despite Bengal's long-standing congestion of population and scarcity of land, the mass migration of Bengalese into the valleys of Assam did not start until after 1900. The census report for 1911 mentions this movement for the first time. At that date, however, only the advance guard of what was to be a huge army had arrived. There were 159,000 persons born in Bengal but living in Assam, excluding those on tea estates. A crescendo of farmer migration was reached in the next decade, for in 1921 there were 348,000 Bengalese in the Province excluding tea estates.[40] The number of Bengali farmers had increased enormously, while the number of Bengali estate workers had declined. Throughout the period of migration to Assam, the intruders from Bengal have come to farm, not to work on estates. The estate laborers have been recruited from more distant places.

The increase in farmer migration between 1911 and 1921 was characterized by a gradual spread up the Brahmaputra valley. At first the cultivators simply spilled over into the nearby district of Goalpara, and, as late as 1911, the other districts of the valley contained only a few thousand Bengali, most of whom were clerks, traders, and professional men rather than farmers. But during the 1911–1921 decade the agricultural expansion was extended far up the valley, and the colonists came to form an appreciable part of the population of all the four lower and central districts. Only the two upper districts (Sibsagar and Lakhimpur) remained practically untouched. A fifth of Goalpara's population was Bengal-born by 1921, a seventh of Nowgong's; Kamrup was filling up fast, and Darrang was being explored beyond the river banks by prospective settlers. All told, in the Brahmaputra valley, the Bengal-born settlers increased fourfold between 1911 and 1921, to attain a total of 258,000 in the valley and 6,000 in the hills. Adding children born, there were probably 300,000 of them.

By 1931 the number of persons born in Bengal had reached the surprising total of 575,000. Thus the influx of settlers from Bengal continued to gain during the 1921–1931 decade, but the influx from other provinces—provinces that furnished laborers rather than farmers—lagged behind (there being 100,000 fewer immigrants from them in 1931 than in 1921).[41] The farm migration into Assam has therefore been a later development than the labor migration—later in getting started and later in stopping. Through 1931 no end of the movement was in sight. By 1941 the density of the Surma valley had reached 404 per square mile, which explains in part why migration to that area had slowed down; but the density in the

much larger Brahmaputra valley was still only 239,[42] which leaves plenty of room for future settlement. It is generally recognized that Assam still contains much good land not yet put to the plow.

Most of the settlers came from a single Bengal district—Mymensingh. Table 44 shows how the people from Mymensingh came to constitute an ever larger percentage of the Bengali horde moving into Assam from 1911 to 1931. Did this movement give any relief to population pressure in Mymensingh? No. Prior to 1911 Mymensingh had the fastest growth of any district in Bengal except the urban areas and three Chittagong districts. During the period of heavy exodus to Assam, its population grew less rapidly, but nevertheless continued to grow. In 1911 its density was 724 per square mile, which was 29 per cent above the density of the average Bengal district. By 1931 the density had risen to 823, which was 34 per cent above the average. The migration to Assam has not therefore helped Mymensingh's population problem. The reason is that the migration has been small compared to Mymensingh's total population. It had 4.5 million inhabitants in 1911, 6 million in 1941. The number of persons living in the Assam Valley in 1931 but born in Mymensingh was only 6 per cent of the district's population at that date. The migration, though large from Assam's point of view, was rather insignificant from the point of view of Mymensingh.

TABLE 44

Growth of Bengal-Born Population in Assam, 1911–1931
(000's omitted) [1]

| Date | Born in Bengal | | Enumerated in Assam Valley (3) | Per Cent of Assam Valley Bengalese Born in Mymensingh (2 ÷ 3) (4) |
	Total [2] (1)	Born in Mymensingh (2)		
1911	194 [3]	37	120	30.8
1921	376	172	301	57.1
1931	575	311	496	62.7

[1] Unless otherwise noted, figures are derived from *Census of India,* 1931, Vol. 3 (Assam), Part 1, p. 50.
[2] *ibid.,* p. 55. Includes those born in Bengal States.
[3] *ibid.,* 1921, Vol. 3 (Assam), p. 38.

How are the settlers from Bengal, and particularly from Mymensingh, regarded in Assam? In certain districts the Bengal-born have become the dominant element in the population, so they cannot be ignored. Here is the way the 1931 census report of the province describes the influx:

"Where there is waste land thither flock the Mymensinghias. In fact the way in which they have seized upon the vacant areas in the Assam Valley seems almost uncanny. Without fuss, without tumult, without undue trouble to the district revenue staffs, a population which must amount to over half a million has transplanted itself from Bengal to the Assam Valley during the last twenty five years. It looks like a marvel of administrative organization on the part of Government but it is nothing of the sort: the only thing I can compare it to is the mass movement of a large body of ants.

"[In Nowgong District] they have opened up vast tracts of dense jungle along the south bank of the Brahmaputra and have occupied nearly all the lands which are open for settlement in this tract. These people have brought in their wake wealth, industry, and general prosperity to the whole district.

[40] *Census of India,* 1921, Vol. 3 (Assam), pp. 38, 40.
[41] *ibid.,* 1931, Vol. 3 (Assam), Part 1, p. 44.

[42] *ibid.,* 1941, Vol. 9 (Assam), Tables, p. 64.

They have improved the health of the countryside by clearing the jungles and converting the wilderness into prosperous villages. Their industry as agriculturists has become almost proverbial. . . .

"Not having sufficient land of their own in their home districts and leading a life of difficulty with the drawbacks peculiar to undertenants of Bengal Zamindars in overcrowded villages, it was quite natural for these industrious agriculturists to be attracted in large numbers. . . . Their hunger for land was so great that, in their eagerness to grasp as much as they could cultivate they not infrequently encroached on Government reserves and on lands belonging to the local people from which they could be evicted only with great difficulty: In the beginning they had their own way and there was frequent friction with the indigenous population who did not like their dealings as neighbours. The appointment of a special Colonization Officer and the adoption of certain definite rules tended much to regularize settlement and prevent friction. Boundary lines had to be fixed restraining the immigrants from occupying lands near Assamese villages by trespass or purchase but even these steps were often found to be inadequate to protect the Assamese villagers. Many immigrants had to be punished with fines and ejectments, sometimes, with the assistance of the police. . . . The local Assamese at first did not like the advent of these peoples in their midst, but gradually as they came to see their better side—their industry, their knowledge of agriculture, their contribution to the general prosperity of the district—their prejudices and dislikes are beginning to disappear." [43]

With their descendants, the Bengali settlers represent a large and permanent addition to the population. Most of them —probably 85 per cent—are Muslim, whereas the original population of Assam was predominantly Hindu with a large tribal element. Mymensingh, the Bengal district furnishing most of the migrants, was 77 per cent Muslim in 1931. Put in other terms, the Muslim population of Assam province increased, between 1881 and 1931, by 109 per cent.[44] The growth of the Muslim population affords the main discordant note in the immigration into Assam. The 1931 census report for Assam says that "the relations between the Hindu and Muslim communities in Assam have undergone a decided change for the worse in the last ten years." [45] These were prophetic words. As a result of the Muslim immigration, Assam lost nearly all of its second largest district by area and its largest in population—namely, Sylhet. In 1891 Sylhet was 47 per cent Muslim; by 1941 it had become 61 per cent so, and in the partition of India it was awarded to Pakistan.

But the agricultural migration had already begun to taper off by the time of partition. Between 1931 and 1941 the growth of the Assam population was mainly a result of natural increase rather than immigration. But since there are still lands available in the province, and since the density of settlement is still low compared with many other Indian provinces, it can be expected that many more will eventually come, restrained only by the new international border between Assam and East Pakistan. "It is sad but by no means improbable that in another thirty years Sibsagar district will be the only part of Assam in which an Assamese will find himself at home." [46]

Assam, having been the center of two kinds of immigration,

has been from a demographic point of view the fastest growing province in the Indian subcontinent. The population figures given at the beginning of the discussion of estate-labor migration show how rapidly the total number of inhabitants has increased. An index of net immigration shows that Assam has had the greatest attractive power of any province.

It seems clear that this migration into Assam is simply extending to that area the same population balance prevailing in the rest of India and Pakistan. Without cities, without industry, depending solely upon colonial or homestead agriculture, the province is destined to become merely another densely settled region with a heavy population eking out an existence on the land. The migration has brought no real or permanent relief to the overcrowded districts from which the migrants have come, and it promises to bring to the new territory conditions virtually identical with those from which the migrants have fled.

THE MOVEMENT TO CANAL COLONIES

A different type of farmer migration is encountered when new territory is opened up by the installation of irrigation. In our earlier discussion of famine it was shown to what extent the subcontinent has become a region of irrigation. Some of the projects have opened up hundreds of thousands of acres to agriculture. The settlement of these areas has been an important factor in permanent migration. As contrasted with Assam, most of the projects are under government control and consequently more supervision is exercised over the conditions of settlement. This has been preeminently true in the Punjab.

The Punjab. The Punjab has seen the development of irrigation on a gigantic scale. In 1887–88 the canals of the Province already irrigated 2.3 million acres. With the opening of the Lower Chenab Canal, the area rose to 6 million acres in 1900–1901. During the 1911–1920 decade the Triple Canal Project materialized, so that by 1921 the total area under canal irrigation amounted to more than 10 million acres, nearly equal to the total plowed area of England and Wales at that time. Later the Sutlej Valley Project was opened, and the total area rose to the unprecedented figure of 12.4 million acres by 1930.[47]

"In 1880 the greater portion of the Punjab consisted of arid waste with a rainfall which varied from 5 to 15 inches per annum, and this desert area was sparsely populated by nomad tribes of camel and sheep graziers. In order to open up some of these waste tracts, and at the same time to relieve the pressure on the land in highly populated areas elsewhere, Government took over these unclaimed lands as Crown waste and embarked on a scheme of colonisation. The country was first surveyed and divided into large squares or rectangles; these in turn were subdivided into smaller squares which varied in area in the first colonies from 22½ to 27½ acres each, but were standardized at 25 acres in all later schemes. Canals were then constructed and village boundaries demarcated, one or more watercourses being allotted to each village. In the first colonies these squares were sold for nominal sums, chiefly in small blocks, to peasant proprietors or given free to military pensioners. The success of these first colonies was so great and the value of land rose so rapidly that Government eventually adopted the principle of auctioning the best lands to the highest bidder. A large area in each colony was, however, set aside for selected peasant proprietors who were allotted one or two squares each on fixed terms; these enabled

[43] *Census of India,* 1931, Vol. 3 (Assam), Part 1, pp. 51–52.

[44] *ibid.,* Vol. 1, Part 1, p. 390.

[45] *ibid.,* p. 197.

[46] *ibid.,* Vol. 3 (Assam), Part 1, p. 52.

[47] *ibid.,* Vol. 17 (Punjab), Part 1, pp. 38–39.

them to acquire proprietary rights after paying for their land by instalments in a stated number of years.

"Colonisation has gradually developed into a fine art. Peasants of the same caste and creed are allotted lands together in the same village. All villages are laid out on a model plan round a central well, with a separate section for servants' quarters. Village roads are aligned ahead, so that each man can get to his holding without trespassing on the land of his neighbour. Concessions are given to those who plant and maintain a shade line of trees along these roads. Once cultivation begins in earnest, market towns are soon established with good district roads radiating into the surrounding country. Cotton factories and oil and flour mills are built by private enterprise. Thus within a very few years a wild desert is turned into a highly cultivated country inhabited by a happy, prosperous people, each man owning his plot of land and living in more sanitary surroundings than are to be found elsewhere in India. . . .

"The success achieved by these schemes led to the construction of the Lower Chenab Canal, one of the largest and probably the most successful and remunerative . . . in India. . . .

"Lyallpur, the capital of this colony, is now a large flourishing town with an enormous export trade. The capital headworks have been remodelled and enlarged and the system now irrigates 2¼ million acres annually. The accumulated surplus of revenue over expenditure is nearly Rs. 400 millions and the return on the capital outlay is about 40 per cent per annum. The value of crops raised annually is nearly five times the original capital cost of the works." [48]

Since the driest areas of the Punjab, and hence the main irrigation projects, are in the West, the center of population in the province has been gradually shifting westward since 1881.[49] The Northwest Dry Area gained population at twice the rate of any other part during 1921–31, and at a much higher rate than the others in both 1911–21 and 1931–41. The particular districts in the dry region which have experienced the greatest jump in irrigated area are the ones that have also had the largest gain in population, as shown below:

PER CENT GROWTH OF POPULATION

	1921–1931 [50]	1931–1941 [51]
Montgomery	45.8	32.9
Multan	32.1	28.0
Bahawalpur St.	26.0	36.2

These rapid rates of growth pertain to a wide area, for the three units in question contain a fifth of the entire Punjab territory.

The main cause of such rapid demographic growth "is the influx of cultivators into these areas as a result of colonization." [52] But there is also a secondary result—namely, a stimulated natural increase. In general the districts that have had the largest increase of agricultural area have also experienced the greatest excess of births over deaths. The coefficient of

correlation between the two series is .90. Thus the opening up of farm colonies in dry areas produces rapid population growth due both to migration and to natural increase. The stepped-up natural increase is doubtless due in part to the migration itself, which brings an excess of people of childbearing age into the region. For instance, in the three districts having a rapid growth of irrigation the proportion of all women who fall in the ages 15–30 is 31.2 per cent, compared with 26.4 per cent in the rest of the Punjab. The fact that the immigrants are in the young ages also reduces the death rate, so that the natural increase turns out to be substantial. Whether or not there is, in addition, a tendency for age-specific fertility to rise is hard to say, but any significant rise seems doubtful.

"The largest wholesale permanent migration within the Province is the migration to canal colonies." The movement is not likely to abate for some time yet. Lyallpur and Shahpur Districts, the first to be colonized, have ceased to be centers of attraction, their places having been taken by Montgomery, Multan, and Bahawalpur State. During the 1921–31 decade it is calculated that no less than 240,400 persons left their home districts to settle in the canal areas.[53] This is a sizable movement to take place within one Province, though the total population of over 28 million makes it relatively small. Most of the migration to the canal colonies has come from the Province itself. Punjab as a whole lost in migration during the 1921–31 decade. Analysis by district shows that those districts more than half under irrigation had only a slight advantage in immigration from outside the Province. They had 2.2 per cent of their population born outside the Province, as against 1.5 per cent for the other districts. The canal colonies of the Punjab have not exercised the magnetic power that the tea gardens and virgin lands of Assam have exercised.

MOVEMENT INTO SIND

The greatest development of irrigation in India has taken place in the Punjab. That province therefore affords the most striking illustration of migration to canal colonies. But Sind has recently been the recipient of the largest single irrigation project in the country, the famous Sukkur or Lloyd Barrage, which is expected to irrigate over 5.5 million acres.[54] Already in 1931 the districts of Sind showed a faster rate of growth than the average district in the Bombay Presidency, although irrigation for this project was not started until 1932.[55] Between 1921 and 1931 Sind's density per square mile increased 19 per cent, whereas the density of the British Districts of Bombay Presidency as a whole increased only 13 per cent.[56] In 1941 the density of Sind was 17 per cent greater than in 1931, whereas that of Bombay was 16 per cent greater. Without the drawing power of cities, Sind has nevertheless grown rapidly. Yet the average density of the irrigable country is officially estimated as 165 per square mile, which leaves considerable room for further expansion.[57] The migration into Sind will probably never be on a very large scale, however. First, the region has already had some irrigation in the form of inundation canals from the Indus. This method was unreliable, both because the floods could not be counted on and because

[48] Sir Bernard Darley, "Irrigation and Its Possibilities," in Radhakamal Mukerjee (ed.), *Economic Problems of Modern India,* Vol. 1 (London: Macmillan, 1939), pp. 157–58.
[49] *Census of India,* 1931, Vol. 17 (Punjab), Part 1, pp. 12–13.
[50] *ibid.,* p. 64.
[51] *ibid.,* 1941, Vol. 6 (Punjab), pp. 11, 14.
[52] *ibid.,* 1931, Vol. 17 (Punjab), Part 1, p. 64.

[53] *ibid.,* p. 117.
[54] Pramathanath Banerjea, *A Study of Indian Economics* (5th ed.; London: Macmillan, 1940), p. 271.
[55] cf. Radhakamal Mukerjee (ed.), *Economic Problems of Modern India,* Vol. 1 (London: Macmillan, 1939), p. 24.
[56] *Census of India,* 1931, Vol. 8 (Bombay Pres.), Part 1, p. 29.
[57] *ibid.,* 1941, Vol. 12 (Sind), Tables, p. 2.

the river beds shifted their location as a result of silting; but it permitted agriculture where it would not have been possible before. Second, "the alluvial soil of the Sind plain is not so rich as that of the Ganges delta."

Yet the economic situation is "being radically changed through the gradual development of the Lloyd Barrage scheme. There has been already an enormous increase in the area under heavy-yielding food crops and a valuable commercial crop like cotton." In the 1934–35 *kharif* season, the total area under cotton amounted to 676,000 acres, of which 670,000 acres were served by the Rohri and Eastern Nara canals. The normal pre-Barrage area under cotton in Sind amounted to only 280,000 acres.[58] In the 1941 census 366,000 persons out of a total population of 4.5 million were born outside of Sind. This represents 8 per cent of the population, which is fairly large but less than that of Assam. The latter, with a slightly larger area than Sind but with a population almost twice as large, had 15 per cent of its population born outside its borders in 1931.

The Punjab and Sind have been selected as exemplars of migration determined by irrigation projects. Since such projects have been developed in many different areas, it follows that a large amount of internal movement has been caused by this factor—though it is impossible to say how much. It may be that the total movement is greater than that caused by estates, but because the latter are concentrated in two limited areas, it is easier to measure their effect, which has seemed more spectacular. In the future the new irrigation schemes now being planned may give rise to new waves of farm migration, but as irrigation approaches the ultimate limit of expansion and as new farm areas become ever more scarce, internal migration will result less from agricultural developments and more from industrial progress.

RELIGION, MIGRATION, AND PARTITION

By all odds the greatest short-term mass migration in the history of the Indian peninsula, and one of the greatest in the world, was that across the borders of newborn Pakistan. The exact magnitude of this exchange of populations will never be known, but official estimates place the figure during the major great wave (within a little more than a year) at about 12 million—roughly half being Muslims entering Pakistan and half being Hindus and Sikhs leaving that country. Initially the greatest part of the movement was between East and West Pakistan, but approximately 1,150,000 non-Muslims left East Bengal for the Union of India.[59] Later, in 1949 and 1950, the main trouble centered in East Bengal, with the result that the Bengal refugees in India were reckoned in June, 1950, at about 3.5 million. The total figure for the entire migration, both ways, may eventually exceed 15 million.

This great mass migration must be measured not only in terms of the numbers involved but also in terms of the damage to crops and industries, the huge relief problems imposed, and the loss of lives, the broken homes, and the human bitterness. "Instead of anticipating developments and preparing a constructive scheme for channelizing the imminent mass movements, Hindu and Moslem leaders in both Dominions persisted in urging the minority populations not to move, promising fullest protection of life and property. These prom-

ises proved to be worthless." [60] Violence became so prevalent that millions had to move, but the movement was so unplanned, unwanted, and strife-torn that hundreds of thousands died and heavy property losses were sustained. Refugee camps were hastily put up, but they were inadequate and costly. The problem of relief was still a large item of expense to the governments concerned two years after the catastrophe. The memory of senseless and brutal bloodshed will possibly remain a permanent source of resentment as between the two countries.

Whatever else it did, the mass migration shifted the position of the religious groups as between the two countries.[61] This in itself represented a sharp historical change because, prior to 1947, there had been little connection between religion and migration. The Hindus and Muslims had been for decades in about the same spots, and neither of them showed a greater propensity to move than the other. Between 1901 and 1931 there was apparently a slight tendency for the Muslims to become more concentrated in their particular areas, but this tendency was reversed in 1931–41, when they became slightly more diffused.

Information on this topic is hard to secure from the censuses, because birthplace data were not regularly cross-tabulated with religion. But, as noted in the discussion of marriage migration, the Muslims seemingly have a lesser tendency to short-run movement. They apparently have not, however, been more heavily represented than the Hindus in the rural-urban migrations, as shown by the data on relative urbanization from 1911 to 1941, as given in Chapter 16. It remains to be seen what the creation of Pakistan and the exchange of religious groups will do to this trend. Do Muslim refugees from the Union of India settle in the cities and thus become more urbanized than they were before they migrated? A census of Pakistan, if taken within ten years after the division of India, will throw light on this and related questions.[62]

ABSENCE OF PAST POLITICAL CONTROL OVER INTERNAL MOVEMENT

Until Pakistan was split off, the whole of India was a land of free migration. There were no restraints upon the movement of people from province to province, from state to state, or from British to non-British India. Indeed, there seemed to be only slight limitation even upon foreign immigration into India, other than that imposed by the foreign countries themselves. Persons from Nepal, French India, and Portuguese India entered the country without let or hindrance. This free movement of people in a land so diverse as India was remarkable, comparable only to the freedom of commerce in the area. It was undoubtedly a help in promoting economic enterprise and in adjusting population imbalances. The fact that there has not been more complaint against it may perhaps be attributed to the smallness of the total movement.

Some criticism has been voiced. The immigration of Nepalese, especially in Bengal and Assam, has been criticized. Also, the estate laborers in Assam have received a low status, and the influx of agricultural settlers from Bengal has sometimes been regarded with resentment by the native Assamese and some governing officials. It is worth going further and examining other expressions of opinion concerning the value or disvalue of migration.

[58] Mukerjee, *op. cit.*, pp. 23–24.
[59] Joseph B. Schechtman, *Population Transfers in Asia* (New York: Hallsby Press, 1949), pp. 18–19.
[60] *ibid.*, pp. 24–25.
[61] See Chapter 20.
[62] The demographic aspects of the division of India into two dominions are treated in Chapter 20.

The 1931 report for Travancore points out that this state has always had a net immigration, and that what has accounted for this net influx has been the entrance of agricultural laborers to work on the estates. If these field laborers had not come in, the immigration and emigration would have balanced each other. "As against 76,699 foreign labourers working in estates, the Travancorean labourers employed therein number only 25,791." This prompted the Census Commissioner to ask "why the estates import foreign labour when there is a large volume of unemployment in the country? If the estates would recruit all their labour from the State itself, more than 75,000 persons could find work, and to that extent the number of the unemployed here would go down." He thereupon calls upon the people of Travancore to "be prepared to migrate to the hills and demonstrate their fitness for work in the tea gardens," thereby gradually replacing the "foreign" workers.[63]

In the United Provinces the situation is different. There one finds a considerable net loss by migration, and the question is raised as to whether this is a benefit or disadvantage for the province. In the 1931 report it is stated that "emigration to the tea-gardens has become unpopular in this province, largely as a result of a deliberate campaign against it by non-cooperators in the early part of the decade." [64] The Report does not state the motive behind this opposition, but doubtless the motive was not the welfare of the province as such. Later this question is raised by the Census Commissioner himself, who says: "I am inclined to think that this outlet is a blessing. The pressure of the population on the soil in this province is severe, and growing heavier year by year. There has been no widespread complaint of shortage of agricultural labour at any time during the past decade, and since the fall in prices of agricultural produce labour has been surplus to requirements in the rural areas. Industrialists in this province have experienced no difficulty in securing all the labour they required, and in fact the development in industries has been far too slow to absorb the surplus labour resulting from a rapidly increasing population and a lessened demand for agricultural labour." [65]

This attitude is but the complement of the Travancorean one. Both reflect the common sentiment that immigration is all right so long as it does not interfere with the employment of local people. Out of this feeling there might, in the future, grow a movement to restrict internal mobility. However, the feeling is not strong, and any such eventuality seems remote, although it is almost certain to play a role as between Pakistan and the Indian Union.

SUMMARY

The population of the subcontinent, like that of most peasant regions, is relatively immobile. The immobility is due not only to the predominance of agriculture, but also to the caste system, to early marriage and the joint family, to the diversity of language and culture, and to the lack of education. This immobility is perhaps loosening a bit, especially for long-distance migration; but on the whole it is hard to find much change since 1891. It requires a major catastrophe, like that attending the partition (in which people were forced to move), to produce much internal migration.

Despite the relative immobility, the absolute numbers in-

[63] Census of India, 1931, Vol. 28 (Travancore), Part 1, p. 87.
[64] ibid., Vol. 18 (United Provinces), Part 1, p. 199.
[65] ibid., p. 201.

volved in the internal movements are large. In 1931 some 12 million were enumerated outside the province or state of birth. The numbers involved, and the economic importance of migration, make the problem worth studying. It is to be regretted that almost the only data on internal migration are derived from birthplace statistics, which give at best only an oblique and distorted picture of actual movements.

The general drift of male migration in the northern part of the subcontinent has been eastward. This is the opposite of the drift of females through marriage migration. Doubtless the eastward drift of the males has been caused by the industrial and urban development around Bengal, the tendency of overseas migrants to leave from the East coast, and the attractive power of the frontier zone in Assam. The westward trend of female marriage migration is surely caused by the custom of hypergamy, coupled with village exogamy. In southern India the most noticeable tendency is a slight northward movement of males, no doubt caused by the same factors that influence the eastward movement across the north.

Between British India and the Native States the migration current has varied. It was directed toward the British territory more often—in 1901, 1911, and 1921—but it went to the Native States more heavily—in 1891 and 1931. There was a great deal of regularity in the states that gained or lost to British territory, and in the provinces that gained or lost to Native territory.

A large part of short-range movement is due to marriage migration. This helps to explain why here, as in most other places, the shorter the migration the more feminine it is. Probably more than 17 per cent of the total interdistrict movement is due to marriage migration.

As between Muslims and Hindus, it would seem that the two have been approximately equal with reference to their migratory tendencies. The Muslims are addicted less to marriage migration and perhaps slightly more to long-range migration.

Rural-urban migration accounts for roughly between 13 and 70 per cent of migration as measured by the persons enumerated outside their district of birth, depending on the province. When the migration is broken down according to distance, it is found, as one might expect, that the cities account for a lesser part of short-range migration and a much larger part of long-range migration.

An important source of internal movement is that caused by the demand for estate labor. The estates are highly concentrated, being located almost exclusively in the northeast corner of India (Assam and Bengal) and the southwest corner (Madras, Travancore, Mysore, Coorg). Of the two areas, that of Assam-Bengal is by far the more important. Migration into this area has gone through the stages of indenture and kangani recruitment, has experienced a history of progressive legal regulation to correct abuses, and has in nearly every way been similar to overseas emigration. There are signs, however, that the region is filling up, and that laborers are being increasingly secured from local sources. Assam has also been the focus of one of the other great migratory movements—the influx of farmers from Bengal (especially the district of Mymensingh) to take up virgin farm land. These twin movements, the one of estate labor and the other of farmers, have made Assam the most powerful magnet of migrants among all the major provinces. The only other farmer movement worth mentioning is that to canal colonies, principally in the Punjab; but this current has produced nothing to equal the Assam phenomenon.

From the political point of view, India has been a vast and diverse area enjoying free migration. This has doubtless had the effect of relieving population pressure in certain parts, of stimulating economic enterprise, of loosening the social organization slightly, and of giving India a somewhat greater unity than she would otherwise have had. There have been murmurs against the policy of letting people come into particular states and provinces, but these have not amounted to much. Now that India is split into two sovereign nations, differing from each other in religion, it can be expected that barriers to migration across their borders will arise. What was internal migration has now become international migration, and throughout the world there is a tendency for international migration to be impeded. To this extent the Indian peninsula has been deprived, so to speak, of one of its degrees of freedom.

PART VI

SOCIAL STRUCTURE AND SOCIAL CHANGE

++

CHAPTER 15

Urbanization: The Growth of Cities

++

It is impossible to understand the population problem of the Indian region without also understanding the social structure. This fact has become abundantly plain in previous chapters. Naturally, then, our discussion turns to an analysis of the social characteristics of the population, and to the social changes that point the way to future demographic developments. There is no better topic to begin with than the growth of cities.

The modern city in Asia is of peculiar significance, because it is the diffusion center for Western traits. The city is where social change begins, where the specialization, talent, and organization necessary for originating and executing new ideas are available. City development is therefore a good index of past economic progress and a safe augury of new progress to come. In many ways what is happening in the city today is what will be happening to all of India in the future.

Because of her agricultural economy, the subcontinent has always been predominantly rural. It has not been rural, however, in precisely the American sense. Instead of a single-farm system with each family dwelling on its land, the region has had a medieval-type village system. Beset for centuries by the dangers of political instability—e.g. organized banditry, confiscatory taxation, military looting, and local tariffs—the agricultural population has banded together for mutual protection in compact villages. The surrounding farm land has been cut into strips to equalize for the villagers the advantages and disadvantages of the surrounding terrain. Some land, of course, was left for common pasture, and some for waste.

The tiny, self-sufficient rural village has persisted until today. At present, because the Pax Britannica long rendered self-protection unnecessary, there is a tendency to move closer to the land being tilled. This saves time, permits more intensive cultivation, and facilitates the protection of crops, particularly if the village was located on a hill or in some other unfavorable (but protected) spot.[1] But as yet the movement has not gone far. Even when the villagers move closer to the land, they tend to do so in compact hamlets. Pakistan and India are still countries of tiny and nearly self-sufficient agricultural villages.

The cities that arose in pre-British India were few in number and archaic in type. They suffered from the same unsettled conditions that prevented the single-farm mode of rural settlement. They did not, for example, rest primarily upon industrial and commercial development, but rather on political and religious functions. The Muslim rulers frequently shifted the seat of government, and when they did so the capital city suddenly dwindled to nothing and a new city arose

around the next governmental site. Cities also arose at strategic points where military necessity required a permanent camp, such as bridgeheads, mountain passes, and cross-roads. Still other cities arose at religious sites, where pilgrimages were made and temples were built. For a long time commerce and industry followed the cities located for non-economic reasons. Only recently has the modern city, based on industry, trade, and natural resources, come into prominence. The emergence of this new type of city means that urbanization can go, and is going, much further than it went under the old conditions. It is this new city that is quickening the pulse of social change in the Indian area.

GROWTH OF THE URBAN POPULATION

Like other modern developments in India, the growth of cities began in a small way and made gradual but recently enhanced progress. The percentage of the population urban since 1881, accepting the census definition,[2] runs as follows:

1881	9.3
1891	9.4
1901	10.0
1911	9.4
1921	10.2
1931	11.1
1941	12.8

The growth has doubtless been steadier than these figures indicate. For instance, the decline in 1911 is accidental, since a plague epidemic in that year caused many cities to be temporarily evacuated. In 1931 the percentage urban was probably lower than it should have been, because both the depression and the non-coöperation movement tended to produce subnormal returns for cities. If so, the growth from 1931 to 1941 was exaggerated, yet there is little doubt that the pace did quicken during this decade, just as it had during the previous one.

Figure 29 compares the trend in the percentage urban in India with the trend in the United States. For purposes of comparability only places of 5,000 or more inhabitants were counted as urban in each case, thus ignoring the smaller places admitted as "urban" by the census. Not only is the urban percentage lower in India than in the United States, but its rate of increase is slower. During the entire period from 1881

[1] *Census of India,* 1931, Vol. 18 (United Provinces), Part 1, pp. 122–23.

[2] The definition of "urban" includes places of 5,000 or larger, but makes numerous special exceptions. So far as possible the figures for various censuses have been made comparable by us. The problem of definition is discussed in detail in Appendix H.

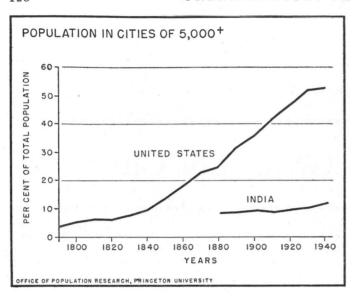

FIGURE 29. Growth of Population in Cities of 5,000 and Over, India and United States Compared.

to 1941 the percentage of the Indian population in urban places increased only 41 per cent, whereas in the United States it increased 111 per cent. Urbanization in India between these dates resembles urbanization in the United States during an earlier period—between about 1790 and 1850. Only in the last decade, 1931–41, did the pace of urbanization in India exceed that in the United States during a contemporary period. The gain was 18.3 per cent in India, as against a gain of only 0.7 per cent in the United States. It appears that India is just beginning a period of rapid urbanization, comparable perhaps to the 1820–30 period in the United States.

Comparative Degree of Urbanization

In 1941 approximately 12.3 per cent of India's population lived in urban places of more than 5,000 inhabitants. As Table 45 shows, this is an extremely low degree of urbanization, compared to most other nations. In 1935 no less than 64.5 per cent of Japan's population lived in such places, and in 1940 no less than 25.8 per cent of Puerto Rico's population did so.

Table 45 gives, for various countries, the percentage of the population in cities of various sizes, and a rough index of urbanization. Only one country in the table, Guatemala, has a lower index than India. Doubtless there are other countries, for which figures were not obtainable, which have a still lower degree of urbanization, but the fact remains that India is quite low in this regard.

If the rate of urbanization should continue as it has been during the last few decades, about 15 per cent of the India-Pakistan population should be living in cities of 5,000-plus by 1951. Even this will represent a low scale of urbanization.[3]

GROWTH OF CITIES OF DIFFERENT SIZE

There are two ways of measuring urban growth. One—the instantaneous method—ascertains the population in all urban categories at each and every census, tracing the changes in each class regardless of the cities that make it up. The other—the continuous method—begins with particular cities and traces the subsequent expansion of these groups. Each method answers a different question. The first shows what is happening to the population in terms of its distribution by

[3] The relative degree of urbanization in Pakistan and the Union of India is discussed in another place. See Chapter 20.

size of city. The second shows what is happening to specific cities as a result of their initial size differences. Since the methods are complementary, both are employed here.

The instantaneous method has the disadvantage of including, at each census, new towns in a given class that were not in that class before. Thus in 1901 the cities 5,000 to 10,000 had 3.4 per cent fewer inhabitants than in 1891. This does not mean that places *of this size in 1891* actually lost population. It means, rather, that some of the cities of this size in 1891 grew so fast that by 1901 they had graduated to a higher category. This is indicated by the fact that the next higher class (cities 10,000 to 20,000) grew 18.2 per cent. But the method does show the actual distribution of the population in urban places of different size at each census.

Figure 30 gives for India a synopsis of the growth of the urban population by the instantaneous method.[4] It demonstrates that the larger categories of city are increasing their proportion of the population faster than the smaller ones. Thus in 1941 the cities of half a million or more had 130 per cent more people than in 1931. This was due mainly to the fact that four new cities (Hyderabad, Lahore, Ahmedabad, and Delhi) entered this class during the decade. In previous decades the "500,000-and-over" class did not show a great increase in its population, comparatively speaking, because no new cities had entered that class since Madras entered it in 1901. During World War II the great impetus to the ur-

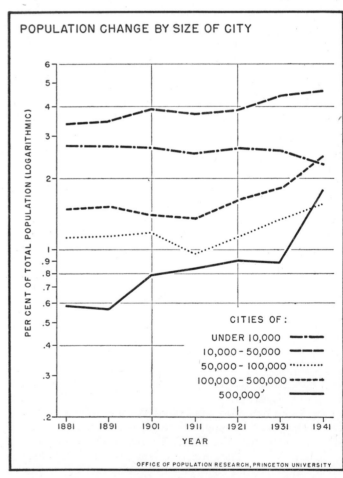

FIGURE 30. Changing Distribution of India's Urban Population by Class of City, 1881–1941.

[4] For 1941 the distribution of cities under 50,000 had to be estimated; the method was to assume that the change in the proportion that each of the three size classes constituted of the total population of cities between 5,000 and 50,000 was the same in 1931–41 as it was in 1921–31.

TABLE 45

Per Cent of Population in Cities by Size Class for Selected Countries [1]

Region and Country	Year	In Cities 5,000+ Per Cent	In Cities 10,000+ Per Cent	In Cities 25,000+ Per Cent	In Cities 100,000+ Per Cent	Index [a]	Per Cent in the Largest City
Africa							
Egypt	1939	[b]	27.0	19.7	13.2	[b]	8.2
Asia and Oceania							
Australia [2]	1939	71.2	67.9	62.1	47.3	62.1	18.4
New Zealand	1941	52.5	49.4	41.5	31.8	43.8	13.7
Japan	1935	64.5	45.8	36.8	25.3	43.1	8.5
INDIA	1941	12.3	10.5	8.1 [c]	4.2	8.8	0.5
INDIA	1931	10.4	8.5	5.8	2.7	6.8	0.3
European Countries							
Great Britain [3]	1931	81.7 [c]	73.6	63.1	45.2	65.9	20.5
Germany [3]	1939	57.4 [c]	51.7	43.5	31.8	46.1	6.3
France [3]	1936	41.7 [c]	37.5	29.8	16.0	31.2	6.8
Sweden	1940	35.9	32.1	25.6	16.1	27.4	9.3
Greece [3]	1937	33.1 [c]	29.8	23.1	14.8	25.2	7.0
Poland [3]	1931	22.8 [c]	20.5	15.8	10.7	17.4	3.6
Latin America							
Argentina [4, d]	1943 [c]	48.9	46.8	42.7	34.0	43.1	18.5
Chile [4]	1940	44.8	41.1	34.3	23.1	35.8	19.0
Cuba	1943	38.8	35.5	28.8	18.8	30.5	13.8
Venezuela	1941	36.2	31.3	23.3	14.8	26.4	10.4
Panama	1940	26.2	24.7	24.7	17.7	23.4	17.7
Mexico	1940	27.5	21.9	16.8	10.2	19.1	7.4
Puerto Rico	1940	25.8	21.2	15.2	9.0	17.8	9.0
Brazil [4]	1940	21.3	18.4	14.6	11.0	16.3	3.8
Columbia	1938	19.0	15.2	12.1	7.1	13.3	3.7
Guatemala	1940	13.2	8.4	6.0	5.0	8.2	5.0
North America							
United States	1940	52.7	47.6	40.1	28.8	42.3	5.7
Canada	1941	43.0	38.5	32.7	23.0	34.3	7.8

[a] The index of urbanization was computed by adding the percentages in the previous four columns and dividing by four.
[b] Figures not available to the author.
[c] Percentages based on estimated population figures.
[d] Data on cities incomplete.
[1] Except where otherwise indicated, the percentages were computed from census data.
[2] Hammond's *New World Atlas*, 1947, p. 82. The figures for cities of 100,000+ include suburbs. The date of the figures is not certain, but it appears to be 1939.
[3] The figures were taken from United States Department of State, Division of Geography and Cartography, *Europe (without U.S.S.R.): Cities of 10,000 Population and Over by Size Categories, circa 1930*, No. 108, April 5, 1944. The percentage for 5,000+ in each case was estimated by us by assuming that the ratio between the percentage in cities 5,000+ and the percentage in cities 10,000+ was the same as the average ratio in the United States and Canada.
[4] The population figures on which the percentages rest were taken from the *Handbook of Latin American Population Data* (Washington, D.C.: Office of Inter-American Affairs, 1945).

banization process tended to push cities into higher classes, with the result that the larger the category, the greater its population gain as seen in the 1941 census. In previous decades the differential changes had been slight, but it is clear that as a whole the classes above 50,000 gained more rapidly than those under 50,000, especially after 1911.

Turning now to the continuous method, one finds that it can be applied either separately for each decade, the cities being taken as those existing at the beginning of each decade, or to a much longer period. The latter, the simpler technique, has been used here. Towns of various sizes in 1891 were traced through the subsequent censuses to 1941. Unfortunately the data were available only for places over 20,000, but

the results are illuminating nonetheless, as Figures 31, 32, and 33 show. With 1891 as the base, Figure 31 gives the growth of the entire group of cities 20,000 and over in 1891, as compared with the growth of the total Indian population. The growth of the cities was of course much more rapid than that of the total population, especially in the later decades. Figure 32 gives the percentage increase for each class of 1891 city throughout subsequent decades, and Figure 33 summarizes the growth for the entire 1891–1941 period in a bar chart. The larger the class of city in 1891, the faster the subsequent rate of growth. There were only two cities (Calcutta and Bombay) over 500,000 in 1891. They never failed to exceed their 1891 total by a larger proportional margin than any

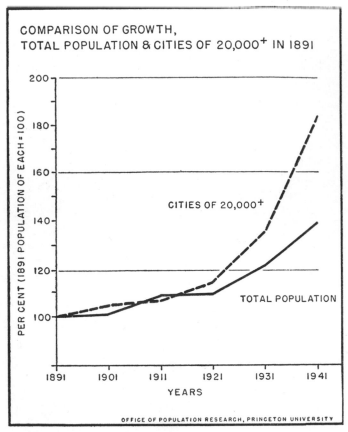

FIGURE 31. Growth of 1891 Cities of 20,000 and Over Compared with the Growth of India's Total Population, 1891–1941. (In each case the population in 1891 = 100.)

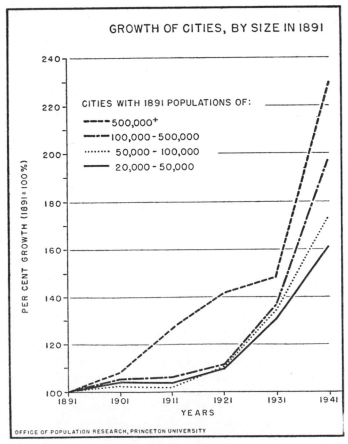

FIGURE 32. Growth of 1891 Cities by Size Classes, India, 1891–1941. (Population of each class in 1891 = 100.)

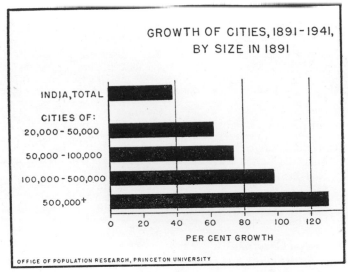

FIGURE 33. Fifty-Year Growth of 1891 Cities by Size Classes, India.

other class. The evidence is clear, therefore, that urbanization is itself a factor in still greater urbanization.

This is what one might expect, because it conforms to the Western pattern of urban development; [5] but precisely for that reason it is of interest to prove it. If urban development in the Indian region is accelerating, if the larger cities are going ahead because they are larger, there is every reason to believe that Westernization itself is going ahead at an accelerating rate.

DEVELOPMENT OF THE FIFTEEN LARGEST CITIES

In 1941 the fifteen largest cities had a combined population of nearly 10 million, or 2.5 per cent of the total population. Sixty years before, in 1891, the fifteen leading cities had only four and a half million inhabitants, or 1.6 per cent of the population. The two lists embraced the same cities, except for three in the 1891 list that were replaced by three new ones in 1941. The fifteen leading cities at each census from 1891 to 1941 are shown in Table 46. It can be seen that there was considerable shifting up and down the scale. In Table 47 the fifteen leading cities in 1941 are shown, together with their population and rank in previous censuses. Calcutta and Bombay have changed places several times, but Madras has always been third and Hyderabad has always been fourth. Lahore, in fifth place in 1941, began in ninth position in 1891 and did not achieve fifth place until 1921. Ahmedabad, now in sixth place, was in fourteenth place in 1891. Delhi's position has remained relatively constant, while Cawnpore's has fluctuated more, and Amritsar's still more. Lucknow has shown a steady decline in rank, as have Benares and Agra. The cities that have shown the greatest gain are Howrah, Karachi, and Nagpur. The three cities that were among the first fifteen in 1891 and subsequently dropped out are Allahabad, Patna, and Jaipur.

THE LOCATION OF INDIA'S CITIES

The percentage of the population in cities of 10,000 and over, by district, is given for 1931 in Map 14. In general it appears that urbanized areas are scattered helter skelter over

[5] cf. Kingsley Davis and Ana Casís, *Urbanization in Latin America* (New York: Milbank Memorial Fund, 1946).

TABLE 46

Rank of the Fifteen Largest Cities, 1891–1941 [1]

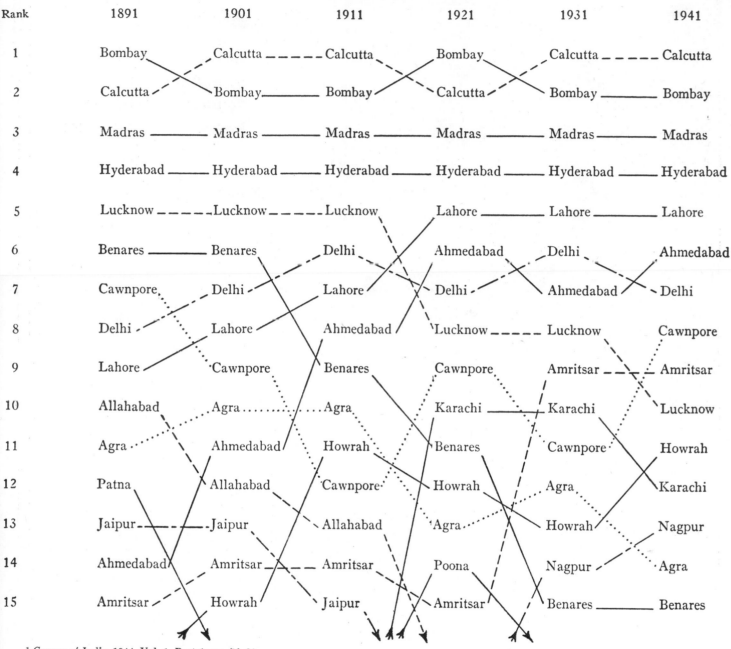

Rank	1891	1901	1911	1921	1931	1941
1	Bombay	Calcutta	Calcutta	Bombay	Calcutta	Calcutta
2	Calcutta	Bombay	Bombay	Calcutta	Bombay	Bombay
3	Madras	Madras	Madras	Madras	Madras	Madras
4	Hyderabad	Hyderabad	Hyderabad	Hyderabad	Hyderabad	Hyderabad
5	Lucknow	Lucknow	Lucknow	Lahore	Lahore	Lahore
6	Benares	Benares	Delhi	Ahmedabad	Delhi	Ahmedabad
7	Cawnpore	Delhi	Lahore	Delhi	Ahmedabad	Delhi
8	Delhi	Lahore	Ahmedabad	Lucknow	Lucknow	Cawnpore
9	Lahore	Cawnpore	Benares	Cawnpore	Amritsar	Amritsar
10	Allahabad	Agra	Agra	Karachi	Karachi	Lucknow
11	Agra	Ahmedabad	Howrah	Benares	Cawnpore	Howrah
12	Patna	Allahabad	Cawnpore	Howrah	Agra	Karachi
13	Jaipur	Jaipur	Allahabad	Agra	Howrah	Nagpur
14	Ahmedabad	Amritsar	Amritsar	Poona	Nagpur	Agra
15	Amritsar	Howrah	Jaipur	Amritsar	Benares	Benares

[1] *Census of India,* 1944, Vol. 1, Part 1, pp. 76–83.

the whole subcontinent, and indeed they are. But, contrary to what one might expect, the western half (excluding Baluchistan) is considerably more urbanized than the eastern half. This is the reverse of the density pattern, which can be seen by turning back to Map 8 in Chapter 3. It appears, then, that in the Indian situation density is not perfectly correlated with urbanization. The functions of a sizable town need to be performed even in sparsely settled regions.

Map 15 gives the location in 1941 of all cities of 50,000 or more, by three size classes. Table 48 gives the distribution by provinces and states. All told there are 95 of these cities scattered over the whole of the subcontinent but with some concentration in the Ganges valley, northern Bombay, and

the extreme south. Their distribution bears a much closer relation to density of population than does the proportion urban (given in Map 14), but even so, the relation is not extremely close. The factors determining the location of the cities seem to be trade, industry, and political function, and these in turn are related to transportation by water and rail, to natural resources, and to provincial and natural boundaries. The chief cities are on water routes, whether by sea or river. They are also, in most cases, provincial capitals. As in the United States, the development of rail transport has not pushed the cities of the interior ahead of those on the water routes, but has rather linked the water-route cities more closely to the hinterland.

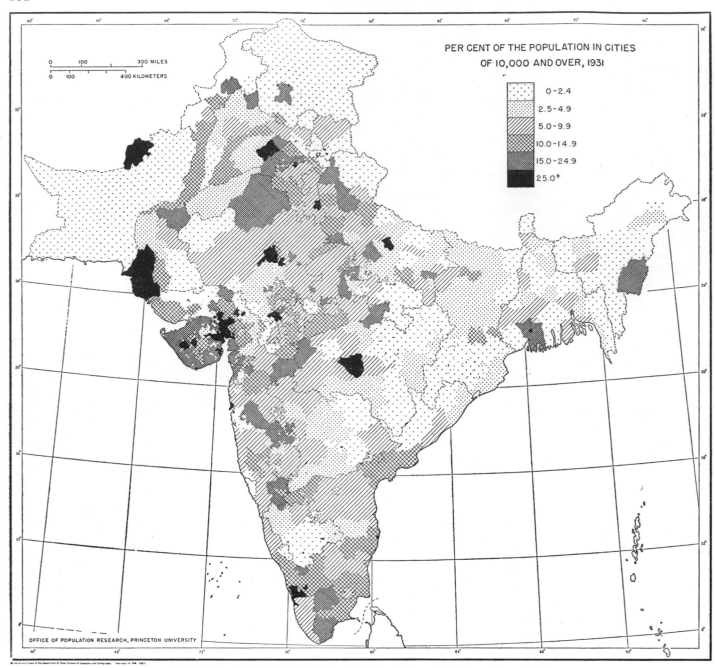

MAP 14. Per Cent of the Population in Indian Cities of 10,000 and Over, 1931.

TABLE 47

The Fifteen Largest Cities in 1941, and Their Rank in Earlier Censuses [1]

City	1891		1901		1911		1921		1931		1941	
	Popu-lation	Rank	Popu-lation	Rank	Popu-lation	Rank	Popu-lation	Rank	Popu-lation	Rank	Popu-lation	Rank
Calcutta, Bengal	744,249	2	921,380	1	1,013,143	1	1,046,300	2	1,163,771	1	2,108,891	1
Bombay, Bombay	821,764	1	776,006	2	979,445	2	1,175,914	1	1,161,383	2	1,489,883	2
Madras, Madras	452,518	3	509,346	3	518,660	3	526,911	3	647,230	3	777,481	3
Hyderabad, Hyd.	415,039	4	448,466	4	500,623	4	404,187	4	466,894	4	739,159	4
Lahore, Punjab	176,854	9	202,964	8	228,687	7	281,781	5	429,747	5	671,659	5
Ahmedabad, Bombay	144,451	14	181,774	11	214,000	8	270,775	6	310,000	7	591,267	6
Delhi, Delhi	189,648	8	206,534	7	229,144	6	248,259	7	347,539	6	521,849	7
Cawnpore, United Provs.	194,048	7	202,797	9	178,557	12	216,436	9	243,755	11	487,324	8
Amritsar, Punjab	136,766	15	162,429	14	152,756	14	160,218	15	264,840	9	391,010	9
Lucknow, United Provs.	264,953	5	256,239	5	252,114	5	240,566	8	274,659	8	387,177	10
Howrah, Bengal	116,606	22	157,594	15	179,006	11	195,301	12	224,873	13	379,292	11
Karachi, Sind	98,195	25	108,644	24	140,511	16	201,691	10	247,791	10	359,492	12
Nagpur, Cent. Provs.	117,014	21	127,734	19	101,415	25	145,193	17	215,165	14	301,957	13
Agra, United Provs.	168,662	11	188,022	10	185,449	10	185,532	13	229,764	12	284,149	14
Benares, United Provs.	223,375	6	213,079	6	203,804	9	198,447	11	205,315	15	263,100	15

[1] *Census of India*, 1941, Vol. 1, Part 1, pp. 76–83.

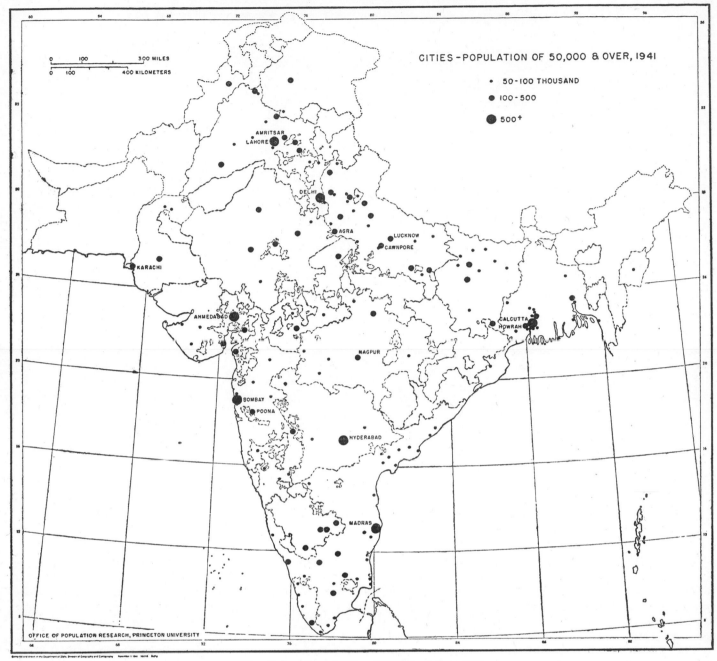

MAP 15. Location of Cities of 50,000 and Over, 1941.

CAUSES OF CITY GROWTH

An inquiry into the causes of city growth raises several kinds of question. Such an inquiry may refer to the problem of why some cities grow faster than others. Again, it may refer to the nature of the economic forces behind the whole urbanization trend. Or it may refer to the demographic question of whether the urban expansion is due to migration or to natural increase. It is this third kind of question with which we shall begin.

NATURAL INCREASE

Our discussion of differential fertility in Chapter 10 showed that, in India-Pakistan as in other areas, the city population has a lower birth rate than the rural population. It also showed that the larger the city the lower its birth rate. Yet, as we have just seen, the city population in India is increasing faster than the rural, and the big cities faster than the small ones. This

being the case, either the cities have an astoundingly low mortality, as compared to the rural areas, or else they are receiving a great number of migrants.

The information on urban mortality, such as it is, does not suggest a low death rate. On the contrary, the registered death rate is generally higher in the cities than in the country. It may be true, of course, that death registration is better in the cities, but if this were true, one would expect birth registration also to be better and the natural increase roughly comparable to that of the country. Actually the natural increase in the cities, as reported by official vital statistics, is lower than that in the rural areas. There is no evidence, then, that urban death rates appear high merely because they are better registered. The cities are known to be unsanitary. They are characterized by bad housing and poor diet to an even greater extent than the rural areas. We cannot, therefore, account for the growth in the urban portion of the population on the basis of a greater natural increase. The only other demographic explanation lies in migration.

TABLE 48

Percentage of Total Population in Cities of 100,000 and over and 50,000 and over, 1941 [1]

Region	Cities 100,000 and over	Per Cent of Population	Cities 50,000 and over	Per Cent of Population
INDIA, Total	58	4.25	155	5.81
Provinces	44	4.63	122	6.50
Delhi	1	56.85	2	67.06
Ajmer-Merwara	1	25.23	1	25.23
Bombay	5	13.06	13	15.45
Sind	2	10.74	4	13.59
Punjab	7	6.23	13	7.36
United Provs.	12	4.76	24	5.89
Bengal	4	4.67	18	6.15
N.W. Frontier Provs.	1	4.31	1	4.31
Madras	6	3.17	27	6.01
Cent. Prov. & Berar	2	2.86	7	4.60
Bihar	3	1.18	11	2.55
Orissa	—	——	1	.85
Others	—	——	—	——
States and Ags.	14	3.05	33	5.25
Mysore	4	9.43	4	9.43
Baroda	1	5.37	1	5.37
Jammu & Kash.	1	5.17	2	6.42
Gwalior	1	4.56	2	6.37
Hyderabad	1	4.52	4	5.73
Rajputana	3	3.14	5	3.98
Central India	1	2.71	2	3.71
Travancore	1	2.11	3	3.89
Western India	1	2.10	4	5.81
Assam	—	——	1	13.74
United Provs.	—	——	1	9.62
Cochin	—	——	2	7.79
Deccan (& Kol.)	—	——	1	3.34
Punjab	—	——	1	1.27
Others	—	——	—	——

[1] *Census of India*, 1941, pp. 56–57, 76–83, 86–94, 116–37.

RURAL-URBAN MIGRATION

Unfortunately there are no precise statistics on rural-urban migration. The most direct evidence is contained in the figures on place of birth gathered at each decennial census. These, however, suffer from at least four defects: (1) They probably underrate the amount of mobility, because children are often recorded erroneously as having the same birthplace as their parents.[6] (2) The figures are affected by purely transitory phenomena, such as pilgrimages, celebrations, and political connivance.[7] (3) They cannot give information on year-to-year movements. (4) They seldom show the number of people living in a city who were born there, but rather the number who were born in the whole district or even the province, and in some cases not even this much. At best, therefore, the statistics on place of birth are a mere makeshift for understanding the amount of rural-urban migration. But they have to be used in lieu of something better.

The Extent of Rural-Urban Migration. In the 1931 census volumes, so far as could be discovered, there are 26 cities for which the home-born population can be separated from the

[6] "When checking enumeration in a railway colony I found that of the six children of a railway employee, five had been born in different districts representing his various halting places in his official progress. Only two of these districts appeared however in the enumerator's original record. This was not so much the enumerator's fault as the effect of a common tendency to attribute to the district of present residence the birthplace of the older children." *Census of India*, 1931, Vol. 14 (Madras), Part 1, p. 75.

[7] The Indian census has always been a *de facto* census.

TABLE 49

Per Cent of Population Out-Born in Cities, 1931 [1]

City	Population	Per Cent Out-Born
All Cities, Average	*180,538*	*37.3*
Bombay	1,161,383	75.4
Cawnpore	243,755	41.4
Baroda City	112,860	38.3
Madras District	647,230	34.8
Fyzabad	65,718	30.7
Muttra	64,029	30.7
Hyderabad City	466,894	30.4
Jhansi	93,112	29.7
Lucknow	274,659	29.6
Etawah	46,948	26.5
Agra	229,764	22.4
Allahabad	183,914	20.5
Farrukhabad	60,354	19.4
Meerut	136,709	18.0
Gorakhpur	71,098	17.6
Saharanpur	78,655	17.5
Budaun	45,455	17.3
Benares	205,315	16.4
Mirzapur	61,184	15.8
Shahjahanpor	83,764	15.7
Koil	83,878	14.6
Hathras	39,784	14.0
Moradabad	110,562	13.7
Bareilly	144,031	11.7
Amroha	44,948	6.3
Sambhal	44,300	4.2

[1] *Census of India*, 1931, Vol. 9, Part 2; Vol. 14, Part 2; Vol. 19, Part 2; Vol. 23, Part 2.

out-born. Table 49 lists these cities, together with the percentage of the population out-born in each case. The average percentage out-born is 37.3 per cent. Thus it appears that more than a third of the inhabitants of India's major cities are born outside the city in which they live. In particular places, however, the percentage may be as low as 4 per cent or as high as 75. There is a tendency, though not pronounced, for the proportion of out-born to be higher the larger the city, despite the fact that it takes a larger stream of migrants to outweigh the greater number of births that inevitably occur in the larger city.

No attempt has been made to trace the historical trend in birthplace returns for the urban population. There is, however, a series for Bombay City, as follows: [8]

	Percentage Born Outside City
1872	68.9
1881	72.2
1891	75.0
1901	76.6
1911	80.4
1921	84.0
1931	75.4
1941	63.5

[8] Through 1931 the figures are taken from *Census of India*, 1931, Vol. 9 (Bombay Cities), Part 1, p. 14. For 1941 the figure is derived from *ibid.*, 1941, Vol. 3 (Bombay), p. 126.

The proportion of out-born residents rose to the phenomenal figure of 84 per cent in 1921, but by 1941 it was down to 64 per cent, the lowest ever recorded. This trend should not, however, be regarded as typical of Indian cities, because Bombay has recently experienced a slower growth than most of them.

Doubtless as the urbanization of Pakistan and the Union of India gains greater momentum, the percentage of out-born in their cities will increase. In other words, there is no reason to expect in the near future any diminution of the rural-urban migration rate. This rate, however large it may seem from the point of view of the cities, is quite small from the point of view of the rural region. As yet it could hardly be said to have any effect in draining off surplus labor from the heavily peopled rural areas.

The Sex of the Rural-Urban Migrants. It is impossible to get the sex ratio of the out-born population for most of the cities. In only four cases is the information available. These show an average ratio of 154 males per 100 females for the out-born population, as against 114 for the home-born population. (Table 50.) The latter figure sounds a bit high. It seems probable that some residents of a city report themselves as born there when in fact they were born elsewhere. If this is true, the real contrast between the sex ratios of the out-born and of the home-born is even greater than the table indicates.

TABLE 50

Sex Ratios of Home-Born and Out-Born Residents in Four Cities, 1931

(Males per 100 Females)

	Home-born	Out-born
Bombay City	137	198
Baroda City	113	148
Hyderabad City	102	142
Madras	104	128
Average	*114*	*154*

As is well known, the movement of females in India is largely a function of the marital customs of village exogamy and patrilocal residence.[9] Hence it is a short-distance movement. The data on the birthplace of city populations tend to substantiate this conclusion. Table 51 gives for a few cities having available data, the sex ratio of the out-born population when broken down by distance of origin. The categories—district in which located, contiguous districts, rest of province, rest of India—are only rough measures of distance, but they are adequate for the purpose. They indicate clearly that in India the urban immigration is more masculine the greater the distance covered. There is possibly an exception in the case of the district immediately surrounding the city, but the data are not conclusive.

Even for short distances, however, the rural-urban stream of migration is predominantly masculine, and for the whole of that stream it is overwhelmingly so. It follows that the sex ratio of any city's population is largely a function of its migration stream—in other words, a function of how fast the city has grown. To test this conclusion, the sex ratios and decade growth rates of the three largest cities were compared for each census. These showed that, in general, the faster the

[9] See material on the sex ratio of migrants in Chapter 14.

TABLE 51

Sex Ratio of Out-Born Population in Cities According to Place of Origin

CITY	PLACE OF BIRTH			
	District in Which City Is Located	Contiguous Districts	Rest of Province	Rest of India
Bombay City				
1931	a	162	175	257
1941	a	b	179 b	247
Hyderabad City				
1931	109	99	156	186
Baroda City				
1931	130	130	139 c	152
Madras				
1931	a	b	124 b	168

a Category inapplicable, because the city itself comprises an entire district.

b No information on contiguous districts. The data on "rest of province" include such districts, but do not include the city population.

c This ratio refers to the whole of Baroda State, excluding the City, because the contiguous districts around Baroda City are all in Bombay.

city had grown during the decade, the more masculine was its sex ratio at the end of that decade.

The Motives of Rural-Urban Migration. As compared to many other peoples, as previously noted, the population of the Indian region is characteristically immobile. The rural-urban movement, strong enough to expand the towns and cities, therefore stands out as peculiar, and it could have been produced only by powerful factors. These factors may be divided into two categories—those at home, in the rural village, which "push" the individual toward the city, and those in the city itself, which "pull" him there. The two are of course mutually dependent, because a "push" in the village might not be so regarded if there were no "pull" in the city, and vice versa; [10] but the classification is convenient.

(1) *Village Pressure.* To Western eyes the plight of the agricultural villages is itself sufficient to explain a mass migration movement. The extremely high density of agriculturalists on arable land, the excessive and hopeless character of rural indebtedness, the progressive subdivision and fragmentation of holdings, the bankrupting recurrence of droughts and crop failures, the inefficient modes of cultivation and stockraising, the uncertainty of foreign and local markets—all conspire to make the peasant's life unbearably hard. Indeed, anyone acquainted with the mass flight of farmers from blighted areas in the United States, would expect an irresistible mass movement in this Asiatic region.

The astonishing thing, however, is the unwillingness of the peasant to move. Until the depression of 1930 there were more complaints in industry of a shortage of labor than of an oversupply of it. Business men had to spend time and effort recruiting labor.[11] Even recently there was still an active recruitment carried on in connection with the Assam tea gardens.

Furthermore, the areas from which migrants come are fairly

[10] Edward P. Hutchinson and Wilbert E. Moore, "Pressures and Barriers in Future Migration," *Annals of the American Academy of Political and Social Sciences,* Vol. 237 (January, 1945), pp. 164–71.

[11] Pramathanath Banerjea, *A Study of Indian Economics* (5th ed.; London: Macmillan, 1940), pp. 292–93. Sir Alexander Murray, "Labour" in Sir John Cumming (ed.), *Modern India* (London: Oxford University Press, 1931), p. 287.

limited in extent, and it is hard to prove that conditions there are much worse than they are in other parts of the subcontinent. "The region comprising Bihar, Chota Nagpur, the eastern districts of the Central Provinces, some of the northern parts of Madras, and a few of the districts of the United Provinces constitutes the largest and the most important source of labour-supply in India. In Bengal, local labour for the mills has always been scarce." [12] Evidently the Indian peasant does not react to adverse conditions in the same way as the American farmer. If conditions of absolute famine prevail he may migrate in large numbers, but as long as the starvation is gradual he tends to remain at home. It is not simply that he is unaware of better conditions elsewhere, but that he defines "good" and "bad" conditions in a somewhat different sense. To him the agricultural way of life in the local village is a superior way of life, and the close association with his relatives, neighbors, and caste fellows is eminently desirable. He is willing to make a considerable economic sacrifice in order to retain these advantages. Homesickness weighs heavily upon him. In short, the rural environment not only pushes him out, but also pulls him in. Certain features of it are to him a burden, but others are an advantage. He wants to live there at almost any price.

(2) *City Advantage vs. City Repulsion.* In the past in India the inducement the city has had to offer has been almost exclusively economic. The "glittering life" of the city, the faster pace, the greater opportunities, the wider social horizon—all have meant little to the average Hindu or Muslim villager or have seemed positively evil. He has generally come to the city for one reason only—to find remunerative work—and since this was a means rather than an end in itself, he has not regarded the city as a permanent place of abode. He has tended to stay in the city only temporarily, until he had an opportunity to return to the village.

Why does the *ryot* thus dislike the city? Why does he go there only under economic compulsion? One reason certainly lies in the traditional ruralism of Indian life. The *ryot's* traditions, associations, and habits are all rural in character. But this is from the side of the attractiveness of the rural village. Is there anything in the city itself which is repellent? The answer is that the rapidly developing industrial city in this part of the world has recapitulated all of the evils through which the industrial city elsewhere has passed. Housing conditions, working conditions, recreational facilities, and sanitary conveniences have all been incredibly bad, and food has been scarce and unwholesome. [13] Even the Westerner who thinks that life begins and ends in the city would find the rural village, for all its filth and monotony, a preferable place to live. The development of industrial cities in India, under conditions of laissez-faire economy in an extremely competitive world, has produced some of the worst urban conditions ever known.

These urban conditions make the peasant want to stay in the city only so long as he has to. Furthermore, they make him reluctant to bring his family there. Wives and children tend to be left at home. Restrictions on child and female labor further reduce the possibility of bringing the family. Hence the Indian and Pakistani cities probably have the most distorted sex ratios of any large group of cities in the world.

The failure of the worker to bring his family makes the city all the more unattractive as a place of residence, and increases the worker's desire to get back to the home village as soon as possible. It also increases the amount of prostitution and demoralizing recreation in the city. [14] To the peasant the city is simply a little bit of hell which fortunately is not eternal.

The Effects of Rural-Urban Migration. As a consequence of his distaste for urban life the peasant who has migrated to the city tends to keep in contact with his local village. He often sends remittances, and returns to the village when he is out of work, when he is needed there, when an important ceremony is taking place, or when he is sick. If he recruits additional labor for his employer, he is likely to get it from his own village. Looked at from the point of view of the migrant, the rural village is a sort of insurance against disaster. He can always return there in time of need. "In sickness and in maternity, in strikes and in lockouts, in unemployment and in old age the village home is a refuge for many." [15]

From the point of view of the village itself, the rural focus of the city worker is a financial and intellectual boon. Not only are the emigrant's remittances of value, but the savings he brings home after several months' absence are a valuable addition to the local capital. Furthermore, the migrant constitutes a direct contact with the city, and helps diffuse to the countryside the urban intellectual ferment—above all, the urban conception of individualism, efficiency, and relativity. The emigration to the city presumably drains off surplus population and thus aids slightly the demographic problem of the rural village, but this is counterbalanced by the fact that the emigration also takes away the able-bodied and capable workers, and leaves the young, the old, and the crippled to carry on agricultural production.

From the point of view of industry the rural focus has the effect of producing an unusually high turnover in the labor force. The peasant works in the factory until illness, unemployment, or nostalgia drives him back to the village, or until he has saved enough money to go back pridefully. In a large number of factories 5 per cent of the workers leave each month. Such rapid labor turnover entails a serious loss of efficiency. "It also means that in most factories there is at hand a supply of substitutes, or 'badlis,' to take the places of those who have gone away with or without giving notice. These 'badlis' form a heavy charge on the wages bill, and their presence in large numbers among the regular labour force gives rise to much irregularity of employment." [16] The high turnover not only lowers the efficiency of labor, as compared to the labor of Europe or Japan, but it also affects adversely the formation of responsible labor unions, the enforcement of labor legislation, the acquisition of skills, and the quest for higher wages. The degree of turnover varies, of course, from one city to another. Generally it is higher in the larger cities than in the smaller. It is extremely high in Bombay and Calcutta, but lower in Ahmadabad, Sholapur, and Madras. [17]

There are evidences, however, that in recent times the laborers have become more accustomed to the city, with many of them expecting to spend their lives there. "Today, the city worker is increasingly reluctant to return to the village, and he, more than his rural cousin, is susceptible to new lines of thought and conduct. Under the guttering gas lights of a city

[12] Banerjea, *op. cit.*, p. 292.

[13] Margaret Read, *The Indian Peasant Uprooted* (London: Longmans, 1931), especially Chapter 2.

[14] B. Shiva Rao, "Labor in India," *Annals*, Vol. 233 (May, 1944), p. 129.

[15] *Report of the Royal Commission on Labour in India*, 1931, quoted by Read, *op. cit.*, p. 5.

[16] Read, *loc. cit.*

[17] Sir Alexander Murray, "Labour" in Cumming (ed.), *op. cit.*, p. 291.

street corner, he listens as a friend reads from the local news-paper, and he hears, too, the familiar gambit of the radio news and entertainment broadcasts: 'Yeh All-India Radio Hai' (This is All-India Radio). He acquires a taste for the motion-picture theater, where rich and poor sit together as the story unfolds imaginative vistas of romance, alien to the stark simplicity of their own lives." [18]

If urbanization continues in Pakistan and the Indian Union, if the cities gradually acquire better housing and better rec-reation facilities, a typical urban proletariat should develop. The high turnover that has characterized Indian industrial labor should begin to diminish, thus leading to greater effi-ciency and improved industrial relations.

THE OCCUPATIONAL STRUCTURE OF THE CITIES

In 1931 there were 89 towns and cities for which data on occupations were obtainable. These were mostly places with more than 50,000 inhabitants; only 15 had less than this num-ber, and only two had less than 30,000. Together they had 12.5 million people, or exactly a third of the total urban popu-lation. They do not represent the whole urban population, but only the most important cities and towns. [19] The occupational structure for the whole urban population, which unfortunately is not obtainable, probably lies somewhere between that for the 89 larger places and that for the rural area, which in turn lies fairly close to that for India as a whole.

OCCUPATIONAL STRUCTURE AND GROWTH OF CITIES

If the cities have grown through migration rather than natural increase, and if their main attraction has depended on economic opportunity rather than way of life or recrea-tional facilities, it could be expected that the most rapid growth would occur in the industrial cities. To test this be-lief, the cities, reduced to 87,[20] were divided into classes in terms of the percentage of the workers engaged in certain occupations. This was done first with reference to Industry alone, and then with reference to Industry, Trade, and Trans-port combined. In both cases it was found, as Table 52 shows, that the cities with the greatest proportion of workers in In-dustry, or in the three occupations combined, tended to grow faster than the cities with the smallest proportion.[21] Thus

[18] Geo. E. Jones, *Tumult in India* (New York: Dodd, Mead, 1948), p. 11.

[19] The representativeness of the sample is discussed in Appendix I.

[20] Bombay Suburban was omitted from the 89 original cities because of area changes between 1931 and 1941. New Delhi City was also omitted because of its very special role in India, the government having been moved there in 1911.

[21] The correlation shows up better if the class averages are not weighted by the populations of the constituent cities. Weighting, as the last column in Table 52 shows, reveals a low average for Group I. This is due to the fact that the largest city in this group, Bombay,

TABLE 52

Growth of Cities, 1921–1941, According to Occupational Composition in 1931

Occupational Composition 1931	Number of Cities	Per Cent Growth 1921–1941 Unweighted Average [a]	Per Cent Growth 1921–1941 Weighted Average [a]
Industry Only	34		
I. Cities with more than 40 % of all workers in industry	16	74.7	60.8 (86.3) [b]
II. Cities with 30–39% of all workers in indus-try [c]	9	64.4	79.8
III. Cities with less than 30% of all workers in industry [c]	9	55.6	75.8
Industry, Trade, and Transport Combined	87		
I. Cities with 70% or more of all workers in these occupations	15	83.8	65.0 (94.0) [b]
II. Cities with 60–69% of all workers in these occupations	28	58.2	67.4
III. Cities with 50–59% of all workers in these occupations	27	48.5	66.6
IV. Cities with 50% or less of all workers in these occupations	17	43.6	55.8

[a] The unweighted average was obtained by adding the percentage growth of all the cities in the group, and dividing by the number of cities; the weighted average was obtained by adding the populations of the cities in each group, getting a total for 1921 and another for 1941 and computing the growth rate from these totals.

[b] With Bombay removed from the class. (See text.)

[c] These are random samples drawn from each class of city, but the other groups in the table are not samples. The entire list is composed of cities for which the data were obtainable. New Delhi was excluded be-cause of its unique role in India, and Calcutta Suburbs in 24-Parganas because of area problems.

there is every reason to believe that in Pakistan and the In-dian Union the cities are growing because of the same eco-nomic factors that prompted urban growth in the Western nations in the early stages. Furthermore, the data furnish independent evidence of the view that the economic opportu-nities afforded by modern economic life constitute the main attraction drawing migrants to the cities.

exercises a disproportionate influence. It has nearly half the total popu-lation of its group in each case, and yet had an unusually slow growth between the dates mentioned.

CHAPTER 16

Urbanization: The Characteristics of Cities

THE significance of urban growth in India is best shown by the characteristics of city populations as contrasted to the rural. The present chapter covers some of the major characteristics, although it cannot cover them all. Throughout the entire book the rural-urban contrast is recurrently treated, this being incidental to other topics. Now, however, it is the contrast itself that is the focus of attention, not the separate topics. Apparently the gulf between city and country is greater in Pakistan-India than in Western countries. This shows up, for example, in the relative degree of literacy and in the sex ratio. It does not show up in certain other traits—such as age composition and housing density—but for understandable reasons.

THE RURAL-URBAN OCCUPATIONAL STRUCTURE

Obviously, as compared to other ways of setting the city off from the country, the occupational pattern affords a sharp distinction. This is true in India as in other countries. If the occupational figures for the 89 cities with available data are subtracted from the occupational figures for all of India, the percentage of workers in Agriculture among the remainder is 76.8 per cent, as against 10.1 per cent for the cities. Were figures for the strictly rural part available, the percentage would undoubtedly exceed 77. In this part of the world, as in other parts, the rural population is distinguished by its virtually complete devotion to a single occupation.

But the difference between the occupational structure of

TABLE 53

Per Cent of Total Workers in Each Occupational Class, for 89 Cities and Rest of India, 1931 [1]

	89 Cities	Rest of India
Exploitation of Animals and Vegetation	10.1	76.8
Exploitation of Minerals	0.4	0.3
Industry	32.2	10.9
Transport	9.7	1.4
Trade	19.1	5.5
Public Force	4.2	0.6
Public Administration	5.5	0.6
Professions and Liberal Arts	6.2	1.6
Persons Living on Income	1.5	0.1
Domestic Service	11.0	2.0
Total	100.0	100.0

[1] Compiled from *Census of India,* 1931, Part 1, pp. 218 ff. and Part 2 of seventeen provincial volumes.

the rural and urban populations, though sharp, is not so great as it is in some other countries. Many towns and even cities in India are still dominated by a rural economy. This fact appears clearly in Table 53 which gives, for the 89 cities and for the rest of India, the percentage of all workers engaged in each major occupational category. One might expect the greatest difference to lie in the first category, Agriculture, and the third, Industry, since the one is typical of rural and the other of urban areas. But the differences with respect to two other occupations—Public Administration and Persons Living on Income—exceed the difference with respect to Agriculture, and all of them, with the exception of Mining, exceed the difference with respect to Industry. Such a result is partly due to the peculiar classification of occupations in the census. Industry, for example, embraces handicraft production in the home, and probably embraces many other activities that would not be classified as industrial in other countries. But the result is also partly due to the fundamental rurality that still clings to many cities in this region. This can be seen more clearly when specific occupations are dealt with.

PERCENTAGE ENGAGED IN AGRICULTURE

The percentage of total workers [1] engaged principally in the exploitation of animals and vegetation (agriculture as broadly defined) is surprisingly high for some cities. In Vizagapatam, for example, it came to 51 per cent, in Gaya to 44, and in Allahabad to 34. At the other extreme, the smallest percentages were 2.5 for Bombay, 3.0 for Calcutta proper, and 4.2 for Kotah in Rajputana. Since the unweighted average was 13.8, and the average weighted by population was 10.1 per cent, the evidence is plain that the percentage in agriculture varies inversely with the size of the city. In the ten largest cities, for example, the weighted average was only 5.9 per cent. [2]

Some of the urban agriculturalists probably cultivate farm land included within the city, but most of them doubtless travel to farms outside the city boundary. Despite the high percentage of these agriculturalists in the towns and cities, the proportion is apparently not so high as would be found in the urban places of some other countries—notably those in the Balkans.

PERCENTAGE ENGAGED IN INDUSTRY

Since the census definition of industrial employment is a very broad one, it is not surprising that rural regions show a

[1] Total workers here excludes those in insufficiently described and unproductive occupations.

[2] Curiously the ten smallest cities in the list were also below the average with 8.5 per cent, but they were nearly all in Rajputana and

substantial percentage of workers in this category. The percentage among the workers outside the 89 cities is one-third of what it is in the cities. With the exception of Mining, the two populations come nearer to being equal in this category than in any other. Also, the variation by size of city is negligible. (Table 54.) A correlation between the percentage in Industry and the rate of growth of the city seems to be present, as already mentioned; but the combination of Industry, Trade, and Transport seems a more significant occupational grouping for the city population.

TABLE 54

Proportion of All Workers Found in Various Occupational Classes, According to the Size of the City, 1931 [1]

Occupational Class	Cities 500,000 & Over	Cities 100,000 to 500,000	Cities 50,000 to 100,000	Cities Less than 50,000
1. Exploitation of Animals & Vegetation	3.6	10.2	17.0	12.2
2. Exploitation of Minerals	0.1	0.1	1.4	0.1
3. Industry	32.4	32.5	31.9	30.7
4. Trade	12.5	9.6	7.7	5.6
5. Transport	20.8	18.8	18.1	17.7
6. Public Force	1.9	5.2	3.8	7.1
7. Public Administration	5.9	5.4	4.5	9.0
8. Professions & Liberal Arts	6.0	6.4	6.2	5.7
9. Living on Income	1.8	1.7	0.9	1.5
10. Domestic Service	14.9	10.1	8.5	10.5
Total	*100.0*	*100.0*	*100.0*	*100.0*

[1] From *Census of India,* 1931, Part 2 of seventeen volumes.

PERCENTAGE IN INDUSTRY, TRADE, AND TRANSPORT COMBINED

In the total sample of 89 cities the proportion of all workers engaged in these three occupations was 61 per cent. The larger the city, the larger the percentage, as follows:

City Size Class	Percentage
500,000 and over	65.7
100,000 to 500,000	60.9
50,000 to 100,000	57.7
Less than 50,000	54.0

A glance at Table 54, however, will show that this differentiation is not so sharp as that of some other occupational groupings. This is because there is, strangely, little differentiation between cities of various sizes with respect to Industry or Transport. There is considerable differentiation with respect to Trade, but it does not carry the weight that the other two do. The net result is a consistently but not markedly higher percentage of workers in the combined category the larger the city.

It was shown above that the more Industry, Trade, and Transport a city had in 1931, the faster it grew between 1921 and 1941. In the section on urban age and sex composition below, it will be shown that a large proportion of workers in

these occupations is conducive, as one might expect, to a concentration of males (and to some extent of females) in the 20–40 age class. Finally, in the section on literacy in urban places, it will be shown that the greater the proportion of workers in these occupations, the more literate the population and the more rapid its future progress in literacy. Nearly every index suggests that in India, as in the Occidental countries, the typically urban characteristics—large size, concentration in the productive ages, high literacy, and low fertility—are associated with the dominance of Industry, Trade, and Transport in the occupational structure. These tendencies have not gone as far as in Western nations, but they are apparently beginning.

THE OTHER OCCUPATIONS

The Professions and Liberal Arts have about the same proportion of workers in each size-class of city. Public Force varies erratically, doubtless because of the presence or absence of army stations. With the exception of cities under 50,000, however, Public Administration, Persons Living on Income, and Domestic Service all have a greater proportion as the city gets larger. The cities under 50,000 surprisingly depart from the pattern, manifesting a proportion in all three of these categories more similar to that manifested by the cities 100,-000 to 500,000 in population. The reason is as follows: These cities are included in the occupational tables because of their importance as minor capitals, not because of their size. There are many cities of this size that are not included in the tables, and hence we have no occupational data on them. The fact that so many of the ones included are capitals tends to swell unduly the proportion of persons in Public Administration, Living on Private Income, and Domestic Service.[3]

THE SEX RATIO IN THE CITIES

If the census figures are to be accepted, the populations of Pakistan and the Union of India, particularly Pakistan, are unusually masculine. Certainly their cities are the most masculine in the world. In 1941 the urban sex ratio was 123 males per 100 females. This might suggest that the rural regions would have an excess of females, especially since it is known that the region as a whole is one of emigration; but in point of fact the rural ratio itself is masculine, being 105 in 1941.

TABLE 55

Sex Ratio of Urban and Rural Population: 1891–1941 [1]

Date	Urban	Rural
1891	112.2	103.7
1901	111.9	103.0
1911	116.9	103.7
1921	120.9	104.3
1931	121.9	104.6
1941	122.8	104.8

[1] From *Census of India,* 1891, 1901, 1911, 1921, 1931, 1941.

A glance at Table 55 shows that the masculinity of the urban population has been increasing since 1891. It has gone from 112 to 123 in five decades. This suggests that the urban masculinity may be related to the economic basis of modern urbanization on the one hand and to the peculiar Hindu-

were consequently not regionally representative. Furthermore, they were not representative in other respects, as explained in Appendix I.

[3] See Appendix I.

Muslim attitude toward female employment on the other. If the cities have been growing by migration, if this migration has been mainly connected with the development of modern industry, trade, and transport, and if there is a prejudice against the employment of women outside the home, one can expect that the faster the cities grow the more masculine would become their sex ratios.

Following this same line of reasoning, one can deduce that the sex ratio will vary directly with the size of the city. Table 56 bears out this deduction. With scarcely any exception since 1881, the sex ratio has been more masculine the larger the class of city. The uniformity of the results is striking. The main exception is in the towns under 5,000. These show a sex ratio consistently larger than that for cities 5,000 to 10,000 and 10,000 to 20,000. This apparently strange result seems fairly easy to explain in terms of census policy in the selection of these towns for inclusion in the "urban" category.[4]

TABLE 56

Sex Ratio in the Towns and Cities, by Size Class, 1881–1941 [1]

Cities with Population of	1881	1891	1901	1911	1921	1931[a]	1941
I. 500,000 plus	162	178	156	171	175	173	161[b]
II. 100,000–500,000	111	115	116	122	131	128	127[b]
III. 50,000–100,000	111	114	111	118	120	120	c
IV. 20,000–50,000	106	109	110	115	121	121	c
V. 10,000–20,000	105	106	106	108	110	113	c
VI. 5,000–10,000	105	104	105	107	108	111	c
VII. Under 5,000[d]	110	110	111	112	113	118	c

[a] The figures for 1931 include cantonments as part of the city. It is not known what was done about this in 1921 and 1911. There are doubtless some elements that prejudice the comparison from year to year, and yet the general trends are probably roughly accurate.

[b] The decline in the rates for the two largest classes in 1941 is attributable to the fact that in this year, for the first time, four cities moved into Class I which had previously been in Class II. This had the effect of lowering the sex ratio for Class I because their ratios were lower than those for the cities which had in the past been in Class I, and it also lowered the ratio for Class II because the cities that left this class had previously contributed such a high ratio. If only the cities traditionally constituting Class I—Calcutta, Madras, and Bombay—had made up this class in 1941, the sex ratio for that class would have been 178, the highest on record since these three cities had been together in this class. The generally lower ratios in 1901 are perhaps due to a large number of males returning to villages devastated and depopulated by the famines.

[c] Information not available.

[d] The high ratios in Class VII are doubtless attributable to the fact that a place under 5,000, to be returned in the census as a "town," must have definitely urban characteristics. In other words, a selective factor is at work.

[1] From *Census of India,* 1891, 1901, 1931, 1941.

As compared with Great Britain, the United States, and other modern countries, the urban sex ratio of this area seems peculiar. In the United States, for example, some cities have high sex ratios and others have very low ones. The cities with heavy industries are predominantly masculine, while those with clerical occupations are mainly feminine. In India-Pakistan, however, the seclusion of women persists as a social institution, and few women are employed in any kind of work

[4] Ordinarily in India a town is regarded as a place having at least 5,000 inhabitants. (See Chapter 15, Appendix H.) Only by the special dispensation of the Provincial Census Commissioner can a town of lesser size be declared a city. To receive this special favor the place must give evidence of urban characteristics. Consequently, the places under 5,000 that are declared to be towns have a more truly urban nature than many places between 5,000 and 20,000 people, and this fact shows up in the sex ratio.

outside the home. At the same time the urban environment makes the support of an idle woman extremely expensive for a working man; consequently, when he goes to work in the city, the peasant tends to leave his wife and other dependents at home. There the women and children are economically productive, because they are not ordinarily excluded from domestic occupations. Thus the urban sex ratio constitutes one more evidence that the Indian area has acquired some of the economic and technological features of modernism, without yet having adjusted all her social institutions to the new order.

TABLE 57

Sex Ratios of Cities in Selected Oriental Countries [1]

Cities with Population of	India (1931)	British Malaya (1931)	Turkey (1935)	Egypt (1937)	West Java (1930)	Japan (1946)
500,000–plus	173	- - -	106	104	- - -	100
100,000–500,000	128	168	124	107	106	96
50,000–100,000	120	169	106	105	103	91
20,000–50,000	121	164	111	105	99	89
10,000–20,000	113	132	108	a	95	a
5,000–10,000	111	167	102	a	91	a

[a] No data.

[1] From *Census of India,* 1931; Turkey, Office Central de Statistique, *Annuaire,* 1940–41; Turkey, Genel Mifus Sayimi, *Recensement Général de la Population,* 1935; British Malaya, *Report on 1931 Census;* Netherlands India, *Census of 1930; Japan, Census of April 26,* 1946; *Population Census of Egypt,* 1937.

The urban sex ratio seems remarkable even when compared to other oriental regions. Of the several countries given in Table 57, only British Malaya has ratios that are higher than those of India, and British Malaya has been affected by heavy international migration. It may be that some other countries for which figures are not available, such as China, Indo-China, or Afghanistan, may have higher sex ratios, but on the whole it looks as though the all-India ratio is outstanding, particularly for a region with virtually no immigration.

As one might expect, the sex ratio is higher in some parts of the city than in others. Occasionally, in highly industrial districts, it rises to very high numbers, as the following figures for Calcutta and Bombay in 1931 demonstrate.

	Males per 100 Females
Calcutta Districts	
I	180
II	249
III	224
IV	190
Bombay Wards	
A	211
B	175
C	180
D	168
E	173
F	172
G	173

On the whole, as we have seen, the rural-urban migration is predominantly masculine. The larger the city, the greater its dependence upon migration, and the lesser its proportion of women. Yet, as already pointed out, the cities do receive some female migrants. This is shown by the age pyramids for cities, as well as by place-of-birth statistics. It is also true that these women come from nearer the cities, on the average, than do the men. In 61 districts the sex ratio outside the cities (70 cities all told) was found to be in 1931, 106.9, whereas the ratio for the rural parts is 104.6. This higher masculinity of the districts surrounding the cities suggests that the latter, despite the predominance of males in their total migration stream, tend to draw females rather than males from their immediate environs.

How long the highly masculine sex ratio will persist in the cities is hard to say. There is certainly some tendency towards the employment of women outside the home, but so far this tendency has been exceeded by the more rapid employment of males in urban industries, with the result that the urban sex ratio has been increasing rather than declining. But there are definite signs that a decline may begin in the near future. This conclusion is based on analysis of the three major cities.[5] In these three cities (Bombay, Calcutta, and Madras) the sex ratio goes up in 1941 rather than down, rising to the very high figure of 178. Yet it is on the basis of these three cities that a future decline can be predicted. If one examines the history of the growth rates and sex ratios for these three cities, one finds that the sex ratio at each census is largely a function of the previous decade's rate of growth. This is what could be expected. But, as Fig. 34 illustrates, the correlation has tended

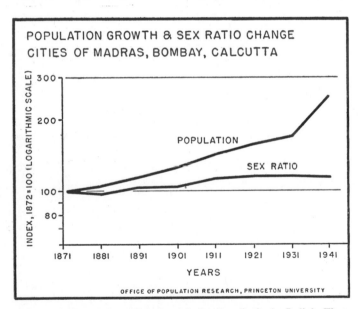

FIGURE 34. Population Growth and the Sex Ratio in India's Three Major Cities: Bombay, Calcutta, and Madras.

to diminish. The high growth rate between 1931 and 1941, for example, did not produce a commensurate increase in the sex ratio. In both Bombay and Madras the ratio declined, and in Calcutta it rose hardly at all. There is reason to believe, therefore, that the rural-urban migration is beginning to contain a larger proportion of women than it formerly did, and that in the future the cities may enjoy a more normal sex ratio. This tendency bespeaks a changed attitude on the part

[5] It is *not* based on the decline in the sex ratio of cities over 500,000 between 1931 and 1941, as depicted in Table 56. This decline comes from the fact that several new cities joined the 500,000-and-over class between the two dates.

of the public, for it means that women are now being given more opportunities in urban economic life.

THE URBAN AGE STRUCTURE

Like most cities in the world, those in Pakistan and the Indian Union have a concentration of people in the productive ages of life. The larger the city the larger is the concentration. Figure 35 shows how much the age distribution of two classes of cities deviates from that of India as a whole. In the

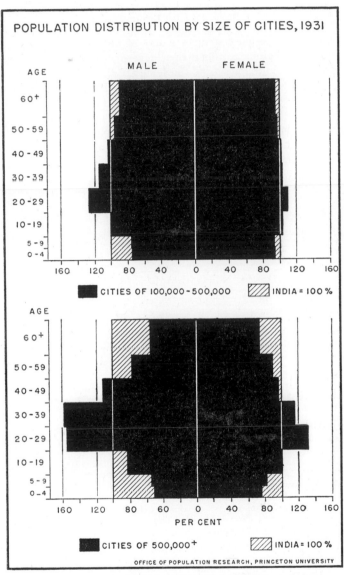

FIGURE 35. Urban Age Distribution in Two Classes of Cities as a Percentage of the all-India Distribution.

cities of 100,000 to 500,000 the age of greatest deviation (about 25 per cent) is 20–29; in cities over 500,000, the age of greatest deviation (about 60 per cent) is 30–39. In both types of city the distortion is less among females than among males. Thus these Asiatic cities, especially the large ones, are plainly behaving as Western cities do by attracting workers aged 20–49. They differ from the Western pattern primarily by their lesser attraction of females.

There seems little likelihood that the age structure of the cities will normalize itself in the near future. The sex ratio of the migrants may tend to rectify itself, but not the age distribution. This is especially true of that part of the age scale lying below ten years of age. If a decline in fertility really begins in India, it will probably affect the cities first. This will compensate for any increased influx of females in the reproductive ages, which might otherwise swell the proportion of children. Continued rural-urban migration, with high urban mortality, will probably keep the proportion of older persons to a minimum. The chances are that Indian and Pakistani cities, therefore, will become more distorted in their age structure before they become less so.

RELIGIOUS COMPOSITION OF THE URBAN POPULATION

One of the most striking points of difference between the various religious groups is their degree of urbanization. Some groups, e.g. the Parsis and the Jews, are almost entirely urban, while others, such as the Tribal and the Sikh, are almost entirely rural. Such differences undoubtedly indicate great variations in the life, outlook, and characteristics of the religious groups concerned. They also imply a contrast between the urban and rural populations with respect to their religious composition.

TABLE 58

The Percentage of the Urban and Rural Population Found in Each Religion, 1911, 1931, 1941 [1]

	1911		1931		1941	
	Urban	Rural	Urban	Rural	Urban	Rural
Hindu	66.43	72.22	66.46	71.09	65.85	69.98
Muslim	28.18	21.78	27.68	22.93	27.79	23.77
Tribal	0.27	3.47	0.16	2.52	a	a
Christian	2.72	1.05	3.22	1.58	3.00	1.75
Sikh	0.70	1.02	0.91	1.33	1.22	1.50
Jain	1.29	0.32	1.16	0.27	1.21	0.25
Buddhist	0.01	0.12	0.06	0.14	a	a
Parsi	0.30	0.01	0.03	- - - b	a	a
Jewish	0.01	- - -	0.04	- - -	a	a
Others	- - -	0.01	0.06	0.13	a	a
India	100.00	100.00	100.00	100.00	100.00	100.00

a Data not available.
b "- - -" indicates less than 0.005 per cent.
[1] Compiled from *Census of India,* 1911, 1931, and 1941, summary volumes in each case, table on "Towns Arranged Territorially with Population by Communities."

Table 58 gives the percentage of the urban population and of the rural population in each religion. It can be seen that in the urban population, as compared to the rural, the Muslims are more numerous and the Hindus less so. The same is true of the Christians, Jains, and Parsis, as against the Tribals, Sikhs, and Buddhists. Table 59 ranks the various religious groups for 1931 according to their percentage in the urban and rural regions. Certain groups occupy different places in the two orders. Thus the Christians are the third most numerous group in the urban population, but the fourth most numerous in the rural. The Tribals are the sixth most numerous in the urban column, but the third in the rural column.

Unfortunately, data were not obtainable for all religious groups in 1941. It is possible, however, to get some data for this year, and it therefore proves feasible to consider the rate of urbanization for the various religions. We find that the

TABLE 59

Rank of the Various Religious Groups According to the Percentage of the Urban and of the Rural Population, 1931 [1]

Per Cent of the Urban Population		Per Cent of the Rural Population	
Religion	Per Cent	Religion	Per Cent
Hindu	66.46	Hindu	71.09
Muslim	27.68	Muslim	22.93
Christian	3.22	Tribal	2.52
Jain	1.16	Christian	1.58
Sikh	0.91	Sikh	1.33
Tribal	0.16	Jain	0.27
Buddhist	0.06	Buddhist	0.14
Jewish	0.04	Parsi	- - -
Parsi	0.03	Jewish	- - -

[1] Same as footnote 1 in Table 58.

TABLE 60

The Percentage of Each Religious Group Urban, 1911, 1931, 1941 [1]

Together with the Increase in Percentage Urban

	1911	1931	1941	Increase 1911–1931	Increase 1911–1941
India, Total	9.4	11.1	12.8	16.9	35.4
Hindu	8.8	10.4	12.1	18.9	38.4
Muslim	11.9	13.0	14.6	9.6	23.0
Tribal	0.8	0.8	a	—2.5 [2]	a
Christian	21.3	20.2	19.9	—5.1	—6.4
Sikh	6.6	7.8	10.7	18.5	61.4
Jain	29.6	34.6	41.4	17.1	40.2
Buddhist	4.6	5.0	a	8.6	a
Parsi	86.5	89.0	a	2.9	a
Jewish	85.4	69.2	a	—19.0	a
Others	4.8	5.2	a	6.8	a

a Data not available.
[1] Same as footnote 1 in Table 58.
[2] The decrease lies in decimals not shown.

rate of urbanization has varied among them in a decided manner. Table 60, in addition to showing the proportion urban in each religious group at three censuses, also shows the increase in the proportion from 1911 to 1931 and from 1911 to 1941. In some groups, e.g. the Christians and Tribals, the tendency has been toward a decrease of urbanism. This does not necessarily mean that members of these religious groups are moving to the countryside. In the case of the Christians it means that new converts are being made in rural areas more rapidly than in urban areas. Actually, there is reputedly a strong tendency for Christians to move to the city, so that the rate of conversion in rural areas exceeds the rate in urban areas by a greater amount than Table 60 suggests. In the case of the Tribals, the decrease in urbanism probably means simply that when members of primitive tribes move to town they become something else—usually Hindus. The Hindus are becoming urbanized more rapidly than the Muslims, but the Sikhs are exceeding both of them. Taking the major religious groups there is a clear, though not entirely consistent tendency, for the most rural groups to increase their urban proportion faster than the least rural groups. This means, in effect, that the differences between the religious groups with respect to the degree of urbanization are tending to grow smaller rather than greater.

LITERACY OF THE URBAN POPULATION

The urban population is much more literate than the rural. Exactly how much more cannot be ascertained, because the Indian censuses do not tabulate literacy according to urban and rural residence. But in 1931 for persons 5 years old or older, the per cent literate in 89 cities was 27.6, whereas for the rest of India it was 7.5 (Table 61). Although these figures

TABLE 61

Literates Age 5-plus as Percentage of Population Age 5-plus, by Sex and by Size of Cities, 1931 [1]

Place	Both Sexes	Males	Females
Cities	*27.6*	*37.2*	*14.0*
500,000 Plus	35.0	41.4	23.4
100,000 to 500,000	25.6	35.5	12.3
50,000 to 100,000	25.0	36.7	11.1
Less than 50,000	19.8	31.1	6.2
India Minus Cities	*7.5*	*12.7*	*1.9*

[1] Compiled from seventeen volumes of the *Census of India,* 1931.

do not accurately reflect either the "urban" or the "rural" literacy,[6] they do indicate that the one is several times greater than the other. Indeed, the writer knows of no other region today where the difference in literacy between city and country is so great. The difference attests the deep gulf that still separates the modern city from the antiquated countryside in this Oriental area.

Literacy in India, as Table 61 reveals, tends to increase according to the size of the city. The cities over 500,000 stand apart as a distinct class, just as they did with respect to fertility ratios.[7] The cities under 50,000, although lowest in the urban scale, still have nearly three times the literacy of the parts outside the cities.

The increase of literacy by size of city is much sharper for females than for males. In the largest cities the male literacy is not quite twice as great as female literacy, but in the cities of less than 50,000 it is five times as great. The greater equality of male and female literacy in the largest cities marks these cities as the focal points of modernization in the Indian region. Everywhere in the West we find female literacy virtually equal or superior to male literacy, but in India and Pakistan this condition is approached only in the three biggest cities.

[6] In 1931 the total urban population of India was 37.5 million. The population of the 89 cities under discussion was 12.6 million. This leaves 24.9 million urban people not in our urban sample but included in the "rest of India." The latter category, which contains only 17 million literates, clearly gives no idea of the true rural literacy in India, which must be much smaller. It is possible, in two provinces, to compare the literacy in cities with that of the rest of the district in which the cities are located. In the case of the United Provinces, the literacy of the cities is roughly seven times the literacy of the rest of the districts. In the case of Madras it is roughly three times. *Census of India,* 1931, Vol. 18 (United Provinces), Part 1, p. 455, and Vol. 14 (Madras), Part 1, pp. 275–76. Of course, it stands to reason that the district in which a city is located will have greater literacy than districts in which no city occurs.

[7] Chapter 10 *supra.*

An additional question is this: Is literacy moving ahead faster in the cities of this area than in the country? The answer is, yes. The evidence consists in returns for literacy by age, as presented in Table 62. Since the age group 5–19 will constitute the most active part of the next adult generation,

TABLE 62

Per Cent Literate for Two Age Groups, in Cities and Outside of Cities, 1931 and 1941

Age and Sex	1931 [1]				1941 [2]	
	89 Cities	Rest of India	10 Cities	Rest of Provinces	10 Cities	Rest of Provinces
Both Sexes						
5–19	23.6	5.9	27.1	5.8	45.3	12.5
20 plus	29.7	8.6	34.0	9.0	47.8	15.1
Ratio [a]	0.80	0.69	0.80	0.65	0.95	0.83
Males						
5–19	30.5	9.3	32.2	9.3	50.7	17.7
20 plus	40.4	15.1	41.0	15.6	54.9	24.2
Ratio	0.75	0.62	0.79	0.60	0.92	0.73
Females						
5–19	14.9	2.2	20.2	2.0	38.3	6.7
20 plus	13.5	1.7	19.9	1.7	33.0	5.0
Ratio	1.10	1.29	1.02	1.14	1.16	1.33

[a] Obtained by the following division: $\dfrac{\%\text{ Lit. Age 5–19}}{\%\text{ Lit. Age 20 Plus}}$. In some cases the ratio appears to be erroneous by a small amount. This is because the figures given here are rounded figures.

[1] *Census of India,* 1931, Part 2 of eight provincial volumes having data.

[2] *ibid.,* 1941, in six provincial volumes.

its degree of literacy holds an important key to the future. In the Indian population the ratio of this age group to the 20-plus age group, with respect to literacy, is generally higher in the cities than in the country. This means that in the future the cities will improve their literacy even faster than the rural sections, and that consequently the gulf between city and country will increase rather than diminish. However, the higher urban ratio holds only for males. For females the position of city and country is reversed, indicating that in the future female literacy will gain faster in the rural than in the urban areas.

TABLE 63

Literacy at Ages 5–19 as a Ratio of That at Ages 20 and Over, by City Size, 1931 [1]

	Both Sexes	Males	Females
Cities 500,000–plus	0.84	0.83	1.05
Cities 100,000–500,000	0.80	0.75	1.16
Cities 50,000–100,000	0.79	0.73	1.18
Cities under 50,000	0.71	0.66	1.16
India minus 89 cities	0.68	0.62	1.26

[1] Compiled from *Census of India,* 1931.

How does this literacy ratio between the generations behave according to size of city? As Table 63 illustrates, the preponderance of the childhood generation is much greater the larger the city. At least, this is true of males and hence of both sexes combined.[8] It is not true of females, however, for with them the ratio between the generations varies inversely as the size of the city. This curious result, which agrees with the rural-urban pattern just described, perhaps indicates that in the larger cities the more stable female population (affected less by migration than the male population) has come nearer reaching a saturation point in literacy, whereas the less stable male population still receives heavy increments of non-literate adult migrants. The educational gain of females, as compared to that of males, is most rapid when the greatest difference in literacy prevails between the two sexes. Outside the 89 cities the females are destined to gain most rapidly, and it is precisely here that their present educational inequality is greatest. In the biggest cities, on the other hand, where they already have the greatest equality with men, they are destined to progress most slowly.

In short, it seems that Indian-Pakistani people are in a very early stage of educational modernization. In the next generation or two the cities, where literacy first began, will continue to advance more rapidly than the rural areas; and the bigger the city, the greater will be the relative advance. At the same time, the females are educationally so far behind in the rural areas that any gain looms large, and they are destined to improve more in the country and smaller cities than in the larger cities. The next step is for the rural areas to begin to catch up with the urban in masculine as well as feminine literacy. This is the stage that Latin America, for example, is in now; it has already been passed in the United States and Northwestern Europe, where there is little difference between urban and rural literacy.

URBAN DENSITY AND THE HOUSING PROBLEM

The distaste of many Indians and Pakistanis for the city is partly attributable to the crowded, dismal, and unhealthful conditions of urban housing. An analysis of census returns throws some light on this problem, though it does not reveal the whole picture. The outstanding facts are these: (1) Some of the cities suffer densities scarcely known even in the heavy industrial nations of the world. (2) These densities are achieved despite an absence of tall, efficient apartment buildings, the bulk of the population living in houses of one or two stories. (3) Most of the tenements contain only one room, with one or more families living huddled in this space. (4) In addition to extreme overcrowding, there is a notable absence of sanitary facilities and other conveniences. (5) The main compensation for such housing conditions lies in the tropical climate, which enables many people to spend most of their time out-of-doors. (6) The urban conditions, bad as they are, are little worse than those in the country; for this region has rural slums scarcely equaled elsewhere. (7) Some effort is being made to alleviate residential overcrowding, though it has not yet progressed far.

DENSITY

Because cities vary widely in the amount of vacant land included in their boundaries, their densities cannot be ac-

[8] The number of male literates is so much greater than the female, that the figures for both sexes combined are governed by the male figures.

curately compared. The figures in Table 64, therefore should not be taken literally; they merely show that the cities of Pakistan and the Union of India rank high in overall density.

TABLE 64

*Density in Selected Cities of India and Pakistan,
United States, and Egypt*

Persons per Square Mile

India, 1931 [1]		Egypt, 1937 [2]		United States, 1940 [3]	
Bombay	48,400	Beheira [e]	26,700	New York, N.Y.	24,900
Jaipur	48,100	Alexandria	24,400	Trenton, N.J.	17,300
Moradabad	29,000	Daqahliya [e]	21,800	Boston, Mass.	16,700
Benares	25,900	Cairo	20,600	Chicago, Ill.	16,400
Amritsar	24,800	Gharbiya [f]	19,900	Philadelphia, Pa.	15,100
Calcutta [a]	24,400	Sharqiya [e]	14,500	St. Louis, Mo.	13,400
Salem	23,100	Minya [e]	13,100	Pittsburgh, Pa.	12,900
Madras	22,300	Beni Suef	11,000	Buffalo, N.Y.	12,600
Trichinopoly	17,700	Gharbiya [g]	8,200	Cleveland, Ohio	12,000
Srinagar	15,800	Faiyûm [e]	8,200	Detroit, Mich.	11,800
Peshawar	13,800	Asyût [e]	6,300	Baltimore, Md.	10,900
Allahabad	12,100	Canal Zone	4,000	Washington, D.C.	10,800
Tinnevelly [b]	11,300	Suez	2,800	Atlanta, Ga.	8,700
Baroda	11,000			Dallas, Texas	7,300
Lahore	10,900			Mobile, Ala.	6,700
Patna	10,600			Kansas City, Kan.	6,700
Rawalpindi	9,500			Memphis, Tenn.	6,400
Hyderabad [c]	8,800			Cincinnati, Ohio	6,300
Jubbulpore	7,900			Miami, Fla.	5,700
Ajmer	7,000			Denver, Col.	5,600
Delhi [d]	6,800			Seattle, Wash.	5,400
Karachi	6,700			Houston, Texas	5,300
Poona	6,400			Akron, Ohio	4,600
				Oklahoma City, Okla.	4,100
				Jackson, Miss.	3,900
				Los Angeles, Calif.	3,400
				Des Moines, Ia.	3,000
				New Orleans, La.	2,500

a Includes Howrah.
b Includes Palamcottah.
c Includes Secunderabad, etc.
d Includes New Delhi, Shahdara, etc.
e The figures are for the Bandars, or provincial capitals, of these districts.
f Bandars: Tanta I and II.
g Bandar: El Mahalla el Kuba.
[1] *Census of India*, 1931, Vol. 1, Part 1, p. 50. The total list includes densities for 35 cities, of which only 23 are given here.
[2] *Population Census of Egypt*, 1937. Table 7, pp. 33–37.
[3] Warren S. Thompson, *The Growth of Metropolitan Districts in the United States: 1900–1940* (U. S. Bureau of the Census, Washington: Government Printing Office, 1948), pp. 27–32. The total list includes 140 metropolitan districts. The ones given here are selected to give representation to different geographical areas. Only the densities of central cities, not the whole metropolitan districts, are given.

As a refinement on overall density, the density by wards in different cities can be compared (Table 65).

Lest it be assumed that crowded living is confined to the cities, it must be stated that many rural villages exhibit an almost equal closeness of settlement. Although exact figures are hard to find, the general view is that the occupied land in villages possesses a high density. Even in tiny hamlets "the houses are as closely packed together as in the main [village] site. . . . If village densities were calculated on the area of the inhabited site or sites, and not on that of the site *plus*

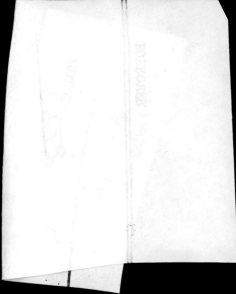

TABLE 65

Density of Urban Wards in Certain Cities, 1931 [1]

City and Ward	Density per sq. mi.
Baroda	
City Ward	79,400
Babajipura Ward	11,400
Fatehpura Ward	10,800
Bombay	
E Ward	72,200
F Ward	21,700
G Ward	27,700
Karachi City	
Rambaugh	39,600
Lyari	28,900
Ranchore	75,500
Calcutta	
District I	61,600
District II	50,900
District III	38,700
District IV	19,500
Lucknow Municipality	
Hassanganj Ward	5,700
Yahiaganj Ward	10,500
Hazratganj Ward	12,900
Cawnpore Municipality	
Civil Lines Ward	8,500
Sadar Bazar Ward	64,000
Collectorganj Ward	16,100
Anwarganj Ward	40,200
Hyderabad	
Ward IV	65,100
Ward VIII	7,300
Ward XI	24,500
Ward I	38,600

[1] Taken from various provincial volumes of the *Census of India*, 1931.

the village lands, they would generally be greater than that of any town. Only in the heart of the larger cities, where two and three-storeyed brick houses may be found, are human beings herded together on a scale which is not general all over the country." [9] Or another comment: "It is by no means sure, however, that the worst specimens of housing in [Madras] . . . do not come from certain rural areas, notably the wealthy delta tracts on the circars coast and in Tanjore. Where land is dear, housing tends to be bad. . . . Every foot of ground is grudged to the village site and even a comparatively well-to-do landowner will exist in an almost squalor that surprises the stranger. If this is so with an actual owner of land it can be imagined what is the condition of the farm labourer who in many cases also belongs to the so-called depressed classes. The depressed people are forced, in the villages and often even in the towns to live in a hamlet apart. Its site is rarely the most attractive and space is grudged." [10]

To check this last statement, the Madras census commissioner asked the tahsildars of certain representative taluks to

[9] *Census of India*, 1931, Vol. 18 (United Provinces), Part 1, p. 123.
[10] *ibid.*, Vol. 14 (Madras), Part 1, pp. 71–72.

give him the densities of village-sites, choosing their samples to illustrate the extremes of congestion. The results he compared with the density of urban wards, as follows: [11]

Taluk in which Villages Located	Persons per Acre	
	HIGH	LOW
Ghumsur	131	54
Sarvasiddhi	97	62
Ramachandrapuram	73	60
Tanuku	92	29
Bapatla	119	36
Koilkuntla	105	16
Arni	89	69
Walajah	65	38
Dharapuram	85	39
Pollachi	66	24
Papanasam	60	16
Tanjore	190	13
Tirumangalam	217	16
Kovilpatti	74	32
Srivaikuntam	96	36
Average	*104*	*36*
City in which wards located		
Madras	175	11
Madura	213	7
Calicut	137	6
Average	*175*	*8*

The average density of the most thickly settled villages is less than that of the city wards, but particular villages equal the urban ward densities. The range is greater in the city than in the village. In Western eyes the village densities must seem phenomenal. "Tanjore taluk produces one village-site of 0.36 acre on which 187 people are packed, equivalent to 519 per acre, and another with 190 people on 0.40 acre, or 475 persons per acre." [12] When it is realized that a density of 100 persons per acre is the equivalent of 64,000 persons per square mile, one can see that the rural density of habitation sites is amazing. Not all of the villages, and certainly not all towns, conform to this pattern of high residential density, but many of them do.[13]

HOUSING

The relatively high crowding in the towns and villages would be partly ameliorated if housing were different. If houses were tall and efficiently arranged, the inconvenience of large numbers per acre would be largely overcome. But the residential buildings are nearly all one or two stories. The large numbers per acre therefore mean extremely crowded housing.

[11] *ibid.*, p. 72.
[12] *ibid.*
[13] In parts of Bengal and most of Travancore the villages are more spread out. In Travancore the towns also do not seem to have an unusual density. In 1931 the 38 towns and cities, having an average population of 13,260, enjoyed an average density of 3,649 persons per square mile. This was high, since it exceeds the figure for a few large cities of the United States, but it was not phenomenal. See *ibid.*, Vol. 28 (Travancore), Part 1, pp. 65–66, 73–74.

TABLE 66

Percentage of Bombay and Karachi City Population Living According to Number of Persons per Room 1911, 1931 [1]

	5 and Under	6–9	10–19	20 and Over	6 and Over
Bombay City					
1911	69 [a]	20	9	3	32
1921	64	22	11	3	36
1931	67	24	8	1	33
Karachi City					
1921	73	21	5	1	27
1931	53	32	12	3	47

[a] This appears as 89 in the text, but it seems clearly an error.
[1] *Census of India,* 1931, Vol. 9 (Bombay Cities), Part 1, pp. 86, 96.

be drawn that the number of houses is not increasing as fast as the number of people.

For the cities of Bombay, Karachi, Lucknow, Cawnpore and Baroda, special information has been gathered on housing accommodations in terms of the number of rooms. It has been shown that by far the majority of the buildings (60 per cent in Bombay and 78 per cent in Karachi in 1931) have only a ground floor; [15] that an amazingly large proportion of the population occupies dwellings that have six or more persons per room (Tables 66 and 67); that in Bombay City 81 per cent of the total tenements are one-room affairs (Fig. 36) and these house 74 per cent of the population, living on an average with more than four persons per room; [16] and that there are numerous one-room tenements containing two or more families,[17] despite the fact that the size of these tenements is normally between 10 x 10 and 12 x 15 feet.[18] Such housing conditions are probably unequalled in occidental

TABLE 67

Percentage of Tenements, Percentage of Population, and Average Number of Persons per Room, for Each Class of Tenement, Certain Cities

	1 Room			2 Rooms			3 Rooms			4 Rooms			5 Rooms			6 Rooms		
	% of T'n's	% of Pop.	Av. No.	% of T'n's	% of Pop.	Av. No.	% of T'n's	% of Pop.	Av. No.	% of T'n's	% of Pop.	Av. No.	% of T'n's	% of Pop.	Av. No.	% of T'n's	% of Pop.	Av. No.
London [1]																		
1911	a	6	1.9	a	15	1.7	a	20	1.4	a	17	1.2	a	11	1.0	a	25	a
Bombay [1]																		
1921	70	66	4.0	14	14	2.1	7	8	1.6	4	5	1.3	3	4	1.1	2	3	a
1931	81	74	4.0	11	12	2.5	3	4	2.0	2	4	1.7	1	2	1.5	2	4	a
Karachi [1]																		
1921	69	58	3.5	22	23	2.2	4	7	2.2	2	4	1.8	1	2	1.8	2	6	a
1931	66	58	3.7	22	24	2.3	6	8	1.9	3	5	1.7	1	1	1.6	2	4	a
Cawnpore [2]																		
1931	a	63	a	a	25	a	a	8	a	a	3	a	a	2 [b]	a	a	a	a
Lucknow [2]																		
1931	a	50	a	a	29	a	a	11	a	a	5	a	a	5 [b]	a	a	a	a
Baroda [3]																		
1931	a	24	a	a	28	a	a	11	a	a	15	a	a	23 [b]	a	a	a	a

[a] No data available.
[b] These percentages are for "5 *or more* rooms."

[1] *Census of India,* 1931, Vol. 9 (Bombay Cities), Part 1, p. 90.
[2] *ibid.,* p. 97.
[3] *ibid.,* Vol. 1, Part 1, p. 58.

The census publishes figures on average number of persons per house. These are not strictly comparable from one census to another, because of changing definitions.[14] At best the data are roughly comparable since 1911, and they reveal a very slight tendency for the number of persons per house to rise, as follows:

1911	4.9
1921	4.9
1931	5.0
1941	5.1

Since the change of definition would be toward regarding a smaller unit as the "house," limited more and more to one family (which itself is becoming smaller), the conclusion may

cities. The figures for London in 1911 are given in Table 67 by way of comparison; they show that, in housing, the Indian cities are considerably more than 20 years behind the times.

Similar statistics are not obtainable for other cities in India. Judging, however, by the figures on density by ward and persons per house, the situation is much the same as in the cities mentioned.[19]

___

living and eating together in one mess with their resident dependents and their servants residing in the house." (*ibid.,* Vol. 1, Part 1, p. 55.) This definition, though used in 1931, could not be applied universally in all parts of India, because of variations in family customs with reference to food and residence.

[15] *ibid.,* Vol. 9 (Bombay Cities), Part 1, pp. 76–77, 95.
[16] *ibid.,* pp. 90–91.
[17] *ibid.,* p. 91.
[18] *ibid.,* Vol. 1, Part 1, p. 57.
[19] The number of persons per house and per room is apparently somewhat independent of the number per acre. Karachi, for example, has a density considerably lower than that of most Indian cities, and yet the crowding of its population per house and per room is quite similar to that of Bombay, which has a much higher density.

___

[14] Initially the census definition was a structural one. The "house" was defined as a dwelling sheltering one or more families and "having a separate entrance whether the entrance be from a public road, compound, corridor, balcony, gallery or otherwise." (Quoted in *ibid.,* Vol. 19 [Baroda], Part 1, p. 48.) Later, especially in 1911, the definition was shifted to more of a familial basis: "the buildings, several, one, or part of one, inhabited by one family, that is by a number of persons

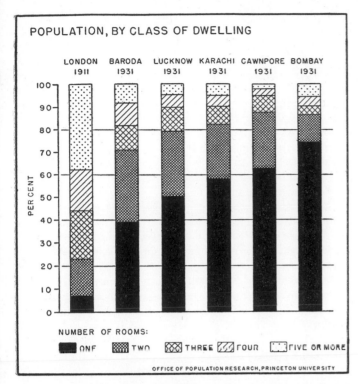

FIGURE 36. Per Cent of the Population in Dwellings by Number of Rooms, Selected Cities.

Connected with such housing conditions, both as cause and as effect, is the floating, or homeless, population of the cities. The mild climate that characterizes most of India, combined with the meager standard of living, makes it possible for many individuals to avoid the inconvenience of a crowded house and confiscatory rent altogether. "A marked feature of Madras is the street-dweller and squatter. A midnight tour of the central and northern parts of the town any fine night would disclose sleeping persons on every sidewalk. These persons are not all tramps by any means; the majority indeed are ordinary citizens in everything but the possession of a roof. Such a possession has no great inducement for a population of floating labour in a mild and pleasant climate, in a city where houses are scarce and rents often exorbitant." [20]

Apparently there are few statistics on the number of persons per room in rural villages. That they would be very different from those in the city is not likely, as indicated by the comparison of densities previously cited. The Baroda census volume for 1941 gives figures for villages.[21] These show the number of persons per room to vary between 4.6 and 5.4 in different parts of the State. These figures are all higher than for cities as given in Table 68.

Lest the figures fail to convey a complete idea of their human meaning, it may be wise to reflect at this point upon the following impressionistic description of housing in the city of Ahmedabad:

"The tap . . . served two rows of workers' tenements. It was the only tap they had. Left and right of me they stretched, and I counted 153 dwellings, of which 140 were occupied. In each was a family, with its lodgers, usually of five or six, occasionally of nine, persons. On this tap seven hundred human bodies depended for the water of life. Here they must drink; here they must refresh their sweating backs; here they must wash their clothes. . . .

[20] ibid., Vol. 14 (Madras), Part 1, p. 69.
[21] ibid., 1941, Vol. 17 (Baroda), p. 124.

TABLE 68

Average Number of Persons per Room for Selected Cities and Groups of Villages

Place	Persons per Room
England	
London [1]	
1911	1.26
Bombay Pres.	
Bombay City [1]	
1921	3.22
1931	3.50
Karachi [1]	
1921	2.86
1931	3.02
Baroda	
Baroda City [2]	
1931	1.84
1941	2.15
Baroda Division	
(16 villages)	
1941	4.58
Mehsana Division	
(21 villages)	
1941	4.70
Navsari Division	
(16 villages)	
1941	5.02
Okhamandal	
(1 village)	
1941	5.02
Amreli Division	
1941	5.43

[1] *Census of India*, 1931, Vol. 9 (Bombay Cities), Part 1, pp. 90. 97.
[2] *ibid.*, Vol. 19 (Baroda), Part 1, p. 83; and 1941, Vol. 17 (Baroda), pp. 17, 45, 120. The figures for Baroda City in 1931 and 1941 are open to some question, but the figures for the City and for the various divisions in 1941 were derived in the same way and should be comparable with those of the City in that year.

"I entered two or three of their dwellings. I paced them; perhaps ten, perhaps twelve, feet square. They had no window, and in the semi-darkness never a through breath of air was blown. They had no chimney, and in some of them I noticed the acrid fumes of the cakes of cow dung which served for cooking fuel. The floors were a foot below the street level, and in heavy rain they must be flooded.

"The roofs were of tumble-down tiles, which certainly would not resist the rains of the monsoon. The two rows stood back to back, and the narrow lane behind them was littered with garbage and green with filthy slime. Each family had only one of these rooms, with a verandah on which there was space for only one person to sleep. But to sleep in such dens is difficult, while the hot weather lasts. Even in Bombay the streets are littered every night with men who have sought refuge in them from their stifling dwellings. They stretch a mat or a bed in the gutter, or even on the pavement, and there amid the roar of traffic and the trampling of feet, they endeavour to sleep. These workers are inefficient. What would you expect? Rarely does sleep bring rest, and rarely do they eat to satisfy hunger. The women fare still worse. They dare not sleep in the open air, and modesty forbids them to bathe naked, as the men will do, under the public water-tap.

"From Bombay to Calcutta I saw many specimens of workers' dwellings. Some few, erected by kindly employers, were creditable: many were worse than the row I have just described. The Report of the Whitley Commission confirms this picture. In Bombay, it states, 97 per cent of the working classes live in one-roomed tenements, with six to nine persons to a room (p. 270). Of the industrial suburb of Calcutta (Howrah) it writes that the overcrowding is 'probably unequalled in any other industrial area of India' (p. 272). Of Ahmedabad it writes: 'The areas occupied by the working classes in Ahmedabad present pictures of terrible squalor. Nearly 92 per cent of the houses are one-roomed: they are badly built, unsanitary, ill-ventilated and overcrowded, while water supplies are altogether inadequate and latrine accommodation is almost entirely wanting. . . .' (p. 277)." [22]

The urban housing situation cannot be due to the speed of urbanization, because the pace has been much slower than in America and Australia. It cannot be due to the inevitable influence of economic progress, because such progress in Argentina, for example, gave rise to no comparable situation. Rather, like many other characteristics of this region, it is due to the social structure combined with the politico-economic situation. Indian existence has been a rural existence, and the social structure reflects this fact. The city and its industry, science, and finance, are alien to the region's folkways and mores. As a result the city wears an aspect of impermanence, and there are few standards that are accepted as fundamental necessities of existence. In addition, the Indian economy has been a semi-colonial economy. The poverty of the masses has made good housing impossible as an investment. The increasing population has deterred a rise in the standard of living, which in turn has prevented any tendency toward a decrease in the rate of population increase. The housing situation is thus a part of the vicious circle that has been cited repeatedly in this study. Industrialization and urbanization in a situation of this sort are extremely costly in human life. Unless a special effort is made to prevent this cost, it tends to be as great as the cost during the initial stages of the industrial revolution in England. But there is this difference—then such cost could not be avoided. Today the knowledge and resources exist to avoid it. This is what makes a tragedy out of what would otherwise be simply a natural calamity.

The Future of the City in India and Pakistan

Although the subcontinent has been traditionally rural, there are undeniable evidences that a change is under way. The acceleration in the growth of cities, the correlation between size of city and rapidity of growth, the trend toward industrial and commercial expansion, the potential development of female employment in urban industries and the consequent normalization of the sex ratio all indicate that urbanization in India is likely to gain momentum as it goes forward, and that within the next few decades, barring major catastrophes, the pace may become extremely rapid.

In so far as this is true, urbanization in this area bears a resemblance to the history of urbanization in other places. In other areas the process was relatively slow at first, gradually gained velocity, and finally tapered off again—the whole

[22] Henry Noel Brailsford, *Subject India* (New York: John Day, 1943), pp. 253–54.

being describable in terms of a logistic curve for population growth. At present Pakistan and the Indian Union appear to be in the early stage of the process.

If the signs are valid, if urbanization is coming on a big scale, then a fundamental revolution will inevitably occur in Hindu and Muslim society. The city is the diffusion center for modern civilization, and as it comes to dominate the countryside, the new will come to dominate the old. The city has so far led in the growth of literacy, in the education of women, in the decline of caste, in the reduction of fertility, and in the development of political awareness. It is therefore playing the same innovating and stimulating role that it has played in Western civilization.

But there is in the cities of this Asiatic area something reminiscent of eighteenth century cities in Europe. Despite the presence of modern industry, modern transportation, and modern ideas, these places have a sprawling, unsanitary, unplanned, and neglected character that is strangely anachronistic. Furthermore, even though modern ideas are in circulation, the extensiveness and persistence of ignorance, disease, overcrowding, and stratification seem appalling. Although postmedieval urbanization in Europe probably exhibited these manifestations in greater abundance than the present-day Indian and Pakistani cities do, it is also true that the latter exhibit them far more than American or Australian cities ever did at any stage.

What, then, gives these Asiatic cities their backwardness? First, they are rising out of a civilization and among a people but lately medieval in type. Whereas the cities of the New World represented a diffusion of urbanism *along with* the diffusion of the whole of Western civilization, the cities of India represent a partial diffusion. They are being built on the basis of Western industry, transport, and commerce; but the people who inhabit them, who do the work and give them life, are not Westerners at all. They are Easterners, and the Western-type city represents an alien borrowing—something that they have only partially absorbed, and that they have altered in the process.

Second, although the very rapidity of city growth is due to the penetration of Western influence into India, the anachronistic character of some features of the city is perhaps due to India's former lack of control over the process. As in other matters, the fact that industry and commerce have been pursued without the limitations that might have been imposed had it been entirely indigenous, has tended to lead to a neglect of the non-economic aspects of life. To a certain extent the Indian population has been used as an instrument—as labor—just as the population in the early history of the industrial revolution in Europe was used. The indigenous culture has served as an element making conditions more archaic; it has not been given a chance on the positive side, because it has not been in ultimate control. Had it been in control, it would undoubtedly have prevented urbanization from developing as fast as it has. Such urbanization as did develop would probably have been even more anachronistic than that we now see, but its lesser scope would have been an extremely mitigating factor. The cities have developed with considerable rapidity, but without the safeguards usually present in recently urbanized Western countries. Now that India and Pakistan are under the control of their own people, it will be interesting to watch the further development of the cities.

It should not be assumed that faster urbanization will simply exaggerate the already hard conditions of life in the cities. There is every evidence that an awareness of urban problems now exists, that the city is becoming a more acceptable place to live, and that improvement is in the air. The Census Commissioner for 1941 says that "city life has begun really to appeal to the ordinary middle class or lower middle class Indian, because for the first time accommodation within his means and to his taste has become available." Blocks of decent flats with the amenities of running water and electric lights, and numbers of cinemas, trams, busses, hospitals, etc., have meant that persons increasingly seek to pass their retirement or their leisure in a city instead of their former home. Also, the best education is available only in the cities.[23] There is evidence of a tendency for families rather than detached individuals to move into the city. Furthermore, the chief change in the age distribution of Bombay and Calcutta from 1931 to 1941 was an increase in the proportion 40 years of age and over. It appears that urbanization is on the way to becoming popular in the two Indian countries.

In the larger cities there are housing trusts, or cooperative housing societies. These are especially prominent in the provinces of Bombay and Madras. These are of two types, one involving individual ownership (Madras) and the other tenant ownership or co-partnership (Bombay). Such developments, however, constitute essentially middle-class enterprises, and are not a solution for the working classes. The Provincial Governments, which had been financing these societies, have been gradually withdrawing that assistance. Since the main requirement of the trusts and societies is long-term cheap financing, this has represented a serious set-back.

Urbanization in India and Pakistan, as it accelerates, promises to become gradually more humane, but there is likely to be a long period when the gains it makes in this direction will be offset by the losses contingent upon the faster rate of growth itself.

[23] *Census of India,* 1941, Vol. 1, p. 26.

++

Education, Language, and Literacy

++

SINCE a wide diffusion of education is indispensable to modern civilization, the extent of a people's enlightenment is highly correlated with other essential traits, such as urbanization, industrialization, and wealth. Consequently, the degree of education is a good measure of progress toward modernization. Exact information on education in backward countries, however, is not always available. The Indian region is fortunate in that it does have passable school statistics on enrolment and attendance and fairly good census data on literacy. These sources enable one to form a roughly accurate picture of educational development.

ILLITERACY STILL PREVAILS

Though the reduction of illiteracy in the India-Pakistan area has been considerable, the end result today is not impressive. In 1931, 91 per cent of those 10 years of age and over could not read and write, and in 1941, according to partial returns, 85 per cent could not do so.[1] This puts the Indian peninsula in the position of being one of the world's most illiterate regions, although it is by no means the worst in this regard. Undoubtedly most of the African continent is worse off, and also certain sections of Asia. But in the whole of Latin America only one or two countries have such a high illiteracy rate, and none in Europe. The illiteracy of the entire world in 1930 is estimated to have been 59 per cent of those aged 10 and over, and it is undoubtedly less now. The illiteracy of Asia exclusive of the U.S.S.R. is estimated to have been 81 per cent at the same date, and the continent of Africa 88 per cent.[2] Even if these estimates are in error by several points, the Indian subcontinent still looms as an extremely illiterate area. Table 69 gives illiteracy rates for selected countries from different areas of the world.[3] India's poor showing is understandable, but it makes one wonder what has been happening there, educationally speaking, during the last century.

THE GROWTH OF LITERACY

In the six decades from 1881 to 1941 the percentage literate of the population aged 10 and over nearly tripled itself (Table 70). Such progress over more than a half century,

[1] The sample basis for the 1941 figure is described in a footnote to Table 69.

[2] Kingsley Davis, "The World Demographic Transition," *Annals of the American Academy of Political and Social Science*, Vol. 237 (January, 1945), p. 10.

[3] Additional rates are given in Walter F. Willcox, *Studies in American Demography* (Ithaca: Cornell University Press, 1940), p. 178; and in Dudley Kirk, *Europe's Population in the Interwar Years* (League of Nations, 1946), pp. 263–77.

TABLE 69

Percentage of Population Age 10 and Over Who Are Illiterate, Various Countries [1]

Country	Date	Per Cent of Population Age 10-Plus Illiterate
U.S.A.	1930	4
France	1931	5
Hungary	1930	9
Italy	1931	22
Bulgaria	1934	31
Spain	1930	32
Greece	1928	41
Colombia	1938	44
U.S.S.R.[2]	1926	50
Philippines	1939	51
Union of South Africa [3]	1936	56
Portugal	1930	60
Venezuela	1936	63
Guatemala	1940	65
British Malaya	1931	70
China [4]	1930	80–89
Egypt	1927	86
Netherlands Indies [5]	1930	91
INDIA	1931	91
INDIA [6]	1941	85

[1] Unless otherwise noted the percentages are computed from census data. The figures for European countries, except Russia, are taken from Dudley Kirk, *Europe's Population in the Interwar Years* (League of Nations, 1946), pp. 263–77.

[2] From Frank Lorimer, *The Population of the Soviet Union* (Geneva: League of Nations, 1946), p. 67.

[3] For all races. Estimated by the author on the basis of data from various censuses.

[4] Estimated by the Office of Population Research, Princeton University.

[5] Age distribution estimated by the author from the rough categories of the census.

[6] Estimated on basis of partial returns. See Table 70.

though gratifying, is not remarkable, considering that the lower the figure one starts with, the easier it should be to register a large percentage increase. If the proportion literate had been 50 per cent to begin with, then it could not have tripled itself. Chile had 23 per cent of its total population literate in 1875, and raised this to 56 per cent in 1930.[4] Russia

[4] *Dirección General de Estadística, Sinopsis Geográfico-Estadística de la República de Chile*, 1933 (Santiago: Universo, 1933), p. 87.

had 24 per cent of its population age 9 and over literate in 1897, and raised this to 81.2 per cent by 1939 [5]—a rate of increase considerably faster than that experienced in India.

TABLE 70

Per Cent Literate, Age 10-plus, by Sex, 1891–1941 [1]

Date	Both Sexes Combined	Men	Women
1891	6.1	11.4	.5
1901	6.2	11.5	.7
1911	7.0	12.6	1.1
1921	8.3	14.2	1.9
1931	9.2	15.4	2.4
1941 [2]	15.1	27.4	6.9

[1] Except for 1941 the values are computed from the table, Literacy by Religion and Age, in Vol. 1, Part 2, of the various Indian censuses.

[2] The 1941 census did not tabulate or publish complete data on literacy. However, in certain provinces and states data were tabulated on this topic. In some of these a 2% sample was taken, in a few the full data were published. The provinces for which information could thus be obtained are Ajmer-Merwara (complete), Rajputana State Agency (complete), Bombay (2% sample, except for Bombay City which had 3⅛% sample), Orissa (2% sample), Delhi Province (complete), Jammu and Kashmir State (2% sample), and Bengal Province and States (2% sample). Although these areas seem to be roughly representative of India, it seemed quite possible that they reported literacy either because, on the average, they were more prosperous or more advanced than the others. Consequently, a correction factor was introduced by taking the ratio of literacy in this group of provinces to the literacy in all-India in 1931. It was found that literacy in the group of provinces exceeded that of all-India in 1931, being 10.76% as against 9.12%. In 1941 the group of provinces had a literacy, for those age 10-plus, of 17.82%. Adjusting this according to the 1931 ratio, we got a 1941 estimated literacy for all-India of 15.10%.

Fig. 37 gives not only the history of India's literacy, but also that of a few other countries. By comparison with other backward regions undergoing a process of modernization, India has *not* experienced such a rapid increase in literacy as the phrase "200 per cent increase" might suggest. It is worth noting, however, that the most rapid increase was experienced in the 1930–40 decade. This may be due in part to error in the 1941 figure, as explained in a footnote to Table 70, but it may also be due to a gradual acceleration in the pace of change.

It should be mentioned that the Indian census long used a very strict definition of literacy. It always defined literacy to include only those persons who were able *both* to read and to write. Thus it differed from a good many countries which merely require that the person be able to read. In India there was traditionally much learning of religious literature by rote, especially in the Muslim schools. The pupils often did not understand the language in which they were supposed to be reading, and were not taught to write. The census definition excluded such "readers." In 1881 and 1891, however, a confusion arose over a tripartite division that was attempted. Each person was to be recorded as falling in one of three categories: those who were *literate*, those who were *learning*, or those who were *illiterate*. The trouble was that the category "learning" was not mutually exclusive with the other two, and there was no sure way of assigning persons so classified to the other two categories. Consequently, the "learning" category was dropped in 1901. There is evidence that people preferred being enumerated as "literate" rather than "learning," and that consequently many literate learners were quite properly (from a later point of view) placed in the "literate"

[5] "Results of the Soviet Census," *The American Quarterly on the Soviet Union,* Vol. 3 (November 1940), p. 97.

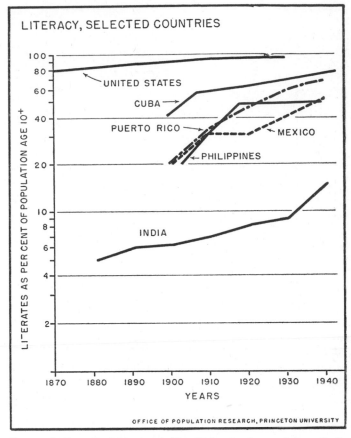

LITERACY, SELECTED COUNTRIES

UNITED STATES
CUBA
PUERTO RICO
MEXICO
PHILIPPINES
INDIA

LITERATES AS PER CENT OF POPULATION AGE 10⁺

YEARS

OFFICE OF POPULATION RESEARCH, PRINCETON UNIVERSITY

FIGURE 37. Growth of Literacy in Population Aged 10 and Over, India and Selected Countries.

category.[6] In fact, it seems likely that this tendency, plus a looser definition of literacy in 1881 and 1891, makes the statistics of literacy at those two dates fairly comparable with the statistics in subsequent dates. In 1911 the definition of literacy was sharpened by defining as literate only those persons "who can write a letter to a friend and read the answer to it." Prior to this date no standard of proficiency in reading and writing had been set forth for the census enumerators. All told, the picture of the growth of literacy since 1891, as given in the census returns, seems satisfactory, although it undoubtedly has some inaccuracies.[7]

[6] *Census of India,* 1901, Vol. 1, Part 1, pp. 157–59. In the 1901 census there was some tendency for enumerators to be influenced by previous instructions and to exclude students from the literate category.

[7] It has been maintained that the Indian statistics exaggerate the amount of literacy, on the following grounds: (1) School children tend to be accepted as literate in many cases when they are not. (2) Adults are often regarded as literate when they have long since lost their ability to read and write. (3) The enumerator does not have time to find out whether or not the person can actually read and write a letter. (4) Since literacy has prestige, people want to appear literate if they can, and the enumerator, for sheer convenience, is tempted to adopt a lenient standard. *Census of India,* 1931, Vol. 8 (Bombay Pres.), Part 1, p. 288. Undoubtedly, there is some truth in this argument. India is perhaps a bit less literate than it is alleged to be. But the same is probably true of most other backward areas, and the proportion of error has likely not changed much in India during the time that censuses have been taken. Therefore, the charge of inflated literacy returns should not be assumed to invalidate international comparisons or studies of trends. In India there is reason to think, especially in the earlier years, that many women described themselves falsely as illiterate because it was not compatible with the ideal of womanhood to have this accomplishment. In some areas, as in the Northwest Frontier, it is not thought manly to admit literacy. On the whole the literacy statistics in India seem to be surprisingly accurate. See R. V. Parulekar, *Literacy in India* (London: Macmillan, 1939), Chaps. 3–5.

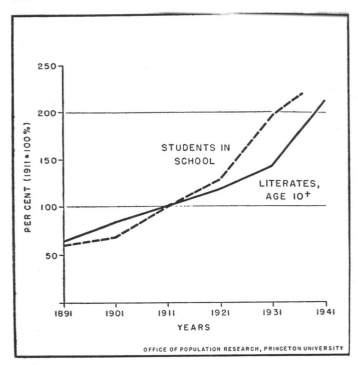

FIGURE 38. Growth of Literacy and School Enrolment in India, 1891–1941. (1911 figures = 100%.)

The role of formal education in the development of literacy is attested by the figures on school enrolment, as shown in Fig. 38. The number of students in school has risen more sharply than the number literate, but this can be expected, since the former include advanced as well as primary students. The striking feature is the fairly close correspondence between the growth in school enrolment and the growth of literacy.[8]

The obstacles to educational progress in the region seem almost overwhelming, and they are all intricately interconnected so that one reinforces the other. The extreme poverty of the masses makes even the small outlay necessary for school expenses difficult for parents to bear. It also hinders the provincial governments in their attempt to support education in the manner required for really rapid gains. The predominantly agricultural character of the economy has made formal education seem of little value, and since the educational ideas have been imported from industrial nations, they have often proved inappropriate to the Indian scene. Parents have often seen little value in sending older children to school when they could be adding to the family income at home. The traditional view that education is the monopoly of particular castes has taken a long time to die. Also, the multiplicity of languages, plus the fact that much of the education has been conducted in a foreign tongue (English), has had a retarding influence. In addition, there is the huge size of the Indian peninsula and the great number of its people, both of which make it difficult to institute modern reforms rapidly. Finally, the rate of population growth, with the inevitably large proportion of the population in the childhood ages, has made education still more of a burden.[9] Reflecting on this network of interrelated

obstacles, one is amazed at the progress that has actually been made. The new governments of the Union of India and Pakistan have a real test ahead of them: Will they be able to accelerate, or even maintain, the recent pace of improvement in literacy?

SEX INEQUALITY IN EDUCATION

The difference between male and female with respect to education is more extreme in this part of the world than anywhere else. This is the outgrowth of an ancient prejudice against the education of women as such, and against the employment of women in pursuits where they would need education.[10] The masculine tradition in the schools is great. Even elementary schools are separate for boys and girls. Some 160 years ago there was not a single girls' school in India. In 1942–43 there were 25,338 recognized girls' schools of all levels in British India alone; but there were 178,047 boys' schools. There were, at this same date, 3.5 million female scholars in recognized schools in British India, as against 11.4 million male scholars.[11] Most of the teachers in Indian schools are male teachers, because of the prejudice against outside employment of women.

No wonder the male literacy exceeds the female literacy. For every literate woman in the population (the sex ratio being held constant) there were in 1931 more than six males literate, and in 1941 approximately four.[12] If these ratios seem remarkable, let us look back to 1891, when there were 21 literate males for every literate female. The truth is that India is gradually overcoming her prejudice. The literacy of females, as Figure 39 shows, has been growing much faster than that of males. If the trend continues, the sexes will eventually become equal in this regard, but it will take a long time yet.

The relative literacy of males and females needs to be broken down according to age. In the last two censuses, for example, the number of males literate for every female in this category (the sex ratio being held constant) was as follows:

	1931	1941 [13]
All ages	6.1	3.8
5–9	3.2	2.2
10–14	3.5	2.4
15–19	4.8	2.9
20-plus	7.6	4.8

In other words, the older the individuals the greater is the inequality between men and women. This fact, which is more pronounced the further back one goes in time, confirms the secular trend depicted in Figure 39. If women have been gaining in literacy compared to men, they can be expected to show greater equality with men in the younger than in the older ages.

In spite of the gains being made by women, the great inequality in literacy that still prevails gives an insight into

---

[8] The relation between school statistics and literacy statistics is discussed in considerable detail by Parulekar, *op. cit.*, Chaps. 3–5.

[9] The number of literates aged 10 and over in 1941 was more than double the number in 1931—i.e. 44 million as against 21.9 million. But if the population had remained at the 1931 figure, the number of literates in 1941 would have yielded a literacy figure of 18.3 per cent instead of 15.1 per cent. Cf. T. A. Raman, *Report on India* (New York: Oxford University Press, 1943), p. 82.

[10] Sir Philip Hartog, *Some Aspects of Indian Education Past and Present,* Studies and Reports, No. 7 (London: Oxford University Press, 1939), pp. 52–55.

[11] *The Indian Year Book,* 1945–46, pp. 363–64.

[12] All 1941 literacy figures are derived from a limited sample. The sample comes mainly from advanced areas and so probably exaggerates the amount of female literacy. See Table 70.

[13] See preceding footnote.

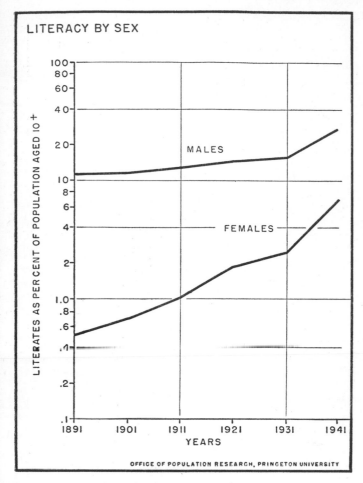

LITERACY BY SEX

OFFICE OF POPULATION RESEARCH, PRINCETON UNIVERSITY

FIGURE 39. Growth of Male and Female Literacy in India, 1891–1941.

the current role of literacy in Indian society. For the mass of people in the Indian peninsula the ability to read and write still apparently has little purpose. For large sections of the population it is an artificial accomplishment. A literacy confined to males is apt to be a special kind of literacy, limited to business or political necessity rather than diffused as a natural heritage through all aspects of life. To have its greatest effect, the ability to read and write must become a domestic necessity, taken for granted by members of both sexes.[14]

THE GEOGRAPHIC DISTRIBUTION OF LITERACY

Concerning the distribution of literacy by political area, two facts stand out: First, the difference between areas is not great; and second, such concentration as exists is found along the coast.

In 1931, the last date when statistics for all political divisions are available, all of the major states and provinces had less than 13 per cent of their people (aged 5 and over) literate. (See Map 16.) The most literate section was Cochin, a small state with 34 per cent of its inhabitants older than 5 able to read and write. The least literate section was in the Central Provinces States, with 2.3 per cent literate. While the difference looks big if stated in terms of literacy, it looks much smaller if turned around and stated in terms of illiteracy. In every province or major state more than 60 per cent of the people over 5 were illiterate, and in none of them were more than 98 per cent of them so. Practically every state and prov-

[14] *Census of India,* 1931, Vol. 1, Part 1, p. 326.

ince falls between 82 and 96 per cent illiterate—a range of only 14 points.

Even with such modest differences, it is nonetheless noticeable that the sections of greatest literacy are all located along the coast, while those of least literacy are located in the interior. This is doubtless explained by the greater development, foreign contact, and urbanization of the coastal areas. It is not due solely to urbanization, because some of the most rural provinces (such as Coorg, Bengal, and Travancore) lie along the coast and yet have a high percentage of literacy, while some of the most urban provinces (such as the Punjab, Rajputana Agency, and United Provinces) lie in the interior and have a low percentage literate. It seems clear that, as in Turkey and other Asian countries, the area of greatest foreign contact, the coast, boasts the greatest amount of literacy. This connection of literacy with the coast is noticeable even by districts—those districts lying to the interior of the coastal states and provinces being less literate than those on the shore.[15]

The extreme differential in literacy is not found between such broad areas as provinces and states, but between groups and sections within these areas—between districts, between males and females, between castes, and between city and country.

RURAL-URBAN LITERACY

The rural-urban differences in literacy have already been treated in the preceding chapter, where it was pointed out that the cities have a tremendous advantage in this respect, and are likely to increase this advantage in the near future. This rural-urban differential suggests that India's modernization is still only skin-deep (i.e. city-deep), and thus reinforces the same conclusion arrived at a few pages back in our discussion of the sex differential in literacy.

LITERACY AND RELIGION

Although there are in the Indian peninsula large inequalities between religious communities with respect to literacy, the largest involve only minor religions. Figure 40 shows, for example, that the greatest inequality lies between the Parsis at the top of the scale and the Tribals at the bottom, both religions taken together constituting only 2.3 per cent of the population. Other groups found near the top—Jews, Jains, and Christians—together with the Parsis constitute only 2.19 per cent of the population. Between the two largest groups—Hindu and Muslim—the difference in literacy is comparatively small though by no means negligible, the Hindus being 91.6, and the Muslims 93.6 per cent illiterate.

As between the Hindus and Muslims, the most significant difference does not appear with reference to the whole region but with reference to specific parts. In areas where the Muslims are town-dwellers and businessmen, while the Hindus are agriculturalists, the Muslims are by far the more literate, and when the positions are reversed, the opposite is true. Table 71 brings this out. Of the 20 political divisions listed, only four fail to show a greater percentage literate in the more urban of the two religious groups. The four exceptions (marked with an asterisk) all have small populations, and

[15] *ibid.,* 1931, Vol. 14 (Madras), Part 1, pp. 266–67; Vol. 8 (Bombay Presidency), Part 1, pp. 290–91; Vol. 5 (Bengal and Sikkim), Part 1, p. 321; Vol. 28 (Travancore), Part 1, pp. 284–85; and Vol. 7 (Bihar & Orissa), Part 1, pp. 214–15. The only place where the relation is not clear is Travancore, all of which lies close to the coast anyway.

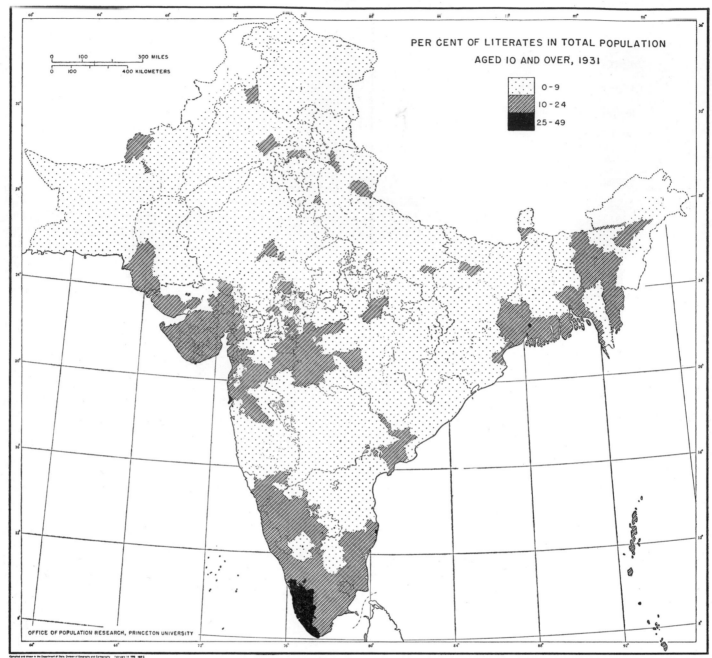

MAP 16. Literacy in India, 1931.

all favor the Hindus in situations where the Hindus happen to be more rural than the Muslims. Thus the literacy of Hindus and Muslims is primarily governed by their degree of urbanization in any given area, but some other factor operates to favor literacy among Hindus as against Muslims. For India as a whole the Hindus are more rural and yet have a greater degree of literacy than the Muslims. What this factor is which favors Hindus we cannot say for sure, but it is probable that it is partly a function of Hindu cooperation with the English-introduced educational system and partly a function of the higher socio-economic status of Hindus in the rural or within the urban habitat. In any case, literacy is apparently a better guide to differential fertility than urbanization, because the Hindus, who are on the whole more rural, are, as is well known, less fertile than the Muslims, who are more urban but also more illiterate. Furthermore, the areas constituting Pakistan are those where the Muslims are more

rural and more illiterate. In Bengal, for example, they are only a fourth as urban and two-fifths as literate as the Hindus, and in the Punjab they are two-thirds as urban and one-third as literate. This has made great difficulty for the Pakistan government, because it has meant a shortage of trained personnel.

To understand the greater literacy of the smaller religions, one must realize how they differ from the larger ones. Whereas the Muslim and Hindu faiths embrace all castes and classes, the Parsis, Jews, and Jains tend to include only a certain stratum of the social hierarchy. This is particularly true of the Parsis, a small trading sect located mostly in Bombay Presidency and enjoying an exceptionally high standard of prosperity. The Jews are in much the same situation, and the Jains, while less concentrated geographically and socially, have a more homogeneous social position than Christians or Sikhs. In contrast to these class-limited sects, the Hindus in-

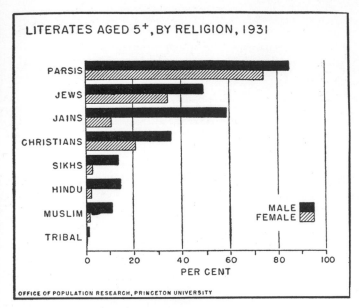

LITERATES AGED 5+, BY RELIGION, 1931

FIGURE 40. Per Cent Literate Aged 5 and Over by Religious Community, 1931.

TABLE 71

Selected Areas: Relation between Proportion Urban and Proportion Literate, Hindus and Muslims, 1931 [a]

Province, State, or Agency	Per Cent Urban [1]		Per Cent Literate Age 5 and Over [2]	
	HINDUS	MUSLIMS	HINDUS	MUSLIMS
INDIA [b]	10.5	13.5	8.4	6.4
Ajmer-Merwara	26.0	55.5	9.4	11.2
Bengal	11.8	3.7	15.7	6.7
Central Provs. & Berar	9.9	45.2	6.4	15.0
*Coorg	4.4	17.8	16.7	11.7
Madras	12.4	25.3	10.4	12.5
United Provinces	7.9	28.9	5.0	5.7
Baroda State	19.1	44.4	19.4	25.0
Bengal States	3.5	1.4	13.2	4.0
Bombay States	12.3	23.9	6.4	7.7
Central India Agency	8.0	47.5	4.5	15.3
Central Provs. States	3.6	25.7	2.7	15.2
Gwalior State	8.7	44.6	3.9	9.2
Hyderabad State	8.6	33.5	3.9	12.0
Madras States Agency [c]	17.0	32.7	12.1	17.6
Mysore State	13.3	42.7	9.3	12.3
*Punjab States	2.0	15.0	4.0	3.1
*Punjab States Agency	10.2	12.3	5.3	1.9
Rajputana Agency	11.2	35.8	3.3	3.9
*United Provinces States	4.7	32.2	5.2	3.0
West. India States Agency	17.4	44.2	10.2	13.8

[a] Asterisks indicate the places in which Muslims are more urban than Hindus.

[b] Includes Burma, but this makes virtually no difference in this table.

[c] Excluding Travancore and Cochin.

[1] *Census of India*, 1931, Vol. 1, Part 1, p. 61. Some areas were omitted either because of lack of data or incomparability between this table and the literacy table.

[2] *ibid.*, p. 340. The source gives the figures by male and female only, with no total. We have added the males and females in each case and divided by 2. This underestimates the total slightly, because the sex ratio is high, but the error is of no consequence here.

clude, for statistical purposes here, every stratum of society, from the outcastes to the most exclusive Brahman ranks.

Some of the Hindu castes pursue occupations that resemble those of the Parsis and Jews, and consequently compare favorably with these in literacy. The same is true of Muslim classes.

It is interesting that literacy is affected by conversion. The Christians, as a group, lost in proportion literate between 1921 and 1931, the reason apparently being that their new converts, coming mostly from the Tribals and lower Hindu castes, were illiterate to a degree which overcame the effects of the Christian zeal for education. The Sikhs in the United Provinces lost in literacy for much the same reason. "The number of Sikhs in the province was more than trebled . . . by a large body of Jats returning themselves as Sikhs for the first time." [16] Elsewhere, for the most part, the Sikhs showed a great gain in literacy.[17] In the United Provinces again, the Arya sect showed a decline as a result of conversions; yet the Arya still had a male literacy over three times as high as that of Brahmanic Hindus, and a female literacy ten times as high.[18] The general rule apparently is this: Not all religious groups with high literacy are proselytizing, but some of them are. In case of a proselytizing religion, the tendency is to make converts in the lower ranks of society, bringing illiterates into a much more highly literate body. This is true of the Sikhs, Christians, Aryas, and to some extent of the Hindus themselves. It follows that the groups that lose converts are the lowest and therefore generally the most illiterate, if not as a religious group, at least as a stratum. Thus the groups that lose most by conversion are the Tribals and the Exterior Castes; but these, when they lose individuals by conversion, tend to lose their best educated members. So conversion, as a type of social mobility in India, enables individuals to jump several ranks (at least along the social scale signified by literacy), though the total distance is not so great when looked at in terms of the individuals being converted as when looked at in terms of the losing and gaining groups as a whole.

Though socio-economic status seems to be the main factor in the degree of literacy in a religious group, we have to ask the additional question of what type of religion is involved. In the case of those religions limited to a single stratum or economic group, it may be legitimately asked if the religion itself does not have some part in giving the group its economic position. Also, we can see plainly that the evaluation of literacy by some religions, independently of socio-economic status, is an independent factor in itself. This is pre-eminently true of the Christians. It is also apparently true of the Hindu as against the Muslim.

TABLE 72

Per Cent of Population Aged 10-plus Who Are Literate, by Religion, 1891–1931 [1]

	Muslim	Sikh	Hindu	Parsi	Jain	Christian
1891	4.2	6.8	6.3	66.2	32.6	26.5
1901	4.4	7.5	6.5	76.2	30.9	26.6
1911	5.2	8.8	7.3	82.7	34.8	28.5
1921	6.2	8.0	8.6	83.7	37.8	31.7
1931	7.2	10.2	9.3	83.0	38.2	30.5
% Increase 1891–1931	70.7	49.9	46.4	25.4	17.1	14.9

[1] Computed from Imperial Table 13, Literacy by Religion and Age, in Part 2 of Vol. 1 of the various censuses.

[16] *Census of India*, 1931, Vol. 18 (United Provinces), Part 1, pp. 459–60.

[17] *ibid.*, Vol. 1, Part 1, p. 329.

[18] *ibid.*, 1931, Vol. 18 (United Provinces), Part 1, p. 459.

Since the turn of the century, when Muslims began to re-alize the handicap of their relative lack of education, they have improved their relative position. Between 1891 and 1931 they made the largest percentage gain in literacy of the vari-ous religious groups (Table 72). The Christians, who have taken in large numbers of Tribals and low-caste Hindus as converts, have made the slowest progress, despite the efforts of missionaries. The school statistics, as depicted in Fig. 41, show that the Muslims have led in the increase of proportion in school, and that both Muslims and Hindus have increased their proportion in school faster than the Christians.

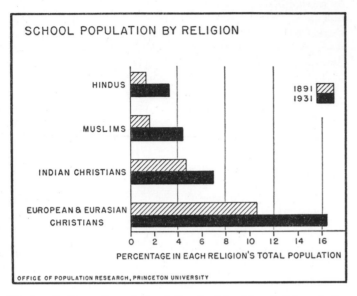

FIGURE 41. Proportion of Population in School by Religion, India, 1891 and 1931.

LITERACY AND CASTE

Within the Hindu, and to some extent within the Muslim and Christian communities, the proportion of literacy varies sharply with caste position. For instance, out of a selected group of twenty-four castes in 1931, the one at the top had a literacy of approximately 63.4 per cent, while the one at the bottom had a literacy of only 0.55 per cent.[19] The rest of the castes were spread up and down the scale between these two extremes. It is not always true that the higher the social status, the higher the literacy. Some castes pursue a type of occupa-tion, such as that of scribe, which requires literacy but does not necessarily bestow the highest social position. (Since the occupation may apply only to one sex or the other, the pro-portion of male literacy may not always be a good indicator of the proportion of female literacy.) But in general there is a rough correlation between social position and degree of literacy. At the top are usually the scribe castes, next the traders, and at the bottom the exterior castes and the tribal groups.

In 1891 it was found that 11 groups of castes or races com-prised just under 14 per cent of the population and just over half the literate population.[20] The next census report had this to say: "The officers of the Education Department, with whom the decision practically rests as to the localities where new schools are to be opened and what grants-in-aid should be given, belong almost exclusively to the small privileged

[19] ibid., 1931, Vol. 1, Part 1, p. 330.
[20] General Report of the Census of India, 1891, Sessional Papers, Cmd. 7181 (London: Her Majesty's Stationery Office, 1893), p. 222.

group of high castes. In Bengal, for example, excluding 44 Europeans and Eurasians, . . . there are 137 officers of the Education Department, of whom no less than 111 are Brah-mans, Baidyas and Kayasths; only 9 are Muhammadans, 5 are Native Christians and 12 belong to other castes. The lower grades of the community are entirely unrepresented." [21]

Granted the inequality of literacy among castes, we can still ask this question: Has the growth of literacy in India meant at the same time a democratization of it? For instance, are the castes becoming more or less equal with respect to literacy? In the Baroda report of 1921 fear was expressed that the spread of education had helped to "enforce and even widen the existing cleavage between the classes in the community."

TABLE 73

Growth of Literacy in Groups of Castes Having High or Low Literacy in 1921 [1]

Groups	Average Literacy per 100 in 1921	Average Literacy per 100 in 1931	Per Cent Increase in Decade
MALE			
64 Castes with 10 or More Literate per 100 in 1921	30.0	38.0	26.7
108 Castes with Less than 10 per 100 Literate in 1921	2.8	4.6	64.3
FEMALE			
16 Castes with 5 or More Literate per 100 in 1921	13.6	19.9	46.3
56 Castes with 0.5–5 Literate per 100 in 1921	1.6	4.6	187.5
100 Castes with Less than 0.5 per 100 Literate in 1921	.1	.3	200.0

[1] Census of India, 1931, Vol. 1, Part 1, pp. 342–45. The castes for which the data are given in the census table are of course only a selected sample of all castes, but there is no indication that the process of selection operated to bias the results as presented in our own table.

But in the Baroda report for 1931 it was shown that this was not the case. Table 73, which compares castes in 1921 and 1931, shows definitely that the castes poor in literacy in 1921 gained more by 1931 than did the others. Similar data are not available for 1941, but the Baroda report for that year indi-cates that the lower castes are rising rapidly in the literacy scale:

"We find several castes (previously intermediate) have now to be found room for in the Advanced section. Some of the big artisan groups like the Soni and the Sutar, have perma-nently pushed into this section and now the Luhar and Darji, and even the humble Mochi, have forced themselves into this hitherto exclusive preserve of Brahmans and Vanias. The Mochis have a male literacy of 56 per cent and quite a respect-able showing in literacy for their females (22 per cent). It may well be that with this progress, the enterprising elements

[21] Census of India, 1901, Vol. 1, Part 1, p. 163.

amongst them will now want a new name for their caste . . . but it is hoped that they will not desert their useful calling. The rate of progress in certain representative castes of the Advanced section with whom education may be said to have reached saturation point is not great, while Darjis show 10 per cent more proportionate increase and Garodas (the only one of the Scheduled Castes now figuring amongst the Advanced) over 8 per cent.

"Of the 18 Primitive Tribes, three were already part of the Intermediate section in 1931 . . . Six others are now in it . . . Gamit is the only one left below: and for the remaining tribes—which are small and unrepresentative,—literacy figures were not compiled. Of the 12 Scheduled Castes, three were there in 1931—Garoda, Chamar and Vankar. The first name is now promoted to Advanced. The remaining two still remain Intermediate. The Bhangi and Shenva have now joined their brother Harijans from below. The other untouchables . . . are small groups not compiled . . .

"The Illiterate section now contains only the most uneducable elements . . . None amongst the selected Scheduled Castes figures in this list. Rabaris and Vaghris are wandering communities, the bulk of them without fixed abodes, and are therefore practically untouched by schooling influences."[22]

Optimistic as these reports seem, it should be borne in mind that Baroda has always been an unusually advanced state. The majority of the census reports in other parts of India suggest that the intermediate and advanced castes are gaining in literacy more rapidly than the untouchables and the Tribals.[23] The untouchables still do not have equal access to educational institutions, and the Tribals are very often handicapped by the additional fact that they must study in a vernacular different from their own.[24] Only when the members of these two classes have joined the Christian community and have thus received the benefit of missionary schooling does their rate of literacy rise rapidly. Clearly the next great step in education lies in the direction of still greater democratization of the educational process.

LANGUAGE, SCRIPT, AND LITERACY

The progress of education has been hindered by the great diversity of language within the Indian subcontinent. There are more than 200 separate languages belonging to four different families of speech. If all of these languages had the same number of speakers, the effect of such diversity would be overwhelming. But fortunately, the great majority of the languages are spoken by relatively small groups, leaving huge blocks of people each of which enjoys the benefits of a common widespread language. Viewed in this way, the problem of linguistic diversity is not so formidable as it at first seems, although it is difficult enough.

All told, there are thirteen languages of outstanding numerical importance, each now having certainly more than 9 million speakers.[25] In 1931, which is the last date when census figures on language for the whole of India are available, over 300 million people, nearly 90 per cent of the entire population, spoke one or the other of these thirteen languages as a mother tongue. The names of these languages, together with the number of speakers and the per cent that each constitutes of the total population with declared mother tongue, are given below in their rank order: [26]

	Number of Speakers (millions)	Percentage of Total Reporting
Western Hindi	71.4	21.2
Bengali	53.1	15.8
Bihari	27.9	8.3
Telugu	26.2	7.8
Marathi	20.9	6.2
Tamil	20.2	6.0
Punjabi	15.8	4.7
Rajasthani	13.9	4.1
Kanarese	11.2	3.3
Oriya	11.1	3.3
Gujarati	10.8	3.2
Malayalam	9.1	2.7
Eastern Hindi	7.9	2.3
Total of 13 Languages	*299.6*	*89.2*
Total Reporting	*335.9*	*100.0*

It will be noticed that Western Hindi is spoken by more than a fifth of the people in what was once India. In the present Union of India this proportion is of course much higher. Western Hindi has been the most important language on the subcontinent since ancient times, important not only as a local vernacular in the heart of northern India but also as a second language, a *lingua franca,* over the whole north and west. It has a rich and varied literature, the cultured form being derived from a particular dialect of Western Hindi known as Hindustani. Furthermore, Western and Eastern Hindi are almost mutually intelligible, although the difficulty of mutual understanding is great.[27] If they are classed together, as is often done by writers wishing to minimize the region's linguistic difficulties, then there are only 12 languages of major importance. Western and Eastern Hindi combined embraced 79 million speakers in 1931, or 24 per cent of the total population. Yet it should always be remembered that each of the major languages tends to have several dialects, some of them mutually intelligible only with practice.

The trouble in this area, however, is not only diversity of language or dialect but also diversity of script. All told, over 40 different forms of writing are in use in India, some of them for the same language. "Many of these scripts have between 200 and 500 characters and furnish a major reason for the enormous stagnation in the lower grades of the schools" and for the slow rate at which pupils in school learn to read.[28]

[22] *ibid.*, 1941, Vol. 17 (Baroda), pp. 95–96.

[23] *ibid.*, 1931, Vol. 14 (Madras), Part 1, p. 272; Vol. 28 (Travancore), Part 1, pp. 295–96; Vol. 8 (Bombay Pres.), Part 1, p. 299.

[24] *ibid.*, Vol. 1, Part 1, p. 331.

[25] The All-India Radio, having an estimated audience of 200,000 radio sets in 1944, broadcast its programs in 16 different languages from nine stations located in different parts of India. Raleigh Parkin, *India Today* (Vancouver: Longmans, 1946), p. 6.

[26] *Census of India,* 1931, Vol. 1, Part 2, pp. 472ff.

[27] Sir John Cumming (ed.), *Modern India* (London: Oxford University Press, 1931), p. 8. T. C. Hodson says, however, that Western and Eastern Hindi "are two quite distinct languages." *India, Census Ethnography, 1901–1931* (Delhi: Manager of Publications, Government of India Press, 1937), p. 25.

[28] Geo. E. Noronha, *Backgrounds in the Education of Indian Girls* (Washington, D.C.: Catholic University of America, 1939), p. 7. See also *Village Education in India* (London: Oxford University Press, 1920), p. 200, cited by Noronha; and Frank C. Laubach, *Toward a Literate World* (New York: World Literacy Committee of the Foreign Missions Conference of North America, 1938), pp. 10–12, 70–71, 75–82.

Western Hindi is written by Muslims in a modified form of the Persian script and by most Hindus in a Sanskrit (Devanagari) script.[29] In the one form it has had so many Persian and Arabic words added to it that it has come to be regarded as a separate language called Urdu; and in the other form it has had so many Sanskrit words added to it, with some use of Persian as well, that it sometimes diverges markedly from its spoken form. Added to the confusion is the fact that the Hindu version of Hindi is not universally written in the Devanagari script. "Historical sentiment and local patriotism alike militate against the abandonment of any of the numerous scripts in use in India, but it seems probable that sooner or later some common script will have to be adopted, . . . Hindustani in the Roman script is already in use in the Army and proves eminently satisfactory, . . ."[30] Numerous attempts have been made to introduce a Roman alphabet for the writing of various Indian languages, or to improve the native alphabets, but custom in this respect [31] is virtually impossible to change.

Another difficulty in the Indian region is the divergence between the spoken and the literary language. This, as just mentioned, is true of Hindi to some extent. It is even truer of Bengali, the language with the second largest number of speakers in the subcontinent, most of whom live in Bengal. As a language for educational purposes Bengali leaves much to be desired, because of the gulf between its spoken and written form. "The literary dialect . . . is never used when speaking, except in formal addresses and the like. Even the most highly educated Bengalis employ the colloquial dialect in their ordinary conversation. The literary form of the language differs from the colloquial not only in its highly Sanskritized vocabulary but in its grammar, in which the dead forms of three centuries ago are retained in a state of fictitious animation. . . . During the past fifty years there has been a movement, with slight success, to reduce this absurd Sanskritization; but, still, at the present day many words current in literary Bengali are mere ideograms. The Bengali vocal organs are not adapted to the pronunciation of Sanskrit words, and so these words spell one thing, and, when read aloud, sound something quite different. Under such circumstances literary Bengali is divorced from the comprehension of every native to whom it has not been specially taught."[32]

Another illustration of the gulf between the spoken and literary language is found in Tamil, a major Dravidian tongue. "In Tamil, for example, newspapers and books print one vocabulary while the illiterate people speak another. In order to read, the illiterate man must practically learn a new language—the language of print. He might almost as well learn English—perhaps better, because Tamil is burdened with difficult rules of rhetoric. For example, there are a dozen synonyms for 'heaven.' It is bad rhetoric to use one of these synonyms twice until the other synonyms have all been used. . . . To a greater or less degree every one of the major Indian languages follows the same custom of over-burdening the *written* vocabulary."[33]

The chief explanation for this exotic tendency in the literary languages of India is the low rate of literacy. When the written language is the possession of a small, specialized class of people, when it is used for religious and literary purposes rather than for the daily information of the masses, it natu-

rally tends to diverge from the spoken tongue. This tendency has an ancient history in India, where dozens of literary languages have risen from the vernacular as a corrective to scholastic traditionalism, only to become themselves dead in turn as they progressively diverged from the mother vernacular. Until general literacy increases still more in India, this old tendency, which is present everywhere to some extent, will continue to manifest itself.

In modern India the question of language, script, and education has long been a bone of contention. When, for example, the first Congress government came into power in Madras, the teaching of Hindi was made compulsory in some classes of secondary schools where the mother-tongue was mainly Tamil or Telegu. The measure "was stormily and obstinately opposed. Though more than 900 persons had been arrested and convicted for disorder, the agitation was still afoot when the Ministry resigned."[34]

The chief conflict over language, however, has been between Hindus and Muslims. In the campaign preceding the 1947 elections, the Moslem League and the Congress party patently disagreed on only two points, one of them being the language issue. "The League pledged itself 'to protect and promote the Urdu language and script', and, though no mention was made of it in its manifesto, the Congress was notoriously bent on making Hindi the national language of India."[35] The Muslims considered the attempt to extend the use of Hindi at the expense of Urdu to be the most insidious feature of Hindu aggression. A Muslim educational survey, the Kamal Yar Jung report, published in 1942, claimed that Urdu primary schools were being closed or amalgamated with Hindi schools. It said, further, that the very languages the Muslims speak were steadily losing their Arabic and Persian words and being "Sanskritised."[36]

The partition of India into Pakistan and the Union of India solved the Hindu-Muslim conflict as far as the question of official language is concerned. In Pakistan the official language is Urdu and the script Persian; in the Union of India it is Hindi and the script, of course, non-Persian. Ironically, the two languages are basically the same. It is mainly vocabulary and script that differentiate them, but for purposes of literacy this is a profound barrier. In effect the two languages now are entirely "foreign languages" to each other. Obviously the adoption of official languages does not in itself eliminate linguistic diversity within each of these new nations, nor does it solve the educational problems growing out of this diversity. The actual languages spoken, both in Pakistan and in the Union of India, are still quite numerous. It is true that the diversity is less in Pakistan than in the neighboring state. But still, in East Pakistan (East Bengal) the people speak Bengali, while in West Pakistan they speak Punjabi, Sindhi, Lahnda, Brahui, Pashto, and others, all with various dialects. In the Union of India nearly all of the languages of the subcontinent are to be encountered.

Under the British, the English language became the intellectual *lingua franca* of India. Now, with independence, the Union of India hopes that Hindi will not only be the official language but will also become the intellectual, as well as popular, *lingua franca* of the country. To what extent this will happen is hard to predict. English has the advantage of using only one script, whereas Hindi is still written and printed

---

[29] Hodson, *op. cit.*, pp. 25–26.
[30] *Census of India,* 1931, Vol. 1, Part 1, p. 356.
[31] Laubach, *op. cit.*, pp. 95–97.
[32] T. C. Hodson, *op. cit.*, p. 32.
[33] Laubach, *op. cit.*, p. 90.

[34] R. Coupland, *The Indian Problem* (London: Oxford University Press, 1944), Part 2, p. 103.
[35] *ibid.*, p. 14.
[36] *ibid.*, pp. 186, 189, 190, 192.

in different scripts in different places. English also has the advantage that it has a wider geographical distribution than any other language in India. And finally, English, more than any native language, opens to Indians the literature of the outside world and provides full coverage of every field of human knowledge—something that no Indian language can yet do. It seems quite likely that Hindi will become the first intellectual *lingua franca* in the Union of India, linking all linguistic groups within the country, but that English will retain a place as the second *lingua franca* connecting the nation with the intellectual world outside.

The Indian censuses have consistently reported the number of persons literate in English. In 1901 data were gathered on literacy by language (any language) but definitions were confused by the enumerators to such an extent that the results are largely without value, except for English.[37] After 1901 all attempts to gather information on literacy according to language (again except for English) were abandoned, on the ground that each person, if literate at all, is almost invariably literate in his mother tongue. Unfortunately, however, since the census tables do not cross-classify literacy by mother tongue of those literate, the relative strength of the various written vernaculars cannot be ascertained accurately.[38] For the whole country we have only the number of those literate in English, and for a few provinces the number literate in other languages.

Literacy in English has risen rapidly in India, more rapidly than literacy in general. In 1931, the last date for which total figures for the entire country are available, there were 3.5 million people in India who could read and write English. This was 15 per cent of the total number of literates. The percentage of all literates who were literate in English at various dates is:

	Per Cent
1901	8.5
1911	10.1
1921	12.9
1931	14.9
1941	18.9 [39]

The population speaking English as a mother tongue (mostly foreign-born and Anglo-Indians) has hardly grown at all, being less than 300,000 in 1931. The gain in English literacy is therefore due to the acquisition of this language by Indians themselves. It seems apparent that the basis has been well laid for the use of English as at least a secondary *lingua franca* in Indian intellectual circles.

Naturally, literacy in English is greatest in the cities. In 1941, Delhi, most urban of all the provinces, had more than 83,000 inhabitants who could read and write English—36 per cent of all the literates in the province. In Bombay City 252,000 could read and write English—42 per cent of the city's literate population (while in the rest of Bombay Province the corresponding proportion was only 13 per cent). In five large cities—Bombay, Ahmedabad, Delhi, Ajmer, and Greater Calcutta—the literate in English constituted 50 per cent of the total literates, whereas in the rest of the provinces of which these cities were parts, the proportion was only 21

per cent. The conclusion seems apparent that not only is literacy itself mainly an urban phenomenon in the subcontinent, but that literacy in English is even more so. Thus the city in this part of the world again shows itself as the primary diffusion center of Western culture.

The various religious groups hold almost the same rank in English literacy that they hold in general literacy. But, as the following figures for 1931 show, one change of rank does occur, the Christians moving ahead a notch in English literacy.[40]

	Per Cent Literate Age 5 and Over		English Literacy as Per Cent of General Literacy
	ANY LANGUAGE	ENGLISH	
Parsi	79.1	50.4	63.7
Jew	41.6	26.4	63.4
Christian	27.9	9.2	32.9
Jain	35.3	3.1	8.7
Sikh	9.1	1.5	16.6
Hindu	8.4	1.1	13.5
Muslim	6.4	0.9	14.4
Tribal	0.7	——[41]	5.7

EDUCATIONAL PROBLEMS

To understand the present status of education in Pakistan-India, we must glance at the forces favoring and the forces opposing its growth.[42] In Western civilization education has represented (at least in part) a channel of vertical mobility in the social scale. It has provided training for urban occupations of high social status and high technological content, adapted mainly to an expanding commercial and industrial society. Much of this educational development in the West has occurred *since* the British entered India, with the result that its spirit has grown progressively away from that indigenous to India. Since the days of Macaulay the British have attempted to diffuse their own educational system to the Indians. The peculiarity of the diffusion has been that the Western model collides with two great realities in Hindu life—ruralism and caste. The rural masses find no real utility in book learning designed for businessmen, scientists, and scholars, and requiring leisured years to master. To them the Western schoolhouse is a nonfunctional institution, a needless expense. At the same time, in the caste order a channel of social mobility is extremely inappropriate and paradoxical, since the essence of caste is the lifetime fixity of social station. We could expect, therefore, that the progress of Western education, as shown by statistics of literacy, would be gradual rather than rapid, and that it would be accompanied by a breakdown of the Indian social order. Actually the progress in literacy has shown some acceleration, especially since 1931, and the Hindu social order has shown a corresponding change.

Just as in other developing areas, so in the Indian region one escape from an exclusively agricultural economy has lain in widespread education, and yet ruralism has itself made this extremely difficult. "Parents are not satisfied that education does their children good, and it deprives them of their services.

---

[37] *Census of India*, 1901, Vol. 1, Part 2, p. 103.

[38] It would be possible, by the expenditure of great effort, to relate the per cent literate to the main language of each district, and thus arrive at a fairly clear idea of literacy by language.

[39] Based on a sample of only six political divisions. The figure is probably too high to represent all of India.

[40] *Census of India*, 1931, Vol. 1, Part 1, p. 339.

[41] This figure is 0.04 per cent.

[42] A glance is all that we can take here. For a fuller coverage of India's educational problems see Hartog, *op. cit.*, together with the references he gives. He describes the pre-British system, gives the history under the British, and discusses current problems.

The Indian peasant has ordinarily no occasion, religious or secular, to read or to write. Such reckoning as he has to do he can do without formal instruction. Education, further, is an expensive luxury. Even free education costs money, and money is a commodity which is very scarce in the Indian countryside. It is not only that the child has to be supplied with books, slates, and other school materials, the cost rising with the stage of advancement; the matter of apparel is even more important. The cultivator's child who would at home spend most of his days in a loin-cloth has to be much more expensively equipped for school-going." [43]

It has been calculated that if the same per capita expenditure on education as in Britain were to be expended on Indian children, the cost would be about eighty times the total now spent in this region, and would exceed the current revenues of the country, central and provincial, by five or six times. Even if the English per capita expense were divided by ten, it would still be greater than India could afford.[44] A rural economy cannot easily support an elaborate educational system.

One fruit of the attempt to develop education in this agricultural territory has been *wastage*. "According to the view expressed by the Indian Statutory Commission a sustained course of instruction for a minimum period of four years is essential to establish a literacy that lasts." [45] If, therefore, we ascertain the number of pupils out of those in Class I who reach Class V, we shall obtain an estimate of the number who drop out before their schooling has reached the point of having any value for them. The Bureau of Education shows that 86 per cent of the boys and 93 per cent of the girls who were in Class I in 1929–30 are not to be found in Class V in 1933–34.[46] (See Fig. 42.) This indeed is wastage.

"The enrolment of primary schools is largely fictitious. Every District Officer knows that boys who will leave these schools before they have learnt to read and write form a big proportion of the total attendance. The parents of such a boy never seriously intend that he should be educated. They send him to school and leave him there so long as he is in the 'preparatory' or even the 'lower' classes, because this is a cheap way of keeping him occupied and out of mischief; because they are pressed to do so by the schoolmaster—or even by his superiors—who want to improve the look of their returns; or perhaps in case he shows a special aptitude for learning. They take him away as soon as the expense increases, and he can make himself useful in field or at pasture." [47] The fact that the girls show greater wastage than the boys is understandable. For them book learning is even less functional than for boys.

A second problem, explaining a good part of the wastage, is *stagnation*, the repetition of the same grade because of failure to pass the first time. R. V. Parulekar roundly condemns the stringency of the examinations in Indian primary schools, holding that a pupil condemned to repeat a grade usually loses interest in education. He cites figures showing that the average number of failures in each of the first four grades is around 50 per cent, varying slightly from one province to another.[48] Doubtless he is right in his criticism. But such a high ratio of failures suggests not only that the administration is at fault but also that both incentives in studying and efficiency in teaching are deficient.

A third problem attributable to the predominantly rural setting is *lapse* of literacy. "Many school children lapse into illiteracy again after they have left school. They return to almost wholly illiterate villages and having nothing to read or write, forget almost all they knew. In many villages it would be impossible to find a post-office, and difficult to find a book or newspaper. Unless a student continues to make use of the knowledge he has gained in four or five years of schooling, he will forget it all." [49] Though there is constant complaint about this problem in the educational literature, with cases being cited, there are few statistics. In Baroda it was estimated that 3.5 per cent of those who had been in Class IV at school were subsequently enumerated in the census as illiterate.[50] This is a very low estimate. Others estimate the proportion at between 20 and 25 per cent.[51] Parulekar, however, believes that the whole problem of "relapse into illiteracy" has been overestimated, and he makes a good case on statistical grounds.[52]

A fourth problem, connected with both wastage and lapse, is *inefficiency*. Though the peasantry is poor, the use made of funds for its education yields insufficient returns in literacy.

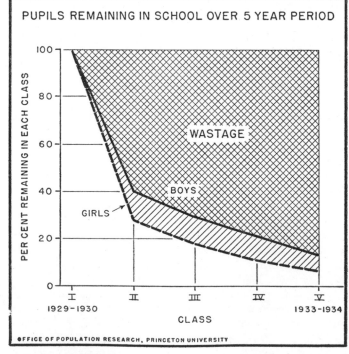

FIGURE 42. Wastage in the Primary Grades in British India, 1929–30 to 1933–34.

[43] J. R. Cunningham, "Education" in L. S. S. O'Malley (ed.), *Modern India and the West* (London: Oxford University Press, 1941), p. 176.

[44] *ibid.*, pp. 177–78.

[45] *Census of India*, 1931, Vol. 17 (Punjab), Part 1, p. 254. For a contrary view, holding that three years usually establishes permanent literacy, see Parulekar, *op. cit.*, Chaps. 3–5.

[46] *Education in India in 1933–34* (Delhi: Manager of Publications, 1936), pp. 40, 56. The tables are not altogether satisfactory, because no clue is given to the time of year at which the pupils are counted. Since it is estimated that a sizable per cent of those who actually pass through Class IV lose their ability to read, it seems better to take presence in Class V as the best gauge of effective education. Wastage varies considerably as between one province and another. See Hartog, *op. cit.*, pp. 34–39.

[47] *Census of India*, 1931, Vol. 18 (United Provinces), Part 1, pp. 468–69. (Quoted apparently from the 1921 report for this same province.)

[48] Parulekar, *op. cit.*, Chaps. 7–8, 11.

[49] Laubach, *op. cit.*, p. 91.

[50] *Census of India*, 1931, Vol. 19 (Baroda), Part 1, pp. 332–33.

[51] *ibid.*, Vol. 1, Part 1, p. 335.

[52] *op. cit.*, Chap. 5.

According to figures given by Cunningham,[53] the cost in rupees has not risen as rapidly as the enrollment. The author, however, attributes this not to increasing efficiency but to a lowering of standards. The Census Commissioner for 1931 speaks of "the inordinate excess of pupils shown by the Education Department as under instruction over the numbers returned as literate aged 5–20 by the census." [54]

In attempting to meet the problems of mass education among an agricultural people, the authorities have become involved in two issues: *educational experimentalism* and *compulsory school attendance*. Cunningham discusses the first of these as follows, speaking of the period before 1921: "One district authority . . . distributed to its primary schools an issue of blacksmiths' anvils. The anvils were an extreme instance of a general tendency. Every reformer sought to ride his hobby-horse in the village school. Sanitation, hygiene, first aid, land tenure, co-operative credit, postal wisdom, and the like pushed their way into the syllabuses. A great deal too much was expected of the teacher. In the ordinary village school the source of all this learning and enterprise was a dispirited drudge, poorly educated and, in most parts of the country, very poorly paid, who was in sole charge of four or five classes of little boys. With an average attendance of two days in three, he was confronted by a different selection of his pupils every day. Unpunctuality added to his difficulties. There are no clocks in the Indian countryside. . . . The lowest class, which gave the whole school a dragging start, was composed of children at many different stages, enrolled at all times of the year according to caprice or the influence of their horoscopes, . . ." [55]

In 1929 the so-called Hartog Committee came out strongly in favor of compulsory education, which had already been *enacted* by all the major provinces. It did so as a corrective of the waste and inefficiency of the voluntary system, holding that there had been no relation between the effort expended and the results attained, especially in the appallingly wasteful primary schools. But compulsion in itself, since it did nothing to alter the underlying conditions which plagued the voluntary system, has apparently accomplished little, most of the statutes having become dead letters. It should be borne in mind that the majority of schools in India and Pakistan are still one-room, one-teacher affairs. The process of consolidation of rural schools has not gone far yet. Under such circumstances the enforcement of compulsory attendance laws is very difficult.[56] In British India in 1941 approximately 23 per cent of the males and 8 per cent of the females of school age were *enrolled* in recognized schools of all levels. If these pupils attended regularly, it would mean a great gain; but still there would be 77 per cent of the males and 92 per cent of the females outside.

Even this brief review of the region's educational problems seems to bear out the statement that "the illiterates for the most part are caught in a vicious circle—they are ignorant because they are poor, and they are poor because they are ignorant." [57] Where to tackle the vicious circle first is a moot point, but common sense would suggest that it must be tackled on several fronts at once. This, in fact, is what is being done. The surprising thing, in view of the overwhelming handicaps, is the amount of progress that has been made. It has apparently been made because education offers the people a way to attain some of the things they want, and once they see the possibility, they grasp at it eagerly. The people in the cities and towns, in the middle classes, in business and industry, and in the army and government have learned the value of education. The government has helped to diffuse this attitude. The unwieldy but persistent drive toward modernization in India is thus reflecting itself inevitably in the demand for widespread education.

The two new governments of Pakistan and the Union of India clearly recognize the necessity of continued effort on the educational front. Prior to partition a drop in the number of pupils in schools was experienced as a result of World War II, but already the Central Advisory Board of Education in its *Report on Post-War Educational Development in India* had announced comprehensive and ambitious plans. It had recommended, among other things, that a system of universal, compulsory, free education for all boys and girls between ages six and fourteen be introduced as speedily as possible, at a cost of approximately two billion rupees. These plans could not have been executed soon, but they show the stress that was being placed on education. The two new Indian nations thus have a legacy of interest in education to go on. Although there will be demands within their own ranks for traditionalism and discrimination, there seems little doubt that the desire for modernization will carry the day. They will realize that national development in the present world depends as much on educational advance as on anything else.

[53] *op. cit.*, pp. 172, 178.
[54] *Census of India*, 1931, Vol. 1, Part 1, p. 335.
[55] *op. cit.*, p. 170.

[56] cf. Hartog, *op. cit.*, pp. 39–41. A somewhat similar situation has arisen elsewhere. In Puerto Rico, for example, there are compulsory attendance laws but the government cannot maintain enough schools to take care of the child population.
[57] Laubach, *op. cit.*, p. 92.

The Demography of Caste

WHEN one thinks of Hindu society one thinks first of caste, because caste is one of the oldest, most peculiar, and at the same time most fundamental features of this society. Despite the common assertion by Indian intellectuals that caste is dead in India, and despite constitutional guarantees that this shall be so, we know that it is not dead. It is dying, but before it dies completely it will long be a force in Indian life. To the great majority of Indians it is still an absorbing focus of attention, and caste affiliation (except in the cities) is a constant means of personal identification. Caste control over the individual's behavior is still strong throughout much of the subcontinent, and caste influence in economic and political matters is still great. We have already seen how in one way and another caste affects mortality, fertility, and migration. Now we wish to approach caste directly from a demographic point of view.

Fortunately, a host of distinguished scholars, both European and Indian, have given their attention to the study of caste. They have done so for at least three reasons: first, because of the obvious importance of caste in Indian life; second, because of the interesting contrast between caste in India and democracy in Europe; and third, because of the obvious hindrance of caste in the modernization of India. Prominent among the scholars who have contributed to this subject have been the census authorities. Indeed, much of what is known about caste in India during modern times comes from the census. The census reports contain some of the most brilliant and best informed discussions of the topic. Census officials such as Gait, Risley, Ibbetson, Enthoven, Russell, Blunt, and Hutton have done more than any other group to give us accurate knowledge of the caste system.

It is therefore surprising that, outside the census volumes themselves (which in the nature of the case must be dedicated primarily to the presentation rather than the manipulation of data) there has been very little demographic analysis of caste. The explanation is that the men interested in caste, despite their connection with the census in many cases, were primarily scholars rather than statisticians. They were more interested in the broad problems of history and interpretation than in the narrow technical problem of securing and analyzing quantitative information.[1]

DEFINITION AND ENUMERATION OF CASTE

The common features, or tendencies, which together distinguish Indian castes from other types of groups are as follows:

(1) Membership is hereditary, and is fixed for life.
(2) Choice of the marriage partner is endogamous.
(3) Contact with other castes is further limited by restrictions on touching, associating with, dining with, or eating food cooked by outsiders.
(4) Consciousness of caste membership is emphasized by the caste name, by the individual's identification with his caste in the eyes of the community, by his conformity to the peculiar customs of his caste, and by his subjection to government by his caste.
(5) The caste is united by a common traditional occupation, although it may be united also by the belief in a common tribal or racial origin, by adherence to a common religious sect, or by some other common peculiarity.
(6) The relative prestige of the different castes in any locality is well established and jealously guarded.

In practice, of course, considerable variation is found. There are a few rare castes that admit new members; there are some that are not strictly endogamous. But any group that is called a caste will exhibit most of these features. The whole can therefore be regarded as a caste complex, and as such, in all its completeness, is peculiar to India.[2]

Although this definition seems clear for theoretical purposes, it is by no means so for statistical purposes. The main trouble is that there are different layers of caste. The word caste, for example, "translates two vernacular terms with different meanings. The first [in Northern India] is zat (breed), with qaum (tribe) as a synonym; the second is biradari or bhaiband (brotherhood). The zat is the caste as a whole; the biradari is the group of caste brethren who live in a particular neighborhood and act together for caste purposes. The biradari, quantitatively considered, is a mere fraction of the zat; qualitatively considered, it is the zat in action." [3] At any time an observer is likely to be faced with several ways of grouping people in a caste context—moving from a class of castes (e.g. Brahman), down to more narrowly delimited caste groups, to subcastes, sections, and sub-sections. It is often hard to draw a line between these different modes of grouping, and the matter has to be decided arbitrarily.

In Mysore, for instance, the so-called Neygi caste embraces half a dozen subcastes. Between these subcastes there are differences of language, sect, and custom, and barriers against interdining or intermarrying. On the other hand, some groups in Mysore that are less different from one another than these "subcastes" are entered as separate castes.[4]

---

[1] J. H. Hutton, Census Commissioner for India in 1931, subsequently published a book on caste that contains surprisingly little quantitative information, despite its very complete sociological treatment. Caste in India (Cambridge: Cambridge University Press, 1946).

[2] Sir E. A. H. Blunt, The Caste System of Northern India (London: Oxford University Press, 1931), Ch. 1. L. S. S. O'Malley, Indian Caste Customs (Cambridge: Cambridge University Press, 1932), Chap. 1.
[3] Blunt, op. cit., p. 10.
[4] Census of India, 1931, Vol. 25 (Mysore), Part 1, pp. 319–20.

Additional confusion arises when the name of an occupation, a locality, or a language is given instead of the proper name of the caste. Errors of spelling and accidents of nomenclature also cause confusion. A similar name in different localities may not indicate the same caste; and two apparently different names may not indicate separate castes but merely two spellings or two synonymous titles of the same caste.[5] Finally, there is widespread effort by caste groups, and often by individuals, to adopt either a new name (not having the invidious connotations of the old one) or the name of a higher caste. The census is erroneously viewed as a place where such claims can be legalized, so that every provincial census office is deluged with petitions reciting alleged historical evidence to substantiate the claim to another name.

To guard against these sources of error and confusion, the census officials have worked out fairly effective techniques. They have often required enumerators to record not only the general "caste," but also the subcaste as well, and in some cases they have called even for a third entry as well—namely "tribe," "section," or what not.[6] They have given such instructions as the following from Bombay:

"Care must also be taken to see that the real caste is entered . . . , and not the name of a sub-caste only, or of an exogamous group or title, or a word merely indicating locality or occupation. Thus Bania is a functional term, including many different castes, such as Agarwal, Oswal, Mahesri etc.; words like Bengali, Hindustani, Madrasi and Nepali must be rigorously refused. . . .

"You should be careful of caste names which are also the names of occupations. In such cases make sure that the man is really of that caste. For instance a man may call himself a Sutar, because he is a Sutar by occupation, whereas by caste he is a Panchal; or a Maratha doing mali's work may return himself as a Mali. You should not accept fanciful names, . . ."[7]

Many provinces have also provided enumerators with a list of castes known to live in the area, to be consulted in doubtful cases. In some cases lists of alternate, subordinate, or unacceptable names have also been provided. Since 1911, for example, the census office in the United Provinces has used a Caste Index, which includes not only a list of castes (with localities where found, chief occupations, religious affiliation, and possible sources of error), but also a list of indefinite or variant names that are *not* to be used.[8] With such aids it is possible both to secure fairly good enumeration and to correct bad returns after they are received in the provincial office.

In spite of all aids some authorities think the caste data are inexact. M. W. M. Yeatts, Superintendent of the 1931 Madras census and Census Commissioner for India in 1941 expressed the view that caste nomenclature was changing too rapidly to make exact and comparable returns possible.[9] Most superintendents, however, believe that it is possible to check and correct the returns on caste in such a way as to make them satisfactory. Satya V. Mukerjea, Census Commissioner for Baroda State and one of the outstanding men connected with census work, says that "the experience of seven censuses in this State confirms the view that the caste return is one of the most accurate of all the census tables, and is far more reliable than age-statistics for instance, or the return of infirmities or occupations."[10]

Beginning in 1881 and continuing through 1931, all the Indian censuses obtained data on caste. In 1941 a question on caste was apparently asked, at least in some areas, but there was never any intention of tabulating the results for the whole of India.[11] The data on caste therefore cover six decades, with fragmentary evidence prior to and after that. This is indeed a rich harvest. It enables us to study the various grades of society in a country where few other indices of socio-economic status are available. It enables us to note changes in the vertical structure of society over time. Doubtless, as caste becomes less important in India, less information will be collected on it. The Census has been criticized for inquiring into caste, on the ground that the information is useless and that it tends to perpetuate caste consciousness.[12] The first allegation is not true, though it may become so; the second is absurd. Nevertheless, we cannot expect that in the future the census material on caste will ever be as full as it has been in the past.

THE PERVASIVENESS OF CASTE

Caste has been virtually universal in India. The people who are not members of some particular caste have been extremely few. Some reform groups, such as the Brahmo Samaj and the Arya Samaj, profess to repudiate caste, but these have only tiny followings.[13] Indeed, though provision was made in the 1931 census for a "nil" return, even the members of these reform groups tended to report their caste. In Baroda 86 per cent of them gave their caste.[13] Although propaganda against the caste question was widespread at the 1931 enumeration, less than 1 per cent of the Hindus in all of India failed to report their caste. Even in these cases the reason for failure was mainly ignorance, error, or unwillingness rather than lack of caste. In some areas, e.g. Central India Agency, not a single nil return was made, though provision was made for such a return if the individual actually lacked a caste affiliation. Undoubtedly, however, more people refused to return their caste or felt themselves to be without caste than in any previous census.[14]

One would expect caste to be pervasive among Hindus, but how about the hundred or so million Muslims? Are they free of caste? In theory they recognize no caste distinctions, for according to their doctrine, all free Muslims are equal. "A Muslim may marry any woman outside the prohibited degrees (which are much the same as in the English law), provided that she belongs to a 'scriptural' or revealed religion; and though some kinds of food are forbidden, commensal restrictions are unknown. The Hindu caste system, therefore, is entirely incompatible with the tenets of Islam."[15] Among Muslims of the northwest, where the foreign element is strongest, caste restrictions are weak; but even in this region the

[5] Blunt, *op. cit.*, pp. 208ff.

[6] Sir Denzil Ibbetson, *Panjab Castes* (Lahore: Superintendent, Government Printing, Punjab, 1916), pp. 31–32. *Census of India*, 1931, Vol. 19 (Baroda), Part 1, p. 391.

[7] *Census of India*, 1931, Vol. 8 (Bombay Pres.), Part 1, pp. 376–77.

[8] *ibid.*, Vol. 18 (United Provinces), Part 1, p. 527.

[9] *ibid.*, 1931, Vol. 14 (Madras), Part 1, p. 336.

[10] *ibid.*, 1931, Vol. 19 (Baroda), p. 393.

[11] *ibid.*, 1941, Vol. 1, Part 1, p. 14.

[12] See G. S. Ghurye, *Caste and Race in India* (London: Paul, Trench, Trubner, 1932), p. 158.

[13] *Census of India*, 1931, Vol. 19 (Baroda), Part 1, p. 397.

[14] *ibid.*, Vol. 20 (Central India Agency), Part 1, p. 219; Vol. 17 (Punjab), Part 1, p. 357; Vol. 18 (United Provinces), Part 1, p. 528; Vol. 28 (Travancore), Part 1, p. 367.

[15] Blunt, *op. cit.*, p. 189.

Muslims descended from converted Hindus have retained a great deal of caste custom. The great majority of Muslims in the subcontinent are descendants of Hindu converts. In 1911 it was estimated that 85 per cent of the Punjab Muslims were of native stock. In the rest of India the proportion must be even greater.[16] It is natural, therefore, that the caste system should permeate Muslim society. The mere switch of religious allegiance, often as a result of compulsion, ulterior profit, or fortuitous circumstance, would hardly incur a complete change of social life.

As is well known, the true Muslims are divided into four large families—Saiyid, Shaikh, Pathan, and Moghul. Though often referred to in India as castes, these are neither castes nor tribes, but merely names given to groups of tribes supposed to be of similar blood.[17] Each of them is subdivided into tribal, sectional, sectarian, or functional groups, in many cases with distinct social status and dubious origin. In addition, the Muslims are divided into two main religious sects—Sunnis and Shias—and this division apparently cuts across some of the others. The result is a bewildering variety of groupings. Between these groups, however, changes of identity are somewhat easier than changes of caste among Hindus, as suggested by the proverb: "Last year I was a Jolaha; now I am a Shekh; next year if prices rise, I shall become a Saiad." [18] Yet, as we shall see, many of the groups have actually come to approximate closed castes.

Into many of these purely Muslim divisions, based as they are upon claims to descent from the Prophet and his kinsmen, have filtered countless Indians having no racial affinity whatsoever with the invaders. They have in many instances retained their caste identity. There are castes that are now entirely Mohammedan, though recruited partly or wholly from Hindu converts. Examples are Atashbaz, Baidguar, Bhand, Bhathiyara, Bhishti, etc.[19] There are others that have both Mohammedan and Hindu branches, but with the Mohammedan element predominant—e.g. Churihar, Darzi, Dhuniya, Kunjra, Manihar. Finally, there are castes with larger Hindu than Mohammedan branches—e.g. Ahir, Baghban, Baheliya, Halwai, Jat, Kahar, Nai, Rajput, Sonar, and Teli.[20]

In addition, there is among Muslims a two-fold division corresponding roughly to the Hindu distinction between interior and exterior castes. In Bengal, for example, it has been said that there are two main social divisions: (a) Ashraf or Sharif and (b) Ajlaf or Atrap. The first, meaning "noble" or "person of high extraction," includes all undoubted descendants of foreigners and converts from higher Hindu castes. The second, meaning "wretches," embraces all other Mohammedans, including the functional groups and low-ranking converts. "Like the higher Hindu castes, the Ashraf consider it degrading to accept menial service or to handle the plough. The traditional occupation of the Saiads is the priesthood, while the Moghals and Pathans correspond to the Kshatriyas of the Hindu regime. In some places a third class, called Arzal or 'lowest of all,' is added. It consists of the very lowest castes, such as the Halalkhor, Lalbegi, Abdal, and Bediya, with whom

no other Muhammadan would associate, and who are forbidden to enter the mosque or to use the public burial ground." [21]

The marriage customs of groups descended from Hindu converts to Islam often exhibit a curious mixture of Hindu and Muslim rites. Contrary to Muslim custom almost all of these groups are strictly endogamous, and many are split into smaller sections that are also endogamous. "Amongst the Bhands, Gujars, and Rangrez, Sunnis and Shias do not intermarry . . . ; and in the Saiqalgar caste there are two endogaous sections, Pathan and Shaikh. . . . Muhammadan Rajputs preserve their Hindu rules of hypergamy; so do the Iraqi and the Gujar, in the shape of refusing to give daughters to families from which they have taken wives. These two castes, with the Kunjra and Meo, also preserve the Hindu exogamous sections." Some castes restrict the Muslim custom of cousin marriage, and many preserve more or less completely the Hindu wedding rites. "The Bhat goes further still; he carries out first a Hindu wedding in its fullest form, and then follows it up by a Muhammadan ceremony." Rules of adoption, inheritance, divorce, and remarriage are often more Hindu than Muslim. "In fact, most of these castes of Hindu converts preserve some trace of their former marriage customs; and many preserve a great deal." [22]

Certain Muslim groups also preserve Hindu commensal taboos and religious rites. "The Ghosi and Kingariya, for instance, will neither eat beef themselves, nor eat in the company of any Musulman who does. . . . Many worship Hindu deities, especially Kali, and observe Hindu festivals. The Bhand worships a deified ancestor. . . . The Dafali bathes in the Ganges in connexion with important ceremonies." The Muslim festival of Shab Barat has been transformed into a *sraddha* ceremony.[23]

In view of these considerations it is not surprising that the census of 1901 listed 133 castes wholly or partially Mohammedan. The census of 1911 showed only 94, but many small castes had been thrown together under a single head. Fifty-four of these castes in 1901, and 41 in 1911, had less than 1,000 Muslim members and can be ignored. Other entries in 1901 can be neglected for various reasons.[24] Yet a substantial number remain, some of them having millions of members. This can be seen by examining the statistics for certain provinces.

In the United Provinces in 1931 it was found that "14 castes account for 81 per cent of all Muslims." Table 74 shows these 14 castes, together with the proportion of each that is Muslim. The table also shows, for the same province, the fourteen castes with the greatest number of Hindus. From the contrast between the two, the Muslim and Hindu, it can be seen that a greater percentage of the Muslims (81 to 70) are concentrated in the fourteen most numerous castes. This suggests that on the average each Hindu caste embraces a smaller percentage of the total Hindu population than is the case with the Muslims.

The Sikh religion, which began in part as a protest against caste, is today almost as caste-ridden as Islam. Indeed, there are many castes that have three branches—Hindu, Muslim, and Sikh. In the Punjab, for example, there are 58 castes important enough to be listed in the Imperial Caste table. These

[16] *Census of India,* 1921, Vol. 1, Part 1, p. 227.

[17] Blunt, *op. cit.,* p. 189.

[18] *Census of India,* 1901, Vol. 1, Part 1, p. 543.

[19] Blunt, *op. cit.,* p. 200. A full list is given by this author. Blunt has the fullest account of Muslim caste, both in theory and practice, that the writer has encountered.

[20] *ibid.,* p. 201.

[21] *Census of India,* 1901, Vol. 1, Part 1, pp. 543–44.

[22] Blunt, *op. cit.,* pp. 201–02.

[23] *ibid.,* pp. 202–03.

[24] *ibid.,* p. 200.

TABLE 74

*The Fourteen Castes with the Most Muslims, and the
Fourteen with the Most Hindus in the
United Provinces 1931* [1]

	Per Cent of Caste Members Adhering to Specified Religion	Per Cent of Total Religious Membership Falling in Each Caste
MUSLIM CASTES		81.0
Shaikh	100.0	21.4
Pathan	100.0	14.7
Julaha	95.5	12.9
Faqir	93.0	5.4
Dhunia	93.5	5.2
Saiyid	100.0	4.2
Teli	25.1	3.4
Nai (Hajjam)	26.9	3.3
Darzi	69.5	2.3
Rajput	4.4	2.2
Qassab	100.0	2.2
Dhobi	14.0	1.5
Manihar	96.4	1.4
Mughal	100.0	0.8
HINDU CASTES		69.9
Chamar	99.7	15.1
Brahman	99.4	10.9
Ahir	99.7	9.4
Rajput	94.2	8.5
Kurmi	99.7	4.2
Pasi	100.0	3.5
Vaishya	92.7	2.8
Kahar	99.1	2.8
Lodh	99.7	2.6
Gadariya	99.6	2.4
Kori	99.9	2.2
Kumhar	98.7	1.9
Teli	74.8	1.8
Kachi	99.9	1.7

[1] Compiled from *Census of India,* 1931, Vol. 18 (United Provinces), Part 2.

58 fall into the following categories with reference to the three main religions of the Punjab: [25]

Hindu	8
Muslim	12
Sikh	—
Hindu-Muslim	9
Hindu-Sikh	10
Muslim-Sikh	—
Hindu-Muslim-Sikh	19

There are thus 29, or half of the 58 castes that have Sikh branches, despite the fact that the Sikhs constituted only 14

[25] *Census of India,* 1931, Vol. 17 (Punjab), Part 2, pp. 282–302.

per cent of the total Punjab population. Yet there are no numerically important castes in this area that are exclusively Sikh. Furthermore, there is still a recognition that Sikhism is somehow opposed to caste. For one thing, it is known that the Sikh population has been growing in the last few decades by virtue of conversion from Hinduism.[26] Most of the converts are from lower Hindu castes, and one of the reasons for their conversion is to get away from their erstwhile caste status. "Except in the case of higher castes such as Jat and Rajput, converts to Sikhism do not as a rule return any caste, being content with the entry of 'Sikh' in the column of caste. . . . Many members of low castes such as Chuhra and Chamar adopt Sikhism in order to escape the inferiority complex. In regard to Sikhs the instructions to enumerators were that they should not be pressed to return their caste." [27]

Even Christianity has not been able to extirpate caste distinctions among its converts. Speaking with reference to southern India, the Madras census report has this to say:

"Intermarriage is practically no more possible between a Christian ex-Vellala in Tinnevelly (or as he would call himself, a Vellala Christian) and a Christian who had come originally (perhaps one or two generations ago) from the depressed classes, than it would be among Hindus of like origin, and boycott would be as sure a consequence if such a union did take place. It is common, among Roman Catholics at least, for a segregation to be made even within the church. . . .

"Christian communities can rarely free themselves from caste differences and prejudices; Muslim converts on the other hand disappear in a couple of generations, probably less, and origins are forgotten. Here perhaps we see the fruits of complaisance and of rigidity. The first Christian missionaries accepted caste, hoping perhaps that in the next or succeeding generation it would vanish. The Muslim methods relied less on persuasion and so could afford to be uncompromising in principle; essential unity in Islam was retained and is never likely to be affected. In Indian Christianity it has been lost and it is unlikely that in the south at least it will ever be recovered. . . .

"There are wide variations in the degree to which these prejudices exist along with alleged Christianity. They are stronger among Roman Catholics than Protestants, possibly because the former have a larger proportion of adherents of higher caste origin; they are worse in the south than in the north or west and in rural areas than in towns. Everywhere, they are present in some degree. . . ." [28]

However, there is evidence that, as with Islam and Sikhism, the doctrinal opposition to caste does exert itself to some extent among the Christians. This is indicated by the fact that the largest proportion of converts is drawn from the low and depressed castes. It is also shown by the fact that a large number of Christians, at least in some parts, do not return their caste. In Baroda, for example, 65 per cent of the Christians did not return their caste in 1931. This compared quite favorably with the Muslims (4 per cent not returned) and with the Aryas (14 per cent).[29]

In conclusion, it seems clear that the caste system is extremely widespread and pervasive in the subcontinent. It is present in all regions. It applies to nearly every person, regardless of his religion. It pervades even those religions, even

[26] *ibid.,* Part 1, pp. 304–09.
[27] *ibid.,* p. 308.
[28] *ibid.,* Vol. 14 (Madras), Part 1, p. 328.
[29] *ibid.,* Vol. 19 (Baroda), Part 1, p. 397.

those reform groups, which have as one of their tenets the social equality of man. It is this pervasiveness that still makes a person's caste one of his most salient characteristics, despite the numerous forces that are now working against the caste principle.

NUMBER AND SIZE OF CASTES

Because of the uncertainty of classifying castes, subcastes, and sections, and because of considerable confusion in names, it is impossible to say exactly how many castes there are in India. In 1901, which was the last year in which an attempt at a complete tabulation of all castes was made, the number of "main" castes and tribes was found to be 2,378.[30] Some of these groups had numbers running into the millions, others had a mere handful. The average number per caste was approximately 120,000, although such a figure is virtually meaningless.

The figure of 2,378 main castes presumably did not include subcastes. How many of these there are cannot even be guessed, but it is safe to assume that any caste whose members run into the hundreds of thousands or millions is divided into a large number of subcastes. In 1891 the subdivisions of caste were recorded in detail, and the resultant lists contained thousands of names. "The Jat and Ahir, for instance, were each responsible for over 1,700 entries; the Kurmi for nearly 1,500."[31] In 1931 Tehri-Garhwal, a tiny state in the United Provinces with an area of 4,180 square miles and a population of only 350,000, had no less than 387 subcastes of Brahmans and 1,025 subcastes of Rajputs.[32] Between subcastes, as noted above, the social barriers are nearly as strong as between castes, little interdining and intermarriage being permitted.

In the 1931 census over 15 million Brahmans were returned. Theoretically they form a single caste, but in practice they are split up into an immense number of separate groups and subgroups. These separate groups even differ markedly in social standing. Some of the exalted Brahman castes rank at the top of the social scale, but others rank so low that even their own clients, members of low castes, will not take food in their houses. Clearly, then, the term *Brahman* designates a very loose class of castes, not a caste in itself.[33]

No caste, strictly defined, is diffused over the whole of India. The Brahmans, as a general class, have an extremely wide distribution, but any particular Brahman caste is more limited as to area. As noted above, the effective caste group is a local group. "The caste council can only act for a limited area, an area small enough for the members of the council to assemble and for members of the caste within the area to have some knowledge of each other."[34] It can be expected, therefore, that the total caste—that is, the widest intermarrying and interdining group—will not ordinarily cover a very extensive territory. The 1901 census provides maps showing the distribution of 36 major castes.[35] They were selected because of their size and dispersion, and yet most of them are confined to one or only a few sections of India. In those provinces that show the distribution of castes by district or other territorial

subdivision, it can be shown that there is a tendency for each caste to be concentrated in a relatively small area.[36]

Since the effective caste group is a local affair, one place to look at the number and size of castes is in the village. For this the census does not help us much, but we are fortunate in having the results of a survey of over 50 villages in the middle Ganges valley.[37] This study found that in the area surveyed there were 52 castes. Not one of these castes, however, was represented in every village. The Chamars, one of the most pervasive, were found in only 32 and the Ahirs in only 30 villages. "And yet, *a priori*, the Chamars should be represented in all villages, as they are the commonest type of *razil* population, supply all the labour in the village and are indispensable to village life." There were Brahmans in 40 per cent of the villages. The Nai, or barber caste, was represented in less than half the villages.[38] The average number of villages in which each caste, taken altogether, was represented was only 9.3.

In most instances the village, if it had any members of the caste at all, had only one family of the caste. The number of instances in which a caste was represented by a given number of families were as follows: [39]

1 family of caste in village	340
2 families of caste in village	80
3–5 families of caste in village	60
6 or more families of caste in village	32

It seems clear that the rural village has by no means a full complement of castes, and that the castes it does have are generally represented by only one or two families. The first fact means that each village must depend to some extent upon the services of persons in other villages, and the second that relations between caste members must be maintained by contact between villages. In this light, the common practice of marrying outside the village can be understood. In short, the rural village is not an isolated social entity, but is intimately linked with others in the immediate area.

Changes in the size of castes are hard to determine, because alterations of name, reversals of tabulation policy,[40] and problems of classification introduce extraneous factors. Therefore, no figures on this are given here.

CLASSES OF CASTES

So many castes jostle each other in India that they must somehow be grouped. Otherwise, neither the scholarly nor the lay mind could find its way through the maze. In practice the people themselves adopt a rule-of-thumb mode of classification and subclassification—a system that makes the caste

---

[30] *Census of India*, 1901, Vol. 1, Part 1, p. 537.

[31] Blunt, *op. cit.*, pp. 37–38.

[32] *Census of India*, 1931, Vol. 18 (United Provinces), Part 1, pp. 9, 572–87.

[33] Sir T. W. Holderness, *Peoples and Problems of India* (New York: Holt, 1910?), p. 98. *Census of India*, 1901, Vol. 1, Part 1, p. 540.

[34] Hutton, *op. cit.*, p. 86.

[35] *Census of India*, 1901, Vol. 1, Part 1, pp. 557–59.

[36] See *ibid.*, 1931, Vol. 20 (Central India Agency), Part 2, Table 17. Even the "principal" castes, selected for their general dispersion, show considerable concentration by area.

[37] S. S. Nehru, *Caste and Credit in the Rural Area* (London: Longmans, Green, 1932).

[38] *ibid.*, pp. 23–31. The table on p. 37 shows 54 castes.

[39] *ibid.*, pp. 37–39, Table C(1).

[40] Since 1901, when a full tabulation was made, not all castes have been tabulated. In 1911 those castes falling below a certain percentage of the provincial population were not included in the tables. In 1921 the percentage necessary was raised, and it was figured on a district basis. (See *Census of India*, 1921, Vol. 1, Part 1, p. 224.) In 1931 the percentage was raised again, from 2 to 4 per cent. Always, however, the exterior castes and primitive tribes have been given full tabulation, at least in the provincial reports. (See *Census of India*, 1931, Vol. 1, Part 1, pp. 432–33.)

structure look much more like our own class order than we would otherwise expect.

CASTE VS. OUTCASTE

The chief line of distinction runs between the twice-born, or "clean," castes on the one hand, and the once-born, or "unclean," castes on the other. The line is by no means uniform from one locality to another, but in some form it seems to be everywhere present. It persists almost independently of religion. It is the deepest cleavage in Hindu society.

Several criteria of membership in the depressed castes are available. If a caste suffers all of the following restrictions, for example, it is certainly depressed: [41]

  (1) Inability to be served by clean Brahmans.
  (2) Inability to be served by barbers, water-carriers, tailors, etc., who serve the caste Hindus.
  (3) Inability to serve water to caste Hindus.
  (4) Inability to enter Hindu temples.
  (5) Inability to use public conveniences, such as roads, ferries, wells, or schools.
  (6) Inability to dissociate oneself from a despised occupation.

Although these criteria would seem to be clear, they do not serve very well for statistical purposes, because they admit of degrees and vary somewhat independently. A caste that suffers food and water restrictions may nevertheless be served by Brahmans of good standing. In Bengal there have been castes whom the barber would shave, but whose toenails he would not cut and whose marriage ceremonies he would not attend.[42] Also, castes are not uniform with reference to particular criteria. "A caste may be untouchable in one district and not in the next; and there are untouchable castes with touchable sections." Finally, the attitudes toward a caste may vary according to which of the twice-born are being dealt with; for "a caste may be regarded as untouchable by some of the twice-born, and not by others." [43]

These circumstances make it difficult to count the number of persons belonging to depressed castes. "It is not possible to say generally that such and such a caste is exterior to Hindu society and to apply that dictum to the whole of India." Although this might be done in the case of a few castes, such as the Dom and the Bhangi, it is not true that a caste depressed in one part of India is depressed everywhere. It was therefore decided in 1931 to allow each province to define the outcastes according to local conditions, with the proviso that only those were to be reckoned as depressed who definitely suffered from "serious social and political handicap on account of their degraded position in the Hindu social scheme." [44]

Bearing in mind possible errors and differences of interpretation, one can cautiously mention some figures on the number of outcaste persons in India (excluding Muslims and Christians). In 1931 the total number came to 50.2 million, which represented a slight drop from the figure for 1921, which was 52.7 million.[45] The proportion of this class among the whole Hindu population in 1931 was 21 per cent, as against 25 per cent in 1921. Figures for 1911 are apparently unobtainable from the general report. It would be unsafe to accept the apparently diminished figure for 1931 as representing a trend, not only because of lack of data for an extended series but also because of changing definitions. Be this as it may, it is worth noting that the number of outcastes is substantial. In a sense this seems to be the largest bottom layer of any class structure in the world. The Negroes in the United States, comparable in some respects (though certainly not in all) to the depressed castes, constitute not quite 10 per cent of the total population. The Eta caste in Japan never constituted anything like 15 per cent of the total Japanese population. The large number of outcastes in India attests the low standard of living in the country. It is the depressed castes that bear the brunt of the struggle for survival in an overpopulated, underdeveloped country.

The emphasis on the line between interior and exterior should not obscure the fact that within each of these groups of castes there are sharp differences of rank. "It is not to be imagined that within the circle of untouchability," for instance, "there are no subgradations, and that all untouchables are equals among themselves. In the Madras Presidency alone . . . there are, it is said, no less than eighty subdivisions, those at the top regarding the less fortunate of their own brethren as untouchable. At the bottom of the scale come some classes, like the *Nayadis* of Malabar, whose very shadow is pollution." An address of Mr. Gandhi contained the following statement: "All the various grades of untouchables are untouchable among themselves, each superior grade considering the inferior grade as polluting as the highest class of the caste Hindus regard the worst grade of untouchables." [46]

BRAHMAN VS. NON-BRAHMAN

But as is the case in other societies, public interest does not center greatly on the gradations of rank in the lowest strata. It centers on those gradations at the top. For this reason considerable attention has been paid to the Brahmans at the top, as distinct from the Non-Brahmans. Although the traditional occupation of the Brahmans is the priesthood, they have been free to abandon this occupation for many centuries. In 1911 the percentage of Brahmans engaged in the traditional profession of the Brahman class was only 13, based on data from 11 provinces and states.[47] A double influence has been exerted to give the Brahmans a wide occupational affiliation. First, the Brahmans, being at the top of the social ladder, were in a position to have no one gainsay them when they chose to take up a lucrative profession. Second, there is apparently a tend-

[41] *Census of India*, 1931, Vol. 1, Part 1, p. 472.

[42] *Census of India*, 1901, Vol. 1, Part 1, p. 541.

[43] Blunt, *op. cit.*, pp. 334–35.

[44] *Census of India*, 1931, Vol. 1, Part 1, p. 473.

[45] The Census Commissioner for 1921 regarded the figure of 52.7 million as a *minimum* estimate, because many members of exterior castes tried to improve their status by changing their caste names or otherwise dissimulating. He estimated the real figure to be between 55 and 60 million. (See *Census of India*, 1921, Vol. 1, Part 1, paragraph 193; also 1931, Vol. 1, Part 1, p. 472.) It should be noted that most other estimates agree fairly closely with those of the census, although there are some that are widely different. Such differences depend primarily on which criteria of outcaste status are used. There is, for example, a difference between untouchability and depressed. In the United Provinces, for instance, untouchability is not prominent, though other criteria are so. The difference between various estimates is therefore due to confusion of definition rather than error of enumeration. In general, the census estimates seem most satisfactory for sociological and economic purposes, because they are generally prepared with several criteria in mind and thus represent a balanced view of the phenomenon. Cf. B. Shiva Rao, *The Industrial Worker in India* (London: Allen & Unwin, 1939), pp. 81–82. The census figures on outcastes exclude persons of non-Hindu religions, such as Christians, Muslims, and tribals. When it is realized that there actually are depressed castes in these categories, the total number in India appears quite sizable.

[46] Reproduced in Rao, *op. cit.*, pp. 81–82.

[47] *Census of India*, 1911, Vol. 1, Part 2, pp. 358–72. The data on Brahmans by occupation were not presented as fully in 1921 and 1931 as in 1911, hence the use of 1911 data.

ency for the lower castes, when they improve their position in some way, to try to call themselves Brahmans, sometimes with success. This would necessarily increase the variety of occupations practiced by so-called Brahmans. It would also have the effect of increasing the total number of Brahmans. However, the Brahmans, as the topmost class of castes, tend to have a lower fertility than do other Hindus.[48] Also, the conversion of new Hindus is primarily at the bottom of the caste scale. Consequently the proportion of Brahmans among Hindus has not been increasing, as shown by the following percentages:

1891	7.14%
1901	7.19
1911	6.71
1921	6.58
1931	6.37

Certain other castes and classes of castes, all smaller than the Brahman, are near the top of the social scale. Their influence is restricted in the main to particular localities, but some of them have an all-India reputation, such as the Kayastha, Vaishya, Rajput, and Baidya. These would have to be classed with the Brahmans as among the aristocracy, but since they are not found over the whole territory, since their status often varies from one place to another, it is impossible to determine the exact number of the upper class by taking those castes that have the highest social precedence. This leaves the alternative of relying upon some more objective criterion—say occupation or literacy—as a method of grouping "clean" castes in a hierarchy of social strata. Suffice it to say, then, that in terms of social distinction, the Brahmans at the top, in 1931, constituted 8.2 per cent of the total *caste* Hindus. Of the rest, a certain number, an unknown percentage, ranked close to the Brahmans as part of the aristocracy, while the others constituted a broad middle class embracing many kinds and degrees of gradation.

DISTRIBUTION OF CLASSES OF CASTES

One would expect the Brahmans to be widely diffused, and this is the case. Yet, as Table 75 shows, they are not evenly diffused. They tend to be strongest in and around their original center, the United Provinces and the Punjab States, and weakest in the outlying tracts settled by non-Aryan peoples. Doubtless "many of the Brahmans of the more remote tracts have been manufactured on the spot by the simple process of conferring the title of Brahman on the tribal priests and local deities." [49] Southern India is relatively free of Brahmans. Madras has only slightly more than a fourth the proportion that the United Provinces have.

The Brahmans are apparently more abundant in the prosperous and urbanized areas. For instance, in Mysore the percentage of all Brahmans who live in the cities is 23, whereas the percentage of all Hindus living in cities is only 5. As the Mysore report says, "the Brahmin lives mainly by occupations which pay his literacy." [50] The same is true of the Central Provinces and Berar. Of course, there are other castes, such as the Mudali, a business caste in Mysore, which follow exclusively urban occupations and who therefore live in cities to a greater extent than the Brahmans.

The exterior castes, the menials and dregs, also show considerable variations of strength from place to place. In general they are more abundant in the North than in the South, although, as seen in Table 75, there are some notable exceptions to this rule. The range varies all the way from 56 per cent in Travancore and 37 per cent in Assam (the result of labor migration into that province) to 0.2 in Baluchistan States. By district there is also found to be considerable variation. In the Central India Agency, for example, the percentage varies from less than 3 in certain minor states to more than 19 in others.[51] In the Central Provinces and Berar the figure varied from less than 1 per cent of all Hindus in some districts, to more than 30 per cent in other districts.[52] In the city of Bombay the proportion of depressed caste members in the Hindu population was 13 per cent.[53] In the Bombay Presidency as a whole the proportion was 11 per cent.

CASTE AND OCCUPATION

If the members of each caste all followed the same calling, it would be easy to group castes according to occupation. Actually this is seldom the case. The common belief that castes are occupationally specialized is due in part to the ideal theory of caste, in part to the patent fact that many castes do follow one occupation predominantly, and in part to the fact that even when a caste has no actual line of work in common it may nevertheless be identified with a *traditional* occupation. Since the so-called traditional occupation is easier to handle statistically than the mixed lines of work usually pursued, castes have often been classified according to traditional calling. Such a classification has little significance, however, unless the traditional occupation is also, at least to a considerable degree, the actual one.

TRADITIONAL VS. ACTUAL OCCUPATION

An analysis of the occupational statistics for 24 selected castes in 1931 showed that only 45 per cent of their members were following the traditional occupation.[54] It is impossible, however, to tell how these castes were selected by the Census Commissioner. A more detailed list of 42 castes in the Punjab revealed that 62 per cent of their members were following the conventional caste occupation.[55] An even more detailed list of 49 castes in Baroda showed that 67 per cent were following the traditional occupation.[56] In the Punjab, 27 of the 42 castes had more than 50 per cent of their occupied males in the historical calling, and 17 had more than 70 per cent in it; while in Baroda 32 castes of the 49 had more than 50 per cent and 17 more than 70 per cent. It appears from these samples, then, that in general more than half the male workers are engaged in a line of work historically associated with their caste, and that in many castes more than 70 per cent are so engaged. Without a doubt the traditional caste occupation therefore still means something.

But it is possible to exaggerate the significance of these figures. It should be remembered that close to 70 per cent of India's gainfully employed males are in agriculture. If the traditional occupation of a caste happens to be agriculture,

---

[48] See Chapter 10, pp. 73–74.

[49] *Census of India*, 1901, Vol. 1, Part 1, p. 540.

[50] *Census of India*, 1931, Vol. 25 (Mysore), Part 1, p. 326. The figures are contained in Part 1, p. 327, and Part 2, p. 226.

[51] *ibid.*, Vol. 20 (Central India Agency), Part 1, p. 215. The percentage is based on total population.

[52] *ibid.*, Vol. 12 (Central Provinces & Berar), Part 1, pp. 383–85.

[53] *ibid.*, Vol. 9 (Bombay Cities), Part 1, p. 40.

[54] *ibid.*, Vol. 1, Part 2, pp. 416–19.

[55] *ibid.*, 1931, Vol. 17 (Punjab), Part 2, pp. 220–24.

[56] *ibid.*, Vol. 19 (Baroda), Part 2, pp. 78–82.

TABLE 75

Percentage of Hindu Population in Various Classes, by Province, 1931 [1]

Province or State	Total Hindu	Brahmans	Other Interior	Exterior Castes	No Cases	Not Returned
INDIA [a]	100	6.4	71.7	21.1	0.79	0.03
Provinces	100	6.5	70.4	22.1	1.06	0.02
Ajmer-Merwara	100	6.4	75.8	17.7	—	0.13
Andaman & Nicobars	100	6.9	85.2	6.7	1.18	—
Assam	100	3.2	59.6	37.1	0.05	—
Baluchistan [b]	100	8.6	77.7	13.8	—	—
Bengal	100	6.7	52.8	32.0	8.39	0.13
Bihar & Orissa	100	6.3	75.0	18.6	0.08	0.02
Bihar		6.4	e	18.9	0.11	e
Orissa		8.4	e	13.7	—	e
Chota Nagpur		3.8	e	22.5	—	e
Bombay [c]	100	4.7	84.8	10.5	—	—
Bombay Presidency	100	4.9	84.6	10.6	—	—
Sind	100	2.5	87.7	9.8	—	—
Cent. Provs. & Ber.	100	3.7	74.3	21.9	0.03	—
Central Provinces	100	3.8	74.2	21.9	0.04	—
Berar	100	3.4	74.6	22.0	0.02	—
Coorg	100	1.9	81.1	17.0	—	—
Delhi	100	12.6	69.0	18.2	0.27	—
Madras	100	3.3	79.2	17.5	0.01	—
North-West Frontier Prov. [b]	100	10.2	86.0	3.8	0.02	—
Punjab	100	12.1	68.4	19.4	0.11	—
United Provinces	100	10.7	61.6	27.7	0.04	0.02
Agra	100	10.2	63.5	26.1	0.05	0.03
Oudh	100	11.9	56.1	31.9	0.02	—
States & Agencies	100	6.2	75.7	18.1	0.02	0.03
Assam States	100	0.2	99.3	0.5	—	—
Baluchistan States	100	1.3	98.6	0.2	—	—
Baroda State	100	5.8	84.8	9.4	—	0.02
Bengal States	100	1.5	93.6	4.8	—	0.13
Bihar & O. States	100	3.3	81.3	15.5	—	—
Bombay States	100	3.4	87.7	8.9	—	—
Cent. India Agency	100	9.8	76.4	13.6	0.05	0.14
Cent. Prov. States	100	1.3	84.5	14.1	0.01	—
Gwalior State	100	9.0	70.2	20.7	0.04	—
Hyderabad State	100	3.1	76.5	20.3	0.07	—
Jammu & Kashmir St.	100	34.4	42.3	23.2	—	—
Madras States Agency	100	2.8	51.8	45.2	—	0.13
Cochin State	100	5.3	78.4	16.1	—	0.21
Travancore State	100	2.2	41.4	56.3	—	0.13
Other Madras States	100	3.1	80.9	16.0	—	—
Mysore State	100	4.1	79.3	16.6	—	—
N.W.F.P. [d]	100	5.7	90.4	4.0	—	—
Punjab States	100	13.0	63.1	23.8	—	—
Punjab States Agency	100	12.4	68.3	19.3	—	—
Rajputana Agency	100	8.9	74.7	16.3	—	0.01
Sikkim State	100	18.2	75.9	4.3	0.72	0.91
United Prov. States	100	16.2	61.8	22.0	0.02	—
Western Ind. St. Ag.	100	6.6	83.6	9.8	—	—

[a] Excludes Aden and Burma.
[b] Districts and administered territories only.
[c] Excluding Aden.
[d] Agencies and Tribal areas.
[e] Data not available.
[1] *Census of India,* 1931, Vol. 1, Part 2, pp. 534–35.

as is true in many cases, it is but natural that a majority of the workers should be found in this occupation. Breaking the samples down according to the nature of the theoretical caste calling, one finds the following: [57]

	Per Cent in Traditional Occupation
Dealers in Food & Drink	37
Agriculture	91
Laborers & Village Menials	14
Pastoral	20
Learned Professions	20
Boating & Fishing	9
Trade & Industry	
Unspecified	70
Specified	51

In Baroda the sample of castes by occupation was classified according to degree of enlightenment, as measured by literacy. It turned out that 63 per cent of the members of the "Advanced Castes" were in the traditional occupation, while 72 per cent of the members of the "Intermediate Castes" were in it. This confirms our view that the higher castes take advantage of their position to enter new occupations.[58] But again, lest the results seem too striking, it should be recalled that the two groups of castes in Baroda were differentiated on the basis of literacy. Since literacy is a comparatively new thing in India, it could be expected that the most literate castes had changed from their traditional occupation more frequently than the less literate castes, many of whom are agricultural anyway.

THE PERSISTENCE OF CASTE

Although its precise form has changed from time to time, the caste system has endured for some thirty centuries. During most of this time the trend was in the direction of a more rigid, more unequal, and more finely stratified order. It reached its peak at roughly the same time that the feudal system in Europe reached its peak. In order to judge the current changes, and what the future may hold, one must weigh carefully both the forces tending to diminish caste and the forces tending to perpetuate it. Both sets of forces are always present, but it is the balance between the two that is crucial.

FORCES TENDING TO DIMINISH CASTE

Too often one thinks that the only forces opposing caste are those modern ones introduced from the West. This is not true. Long before the Muslims or the British there were factors in India that worked against the system. These were factors that will militate against a complete caste system in any society. If the Hindu social order could be summed up in a single sentence, it would be this: It is the most thoroughgoing attempt known in human history to introduce absolute inequality as the guiding principle in social relationships. Such an attempt

cannot completely succeed, any more than an attempt to introduce absolute equality.

Inherent Contradictions. In the first place, any system of stratification must have certain standards of excellence that form the basis of its invidious distinctions. Hindu culture, like any other, has such standards. It places a high value on restriction of women, celibacy of widows, purity of diet, cleanliness of occupation, freedom from manual labor, knowledge of sacred literature, and economic security. It follows that any group (be it a local caste brotherhood or even a family) that manages to improve itself with respect to any of these standards, will also improve its social status. Inevitably some groups will strive to improve themselves, because they and their fellows believe in these standards. But in so far as a group achieves a greater conformity to the standards and thus improves its social position, it overcomes the main principle of caste, the fixity of inherited status.

Blunt and Hutton, as well as other observers, give numerous examples of changes of status by change of occupation.[59] They also give examples of changes of status by the greater or lesser observance of certain taboos and moral rules.[60] Since the observance of most such rules is expensive, the more successful the caste is in an economic sense, the more it can improve its conformity. In no society can economic competition be wholly eliminated. In India, prior to British rule, the untouchable castes in many areas were not allowed to own land. They are still handicapped in education, occupation, and health, and so do not have an equal chance to acquire wealth. Nevertheless, in so far as there are rights in property not completely governed by inheritance, the possibility of acquiring or losing wealth is present, and with it the possibility of rising or falling in the social scale. In India even unclean occupations may in some cases afford a nice income. Customarily the profits are invested in land; the families thereupon become landholders, abandoning their old occupation and achieving a new station in life. Some of the marks of high status may, on the other hand, carry an economic penalty. It is said that one can always tell which farms belong to Brahmans and which to non-Brahmans, because the Brahmans, forbidden by their caste to do manual labor, must hire their work done by others, and the work is always inferior to that which a farmer would do for himself.

It seems clear, then, that the Hindu attempt to construct a system of absolute social inequality is inherently contradictory. The very scale of values, or standards, by which one stratum is judged better than another motivates people to try to improve themselves with reference to these standards; in so far as they succeed, the community is bound to recognize

---

[57] Blunt, *op. cit.,* pp. 251–52. The figures are taken from *Census of India,* 1911, United Provinces volume. They refer to male workers only, and if the traditional occupation was given either as the primary or subsidiary occupation, the person was listed as following his traditional line of work.

[58] This of course conforms to ancient historical tradition in India. In the Post-Vedic period the rule was that "in times of distress one might follow the occupation peculiar to the lower orders, but never that of the higher, and preferably the one prescribed for the caste next in status to one's own." Ghurye, *Caste and Race in India,* p. 74.

[59] The Pasi caste practiced the despised occupation of hunting and fowling. A part of the caste turned to cultivation and fruitselling, a more honorable calling. Consequently, this part became a new caste, adopting a new name (Phansiya) and acquiring a higher social status. "The Kayastha caste, as a whole, stands in high repute. But the numerous class of *patwaris* (keepers of the village revenue records) consists almost entirely of Kayasthas: and as the *patwari* has a bad name for chicanery, the better class Kayasthas affect to despise this occupation. Some years ago many Srivastava [Kayastha] families . . . refused to have any relations, whether connubial or commensal, with *patwari* families; and the Kayastha *sabha* [association] had some difficulty in preventing the consequent formation of a 'patwari' subcaste." Blunt, *op. cit.,* p. 222. cf. Hutton, *op. cit.,* pp. 98–99.

[60] The Biyahut, or "Married" Kalars, are a particular branch of the Kalars, distinguished by the fact that they prohibit the remarriage of widows. As a consequence they rank a little higher than the other Kalars, who permit widow remarriage. Robt. V. Russell, *Tribes and Castes of the Central Provinces of India,* Vol. 1 (London: Macmillan, 1916), p. 85.

their achievement by giving them more or less prestige. A change of occupation, a shift of economic fortune, an alteration in moral conduct—any or all of these will affect the standing of the group in the eyes of the general community.

In theory the caste system is a hierarchy of strata in which each makes a functional contribution to the whole, deriving its prestige from the nature of that contribution. But the idea of exclusiveness and ritual taboo has overriden this concept. Some groups are too exalted or too lowly to enjoy the services of other groups, despite the necessary nature of these services. The Brahmans, for example, are supposed to be the priestly class and to perform the religious functions. But they cannot perform these services for the untouchables. Consequently millions of depressed peoples must find priests in their own ranks. New castes of priests, having a much lower rank than the Brahmans, are thus created. The Bhangis of Baroda, for example, have priests (Garodas) from their own caste.[61] Similarly the barber castes among the caste Hindus will not serve the outcastes. Each depressed caste must then supply its own barbers, and new castes or subcastes of barbers are thus created, with a lower rank than the others. In Travancore the Ilavathi are the barbers for the Liava, a depressed caste of which they claim they were formerly members.[62] There is then a tendency in India for the idea of exclusiveness to create closed communities, each having groups that are functionally interdependent, the whole Hindu polity thereby acquiring a fundamental lack of unity. Again we see that there is an inherent contradiction in the theory of a social system built on the principle of absolute inequality.

Incompatibility with Change. In addition to inherent contradictions, it can now be shown that the ideal of absolute inherited inequality is incompatible with societal needs. To be practicable the ideal calls for a completely static social order. But there is, and can be, no such thing. Every society generates internal frictions that lead to change, and every society lives under conditions that themselves change. The moment there is social change there is also social mobility, and hence fixity of hereditary status becomes impossible.

To have each caste performing its own unique occupation and occupying the same rung generation after generation, a uniform rate of population replacement would be necessary for every caste. But the very notion of caste implies that there are different caste customs, and some of these customs will unavoidably affect fertility and mortality, and hence natural increase. Some castes will expand in population and others will contract. For those that expand, some new occupations must be found, because their increased membership could not all find employment in the old. For those that contract, replacements from other castes must be found to carry on the occupation. Thus the demographic variable alone prevents absolute immobility.

In addition, there is the political variable. Political sovereignty is associated with territory, but a territorial basis of cohesion cuts across caste lines. Only when the entire caste society is embraced in one political entity are caste and sovereignty wholly compatible. India, however, has never been united as one political entity. The nearest it has come to it is under the hegemony of the British, a foreign regime. The very weaknesses of a caste society make it incapable of political unity over a large territory, and virtually helpless against an invader. As a result, political conflict develops, which not only turns caste against caste but also area against area. The moment one territorial unit is pitted against another, in war or civil strife, the principle of caste has yielded to another principle—that of territorial solidarity—and the lowest caste in one territory is theoretically superior to the highest caste in another. This is simply the old principle that national interest, if there is to be any national interest, must transcend class interests. India's history is full to the brim with accounts of dynastic wars. Such wars threw aside the principle of caste as the dominant motif, and substituted the principle of national political unity. They also introduced a dynamic, almost chaotic, element, which made the social system anything but fixed. A battleground is hardly an ideal setting for a static caste order, and much of India has been precisely that throughout history.

Geographical changes should also be mentioned. Hindu society has from its inception been agricultural and pastoral. The practice of these arts changes the physical setting. Forests are depleted and fields eroded. As the population reaches the limit afforded by the given organization and technology, new developments must take place or else the death rate will rise. In so far as the social system adjusts to changing necessities, it facilitates social mobility.

The conclusion emerges, then, that the caste system has never been perfect. It has had to fight for its existence. It has had to contend constantly with social forces inherently contradictory to the caste principle. So the theory that the loosening of caste came only with the advent of Europeans in India, is wrong. The system was already loose. What the Europeans did was give an impetus to some of the old factors opposing caste, and add some new ones of their own.

THE IMPACT OF MODERN CONDITIONS

The ways in which modernization is dissolving caste have been detailed by many writers. All that we shall attempt is a brief summary.

The Spread of Education. Two mainstays of the caste order are, first, the content of its learning—mystical, religious, and traditional—and second, the distribution of this learning, limited mainly to the priestly class. The mysticism helps to rationalize and strengthen the superstitions of the masses, thus holding them ideologically under control, while the monopoly of the Brahmans restrains competition for spiritual leadership. Both features of the system place an effective brake on technical and scientific progress. Western education, on the other hand, is directed along technical lines and is meant for all the people. It serves as an avenue of individual advancement, on the theory that productive achievement is to be rewarded with enhancement of status. It is precisely contrary to India's medieval view of education. In so far as it has gained ground in the subcontinent, it has tended to upset the caste system.

Literacy, which in India tripled between 1881 and 1941, increased faster among the lower than among the higher classes. This trend indicates that education is spreading, and the history of Indian politics during the last half century shows that Western ideals and methods are being introduced by it. The slogans, premises, aims, and techniques of the Indian nationalist movement were clearly inspired by the West. Most of the leaders had received a Western education, often in Western countries; most of them were emancipated from the narrow rituals and superstitions of Hinduism; most of them wanted India to modernize; and most of them thought in terms of democracy. Gandhi may seem an exception, but actually he was influenced by the West more than he realized.

[61] *Census of India,* 1931, Vol. 19 (Baroda), Part 1, p. 437.
[62] *ibid.,* Vol. 28 (Travancore), Part 1, p. 382.

Political Democracy. One effect of British rule was to remove much of the local autonomy that once prevailed. Since the stronghold of caste is the isolated and nearly self-sufficient rural area, where the caste *panchayat* and the village *pachayat* govern most of life, the centralization of government inevitably affected caste adversely.

In addition, the British progressively allowed greater measures of representative self-government to India. At the time of the Montagu-Chelmsford Reforms in 1919 the number of Provincial voters was about 5.5 million.[63] This was not many in a population of some 240 million, but it represented progress. The number was subsequently enlarged; by 1937, with a franchise based on literacy and/or property, some 30 million were reportedly placed on the electoral rolls, and later, by 1943, over 35 million.[64] The new government of the Indian Union has completed the trend by inaugurating universal suffrage.

The question of representation raised, of course, the problem of the *basis* of representation. Many of the main cleavages in India were not territorial, but religious and cultural. It was natural that representation on a communal basis should be suggested, and that the first separate electorates should be for Muslims and Hindus (beginning in 1909). Later special electorates were also provided for Sikhs in the Punjab, for Europeans in all but three provinces, for Anglo-Indians in two, and for Indian Christians in one.[65] It soon became clear that the lower castes were not wielding the power in elections that the upper castes were wielding, and the clamor arose for special electorates along caste lines.

At the first Round Table Conference (1930), Dr. Ambedkar, leader of the Depressed Classes, demanded that the untouchables be treated as a separate community for electoral purposes. His proposal was accepted in principle in the third Conference, but on the ground that such a measure would split the Hindu ranks and perpetuate untouchability, Gandhi vigorously opposed the plan, beginning a "fast unto death." A new scheme was then drafted whereby the number of seats reserved for the Depressed Classes would be substantially larger than that provided in the proposed Award, but the principle of separate electorates would be applied only in a preliminary stage of the elections. "The Depressed Class voters would first elect a panel of candidates, and from this the members of the legislature would be elected by the general body of Hindu voters, including those of the Depressed Classes." This, the so-called "Poona Pact," was accepted.[66]

In some provinces the Depressed Classes wielded considerable influence, occasionally acting as a cohesive group and sometimes split up between various parties. Curiously, their first objective was not economic improvement but the removal of their disbarment from Hindu temples. The campaign met with some success, as new laws in Madras, Bombay, the Punjab, and Travancore demonstrated. In Travancore, one of the most caste-ridden parts of India, a great campaign was waged with Gandhi's participation, using modern methods of propaganda, passive resistance, and mass expression.[67]

The Scheduled Castes were represented by two men at the Cripps hearings. They condemned the Cripps proposals, because these left open the possibility of Pakistan. This, they said, would do the greatest harm to the Depressed Classes, because it would place them under an unmitigated system of Hindu rule. Clearly the Depressed Classes had acquired a vested interest in their special representation.

In addition to the Poona Pact, there was a movement to reserve government posts for the untouchables. Some of the provinces undertook to reserve a definite percentage of posts for non-Brahmans, provided they have the minimum qualifications.

The policy of special electorates and reserved posts cuts both ways with reference to the persistence of caste. On the one hand, by giving special favor to one class, it emphasized the separateness of that group as against the rest of the Indian polity. If such a policy had been pursued to its bitter end, the voting public would have been cut up into so many special groups that concerted action would have been utterly impossible. On the other hand, the avowed purpose was to give equality to people who were not equal—in other words, to make it possible for the scheduled castes to make their political voice heard and in this way to improve their social and economic position. In analogous fashion the laws of various lands protect children, wives, aments, and primitive peoples.

Legal Democracy. The British at first made no attempt to impose their entire legal structure on India. In the personal sphere, especially, they left things alone—the courts simply applying the Hindu and Muslim law as it stood. Until 1864 "the judge was merely the Pandit's mouthpiece and accepted without question the opinion which was given him, . . ."[68] Since most of the usages maintaining caste came under personal law, it is clear that at first British law contributed very little to the decline of caste. After 1864, however, more interpretation became possible, and other changes became noticeable.

One important change was the dissolution of the Brahman's legal monopoly. Whereas the Brahmans, as sole custodians of the law, had presented it to the lower orders as a divine creation, the British treated it as a secular institution, made by man for the benefit of man and not to be monopolized by any particular caste. This had a powerful effect in undermining the power of the Brahmans and hence the caste system.

Another change was the unwillingness of the courts to take notice of, or enforce, rules giving jurisdiction or power to castes as such. In the Mughal empire the Court at Delhi had been a supreme authority in these matters. The British government at first continued this practice, but in 1769 it was abandoned, and after a few years the special Court in Calcutta, known as the Caste Cutcherry, was abolished.[69]

In 1850 the Caste Disabilities Removal Act was passed. It was intended only to protect converts to Christianity or Islam, having no effect on those who remained in caste—virtually the whole Hindu population. But it did protect the individual's property rights in case of outcasting, and thus deprived the caste of a powerful instrument of control.[70]

A greater blow to caste was the adoption of the Western principle of equality before the law. Modern India is notorious for the amount of litigation that occurs. Even peasants resort to the courts for small grudges. This excessive litiga-

[63] R. Coupland, *The Indian Problem* (London: Oxford University Press, 1944), Part 1, p. 62. See also Sir George Schuster and Guy Went, *India and Democracy* (London: Macmillan, 1941), pp. 72–73.

[64] T. A. Raman, *Report on India* (London: Oxford University Press, 1943), p. 170.

[65] Coupland, *loc. cit.*, Part 1, p. 62.

[66] *ibid.*, Part 1, p. 128; Part 2, p. 143.

[67] Mahadev Desai, *The Epic of Travancore* (Ahmedabad: Navajivan Karyalaya, 1937).

[68] Sir Benjamin Lindsay, "Law" in L. S. S. O'Malley (ed.), *Modern India and the West* (London: Oxford University Press, 1941), pp. 128–29.

[69] O'Malley, *op. cit.*, pp. 368–69.

[70] *ibid.*, p. 369; Ghurye, *op. cit.*, p. 152.

tion is the natural result of a changing social order. The courts, by making the Brahman and the sweeper equal, are the agencies of change; they offer an escape from the restraints of the old social order.

The courts have also replaced caste jurisdiction. Formerly the caste *panchayat* protected the interests of the caste group and prevented disobedience to caste rules. Now, however, the caste member can appeal to outside authority. "The power of caste panchayets has thus greatly weakened in the last few decades, and is now almost extinct. If a panchayet decreed a fine or penalty in the past it could enforce its decision. If the offender were recalcitrant it could prevent his intercourse with the community without fear of itself getting into trouble. Now such a recalcitrant member can file a suit in the civil court against the members of a Panchayet or prosecute them for defaming him." [71]

The caste has lost legal control over the very essence of the caste system—intermarriage. Although the British courts at first supported the ban on intermarriage, they later reversed this policy. The Special Marriage Act of 1872 made it possible for an Indian of whatever caste or creed to marry a person of any other caste or creed, "provided the parties registered the contract of marriage, declaring *inter alia* that they did not belong to any caste or religion." This proviso was considered a great hardship, so finally, in 1923, the Special Marriage Amendment Act made the renunciation unnecessary. But at the same time it exacted a substantial sacrifice: "If two Hindus belonging to different castes marry under this Act they are not required to renounce their religion in declaration but have to forfeit certain of their personal rights as Hindus. They cannot adopt. On their marriage they cease to be the members of the joint family to which they previously belonged. Whatever rights in the property of the family would have accrued to them by survivorship under Hindu Law cease." [72] Clearly the legalization of intercaste marriages was not entirely accomplished, but the law was far ahead of custom. Although in the cities there is a tendency for romantic love among the younger generation to break down caste barriers, the rule of endogamy is still observed more scrupulously than any other caste usage.

Another legal blow at the caste system is the effort to abolish untouchability. Some of the provincial or central laws along this line, as already seen, free the untouchables from particular disabilities—such as temple pollution or separate schools. The most drastic legislation, however, was that of the Indian Constitutent Assembly on November 29, 1948, which adopted with acclamation an article in the Constitution making illegal *any* kind of disability for untouchables. The article states: "Untouchability is abolished and its practise in any form is forbidden. Enforcement of any disability arising out of 'untouchability' shall be an offense punishable in accordance with law." The adoption of this article was acclaimed in the world press, and in the United States it was compared to the abolition of slavery. [73] This comparison is worth noting, not only because it suggests the importance of the step, but also because it indicates the impotence of mere legislation. The slaves of the South were "emancipated" in a legal sense, but they have not yet been completely emancipated in a social sense. Nevertheless, the legal phase is a necessary part of social change in this regard, and the step in India has been appropriately recognized as important. One sign of its im-

portance was the protracted picketing of government buildings by diehard caste Hindus when the Assembly passed the measure.

Western Economic Influence. Three aspects of caste are particularly susceptible to modern economic influence: (a) the association between occupation and caste, (b) the local character of caste unity, and (c) the joint family system. These will be discussed in turn.

(a) The caste order always held, but did not thoroughly practice, the principle of hereditary occupation. Modern influence, because of its fast rate of change, has made the principle much more difficult to practice. Old occupations have gone and new ones come so rapidly that decisions were not made on a caste basis, but by individuals, with the result that the members of given castes have become occupationally dispersed. [74] Furthermore, modern technology is so complex that many occupations require elaborate education, which cannot be supplied simply by one's parents, or given to people below a certain capacity. Hence entrance into such occupations cannot be purely on the basis of birth. Finally, the modern specialization of labor is carried to such a degree that the particular occupational task may not be known to the public. This makes the identification of a caste with the special task virtually impossible.

(b) It was the local area where caste found its function and its unity. Nowadays, however, even the remotest village of India must submit to economic developments far beyond its horizon. Its economy is no longer in its own hands or in the hands of its castes. The large-scale business or industry draws its workers to central workshops, and generally hires them on an individual basis. It pays little respect to the unity of caste.

(c) Where hereditary status is strong the family also must be strong. But modern economic enterprise pulls people away from the homestead and pays them as individuals. Consequently, the joint family in India is disintegrating. "In 1861 it was noticed that, however divisible the possessions of a Hindu family might be theoretically, they were in fact so rarely distributed that many generations constantly succeeded each other without a partition taking place. Twenty years later fissiparous tendencies were seen in operation. Partition had become very frequent, and a family which had lasted for more than two generations was said to be rare. . . . The process of disintegration has gone on steadily and without check since then, and it is becoming increasingly common for families to be dissolved into their component parts on the death of a father, . . ." [75]

Urbanization. The anonymity, congestion, mobility, secularism, and changeability of the city makes the operation of caste virtually impossible. As far back as 1818, and again in 1883, it was observed that in Bengal cities the rules of castes were honored more in the breach than in the observance, and it was thought that the caste system was on the verge of disappearing. Nowadays the violation of caste rules is even more

[74] Blunt, *op. cit.*, pp. 52–53, 241–42. In the 1931 census report for Baroda a tabulation was made which illustrates neatly the hiatus between the traditional and the modern occupational structure. It showed that in Baroda there were far more agriculturalists, professionals, and village servants than there were people having these as a traditional caste occupation. On the other hand, there were far fewer persons employed in military, religious, janitorial, and trade occupations than were traditionally destined for such employment. It would be utterly impossible to meet modern conditions if everyone simply practiced his traditional occupation. *Census of India*, 1931, Vol. 19 (Baroda), Part 1, p. 401.

[75] O'Malley, *Modern India and the West*, pp. 382–83. See also, *Census of India*, 1931, Vol. 14 (Madras), Part 1, pp. 340–41.

[71] *Census of India*, 1931, Vol. 25 (Mysore), Part 1, pp. 330–31.
[72] Ghurye, *op. cit.*, pp. 152–53.
[73] *India Today*, January, 1949, p. 3.

open than it was then. "The growth of city life with its migratory population has given rise to hotels and restaurants. The exigencies of office work have forced city people to put aside their old ideas of purity. Caste-Hindus have to eat articles of food prepared by Christians, Musalmans, or Persians, because Hindu restaurants have not been easily or equally accessible during office hours. In Hindu hotels, they have to take their meals in the company of people of almost any caste—as the hotel-keeper cannot manage to reserve accommodation for members of different castes. What was originally done under pressure of necessity has become a matter of routine with many in their city life." [76]

The Census gets poor caste returns from the cities. Some persons refuse to return their caste at all, others refuse to return their subcaste, while still others give a false return. Many are not interested in caste at all. [77]

However, this urban freedom from caste-restrictions "is a mere garb that is usually cast aside by city people when they go to their villages." Back with their village folk, they tend to observe the old restrictions, especially in private. [78] Furthermore, the urban setting, by virtue of its very size and fluidity, gives an opportunity for castes to segregate themselves residentially more completely than in the village. It affords a greater opportunity for caste associations to operate and a modern type of caste patriotism to develop. [79] Clearly the city's influence on caste is not all one-way, but on the whole there seems little doubt that it is a powerful solvent of the old system.

New Technology. Technological innovations create new situations not defined by the previous folkways. In reaching a new definition of the situation, people are likely to make convenience the guiding principle, even when, from a logical point of view, it conflicts with the spirit of the old law. Thus in Calcutta, for Hindus, the practice of taking water from municipal pipes was open to possible objection, because the pumps were manned by Christians and Muslims and the taps were open to persons of every caste. The problem was solved by the pious fiction that the water-rate was a penance atoning for the use of the taps. [80] Travel on trains was questioned by orthodox Hindus, but rationalizations were found to justify it from the very first.

Observers have often noted the effect of trains, buses, highways, hotels, etc., in breaking down caste barriers in India. The effect has not been sudden or uniform, but it has been persistent, as the case of the river and canal ferries of the Telugu delta in Madras illustrate. As late as 1919 members of the Depressed Castes had to wait for hours before being accommodated on these ferries. "In the bigger boats plying on the two rivers and larger canals there is now no such preference; any person waiting is admitted on board. Depressed classes however have to keep to a different end of the boat from Brahmans. In the cross-river ferries the disappearance is not so complete. . . . The extent to which prejudice and preference have scope varies from village to village and with the importance of the Brahman or enlightenment of the depressed. It has been noticed that Christians of depressed class origin make no bones about getting into the boat whether a Brahman is waiting or not." [81]

The effect of rapid travel is not only the necessity of rubbing elbows with all sorts of persons, not only the difficulty of maintaining food and drink taboos, but also the removal of the individual from local caste control. Also, through returning travelers, through foreign goods, through mail, telegraph, and telephone, new ideas gain rapid dissemination.

Religious Conversion. The presence in India of proselytizing religions that do not in principle recognize caste has two effects. First, it affords a means by which members of lower castes can partially lose the stigma attaching to their status. Second, by virtue of this possibility, it forces Hinduism itself to inaugurate certain reforms in order to meet the competition of the more liberal religions.

It was estimated that in Madras, between 1921 and 1931, there was an increase of about 275,000 Christians and about 170,000 Muslims attributable to conversion, virtually all of them from the depressed classes. In fact it appeared that over half the natural increase of the depressed classes was absorbed by conversion to these two religions. [82] In the Punjab the strength of the Aryas rose from 82,488 in 1911, to 199,089 in 1921, to 341,390 in 1931, "in no small measure due to accretions from the low castes including Chamar." Between 1921 and 1931 the Hindu Chuhras decreased by 47 per cent, while Chuhras in other religions showed a substantial increase (300 per cent for the Sikh Chuhras and 16 per cent for the Muslim Chuhras). In some districts the percentage gain of Sikh Chuhras was as high as 1,000 to 5,000 per cent, and in a few places there was a struggle between the Sikhs and the Ad-Dharms to appropriate the Chuhras. [83]

Of course, it is easy to exaggerate the role of conversion as an escape from low caste status. As has been mentioned before, the caste identification may persist after conversion. This is particularly true when large numbers have been converted, for a point of diminishing returns is reached in terms of the gain in status. It must be remembered that Pope Gregory XV published a bull sanctioning caste restrictions in the Indian Church, and that in general caste divisions tend to reappear even in religions doctrinally opposed to caste. [84] But even though the gain is not complete, there is an improvement of status in most cases, especially in the second and third generation after conversion. Furthermore, it is significant that the number of persons returning *no* caste in these religions is higher than it is in Hinduism. [85] The non-caste religions in India thus do serve as a genuine, if only partial, escape from low status.

In addition to their direct effect through conversion, these religions have an indirect effect through the competitive attitude induced in Hinduism. In Travancore it appears that one stimulus that finally brought the government, and indeed most of the caste Hindus, around to granting the right of temple entry was the presence of proselytizing religions in the State, and specifically the plea of Dr. Ambedkar at a conference of Harijans (untouchables). This leader asked the Harijans to break away from the Hindu fold altogether. His

[76] Ghurye, *op. cit.*, p. 173. Also, O'Malley, *op. cit.*, pp. 365–66.

[77] *Census of India,* 1931, Vol. 9 (Bombay Cities), Part 1, pp. 38–39.

[78] Ghurye, *op. cit.*, pp. 173–74.

[79] *ibid.*, pp. 176–77.

[80] O'Malley, *Modern India and the West,* p. 367.

[81] *Census of India,* 1931, Vol. 14 (Madras), Part 1, p. 344.

[82] *ibid.*, p. 346.

[83] *ibid.*, Vol. 17 (Punjab), Part 1, pp. 334–35. The members of these anti-caste religions were not pressed for a return of caste, and hence the percentage increase was undoubtedly higher than it actually appears to be.

[84] Ghurye, *op. cit.*, p. 164. *Census of India,* 1931, Vol. 28 (Travancore), Part 1, pp. 367–68.

[85] *Census of India,* 1931, Vol. 19 (Baroda), Part 1, p. 397. The percentage of Indian Christians for whom caste was unspecified was 65; of Hindu Aryas, 14; of Hindu-Brahmo, 23; and of Muslims, 4—as against only 0.1 per cent of regular Hindus.

plea was followed by a special effort of the non-Hindu missionary organizations to make converts among the Harijans. The reaction of the caste Hindus was to take a more favorable attitude toward temple entry. In fact, an important talking point throughout the campaign was the danger and misfortune of conversion to a strange religion unless the Hindu elite bestirred themselves. Shrimata Nehru, speaking to a large audience, had this to say: "I am amazed to find missionaries of every religion rushing into Travancore thinking that the Ezhavas [a depressed caste] can be converted to one religion or the other. This is a very sad and humiliating spectacle. . . . I cannot promise you anything so big [as leadership] if you remain loyal to Hinduism. I can only promise you our heartfelt repentance for the past and our tireless service in the future. . . . Whether Ezhavas and Harijans go away or stay with us, we shall continue the holy task of purifying Hinduism and Hindu society, of purging them of the evils of untouchability and of the distinctions of high and low."[86] A clearer expression of the effect of competition could hardly be found.

The fact of partition itself will doubtless accelerate the breakdown of caste. The presence of an extremely Muslim state on the subcontinent, anxious to dissociate itself from Hinduism and Hindu institutions, should not only have the effect of purging caste distinctions from the territory it occupies but also of setting a nearby example for the Union of India. The latter should feel some pressure to modify its own institutions so as to avoid criticism by public opinion in Pakistan.

FORCES TENDING TO MAINTAIN CASTE

So many forces oppose caste in India that one may wonder how it ever got started and why it persists. But we know that certain conditions facilitate a caste organization. One of these is a settled agricultural economy. India has seen the growth of cities and industry to some extent, but it is still an agricultural area. As long as the village predominates, caste will be hard to eradicate, especially since it is now deeply rooted in the religion and mores of the Hindus.

In addition, castes are showing a certain amount of adaptability to modern conditions. Since about 1900 they have been forming associations that use modern methods in pursuing the interest of the caste. The associations consist of caste members who speak the same language. Their purpose is "(1) To further the general interests of the caste and particularly to guard its social status in the hierarchy from actual or potential attacks of other castes; (2) to start funds to provide studentships for the needy and deserving students of the caste, . . . ; (3) to help poor people of the caste; (4) and sometimes to try to regulate certain customs of the caste by resolutions passed at the annual meeting. . . ."[87]

"With the quickening of caste-consciousness and the fostering of caste patriotism, philanthropic persons have been building houses and chawls to be rented only to their caste-members at moderate rents. Charity, intending to further the educational interests of a caste, has found expression also in providing free hostels to the student members of the caste. As a result, in those areas of Bombay which are largely inhabited by the middle classes, we find today whole chawls which are occupied by members of one or two castes with close affinity, whole buildings rented at moderate or even nominal rents only to the members of a particular caste, and hostels giving free accommodation to the students of a particular caste. . . .

Even the colleges and the University are infested with endowments from which scholarships are to be paid to students of certain specified castes.

". . . Co-operative housing more than any other aspect of co-operative undertaking, has appealed to the caste-spirit, though credit societies of individual castes, like that of the Reddis, are not altogether unknown. In fact it would be true to remark that only those co-operative housing societies have succeeded most which have restricted their membership to their caste-fellows. Even in business this tendency to restrict the holding of shares to the members of a particular caste is sometimes apparent."[88]

In the past it was the caste panchayat that directed the affairs of the caste, and this embraced the local brotherhood rather than the caste as a whole. The new emphasis on associations reflects an increasing solidarity of castes over large geographical distances, and as such has led in some ways to a strengthening of the caste spirit. Yet this spirit now has a new element in it. It is competitive, pointed in the direction of social mobility, and is therefore contrary to the old static conception of caste. Also, it implies a lack of acceptance of one's position in the hierarchy. Today hardly any caste accepts its alleged status or concedes the precedence of another caste, though it may demand acknowledgment of its own superiority from a caste considered lower in the hierarchy.

Allied with the formation of caste associations is the tendency toward consolidation of sections and subcastes. Such a movement is noteworthy, because the thing that has been evident in the past is the ease with which new subdivisions are formed. The consolidation, of course, results from new means of communication and broader horizons. It has gone farther in some places than in others. In the United Provinces in 1931 it was pointed out that fissions and fusions are both quite rare.[89] In Travancore, on the other hand, "the fusion of subcastes is a common creed of all caste associations and is the one subject which is engaging their most prominent attention." It is advocated on both social and political grounds. "Socially, it is considered desirable that all petty differences between sub-divisions should be wiped out and one common caste formed. Politically, such a fusion will increase the numerical strength of the caste and enhance its importance in the body politic."[90]

The fusion of subcastes, if carried far enough, will tend to alter the caste system. Like caste associations, it is a movement to strengthen the caste in its competitive fight with other castes, and like them it disturbs the fixed hierarchy. If carried to the point of fusing castes rather than merely subcastes, it will tend to create broad classes, and thus the caste system will be transmuted into a class system.

THE BALANCE OF FORCES: THE DECLINE OF CASTE

Our discussion indicates that the forces now opposing caste are more numerous and definite than those favoring it. This conclusion can be reached in another way—namely in the actual evidences of the decline of caste. Foremost among such evidences are these: (1) the noticeable loosening of restrictions on interdining; (2) the widespread violation of food taboos; (3) the slight tendency to ignore intermarriage barriers; (4) the gradual removal of untouchability; (5) the pronounced growth of social mobility.

[86] Desai, op. cit., pp. 38–39. See also p. 33.
[87] Ghurye, op. cit., pp. 177–78.

[88] ibid., pp. 176–77.
[89] Census of India, 1931, Vol. 18 (United Provinces), Part 1, pp. 538–39.
[90] ibid., Vol. 28 (Travancore), Part 1, p. 364.

In Bombay "it would be almost true to say that the younger generation observe no distinction in the matter of offering and accepting hospitality among members of the various sub-castes within a major caste, but . . . members of different major castes would not, except in very special cases, meet at a common dining table." [91]

That untouchability is being removed to an ever greater degree—in schools, in temples, in modern means of transport, in cities, and in various services seems undeniable. Concerning the United Provinces, Blunt says: "There are untouchables, but they convey pollution only by contact; whilst the superstition is now moribund, few take any account of it save the Brahman, and even he deals with a case of pollution in a practical manner that suggests that he will before long ignore untouchability altogether." [92] The untouchable now has various escapes from his status—by conversion to a non-caste religion, by passing, by the adoption of a new occupation and a new caste name, and by migration. It is no longer true that once an untouchable, always an untouchable.

Mobility is prevalent all up and down the caste hierarchy. There is growing up today a new middle class, based on professions such as law, medicine, and business. This new middle class is drawn from all castes, some more than others to be sure, but certainly from no particular caste.

Though the balance is in favor of the dissolution of caste, it should not be thought that the caste system is disappearing rapidly. An institution that has endured for thirty centuries is not likely to pass overnight. The central and most essential trait—caste endogamy—remains almost as vigorous as before, being nibbled at only slightly by the modern notion of romantic love and individual choice. Moreover, the caste system is adapting itself to new conditions; it has a certain fluidity. "A fluid takes the shape of the vessel within which it is contained but does not alter in volume or quality. Much the same applies to Hinduism and the Hindu caste system. . . . It is this fluidity which gives [them] their strength and which has ensured and will ensure their survival." [93] Yet, when adaptation is carried beyond a certain point it ceases to be adaptation and becomes change. The modes of caste adaptation—the growth of caste associations, the tendency toward fusion, the adoption of needed reforms—presage the end of caste. It shows every sign of turning into a system of classes, "rather more rigid perhaps in the beginning than their prototypes in modern European countries," [94] but similar nonetheless.

Doubtless there will be remnants of caste in Indian life for centuries. On the other hand, some aspects may be gone before another generation has passed. The separation of Pakistan will probably eliminate caste from that large area of what once was India. The importance that government planning must assume in the new Union of India will doubtless hasten the decline of caste there. If industrialization proceeds rapidly in that nation, the caste system will have essentially disappeared by the end of this century.

[91] *ibid.*, Vol. 8 (Bombay Pres.), Part 1, p. 382.
[92] *The Caste System of Northern India, op. cit.*, p. 334.

[93] *Census of India*, 1931, Vol. 14 (Madras), Part 1, p. 339.
[94] *ibid.*, Vol. 19 (Baroda), Part 1, p. 412.

CHAPTER 19

Religion: Numerical Aspects

SINCE religion is still taken seriously on the Indian subcontinent, it plays an important role in the life of the people. Among its effects the following two may be noted.

(1) *Technological backwardness*. Whether Muslim, Hindu, Sikh, or Jain, religion in India is not limited to the vague and ultimate affairs of life, not confined to one hour per week, but is practiced every day and with minute and literal detail. The people are still living in a sacred society where both means and ends are viewed in a religious light, and ritual and magic are regarded as efficient. This means that the scientific, empirical, and businesslike approach to the world is subordinated to a multiplicity of specific and relatively rigid beliefs and rituals. The result is a strong resistance to technological change.

If it is a question of agriculture, technological advance is hindered by caste restrictions on types of labor, by dietary taboos, by the ritual value of dung, and by the veneration of the cow.[1] If it is a question of medicine, progress is retarded by the taboo on the treatment of women by male physicians, the prejudice against women entering the nursing profession, the definition of midwifery as an "unclean" occupation, and the taboo on contact with dead bodies and hence dissection. If it is a question of business, economic advance is handicapped by the Muslim taboo on moneylending, heavy borrowing for ceremonial rather than productive purposes, by obligations within the joint family, and by the occupational restrictions of caste.

To regard as sacred what are really unimportant matters is a familiar pattern in any society. The United States can furnish numerous examples in the attitudes of some groups toward contraception, feminine smoking, and Sunday baseball. But in India this religious grip on the details of life is much stricter than in Western nations.

(2) *Political conflict*. When religion is taken seriously and is applied to all aspects of life, the adherents of different faiths become peoples set apart. Each group tends to have its own folkways and mores, its own outlook, and its own allegiance superior to all others. Each faith thus becomes a nation within a nation. The Hindu term for religion, *dharma*, is much broader than our term. It "covers the whole field of conduct in all its wide relations."[2] Similarly, "Islamic civilization is centered around the religion of Islam." Its doctrine "makes a

bifurcation of civilizations into the Islamic, which fundamentalist Muslims regard as God-inspired and the only true and defensible civilization, and all other civilizations, which are by nature heterodox and false."[3] Despite their similar emphasis on religion, the two faiths, and hence the two civilizations, are distinct in many fundamental respects. As a result there has always been conflict between the two, flaring up at different times. Years ago it was said that the Muslims in India "are for many purposes a nation."[4] This conception served the Muslims as a basic reason for demanding Pakistan, so that they could fulfill their national faith by territorial sovereignty.

QUANTITATIVE INFORMATION

Recognizing the importance of religion in India, the census authorities have included religious affiliation on the schedule of every census. They have thus differed from American census procedure, which ignores the subject, and have accumulated a wealth of invaluable information. In nearly every chapter of the present book the religious groups are compared with reference to their demographic and social characteristics. In the present chapter the purpose is not to repeat or extend these comparisons, but to put together the most essential information about each group. In this way a sort of case study, or population profile, is made, enabling the reader to see each religious body as a whole. Comparative data are provided in the first section, giving the numerical strength and relative growth of the various groups. It goes without saying that there are many aspects of religion that cannot be dealt with here, either because the data do not exist or because they are not relevant to our main interest.

STRENGTH AND GROWTH OF MAIN RELIGIONS

From a numerical point of view the only two religions important in geographical India are Hinduism and Islam. In 1941 these together included 94 per cent of the total population. Hinduism claimed 70 per cent and Mohammedanism 24 per cent (Table 76). The third most important religion, Christianity, came far behind with less than 2 per cent of the population. The designation "Tribal" does not refer to any one religion, but to hundreds of different religions, all primitive in one way or another. The fact that more than 2 per cent of the population still came under this category at-

---

[1] The principal draft animal and source of animal food, the cow, according to Hinduism, cannot be killed when old or crippled, used for food, or scientifically bred. It consequently has far less value to the people than it would otherwise have. See G. T. Garratt, *An Indian Commentary* (New York: Cape & Smith, no date), pp. 36–37. For resistance to technological change in general, see F. L. Brayne, *Socrates in an Indian Village* (London: Oxford University Press, 1929).

[2] *Census of India*, 1931, Vol. 19 (Baroda), Part 1, p. 373.

[3] W. Norman Brown, "India's Pakistan Issue," *Proceedings of the American Philosophical Society*, Vol. 91 (1947), pp. 167–68.

[4] Sir T. W. Holderness, *Peoples and Problems of India* (New York: Henry Holt, 1910), pp. 127–28. Cf. *Census of India*, 1931, Vol. 14 (Madras), Part 1, p. 319.

tests the resistance and vitality of the primitive tribes, but reveals little else. The truth is, as we shall see, that numerical and social importance are not equivalent. The Christians, Sikhs, Jains, Parsis, and Jews have played a role in Indian affairs out of all proportion to their numerical strength.

TABLE 76

Per Cent of Total Population in Each Religion, 1881–1941 [1]

	1881	1891	1901	1911	1921	1931	1941
Hindu	75.09	74.24	72.87	71.68	70.73	70.67	69.46 [a]
Muslim	19.97	20.41	21.88	22.39	23.23	23.49	24.28
Tribal	2.57	3.26	2.88	3.17	2.97	2.26	2.26 [a]
Christian	.71	.77	.98	1.21	1.47	1.77	1.91 [a]
Sikh	.74	.68	.77	1.00	1.06	1.28	1.46
Jain	.49	.51	.47	.41	.39	.37	.37
Buddhist	.07	.09	.10	.11	.12	.13	.12 [a]
Parsi	.03	.03	.03	.03	.03	.03	.03
Jewish	— [b]	.01	.01	.01	.01	.01	.01
Others	.32	—	—	—	—	—	.11

[a] Because of a change of classification in the 1941 Census, many persons who would formerly have been enumerated as Hindu were classified as Tribal. This resulted in only 65.54 per cent of the population being reported as Hindu, and as much as 6.54 per cent being reported as Tribal. On the basis of certain assumptions, an adjustment was made which renders the figures for Hindus, Christians, and Buddhists more comparable with previous censuses. The method of making the estimates is given in Appendix J.

[b] A dash, "—", indicates that the number is less than .005 per cent.

[1] Each figure is a percentage of the total population for whom religion was reported. The data were obtained from the various census reports, and the absolute numbers will be found in Table 77 of this chapter.

Table 76 gives the per cent of the population in each religion from 1881 to 1941. It is derived from Table 77, which gives the absolute figures. Figure 43 depicts the growth of the six major groups on a logarithmic scale. It shows correctly the relative rates of growth but not the absolute numbers. As one might expect, the Christian religion has had the most phenomenal growth, but the Sikhs have not been far behind. The growth in the Muslim percentage, though smaller in proportion, has perhaps been more important than either of these, because of the greater absolute size of this body. The significance of these trends will be better understood by considering each religion separately. The reader is advised to refer to these tables and the chart as he reads the following sections.[5]

[5] The question of definition must be raised in comparing religious figures from different censuses. The most troublesome distinction has been that between Hindus and Tribals. In 1941, for example, the definition of "Tribal" was changed in such a way as to put approximately 17 million people into that category who did not belong there according to previous definitions. It has consequently been necessary to *estimate* the number of Hindus, Christians, Buddhists, and Tribals in 1941 according to the previous definition, in order to make legitimate comparison possible. The method is described in Appendix J.

Except for the case of Hindus and Tribals in 1941, the census definition of religious groups is thought to be reasonably consistent and accurate. In the Bengal report for 1931 (Vol. 5, Part 1, p. 382) it is claimed that the accuracy of the returns on religion is roughly the same as that of the figures on general population by age. To be sure, there are always problems in particular provinces. It is sometimes difficult to tell whether a given sect is Muslim or Hindu; sometimes Jains classify themselves as Hindu; sometimes untouchables return a new religious name rather than Hinduism; and sometimes there is deliberate falsification for political purposes. But most of these errors are minor, and many of them are corrected in the census office.

The Hindus

With now over 280 million adherents in geographical India, not to mention a few million in other places, Hinduism holds third place among the world's great religions, being exceeded in numbers only by Christians and Confucianists-Taoists.

Because of its pervasive influence and its complex nature, there is no single criterion by which Hinduism may be defined. It can be distinguished from other religions only by multiple criteria, most of which are useless for census purposes but which nevertheless give meaning to the census figures. On the level of its *supernatural content* it possesses three outstanding characteristics: first, a doctrine of radical immanence (pantheism) which finds God in everything; second, a tendency toward tolerant syncretism, which allows it to incorporate almost any ritual or deity into its own system; and third, a complex conception of individual destiny, contained in the doctrines of karma, reincarnation, and moksha. On the level of its *social content*—that is, its manifestation in social behavior—Hinduism becomes even more distinct. To an exceptional degree it is bound up with a specific social order, the outstanding institutions of which are the caste system, the joint family, and the rural village (themselves mutually related and interdependent). Indeed, since it is this order to which its supernatural content refers, the social system forms the fundamental basis of Hindu unity.

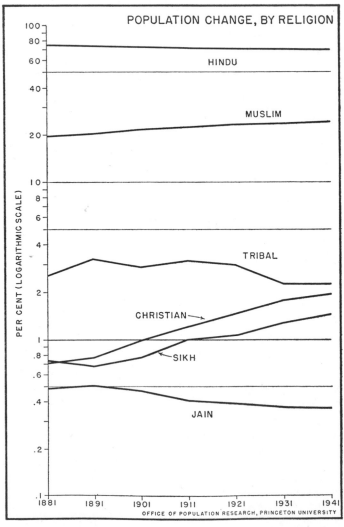

FIGURE 43. Growth of Population in Six Main Religions, 1881–1941.

TABLE 77

India: Population by Religion, 1881–1941 [1]

	1881	1891	1901	1911	1921	1931	1941
INDIA	250,155,050	279,575,324	283,867,584	303,004,354	305,726,528	337,675,361	388,997,955 [a]
Hindu	187,849,261	207,560,150	206,861,542	217,197,213	216,249,436	238,624,187	270,187,283 [b]
Muslim	49,952,714	57,068,133	62,118,631	67,835,078 [c]	71,005,307 [d]	79,305,543 [e]	94,446,544 [b]
Tribal	6,426,511	9,112,018	8,184,758	9,593,695	9,072,024	7,629,959	8,791,354 [b]
Christian	1,778,407	2,163,612	2,775,716	3,666,122	4,496,958	5,965,657	7,427,243 [b]
Sikh	1,853,426	1,904,669	2,188,743	3,007,773	3,233,960	4,324,864	5,691,447
Jain	1,221,880	1,416,638	1,334,055	1,247,687	1,177,461	1,251,384	1,449,286
Buddhist	167,311	243,286	292,638	336,874	369,325	438,769	457,551 [b]
Parsi	85,314	89,808	93,945	99,796	101,398	109,333	114,890
Jewish	11,805	16,843	17,543	19,956	20,643	22,923	22,480
Others	808,421	167	13	160	16	2,742	409,877

[a] Includes 2,331,332 persons in N.W. Frontier Prov. not enumerated by religion but believed to be Muslim.

[b] See Appendix J. These figures are estimates.

[c] Includes 1,608,556 persons in N.W. Frontier Prov. not enumerated by religion but believed to be entirely Muslim.

[d] Includes 2,770,666 persons in N.W. Frontier Prov. not enumerated by religion but believed to be Muslim.

[e] Includes 2,212,837 persons in N.W. Frontier Prov. not enumerated by religion but believed to be Muslim.

[1] Data taken from Imperial Table XVI in summary volume of each census. For 1941 see Appendix J of this chapter.

GEOGRAPHICAL DISTRIBUTION OF HINDUS

Map 17 shows the distribution of Hindus by district in India for 1931.[6] It will be observed that a very large portion of the subcontinent is 75 to 100 per cent Hindu. The main exceptions are the Muslim areas in the northwest and the northeast, which exclude even a Hindu majority, and the partially tribal areas (center) and partially Christian areas (extreme south). Outside of the Muslim-dominated areas, there is only a very small portion of the area that has less than 50 per cent Hindu, and this portion has less than its share of the population. The map displays in graphic manner the solid and wide dispersion of Hinduism in India.

GRADUAL DECLINE IN THE PROPORTION HINDU

Prior to partition, three forces were gnawing at Hindu hegemony in India. One was the inevitable secularization attendant upon Westernization; another was the accompanying alteration of the social system; and the third was the growing size and power of other religious groups. The result was a weakening of religious sentiment and a decline in the proportion of the population Hindu. The percentage of Hindus in the Indian population showed a slight decline at every census, as follows:

Year	Per Cent of Population
1881	75.1
1891	74.2
1901	72.9
1911	71.7
1921	70.7
1931	70.7
1941	69.5

At first it might seem that Hinduism would enjoy a demographic advantage. By far the majority of the millions who

[6] A similar map could be prepared for 1941, but it would not be comparable with any previous situation in India because of the change of definitions at that census. It seems better to use 1931 proportions, because, up until the migrations connected with the formation of Pakistan, the geographical distribution by religion remained very constant.

leave the tribal religions do so by drifting into Hinduism.[7] Hinduism probably receives more accretions, therefore, than any other religion in India. But against this must be balanced several adverse factors. In the first place, though Hinduism gains by accretion more in absolute numbers than any other religion, it probably also loses more. Many of the converts to Christianity, for example, are from the Hindu fold. Up until recent times the Hindus did not, and in many areas still do not, regard the untouchables as properly among the faithful, and did not admit them to Hindu temples. Among these semi-Hindus, therefore, the Christians found proselytizing fairly easy, as indeed the Muslims did also. In the second place, the Hindus apparently have a low fertility compared to Animists, Sikhs, Christians, and Muslims.[8] This low fertility is due partly to the high proportion of widows in the Hindu population—a proportion that is higher than for any other religious group except the Jains. At the same time, however, due to the young age at marriage of the Hindus, fewer of their women 15–39 are single than in any other group except the Jains. Yet it is thought that this young age at marriage itself has an adverse effect on fertility; and in any case it is worth noting that the ratio of children 0–4 per 1,000 *married* women among the Hindus is just as low, compared with other religions, as the ratio per 1,000 of *all* women.

Whether or not Hindu mortality is low or high is unknown. On the basis of the general characteristics of the Hindu population, and the age structure found for them, it would be reasonable to assume that the Hindus have a slightly lower mortality than all other groups in India, with the exception of the Sikhs. If so, this may be due in part to the fact that the Hindus, except for the Sikhs, are also the most rural. (Although it cannot be definitely established that the country is more healthful than the city, there would seem to be reason, by analogy with other areas, for believing it to be so.)

With a hypothetically low mortality and an advantage in the recruitment of new members, the fact that the Hindus are gradually declining in their portion of the total population indicates a considerable loss through conversion to other religions (either Christianity or Sikhism) or a comparatively low fertility. In the nature of the case the latter must be the

[7] *Census of India,* 1931, Vol. 7 (Bihar & Orissa), Part 1, p. 254.

[8] See Chapter 10, *supra.*

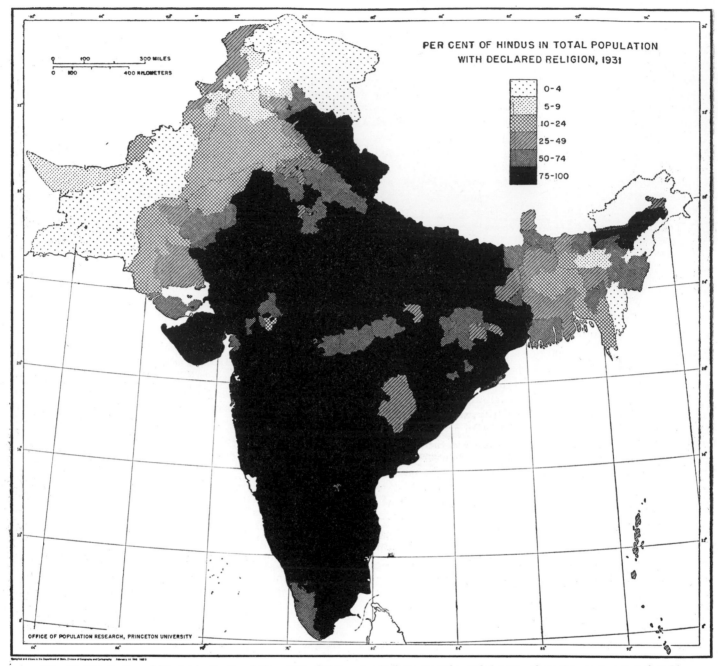

PER CENT OF HINDUS IN TOTAL POPULATION
WITH DECLARED RELIGION, 1931

	0-4
	5-9
	10-24
	25-49
	50-74
	75-100

OFFICE OF POPULATION RESEARCH, PRINCETON UNIVERSITY

MAP 17. Distribution of Hindus in the Population, 1931. (White areas indicate sparsely settled parts where data were not gathered.)

main factor, although it should not be deduced that the Hindu fertility is low in any absolute sense.

Before the formation of Pakistan there were signs that the Hindus were awakening to their decline. They had begun to take a more active role in behalf of their religion. Political associations such as the Mahasabha (later banned temporarily after the assassination of Gandhi), reform sects such as the Arya Samaj, and proselytizing movements such as the Hindu Mission were all giving Hinduism a more modern approach to the pursuit of its own interests. The effect of the partition of India was of course to increase the proportion of Hindus in the Union (now approximately 81 per cent Hindu instead of 69 per cent) and to create a Hindu minority problem (approximately 17 per cent of the population) in Pakistan. In Pakistan the Islamic religion already has a strongly nationalistic flavor, because the new state was created specifically for religious ends. It is quite possible that Hinduism will also

move further and more rapidly than in the past in the direction of a nationalistic religion, since Hinduism is one of the things that most distinguishes the Indian Union.

HINDU SECTS

Who are included among the Hindus? Obviously the great divisions of Hinduism which worship one of the five principal manifestations of the divine spirit are to be included. The two principal ones are Vishnavism (or the worship of Vishnu) and Sivaism (or the worship of Siva). Any Hindu whose main worship is addressed to one of the major Hindu deities may be considered to be "orthodox," and this embraces a very high percentage (perhaps 90 per cent) of those who call themselves Hindu.

There are other sects that are less completely a part of Hinduism, such as the Left-hand Saktas and the Lingayats;

yet these are generally counted as being within the orthodox fold. The Census has generally classified Hindus into only three divisions: Brahmanic, Arya, and Brahmo. The Arya Samaj and the Brahmo Samaj, both recently formed liberal sects, have small memberships, the first with 990,000 and the second with 5,000 adherents in 1931. In 1931 an "Others" category was added to the classification of Hindus. It evidently included a large number of Tribals, because the Census explained as follows: "The term 'Brahmanic' has been used for those Hindus who were not returned as belonging to either the Arya Samaj or the Brahmo Samaj or to certain other reforming or segregative bodies, which have been shown together in 'Other Hindus'. These bodies consist of Deo-Samajists, Adi-Hindus, Adi-Dravidas, Adi-Karnatakas and such persons of the Stnami, Sanjogi, Kabirpanthi and Dadupanthi sects as returned themselves by these terms in place of the term Hindu." [9]

Many of these names are ones that Tribalists adopt when they switch to Hinduism, or that untouchables adopt when they try to raise their status. Hence the new category "Others" must be mainly responsible for the enormous drop in the percentage of Hindus listed as Brahmanic between 1921 and 1931. The percentage of all Hindus listed as Brahmanic in the various censuses was as follows: [10]

Year	Per Cent Brahmanic
1891	99.98
1901	99.95
1911	98.89
1921	99.78
1931	91.68

The loss of nearly 10 points in the percentage of Brahmanic Hindus in 1931 could possibly be due to a growing unorthodoxy, but it seems that the main explanation lies in the use of a stricter definition that excluded some of the new names being adopted by adhering Tribalists and socially climbing untouchables.

THE SIKHS

At the time of their foundation in the sixteenth century, the Sikhs were a Vishnava sect. They retained the Hindu pantheon, as well as the Indian social system and the doctrines of karma and reincarnation. Their chief difference lay in their denial of divine incarnations, their condemnation of idolatry (which prevented their worshiping in Hindu temples), and their distrust of asceticism. "Sikh" means *disciple,* and "guru," the name given by the Sikhs to their spiritual leaders, means *teacher.* There were ten successive *gurus,* the succession being stopped by the declaration of the last, who died in 1708, that the sacred literature (the Granth Sahib) written primarily by the first and tenth *gurus,* should be sufficient.

It was not until the end of the 17th century that the sect began to diverge markedly from the Hindu pattern. By virtue of its geographical location between Muslim and Hindu areas, Sikhism had long shown a certain tendency toward militant solidarity. As a result it had frequently aroused the suspicion of the Muslims. The last great Mughal emperor, Aurangzeb,

put to death the ninth *guru* in 1675 and continued to persecute the sect, as did his followers. It was hatred of the Muslim that served to unite the Sikhs. In the crisis the tenth *guru* invited all Sikhs to form by mutual covenant a sacred league (*Khalsa*) within which caste would disappear, and each man would become a warrior, would regard every other member as a brother, and would vow to fight to the death for his faith. Calling themselves "Lions," each adding the word Singh ("lion") to his name, a great number of Sikhs responded to this call and formed themselves into a redoubtable army of heroes. The Khalsa, however, was not at first successful. The Sikhs were beaten and scattered during most of the 18th century. But the ideal of the Khalsa lived on, and eventually the faithful were remarkably successful. As the Mughal Empire gradually crumbled, Sikh bands gained power and prestige. They organized two small democratic republics, later twelve petty states, and finally, under Ranjit Singh, who ruled from 1800 to 1839, they were united in a monarchical nation called Punjab.

The Sikh nation went to war twice with the British, in 1845 and 1848. In consequence they lost their sovereignty, and settled down under British rule as simply another religious minority seeking political advantages and economic improvement. They did have the advantage of being a third party in the struggles between Muslims and Hindus. They also possessed a strong military tradition, and were consequently used heavily in the Indian Army, where they gained not only financially but educationally.[11] It is not surprising that in political strife they have generally been pro-British. This was true, for example, in the so-called Sepoy Mutiny of 1857.[12]

GEOGRAPHICAL LOCATION

The Sikhs have always resided mainly in a small section of India—a part of central-eastern Punjab, which is their original homeland. The bulk of them have resided within a triangle whose points were near Lahore, Kangra, and Patiala respectively, and whose area was less than 10,000 square miles.[13] The degree of concentration is shown by the fact that 90 per cent of all the Sikhs in India in 1941 resided in the Punjab. Map 18 shows the location of Sikhs in 1931.

Within their restricted area, however, the Sikhs did not represent anything like a majority. In 1941 there was only one political unit, Faridkot (a small Punjab State), where they had a majority (58 per cent). Everywhere else they were a minority. In the Punjab as a whole they represented

---

[9] *Census of India,* 1931, Vol. 1, Part 2, p. 513.

[10] In 1941 no such classification of Hindus was made. The only division was between Scheduled Castes (Untouchables) and "Others" (meaning all Caste Hindus).

[11] For a long time the British thought that only certain "races" had military capacity, and the Sikhs and Muslims were counted among these. Consequently virtually all the recruits for the Indian Army came from the northwestern region. During World War I, for example, the Punjab, with a population of 20 million, provided 350,000 combatant recruits, or *more than 50 per cent of the total,* while Bengal, with a population of 45 million, provided only 7,000 recruits! [Indian Statutory Commission, *Report* (London: His Majesty's Stationery Office, 1930; Cmd. 3568), Vol. 1, pp. 96–98.] As late as 1944, when the Indian Army numbered over two million, 10 per cent of the Indians recruited were Sikhs. This was nearly seven times their proportion in the total population. In other words, the Sikhs have been many times more heavily represented in the army in proportion to their population than any other religious or ethnic group in India. The Ghurkas, Hindus from Nepal, have always been outnumbered by the Sikhs in the army. See Raleigh Parkin, *India Today* (New York: John Day, 1945), pp. 89–90.

[12] A recent and full account of the Sikhs is that given by John Clark Archer, *The Sikhs* (Princeton: Princeton University Press, 1946). A shorter account is contained in J. N. Farquhar, *Modern Religious Movements in India* (New York: Macmillan, 1915), pp. 336–43.

[13] Archer, *op. cit.,* p. 274.

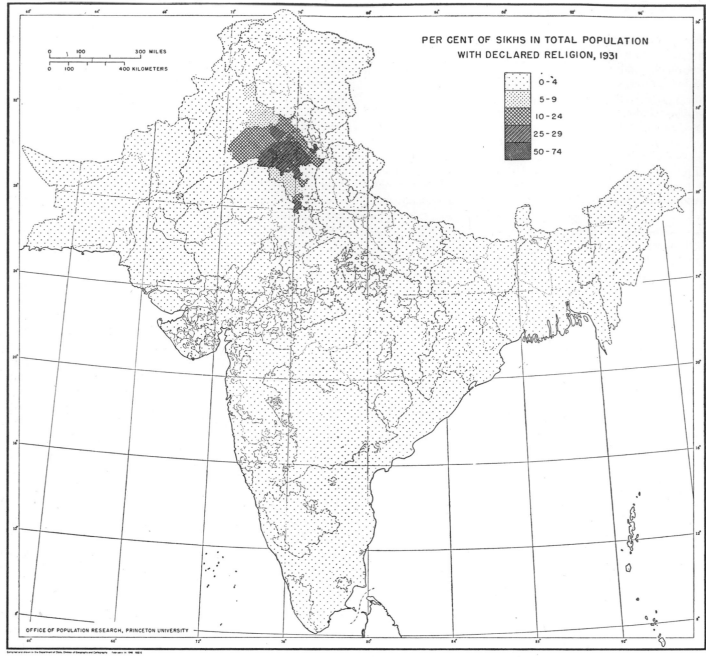

MAP 18. Distribution of Sikhs in the Population, 1931.

15 per cent of the population in 1941—13.2 per cent of the British Territory and 24.4 per cent of the Punjab States. There is a light sprinkling of Sikhs all over India, but in most districts they constitute less than 1 per cent of the population.

The formation of Pakistan has undoubtedly served to concentrate the Sikhs still more. The boundary that was drawn between the two new nations cut directly through the Sikh territory. According to 1941 figures, if the Sikhs had remained where they were and the population had not changed, there would have been approximately a million and a half of them in Pakistan and four million in the Union of India. But it is believed that every Sikh who was in Pakistan left there, either by death or by migration. As a consequence the Sikh community is now entirely in the Indian Union, and presumably concentrated close to the boundary. Some Hindus have gone back to their homes in Pakistan, but there is no indication that the Sikhs will ever do so.

GROWTH OF THE SIKH COMMUNITY

During the period since 1900 the Sikhs have had a remarkable growth in numbers, second only to the growth of Christianity. Within four decades they nearly tripled their membership. They have steadily increased their percentage of the total population. The figures are as follows:

Year	Number (000's)	Per Cent of Population
1881	1,853	0.74
1891	1,905	0.68
1901	2,189	0.77
1911	3,008	1.00
1921	3,234	1.06
1931	4,325	1.28
1941	5,691	1.46

What has caused this rapid increase? As a religious body the Sikhs practice a few peculiar customs that set them apart from other Indian religions. Some of these customs apparently have little to do with an increase in numbers, while others apparently do. The true Singhs are not supposed to cut their hair, to use tobacco, or to eat flesh improperly slain. Properly slain, nearly any kind of meat is admissible in the diet. Infanticide, suttee, child marriage, and pilgrimage are forbidden. But more important from our point of view are two related facts: first, the Sikhs forbid distinctions of caste within their own ranks; and second, they accept converts to the fold. Actually, as one might expect, there are caste distinctions among the Sikhs, just as there are among Christians,[14] but they are not so pronounced as among Hindus. Also, there is some prejudice against the recent converts to Sikhism, but not so much that low-caste Hindus and even Muslims cannot gain in social status by turning Sikh. The result has been a very high rate of conversion to the Sikh community. Anyone can be initiated into the religion by a kind of baptismal ceremony (*pahul*). The proselytizing drive, the so-called *Akali* movement, has brought in many recruits. "Such persons for the most part comprise members of the depressed classes, agriculturalists, and artisans in rural areas, who obviously consider that they gain in status as soon as they cease to be Hindus and become Sikhs."[15] Proof of both the character and the number of the recruits is obtainable from census figures. The Saini (in central Punjab) and the Mali (in eastern Punjab) are two branches of an agricultural caste. In 1911 these two branches together were 30 per cent Sikh (the rest being Hindu), whereas in 1931 they were 57 per cent Sikh. Actually such figures underestimate the movement into Sikhism, because "converts to Sikhism do not as a rule return any caste, being content with the entry of 'Sikh' in the column of caste. . . . In regard to Sikhs the instructions to enumerators were that they should not be pressed to return their caste." In spite of this, certain low castes were much more numerous in the Sikh fold in 1931 than in 1921. Dhobis (washermen), *darzis* (tailors), carpenters, masons, and goldsmiths were switching religions, as shown by the fact that the decrease in the number in one religion can be matched by a corresponding increase in the number in the other. The Chuhra increased their number in the Sikh community by 300 per cent during the decade, and the Saini by 61 per cent. But the influx into Sikhism also characterizes some of the higher castes. During the 1921–31 decade the Rajputs, for example, enlarged their numbers in Sikhdom by 73 per cent.[16] In view of these facts it seems highly probable that the Sikh willingness to accept converts and the Sikh denial of caste (which makes conversion attractive) both account for the major part of the rapid growth of the Sikh community as compared to the rest of India. But there are other factors that may also contribute.

The Sikhs, though an offshoot of Hinduism, do not oppose remarriage of widows. They have a smaller proportion of *widows* among the women 15–39 than does any other religious group in India except the Parsis. They also have relatively few *single* women in these ages, though because of their late age at marriage, they have a larger proportion than Muslims, Hindus, and Jains. The net result is that they have a greater ratio of *married* women 15–39 than any other religious group. At the same time they have, as indicated by the child-woman ratios, an exceptionally high fertility per married woman, being ahead of all other groups (including Tribalists) in this regard.[17]

Not only do the Sikhs apparently have a high fertility, but also, on the basis of slender evidence, they have a low mortality. They have a far larger percentage of persons in the older age brackets than any other group. This may be due in part to proselytizing, but if so, one would expect the Christians to have a similar age structure, but they do not. If mortality is lower in the country than in the cities of India, as many believe, the Sikhs would have a favorable position because, with the exception of the Tribals, they are the most rural of any major religious group. Only 7.8 per cent of them were urban in 1931, as against 10.4 for Hindus and 13.0 for Muslims.

It seems, then, that a large natural increase is, along with conversion, a factor in the rapid increase of the Sikh community.

REFORM AND EDUCATION

Toward the end of the last century Sikhism showed some tendency to lose its distinctiveness and solidarity. The mode of worship was beginning to resemble that of the Hindus, internal caste divisions were getting stronger, and idolatry was creeping in. Under Western influence, however, a reforming spirit set in about 1905 which revived and purified the sect to some extent.[18] Sikhs took more seriously to education. They prospered as farmers and soldiers. Now, despite their rurality, they are more literate than either the Hindus or the Muslims. In 1941 in the Punjab the Sikhs were 17 per cent literate (all ages), the Hindus 16 per cent, and the Muslims 7 per cent. Their high percentage in the Indian Army has doubtless helped their literacy.

The conflict accompanying the partition of India has doubtless set back the Sikhs economically and numerically, but there is no indication that this vigorous and unusually adaptable religious community will cease to grow and develop in the near future.

THE JAINS

The Jain sect is far older than the Sikh, and slightly older than Buddhism, having arisen within Hinduism in the sixth century B.C. It retains most Hindu doctrines, but is distinguished by carrying to an extreme the doctrine of radical immanence. This doctrine, the concrete expression of which is *ahimsa* (non-injury), would result in extreme asceticism, were it not for the sharp distinction among Jains between the laity and the monks. The Jains possess one of the most ancient monastic orders in India, and one of the most ascetic. The Jain laity, on the other hand, has always been remarkably successful in worldly affairs. They were already wealthy and prominent in the old regimes, and they were one of the first religious groups to take advantage of Western education, prospering exceedingly in business under British rule.[19] They seem to exemplify the symbiotic relation that may exist between religious asceticism and worldly success, resembling in a vague way the Christian Puritans.

---

[14] See Chapter 18, *supra*, p. 165.

[15] *Census of India*, 1931, Vol. 17 (Punjab), Part 1, p. 293.

[16] *ibid.*, p. 308. A table is given here showing for several castes and tribes the percentage who were Sikhs at the various censuses from 1891 to 1931. cf. the section on "Religious Conversion" in Chapter 18 on Caste in the present book.

[17] The position of the Sikhs with reference to fertility is more fully presented in the section on "Religious Differentials" in Chapter 10, "Differential Fertility," *supra*.

[18] Farquhar, *op. cit.*, pp. 340–43.

[19] *ibid.*, pp. 324–26. H. De Witt Griswold, *Insights into Modern Hinduism* (New York: Henry Holt, 1934), pp. 144, 147, 150.

Worldly success, however, is not causing the Jains to grow in numbers. On the contrary they seem to be numerically stationary, and to be declining as a portion of the total population, as the census returns show:

	Number (000's)	Per Cent of Population
1881	1,222	0.49
1891	1,417	0.51
1901	1,334	0.47
1911	1,248	0.41
1921	1,177	0.39
1931	1,251	0.37
1941	1,449	0.37

As a partial explanation of the stagnation one may note that, because they observe the taboo on widow remarriage more strictly than any other religious group, the Jains have a low percentage of their women 15–39 married. A fifth of their women in this age group were widows during the period 1911–31. If they permitted widows to remarry to a degree that would give them the same proportion widowed as the United States had in 1930, their fertility would be increased more than 20 per cent.

Not only does widowhood cut down Jain reproduction, but the sect also has a low fertility within the marital relation. They have next to the lowest ratio of children to *married* women of any religious group, being outdone in this respect only by the Parsis, who have roughly the same socio-economic position as the Jains.[20]

The low marital fertility of the Jains is doubtless connected with their social position. They are the third most urban religious group, the third most literate, and the second or third most prosperous. The price they are apparently paying for their high social position is a low fertility. Since they do not acquire new converts, this low fertility helps to prevent any growth in their number.

Low fertility is probably not the only factor, however. This is indicated by the case of the Parsis. The latter have, by all signs, a lower fertility than the Jains, but are slowly increasing in population. There is some evidence that the Jains are losing some members who drift into Hinduism.[21] It will be noticed, from the figures given above, that the Jain population reached its low point in 1921, and began to climb thereafter. In this connection it is interesting that the Jains made the greatest improvement of any group in lowering the amount of widowhood. In 1921 the proportion of widows among women 15–39 was 20.8, whereas in 1931 it was down to 16.9. It is also interesting to note that vigorous reform movements began within the sect around the turn of the century. It may be that the Jains will steadily increase in numbers in the near future. In any case they will long retain their place as the sixth most numerous religious group in India, though there is little chance of their catching up with the fast-growing Sikhs, the nearest group ahead of them.

[20] See section on religious differentials in Chapter 10.

[21] "In respect of Jains it is always doubtful whether the numbers recorded are really accurate as many return themselves as Hindus. Sometimes there is no uniformity about this practice so that the comparative figures of Jains and Hindus are always liable to a certain amount of disturbance by influences which cannot be gauged statistically." *Census of India,* 1931, Vol. 9 (Bombay Cities), Part 1, p. 11.

THE BUDDHISTS

It is ironical that Buddhism, which has permeated Asiatic culture from Tibet to Japan, has all but vanished from the one Asiatic country where it originated and flourished. It began in India in the sixth century B.C. as a reform movement against Brahmanism. Differing from Brahmanism mainly in its denial of caste and its advocacy of universal brotherhood, its strength lay in its communal monasticism, which gave it a powerful missionary agency. The view was fostered that the laity, less sacred than the monks, acquire secondary merit by financially supporting the monasteries. Buddhism quickly became a great influence in India, apparently reaching its peak during the reign of Asoka (c. 269 to c. 232 B.C.). This was also the period of India's greatest influence abroad; with Asoka's zealous encouragement, Buddhist missionaries traversed continents and seas. Within a few centuries it permeated most of southern Asia. During the first five centuries of the Christian era it spread to Central Asia and the Far East. It reached China in the first century A.D., Korea in the fourth century, Japan in the sixth, and Annam about the tenth. In the meantime, however, it yielded to a revived Brahmanism in India, and by the tenth century had disappeared there as an active religion. Today its influence is overwhelming in nearby Tibet, Burma, and Ceylon, but in India it is a minor religion professed by a handful of people who are mostly foreign. In 1941 its followers were less than 1 per thousand of the total population.

The census figures show a rapid growth in the number of Buddhists, as follows:

Year	Number (000's)	Per Cent of Population
1881	167	0.07
1891	243	0.09
1901	293	0.10
1911	337	0.11
1921	369	0.12
1931	439	0.13
1941	458	0.12

That most of these Buddhists are basically non-Indian can be gathered from their distribution. The bulk of them are found in Sikkim and the adjoining hills. "There are a few in Assam, the descendants either of ancient immigrants from Burma *via* the Hukong valley or of isolated parties left behind by the army of invasion in the early 19th century." [22]

The Buddhists in India are slightly better educated than the Hindus, and slightly less so than the Sikhs. Judging by their fertility ratios they tend to reproduce about as rapidly as the general population. They have a very low proportion of widows, but a high proportion of single (i.e. never-married) women. This latter fact, despite what is apparently a high fertility for married women, brings the fertility ratio down to about the general average.

There is little reason to believe that Buddhism will ever be strong again in India. Its strength there will probably continue to be cultural only, for Hinduism has absorbed a good deal from Buddhist teachings.

[22] *ibid.,* Vol. 1, Part 1, p. 389.

THE JEWS

India has practically no Jews. The number in 1941 was 23,000—less than one Jew for every ten thousand inhabitants. For the most part, however, they are native Jews, their forefathers having been in India for centuries. They have remained a closed body, receiving practically no recruits by conversion. In spite of long residence in the country they have resisted the process of Hinduization. The two main signs of Hindu influence among them are the addition of a Hindu name after the Hebraic one, and the formation of two mutually exclusive Jewish castes—the White Jews and the Black Jews. The White Jews have apparently retained their Caucasian blood, while the Black have mixed with the Indian population until very similar to the ordinary Indian.

The Jews are predominantly urban. More than a third live in Bombay City, and the rest mostly in other urban places. The Bombay Presidency, the most urban province in India, contains well over two-thirds (17,739 in 1931) of all Jews. The second largest concentration (1,451 in 1931) is in Cochin. In each place both castes are present.

The Jews have the second highest literacy rate of any religious group. Yet, despite their urbanism and their literacy, they seem to be maintaining themselves. It is alleged that the White Jews in Cochin are dying out,[23] but the Jewish group as a whole has increased about as fast as the total population. The figures are as follows:

Year	Number	Per Cent of Population
1881	11,805	0.005
1891	16,843	0.006
1901	17,543	0.006
1911	19,956	0.007
1921	20,643	0.007
1931	22,923	0.007
1941	22,480	0.006

In view of the small size and modest growth of the Jewish population, it seems unlikely that to India's religious conflicts will ever be added a Jewish problem.

THE PARSIS

When Persia was conquered by the Islamic Arabs, a sizable group of Zoroastrians escaped to India, where they settled in Gujarat and became known as "Parsis." In their new home they prospered and became an outstanding commercial group, influential far beyond their numerical importance. Their religion had the same remote origin as Hinduism (deriving from the branch of Aryan culture that went to Persia instead of India). It was the faith of a people shifting from pastoralism to settled agriculture, its mythology, ritual, and morality all centering on the virtue of agricultural pursuits. The cow was venerated, the ox featured in the creation myth.

The Parsis remained an exclusive group in India, but they found Hinduism congenial and soon adopted many of its practices. "Child-marriage and the Zenāna became universal among them. Polygamy was not uncommon. The men ate separately from the women. Many were ready to recognize Hindu festivals and worship. The Parsee priesthood became a hereditary caste. Religious, social and legal questions were settled, according to Hindu custom, by a . . . Panchayat." In 1843 a book on the Parsi religion appeared, written by John Wilson, a Christian educator in Bombay. It exposed the degree to which the Parsi community was ignorant of its own religious background and literature. After the first wave of resentment, the Parsis took the accusations to heart and began an educational and reform program that has reputedly had considerable effect.[24]

Of all the religious groups in India, the Parsis are the most literate (nearly 80 per cent of all persons age 5 and over),[25] the most urban (89 per cent),[26] and probably the wealthiest. Their position resembles that of Jains and Jews. Somewhat like the Jains, they ironically combine a simple agrarian religion with a high worldly position. Like the Jains, too, the Parsis, although increasing gradually in absolute numbers, are not growing quite so fast as the general population.

Year	Number (000's)	Per Cent of Population
1881	85	0.034
1891	90	0.032
1901	94	0.033
1911	100	0.033
1921	101	0.033
1931	109	0.032
1941	115	0.032

That they are growing as fast as they are is surprising, because, being at the top of the economic ladder, and being the most literate and urban of all the religious groups, they can be expected to have the lowest fertility. Actually, a curious circumstance may be noted. Of all religious groups the Parsis have the fewest widows between the ages of 15 and 39 (Fig. 21 in Chap 10). But on the other hand they have far the greatest number of single (never-married) women in these ages. Indeed, they have more than double the percentage of the next highest group (the Buddhists). The result is that they have the smallest percentage of married females in the reproductive ages of all religious groups. In addition, as measured by the fertility ratio, they have the lowest reproduction per married woman.[27] Their total fertility must therefore be extremely low for India, and this doubtless explains their slow population growth. But the fact that they are growing at all suggests that they balance their low fertility with an exceptionally low death rate.

Having entered India from the west, the Parsis have remained concentrated in western India. More than four-fifths of them live in Bombay Province, and more than half live in Bombay City (where they approximate 5 per cent of the city's population). In connection with their commerce, however,

[23] ibid., p. 197.

[24] Farquhar, op. cit., pp. 81–84.

[25] Their literacy in English is even more remarkable than their literacy in other languages. In 1931 over half the Parsis age 10-plus knew English, almost twice as large a proportion as the nearest rival, the Jews, with 26 per cent. Even the Christians had only 9 per cent literate in English, and the Jains only 3.4 per cent. See p. 159 in Chapter 17.

[26] How well they have adapted to urban life is shown by the fact that their age structure in Bombay is more normal than that of any other religious group in the city. Census of India, 1931, Vol. 9 (Bombay Cities), Part 1, p. 29.

[27] C. Chandra Sekar stresses the declining fertility of the Parsis. See his "Some Aspects of Parsi Demography," Human Biology, Vol. 20 (May, 1948), pp. 47–89.

they have taken up residence in all the principal cities of India.

THE CHRISTIANS

Christianity shows the fastest growth of any religion in India. Between 1881 and 1941 it more than quadrupled its adherents, and more than doubled its proportion of the total population. Already by 1891, at which time it outstripped the Sikhs, it had become the third most popular religion in the country (leaving aside the artificial "Tribal" category). To-day, with 7.5 million adherents, it is still far behind the Muslims, but shows little sign of ceasing its growth. The trend is as follows:

Year	Number	Per Cent of Population
1881	1,778,000	0.71
1891	2,164,000	0.77
1901	2,776,000	0.98
1911	3,666,000	1.21
1921	4,497,000	1.47
1931	5,966,000	1.77
1941 [28]	7,427,000	1.91

Christianity came into India many centuries before either the Portuguese or the British. Christian congregations, off-shoots of the Mesopotamian church, existed in southwest India in the third century and "persisted with many vicissitudes until their 'heresies' shocked the orthodox Portuguese ecclesiastics who came to Goa in the sixteenth century." [29] Later came Nestorian Christianity. The Portuguese pursued an active policy of converting to Catholicism all and sundry, including the Nestorian Christians. The British, held back by the reluctance of the East India Company to mix religion with business, did not seriously begin missionary work until 1813.[30] The Americans came actively into the field from 1880 onwards. Not restrained by the official British fear of offending the religious sentiments of the people, they devoted themselves to proselytizing, rather than merely teaching and preaching. They worked particularly among the depressed classes.

The census of India has long enumerated the Christians by "race," dividing them into three categories: (1) Europeans and Allied Races, (2) Anglo-Indians—descendants of mixed unions, and (3) Indians. Since 1891 the first two categories have steadily become a smaller portion of the total Christian population, the third category a larger portion. The percentages are given in Table 78. In 1911 the first two categories together constituted 11 per cent of all Christians, but by 1941, less than 4 per cent. Christianity is obviously not a hot-house flower in India depending on the presence of Europeans, but a native plant.

In view of the large native membership and the well-known

---

[28] This is an estimate. The census figure, which excluded Christians of tribal affiliation and Europeans, came to only 6,181,000. See Appendix J for the method of estimate.

[29] W. H. Moreland and Atul Chandra Chatterjee, *A Short History of India* (London: Longmans, 1936), pp. 83–84.

[30] A. I. Mayhew, "The Christian Ethic and India" in L. S. S. O'Malley (ed.), *Modern India and the West* (London: Oxford University Press, 1941), p. 322.

TABLE 78

Christians by "Race," 1891–1941 [1]

	Total Christians (000's)	Number in Each "Race" (000's)			Per Cent in Each "Race"		
		Euro-pean	Anglo-Indian	Indian	Euro-pean	Anglo-Indian	Indian
1891	2,284	168	80	2,037	7.4	3.5	89.2
1901	2,923	170	89	2,664	5.8	3.1	91.1
1911	3,876	200	102	3,575	5.2	2.6	92.2
1921	4,753	176	113	4,464	3.7	2.4	93.9
1931	6,297	168	138	5,990	2.7	2.2	95.1
1941 [2]	7,427	135	140	7,151	1.8	1.9	96.3

[1] Compiled from table on religion in various censuses, except for 1941. The figures included Burma, which explains why the totals differ from those in the text table. However, Burma has never had many Christians: in 1931 there were 331,000. The inclusion of Burma should not greatly affect the results.

[2] Total Christians estimated for 1941 (see Appendix J). It was assumed that all Christians added by this estimate were Indian Christians.

absorptive tendency of Hinduism, it is worthwhile to ask how unalloyed Indian Christianity has remained. Hinduism is so largely a social system, and the Indian Christians so definitely a part of it, that Christianity has certainly had to effect some compromises. The early Jesuits adapted themselves to Indian customs to attract converts. Some Indian Catholics still observe caste, employing caste marks in some cases; they also use the *tali* instead of a ring in marriage and retain other Hindu customs.[31] Even the Protestants observe restrictions on interdining. The fact that most of the Christian converts have come from the untouchables and the primitive tribes has not increased the likelihood of their having a firm grasp of Christian principles. "Social customs, such as early marriage, treatment of women, etc., do not change with the change of one's faith." [32]

Some of the Hindus, in turn, have borrowed Christian practices. The Lingayat sect has taken over the belief in the virgin birth and the practice of burying the dead.[33] Willy nilly, many cultural traits associated with Christian civilization, while not necessarily specifically religious in character, have become a part of Indian thinking, especially on the intellectual level.

GEOGRAPHICAL LOCATION

Most of the Christians, as Map 19 shows, are located in South India, where missionary work first started. In 1931, of 6.3 million Christians in India (without Burma), 3.8 million, or about 60 per cent, resided in Southern India. More than a fourth of the total, or 1.6 million, resided in Travancore State.[34] Travancore, with 32 per cent of its population in this religion, is the most Christian of any major political division. It contains two large taluks with more than 55 per cent Christian, and four others with more than 45 per cent. The next most Christian state is Cochin, with approximately 29 per cent of its population so identified. Of the provinces, Madras leads in percentage Christian, with roughly 4 per cent. Here as well as elsewhere the Christian areas have foci where

---

[31] O'Malley, *op. cit.*, pp. 51–52.

[32] *Census of India*, 1931, Vol. 28 (Travancore), Part 1, p. 329.

[33] *Census of India*, 1931, Vol. 1, Part 1, p. 380.

[34] *ibid.*, Vol. 28 (Travancore), Part 1, p. 330.

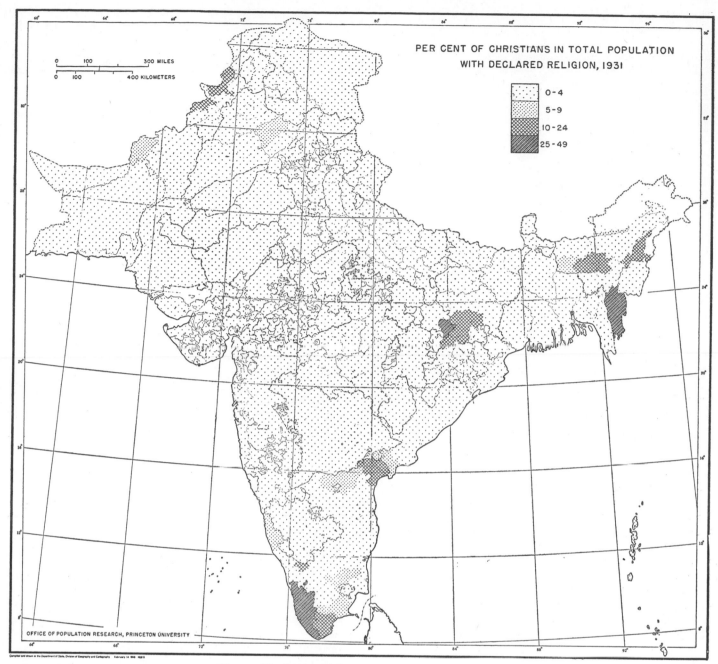

OFFICE OF POPULATION RESEARCH, PRINCETON UNIVERSITY

MAP 19. Distribution of Christians in the Population, 1931.

there has been some historical contact with Christianity. From these foci, or initial communities, dating in many cases from Portuguese or pre-Portuguese times, Christianity has spread, the percentage of adherents tending to be greater nearest the center and less as distance from the center increases.[35]

In northern India the Christians tend to be found where missionary work has been particularly active among tribal peoples or members of the depressed classes.

CHRISTIAN SECTS

The Christians were enumerated by sect at each census through 1921, but in 1931 this policy was abandoned as too cumbersome and too inaccurate. Some provinces did enumer-

ate by sect in 1931, but not with any feeling of satisfaction. In that year the Cochin census superintendent said: "From a review of the statistics for five censuses, we cannot but draw the conclusion that the figures of Christian sects recorded at every census (including the present) are utterly inaccurate, unreliable and worthless." [36] It is therefore with considerable reservation that the strength of the main sects in 1921 is given below: [37]

[35] ibid., Vol. 14 (Madras), Part 1, pp. 323–26.

[36] ibid., Vol. 21 (Cochin), Part 1, p. 239. As evidence of inaccuracy, this superintendent compared the returns at different censuses for the same sect and found impossibly high fluctuations, which he knew by first hand acquaintance did not occur. In addition, he compared the census returns with the church records, and found enormous discrepancies. He adduced two major reasons for the inaccuracy of the returns: first, ignorance on the part of enumerator and enumerated, and second, deliberate falsification for political and other reasons.

[37] Census of India, 1921, Vol. 1, Part 2, p. 184.

	Per Cent
Protestant	41.7
Anglican Communion	11.4
Baptist	6.3
Presbyterian	5.6
Lutheran	5.4
Methodist	4.6
Congregationalist	2.7
Salvationist	2.0
Other and Unspecified	3.7
Roman Catholic	39.0
Syrian	17.6
Romo-Syrian	9.4
Jacobite	5.6
Reformed	2.5
Other and Unspecified	0.1
Armenian	— [38]
Sect not returned	1.7
TOTAL, ALL CHRISTIANS	100.0

Assuming the accuracy of these figures in 1921, one has little reason to believe that the proportions have changed substantially since then. Protestants and Catholics are almost equally numerous, with Syrians a poor third.

POPULATION CHARACTERISTICS OF CHRISTIANS

The Indian Christians are in general more fertile than the Indian non-Christians. Their high fertility is not due, as one might expect, to a higher marriage rate. They of course permit remarriage of widows more freely than do Hindus and Muslims, thus lessening the proportion of widows at any given time; but on the other hand, they have a greater percentage of single women, due apparently to a later age at marriage than is generally customary in India. What gives the Christians their high birth rate is their exceptional fertility per married woman. Their marital fertility exceeds that of all other groups except the Tribals.[39] This means that their crude birth rate is high, being exceeded, it seems, only by that of the Tribals, Sikhs, and Muslims.

Ironic as it is, in view of the propensity of Christians elsewhere in the world to limit their fertility, this high birth rate among Indian Christians is understandable. Not only are Christian converts drawn heavily from the lower strata of the caste society (already seen to be more fertile than the higher), but also the Christian group is dispensing with many of the birth-limiting customs of the Hindus without yet adopting the Western pattern of birth control. The Indian Christians therefore stand in the vanguard of a trend that is seemingly coming to characterize the population of the entire peninsula.

The Christians show a considerably higher percentage literate than either the Hindus or Muslims, as shown in Chapter 17. In 1931 they were more than four times as literate as Muslims and over three times as literate as Hindus. In English, of course, the discrepancy is even greater. In 1931 the Chris-

tians were ten times as literate in this language as the Muslims, and 8 times as literate as the Hindus. The Christians, furthermore, are just behind the Parsis and the Jews in female education. Their masculine literacy is less than twice that of their female literacy, in contrast to the much higher ratio of India in general.

The Christians are also more urban than most of the other religious groups. In 1931 more than 20 per cent of their number lived in urban places, as against 13 per cent for the Muslims and 10 per cent for the Hindus.

On the whole the Christian group, despite the lowly origin of most of its members, shows the results of intensive Westernization. The Christian community ranks above the general population in several major indices of social and economic development, such as literacy, urbanization, age at marriage, command of English. Thus, although the Christians no longer have the advantage of a Christian Raj over India, there is reason to believe that their future influence, at least in the Union of India, may increase even faster than their number.

TRIBAL PEOPLES

The most inaccurate figures on religion in India are those covering the "Tribals" (or "Animists" as they were called prior to the 1931 census). One source of error is unintentional, having to do with the difficulty of classification. It is hard in practice to draw a line between advanced primitive religion on the one hand and backward Hinduism on the other. As noted previously, Hinduism is so syncretistic that it embraces almost every conceivable religious practice, and the Hindu social order is so pervasive that it infiltrates nearly every group. "Traces of Hindu influence," for example, "can be detected in every tribal religion practiced in Madras." [40] Nearly always, therefore, there is some remote basis for labeling a primitive tribesman as Hindu, and he, being illiterate, is often incapable of asserting himself in the matter. Moreover, because of the vagueness and inclusiveness of Hinduism, the enumerator tends to regard it as a residual category. Any person in India is thus a Hindu unless he definitely proves that he is something else, say a Muslim or a Christian. "The process of thought is something as follows: 'This land is called Hindustan and is the country of the Hindus, and all who live in it must be Hindus unless they definitely claim another recognized religion.'" [41] The term "Hindu" thus tends to designate not only a religion but also a country and a people.

Another source of error, especially prominent since separate religious electorates were inaugurated in 1909, is deliberate misrepresentation. There has been an increasing pressure on the part of religious groups to swell their numbers in the census. The once-militant Hindu organization, the Mahasabha, virtually took the point of view that everyone whose religion did not originate outside of India—practically everyone but Muslims, Christians, Parsis, and Jews—should be counted as Hindu. In 1931 it propagandized actively among certain tribes, and instructed Hindu enumerators to return everyone of doubtful status as a Hindu. When the enumerator failed to make the desired entry, the supervisor or check officer sometimes "corrected" his return.[42]

As a result of these sources of error, the data on Tribals are among the most inaccurate of all those gathered by the

[38] The figure is 0.03 per cent.

[39] In Travancore the special 1931 investigation of fertility revealed that the Christians had a rate of reproduction for completed marriages considerably in excess of that of any other group. *Census of India, 1931*, Vol. 28 (Travancore), Part 1, pp. 139–60.

[40] *ibid.*, Vol. 14 (Madras), Part 1, p. 318.

[41] *ibid.*, Vol. 8 (Bombay Pres.), Part 1, pp. 356–57. See also Vol. 14 (Madras), Part 1, p. 318.

[42] *ibid.*, Vol. 1, Part 1, pp. 384–87.

Census.[43] The net effect is to understate the number of Tribals, and correspondingly, to overstate the number of Hindus. The extent of the error can be gauged by reference to particular provinces. In Bombay it is said that "the real figure of Tribals in British Districts is in the vicinity of one million as against 129,135, the figure returned." [44] In Madras "the number who could reasonably be classed under 'tribal' is at least twice the number actually so returned." [45] In Baroda the Census Commissioner believes that the recorded figure is substantially correct, as does the Commissioner for Central Provinces and Berar,[46] but the Commissioner for Bihar and Orissa points out that to a large extent the classification of primitive peoples as Hindus is purely arbitrary.[47]

THE ABANDONMENT OF THE TRIBAL RELIGION CATEGORY IN 1941

In view of this widespread tendency to understate the number of Tribal religionists, it is understandable why in 1941 no figure for them was published. Instead, the number of all persons of "tribal origin" was given, no matter what religion they professed. No explanation was provided of how "origin" is defined. Presumably it refers to persons who give a tribal name instead of a caste name, and if so it should be comparable to statistics of tribal peoples obtained in past censuses quite apart from religion. In fact, tribes are to be found in all religions, including Muslim, Hindu, and Christian.[48] It should be borne in mind, furthermore, that a great proportion of the Indian people was of tribal origin only a few generations ago. Being aboriginal is not a racial but a cultural phenomenon. It is hard to discover, therefore, what, if anything, tribal origin has to do with either religion or community, and the procedure of the 1941 Census whereby the table on Community [49] lists Hindus, Muslims, Christians, and other religions, and then along with them "Tribes," is illogical, a backward step rather than an improvement.

The figure on Tribes belongs with the usual figures on race, tribe, and caste, rather than in the religion or community table. The changed procedure in 1941 leads to the conclusion that 66 per cent of the population is Hindu, when it is obvious that there are many Hindus (in the sense of both religion *and* community) in another category. It leads to such results as those in Assam, which, though it had 249,246 Christians (2.7 per cent of the total population) [50] in 1931, had only 67,184 Christians (or 0.6 per cent of the total population) in 1941. The 1941 census wanted to give data on communities rather than religions,[51] but "community" is even

vaguer and harder to determine than "religion." In what sense do the Muslim, Hindu, and aboriginal tribes constitute a single community? The best measure of community, if that word means anything in India, is still religion.

The new procedure results in three times as many people in 1941 under "Tribal" as were so reported in the same table in 1931. A large part of this enormous increase in the Tribal category, of course, has come out of the other religions, mainly Hindu and Christian. Obviously the changed system makes it impossible to compare the 1941 figures with those for previous censuses, and consequently some means of rectification must be found.[52]

PERSISTENCE OF THE TRIBALS

Looking back at the history of the Tribal religion category, one can see that, with the possible exception of the Sikh, it has been more irregular than any other category. (Table 76, Fig. 42.) It has shown no consistent trend, nor any marked stability, but simply irregularity. All of its variation can hardly be attributed to the vagaries of conversion, migration, or territorial changes; instead, some of it must be due to arbitrary changes of classification. A common belief in census circles is that the political maneuvers of the Hindus to have the aboriginals classified as Hindu were stronger and more successful in 1931 than in any previous census. In fact those reporting Tribal religion decreased from 9.1 million in 1921 to 7.6 million in 1931. But how much of this was due to genuine absorption into other religions, and how much to political artifice, is hard to say. It is generally thought that the rate of assimilation of the aboriginals has risen in recent years, due to a greater penetration of railways and highways, traders and teachers. It seems best, therefore, not to undertake to change the 1931 figure, but, on the theory that assimilation has been continuing, to adjust the 1941 *proportion* to agree with that of 1931. On this basis we assume that the actual number of Tribal religionists rose to 8.8 million in 1941, but that their percentage of the total population remained the same (2.26 per cent). This estimate for 1941 may conceivably be more accurate than the census return for 1931, but we have no way of knowing.

With the figure for 1941 adjusted, the resulting history of the returns for Tribal religion is as follows:

Year	Number (000's)	Per Cent of Population
1881	6,427	2.57
1891	9,112	3.26
1901	8,185	2.88
1911	9,594	3.17
1921	9,072	2.97
1931	7,630	2.26
1941	8,775	2.26

The surprising thing revealed by these figures is the extent to which the Tribal religionists have held their own. Despite all the efforts to induce the aborigines to change their religion, or at least to *say* it is something else, there are still millions of them who are recorded as following an aboriginal creed. Yet the fact remains that they have not increased as fast as the general population. Two questions therefore need answering: first, why have peoples with aboriginal religions not held their

---

[43] *ibid.,* Vol. 8 (Bombay Pres.), Part 1, p. 355.

[44] *ibid.,* p. 358.

[45] *ibid.,* Vol. 14 (Madras), Part 1, pp. 318–19.

[46] *ibid.,* Vol. 19 (Baroda), Part 1, p. 377; and Vol. 12 (Central Provinces and Berar), Part 1, p. 324.

[47] *ibid.,* Vol. 17 (Bihar & Orissa), Part 1, p. 254.

[48] In 1931 a careful analysis revealed a total of 24,613,848 members of primitive tribes in India and Burma. (*ibid.,* Vol. 1, Part 1, pp. 502–03.) Omitting the ones in Burma, as derived from Vol. 1, Part 2, pp. 522–33, and Part 1, p. 503, the remainder is 22,615,708, or roughly 2½ times the number for whom primitive religion was returned. In 1941 the number of persons of "tribal origin" as given in the Community table is 25,441,489. According to these two figures, the growth in the number of aborigines would be 12.5 per cent, or slightly less than that of the total population. There is no reason, then, not to accept the 1941 figure as representing approximately the number of persons with primitive culture in India, but that it has nothing to do with religion is equally apparent.

[49] *Census of India,* 1941, Vol. 1, pp. 98–105.

[50] *ibid.,* Vol. 3 (Assam), Part 1, pp. 194–95.

[51] *ibid.,* Vol. 1, Part 1, pp. 28–30, 97.

[52] Appendix J explains how this is done, and throughout the present chapter the estimated figures have been used.

own, and why, despite their loss, have they done as well as they have?

WAYS IN WHICH NUMBERS ARE REDUCED

There is evidence that the aboriginal religionists have been losing by four different processes: (1) By a gradual drift or assimilation into Hinduism; (2) by definite conversion to one of the main religions; (3) by political maneuvering to have them recorded as Hindu; and (4) by high mortality.

(1) In India, as in other parts of Asia, the aboriginals are to be found mainly in inaccessible places—notably hills and forests. This is not simply because they have retreated to those places to escape disease and death at the hands of the more civilized invaders, but also because those of their numbers who were in other areas were assimilated. Today it is known that when certain members of a primitive tribe move down into the plains they tend to become assimilated, in contrast to the other members who remain behind. In Travancore, for example, there are two tribes (the Kuravan and the Vetan) each of which has two sections, one living in the jungles and the other in the plains. The jungle section is generally distinguished from the plains section by the addition of the prefix "Mala" to the tribal name, a prefix which disappears when they come down and settle in the plains. "From very early times there has been a constant migration of these tribes from the jungles to the plains and hence we find large numbers of them included under Hindus." [53] The plains, coasts, and river valleys have been the arteries of civilization in India, and peoples who have remained in these places or have moved to them have tended to become civilized.

Nowadays, however, civilization is moving even into the jungle and the hills. Forest products such as tea, cardamom, rubber, coffee, and lumber have been found profitable. The growth of population has caused a movement of agriculturalists into areas formerly disdained for such purposes. Deforestation and the government efforts to preserve the forests have changed the mode of life of many primitive groups who lived by hunting and fishing or by the slash-and-burn system of nomadic agriculture. Traders and adventurers, land speculators and moneylenders, missionaries and educators have invaded their domains, so that assimilation no longer depends solely on the slow process of migration into the plains.

The evidences of assimilation are in many cases tragically apparent. Certain Santals of Bengal, for instance, give distinctively Hindu names to their children, practice child marriage before the age of seven, revere the *tulsi* plant, observe the *paus parbban* festival, abstain from beef, "cleanse" their living quarters with cow-dung, decline food cooked by Muslims, wear the occipital tuft of hair, cremate their dead, and place the vermilion mark and the iron bangle upon their wives.[54] The following passage depicts the economic side of their assimilation:

"The pacification of the Santals . . . led to the penetration into Santal villages of numbers of Hindu traders and shopkeepers. The ignorance and honesty of the Santal enabled the first adventurous traders from the plains to make rapid fortunes out of the hill-men, and they were followed by numbers of others bent on making a similar rapid fortune by any means whatsoever. . . . Even legitimate trade is said to have yielded a profit of cent per cent., but the Hindu trader was an adept at cheating, and the simple hill-man was too easy to cheat. Even if he detected that the salt he purchased was weighed light, he was told that salt was excisable and therefore subject to special weights and measures, and he believed it. Moreover, opportunities for trade made opportunities for usury. . . . If the Santal accepted an advance, he became forthwith virtually the slave of the usurer. Whatever he reaped, the lender contrived still to show a balance outstanding—a balance which ever grew instead of decreasing, until the annual crop, however large, was always pledged beforehand to the usurer, who then returned to the cultivator just enough grain to live on till the next harvest, and retained his debtor on these terms until it suited him better to dispossess him of his land. Meanwhile, his cattle and his goats, his wife's ornaments, and all his treasured possessions were sold to make payment towards the exorbitant interest accumulating against him, and the land itself became the property of the shopkeeper, while the owner who had cleared it of jungle and tilled it to fertility became the mere tenant-at-will, fed by his landlord for just so long as he was strong to labour and a willing tool." [55] Sometimes the chiefs of a tribe are converted to Hinduism. These chiefs then either intentionally or unintentionally assign the revenues from the tribal lands to Hindus, who wind up by owning the land, dispossessing the natives or else making virtual serfs out of them.[56]

British rule hastened the process of tribal disintegration by introducing more system and efficiency into the process of invasion and subjugation.[57] Regardless of whether the change was beneficial or not, the effect was to eliminate the tribe as an effective unit. It could no longer fight to retain its own existence and to preserve its customs. Hence assimilation was hastened.

Gradual assimilation, sometimes painful, sometimes unconscious, is probably the chief way in which the tribal religions are losing ground in India. In the nature of the case it is chiefly a gain to Hinduism, because the Indian way of life is a Hindu way of life, and except under special circumstances, assimilation implies change toward Hinduism.

(2) Definite conversion is mainly the instrument of Christianity. Hinduism, through the Hindu Mission movement begun in 1925, has made some use of it, but since the official Hindu doctrine has long been that all who follow any religion originating in India are basically Hindus, the ceremony of conversion is viewed merely as a "reclamation" or "purification" of people who have *strayed away* from the true religion.[58] The Muslims have apparently been inactive with reference to proselytizing among the aborigines. The field has been virtually left to the Christians, who are particularly active in Assam, where their number increased 90 per cent between 1921 and 1931, mainly in the aboriginal districts,[59] but who are also working in most other provinces where aboriginals live, including Bihar and Orissa, where the number of Christians in the four main aboriginal tribes increased 39 per cent between 1921 and 1931.[60] Yet despite the importance of this movement for the growth of the Christian community in India, it is probably secondary to the infiltration into Hinduism as a factor reducing the tribal religionists of India.

[53] *Census of India*, 1931, Vol. 28 (Travancore), Part 1, p. 333.
[54] *ibid.*, Vol. 5 (Bengal & Sikkim), Part 1, p. 383.
[55] J. H. Hutton, "Primitive Tribes," in L. S. S. O'Malley (ed.), *Modern India and the West*, pp. 422–23.
[56] *ibid.*, pp. 415–17.
[57] *ibid.*, pp. 417ff.
[58] *Census of India*, 1931, Vol. 7 (Bihar & Orissa), Part 1, pp. 247–48.
[59] A discussion is contained in *ibid.*, Vol. 3 (Assam), Part 1, pp. 194–96.
[60] *ibid.*, Vol. 7 (Bihar & Orissa), Part 1, pp. 256–57.

(3) The factor of political maneuvering to have aborigines *counted* as Hindu has already been discussed. It has undoubtedly been effective in some areas but not in others. It is interesting that one of the places where it was most successful was Assam, where the Christian missionaries have also been most active in making converts.[61] On the whole it seems to have been more important in 1931 than in any other year, although it should be remembered that this was also the time when noncooperation with the census authorities reached its peak, undoubtedly causing some underenumeration among Hindus in general. Probably the 1931 figures for Tribal religionists are too low for this reason, and those for Hindus slightly too high, but as previously remarked such a distortion probably represents the reality of the future anyway.

(4) A factor of a different order from the three mentioned is the effect of high mortality in reducing the number of Tribals. There is some evidence that in the past the aboriginal population grew faster than the normal population in good times, but declined faster in bad times. If true, this is a situation that one might expect, because the primitive peoples live closer to nature, and their mortality is more quickly and completely affected by changes in the external environment. Famines therefore affect them with extreme severity.[62] Furthermore, they have been the victims of what is probably a high disease rate because of their increasing contact with more civilized peoples. This contact affects them adversely not only because they have not yet built up natural immunity to the new diseases but also because their standards of living are likely to be lower than those of the peoples from whom they get the diseases. Although not much can be directly obtained on the subject of mortality among the aborigines, their age distribution strongly suggests a high mortality. They begin with the highest percentage of their population in the 0–4 ages, but they quickly lose after that and from age 15 on tend to have either the lowest or next to the lowest percentage in each age group. Until further evidence is available, the tentative conclusion seems justified that the Tribal religionists have the highest mortality of any religious group in India.

WHAT SUSTAINS THE NUMBER OF TRIBALISTS?

After this description of factors tending to reduce the Tribal religionists in India, the reader may be still more amazed that, since 1881 at least, these people have virtually maintained their number. The explanation lies in their exceptionally high fertility, which was described in Chapter 10. If it is asked why the aboriginals have such a high fertility, the answer is that their folkways and mores, as is usual in primitive society, are adjusted to compensate for a high mortality under savage conditions of life. Today deaths from famine and some other causes have been reduced. Although deaths from new causes have come in, the net effect has probably been to reduce mortality more than fertility. In this way, so far as the balance of births and deaths is concerned, the Tribals show the characteristics of India as a whole, except more so. If other factors did not intrude, the balance of births and deaths would probably give them a greatly expanding population. As it is, they are contributing a great deal racially and culturally to India, because they are being constantly assimilated into the general population. This process has gone on for centuries, and has helped to make the Indian people and their civilization what they are today.

[61] *ibid.*, Vol. 3 (Assam), Part 1, pp. 190–91.
[62] *ibid.*, Vol. 8 (Bombay Pres.), Part 1, pp. 357–58.

DISTRIBUTION OF THE TRIBALS IN INDIA

As already mentioned, the Tribal religionists are located in the most out-of-the-way places in India. Map 20 shows that these places are chiefly in the central and northeastern highlands. This dispersion in inaccessible places is truer of the Tribal religionists than of the Tribals in general. Those who, despite all the forces to the contrary, are described as practicing a tribal religion are the most truly primitive people that can be found in India. Their primitiveness is a function of their remoteness.

THE FUTURE OF THE TRIBAL RELIGIONS

In India, as elsewhere in the world, the primitive cultures are probably soon destined to disappear. This does not mean that the peoples will disappear in a biological sense. On the contrary, some of them will probably represent by far a greater proportion of future generations. But it does mean that the diffusion of advanced civilization to these tribes is progressing at an accelerated rate today, so that before many more decades the category "Tribal" in the religion table—or for that matter in any other table—will no longer be necessary in India.

THE MUSLIMS

Although the youngest of the world's great religions, Islam has flowed widely over the world. With extraordinary rapidity it spread from Medina to Spain on the West and to China, Java, and the Philippines on the East. It first came to India about 650, only a few years after Mohammed's death, and from that time continued to occupy certain Western parts of the region. Not until A.D. 1000, however, did Islam really take hold in India. After that date, beginning with the Mahmud kingdom and ending with that of Jahangir, large portions of India were controlled by a succession of Muslim dynasties.

Yet "Hindu civilization maintained its vitality under Muslim rule, and India never became a Muslim country." Islam never achieved complete territorial dominance over the peninsula, for there were always some areas beyond its control and others where control was exercised only through Hindu princes and nobles. Furthermore, although there were mass conversions, "the country was too vast, the invaders too few, and the volume of immigration too small to change the social complex. The Muslims were not so much colonists as rulers. . . . They depended on Hindus for much of their labour and clerical work." The Hindus, handling much of the small bookkeeping and trading, gradually improved their position until finally they were "holding the power of the purse as financiers, bankers, merchants, and traders."[63] India, therefore, never became a Muslim nation, but remained simply a Hindu country in which Muslims were numerous. The partition of the region into Pakistan and the Union of India was the admission of final defeat so far as the Muslim conquest of India is concerned.

Today there are more than 100 million Muslims in the Indian peninsula, or better than one-fourth of all the Muslims in the world, and far more than any other country contains. Despite their numerical ascendency, however, they do not enjoy, and have never enjoyed, ascendency in the Islamic world at large. They have never originated any great Islamic movement. They have been "content, if of the Sunni sect, as

[63] O'Malley, *op. cit.*, p. 5.

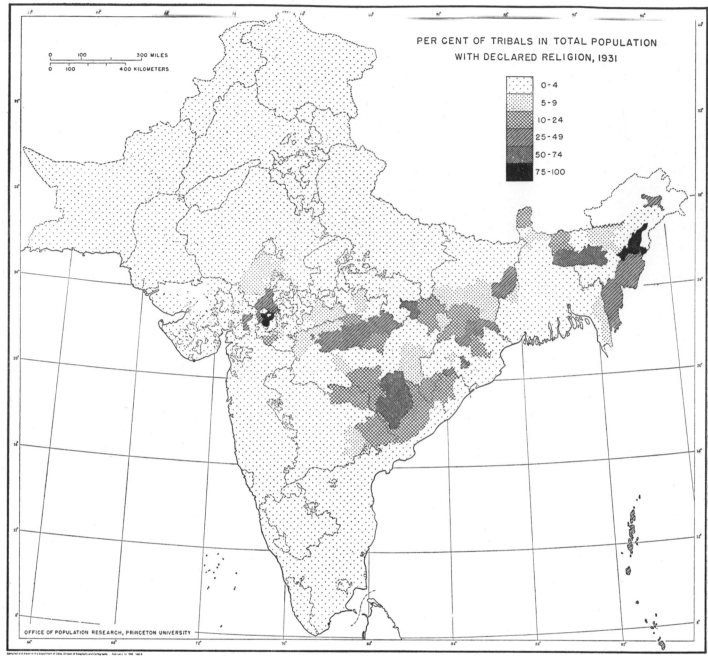

MAP 20. Distribution of Tribal Religionists in the Population, 1931.

the majority are, to look up to Turkey for spiritual leadership; and, if Shias, to turn for guidance to Persian theologians and mystics." [64] The cause of this backwardness has lain partly in the isolation of Indian Muslims, and partly in the superficiality of their Indian diffusion. Long ago, with the first conquest of Sind, the rule that the conquered must either embrace Islam or be killed or enslaved was waived. The Hindus were given the same privilege that the Jews and the Christians were given—namely, they were treated as "people of the Book," which meant that if they submitted to Muslim rule and paid a special tax (*jizya*), they would be allowed freedom and protection in their religion.[65] This meant that though force was occasionally used to secure conversion, most conversion was voluntary in character. It meant, too, that

millions of Hindus were left undisturbed in their social and religious life. Granted the well known absorptive power of Hinduism, it is not surprising that many of the nominal converts retained much of their former religion, and that indeed Islam underwent considerable Hinduization in India. Because of conversion and because of interbreeding between Muslim men and Hindu women, the Muslims became racially indistinguishable from the Hindu population. Even the Muslim rulers were in many cases descendants of Hindus, having Hindu mothers and grandmothers. In the Islamic world at large, then, it is not surprising that the Indian members of the faith usually counted as a group apart, subsidiary and somehow alien. Yet in India itself, because Hinduism and Islam were extreme opposites, fusion of the two never occurred. A certain amount of overlapping did develop, but the two groups settled down in an uneasy mutual accommodation with the seeds of potential conflict always present.

[64] Holderness, *Peoples and Problems of India*, p. 131.
[65] Moreland and Chatterjee, *op. cit.*, pp. 145–46. Cf. Joseph Schacht, "Islam," *Encyclopaedia of the Social Sciences*, Vol. 8, pp. 338–39.

GROWTH OF THE MUSLIM POPULATION

The growth in the number of Muslims is unknown prior to the inauguration of the censuses. It is known, however, that since 1881 the proportion of the Indian population which is Muslim has increased gradually but steadily, as the following figures show:

Year	Number (000's)	Per Cent of Population
1881	49,953	19.97
1891	57,068	20.41
1901	62,119	21.88
1911	67,835	22.39
1921	71,005	23.23
1931	79,306	23.49
1941	94,447	24.28

As against the 94 million Muslims in 1941, there were 270 million Hindus. The former were 24 per cent, the latter 69 per cent, of the population. The others (mostly Tribal, Christian, and Sikh) constituted 6 per cent. In 1881, however, the Muslims formed only 20 per cent and the Hindus 75 per cent. Thus in six decades the percentage difference between the two was cut by more than one-seventh. In addition to its gradualness, this gain by the Muslims has been remarkably constant. At no census have the Muslims failed to improve their percentage, or the Hindus failed to lose.

The source of the gain apparently lies not in conversion but in the greater fertility of the Muslims, which in turn is attributable primarily to their greater tolerance of widow remarriage. Muslim women marry almost as universally as Hindu women, and they remarry considerably more frequently. (Chapter 10.) The result is that a higher proportion of women in the reproductive ages are married, and this accounts for a portion of the higher fertility of Muslims. But at the same time, as judged by the fertility ratios, the married women among the Muslims are more fertile than they are among the Hindus. This is a condition that has existed at every census, as Table 79 indicates. It is clear from the table that the difference between the number of children per 1,000 of *all* women 15–39 and the number per 1,000 *married* women is greater in the case of the Hindus than in the case of the Muslims. This indicates that the greater proportion married among the Muslims explains a part of the higher Muslim fertility, but not the whole of it. Not only is there a greater

TABLE 79

Fertility Ratios for Hindus and Muslims, 1891–1941

Year	Children 0–4 per 1000 Women 15–39		Children 0–4 per 1000 Married Women 15–39		Married Women Ratio as Per Cent of All-Women Ratio	
	HINDU	MUSLIM	HINDU	MUSLIM	HINDU	MUSLIM
1891	723	826	936	1,017	130	123
1901	626	748	769	884	123	118
1911	669	768	799	894	119	116
1921	626	715	765	842	122	118
1931	739	827	885	965	120	117
1941 [a]	670	751	804	874	120	116

[a] Compiled from *Census of India*, Part 2, for each year. The figures for 1941 are based on a sample including only those provinces for which data were obtainable.

proportion of the Muslim women married, but those who are married also have a higher fertility. The consistency of the Muslim advantage in past years suggests that it is deep rooted and likely to continue for some time.

In searching for a reason for the higher marital fertility of Muslims, one could point out that the Muslims are less literate than the Hindus. It is well known that even when they ruled India the Muslims paid relatively little attention to education and depended to a great extent upon literate Hindus to carry on their paper work. It is also known that the Muslims, after the coming of the British, resisted Westernization and the advantages of modern education more stolidly than did the Hindus. They were in the position of being dispossessed by the British. "Owing to loss of power and dignity, loss of honourable employment and the comforts of material life, owing to poverty and injured pride, there was a degradation in Muslim standards, . . . In British India this continued till after the Mutiny." [66] By the latter half of the nineteenth century it had become apparent to the Muslims, however, that they were losing out in the quest for government positions and social and economic advantages. The Hindus, for whom the presence of the British represented merely a change of rulers rather than a loss of leadership, had reaped many rewards for having taken to modern education with alacrity. The Muslims saw that they had fallen into a position of inferiority to the Hindus, and they therefore began to change their policy. By 1891 the per cent of the Muslim population who were in elementary schools exceeded the percentage of Hindus who were, and the advantage increased slightly by 1931. The literacy figures, however, being a reflection of past as well as current trends in educational policy, still showed the Hindus to be ahead in 1931. It seems likely that eventually the Muslims will catch up with the Hindus in this respect, but in the meantime their lack of Westernization, as indicated by their greater illiteracy, has apparently had the effect of giving them a higher fertility than the Hindus have had.

The fact that the Muslims are more urban than the Hindus would theoretically operate to give them a lower fertility. In 1931, 13 per cent of the Muslims lived in urban places, as against 10.4 per cent of the Hindus. But if the statistics for cities 500,000 and over are examined, it will be found that the Muslims have a lesser proportion there than their general average in the population. The "urbanism" of the Muslims seems to be therefore due to their slightly greater concentration in smaller towns and cities than in the country. Perhaps this explains why urbanism has not greatly affected their high marital fertility.

Sometimes the belief was expressed that the Muslims in India would eventually attain numerical equality with the Hindus. This was possible but not probable. The rate of gain has been so gradual that if the two religious groups had continued the same rates of growth that they averaged between 1891 and 1941, 263 years would have been required after 1941 for the Muslim population to equal that of the Hindus. In other words the two groups would not have become even until the year 2204. In the interim it hardly seems likely that the current conditions governing growth would have remained the same, so that the assumption underlying the calculation— namely, that the 1881–1941 rates of growth would continue— is not realistic. It is likely that the Muslims would have continued to be a minority in India for hundreds of years. But in view of the 50–60 million untouchables who are mostly re-

[66] Ali, *loc. cit.*, p. 396.

garded as Hindu, but who might form a mass movement into Christianity or Islam, the future was not necessarily assured.

Summary: The Situation before Partition

This chapter has given the quantitive history, position, and location of the various religious groups in India so far as census data allow, up to 1941. It has shown that the Hindus remained the great majority, although gradually losing to their main competitor, the Muslims. Of the remaining groups, none of which loomed large in numerical terms, the Sikhs and Christians showed the most rapid gains. Small religious groups at the top of the social ladder, such as the Jains, Jews, and Parsis, were either just barely holding their own or were losing ground in terms of numbers.

The partition of India in 1947 affected religion, as it affected everything else in the country. Because it was motivated primarily by religious considerations, and because in India religion is still highly important to the people, the partition had more to do with religion than with nearly any other matter. It had a considerable effect, among other things, on the geographical distribution of members of different faiths, especially upon the distribution of Muslims, Sikhs, and Hindus. Quite properly, therefore, the partition is thought of in religious terms. For this reason, the analysis of the Muslim population, and of its relation to the Hindu population, has been cut short in the present chapter, to be taken up again in the next chapter, which deals with the demographic aspects of partition. It seems appropriate, indeed, to place the treatment of partition immediately after the discussion of religion. The one is a natural continuation of the other.

+++

Population and Partition

+++

HINDUISM and Islam, embracing together 94 per cent of the people, were by far the most important religions in undivided India. Conflict between them was the most important domestic issue. It rested on sharp differences of belief, ritual, and social philosophy, and on remembrance of Muslim military conquest and political ascendancy.

Two more contrasting religions would be difficult to find. Meeting in India by historical accident, Islam was rigorously monotheistic, Hinduism profusely polytheistic. Islam abhorred idolatry, Hinduism adored it. Islam had one sacred book, Hinduism had a variegated and conflicting literature. Islam had a clear-cut and relatively uniform dogma and was intolerant of all other religions, conceiving itself to have a divine mission to conquer the world in the name of the one and only true god. Hinduism, embracing nearly every form of belief and ritual known to man, had no definite or uniform dogma and was tolerant and passive with respect to other religions. Islam gained by military conquest and aggressive proselytism, Hinduism gained by passive resistance and peaceful absorption.

On the side of ritual the contrast was equally great. Not only did the Muslims eat beef, but once a year (at the ceremony of Baqr Id) they sacrificed cows, to the horror of the cow-venerating and beef-abstaining Hindus. The Muslims buried their dead, the Hindus burned theirs. The Muslims worshipped by one calendar, the Hindus by another, with the result that ceremonies of special importance to each group occasionally coincided—an anniversary of Muslim mourning, for example, synchronizing with a day of Hindu rejoicing. The Muslims abhorred music in connection with sacred ceremonies, the Hindus liked it; hence resentment arose when Hindu processions, with band playing and an idol aloft, would pass before a mosque where Muslims were worshipping. To express hostility, the Muslims would sometimes slaughter cows deliberately or destroy a Hindu temple; the Hindus would throw a pig into the Muslim quarter or desecrate the mosque.

"The social restrictions of both religions prevented friendly contact.

"The Turks kept their women in strict seclusion, so that the opportunities for what we think of as social intercourse were reduced by half. [Furthermore] . . . , the convivial propensities of the Turks were incompatible with the restrictions imposed by the system of caste, which prevented anything in the way of common meals, while their taste for beef was an offence to all Hindus." [1] Intermarriage was tabooed in theory by both sides, although Muslims took non-Muslim wives, often forcefully.

Each religion fitted a different social order. Islam maintained in theory an ethical and social equality of all believers, Hinduism upheld absolute inequality. Islam had no priestly caste set apart from and above the rest of society, Hinduism did have. Islam conceived the state as theocratic—a society of supernatural origin, whose every branch (administrative, legal, military) was dedicated to the propagation of the faith in the face of all opposition. It was a militantly aggressive and proselytizing society of believers, glaringly realistic and boldly fanatical. Hinduism conceived the state as limited in function and of secondary importance; the Hindu community maintained itself without the help of a state or an army. It lapped away at any intrusive system as the sea laps away at a sand bank.

The cleavage between the two groups was kept alive by memories, myths, and current grievances. The Muslims never forgot that they were a race of conquerors; sometimes they talked of restoring their former ascendancy by the sword.[2] Hindu textbooks told of invasions by hordes from outside, and of gruesome oppression, pillage, and rapine.[3] Their own practice of purdah was explained as due to the necessity of saving their women from rape when the Muslims were invading India.[4]

With the coming of Western influence, new tactics of conflict and competition were developed. The British were accused of deliberately exacerbating the mutual distrust by inaugurating in 1909 the system of separate communal electorates. By this system the adherents of each creed were registered in distinct religious constituencies that voted apart, each constituency electing its own representatives. The system has been severely criticized because it frees political leaders from any necessity of compromising. Their constituents are all fanatics of the same persuasion.

As India moved in the direction of independence, the religious conflict became intensified. Each side jockeyed for position as the time drew near. The Muslims feared oppression by the Hindu majority once independence was obtained. The Hindus feared that the Muslims would somehow block independence. Between 1930 and 1937 the idea of a separate Muslim state was born and took hold of the imagination of the Muslims.[5] In 1930 the demand had been merely for a regroup-

---

[1] Moreland and Chatterjee, *A Short History of India* (London: Longmans, 1936), p. 185.

[2] Henry Noel Brailsford, *Subject India* (New York: John Day, 1943), p. 95.

[3] Humayun Kabir, "Influence of Islamic Culture on Indian Life," *Annals of the American Academy of Political and Social Science,* Vol. 233 (May, 1944), p. 24.

[4] Actually, of course, Hindu purdah represents a culture trait borrowed from the Muslims.

[5] The name "Pakstan" was originally coined by young Indian Muslims in Cambridge, England—"P" for Punjab, "A" for Afghan Province (North-West Frontier Province), "K" for Kashmir, Sind, and Baluchistan. It was later spelled "Pakistan," which means "land of the

ing of provincial boundaries, to give the Muslims a separate unit in a federated India. By 1937 the demand was for a full-fledged independent nation. Ten years later, August 1947, the reigns of government were at last turned over to a divided India.

Accompanying the partition, beginning before and lasting for months afterward, was a wave of religious rioting, murder, and arson, together with mass migrations across the newly established borders. Order was not restored until spring, 1948. A year later, fighting still continued in the disputed state of Kashmir, but the other states had been distributed, by agreement or by force. Sporadic riots and forced migrations were still occurring in 1950.

The Demographic Basis of Pakistan

In 1941 the Muslims comprised 24.3 per cent of the total population, the Hindus 69.5 per cent. Since these proportions change slowly, they effectively describe the situation on the eve of partition.

The only fact that made partition possible was the concentration of Muslims in certain parts of India. If the 94 million Muslims had been equally numerous everywhere, if they had constituted 24 per cent of the population in every district and province, they would have had real strength nowhere. The idea of Pakistan would have been utopian. Actually there was a high degree of concentration. Out of a total of 435 districts or other comparable divisions in India in 1941, there were 76 whose population was more than half Muslim. These, representing only 17 per cent of all districts in India, contained 60 per cent of the entire Muslim population. Among the 76 Muslim-majority districts, there were 50 whose population was more than three-fourths Muslim; and these, representing only 11 per cent of all districts, contained 39 per cent of all Indian Muslims. How stable this distribution was can be seen from Table 80, which compares the 1931 figures with those of 1941.

Table 80

Concentration of India's Muslims by Districts, 1931 and 1941 [1]

	Per Cent of all Districts	Muslim Population (000's)		Per Cent of All Muslims	
		1931	1941	1931	1941
50 Districts three-fourths or more Muslim [2]	11.5	26,243	30,785	33.1	32.6
76 Districts half or more Muslim	17.5	47,502	56,416	59.9	59.8
All 435 Districts	100.0	79,306	94,389	100.0	100.0

[1] Compiled from data on population by religion for districts in the 1931 and 1941 census reports.
[2] Actually there were 436 districts in 1941. An extra district was created between the two censuses by splitting a district in Sind. This district happened to be one that had more than three-fourths Muslim, and when split, its two parts also had three-fourths Muslim. But the two were treated still as one district in 1941 in order to simplify the table.

If these predominantly Muslim districts had been scattered over the whole of India, there would have been no effective concentration. But it so happened that *all* of the 76 Muslim-majority districts were grouped together in two clusters. As

pure." R. Coupland, *The Indian Problem,* Part 2 (London: Oxford University Press, 1944), pp. 188–99.

Map 21 shows, one cluster was in northwest India and the other in northeast India. Not a single Muslim-majority district existed apart from these two clusters, nor did either cluster completely contain a Hindu-majority district. Consequently, the two clusters, embracing some 56 million Muslims in 1941, formed the geographic and demographic reality that made the idea of Pakistan feasible.

The territory actually allotted to Pakistan by Sir Cyril Radcliffe's Boundary Commission followed very closely the boundaries of the two Muslim-majority clusters. But mainly because Kashmir was left in dispute, Pakistan did not acquire all the Muslim-majority districts. It acquired enough of them to have 53.8 million Muslims, or 57 per cent of all the Muslims of India, as of 1941; but the two groups of Muslim-majority districts contained 56.4 million Muslims at that date, or 60 per cent of all the Muslims in India. The difference is almost wholly due to Kashmir, for that state contained in 1941 five Muslim-majority districts with 2.8 million Muslims all told. If these districts were added to the territory that Pakistan actually received, the total number of Muslims in Pakistan, as of 1941, would come to 56.5 million, which is almost identically the same number we calculated for the two clusters of Muslim-majority districts. Except for the case of Kashmir, then, we may conclude that the award of territory to Pakistan was as fair as could be expected, and that it followed the natural lines of geographical concentration of Muslims in India. It was this concentration that made Pakistan possible.

But while the geographic concentration of Muslims was great enough to enable Pakistan to be created, it was not great enough to ensure either that the new Muslim country would contain all the Muslims in India or that it would contain no non-Muslims. In 1941 no less than 40 per cent of all Muslims (38 million, to be exact) lived outside the two clusters of Muslim-dominated districts. At the same time the Muslim-dominated districts themselves contained 20.2 million non-Muslims, which was more than a fourth of their total population. These twin facts—the existence of 38 million Muslims outside the concentrated areas and the presence of 20 million non-Muslims inside those areas—represented the great demographic obstacle to the realization of the Pakistan idea. The contention was absolutely true that partition would create two minority problems where there had been only one before, and this was only partly balanced by the fact that in each case the minority would have a contiguous nation to speak for it. If the minority problem were to be avoided, and if the ideal were to create a religiously homogeneous Mohammedan state, the only conceivable policy would be one of mutual exchange of populations as between Pakistan and India. In other words, the Pakistan of the future could have exchanged its 20 million non-Muslims for 20 million Muslims from India. This would have had no less than three disadvantages: first, the difficulty of matching the people exchanged with reference to occupation, rural-urban residence, education, etc.; second, the difficulty of inducing the individuals to move; and third, the circumstance that even after the exchange, there would still be 18 million Muslims living outside of Pakistan, whom it would have been impossible to bring in because of their effect on the Pakistan economy. In other words, it was theoretically conceivable that Pakistan could be made a religiously homogeneous Mohammedan state; it was not conceivable that it could accommodate all the Muslims of India. But even so, the exchange of minorities, involving the migration across the international border of 40 million people, would have been by all odds the largest mass migra-

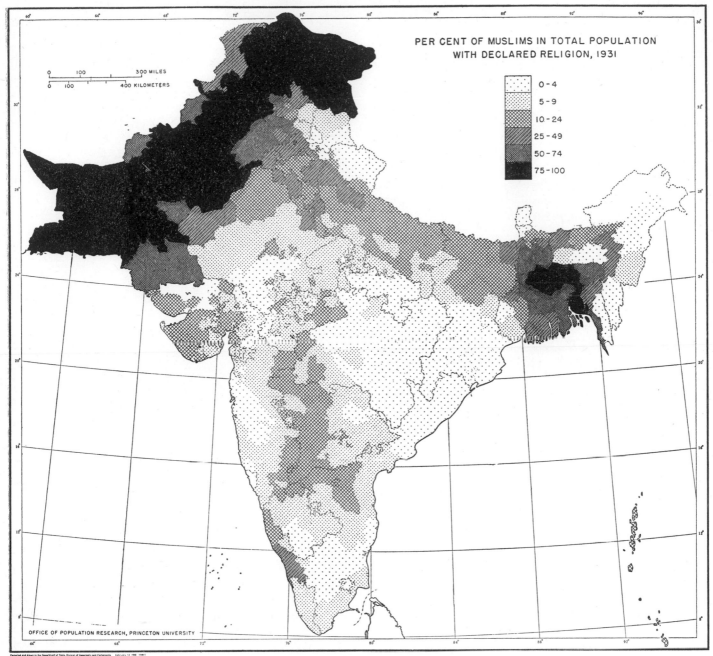

PER CENT OF MUSLIMS IN TOTAL POPULATION
WITH DECLARED RELIGION, 1931

0 - 4
5 - 9
10 - 24
25 - 49
50 - 74
75 - 100

MAP 21. Distribution of Muslims in the Population, 1931.

tion in human history, granted the brevity of the time and the smallness of the region. The costs in a poor region such as India would have been staggering. Furthermore, the first two difficulties mentioned above—the problem of matching persons exchanged so as not to upset the economy on either side of the border and the question of inducing them to move—were very real obstacles. No one seriously believed that the absolute ideal of Pakistan—the ideal of a religiously homogeneous state—could be realized in practice.

What actually happened is interesting. As we have seen, Pakistan did not, or has not yet received, all the Muslim-dominated territory, because Kashmir is still in doubt. But it got most of this area, so that its population was composed, as of 1941, of about 77 per cent Muslims—which is an impressive degree of religious homogeneity in itself. In addition, however, there arose spontaneously one of the largest and quickest mass migrations in human history. No one knows

and no one will ever know the exact figures, but it appears that about 6 million Muslims came into Pakistan and about 5 to 6 million non-Muslims left it.[6] Something like one million of the total died in the process, from starvation, exhaustion, disease, or murder. In the light of the difficulties mentioned above, how did this migration happen? Being unplanned, it of course involved no matching of immigrants with emigrants. On the contrary, Pakistan is suffering today from the fact that it lost educated Hindus in clerical and professional positions (of which it had great need), and gained additional Muslim peas-

[6] Joseph B. Schechtman, *Population Transfers In Asia* (New York: Hallsby Press, 1949), Chap. 1, "The Hindu-Moslem Exchange of Population." Most of the migration took place with reference to West Pakistan, and this is the only movement treated by Schechtman. The movement across the border of East Pakistan was apparently minor. Higher estimates have of course been made—6 million from West Pakistan, 1.5 million from East Pakistan coming into India. See "Refugee Problem," *Indian Review,* Vol. 50 (February, 1949), p. 76.

ants (which it did not need). Nor was there any provision in advance for resettling the migrants, with the result that there have been serious refugee and relief problems.[7] As for the question of motivation, the migrants were induced to move by fear for their lives. The wave of religious fanaticism and intolerance was spectacular in its bloodthirsty violence.[8] It took care of the incentive problem automatically. If the frenzy had not eventually burned itself out and the governments gained control of the situation, the total migration each way might have equalled 20 million and Pakistan might have become a 100 per cent Muslim state, but an economically and politically bankrupt one.

The mass migrations, although they did not bring all the Muslims into Pakistan or all the non-Muslims out, did change the religious composition of the two countries substantially.

TABLE 81

Estimated Religious Composition of India and Pakistan, 1941 and 1949

	1941 [1]		1949 [2]	
	Number (millions)	Per Cent	Number (millions)	Per Cent
Indian Union	318.9	100.0	356.2	100.0
Muslims	40.7	11.9	39.6	11.1
Non-Muslims	278.2	88.1	316.6	88.9
Pakistan	70.1	100.0	79.6	100.0
Muslims	53.8	76.7	66.3	83.3
Non-Muslims	16.3	23.3	13.3	16.7

[1] Computed from *Census of India,* 1941, by method described in footnote 1, Table 82.
[2] Estimated by assuming that the population of all groups increased between 1941 and 1949 by a percentage that was four-fifths the percentage increase between 1931 and 1941, and that six million were added to the Muslims in Pakistan by immigration and five million were added to the non-Muslim population of India by the same process. The estimated absolute figures doubtless contain a large margin of error, but the proportions should not be so liable to error.

As Table 81 shows, the estimated per cent Muslim in Pakistan territory rose from 77 per cent in 1941 to 83 per cent in 1949. In other words Pakistan approached nearer to its ideal of being a completely Islamic country. In the Indian Union, correspondingly, the number of Muslims still remains as high as about 40 million, but this is only 11 per cent of the population (about the same proportion as the Negroes in the United States). In the proportional sense, therefore, the minority problem has diminished in both countries as a result of the migrations, but it has diminished far more in Pakistan. Nevertheless, if we judge the value of partition in terms of the degree to which it has provided a separate national home for each religious group, it has not succeeded. There are still millions of non-Muslims in Pakistan and tens of millions of Muslims in India. What partition has accomplished is the creation in Pakistan of a "national home" for the Muslims of the Indian subcontinent, vaguely analogous to the creation in Israel of a "national home" for the Jews of the world. Not all of the Muslims could live in Pakistan, any more than all of the Jews could live in Israel.

[7] T. Walter Wellbank, "India: Trial Balance," *Current History,* Vol. 16 (April, 1949), pp. 203–209. Schechtman, *loc. cit.*
[8] See the graphic account in Geo. E. Jones, *Tumult in India* (New York: Dodd, Mead, 1948), Chaps. 11–12.

POPULATION, AREA, AND DENSITY

Map 22 shows the boundaries of Pakistan and of the Indian Union, with the disputed area of Kashmir. One should note the similarity of this map with Map 21; for the similarity illustrates the high degree to which Pakistan was based on the two clusters of Muslim-majority districts.

In 1941 the area now occupied by Pakistan had approximately 70 million inhabitants. Since that date the number has been augmented by natural increase and possibly by a slight net immigration, which should give it close to 80 million today. By contrast, the 1941 population of what is now the Indian Union (including Kashmir) came to approximately 319 million, and by now must have risen to about 357 million. Table 82 shows the areas and average 1941 density of the two countries.

TABLE 82

Population and Density in Pakistan and India, 1941

	Population [1] (000's)	Area [2] (000's)	Persons per sq. mi.
Union of India	318,863	1,220.5	261
Kashmir	4,022	82.3	49
Without Kashmir	314,842	1,138.2	277
Pakistan	70,135	361.0	194
West Pakistan	28,169	307.0	92
East Pakistan	41,966	54.0	777

[1] Computed from 1941 census volumes by the writer. For districts split by the boundary between Pakistan and India it was assumed that Hindus and Sikhs all went to India, the Muslims to Pakistan. The remaining religious groups were split according to the percentage of Muslims in the district population. (Failure of figures to add is due to rounding.)
[2] Adapted from O. H. K. Spate, "The Partition of India and the Prospects of Pakistan," *Geographical Review,* Vol. 38 (January, 1948), p. 17.

One should note that although the population of India is more than 4½ times that of Pakistan, its area is only 3 times the area of the latter. This means that the overall density of Pakistan is lower than that of India (194 as against 261 persons per square mile), but no conclusion concerning differences in living standards or future potentialities should be drawn from this difference. In the Indian subcontinent density varies primarily according to rainfall. The dry areas are as overpopulated as the wet areas, although the difference of density may be striking. It happens, as Table 82 shows, that Pakistan is divided into two parts separated by over 1,000 miles of foreign territory and differing markedly in climate, crops, population density, and general culture. Whereas Western Pakistan, comprising the northwest part of the subcontinent, is made up mostly of dry areas, Eastern Pakistan, comprising the eastern part of Bengal and one district in Assam in the northwest, is extremely wet. This means that the agricultural resources of Eastern Pakistan, per square mile, are far greater than they are in Western Pakistan, but because the population is more dense, the poverty is as great or greater. Because of the rather recent development of large-scale irrigation schemes in Sind and West Punjab, these areas have not yet had time to achieve quite as high a ratio of population to resources as has East Bengal.

In the partition of India, the Indian Union received most

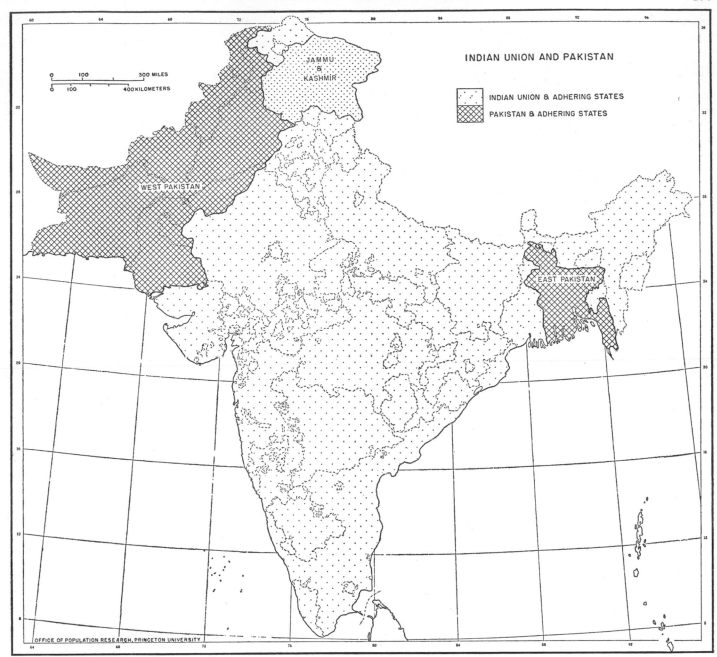

MAP 22. Pakistan and the Union of India with the Disputed State of Kashmir. From O. H. K. Spate, "The Partition of India and the Prospects of Pakistan," *Geographical Review*, Vol. XXXVIII, No. 1 (January, 1948), p. 6.

of the existing industrial plants and industrial resources. In Western Pakistan, for example, the fact that the accessible areas are composed of almost unaltered sedimentary rocks free from igneous intrusions, precludes over wide tracts the occurrence of many of the more valuable metalliferous and other mineral deposits.[9] East Pakistan, made up mostly of low-lying alluvial lands in the Ganges and Brahmaputra delta area, is also singularly devoid of industrial resources. The only major industrial resource that Pakistan has is oil, and this does not occur in impressive quantities. A second asset is potential waterpower, but on the whole the industrial resource base is anything but impressive.[10]

[9] E. R. Gee, "The Mineral Resources of North-Western India" (read at meeting of National Institute of Sciences of India, November, 1945, mimeographed.)

[10] See Maneck B. Pithawalla, *An Introduction to Pakistan: Its Resources and Potentialities* (Karachi: 1948).

The Union of India, on the other hand, has the rare good fortune of possessing immense coal and iron deposits lying close together. It has been estimated that the iron ore deposits in the Bihar-Orissa-Bengal region are sufficient for a thousand years at a pig iron output rate of a million and a half tons annually. Of extremely high quality, these ores are located at a distance of only about 125 miles from the rich coal deposits of West Bengal and central Bihar and about 400 miles from the coal deposits of the Central Provinces. The coal is of lower quality than the iron ore, but it is nevertheless suitable for steel production. Also, deposits of iron ore occur in the south of India (Mysore); these furnish a basis for a steel industry there, with nearby limestone deposits used for flux and local forests used for fuel in the form of charcoal.[11] With

[11] Tulsi Ram Sharma, *Location of Industries in India* (Bombay: Hind Kitabs, 1946), Chap. 5, "Factors Governing the Distribution of Iron and Steel Industry."

a wide distribution of other metallic ores, India therefore possesses the minerals necessary for large-scale heavy industry. In fact, her industrial resources are greater than those of any other country except the United States and Soviet Russia.[12] "The Tata Iron Works at Jamshedpur is the producer of the lowest-cost pig iron in the world; its plant is the largest and most modern in the British Empire." [13]

With the great difference in industrial potentialities, the future prospects of Pakistan and the Indian Union stand in vivid contrast. Both countries are trying to industrialize rapidly, but the chances are that India will succeed earlier and more abundantly than Pakistan. If so, India's population may grow more rapidly than Pakistan's for a while, but will stop growing at an earlier time. In both countries the population is already so dense in relation to developed resources that the industrialization process is being impeded by the prevailing poverty and inability to raise capital.

Of course, natural resources and population density are not the only factors in economic progress. Perhaps equally important is the potential population growth, the kind of social organization, and the character of the people that a country has to work with. Some insight into these matters is provided by statistics on the basic characteristics of the population. Let us therefore turn to a consideration of future growth and of the rural-urban, educational, and occupational differences between the two countries.

PROSPECTS OF POPULATION GROWTH

Since the data of the last chapter showed a consistent gain of the Muslim population as contrasted with the Hindu, one might expect the new Muslim state (83 per cent Muslim) to show a faster gain in population than the Union of India (90 per cent non-Muslim). But there is no reason to believe that after partition religion will necessarily have the same effect on population growth that it had before. Religious customs are changing rapidly, and other differences between the two countries will undoubtedly become increasingly important in determining the future course of population growth.

If India undergoes a more rapid industrialization than Pakistan, the chances are that this will reduce its mortality to a lower level and that consequently its population will grow faster. By the same reasoning, the Pakistan population will have its rapid growth phase later than India.

In the meantime both countries have all the people they need. Yet there is a possibility that they may try to encourage population growth as a means of "demographic armament." Both of them are currently spending huge portions of their national budgets for military purposes. It is conceivable, therefore, that they might adopt the mistaken view that military efficiency would be increased by an expansion of numbers.

It hardly seems likely that, once the frenzy of religious intolerance is over (possibly with the removal of nearly all non-Muslims from Pakistan), mass migration between the two countries will recur. It appears more probable that, like other nations in the modern world, India and Pakistan will become increasingly selective of the immigrants they admit. In short, neither population is likely to gain or to lose much by future

migration. Only a war between the two countries would seem likely to disturb the present equilibrium.

URBANIZATION

Pakistan has fewer cities and a smaller proportion of urban inhabitants than does the Indian Union. In 1931, in the area that is now Pakistan, only about 6.5 per cent of the population was defined as urban, while the area that is now the Union of India had about 12.1 per cent of its population so defined. As Table 83 shows, this was mainly due to the extremely rural character of East Pakistan (only 2.7 per cent urban), for West Pakistan was fully as urban as the Indian Union.

TABLE 83

Rural-Urban and City Populations, Pakistan and Union of India Territory, 1931, in Percentages [1]

		PERCENTAGE IN EACH CLASS OF PLACE				
	RURAL PER-CENTAGE	Places under 5,000	Places 5,000 to 50,000	Places 50,000 to 100,000	Places 100,000 and over	Total
Union of India	88.0	86.2	9.5	1.4	2.9	100.0
Kashmir	90.6	91.9	3.2	—	4.6	
Without Kashmir	87.9	86.1	9.5	1.4	2.9	100.0
Pakistan	93.6	89.5	7.9	1.0	1.6	100.0
West Pakistan	88.0	84.4	11.7	2.4	3.6	100.0
East Pakistan	97.3	92.6	6.9	0.1	0.4	100.0

[1] Compiled on basis of *Census of India*, 1931, Vol. 1, Part 2; Vol. 17 (Punjab), Part 2, and Vol. 3 (Assam), Part 2.

Since, however, there is considerable variation from one area to another in the definition of "urban," it is safer to take the people living in places of 5,000 or more as urban. On this basis, in 1931, the Pakistan area turns out to be 10 per cent urban, the Indian area 14 per cent so. Available evidence suggests that the relative position of the two areas had not changed essentially by 1941. For instance, East Bengal had at that date 13 per cent of its people in places of less than 5,000, whereas West Bengal had 22 per cent of its people in that category.[14]

Pakistan is notably deficient in large cities, as Fig. 44 shows. Of the 25 largest cities in India in 1941, only four were in what is now Pakistan, as follows:

	Population (000's)	*Rank*
Lahore	672	5
Karachi	359	12
Dacca	213	19
Rawalpindi	181	25

These were the only cities in Pakistan territory that were above 100,000 in population. Together they comprise only 12 per cent of the total population of India in cities over

[12] Robert Strausz-Hupé, *The Balance of Tomorrow* (New York: Putnam, 1945), Chap. 8, "Geography of Coal and Iron."
[13] *ibid.*, pp. 135–36.

[14] Of course, one reason why West Bengal is so urban is that, in the partition, it received the Calcutta metropolitan area. If Calcutta and the urban part of 24-Parganas are removed from consideration, West Bengal (including Sikkim) turns out to have only 11 per cent of its population living in places more than 5,000—in other words, less than East Bengal. But the fact is that the Union of India did get Calcutta, as well as most of the other large cities.

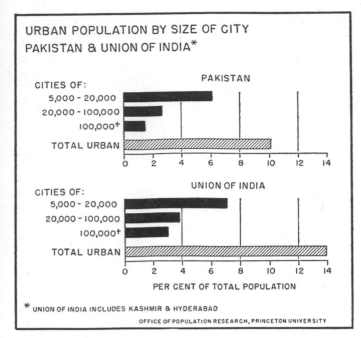

URBAN POPULATION BY SIZE OF CITY
PAKISTAN & UNION OF INDIA*

PAKISTAN

CITIES OF:
5,000 - 20,000
20,000 - 100,000
100,000⁺

TOTAL URBAN

0 2 4 6 8 10 12 14

UNION OF INDIA

CITIES OF:
5,000 - 20,000
20,000 - 100,000
100,000⁺

TOTAL URBAN

0 2 4 6 8 10 12 14

PER CENT OF TOTAL POPULATION

* UNION OF INDIA INCLUDES KASHMIR & HYDERABAD

OFFICE OF POPULATION RESEARCH, PRINCETON UNIVERSITY

FIGURE 44. Urban Population by Size of City in Pakistan and the Union of India, as of 1931.

100,000 in 1941, whereas the general population of the Pakistan territory was 18 per cent of that of India. India received not only the four biggest cities—Calcutta (2.1 million), Bombay (1.5 million), Madras (777 thousand), and Hyderabad (739 thousand)—but also most of the other large ones.

This lower degree of urbanism in Pakistan is interesting in view of the fact that in the Indian subcontinent as a whole the Muslims are more urban than the Hindus. In 1931, for example, 13 per cent of the Muslims lived in urban places as against 10.4 per cent of the Hindus. This suggests that the Muslims have been most urban where they were least concentrated. Even so, however, it is true that the Muslims have not been present in large cities in as great a proportion as the non-Muslims. The net result of the fact that Pakistan received the territory where Muslims were most concentrated and least urban is that the country as a whole is less urban than the Union of India. In the migrations attending partition it was the more urbanized Hindus and Sikhs who left, and the less urbanized Muslims who came, thus tending to exaggerate the rural-urban differences between the two countries.

LITERACY

Literacy and urbanism are generally correlated. But, despite the fact that they are more urban, the Muslims of the whole Indian subcontinent have always shown a lower rate of literacy than the Hindus. The Muslims, as we have seen, have however shown the most rapid gain in literacy of any religious group.

One of the reasons for the low percentage of Muslims literate, as compared with other religious groups in India, is their tendency to neglect the education of females. India as a whole, as we have seen, has probably shown the greatest discrepancy of any country in the world between male and femal illiteracy, but this discrepancy is carried to its greatest extreme by the Muslims. The following figures for Bengal in 1941 tell the story:

PER CENT LITERATE, ALL AGES

	Males	Females	Ratio of Females to Males
Muslims	18.4	4.6	.25
Hindus	33.0	11.4	.35
Christians	51.4	45.7	.89

Since the Muslims are slightly less literate than other religious groups in India, and since the areas incorporated into Pakistan are less urban than those incorporated into the Indian Union, it can be surmised that Pakistan is the less literate of the two countries. This can be documented by the figures for 1931, which show that the territory now constituting Pakistan was approximately 8.6 per cent literate for ages 10 and above, while the territory now constituting the Indian Union was 9.0 per cent literate. The difference is small, but the loss through migration of a substantial proportion of the educated Hindu and Sikh minorities from the Pakistan area may have increased the difference—perhaps overbalancing the tendency of Muslims to gain in literacy vis-à-vis both these groups.

TABLE 84

Per Cent of All Gainfully Occupied Males Found in Each Occupational Class, 1931 [1]

Occupational Class	Pakistan	Indian Union
Exploitation of animals and vegetation	70.8	68.9
Exploitation of minerals	—— [2]	0.3
Industry	9.7	11.2
Transport	2.2	2.0
Trade	6.6	5.9
Public Force	1.3	0.7
Public Administration	0.7	1.0
Professions and Liberal Arts	2.2	1.9
Persons Living on Income	0.2	0.2
Domestic Service	2.2	2.0
Insufficiently Described	2.7	5.0
Unproductive	1.4	1.0
	100.0	100.0

[1] Compiled from *Census of India,* 1931, Vol. 1, Part 2, and Vols. 3, 5, 8, 17—tables on occupation. The figures include both main and subsidiary occupations.

[2] Less than 0.05 per cent.

OCCUPATIONAL DIFFERENCES

Both Pakistan and the Union of India are such heavily agricultural countries that there is relatively little difference between their occupational profiles. However, such differences as do exist suggest that India is slightly more industrial (Table 84). For 1941 there is little evidence available, since occupational statistics were reported for very few areas. At that date the two parts of Bengal showed the following percentages of occupied males in the major occupational classes: [15]

[15] Compiled from *Census of India,* 1941, Vol. 4 (Bengal), pp. 121–27. The figures refer to all of Bengal.

	Production of Raw Materials	Preparation and Supply of Material Substances	Public Administration and Liberal Arts	Miscellaneous
East Bengal	75.0	13.0	3.4	8.2
West Bengal	53.3	27.3	4.9	14.6

In northwest India the provinces and districts that went to Pakistan are known to be primarily agricultural and pastoral. Putting this information together with what we know about the distribution of industries and industrial resources in the subcontinent, we can only conclude that, as between the two nations, Pakistan is less industrial than the Union of India. But the outstanding fact is that both of them are only slightly industrialized as yet. It would be a mistake to conclude that because in absolute terms it does have considerable industrial production, the Union of India is far along the road to industrialization in relative terms—relative, that is, to its huge population.

Conclusion

This chapter was designed to give some statistical facts about the new nations of Pakistan and India. Since the countries are so new, it requires painstaking analysis of the 1931 and 1941 census volumes to ferret out the essential facts—district data being assembled in cases where the new boundaries cut through provinces. The 1931 and 1941 data are now out of date. The absolute figures would be out of date anyway, but the great migrations attending the partition render even the proportions out of date. As a consequence, only indirect approaches to the present picture can be utilized. These document in a somewhat more precise manner the conclusions generally known already. Among these is the fact that Pakistan has achieved a high degree of religious homogeneity, being now about 83 per cent Muslim; but it still has within its borders only 63 per cent of the Muslims living in the subcontinent, because about 40 million still reside in the Indian Union. The Muslims have shown a steady gain in population throughout the period of Indian censuses, but this does not mean that Pakistan is necessarily destined to increase faster than India. India has the greater industrial resources and is already slightly more industrialized. It is also more urbanized and literate. As a consequence we may expect that the population of India will enter the rapid growth phase attending industrialization earlier than that of Pakistan, but that, by the same token, its demographic growth will decline at an earlier period.

++

Economic Achievement:
Population and Agriculture

++

THE tragic fact that Pakistan and the Union of India contain many millions of desperately poor people raises two inevitable questions: First, why does this poverty exist? Second, when and under what circumstances will it cease to exist? The present and the following chapter deal mainly with the role of population in the answers to these questions. At the outset a theoretical discussion of the "overpopulation" debate is given. Then the facts are brought to bear on the questions raised. Evidence is given concerning the level and trends of real income, and, in an effort to explain the findings in empirical terms, the conditions of Indian agriculture and industry are examined. Finally, an exploration is made of possible avenues of increased living standards. Warning should be given in advance that no easy solutions appear likely, and none is offered in either of the two chapters.

THE "OVERPOPULATION" DEBATE

The belief that India is overpopulated dates from long ago. It is an interpretation that flows naturally from Malthusian principles, because according to Malthus any long-settled country must necessarily be pressing on the means of subsistence. Malthus wrote a chapter on "The Checks to Population in Indostan and Tibet," in which he admitted that certain customs, such as the taboo on intercaste marriage and on widow remarriage and the asceticism of the Hindu religion, constitute preventive checks to population growth, but he thought that the universality of marriage in India and the prevalence of child marriage offset these preventives and that India was therefore suffering from the baneful effects of the positive checks—poverty, undernourishment, and famine.[1] Since that time disciples of Malthus have pointed *ad nauseam* to India as a place where "the Malthusian law applies."

This view was reflected by the Abbé Dubois, a remarkable observer of India in the years around 1800, who wrote as follows:

"Of these causes [of the misery of the lower classes] the chief one is the rapid increase of the population. Judging by my own personal knowledge of the poorer Christian populations in Mysore and in the districts of Baramahl and Coimbatore, I should say that they have increased by twenty-five per cent. in the last twenty-five years. During this period Southern India has been free from the wars and other decimating

calamities which had been dealing havoc almost uninterruptedly for centuries before.

". . . I have every reason to feel convinced that a considerable increase in the population should be looked upon as a calamity rather than as a blessing."[2]

Since then other writers have continued to explain India's poverty in terms of overpopulation, and to give evidence for their interpretation. Baden-Powell noted in 1882 that a lowering of the land tax in any section tends to be followed by such a fast increase in population that the potential rise in prosperity is soon neutralized.[3] Darling claimed in 1925 that the natural increase of the new irrigation colonies of the Punjab was so rapid that the initial prosperity was giving way to overcrowding and indebtedness.[4] More recently, Vera Anstey expounded the overpopulation view with emphasis and authority. She placed population at the head of the list of obstacles to economic progress. "First and foremost," she said, "it must be definitely recognized that general prosperity in India can never be rapidly or substantially increased so long as any increase in the income of individuals is absorbed not by a rise in the standard of life, but by an increase in the population. The population problem lies at the root of the whole question of India's economic future, and it is useless to try to bilk the fact."[5]

All of these authors expressed their opinion prior to the census of 1931. They were therefore all writing at a time when the Indian population had not shown a very rapid rate of growth. It was, as already shown, the censuses of 1931 and of 1941 that revealed the fastest population growth in India's history. The decade increase was found in 1931 to be 32 million and in 1941, 51 million, whereas the average increase for the five previous decades had been only 10 million. If the belief in India's overpopulation was strong before the new facts were revealed in 1931, one can imagine how much stronger it has been since that date. In fact, in very recent years the attention given to population by students of the

[1] T. R. Malthus, *An Essay on Population,* Vol. 1, Book 1 (7th ed.; London: Dent, 1914), Chap. 11.

[2] *Hindu Manners, Customs and Ceremonies,* translated and edited by Henry K. Beauchamp (3rd ed.; Oxford: Clarendon, 1924), pp. 93–94.

[3] B. H. Baden-Powell, *Land Systems of British India,* Vol. 1 (Calcutta: Office of the Superintendent of Government Printing, 1882), p. 346.

[4] M. L. Darling, *The Punjab Peasant in Prosperity and Debt* (London: Oxford University Press, 1925), pp. 252, 286–88.

[5] Vera Anstey, *The Economic Development of India* (London: Longmans, 1929), p. 474. See also pp. 39–41. She cites both Baden-Powell and Darling.

Indian scene has increased remarkably, and the cry of over-population has grown louder.[6] Before that, some authors, looking at wild territories or industrial opportunities in India, had thought that India was not overpopulated,[7] and some had simply paid no attention to the population question.[8] Nowadays almost anyone who deals with India feels it necessary to consider the matter, pro or con.

In recent years a newer form of opposition to the overpopulation view arose. It came from certain intellectuals of the nationalist movement. These critics concentrated their fire on alien political and economic dominance. They apparently felt that the population problem was a red herring thrown across the trail (for the British could hardly be held responsible for excessive population growth in India, except in the laudable way of reducing the death rate). They seemingly thought that the British were all too ready to use population as an excuse for a do-nothing policy, a rationalization of India's bad state. The nationalists wanted quick action, immediate political and economic reforms. Population was a long-range and unmanageable phenomenon that did not promise swift results. Consequently they were inclined to emphasize the political and economic problems and to play down the population problem.[9]

Some of the pro-nationalist writings followed a standard pattern in treating the population question.[10] They began by branding as a "myth," "fable," or "fallacy" the view that India is overpopulated. This "myth" was then attributed to Malthus, and Malthus was personally abused as the tool of capitalism and the prophet of reaction. Next it was shown that, contrary to Malthus and subsequent British apologists, the population of India had not been growing very fast. Curiously, the growth was compared with European and American countries and with Japan at the peak of their industrial revolutions. Also the writers tended to cite only India's earlier decades, forgetting the later ones when growth was faster. Miss Mitchell, who used the preliminary returns from the 1941 census on page 13, ignored them when talking about the myth of overpopulation on page 45. Dutt mentioned the 1941 increase but played it down and gave the reader a misleading impression. Goshal, writing in 1944, stopped his analysis of the slow growth of Indian population with 1910. He mentioned 1933, but in another connection. These authors also shied away from absolute increases. They resisted letting the reader know that the mere 10.6 per cent growth in 1921–31 involved an accretion of over 32 million, the 15 per cent growth in 1931–41 an accretion of 51 million. Since these absolute additions would seem staggering to the ordinary reader, he must presumably be shielded from seeing them and thinking that

perhaps Malthus was right after all. A fortiori the discussions ignored the question of future growth in the population.

Having proved to their satisfaction that the Indian population had not grown fast, the authors in question then unveiled another fact designed to explode the fallacy of overpopulation. They tried to show that actually the food supply has been increasing faster than the number of people, ignoring their own claims that the level of living had declined under the British. Finally they ended their discussion by pointing out that the cause of the Indian poverty was not an excessive population but an "arrested economic development" due to the attempt by the British to make India an agricultural satellite, a vassal state, for industrial England.

In this discussion Gandhi occupied a peculiar position. Like some of his colleagues in the nationalist movement he disliked giving attention to the population question; but unlike them he favored a return to handicraft production rather than a march to greater industrialization. The trouble was that an insurmountable obstacle to his handicraft dream was precisely India's gigantic population, which could not now survive in the old economy. Furthermore, he found himself in a further dilemma because he did not favor birth control. The present and future population of India was obviously for him a bitter fact which he would prefer to forget.[11]

Only some of the nationalist sympathizers, however, were cavalier in dismissing or ignoring the population problem. Those who had made a study of population were particularly concerned about it and wanted to work on both the demographic and economic fronts at the same time. Gyan Chand, for example, who agreed with the nationalist aspirations, said bluntly that the population problem "exists and cannot be solved merely by denying that it is there." Later he said that the control of fertility is "one of the most imperative needs of the country."[12] S. Chandrasekhar, who is far from pro-British, recommended a Ministry for Population Affairs for the Government of India, which would, among other duties, help to diffuse birth control knowledge.[13]

Since partition there has been insufficient time for enough Indian literature to emerge to establish a climate of opinion with reference to the population problem. It is possible that, with the British bogy out of the way, fewer writers will find it distasteful to admit the existence of a population problem. On the other hand, it is possible that Pakistani writers, under the impression that their country has an agricultural surplus and needs manpower, may say that no population problem exists. Perhaps mistaken views concerning the relation of numbers to military power may influence intellectuals in both countries to combat the theory of overpopulation, though this does not seem so likely in the Union of India. In any case, the old debate will continue; the only question is which side will have the greater following.

Since there is genuine truth on both sides, the dispute seems to hinge, as many disputes do, on ambiguity and bad logic. The term overpopulation obviously implies a relationship to something else, just as too hot, too high, or too thin do. It also implies a norm, or standard, by which different degrees of the relationship are to be judged. Unless the "something else" in the relationship is specified, and unless the standard is defined, the term itself is meaningless. Usually one has in mind

[6] e.g., A. V. Hill, "Health, Food and Population in India," International Affairs, Vol. 21 (January, 1945), pp. 40–50. T. A. Raman, Report on India (London: Oxford University Press, 1943). John Fischer, "India's Insoluble Hunger," Harper's Magazine, Vol. 190 (April, 1945), pp. 438–45. Gyan Chand, India's Teeming Millions (London: Allen & Unwin, 1939). The Government of India, the Famine Inquiry Commission, Final Report, Part 2 (Madras: Government Press, 1945), Chap. 1.

[7] Sir E. A. Gait, "Population," Imperial Gazetteer of India, 1907, Vol. 1 (Oxford: Clarendon, 1907), pp. 461–62. A contrary view is expressed in the very next chapter, "Public Health and Vital Statistics" by A. E. Roberts, in the same volume, p. 502.

[8] Romesh Dutt, The Economic History of India in the Victorian Age (2nd ed.; London: Paul, Trench, Trübner, 1906).

[9] For a brief discussion of the controversy see Chand, op. cit., pp. 6–9.

[10] e.g., R. Palme Dutt, The Problem of India (New York: International Publishers, 1943), pp. 34–39; Kumar Goshal, The People of India (New York: Sheriden House, 1944), pp. 144–46; Kate L. Mitchell, India Without Fable (New York: Knopf, 1942), pp. 44–46.

[11] See his highly instructive remarks in Louis Fischer, A Week with Gandhi (New York: Duell, 1942), pp. 89–90.

[12] Chand, op. cit., pp. 15, 76–77.

[13] "India's Human Resources," in Annals of the American Academy of Political and Social Science, Vol. 233 (May, 1944), pp. 76–77.

a relationship between economic production and population, and one measures the relationship in terms of some index that involves both, such as per capita food consumption, per capita income, or per capita wealth. It is further assumed that the higher this index goes, the better off the people are. There are of course other relationships and other indices—e.g. political power, religious beatitude, cultural purity—in which population may be involved in a way contrary to economic maxima, but it will simplify the argument to stick simply to the economic case.

If the economic index in a country is falling, one may inquire whether or not population has anything to do with it. Clearly it has something to do with it in a formal sense, because the population enters into the very computation of the index. Thus if, while the index is falling, population is also declining, one might be tempted to say that the number of people is moving away from a theoretical optimum in the direction of *under*population. If, on the other hand, the decline of the index is accompanied by an increase of population, one might try to say that the number of people is moving in the opposite direction toward *over*population. Such reasoning may be correct, but it is more probably erroneous, simply because in most cases the causal factors determining variations in economic indices are not demographic at all. Most economic oscillations are short-run and temporary as compared with demographic oscillations, and they cannot therefore be the results of population trends.

In short, the two variables—population and economic production—are to a certain degree independent of each other in their movements. Population trends arise from family institutions, health measures, popular customs, etc., as well as from economic conditions. The speed of their alteration is limited not only by cultural inertia but also by the nature of biological processes. Economic trends (related, of course, to the factor of resources) arise from business institutions, market opportunities, political control, technological invention, etc., as well as from population trends. The speed of their alteration is limited primarily by cultural factors, not by the nature of biological processes. With this mutual independence and difference of tempo, it is dangerous to interpret a change in a per capita economic index as due to population. One would be saying that a country is overpopulated in one year, but underpopulated the next, simply because business conditions suddenly improved. But once having lopped off the heads of a population because it was temporarily too numerous, it would be impossible to get them back the next year. Human reproduction and human maturation are too slow for that.

To prove that population *per se* is having a given economic effect is extraordinarily difficult; but to prove that it is having no effect at all is equally hard. It certainly will not do to say, as some writers on India have said, that a rising economic index proves that population growth is having no deleterious effect. For all that is known, the index might be rising *faster* if the population growth were less. Nor will it do to say that a declining index is a sign that population growth is excessive, because the decline may be due simply to short-run factors that will endure only temporarily.

Behind our effort at sensible thinking is the implication that somehow the number of people makes a difference only in the normal or long-range functioning of the economic system. For population to be considered a causal agent, the phenomenon in question must be of sufficiently long duration to be responsive to population changes.

Numerous writers have pointed out that if economic production can advance faster than population can grow, over-population need not occur. This is absolutely true. But the conclusion that we can concentrate on economic development and ignore population does not follow in the least. Since the two variables in question affect each other, economic production cannot *permanently* be advanced in the face of an ever-increasing population. There must come a point when further population increase in a finite world will bring curtailment of per capita production. Quite apart, then, from the feasibility and possibility of economic reforms in a given country, there is the additional consideration that any kind of economic system has its optimum population, beyond which numbers cannot rise without penalty.

THE LEVEL OF LIVING

Applying what has been said to India, we find that there is one economic fact of sufficient duration to have some connection with population. This is India's poverty. If, as previously mentioned, India is so poor now, her level of living could not have risen much. It would be more likely to have declined, but there is no evidence of this.

Pelsaert, a Dutch commercial agent in India between 1620 and 1627, wrote of "the utter subjection and poverty of the common people—poverty so great and miserable that the life of the people can be depicted or accurately described only as the home of stark want and the dwelling-place of bitter woe." [14] Since then nearly every observer has been struck by the same fact, and it is generally admitted that even in recent decades the standard of living, if it has risen at all, has risen very little.

For the modern period there is more evidence with respect to level of living, but the statistical measures of real income are inconclusive. The wage statistics are incomplete, faulty, and not available for the largest class of workers, the agricultural, although there are some good family budget studies. Estimates of national income are also shaky. But such evidence as exists gives a picture of poverty exceeded in few other civilized areas. As late as 1940 the average wage, admittedly an artificial construct, was said to be 6 annas, or about 14 cents per day for an able-bodied unskilled laborer. [15] The average per capita income in British India in 1931–32 was given as 65 rupees, or roughly $23.40, per year. [16] If correct, this means that the average person in the United States had 22 times the wage of the average Indian; the average Englishman, 15 times; and the average Japanese, 4½ times. Below are comparative figures given by Ghosh: [17]

[14] *Jahangir's India: The "Remonstrantie" of Francisco Pelsaert,* translated by W. H. Moreland and P. Geyl (Cambridge: Heffer and Sons, 1925), p. 60. Not all observers agree that India is poverty stricken. e.g., A. W. T. Webb, *These Ten Years: A Short Account of the 1941 Census Operations in Rajputana and Ajmer-Merwara* (Bombay: British India Press, 1942), pp. 27–32.

[15] Pramathanath Banerjea, *A Study of Indian Economics* (5th ed.; London: Macmillan, 1940), pp. 129–30. A series of wages in different industries occurs in S. Subramaniam, *Statistical Summary of the Social and Economic Trends in India,* 1918–39 (Washington, D.C.: Government of India Information Services, 1945), p. 39. The same source gives data on prices and costs of living.

[16] V.K.R.V. Rao, "National Income of India," *Annals of the American Academy of Political and Social Science,* Vol. 233 (May, 1944), p. 104. Estimates for other years and for rural and urban people are cited in Baljit Singh, *Population and Food Planning in India* (Bombay: Hind Kitabs, 1947), p. 40.

[17] D. Ghosh, *Pressure of Population and Economic Efficiency in India* (New Delhi: Indian Council of World Affairs, 1946), p. 29.

	Per Capita Annual Income (rupees)
U.S.A	1,406
Canada	1,038
Australia	980
France	621
Germany	603
Japan	281
British India	65

Of course, these monetary comparisons exaggerate the inequalities. An American could not live on $23.40 per year or work for 14 cents per day without starving. Figures on real income are therefore needed but are hard to get. Patterns of food consumption, however, afford some evidence.

The average Indian spends a high proportion of his income for food but gets in return an inadequate diet. In order to keep alive, the Indian farmer must consume most of what he grows.[18] The urban working man, whose income is substantially above that of the peasant, spends half to two-thirds of his budget on food.[19] Yet, in spite of this great effort, the average Indian gets little to eat. "An insufficient and ill-balanced diet giving only about 1750 calories per day (as against the needed 2400 to 3000 calories) is typical of diets consumed by millions in India."[20] The deficiency in food supply has been estimated as 17 per cent in terms of calories, 38 per cent in terms of proteins, and 64 per cent in terms of fats. Between a third and a half of Indian families are undernourished.[21] As previously shown,[22] the deficiencies in the quality and quantity of food are partly responsible for India's high death rate. Such deficiencies, in spite of high food expenditures, clearly demonstrate a low real income.

Other evidence of low living levels is found in respect to housing (overcrowded, unsanitary, and unsightly), working conditions (bad for children, women, and men), medical service (non-existent for most of the population), and education (also non-existent for most).

Since India's average level of living is so low today, it can hardly represent much gain over the past. Some Indian authors dispute that the level has risen at all.[23] Yet the estimates suggest a slight but erratic rise during the last eight decades. A series of estimates is given at the top of the next column. The important feature of these figures is the absence of much change. Yet we know that during the period covered the people of the subcontinent were greatly influenced by Western culture and Western control. Their isolation in the local village was overcome, their handicraft system was depressed, manufactured goods became increasingly abundant, transport, communication, and trade increased. Consequently, it should be stressed, as Fig. 45 demonstrates, that urbanization, literacy, and manufacturing have all grown faster than population. Such progress implies a rise in the standard of living. But Fig. 45 conveys a better impression at first sight than it does under

[18] Baljit Singh, op. cit., pp. 38–41.
[19] Banerjea, op. cit., p. 199.
[20] Health Survey and Development Committee, Report, Vol. 4 (Delhi: Manager of Publications, Government of India, 1946), p. 23.
[21] Rao, op. cit., pp. 104–05. See also Singh, op. cit., p. 101, who estimates India's calorie shortage as 21.6 per cent.
[22] Chapter 6.
[23] J. C. Kumarappa, "Handicrafts and Cottage Industries," Annals of the American Academy of Political and Social Science, Vol. 233 (May, 1944), pp. 106–12.

Estimator [24, 25]	Period [24]	Annual Income per Head [24] (rupees)	Adjusted for Price Changes [26]
D. Naoroji (U)	1868	20	22
Baring and Barbour (O)	1881	27	27
Lord Curzon (O)	1897–98	30	27
W. Digby (U)	1899	18	16
Findlay Shirras (O)	1911	49	38
Wadia and Joshi (U)	1913–14	44.5	31
Shah and Khambata (U)	1921–22	74	28
Simon Report (O)	1921–22	116	43
V. K. R. V. Rao (U)	1925–29	78	37
Findlay Shirras (O)	1931	63	45
Sir James Grigg (O)	1937–38	56	40

closer scrutiny, for it must be recalled that in each of the four trends depicted there—except population—the region is starting from a small figure. The percentage gain can therefore be made rather easily, and it masks a low absolute gain. Even so, other countries, starting from much higher proportions ur-

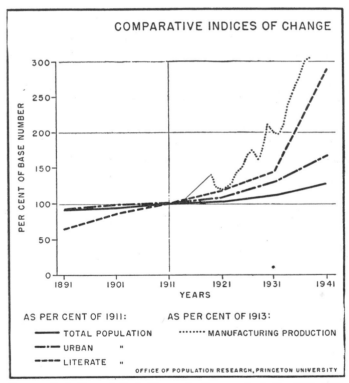

FIGURE 45. Indices of Socio-Economic Progress in India, 1891–1941.

banized, literate, and engaged in manufacturing, have made much higher percentage gains. The Indian level of living has risen, and this clearly implies that social and economic progress has somewhat exceeded population growth, but it has not risen fast.

[24] From R. Palme Dutt, The Problem of India (New York: International Publishers, 1943), p. 29. Dutt gives source in each case. See also K. T. Shah and K. J. Khambata, Wealth and Taxable Capacity of India (London: King, 1934), pp. 63–67; and Rao, op. cit., p. 104.
[25] "U" designates an unofficial estimate, "O" an official one.
[26] Changes in price levels are calculated from data given in S. M. Akhtar, Gurucharan Singh, and K. K. Dewett, Indian Economics (Lahore: S. Chand, 1946), pp. 623–29. Their data are incomplete and it is not altogether clear that they refer to the same series, but presumably the levels are based on retail prices. The adjustment should be regarded as extremely rough, as indeed are the estimates of income.

If one seeks to learn why the Indian level of living did not rise faster, several factors suggest themselves. First, there were certain circumstances that retarded India's industrialization, despite her rather early start. Second, her agriculture was, and still is, in a static and relatively inefficient condition. Third, her already dense population was growing. Behind these three factors lay many others—not the least of which were the Indian social order and the satellite relation to the British economy. The factors are of course interwoven in a complex way, but since our interest lies in population, we shall try to examine the relation of numerical increase to the level of living, first in terms of agriculture and then in terms of industry.

Agriculture and Population

In the countries that have made the greatest economic advance, a shift in the occupational structure has taken place. A greater and greater proportion of the population have found their living in manufacturing, transportation, merchandising, and professional and service occupations. This has meant that, despite the growth of population, there has been little increase in the ratio of farm population to the supply of land. In India, on the other hand, it is well known that such a shift in the occupational structure has not taken place and that, consequently, with the growth of population more and more people have sought to find a living in farming. Ghate shows, for example, that the number of males engaged in agricultural and pastoral pursuits in three censuses was as follows:[27]

	Males in Agriculture and Pasture (000's)	Per Cent Increase
1911	71,834	
1921	71,824	—
1931	79,874	11.1

It will be recalled that from 1911 to 1921 the population of India grew scarcely at all (due to the influenza epidemic) and that between 1921 and 1931 it grew approximately 10.6 per cent. The males in agriculture and pasture grew at virtually the same rates.[28] Therefore, it appears that India is having difficulty in shifting to another type of occupational structure. Its population increase, in the absence of industrialization, is causing an ever larger number of people to try to get a living from the land.

At the same time there has been, and can be, no great increase in the total supply of cultivated land, and there has been no real rise in the farm land's productivity. Between 1920 and 1941, for example, as Table 85 shows, the net area sown and the area characterized as culturable waste remained approximately the same, despite the gain in persons dependent on agriculture. In British India the population grew by 27 per cent during the period mentioned, whereas the net area sown

[27] B. G. Ghate, *Changes in the Occupational Distribution of the Population* (Delhi: Manager of Publications, 1940), p. 21. This author has made a careful study of the occupational statistics in India from 1911 to 1931. His discussion of changing definitions and his conclusions as to trends deserve attention.

[28] There are some occupational statistics for 1941 in a few of the census volumes for particular areas. By comparing data for five areas—Baroda, Mysore, Jammu and Kashmir, Rajputana, and Ajmer-Merwara—the writer found virtually no change in the proportion of gainfully occupied males who are in agriculture. This affords some evidence that between 1931 and 1941 the population dependent on agriculture increased as fast as the total population.

increased by only 8 per cent (and much of this growth was at the expense of cultivable waste and fallow, for the total cultivable land increased by only 4 per cent). Doubtless some expansion of agricultural land in both India and Pakistan is still possible by taking over remote unused areas (such as still exist in Assam) and by extending the area under irrigation. But neither of these methods promises great expansion, and certainly nothing to match the current increase in the population.

TABLE 85

Cultivated Land in British India and the States, 1920–21 to 1940–41 [1]

(000's of acres)

Country	1920–21	1924–25	1928–29	1932–33	1936–37	1940–41
British India						
Net Area Sown	197,279	209,934	210,631	210,070	213,719	213,963
Cultivable Waste[a]	146,429	135,939	139,361	141,686	137,065	143,113
Total	*343,708*	*345,873*	*349,992*	*351,756*	*350,784*	*357,076*
States						
Net Area Sown	b	64,321	66,520	70,029	69,691	b
Cultivable Waste[a]	b	28,546	27,618	30,092	31,444	b
Total		*92,867*	*94,138*	*100,121*	*101,135*	

[a] Includes culturable waste and current fallows.
[b] Figures not available in source used.
[1] S. Subramaniam, *Statistical Summary of the Social and Economic Trends in India, 1918–39* (Washington, D.C.: Government of India Information Services, 1945), pp. 7, 9.

The most favorable places for irrigation have already been subjected to this improvement, and the remote but cultivable corners of the peninsula are now very few. Indeed, because of excessive deforestation, over-grazing of pastures, and waterlogging from irrigation, it is probable that in the future the loss in cultivable land, or at least in its fertility, will be about as great as the gain, unless heroic conservation and expansion measures are undertaken.

THE MAN-LAND RATIO

If the population has grown more rapidly than the area sown, while the proportion engaged in agriculture has remained approximately the same, there must be a trend toward less and less land per cultivator. Indeed, this is the situation. Figure 46 gives the trend in the number of acres per person engaged in agriculture for selected areas of British India, 1891 to 1940. The figures are broken down according to type of tenure.[29] The figures, compiled from the *Statistical Abstracts*, should be representative and fairly comparable (the areas covered were made standard so far as possible). Altogether some 103 million people were included in 1891–92 and some 118 million in 1934–40. The results show that no matter what the kind of tenure, the number of acres per person has diminished. The average number of acres per person was 2.23 in 1891–92, as against 1.90 in 1939–40. This represents a 15 per cent decline.

[29] *Ryotwari* is a freehold tenure in which the cultivator pays his tax directly to the state rather than giving revenue to a landlord. *Zamindari* refers to various kinds of tenancy, the landlord being responsible for paying taxes to the state. Some of the Zamindari areas, under the British, had their rates permanently settled, others did not—hence the distinction between the two kinds of Zamindari holding in the statistics.

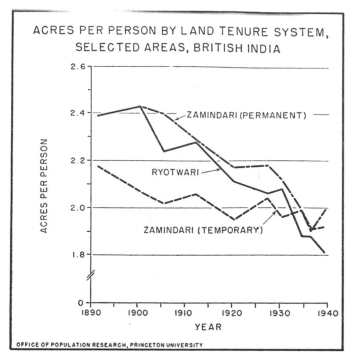

FIGURE 46. Number of Acres of Agricultural Land per Person Dependent on the Land, Selected Areas of British India, at Various Dates from 1891–92 to 1939–40.

PRODUCTIVITY OF THE LAND

The increasing ratio of agricultural population to farm land could have been compensated for if productivity per acre had grown proportionately. It is well known, however, that the productivity of land in the Indian subcontinent has not been improving and that at present it is far below that of most other agricultural areas. Statistics to demonstrate these two facts will be given presently, but first let us analyze the causes.

India's disadvantage in this matter is *not* due to the natural deficiency of the land itself. As previously noted, the subcontinent includes great tracts of the richest land in the world. The low productivity is due rather to the way the land is handled—to the low proportion of capital invested in it—and hence is correlated with the farmers' poverty and density on the land. The smallness of the capital investment in farming is shown in numerous ways—in the absence or inadequacy of conservation measures, in the primitive techniques of cultivation, in the non-use of both natural and artificial fertilizers, in the failure to improve the breeds of plants and animals. The inevitable consequence is that the land does not produce as much as it otherwise could.

LOSS OF AGRICULTURAL RESOURCES

Since conservation cannot be adequately carried out by the individual farmer, it requires planning and capital investment by the community at large. In India, however, neither the individual farmer nor the state has done well at conservation; yet the need has been great. It must be remembered that the subcontinent has a tropical climate, with a combination over much of its area of strong sunshine and alternating torrential rains and drought. This is the sort of climate that quickly ruins soil after its natural covering has been removed. In the Indian region, because of the growth of population, the expansion of cultivation, the excessive grazing of goats and cattle, and the demand for wood, drastic deforestation has occurred. Despite conservation measures taken in 1855 and

1878 the process has gone so far that cowdung must generally be used for fuel rather than for fertilizer. The loss of the forest cover on mountains and hills has brought increasingly destructive floods and has worsened the effects of drought.[30]

With more than a quarter of the world's bovine population but only one-thirtieth of the earth's land surface, the Indian subcontinent suffers severely from the overgrazing of its pastures. Nutritious grass has been replaced by grasses of lower grade and by unpalatable or poisonous bushes. "Most village pastures are pastures only in name, and serve mainly as an exercise ground for cattle, and year by year the soil is eroded away until the land becomes a dreary waste. More and more animals are kept and there is less and less for them to eat. It is small wonder then that the village cows are poor, thriftless beasts with a phenomenally low milk yield."[31]

Finally, Indian farming methods are destructive of fields. On sloping surfaces rows often run straight up and down hill; terracing and contour plowing are only sporadic. In irrigated sections millions of acres have been ruined by alkali deposits.[32]

As a result of this abuse, the Indian region now exhibits the classic effects of poor conservation. In peninsular India, where the land is generally sloping, the soil has long since been washed away from the ridges and the fields made shallow and less fertile. In the Punjab the canals and rivers used for irrigation and water power show decreasing strength in the dry season. Around the Siwalik Hills the subsoil water-level is falling and, due to sand deposition, deserts are destroying "hundreds of thousands of fertile cultivated fields in the plains."[33] In the Indus valley wind erosion has been destructive. In some areas the rivers are silting and becoming useless for irrigation and transportation.

Although generally ignored, this deterioration has economic and demographic importance. It means a loss on the side of renewable resources which, if not remedied, must be compensated for by other means. It is commonly claimed in India and Pakistan that soil fertility can be greatly increased. This is true. It *can* be increased, but the more soil deterioration is allowed to take place, the greater will be the cost and the longer will be the time required to achieve such an increase. It is also claimed that a great expansion of the cultivated area in the two countries is possible,[34] but plainly the past record shows the danger of extending cultivation to forested, hilly, or dry areas without first meeting the costs and expending the energy for adequate conservation. It requires capital and labor merely to conserve agricultural resources, and the more marginal the land, the greater the relative costs.

SHORT-RUN INEFFICIENCIES

India's soils are protected from absolute disaster by the fact that the Indo-Gangetic plain is rich and level, and that its rivers, starting in the high Himalayas, constantly deposit new sediments. But even in the river basins the soil is in a depleted state, not so much from erosion as from constant use. "In spite of the increasing use of improved seeds, the yield per acre does

[30] Sir Harold Glover, *Soil Erosion,* Oxford Pamphlets on Indian Affairs, No. 23 (London: Oxford University Press, 1944), pp. 8–10. This excellent pamphlet is the main source for the present section.

[31] *ibid.,* p. 11.

[32] William Vogt, *Road to Survival* (New York: Sloane, 1948), pp. 225–26.

[33] Glover, *op. cit.,* p. 14.

[34] The National Planning Committee, in the report of its Population Subcommittee, *Population* (Bombay: Vora, 1949), pp. 25–26, estimates that in pre-partition British India the area under cultivation could be increased by more than 60 per cent and that this would increase the food supply by 50 per cent.

not seem to improve permanently. . . . It has been a common experience that after a few years the yield per acre from improved varieties begins to decline rapidly."[35] The reason is that heavier-yielding varieties remove nutrients from the soil at a higher rate. Unless the soil is reinforced somehow, the net result is to reduce its fertility to the point where the new variety no longer yields a greater return than did the old variety.[36] In short, the present low productivity of the Indian soil cannot be increased without improving the soil itself.

In order to help his land maintain its fertility the Indian or Pakistani farmer takes the way that requires least immediate capital but which in the long run is wasteful—he lets the land lie fallow. "In 1930–31, nearly a fifth of our land under cultivation was current fallow; fields were taking rest to regain their natural fertility."[37]

ACTUAL PRODUCTIVITY

For these and other reasons, the per acre productivity of Indian farms is lower than that of most other countries, as Table 86 shows.

TABLE 86

Indices of Comparative Yields in Six Crops, Various Countries
(British India = 100)

Country	Rice	Wheat	Barley	Maize	Potatoes	Cotton
British India	100	100	100	100	100	100
Siam	116[b]	112[b]	. . .	. . .	. . .	. . .
Egypt	241[c]	. . .	. . .	. . .	. . .	500[c]
China	293[c]	152[c]	. . .	. . .	. . .	. . .
Japan	256[b]	180[b]	. . .	. . .	. . .	. . .
	277[c]					
Italy	337[b]	154[b]	. . .	. . .	. . .	. . .
	361[c]					
United Kingdom	. . .	313[a]	257[a]	. . .	276[a]	. . .
Australia	292[a]	116[a]	106[a]	189[a]	134[a]	. . .
		109[c]				
Canada	. . .	141[a]	153[a]	241[a]	142[a]	. . .
		150[c]				
United States	155[a]	140[a]				
	161[b]	133[b]	131[a]	230[a]	146[a]	167[c]
	181[c]	131[c]				

[a] Figures marked with "a" indicate percentages calculated on the basis of data given in Baljit Singh, *Population and Food Planning in India* (Bombay: Hind Kitabs, 1947), p. 59. The data were computed from the *Statistical Yearbook of the League of Nations, 1942–44* and refer to the year 1943–44.

[b] Figures marked with "b" indicate percentages calculated from D. Ghosh, *Pressure of Population and Economic Efficiency in India* (New Delhi: Indian Council of World Affairs, 1946), p. 44. The data on rice production refer to an average for the years 1931–32 to 1935–36, and those for wheat production to an average for the years 1924 to 1933.

[c] Figures marked with "c" indicate percentages calculated on the basis of data given in P. C. Malhotra, "Agricultural Possibilities in India," *Indian Journal of Economics*, Vol. 25 (April, 1945), p. 559. Malhotra took his data from a report of the Post-War Reconstruction Committee of the Government of India, entitled "The Technological Possibilities of Agricultural Development," by W. Burns.

Turning to the history of Indian yields, we get an ambiguous picture, but the most likely conclusion seems to be that the average yield has not risen much since 1910. Figs. 47 and 48 give, in index form, the per acre yields of twelve of India's

[35] Ghosh, *op. cit.*, p. 46.
[36] Singh, *op. cit.*, pp. 57–58.
[37] Ghosh, *op. cit.*, p. 46.

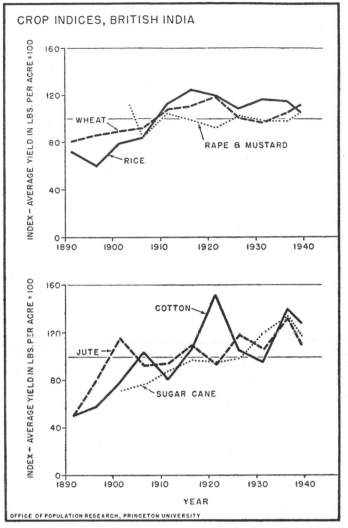

FIGURE 47. Indices of Yields for Six Crops in British India, 1891–92 to 1939–40. (Burma is included except for the year 1939–40).

major crops.[38] A first glance suggests that there has been a general rise in productivity from 1891–92, but this impression is largely given by the earlier period and by some of the commercial crops such as coffee, tea, sugar, which have an exceedingly small acreage compared to the big crops. The big crops are rice, wheat, and cotton, which have not done well. The

[38] Unfortunately the statistics for Figs. 47 and 48 include Burma, except for the year 1939–40; but the cultivated area of Burma was such a small proportion of the total that it should not greatly influence the result, and there is little reason to think that the changes in soil productivity there were much different from those of India.

These figures from the *Statistical Abstract* differ from those given in Subramaniam, *op. cit.*, pp. 7–8. The latter shows an increase in per acre yields since 1920–21 for everything except rice, other cereals (except wheat), and groundnuts. In 1940–41 the weighted average was 103 per cent of that for 1920–21. Although this is more optimistic than the other figures, it still does not represent much growth in productivity. One difference between the two sets of figures is that Subramaniam omits Burma throughout. He has perhaps corrected for the *Abstract's* error of giving the acreage of crops for British India only but the estimated yields for the States as well. Unfortunately, Subramaniam does not give the figures for dates earlier than 1920–21. He does, however, give separate figures for the Indian States, and these show much the same trend as those for the Provinces: rice and wheat have declined in per acre production while most other crops have increased, but since some other crops have larger areas, especially "other cereals" (jowar, bajra, and maize), the result is an increase in the weighted average, which in 1940–41 was 127 per cent of what it was in 1920–21.

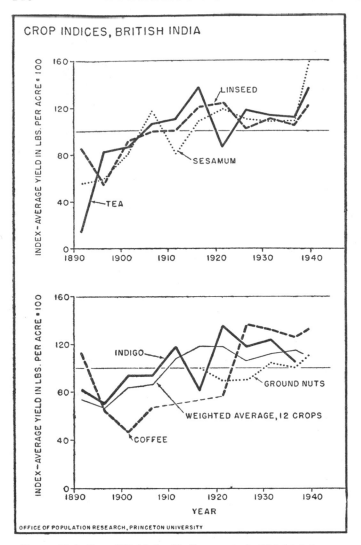

FIGURE 48. Indices of Yields for Six Crops and of a Weighted Average for Twelve Crops in British India, 1891–92 to 1939–40. (The Weighted Average relates to the six crops depicted here and the six crops depicted in Figure 47. Burma is included except for the year 1939–40.)

line to watch, therefore, is the one in Fig. 48 which indicates the *weighted* average index. This shows a rise from 1901–02 until 1920–21, and a decline after that. In 1939–40 the index stood six points below what it had been in 1920–21. The statistics of crop yields therefore, bear out the conclusions of soil scientists to the effect that the Indian land, under present conditions of low capital investment, is in virtually a static condition. Others, using the same basic data, have come to similar conclusions.[39]

RURAL ECONOMIC PROBLEMS

To understand the lack of capital in Indian farming and the role of population pressure in this lack, one must consider some of India's rural economic problems, among them unemployment, indebtedness, and tenancy. If the agricultural population is growing faster than either the supply or the productivity of agricultural land, rural unemployment and underemployment can be expected to increase. This has apparently

[39] E.g. H. Venkatasubbiah, *The Structural Basis of Indian Economy* (London: Allen & Unwin, 1920), pp. 85–89; Singh, *op. cit.*, pp. 38–41, 59; Ghosh, *op. cit.*, pp. 44–57, cites several additional sources; Michael Brown, *India Need Not Starve!* (London: Longmans, 1944), pp. 152–56.

been happening. Although the rural villages have furnished millions of low-paid workers to cities, industries, and foreign areas, they still have far more farmers than they need for efficient tillage. In other words, most rural areas have long since passed the point of diminishing returns so far as the application of labor to land is concerned. The elimination of the surplus agricultural population would greatly increase the per capita product and would not seriously reduce the total agricultural product. Just how large this surplus is cannot be determined, and indeed it depends upon how much capital is assumed to be utilized in agriculture. Under the present conditions of extremely low capital investment the surplus can be very roughly estimated by assuming the average size holding to be one that could conveniently be worked by a farmer and his family, using one bullock team and one plow.[40] Let us say it is half again as great, or 1.5 times the present average holding. This would mean a one-third reduction in the population dependent on agriculture—that is, in 1941, a withdrawal of something like 91 million people from farms over all of India. If, on the other hand, we assumed heavy capitalization of farm enterprise, still more agriculturalists could be dispensed with. In the United States in 1940 the average per capita number of farm acres for the farming population was approximately 35, as compared with India's approximate 2. This suggests that India might, with a similar degree of capitalization, eliminate some fifteen-sixteenths of its agricultural population, all other factors being equal. By a conservative estimate, over 200 million might be withdrawn from Indian agriculture with a net gain in per capita agricultural production. These results certainly seem astronomical, and doubtless they are extremely inaccurate; but they give some idea of the numbers of people who are unnecessary on Indian farms— some idea of the excess agricultural population.

Another well known problem of Indian agriculture is indebtedness, the subject of much literature and some legislation. Both the proportion of cultivators who are in debt and the size of the debts are generally considered high. An intensive village study in the United Provinces showed about two-thirds of the families to be in debt,[41] and another in Gujarat showed nearly three-fourths of them to be so.[42] The latter implied that the situation is worse than these figures sound, because a good proportion of the debt-free families are migratory, have but one or two individuals in them, or are otherwise anomalous. The size of indebtedness is best judged by its relation to the debtor's annual income. The Gujarat study found it to be about 67 and 60 per cent of the annual income for the upper and middle groups, but 110 per cent of the annual income for the lowest group.[43] These studies relate to predepression conditions. There is a belief that the scope of indebtedness has risen since then.[44] In any case, interest rates are notoriously high, ranging from 9 to 300 per cent, depend-

[40] For a discussion of the economic holding for the Indian farm family see G. B. Jathar and S. G. Beri, *Indian Economics* (5th ed.; London: Oxford University Press, 1937), pp. 217–21.

[41] S. S. Nehru, *Caste and Credit in the Rural Area* (London: Longmans, 1932), p. 106.

[42] G. C. Mukhtyar, *Life and Labour in a South Gujarat Village* (Calcutta: Longmans, 1930), pp. 247–49.

[43] *ibid.*, p. 250. M. L. Darling, *The Punjab Peasant in Prosperity and Debt* (London: Oxford University Press, 1925), p. 11, finds the debt to be about three times the annual *net* income. He also noted, pp. 18–19, that the rural indebtedness in the Punjab was more than 17 times the land revenue of the province.

[44] P. J. Thomas, "Rural Indebtedness" in Radhakamal Mukerjee (ed.), *Economic Problems of Modern India*, Vol. 1 (London: Macmillan, 1939), pp. 173–78.

ing on the type of security and the kind of moneylender.[45] Sometimes the moneylenders have been blamed, and doubtless the behavior of some of them, especially those using physical force to collect their loans, is reprehensible; but the truth is that the moneylender is a symptom rather than a cause. The true causes lie in the conditions that keep the peasant on the margin of subsistence. As long as he tills a plot too small to make an income, as long as his agricultural activity is primarily for subsistence, as long as he can accumulate no capital in advance, he will be forced to borrow; and, since his collateral is poor, he will be forced to borrow from a moneylender, who, perforce, will have to charge him high interest rates.[46] The functional role of the moneylender in the situation is shown by the fact that government cooperative loan agencies have not been able to compete with him. Also, government legislation aiming to restrict or control the moneylender has often had the effect, so far as the cultivator is concerned, of making the moneylender's loan still more costly to get. It is frequently maintained (and this is one test of poverty) that one cause of heavy indebtedness is the tendency of the agriculturalist to borrow for non-productive purposes—for weddings, funerals, pilgrimages, litigation, and the feeding of the caste brotherhood. This is particularly true of long-term loans and of the higher castes, and there seems little doubt of its importance.[47] Again, however, it seems to be the conditions facing the cultivator that are responsible. If he wants to live socially as well as physically, he must borrow because of the pressure of numbers on the means of subsistence. It is for this reason that attempts to extricate him from his indebtedness are not likely to succeed unless his basic economic and demographic position is changed.

A third agricultural problem in which population pressure plays a role is that of subtenancy, sometimes called subinfeudation. India has a variety of tenancy laws which in *zamindari* areas (e.g. Bengal and the United Provinces) protect the tenant against the landlord and in *ryotwari* areas protect the actual cultivator against the absentee *ryot* owner.[48] But the laws have been combatting an irresistible force—the steady growth of population and the consequent rise in the value of land. Everywhere in the country, whatever the legal system, there seem to be complaints over the multiplication of subtenancies of various kinds. "The process of subletting by the peasantry inevitably paves the way for the pernicious cottier system. This happened in Ireland where, in some areas, as many as five or six degrees of interests intervened between the proprietor and the actual cultivator. This array has been far out-stripped in Eastern Bengal, where proprietary rights are quite commonly found seven and eight deep and in some cases 12, 15 or 17. In India as a whole agrarian history is repeating itself, . . . A greater population pressure has led to a more acute situation. . . ."[49] In many areas the *ryot*, the "legal peasant," has been transformed into a petty landlord or a

middleman, and the under-*ryots* often outnumber the *ryots* proper.[50]

In *zamindari* areas, in order to protect the tenants, the government long ago fixed rents by careful assessment. The *zamindar* was supposed to pay one-half the rents he collected to the government, a small portion for local costs, and to keep the rest. Steadily, however, the fraction the government obtained has been reduced.[51] In the meantime the powerful landlord class, in addition to putting pressure on the government to reduce its taxes, has pursued various devices to increase its revenue from the tenants. The *zamindar* has above all exacted illegal rent in the form of *nazarana* (payment in kind), *begar* (payment in labor), fines, fees, etc. "Some of the landlords keep their own private records in which the real rent-rate, which is sometimes 50 per cent more than the rate in the *patwari's* books, is recorded." [52] In addition, the *zamindar* has encouraged subletting on the part of his tenants, because it proved profitable to him. The tenant's rights have still been of sufficient value to enable him to sublet the land. Nothing illustrates so clearly the desperate necessity of people to find some scrap of land on which to try to make a living. To the man at the bottom the value of land is not so much that it offers a chance to make money but that it offers the possibility of subsistence, a chance to live.

In *ryotwari* areas, as already mentioned, the same subletting tendency has taken place. The Bombay census of 1931 found the number of tenant cultivators to exceed that of cultivating owners, and an increase of tenancy has been noted in the Punjab, the alleged stronghold of the peasant proprietor.[53]

Like rural underemployment and indebtedness, subtenancy would hardly develop were it not for the growing agricultural population. The struggle for life expresses itself as a struggle for land at any cost. The effect of subtenancy is to decrease efficiency in several ways. First, it causes a further reduction in the size of holdings; for as the value of land increases, the amount of it that an ordinary man can command decreases. Second, it means that the efficiency of employment on the land declines, not only because of the small holding but also because of the tenant's lack of long-run security, incentive, and capital for improving the land.[54] Third, although theoretically a landlord class can accumulate large sums of capital and invest them in agricultural improvement or industrial enterprise, it does not seem to work that way in India. The gains tend to be dissipated in lavish consumption of foreign goods, in the support of large joint families, and in sports and travel. Because he is divorced from the actual work and is habituated to profit by "squeeze" rather than by technical competence, the landlord devotes little attention to agricultural modernization.

CONCLUSION

The Indian population is believed to have grown substantially, albeit by fits and starts, from what it was when Pelsaert made his observations on poverty. This increase could have come only as a result of enhanced national productivity, not as a result of lowering the standard of living, because the latter was already, it seems, at rock bottom. What would have happened if the national productivity had grown as it did but the

[45] *ibid.*, pp. 169–70. Mukhtyar, *op. cit.*, pp. 252–54.

[46] T. N. Ramaswamy, *Economic Stabilisation of Indian Agriculture* (Benares: Nand Kishore, 1946), pp. 132–36, emphasizes the conditions with which the agriculturist is faced, rather than his "irrationality" or the money lender's rapacity.

[47] C. G. Chenevix-Trench, "The Rural Community" in Sir Edward A. H. Blunt, *Social Service in India* (London: His Majesty's Stationery Office, 1939), pp. 107–08. Sam Higginbottom, *India's Agricultural Problems* (New York: Institute of Pacific Relations, Eighth Conference, 1942), p. 31.

[48] For explanations of these terms, see footnote 29.

[49] Radhakamal Mukerjee, "Land Tenures and Legislation" in Radhakamal Mukerjee (ed.), *op. cit.*, pp. 237–38. For more examples see Chenevix-Trench, *op. cit.*, pp. 93–94.

[50] Mukerjee, *op. cit.*, pp. 228, 230.

[51] Chenevix-Trench, *op. cit.*, pp. 86–87; Higginbottom, *op. cit.*, p. 26.

[52] Mukerjee, *op. cit.*, p. 226.

[53] *ibid.*, pp. 233–34.

[54] Glover, *op. cit.*, p. 12.

population had remained fixed? It seems likely that the standard of living would have risen instead of remaining virtually stationary.

This deduction assumes, of course, that the extra national productivity was not merely a function of the additional labor furnished by the augmented population. The evidence of the present chapter favors this assumption. It has been shown that the farm unit has moved toward a smaller and less economical size, that pressure on the land has prevented adequate capitalization for soil and technological improvement, that consequently soil productivity has not increased and loss of natural resources has resulted, and that indebtedness, underemployment, and subinfeudation have further thrown obstacles in the way of agricultural improvement. Most of these conditions are traceable, at least in part, to an increased number of people on the land. Today, if the subcontinent had millions fewer farmers, the agricultural product would probably be increased rather than decreased. It would seem, then, that the growth in productivity of the total economy has come from a certain amount of industrialization, from commercial stimulation, and better distributive machinery. Such improvements have been especially prominent in recent decades, and it is precisely in these decades that population growth has accelerated. The population growth seems therefore to be more of a result than a cause of the enhanced productivity; if it has not impeded economic achievement, it has almost certainly caused the fruits of it to be divided among so many people that the per capita gain has been very slight.

++

Economic Achievement: Population and Industrialization

++

THE agricultural situation in India and Pakistan is obviously a vicious circle in which population density, fragmentation, inefficiency, soil mining, lack of capital, low productivity, and countless other features mutually reinforce one another. This vicious circle cannot be broken by agricultural reform alone. It can be broken only by the *deus ex machina* of industrialization. It is therefore with some hope that we turn, as the people themselves have turned, to the prospects of industrial growth in the two countries.

The gist of Indian industrialization can be summed up in four general propositions: (1) There is no doubt that industrialization has been moving ahead in this region, growing faster than population. (2) But there is also no doubt that it has moved ahead more slowly than it might have done. (3) Among the reasons for retardation are apparently the Indian social organization, the long sway of Britain, and the gradually evolving demographic situation. (4) By now, with independence attained, the major obstacle to rapid industrial growth is the excessive population, although other obstacles are also present. These propositions receive documentation in the following paragraphs.

EVIDENCE OF INDUSTRIAL GROWTH

Apart from scattered and rather unsuccessful earlier attempts, industrialization (i.e. the application of mechanical power to manufacture and transport) began in India about 1850. During the first five years thereafter "railways reached out from Calcutta, Bombay, and Madras; coal mines began to be seriously worked in Bengal; and the first cotton mills in Bombay Presidency and the first jute mill in Bengal were started."[1] From these beginnings, in less than a century, India became in absolute though not in per capita terms one of the great industrial nations, and the Union of India today remains in that category.

Evidences of industrial growth are many. Despite set-backs during the depression and World War II, the per capita volume of both imports and exports tended to rise. Furthermore, the character of these imports and exports changed—manufactured goods were increasingly exported and decreasingly imported, as follows:

[1] Daniel H. Buchanan, *The Development of Capitalistic Enterprise in India* (New York: Macmillan, 1934), p. 129.

Percentage Composition of Exports and Imports [2]

Principal Groups	Before World War I		After World War I		1940–41	
	EXPORTS	IMPORTS	EXPORTS	IMPORTS	EXPORTS	IMPORTS
Food, drink, and tobacco	29	15	21	20	22	15
Raw materials	47	7	50	33	33	26
Manufactured articles [a]	23	76	27	43	43	57
Miscellaneous	1	2	2	4	2	2
Totals	100	100	100	100	100	100

[a] Articles mainly or wholly manufactured.

Also, there was a large increase in the importation of machinery and chemicals required by industry.[3]

Industrial production itself has surely risen faster than population. This is illustrated by Figure 49, which shows the trend of industrial production. It is also shown by reference to specific kinds of production (Figures 50 and 51). With reference to the textile industry, for example, between 1920–21 and 1943–44 in India as a whole (excluding Burma) the output by weight of cotton piecegoods increased 223 per cent, and of cotton yarn by 152 per cent.[4] Between 1920–21 and 1939–40, the number of looms in the textile industry (cotton, jute, and woolen mills combined) increased by 66 per cent and the number of spindles by 47 per cent. Between 1938–39 and 1943–44 in British India the total energy generated by electric power plants increased by 45 per cent.[5] Another indication of enhanced industrial activity lies in the output of industrially useful minerals. Figure 49 shows that the gains since 1921 have been startling. Iron ore production, for example, has more than tripled since 1921. Almost any other index of economic activity, such as freight-car loadings, postal receipts, urban growth, will show the same upward trend.[6] The impetus behind industrialization is shown by the remarkable fact that while industrial production in most coun-

[2] General Motors India, *Economic Survey of India* (New York: 1945), p. 115.

[3] John Matthai, *Tariffs and Industry,* Oxford Pamphlets on Indian Affairs, No. 20 (London: Oxford University Press, 1944), p. 18.

[4] Subramaniam, *op. cit.,* p. 15.

[5] *ibid.,* pp. 16–17.

[6] See Buchanan, *op. cit.,* especially Chs. 7–13; and P. S. Lokanathan, *Industrialization,* Oxford Pamphlets on Indian Affairs, No. 10 (3rd ed.; Bombay: Oxford University Press, 1946).

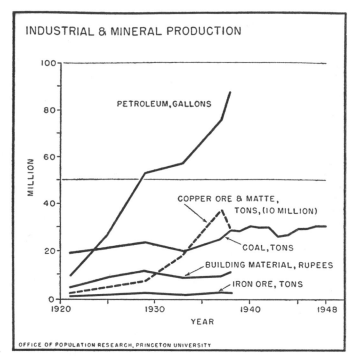

FIGURE 49. Industrial and Materials Production in India.

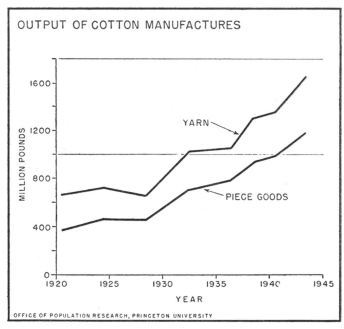

FIGURE 50. Output of Cotton Manufactures, India, 1920–21 to 1943–44.

tries showed a heavy decline during the period of the great depression which started in 1929, the output of the principal industries in India showed a steady and, in some cases, a marked increase.[7]

The necessary accompaniments of industrialization have also manifested themselves. For instance, in spite of the pronounced tendency of Indian industrial labor, drawn from rural villages, to be transitory (as noted in Chapter 14 above), there is now coming to be a settled industrial population in manufacturing cities such as Jamshedpur, Madras, Nagpur, and Ahmedabad. This new class of industrial workers has developed skills that enable finer products to be produced. Ma-

[7] Matthai, *op. cit.*, pp. 12–13.

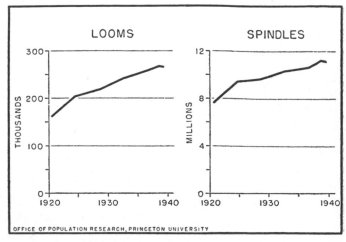

FIGURE 51. Number of Looms and Spindles in Textile Mills, India, 1920–21 to 1939–40.

dras cotton drills now compare favorably with English drills. "The finer types of saris, dhoties and shirtings from Ahmedabad, Sholapur, Bombay and Nagpur and coatings from Madras have practically driven out of Indian markets similar foreign products." In the Tata Steel Works laborers who only a few years ago were primitive tribesmen in the Santal jungles " 'are handling now red hot steel bars, turning out rails, wheels, angles of iron, as efficiently as you can get it done by any English labourer.' " An industrial manager reports that in his machine shop at least 20 per cent of the men "can use the micrometer and know what it means to machine to 1/2000th to 1/3000th of an inch and can do it as people in England can."[8]

"Not only are skills developing in the settled industrial population, but these skills are a factor in vertical social mobility. The skilled workers in various categories have been generally drawn from the ranks of unskilled workers and now form a considerable proportion of workers in India, estimated at 26.9 in 1921 and obtaining wages at a higher rate than that for unskilled workers. Intelligent skilled workers, as soon as they pick up skilled work, are promoted from lower to higher ranks. Many women workers join the cotton mills in Bombay as half-timers drawing only Rs. 4–8 a month, then pick up skill and are admitted as full-time workers earning Rs. 25 a month within three to five years. Boys begin as half-time doffers earning only Rs. 3–8 a month and become full-time workers in the same department earning double the wages within the same period. Then they become siders in the throstle department and end as doffer jobbers earning Rs. 50 a month within another five years. Similarly in the jute mills in Bengal a boy starts learning weaving by going in his recess to the Weaving Department to help his associates from his own village, ends as a skilled weaver, earning Rs. 10 a week."[9] This opportunity to climb in accordance with manifest ability means that India is beginning to develop the kind of society characterizing an industrial system.

In addition, the habit of investment in industry is apparently growing. At least this is the impression that economists derive from the amount of deposits in banks, cooperatives, and post offices, and from the purchase of government securities and industrial stocks. New industries have found it sur-

[8] Tulsi Ram Sharma, *Location of Industries in India* (Bombay: Hind Kitabs, 1946), pp. 191–92.
[9] *ibid.*, p. 193.

prisingly easy to draw capital from Indian investors.[10] A well known case is that of Tata. When commencing to finance their steel plant, Doraji Tata and B. J. Padshah tried in vain to get London backing under conditions satisfactory to the Indians. They then turned to the Indian public and met an enthusiastic response. "The Tata offices in Bombay were besieged by an eager crowd of native investors. Old and young, rich and poor, men and women, they came offering their mites; and at the end of three weeks, the entire capital required for the construction requirements, £1,630,000 was secured, . . ."[11]

The habit of investment, however, is not fully developed in India. The public still has a strong liquidity preference, finding bank facilities either inadequate or, in its eyes, untrustworthy.[12] But the propensity is capable of being awakened.

The bogy of a tropical climate is also being overcome. Not long ago it was generally believed that countries such as India suffer *permanent* climatic disabilities in the establishment of large-scale mechanized industries. To be sure, in the diffusion of heavy industry from a temperate to a tropical climate, certain adjustments must be made which require time and experience to work out. But the same science and technology which invented the industries in the first place can certainly perform the relatively minor task of adjusting it to another climate. "Fifty years ago an industry involving operations at high temperature, such as the sheet iron industry or the tin-plate industry, would have been considered impossible in India. But the introduction of suitable cooling arrangements and the construction of factories with high roofs and good ventilation have eliminated this difficulty and have enabled these industries to establish themselves. Similarly artificial humidification has enabled the cotton textile industry to operate efficiently in regions where the existence of a relatively dry climate might otherwise have proved a serious handicap."[13]

SLOWNESS OF INDUSTRIAL GROWTH

Although the evidence seems clear that industrialization is moving ahead in the Indian subcontinent, virtually no one seems satisfied with the *rate* at which it is moving. This feeling is not due to mere impatience, but rather to a threefold consideration. First, the urgency is very great. India and Pakistan need industrialization about as badly as any country in the world, and they need it quickly. Second, the potentialities of this region for industrial development are great, so that its actual performance in this field seems tragically below what might be expected. And third, comparison with certain other countries that have *recently* become industrialized— Japan, Russia, Australia, Argentina—suggests that in the modern world, where industry does not have to be invented but can be quickly borrowed, India is definitely lagging. No inquiry is superfluous which promises to reveal why.

COMPARISON WITH NEW INDUSTRIAL AREAS

A puzzling fact about India is that it was "the first of the oriental countries to feel the impact of industrialism"[14] and

yet never completed the transition; whereas Japan, starting later and with fewer resources, did complete it. Japanese industrialization did not begin until several years after the Meiji Restoration in 1868, and it was behind India's industrial development until 1880. But then the process in Japan began to gain momentum, with the result that the entire industrial revolution was accomplished within the lifetime of the young planners of 1868. Not only did Japan become in a few short decades the first and only industrialized oriental country, but she became one of the world's major powers, vying with Britain and America for trade and empire. By the 1930's her economic system was already that of a modern industrialized nation.[15]

The demographic and social changes were no less spectacular than the economic. The population grew from 35 million in 1870 to 73 million in 1940, but due to urbanization, the population dependent on agriculture remained virtually unchanged. By 1940 half the population lived in places of 10,000 or more, 29 per cent in cities of 100,000 or more. Indeed, in sharp contrast to India, Japanese urbanization was faster than that of the West. "The relative growth between 1920 and 1935 alone was practically as great as that which occurred in the United States between 1900 and 1940."[16] At the same time, despite the handicap of an ideographic script requiring the learning of some 2,000 characters for literacy, Japan speedily changed from an illiterate to one of the most literate countries in the world. The basic education law was passed as late as 1872, but by 1938 the country was 95 per cent literate and had nearly 12 million pupils in primary schools as compared to something over 9 million in British India (which had a population four times as great).[17] The industrial transition was therefore a full-blown social revolution in Japan, and the speed of its accomplishment seems undeniable.

How can one explain India's slower and much less complete development despite her earlier start? Population cannot explain it, because both countries were already densely populated in the 1850's. Inequality of resources cannot explain it, because India had, and still has, incomparably greater resources. In 1936, 90 per cent of Japan's crude oil, 88 per cent of her iron ores, 71 per cent of her tin, and 11 per cent of her coal were imported. Textiles have long been Japan's principal industry, yet apart from silk and rayon, she must import the raw materials. "Japan Proper produces no cotton and grows no wool."[18] Nor can the access to transportation explain the difference, because India sits astride some of the world's oldest ocean trade routes and is nearer to the oldest centers of commerce and industry.

At bottom there seem to be only two explanations. First, although both countries were oriental, their cultures were different and that of the Japanese was more compatible with

[10] Lokanathan, *op. cit.*, p. 23. Also General Motors, *op. cit.*, p. 129, and Matthai, *op. cit.*, p. 15.

[11] Quoted in Sharma, *op. cit.*, p. 96.

[12] Lokanathan, *op. cit.*, p. 23. Matthai, *op. cit.*, pp. 15–16.

[13] Matthai, *op. cit.*, p. 17.

[14] Herbert Heaton, "Industrial Revolution," *Encyclopaedia of the Social Sciences*, p. 9.

[15] Japan adopted anti-depression and anti-inflation controls prior to their adoption in the United States and simultaneously with their adoption in England. John F. Embree, *The Japanese Nation* (New York: Rinehart, 1945), pp. 57–58.

[16] Irene B. Taeuber and Edwin G. Beal, "The Demographic Heritage of the Japanese Empire," *Annals of the American Academy of Political and Social Science*, Vol. 237 (January, 1945), pp. 65–66.

[17] Embree, *op. cit.*, pp. 131–40; Edwin O. Reischauer, *Japan, Past and Present* (New York: Knopf, 1946); Sir Philip Hartog, *Some Aspects of Indian Education Past and Present*, University of London Institute of Education, Studies and Reports, No. 7 (London: Oxford University Press, 1939), p. 33.

[18] Harold G. Moulton and Louis Marlio, *The Control of Germany and Japan* (Washington, D.C.: The Brookings Institution, 1944), pp. 66–67.

modern industrialism. Second, Japan entered the process of industrialization as a sovereign nation, whereas India entered it as a subject people. Both explanations merit brief discussion.

CULTURE AND SOCIAL ORGANIZATION

To show historically the social obstacles to industrialization, one cannot simply cite the feudal or other institutions of an agrarian society. Obviously such a society is not conducive to industry. The task, rather, is to find the peculiar features which lead one agrarian society toward or away from industrialism as contrasted to another. Put in these terms, the Indian case is not easy to diagnose, but certain facts stand out. The caste system, for example, introduces unusual rigidities into the social order. It requires a strong reliance on custom to maintain, because otherwise people will not remain in their hereditary status. Also, the conception of a hereditary occupation is exactly the opposite of the idea of open opportunity, free competition, increasing specialization, and individual mobility associated with a dynamic industrial economy. Caste adds another primary group, in addition to the joint family and the rural village, to the custom-bound control of the individual. Its divisive and exclusionist character—with commensal, marital, religious, and other taboos separating different groups, is an effective brake on geographical mobility, ready contact with strangers, and the formation of large-scale business organizations. The fact, therefore, that India had a much more developed caste system than did Japan, helps explain why Japan could industrialize more rapidly.

Another feature of Indian social organization distinguishing it from 16th century Europe (though not from Japan) and militating against industrialization was the joint family system. Such a system, like caste, strongly limits social mobility and social change because it binds the individual to others on the basis of birth, forces him to contribute to the support of a large group independently of their ability, introduces nepotism into both business and politics, and assures control of the younger generation by the elders. The Hindu and Muslim tendency to seclude women, itself a factor in immobilizing the economy and strengthening tradition, could be carried out only within the joint family household. In both China and Japan the joint family has been an obstacle to industrialization, but more so in China because there the family was the main focus of social organization whereas in Japan there were other principles that on occasion could override the family.[19] In India, too, there were other aspects of social organization that could override the family, but for the most part these were embodied in caste and therefore were even more inimical to industrialization than familism itself. Agrarian Europe, prior to the great economic transition, was remarkably free from strict familism (the Catholic Church with its wide-flung organization and its celibate clergy being a factor), from the seclusion of women (bilateral rather than unilateral kinship being emphasized), and from the caste principle. It is no accident, therefore, that Europe rather than the orient originated the industrial revolution.

The Hindu religion in India was also an obstacle to modernization. It was integrally related to caste by giving divine sanction to caste divisions, by rationalizing caste immobility in terms of transmigration (supernatural mobility resting on observance of caste customs while alive), by putting untouchables beyond the pale, and by giving a central religious posi-

tion to the Brahman caste. The religion was also bound up with the joint family by containing a strong tinge of familistic worship and giving sanctions for paternal authority in marriage and all other matters. In addition, it was a highly eclectic religion having no central organization, taking on local coloring in different areas, and admitting a maximum number of magical practices. At the same time it placed great value on asceticism of an individualistic and functionless kind, gave an extreme rationalization for ignoring the material world, and had a strong agricultural bias (as witness the veneration of cows). Islam, as we have seen, was a quite different religion, but in India it was greatly influenced by Hinduism and by the fact that its bearers were militaristic and feudalistic conquerors averse to commerce and practical arts.

A full exploration of the antinomy between Indian social organization and economic change would require many chapters. But even with brief mention it can be seen that the combination of caste, familism, and Hinduism was a formidable block to modernization, though not necessarily an insuperable one. Some of the same factors were present in other oriental civilizations, but least so in Japan and perhaps less in China than in India. Far back in feudal times Japan had apparently a more disciplined population, a more orderly government, a more industrious ethic than did India.

The factors described are of course still present today and are still interfering with modernization, but they are becoming attenuated. They will doubtless change in form until they have either disappeared or have accommodated themselves to modern technology and modern economic life. It would be foolish to think, however, that India will ever have a social organization closely resembling our own, not simply because she will retain vestiges of her own institutions but also because, by the time they have changed radically, industrial civilization in general will be quite different from what it is in Western countries today.

POLITICAL AND ECONOMIC DEPENDENCE

All historians stress the degree to which industrialization in Japan was the consequence of conscious effort and planning by her statesmen for the purpose of building a powerful nation. Borrowing from the West was not a random diffusion or a foreign invasion, but rather a strategy of nationalistic statesmanship. Industrial development was not the unplanned outgrowth of unfettered private enterprise but rather the result of paternalistic government control over, and collaboration with, business empires. Strong governmental guidance and control, even in the Tokugawa regime, persisted straight through. More reminiscent of Germany than any other nation, it combined nationalistic and imperial aims with the technology of industry and the acumen of commerce to build a modern industrial and militaristic nation in the brief span of half a century.[20]

India, on the other hand, was in many ways an economically vassal state. England's policy toward her, while always mixed with other motives and interests, was the policy of an industrial nation towards an agricultural colony. She tended to use the area as a source of raw materials for her industry and as a market for the products of that industry. Such industry as was allowed to develop in India was often for the profit of citizens of the paramount power. The evidence of this economic vassalage, amassed and reiterated by both Indian and

[19] Marion J. Levy, Jr., *The Family Revolution in Modern China* (Cambridge: Harvard University Press, 1949), p. 351.

[20] Reischauer, *op. cit.*, Chs. 9–11; John M. Maki, *Japanese Militarism: Its Cause and Cure* (New York: Knopf, 1945), Chs. 2–7; Embree, *op. cit.*, Chs. 2–6, 8, 10.

British economists,[21] need not all be repeated here. One need mention only the following:

(1) The British men who ruled India were not of the type, even had they been so motivated, to develop Indian industry. They were Europeans who did not understand, who looked down upon, and who were aloof from their oriental subjects. Being aliens, they feared to tamper with the essential social organization and customs of the people. They could not undertake vigorous policies of innovation, because they could not marshal the sentimental support or trust of the masses. Furthermore, "though coming from the most advanced industrial country of the world, they were not trained in industry, or even conversant with its problems. They were nearly all men of aristocratic background who not only knew nothing about business but openly despised it." [22] Finally, they held fast to the economic doctrine that "Adam Smith, Ricardo, and J. S. Mill had developed and which it is now generally conceded was largely determined by the particular conditions then prevailing in England," not the ones now prevailing in India.[23] They viewed their task as the maintenance of law and order and the facilitation of trade. Inevitably their allegiance was with their home and their own kind. They were hardly the men to use their statecraft to mold India into a powerful modern industrial nation in the shortest possible time.

(2) The tariff policy in England and India has been admittedly influenced by strong demands from British economic interests. From 1700 to 1825 Britain levied high protective duties on the excellent textiles made by Indian handicraft, while insisting that British goods enter India almost duty free. When England began manufacturing textiles from American cotton with power machinery, she no longer needed protection from Indian textiles. Instead, insisting on "laissez faire," she flooded the unprotected Indian market with cheap cloth and ruined the native handicraft industry. "Between 1818 and 1836 the twist imports into India rose in the proportion of 1:5200. In 1824 the exports of British muslin to India hardly amounted to one million yards. By 1937 they exceeded 64 million yards. At the same time the population of Dacca, world famous for its muslins, decreased from 150,000 inhabitants to 20,000." [24] Later, from 1927 onwards, when the conditions of British advantage changed, the benefits of laissez faire were conveniently forgotten. Instead the policy of Imperial Preference, "which gave British products an advantage over both non-empire and Indian production in the Indian market," was thrust upon an unwilling India.[25]

(3) In order to get raw materials out and manufactured goods into India, Britain needed efficient transport into the interior. Consequently, for this and military and administrative reasons, she built an elaborate system of railroads in India. The organization and rate structure of the system, however, "favoured unduly the port towns and the foreign trade as against the interests of the inland towns and a uniform general industrial development of the country." Among the most inequitable practices was the custom of charging lower rates for hauls between seaports and the interior than for hauls between different centers within the interior. For example, "the rates charged from cotton growing tracts to some of the western ports were lower for longer distances than for shorter distances to inland industrial centres." The rate for shipping hides was 50 per cent less on hauls to ports than on hauls between interior towns. The situation was much the same for sugar and wool.[26] Apart from rates, the location of the railroads was not suitable for the interchange of products between industrial and market centers within India. Relatively short shipments of cotton to interior manufacturing centers sometimes took months, whereas the ginners could ship with great ease to the ports.[27]

(4) The Indian government did not guide and control the exploitation of natural resources for the purpose of maximizing the long-run national interest. Instead, it tended to give foreign enterprises a free hand to reap quick profits at the expense of future production. Perhaps the outstanding example of this is the coal industry, where the structure of the business (the managing agent system), a rising economic demand, and wasteful working methods have been conducive to the taking of huge profits in the shortest possible time, without much regard for the eventual lowered productivity of the collieries. The Indian government, committed to a laissez faire policy, has kept its hands off rather than introduce regulations for the benefit of future generations.[28]

(5) Neither did the Indian government lend much support to the native producers of raw materials as against the foreign manufacturers in India who used these raw materials. An outstanding example is the exposed position of the Indian jute grower, who, unorganized and inarticulate, bore the brunt of set-backs in the jute industry, while the Indian Jute Mills' Association, heavily represented by Britishers, enjoyed a monopolistic position both with reference to the export market and the price to the growers.[29]

(6) Another source of deep suspicion was the purchase of stores by the Government of India—equipment for the army, materials for city utilities, supplies for hospitals, tracks and rolling stock for railroads, etc. It was believed by Indians that contracts were let to British firms when Indian firms could have supplied the goods, and that an opposite policy would have helped to build up Indian industry.[30]

(7) There is also reason to believe that currency regulation and banking practice have been handled in a way prejudicial to Indian interests. But probably a still greater complaint is that the British government of India, collaborating with British economic interests, ruined the handicraft industries of India, and thus impoverished and forced into an already crowded agricultural situation countless thousands of artisans. It will be readily admitted that handicraft industry would have had to decline eventually under any program of industrialization, but the point is that the British did not create a new industry in India to take the place of the handicraft. Nor did they make any effort to blend the old handicraft system into a new industrial order. Above all, the development of a peculiar adaptation such as that which occurred in Japan did not take place. It is well known that Japan's preindustrial

[21] Perhaps the soberest and most penetrating discussion of this subject ever published was written by an American, Daniel H. Buchanan, in the final chapter of his great book, *The Development of Capitalist Enterprise in India,* already cited.

[22] The Indian Civil service was recruited in London on the basis of tests in classical learning. Economic proficiency was not a desideratum.

[23] Buchanan, *op. cit.,* pp. 456–59.

[24] P. A. Wadia and K. T. Merchant, *Our Economic Problem* (Bombay: New Book, 1946), p. 292.

[25] *ibid.,* p. 297. See also Buchanan, *op. cit.,* pp. 464–71, and Kate L. Mitchell, *India Without Fable* (New York: Knopf, 1942), pp. 125–27, 171–75.

[26] Sharma, *op. cit.,* pp. 175–77.

[27] *ibid.,* pp. 179–81. See also Wadia and Merchant, *op. cit.,* pp. 289–90.

[28] H. Venkatasubbiah, *The Structural Basis of Indian Economy* (London: Allen & Unwin, 1940), pp. 124–31.

[29] *ibid.,* pp. 131–40.

[30] Buchanan, *op. cit.,* pp. 471–73.

handicraft shops were turned into industrial shops. "Almost half the people in Japanese industry operate in work places with under five persons and two-thirds in work places with under fifty persons." [31] The gradual blending of handicraft into manufacturing did not prevent the Japanese from industrializing. Rather, granted the strength of the old organization, it is hard to see how industrialization could have been accomplished any other way. But in Japan the economic development was guided by an indigenous government, the interests of which were identified with the nation itself.

These evidences of economic vassalage are not presented in order to "blame" the British. Actually, because of the weakness of India at the time (due to political chaos, feudal backwardness, and archaic customs) if the British had not come to rule, some other foreign country would have done so. In other words, India's peculiar culture and social organization are not entirely separable from her subjection to British rule. In all probability the British did a more efficient and a fairer job of governing India than any other foreign nation would have done. Our purpose has been merely to explain the apparent blocks to industrialization created by the presence of an outside ruler. Seemingly the enormous task of transforming a people from a peasant economy to an industrial nation in a short time is one that only an indigenous government can perform.

Our comparison has been primarily with Japan, because this seemed the most cogent comparison to make. The industrialization of Australia, Canada, and Argentina adds little to the picture except to show the advantage of a sparse population as well as governmental autonomy. The industrialization of Russia is more instructive, because there too there was a transformation from a peasant regime. The Soviet experience illustrates more emphatically the necessity of an extremely strong central and indigenous government (even if dictatorial) for this kind of great but rapid transformation. The next chapter will deal more fully with the requirements of industrialization in India and Pakistan as things now stand—especially with the revolutionary and drastic policies that seem required. But to understand the straits to which economic policy must now address itself, it is first necessary to return to our main theme, the role of population in the economy of the region.

POPULATION GROWTH AND INDUSTRIALIZATION

The slow rate of industrialization has seemingly caused India's population to grow more slowly than it would otherwise have done (as shown by comparison with Japan, England, Australia, and the United States during their periods of fast industrialization). [32] But because of Western medical effort, better transport, and more commerce, as we have seen, the population did grow, and its growth accelerated with time. Consequently India now faces the prospect of large potential industrialization with a population more crowded than that of any past country on the eve of its industrialization. That such agrarian density together with the prospect of rapid growth tends to impede industrialization there can be little doubt. The following seem to be some of the main ways it tends to do so.

(1) In general the consequence is to focus economic effort on consumption goods rather than heavy industry, and thus to discount future advantage against present advantage. The swollen masses are so deprived of the immediate necessities that everything is expended on sheer maintenance of life. As bare necessities are met, the population multiplies so fast that the supply of immediate necessities must be constantly expanded. This makes it hard to accumulate the surplus and invest the energies necessary to develop large-scale basic industries, even though in the end these industries would yield a greater volume of consumption goods. Most individuals are so near the subsistence point that they cannot save; instead they tend to borrow for consumption purposes and thus fall into the vicious circle of personal indebtedness. Even when they can save they feel so insecure that they prefer a high liquidity of their assets to a modest interest through investment. In this way the amount of investment capital produced by the population tends to be small. At the same time the business firm finds the demand for consumption goods so insistent that it sees greater profit in immediately satisfying this demand with inefficient equipment than in making long-run expenditures on new basic equipment. The government feels the same pressure. Especially if democratic, it finds difficulty in ignoring the pressing wants of the majority of its citizens in order to build heavy industry for the future. It must use its economic means to feed, clothe, and house the people when they are in dire poverty and when there will be many more of them tomorrow than today. Its labor is like the labor of Sisyphus, except that the stone grows constantly larger.

(2) The evil of low capitalization, as we have seen, first shows itself in agriculture, where the chief instrument of production—land—becomes ever more scarce and hence ever more dear.

"The great demand for land from people, most of whom have no alternative source of income, has driven up the price of farm land out of relation to its income-earning capacity. In many parts of the country farming is a deficit undertaking. Yet the value of land rules high, because the mass of the people must have some land, if they are to subsist at all. [The high price of farm land in India is thus an index of population pressure rather than of agricultural prosperity.] . . . The high price of land absorbs a good proportion of the farmer's capital resources leaving him a residue that is hardly sufficient for its improvement or efficient operation. Hence the Indian farmer relies as much as possible on human labour and on poor cattle that costs him little to maintain, uses the simplest and the cheapest implements, draws as much as he can on the natural fertility of the soil and secures from his enterprise a yield that keeps him and his land on the margins of subsistence." [33]

We have already seen how the amount of land per cultivator has steadily declined, and how this has tended to increase poverty, to limit investment in the soil, and thus to hold down productivity. We have seen how the crowding on the land has led to underemployment in agriculture, to non-productive indebtedness, and to functionless subinfeudation. Caught in this vicious circle, the over-numerous farm population is in no condition to furnish the economic surplus with which an industrial system can be built.

(3) A high ratio of farm population to agricultural resources means that most of the land is devoted to food crops for sustenance rather than to export crops for an investment surplus. The economy cannot compete successfully in world markets with other agricultural countries where the amount of land, equipment, and technology is greater per worker. The situation reaches its ultimate futility when the food requirements

[31] Embree, op. cit., p. 53.
[32] See Chapter 4.
[33] Ghosh, op. cit., p. 47.

of the swollen population become so great that an agricultural country becomes an importer of agricultural produce—that is, when the total value of agricultural imports exceeds the total value of agricultural exports. India has not reached this condition yet, and she can reach it only if she industrializes (in which case she is no longer an agricultural country) or if the rest of the world feeds her out of charity.

(4) In a dense agrarian economy, labor is immediately cheaper than machinery. The entrepreneur cuts his costs by selecting labor-using methods in preference to capital-using ones. The government fosters this attitude by attempting to maintain full employment in the face of surplus labor. Planning experts call for a development of those industries in which labor is a big portion of the cost of output. But the truth is that a low ratio of capital to labor means a low level of living, a low output per head, and a low national income. In so far as labor is immediately employed because it is cheap instead of machinery because it is dear, the future is sacrificed for the present.[34] In short, the measure of industrialization is precisely the degree to which machinery is substituted for human labor; to the extent that a dense agrarian economy impedes this substitution, it impedes industrialism.

(5) A rapid population growth attributable to an extremely high fertility and a high but somewhat lower death rate, produces an unusual burden of young-age dependency. As seen in Chapter 11, India has approximately 47 per cent of her population in the productive ages (20–60), whereas the United States has 55 per cent in these categories. Much of the dependency is wasted. Indian women are pregnant, give birth to and nurse millions of babies each year who die before they reach a productive age. Energy, food, and supplies are wasted on them. Thus the young-age dependency is a greater drain on the economy than the sheer proportion of dependents would indicate.

(6) The high mortality—high but not high enough to cancel the birth rate—is associated with a high morbidity. Disease, undernourishment, malnutrition, and injury lead to lethargy, absenteeism, and inefficiency. As a consequence the productivity per worker is low, independently of capital equipment.

(7) Finally, in a heavily peopled agricultural country suffering from the conditions mentioned, the state of public enlightenment is so low and the poverty is so great that political stability is hard to maintain. The citizenry is a prey to any rumor or illusion that will promise relief from the round of disaster and despair. *Personalismo,* intrigue, corruption, and revolts tend to thrive. Under disturbed political conditions, industrial enterprise cannot thrive. As yet both Pakistan and India have maintained the political stability that was present under the British, but there is a possibility that this stability will melt away as insuperable problems reappear and disillusionment follows independence.

No one should construe this discussion as arguing that population density makes industrialization in India impossible. At the beginning of its industrial expansion (1870) Japan, with approximately 35 million people, had a density of about 235 per square mile—higher than any other country ever had at the beginning of its industrial career. Today in the Indian subcontinent the average density has already surpassed the Japanese figure of 1870. However, in both countries large parts of the terrain are unsuitable for agriculture. Assuming Japan had, in 1870, the same proportion of arable land she

had in 1936 (15.8 per cent),[35] the density per square mile of arable land was then approximately 1,500, far higher than that in India today (about 602 per square mile of cultivated land in the surveyed area of British India in 1940).[36] So, in terms of average density the Indian subcontinent is slightly more crowded than Japan was at the beginning of her industrial career, but in terms of agricultural land it is less so.

This comparison shows the fallacy of relying on population density alone to prophesy the impossibility of industrial transition. But certain other considerations must be mentioned. First, the productivity of Japanese agriculture was probably higher in 1870 than is that of India today. Second, even though Japan industrialized despite her initial high density, the beginning figure plus the subsequent population growth (which by 1940 brought the number to 73 million in the home islands) doubtless caused the standard of living to rise much more slowly than it would otherwise have done. India now faces the same prospect. Her standard of living will not rise with industrialization as fast as if she had a smaller initial density and faced a less rapid population growth. Third, Japan became a colonial power and bolstered her economic life by colonial exploitation, whereas there is little chance that either India or Pakistan will be able to do this. Both India and Pakistan are far larger countries than was Japan at the inception of her industrial career. Although bigness has the advantage of possibly providing a huge internal market for industrial products with the resulting economies of mass production, it has several disadvantages ably discussed by George Rosen.[37] Any product sold by India on the world market in sufficient quantity to help measurably the Indian economy will represent a substantial portion of the world trade in that commodity. It will therefore affect seriously the other major countries exporting the same or similar products, and they may be expected to protect themselves by various measures, including possible price reductions. In trying to pay for imported food for a growing population, an area the size of India and Pakistan (which, remember, increased its population by 83 million in two decades) will have to purchase so much food from abroad that the prices of food products on the world market may rise sharply. Thus a region as large and populous as the Indian subcontinent may find its attempted industrialization jeopardized by declining prices of manufactured products on the one hand and increasing costs of agricultural products on the other. For this reason, if for no other, any program of industrialization must be sufficiently far-reaching to involve an agricultural revolution as well.

The case of Japan is thus not conclusive in showing that India can industrialize in spite of her demographic position. But neither is it conclusive in showing that she cannot. The writer has already stated his belief that India will eventually become industrialized. This is based on the fact that no new technological level that has emerged in human culture has failed to diffuse widely over the world, and of all the levels that have thus far emerged, industrialism has diffused more rapidly than any. In a sense industrial civilization is still in its infancy, and as it comes to characterize greater portions of the world, it will be capable of quicker transmission to the

[34] Ghosh, *op. cit.,* p. 40; Buchanan, *op. cit.,* p. 378.

[35] E. B. Schumpeter (ed.), *The Industrialization of Japan and Manchukuo, 1930–1940* (New York: Macmillan, 1940), p. 75.
[36] Computed from *Statistical Abstract for British India,* 1930–31 to 1939–40, pp. 550, 558.
[37] *The Long-Run Effects upon the United States of the Large-Scale Industrialization of India and China* (unpublished doctoral dissertation, Princeton University, 1949), Ch. 3.

rest. India is already partially industrialized; it is moving ahead now. Eventually it will go the whole way.

But the problem is not so much one of "eventually" as of "soon." Every decade that India tarries in its industrial development, there is danger that, through population growth, it will lower by that much the level of living the people will enjoy after the region has passed the economic transition. Viewed in this light the demographic and other handicaps are real. To overcome them, India and Pakistan will have to use an amount of ingenuity roughly equal to that heroically shown by the Japanese. The Indian Union will have to use her advantage in resources to compensate for other numerous disadvantages, and Pakistan, with far fewer resources, will have to use to the utmost her slight agricultural advantage.

Summary

The threads of this chapter can be drawn together by relating them to the problem of poverty in India. We have seen that the per capita income of the people is low, and that it has not risen much in the past 80 years. The simplest explanation is that the country has remained predominantly agricultural, for no predominantly agricultural country is wealthy in comparison to any industrial nation. But why has the Indian subcontinent remained so agricultural? It has done so in part because of the kind of social organization it had and in part because of its dominance by an alien industrial power. It long ago began the industrial transition, but it has dawdled and still remains in the early stages. In the meantime the population has grown until the rural density has made agriculture an insecure basis for further industrialization. Some of the old obstacles to industrialization continue in attenuated form, while population growth has become a frankenstein. As a result, although eventual industrialization seems inevitable, a quick achievement of the transition seems likely only with the strongest and most skillful policy to that end. At this point we leave the problem, only to come back to it in the next and final chapter, which deals with policy.

++

Population Policy and the Future

++

IF A "policy" is an official program for organized action, it involves two elements: an end to be attained and the means for attaining this end. A "population policy," then, must be one that conceives a possible but currently non-existent demographic condition either as an end in itself or as a necessary means to some further end. It implies that the actual demographic situation is not satisfactory, and that a more favorable one could be attained by pursuing the policy in question.

As for India and Pakistan, few observers regard the existing situation as satisfactory, because poverty is conjoined with a high density and with a fast rate of growth based on extreme fertility and a lower but still high mortality. Whether or not one desires a population policy, however, depends both on the goal that one has in mind and the supposed connection of the demographic situation with the goal.

POLICY GOALS

Since India and Pakistan are comparatively poor, the goal that receives most attention is greater real income. Yet each of these nations, just emerged from a struggle for its independence, is imbued with another aim, the attainment of national power. Although usually regarded as mutually beneficial, these two goals may occasionally conflict. Both the Soviet Union and Nazi Germany in peacetime, and all countries in wartime, have shown that an increase in industrial and military power does not necessarily require a corresponding rise in purchasing power. Rigid consumer controls, forced labor, enforced saving, and subsidy of armaments industries may all increase national power at the expense of living standards for the masses.

"A higher standard of living is, all else being equal, a positive factor in a country's military strength vis-a-vis another country. However, this holds true only within limits. It does not [necessarily] hold true . . . of an industrial establishment devoted principally to the satisfaction of certain strata of society, as for example, bureaucracy, skilled labor, and the army, at the expense of the living standards of the population as a whole. It does not follow as a matter of course that such a state will be militarily 'inefficient.' Such a maldistribution of national income can be perpetuated indefinitely without causing much distress to the ruling groups, and may be accepted stoically, perhaps even enthusiastically, by the masses. . . ." [1]

In 1949 Pakistan was spending, according to the *New York Times*, 67 per cent of her estimated annual revenues for national defense and was planning to spend still more, in spite of the fact that her need for economic development was very great.[2] India was spending a lesser but still high proportion of her budget (about 45 per cent) on military affairs.

Another end that may conflict with both national power and higher income is individualistic democracy. Such a social order, as the case of France shows, may impede concerted action both in the military and the economic spheres.

The truth is, of course, that no public policy can pursue one end to the exclusion of all others. Some sort of balance must be struck between different goals, and much of the dispute as to policy concerns not the exclusion but the relative emphasis that will be given the various major goals. What policies are favored with respect to population depends in part on which goals are stressed.

But with respect to population another complication arises. Because the customs and institutions governing demographic behavior are deeply rooted in the mores, such behavior is seldom regarded simply as a means to an ulterior end. For instance, the reduction of mortality is universally considered an end in itself; consequently an increase in mortality is not acceptable as a means to a given goal, even though in fact it could serve in this way. Only on occasion, as in the case of a war declaration, is an increase in mortality accepted as an inevitable but undesirable consequence of a given policy. Similarly, a high fertility or the customs that inevitably lead to a high fertility may be considered as an automatic good and therefore not a means to any other aim.[3] Such goals set a narrow limit to population policy. As yet it is not clear to what extent the governments and peoples of the Indian subcontinent will be willing to treat demographic matters as means.

For the sake of our present discussion, however, let us assume that the major though by no means exclusive goal is a higher per capita income, and that the question of population policy is thus oriented toward the problem of mitigating Indian and Pakistani poverty. This allows us to analyze different possibilities in the light of conditions in the region.

---

[1] From *The Balance of Tomorrow* by Robert Strausz-Hupé, p. 235. Copyright 1945 by Robert Strausz-Hupé. Courtesy of G. P. Putnam's Sons.

[2] "It is most unfortunate in the eyes of impartial observers that the new nation should believe it necessary to spend so much of her income for national defense. When one asks against whom Pakistan is preparing to defend her borders, the answer is not Afghanistan, but India. That such a situation should exist does not make sense to foreign observers, since both nations are in the British Commonwealth and their mutual interests inevitably will force them toward joint defense arrangements. . . . The amount is out of all proportion to what is in accordance with reasonably sound accounting principles." Robert Trumbull, "Pakistan Is Facing Economic Pitfall," *New York Times*, May 6, 1949, p. C-9. Other reports cite a slightly smaller military expenditure—around 50 per cent for Pakistan. See Daniel Thorner, "Prospects for Economic Development in Southern Asia," *Foreign Policy Reports*, Vol. 26 (April 15, 1950).

[3] For an interesting analysis of the emotional resistances to a rational consideration of population matters see J. C. Flugel, *Population, Psychology, and Peace* (London: Watts, 1947), Ch. 2.

IS A POPULATION POLICY NEEDED?

Assuming a willingness to regard demographic behavior from an instrumental point of view, one may still ask if it is necessary to do so. Do population density and rate of growth have anything to do with poverty? If not, a population policy is hardly necessary. Previous chapters have already dealt with the relation of population to poverty, but a few more words on it seem necessary from the policy standpoint.

Since per capita income depends upon resources, technology, and economic organization as well as upon population, the question is whether or not one needs to worry about population at all. Why not simply accept the expanding population as a basic fact and direct one's policies toward improving the economic situation? This point of view has been repeatedly maintained in India, though less often than in some other countries. Its basic difficulty, the reader will recall, is that population change and economic development are interlinked. Economic expansion cannot forever compensate for a constant increase of population, because economic potentialities are affected by population. The people of the Indian subcontinent have apparently already reached the point where density and rapid growth are impeding economic development. Therefore, it seems somewhat unrealistic to attempt to do something on the economic side and yet do nothing on the population side. To make the discussion more concrete, let us take a recent example of the exclusively economic point of view.

An Indian economist, Dr. Baljit Singh, published a book [4] showing that the Indian diet is 22 per cent below physical requirements. The shortage, he showed, is not due to an absolute lack of food potentialities, but rather to other conditions. A considerable amount of food is wasted in wedding feasts and other celebrations. A great amount is lost in the fields and in storage due to animal, bird, and insect pests. Still more is lost through poor distribution and class inequalities. Inefficiency also arises from the inflexible nature of Indian food habits, the people being divided into rice-eaters and bread-eaters, unwilling to use substitutes. Some food is exported. And Indian agriculture is so undercapitalized and badly organized that the land produces far less than it is capable of producing. For this reason Dr. Singh, although he acknowledged the massive population growth in India, rejected the idea of trying to stop this growth by direct measures. ". . . There is no call for the pessimism implied in the demand to consciously curtail and limit the country's population by a wide-spread adoption of the so-called neo-Malthusianism. . . . The right course would be to husband economic resources in agriculture, industry and trade with the aid of science and modern inventions to realize optimum conditions of living for the growing population." [5] He maintained that by cutting wastes, stepping up production, and changing eating habits, the food problem could be solved. To this end he would stop feasts, kill pests, ban food exports, make rationing universal, consolidate agricultural holdings, shift the Indian dietary in the direction of potatoes, and import foodstuffs.

Clearly, so far as the *existing* population is concerned, Dr. Singh is right. If his proposed measures were taken, this population could eat very well. But in the long run (and a not very extended "long run") his solution is no solution at all. As soon as the food situation improved, the population would grow even faster than it has been growing. Soon the time would be reached when the food supply would again be deficient, not because of waste or bad habits, but because of increased numbers. At that point no further remedial measures could be taken on the food side, except at greatly increased cost, because they would already have been taken. The kind of relief offered, therefore, would be at best a temporary relief, and it would result in a larger and more insoluble problem later on.[6]

Although the author admitted that some of his proposals, such as pig and poultry raising and potato-eating, are probably too radical for his countrymen, none of them is so radical as to cause the food supply to keep pace indefinitely with rapid population growth. Furthermore, he said nothing about the effect of a redundant population in preventing some of the very food reforms by which he proposed to alleviate the situation. The conclusion seems inevitable that something must be done on the population side if Indian poverty is to be reduced. As Notestein has said: "It is not the problem of doubling, or perhaps even tripling, the product of backward regions that staggers the imagination; it is the need for an indefinite continuation of such an expansion in order to keep up with an unending growth. The demographic problem is not that of putting an immediate end to growth, but of checking growth before the populations become unmanageably large—for example, before the present numbers are doubled." [7]

Dr. Singh's neglect of the population variable placed him in a queer position, a position that one might call totalitarian Puritanism. He would abolish feasts by law, require the eating of potatoes, regulate the milling of rice, make rationing universal, abolish moneylenders and restrict middlemen, encourage sexual abstinence, close the bazaars, and kill most of the wild animals. To what purpose? Not, in the long run, so that Indians could eat better, but rather so that there could be more of them. This strange view, that the purpose of life is to sweat and strain in order that the maximum number may be supported, is completely at variance with the goal of a higher standard of life.

In the end any attempt to compensate indefinitely on the economic side for population increase is bound to fail, because human beings live in a finite world. Atomic energy, use of the sun's rays, harnessing of the tides, all may enormously increase the food supply, but they cannot forever take care of an ever growing population. To see this one has only to put it in an extreme form. If the human species is 200,000 years old, and if from an initial pair it had increased at the modest rate of 1 per cent per annum, the number of human beings would now run to approximately 10^{1720}. If each of these individuals weighed on an average 100 pounds, their total weight would be 10^{1722} pounds. Since the weight of the entire earth is only about 10^{25} pounds, it can be seen that the human species would long since have reached the point where *all the substance of the earth would be in their bodies*. It would be idle to talk about feeding them, because there would be absolutely nothing to feed them with. But long before this point were

---

[4] *Population and Food Planning in India* (Bombay: Hind Kitabs, 1947), p. 101. Another example of a refusal to consider population policy is Bimal C. Ghose, *Planning for India* (Calcutta: Oxford University Press, 1945), pp. 81–86.

[5] Singh, *op. cit.*, pp. 127–28.

[6] The frequent habit which people have, when faced with the population question, of saying that agricultural possibilities are not yet exhausted needs serious and immediate challenge. Ghose, *op. cit.*, p. 84, says, for example, that "the crucial problem in this question of overpopulation is the potentialities of Indian agriculture." There are no conceivable potentialities of Indian agriculture that could indefinitely take care of a population expanding at its present rate. Why therefore is not population itself the "crucial question"?

[7] Frank W. Notestein, "Problems of Policy in Relation to Areas of Heavy Population Pressure" in *Demographic Studies of Selected Areas of Rapid Growth* (New York: Milbank Memorial Fund, 1944), p. 152.

reached the growth rate would have stopped, because the piling up of human beings in layers would have smothered those lying a few feet below the human surface. In long-run terms, then, it is preposterous to talk about economic measures being able "to take care of" population growth. The latter, if continued steadily, would in only a few centuries use up all the resources that even the wildest technological enthusiast might conceive.

It may be urged, however, that the problem of population growth in the Indian region is not a matter of 200,000 years or several centuries, but of here and now. This is exactly the point. In the Indian subcontinent, given world conditions as they are and not as a utopian might wish, the existing density and growth rate leave doubt that the standard of living can be raised if the growth is continued. Under ideal economic conditions, with the whole world focused on the problem of maintaining Indians and Pakistanis, a population of more than two billion could probably live in this area. But the populations in other parts of the world are growing too. The world economic system is not and cannot be focused on India alone. Even over a short period, say thirty to forty years, it is questionable that the Indian rate of population growth can be maintained and at the same time a significant rise in the standard of living be achieved. In any case it will take a herculean effort. Since the demographic situation is thus apparently handicapping economic progress, it seems foolish to forswear any demographic policy and simply try to step up economic production. This would be as foolish as simply forswearing any economic policy and trying to do it all on the population side. The task of raising the standard of living in India and Pakistan will be hard enough without making it even harder by a blind unwillingness to deal with relevant factors. Both countries desperately need a population policy. Of course, when economic plans are undertaken with a view to, and in a way susceptible of, affecting the rate of population growth, they become a part of population policy (as shown below). But pursued without reference to population or as a perpetual compensation for population change, purely economic measures do not constitute a population policy.

ALTERNATIVE POLICIES

To the extent that the Indian region has a population problem, it is obviously a problem of over- rather than underpopulation. The logical approach to improving the Indian living standard would therefore be to slow down the growth rate. Demographically speaking, there are only three ways of doing this—by raising the death rate, encouraging emigration, or lowering the birth rate.

MORTALITY AND POPULATION POLICY

Not only are health and longevity ends in themselves, but they are part of a high living standard. Therefore it would be self-contradictory to say that the death rate should be increased in order to improve the standard of living. It is precisely a high death rate, among other things, that a population policy is designed to avoid. If people get poorer and poorer they will inevitably begin dying off faster and faster until their number fails to grow. At that point the problem of population growth will have been solved, but not the problem of poverty. Countries like India and Pakistan face the question of (a) how to stop population growth before a rise in mortality automatically stops it, and (b) how to lower mortality

still more without defeating this aim by a corresponding rise in numbers.

Yet low mortality is not the only element in a high standard of living. There are other elements having little or nothing to do with longevity. Therefore, a *temporary* rise in mortality would not necessarily represent a regression in the *total* standard of living. Its effect would depend largely on the duration, causes, and circumstances of the rise. For instance, as mentioned before, a sudden epidemic that quickly killed 50 million people in India and Pakistan would greatly increase the average real income of the remaining population, especially if its incidence were highest in the non-productive ages. Such a sudden increase in deaths would only temporarily disrupt the economy, and it would in one stroke eliminate a huge portion of the surplus population. Conceivably it might open the way to social reforms that would otherwise be more difficult and thus help to break the vicious circle of poverty.

This is what Gandhi probably meant when, pushed into a corner by a journalist's insistence on the population problem, he said, "Then perhaps we need some good epidemics." [8] Gandhi laughed when he said this, because he recognized that a policy of promoting epidemics could not be seriously envisaged. It is important, however, to distinguish between the negative evaluation of high mortality on the one hand and its actual consequences on the other. Notestein seemingly confuses the two. "Policies designed to yield [a rising death rate] are occasionally suggested as a temporary expedient to obtain release from pressure, pending a decline in fertility. However . . . the suggestion is based on a misconception of the factors governing growth. A period of increasing mortality would in fact impede the developments essential to induce a decline in fertility. Rising mortality in the areas under consideration means in reality rising population pressure, and not a solution of that pressure." [9]

This and similar passages imply that a heightened death rate is rejected as policy because it always reduces economic efficiency. But increased mortality may not have a net adverse economic effect. Whether it does or not depends on how long it is sustained and what its causes are. If it is sustained or rises over a long period, it is a sign that conditions are getting worse. If it is sudden but temporary, as in the influenza epidemic of 1918 or the earlier famines, it may bring unusual prosperity through relief from excess numbers until the population builds up again to its former level. Even the immediately bad effects of a civil war may be compensated for by a subsequent period of lessened population pressure. This being true, the rejection of increased mortality as a policy does not rest on its economic effects. It rests on the fact that human life, except under extreme group necessity, is viewed as an end in itself and not as a means to an end. This reason explains why official domestic policy with reference to deaths is nearly always in one direction—limitation. [10]

The limitation of deaths by health measures, although not pursued as a population policy, nevertheless has demographic

[8] Louis Fischer, *A Week with Gandhi* (New York: Duell, 1942), p. 89.

[9] Notestein, *op. cit.*, pp. 148–49.

[10] Of course, increased mortality is used as a policy with respect to real or fancied enemies, as in war or genocide. But this simply illustrates its negative evaluation *within* the ethnocentric group. It is a peculiarity of human populations that their growth (apart from migration) must be gradual, but their shrinkage can be sudden. Every group therefore must guard against being wiped out by catastrophe or enemy action. It must place a very high evaluation on keeping alive. For a much fuller exposition of the role of mortality in human culture, see Kingsley Davis, *Human Society* (New York: Macmillan, 1949), Ch. 20.

effects. In so far as it succeeds while other demographic variables remain fixed, it tends to increase the population. Consequently, a policy of reducing deaths but not reducing births can lead to an unbalanced situation. The United States may seem to be an exception, because here public health has advanced rapidly, there has been no *official* policy favoring birth control, and yet the rate of population growth is declining. There has, however, been an unofficial or *private* policy of limiting offspring, and it is precisely this factor that makes possible the continued success of public health work. If it were not for birth control in the United States, the great reduction in mortality would soon produce such excessive population that the death rate would be forced up. Public health success would thus defeat itself.

We have seen that India's semi-colonial position has seemingly resulted in an unequal acquisition of Western culture. Scientific techniques of preventing death have been imported and accepted with enthusiasm. By a combination of these techniques and a minimum disturbance of the Indian way of life, the spectacular causes of death (famine, epidemic, war) have been considerably controlled. But because the texture of Indian life was left relatively unchanged, and because India's industrialization and urbanization were slow under the British, the birth rate has not changed. Hence the demographic situation has got out of balance, even compared to the imbalance usually produced by the industrial revolution. Instead of going through the growth phase of the population transition rather quickly (as recent industrial countries are doing) the Indian subcontinent seems, through the force of circumstances, to have reached this phase prematurely and to be lingering in it overlong. Having neither a public nor a private policy of birth limitation to accompany the improvement in mortality, public health work in India and Pakistan is now up against greater and greater obstacles. Unless birth control begins to occur on a wide scale or a miraculous outlet in emigration occurs, the death rate must ultimately rise again and public health policy fail.

EMIGRATION AS A POLICY

The Union of India would undoubtedly benefit if six million of her people, grouped in families, could emigrate each year for the next thirty years. Similarly Pakistan would benefit if about two million left from there each year. Such emigration would remove the annual population increase and would reduce the present population by a little. It would thus give the two countries a 30-year breathing spell in which to industrialize. But in all probability neither government would favor that much emigration; if either one did, it would insist that the emigrants be well provided for, that they retain their cultural, religious, and national allegiance, and that they not remove essential skills or much wealth from the country. Such conditions would effectively prevent mass emigration of the size mentioned.

Although neither government is likely to favor or carry through a huge emigration policy, there is a current of thought in Indian circles (though apparently not in Pakistan) which definitely favors large-scale emigration—or at least the *right* to make such an exodus. One prominent exponent of this view is Radhakamal Mukerjee, whose ideas are worth examining.

Like many Indians and a few Westerners,[11] Mukerjee feels that the European peoples have acquired the major share of the world without settling it as fully as the Asiatic peoples

could settle it. From most of these domains, particularly the comparatively "empty" ones (e.g. Australia, western North America, parts of Africa) Asiatics are excluded by the color bar. At the same time, by virtue of their economic and political ascendancy over Asiatic countries, the Western peoples have achieved a higher standard of living than the Oriental peoples. The net result is that comparatively small numbers command the greatest area and wealth of the world, while the bulk of humanity is compressed into a relatively small area and suffers from extreme poverty. The obvious solution of this inequality is to open up the empty spaces, especially the tropical areas, to mass emigration from India, China, Java, and Japan. Unless such equalization occurs fairly soon, war will be inevitable.

"The Pacific is, to a large degree, an Asiatic Ocean, and the islands, large or small, including the sub-continent of Australia and New Zealand, may be said to belong to a pan-Asiatic system. In this part of the globe, which is largely uninhabited, the doctrine of Asiatic *Lebensraum* cannot be dismissed offhand nor the doctrine of the White Man's reserve taken for granted. . . . The acid test of the Atlantic Charter will be the satisfactory settlement of the racial issue of the Indians in South Africa and the revision of the White Australian Policy. The British Empire, which comprises the largest empty spaces of the globe, has now evolved into a Commonwealth of Nations. . . . The essence of the commonwealth idea is utterly incompatible with the color-bar in respect of Oriental migration to the open lands. . . .

"In one part of [the Pacific basin] millions live on 3 to 5-acre holdings and go on subnutritional and subphysiological standards; while in another, tractors, sheep, and cattle luxuriate on the open spaces and men's artificially bolstered-up standard of living is protected by government tariffs, subsidies, and bans on foreign immigration. Such an economic and social contrast is entirely incompatible with world peace."[12]

Although these quotations concern the Pacific area, Mukerjee's vision goes beyond that region to huge territories in South America, North America, and Africa. And his conception of the "carrying capacity" of these areas is by no means modest. "Rice grown in the tropical rain forests of South America may support about 2,400,000,000, and again in the forests and savannas of Africa with a population capacity of another 2,300,000,000."[13] He seemingly accepts Matsuoka's belief that Oceania could support 600 to 800 million persons,[14] and he thinks that the Philippines could take 90 million settlers.[15] He apparently feels that hundreds of millions of Asiatics could settle in the United States and Canada. "Vast arid areas in North America which are now settled only by cattlemen can be brought under the plough and the harrow if Chinese and Indian immigration is encouraged on a reasonable scale."[16] Obviously, this view of the world's carrying capacity implies that the annual emigration of 7 million from the Indian subcontinent could be easily sustained for a very long time—a mere drop in the bucket in a world capable of supporting about ten billion people.

A pertinent question, however, is how *well* would these people be supported? What would be their level of living? On this matter Professor Mukerjee is optimistic, saying that

[11] e.g. Warren S. Thompson, *Population and Peace in the Pacific* (Chicago: University of Chicago Press, 1946).

[12] Radhakamal Mukerjee, *Races, Lands, and Food* (New York: Dryden Press, 1946), pp. 7, 39. See also p. 82. Similar ideas were expressed in an earlier work, *Migrant Asia* (Rome: Tipografia Failli, 1936).

[13] Mukerjee, *Races, Lands, and Food*, p. 28.

[14] *ibid.*, p. 68.

[15] *ibid.*, p. 66.

[16] *ibid.*, pp. 29–30.

Asiatic migrants acquire a higher standard of living in the new areas to which they go.[17] Since he cites no evidence, one may question the statement. Certainly for a time, until the usual Indian population pressure develops, the real income may rise. This is the case in Fiji. And if, as in South Africa, the Indians form a commercial and urban minority, they may well enjoy a higher income than Indians generally; and the same will be true if, as in Burma, they manage to dominate the local population. But if they take to peasant agriculture, growing rice under subsistence conditions, and living together by the tens of millions, it seems only a question of time until they will overflow the land and sink back to the usual Indian standard. Certainly a place like Mauritius does not reveal descendants of Indian immigrants having a high standard of life.

How low a living standard our author would deem satisfactory for the Indian migrants is shown by the following passages: "In the case of Asiatic subsistence farmers who would settle in the pioneer lands, substantial capital investments for planned railway development and supply of social services will not be required as a precondition of colonization. For the Asiatics, unreclaimed land is for potential subsistence and arable land is food. With European colonists land is . . . merely one factor in the complicated problem of keeping up a standard of living on the land so as not to sink . . . to the level of peasants.

"The European colonist . . . is a farmer. The Asiatic colonist is a peasant. He belongs to the land. No title is more accurately given.

"There is no doubt that the entry of Indian or Chinese agriculturalists as small-scale subsistence farmers depending upon family labor will speed up the change from the European estate-system to subsistence agriculture." [18]

To Western ears this does not sound like a high standard of living but more like what is now prevalent in teeming Asia. Indeed, one begins to see on what basis Professor Mukerjee assumes such huge carrying capacities for the various parts of the world. If Asiatics settled there at their customary standard of living, these areas could indeed hold additional hundreds of millions. But in this case what would be the purpose of settling them there? Professor Mukerjee never clearly states the goal he has in view, other than equalizing the world's wealth between Asiatics and non-Asiatics. One is entitled to suspect that there is an implicit imperialistic aim. He seemingly wants to see Asiatics spread over the world because he prefers Asiatics to Europeans. If there is no such implicit aim as this, then one may ask the same kind of question that was previously asked in connection with Baljit Singh's views: Why use more of the earth's surface merely to support more people at subsistence?

As the *sole* relief for population pressure, emigration is a palliative rather than a solution. To be effective it must not only remove people from the region but, by hastening social change, aid in reducing fertility. Even as a palliative, however, it is hardly suitable to India and Pakistan. Their populations are so large that outlets for their total natural increase would be impossible to find. The rest of the world would become filled with Indians and Pakistanis. Minority problems and conflicts would develop. Moreover, the proud governments of the two countries would not admit the failure implied by such mass emigration, nor would they tolerate an undignified status for the emigrants in new areas. A palliative emigration large

enough to carry off the natural increase of the Indian subcontinent therefore seems extremely unlikely as either a policy or a fact.

When used in conjunction with other measures, emigration may in some cases assist in alleviating the basic situation. If it can remove population in sufficient proportion, it may give an impetus to reform at home, to a rise in the standard of living, and to industrial expansion. It will have this effect still more if the emigrants are negatively selected with reference to skills, if the cost of emigration is borne by someone else than the sending country, and if, once abroad, the emigrants remit large capital funds to the people at home. However, in practice such ideal conditions of emigration are virtually never encountered. Seldom do emigrants leave in sufficient number to make a serious dent in the population.[19] They often have higher skills than the average among the population that remains.[20] And their remittances are usually too small to represent a powerful stimulant.[21] Furthermore, emigration is much more feasible as a help for overpopulation in small countries like Ireland, Puerto Rico, Norway, and Jamaica than it is in large ones like India, Pakistan, China, Java, Japan, and Italy.[22] Certainly there is little indication that the movement of Indians to overseas areas, as discussed in Chapter 14, had any effect in easing India's population problem. The volume of emigration was for many years quite substantial in absolute numbers, yet in relation to the total population of India it was insignificant. It brought very little financial return to India, nor did it stimulate much foreign trade. Conceivably future migration might have a different effect, but, for reasons given above, the volume of emigration will probably be insufficient to have much effect on the masses left at home. As either an exclusive or an ancillary solution, therefore, emigration would seem a weak reed for India and Pakistan to lean on in their population policy. This is realized by nearly all Indian students themselves.[23]

BIRTH CONTROL

The promotion of birth control as an official population policy has been rare in human society. Most governments have tolerated it as a private practice (in spite of restrictive laws), and some have favored it in one way or another.[24] But an official campaign to teach, encourage, and spread the use

---

[17] *ibid.*, p. 79.
[18] *ibid.*, pp. 31–32, 35.

[19] The major exception is the case of Ireland, where numbers have fallen from 6,548,000 in 1841 to 2,953,000 in 1946. See Wm. Forbes Adams, *Ireland and Irish Emigration to the New World* (New Haven: Yale University Press, 1932) and Conrad M. Arensberg and Solon T. Kimball, *Family and Community in Ireland* (Cambridge: Harvard University Press, 1940), Ch. 6.
[20] See, for example, C. Wright Mills, Clarence Senior, and Rose Kohn Goldsen, *The Puerto Rican Journey* (New York: Harper, 1950).
[21] For the economic effects of emigration on the home country see Julius Isaac, *Economics of Migration* (New York: Oxford University Press, 1947), Chs. 3–7.
[22] For the volume of emigration in relation to population pressure, see Kingsley Davis, "Puerto Rico's Population Problem: Research and Policy" in *International Approaches to Problems of Undeveloped Areas* (New York: Milbank Memorial Fund, 1948), pp. 60–65.
[23] Gyan Chand, *India's Teeming Millions* (London: Allen & Unwin, 1939), pp. 291–295; Lanka Sundaram, *India in World Politics* (Delhi: Sultan Chand, 1944), pp. 234–36. Two recent works on Indian population do not discuss emigration as a likely population policy: D. Ghosh, *Pressure of Population and Economic Efficiency in India* (New Delhi: Indian Council of World Affairs) and S. Chandrasekhar, *India's Population, Fact and Policy* (New York: John Day, 1946).
[24] On the growth of contraception as a private practice see A. M. Carr-Saunders, *World Population* (Oxford: Clarendon, 1936), Chs. 8, 9, 11, 17. Certain primitive societies, especially those living on small

of contraception among the general public has been conspicuous by its absence. Governmental policy with reference to births has thus generally been the opposite of the policy with respect to deaths. Public funds have been liberally expended for public health, including medical research, education, treatment, and prevention. These efforts have yielded large dividends in the saving of lives. But the idea of lowering birth rates by similar expenditures has met either with hostility or with indifference in official circles.

The reason for this extreme contrast in public policy is rather clear. Prior to the Industrial Revolution all human societies had a high death rate, as judged by modern standards. In order to survive they therefore had to have a high birth rate. Their high death rate, however, was primarily involuntary. All peoples wished to enjoy good health and a long life; their failure to achieve this end was due to an inability to control deaths beyond a certain point. In general those societies that managed to reduce deaths below the world average gained in their competition with other societies for survival. At the same time a high birth rate was also an advantage in survival. It follows that throughout human history the societies that managed to control their deaths reasonably well and to have at the same time a high birth rate were the ones that continued to exist. The others fell by the wayside. As a consequence, the customs and institutions of the surviving societies express both a high evaluation of health and longevity and a high evaluation of fertility.[25]

When the Industrial Revolution made it possible for Western societies to make extraordinary gains in the control of vital processes, the application of this control was naturally guided by the traditional values. Since death control was already an established value, the new science and technology were put to work for this purpose. But on the fertility side the established value was in the direction of more rather than fewer births; consequently the new science and technology were not directed toward lowering fertility but rather, if anything, toward raising it. In other words, the movement to limit fertility in unaccustomed ways met with strong opposition as being contrary to an established value, whereas attempts to preserve life, even in unaccustomed ways, met with approval.[26] It was only after the successful preservation of life had resulted in larger families, and these larger families had proved an embarrassment to the individual in the highly urbanized and mobile structure of modern society, that he sought a way around the full practice of his high fertility

mores. He left the customary evaluation intact, but tended to violate it to a certain degree in his own private behavior.[27] Thus the lag of birth control behind death control—a lag which gave a tremendous spurt to population growth—was implicit in the growing rationalism of modern life, which first attacked the negative value (death) and only later the positive value (high fertility).

Since the lag has almost invariably accompanied the industrial revolution, its presence now in India and Pakistan is not strange. And because it eventually disappears, it will someday disappear in India. The case of Japan indicates that it can happen in an Oriental as well as a Western country, given the industrial basis. But from a policy standpoint the crucial question is whether the change of attitude as regards fertility must wait upon the gradual unfoldment of the industrial revolution or whether it can be induced more quickly. Evidence in Chapter 10 gave no indication that the high fertility in India and Pakistan will soon be reduced by any automatic process. If fertility is to be substantially lowered soon, it will be only by some strong and unique policy.

Theoretically, there are two conceivable ways of reducing fertility quickly. One—the direct method—is to bring birth control immediately to the people. The other—the indirect method—is to industrialize at once and thus create overnight the conditions that will cause people voluntarily to limit their fertility. Although the two are not necessarily antithetical, we shall discuss them separately—the first method in the present section and the second method in the section that follows.

Those who zealously wish to start an all-out birth control campaign in India and Pakistan are impelled not only by humanitarian motives but also by a greater appreciation of technology than of sociology. Forgetting the cultural obstacles, they are tempted to believe that if a quick, easy, inexpensive, and semi-permanent contraceptive could be found which, like an injection or a pill, would produce harmless sterility for six months or more, it could be brought to the Indian and Pakistani population much as smallpox vaccination has been brought to them. From a purely physical point of view birth control is easier than death control. It involves the management of only one type of germ and only one kind of contagion, as against hundreds of types in health work. It involves only one period of life, as against all periods subject to disease; and only one type of medical specialist, as against dozens in fighting sickness. It involves relatively simple and easy principles that the layman can grasp, as against complicated ones that he cannot grasp in general medicine. The money it requires cannot compare to that required for other kinds of medical attention. Indeed so simple is the process of contraception, so clear the principle, that it is absurd to think that science, which has accomplished so much in so many more complex matters, cannot find suitable techniques for accomplishing this goal. In fact, we know that when there is a will to limit family size, even crude techniques will greatly reduce fertility.[28]

But the simplicity of the problem from the *physical* point of view merely underlines the fact that the obstacles are not primarily technological but sociological. An immediate birth control campaign in countries like India and Pakistan would leave social conditions the same. The peoples' old values and

---

islands, have deliberately limited their numbers for demographic reasons —see, e.g., Raymond Firth, *We, the Tikopia* (London: Allen & Unwin, 1936), pp. 414, 415—but in most cases the method used has not been contraception but abortion and infanticide. Contemporary examples of government sponsored birth control are the maintenance of health clinics with contraceptive services in Puerto Rico and in some states of the United States. See Christopher Tietze, "Human Fertility in Puerto Rico," *American Journal of Sociology*, Vol. 53 (July, 1947), pp. 34–40, and G. M. Cooper, "Four Years of Contraception as a Public Health Service in North Carolina," *American Journal of Public Health*, Vol. 31 (December, 1941), pp. 1248–52. In the early nineteenth century French public policy seemed to favor limitation of offspring, although at most other times France favored population growth—see D. V. Glass, *Population Policies and Movements* (Oxford: Clarendon, 1940), pp. 146–47.

[25] For a fuller analysis of the role of fertility in social organization, see Kingsley Davis, *Human Society, op. cit.,* Ch. 20.

[26] Of course, there are plenty of instances in which new methods of preventing death were rejected, but these were nearly all instances in which the people believed that the method did not in fact achieve the result claimed. They distrusted the motive of the physician or the efficacy of the remedy. Once they came to believe that the innovation really promoted health, they generally accepted it.

[27] cf. E. F. Penrose, *Population Theories and Their Application* (Stanford University: Food Research Institute, 1934), pp. 115–20.

[28] Regine K. Stix and Frank W. Notestein, *Controlled Fertility* (Baltimore: Williams & Wilkins, 1940), Chs. 1, 6, 15.

sentiments would remain intact, as would their old illiteracy and conservatism. They would therefore lack the incentive to adopt contraception even if it were handed to them. They would not have the habits and personal circumstances that go with family limitation. In other words, the very forces responsible for the current high fertility would make the adoption of such a policy difficult and unlikely, in spite of its demographic advantages.

This negative conclusion, however, should not be maintained dogmatically. It is true that as yet the technique of contraception has not been perfected. Very little medical and biological research has been expended on improving contraceptive technology, and the existing techniques, evolved in the middle class cultures of industrial countries, are not very well suited to the Indian and Pakistani populations.[29] A marked improvement in this sphere—a technological revolution in contraception—might considerably enhance the success of a birth control campaign. Furthermore, since no all-out government campaign using every available educational and propagandistic resource to bring contraception to an agricultural people has ever been tried, we do not know simply on *a priori* grounds that it will not work. We do know that in cases where birth control clinics have been set up in backward communities, the response has not been satisfactory.[30] We know that the cost of an adequate birth control service for a population of 420 million would be enormous and would strain the exchequers of both India and Pakistan. And finally—most relevant of all—we know that the people of the Indian subcontinent have already had some exposure to contraception and have thus given some evidence of what their reactions to a large-scale campaign might be.

In the cities and among the intellectual classes of the Indian subcontinent, modern contraception has been an imported culture trait for some time. Prior to the modern period, and still among the rural population, folk methods (mainly magical) were in use.[31] But the international birth control movement, epitomized by Margaret Sanger, did not fail to penetrate to India. In 1911 the President of the Calcutta Municipal Council, Babu Nilambara Mukerji, strongly advocated instruction in birth control. In 1928 the Madras Neo-Malthusian League was founded. Sometime prior to 1936 a Birth Control Information Centre was founded at Calicut, and clinics were in existence in Delhi, Nagpur, Lahore, Lucknow, Akola, Satara, Indore, Calcutta, Poona, Mysore City, and Bangalore. In 1934 the journal, *Marriage Hygiene,* was started in Bombay and fought valiantly for birth control in India. Mrs. How-Martyn, an English birth control advocate, toured India three different times, the first time in 1935. On her third tour, in 1936, she addressed the All-India Medical Conference, the Institute of Population Research at Lucknow, the Marriage Welfare and Child Guidance Association in Calcutta, the Bombay Women's Work Guild, the All-India Women's Conference at Ahmedabad, as well as many other groups and associations. She also broadcast from a Bombay radio station. On her first tour Mrs. How-Martyn was ap-

parently part of the entourage of Mrs. Sanger when the latter first visited India. Also accompanying Mrs. Sanger was a Miss Phillips. Mrs. Sanger and Miss Phillips travelled over 10,000 miles in the country, visited 18 cities and towns, and addressed 64 meetings. Mrs. Sanger saw scores of government and city officials, and met most of the leaders of Indian public opinion. Mrs. How-Martyn travelled about 6,500 miles and addressed 41 meetings. Altogether the three women also addressed 32 medical organizations. They could not meet all the requests to speak, so great was the interest in their work. At Mrs. Sanger's suggestion, films on contraception were made, and these were subsequently shown to hundreds of doctors in India. On her third visit Mrs. How-Martyn reported that the Bombay Mofussil Maternity Child Welfare and Health council had accepted the birth control programme as a part of its welfare work and had required most of its medical staff to get training in the technique of contraception.[32]

What has been the Indian reaction to birth control? Apparently it has been mixed. Among the intellectuals and in the newspapers, to judge by reports, interest has been great. In certain quarters there has been opposition, especially when it came to policy resolutions and to the initiation of action. As for the Indian masses, they have not been sufficiently exposed to the movement to express their reaction, but one observer, director of the Maternity and Child Welfare Bureau, New Delhi, believes that a common error among birth control enthusiasts in India is in believing "that the women of India are crying out for it."

"Nothing could be further from the truth. In a dumb sort of way thousands, even millions of women do desire release from perpetual child bearing and the misery which so often accompanies it, but that is not synonymous with a desire for birth control. Some of those who want to escape child bearing might be shocked or horrified at the thought of contraception. Moreover the vast majority know nothing whatever about it in the modern sense though they may have a nodding acquaintance with the Indian counterpart of the professional abortionist."[33] This of course is but one person's impression. There has not yet been enough depth-interviewing and public opinion analysis to speak with confidence about the thinking of Indian and Pakistani peasants on birth limitation. One modern study, cited in Chapter 10, throws some light on the matter.[34] It showed the following results:

	Attempted Contraception (per cent)	Desired, but no Attempt (per cent)	No Desire (per cent)	Total Women
Rural section	0.3	4.0	95.7	1,459
Lower middle class city area (Muslim)	3.3	0.3	96.4	1,499
Lower middle class city area (Hindu)	13.2	7.0	80.0	1,265
Upper class city area (Hindu)	38.0	1.0	60.3	1,452

[29] Ruth Young, "Some Aspects of Birth Control in India," *Marriage Hygiene,* First Series, Vol. 2 (August, 1935), p. 40. Gyan Chand, *India's Teeming Millions* (London: Allen & Unwin, 1939), pp. 343–45.

[30] See Gilbert W. Beebe, *Contraception and Fertility in the Southern Appalachians* (Baltimore: Williams & Wilkins, 1942). Also Gilbert W. Beebe and Jose S. Belaval, "Fertility and Contraception in Puerto Rico," *Puerto Rico Journal of Public Health and Tropical Medicine,* Vol. 18 (September, 1942), pp. 3–52.

[31] Norman E. Himes, *Medical History of Contraception* (Baltimore: Williams & Wilkins, 1936), pp. 131–32.

[32] C. V. Drysdale, "The Indian Population Problem," *Marriage Hygiene,* Second Series, Vol. 1 (November, 1947), p. 100; also news notes as follows: "Mrs. Margaret Sanger in India," *ibid.,* First Series, Vol. 2 (May, 1936), pp. 461–64; "Birth Control in India: Mrs. How-Martyn on Her Tour," *ibid.,* Vol. 3 (February, 1937), pp. 241–42.

My account is not meant to be definitive and the sources may not be completely accurate in detail; the aim is rather to suggest the kind of birth control work that has been undertaken.

[33] Young, *op. cit.,* p. 39.

[34] C. Chandra Sekar and Mukta Sen, "Enquiry into the Reproductive Patterns of Bengali Women," under the auspices of the Indian Research

These returns suggest there is a slight desire for birth control in rural areas, but that the higher classes in the large city are the ones who have definitely adopted the practice. As for the methods used, the following are instructive:

	Con- tinence	Safe Period	Coitus Inter- ruptus	Hus- band Uses	Wife Uses	Total Cases
Rural section	4	—	—	—	—	4
Lower middle class urban (Muslim)	11	22	10	24	4	50
Lower middle class urban (Hindu)	56	17	32	100	7	167
Upper middle class urban (Hindu)	130	237	235	251	37	551

Obviously a number of couples used more than one method. The most popular methods were those used by the husband (possibly condoms). Next in importance were "coitus interruptus" and "safe period." The frequent use of "continence" is of interest. "The enquiry also collected information as to what was considered the safe period. Although the data have not been tabulated, the feeling among the women seemed to be that the period of risk was either immediately preceding or succeeding the menstrual period—which is contrary to the current scientific view." Among the reasons given for family limitation, inability to look after more children was slightly in the lead, with woman's health a close second, and economic reasons a close third. The age group most disposed to practice contraception in the two Hindu areas of the city was the one 25–29. The main reason for not attempting family limitation although desiring it, was given as lack of knowledge of methods. The percentage of women having a "fatalistic" attitude toward family size was as follows for each group:

Rural section	86.8
Lower middle urban (Muslim)	91.0
Lower middle urban (Hindu)	46.3
Upper urban (Hindu)	30.1

In answer to the question, "How many living children should a woman have when she is 40?" the following answers were given:

	nil	1	2	3	4	5	6 & Over
Rural section	3	110	353	353	299	102	147
Lower middle urban (Muslim)	1	1	21	49	181	332	106
Lower middle urban (Hindu)	4	45	289	431	217	89	113
Upper urban (Hindu)	1	27	243	397	312	81	85

In each case the highest number (in italics) suggests a tendency toward a relatively small family, with the exception of the Muslim group. The rural women show the least concentration

on any one family size but, curiously, seem generally to prefer a size smaller than do the urban groups. More studies of this type will reveal, perhaps, that more Indian women use and desire family limitation than has generally been believed.

It has been said that Indian opinion is receptive to birth control education because neither Hinduism nor Mohammedanism has definite tenets against contraception and because the Indians are less prudish in matters of sex than are Europeans. But both of these allegations are offset by other factors. In the first place, there is in Hinduism a strong ascetic element that may be, and already has been turned against birth control. This is pointedly illustrated by Gandhi, who may be taken as the symbol of the modern Hindu ethos.

Gandhi readily admitted that there were too many people in India for the existing economy. Since he disliked industrialization, there were also too many for his ideal economy. One would think, then, that he might seize upon birth control as the way out, and this he did—but in a peculiar way. "There can be no two opinions about the necessity of birth control. But the only method handed down from ages past is self-control or Brahmacharya. It is an infallible sovereign remedy doing good to those who practice it. The union is meant not for pleasure but for bringing forth progeny. And union is criminal when the desire for progeny is absent." [35] Thus for Gandhi, reflecting Hindu asceticism, sexual pleasure is inherently sinful. It is justified only when it serves a higher purpose—reproduction. It follows that the only permissible form of birth control is abstinence, which implies self-control (i.e. the foregoing of bodily pleasure) and is therefore good. Gandhi's position is the same as that of the Roman Catholic Church, except that he did not get into the complexities of intermittent abstinence and the so-called safe period.

That Gandhi's views are congenial to the Indian people need hardly be said. Up to now birth control has been debated mainly among the Westernized intellectuals. If it is carried to the more orthodox by encompassing a larger circle, it will certainly run the risk of attack from an ascetic point of view. It may be felt that contraception allows people to have sexual pleasure without risking the penalty of having children,[36] that birth control is a materialistic Western innovation, and that it promotes immorality. However, as yet there has been no crystallization of opposition. The main opposition has come from the Roman Catholic Church in India. Certain Hindu scholars, such as Sir S. Radhakrishnan, favor birth control as a help in alleviating India's poverty.

The statement that Indians are less prudish than Westerners in matters of sex is, like the supposed absence of religious attitudes on birth control, open to question. In certain ways the Indians may be less prudish, but in other ways (some bearing directly on birth control) they are not. The seclusion of women (*purdah*) is a Mohammedan institution borrowed by the Hindus; it implies an extreme hypersensitivity in matters pertaining to sex. This hypersensitivity manifests itself in the resistance to having male doctors treat female patients,[37] in the unwillingness of women to enter the medical and nursing professions, and in the hesitancy of female doctors to discuss sexual matters in the presence of male doctors.

Fund Association and the All India Institute of Hygiene and Public Health. The study is not yet published, but some of the tentative results were kindly shown to the writer. The urban groups were all in Calcutta, the rural group about 20 miles from the city.

[35] Quoted by Chand, *op. cit.*, pp. 328–29, taken from *Young India*, April 26, 1928.

[36] This idea of children as a penalty for pleasure has been criticized by Chand, *op. cit.*, pp. 331–37. Chand also speaks of the utter impracticability of absolute abstinence.

[37] This feeling seems to be present to some degree in any peasant society, but it is especially strong in India and Pakistan.

In 1937, after a tour of South India in behalf of birth control, one M.D. summed up his conclusion on the medical aspects as follows:

"My impressions of the tour are very uncomplimentary to the medical profession. No contraceptive advice whatever is being given except in some of the Mission Hospitals, the male doctors are indifferent or timid to take up the work, asserting that Indian women will not practise birth control methods and that there is no demand for the same. The lady doctors believe just the contrary but are equally timid to seek the required knowledge and are often domineered by anti-birth control superiors. It was distressing to hear from a reliable source that in one station, the lady doctors to whom women were referred for advice told them that birth control methods were harmful, apparently just to cover their ignorance of the subject!

"The doctor to tour the country can be male or female, but I think males would be better. . . . Over 95 per cent of the doctors in this country are males and it will be difficult to get lady doctors in India who would agree to demonstrate and talk on birth control methods to the men doctors and take up the matter with administrative bodies and officials. . . . In a few stations I visited, the lady doctors would not attend the demonstrations *along with* the male doctors." [38]

Opposition to birth control in India and Pakistan may therefore be expected on both religious and moral grounds. To date, this opposition (except for the Catholic community) is not highly organized, but neither are the proponents of birth control. As the birth control movement gains strength and vociferousness, the opposition will doubtless crystallize and gain strength as well. This capacity of a movement to evoke opposition is inevitable. It does not mean that the movement itself will fail. The very controversy itself will tend to spread contraceptive knowledge. In no country of the world has religious opposition been able to stop the diffusion of birth control, any more than it has been able to stop the use of tobacco or alcohol. The practice will eventually come to India in spite of opposition. But as for the government taking the initiative and speeding the diffusion by a vigorous birth control policy, the probability seems remote. "In no country of the world have the politicians openly associated themselves with birth control." [39] But it is precisely this sort of government policy that would be necessary if reliance were placed on birth control alone as the means of quickly reducing the rate of population growth. If it were tried and if it succeeded, it would be (assuming normal economic development) a powerful factor in the rise of the Indian standard of living. But it is safer to predict that it will not be tried than to say that it would not succeed. The speed of birth control diffusion on the Indian subcontinent will probably depend on the enthusiasm and skill that its proponents, in their private capacity, bring to the problem rather than upon official governmental action.

RAPID INDUSTRIALIZATION

Already in this chapter industrialization has been considered as an alternative to any population policy at all. The conclusion was reached that no conceivable economic development could support indefinitely a steadily growing population. Now we are considering rapid industrialization as a population policy. As such it is really a means of reducing fertility, not directly through officially diffusing contraceptive material and information, but indirectly through changing the conditions of life and thus forcing people in their private capacity to seek the means of family limitation. As a population policy, industrialization obviously means something more than merely allowing social evolution to take its course; if this were all that were implied, it would represent no policy at all. It implies rather an attempt to speed industrialization beyond what it would otherwise be and to emphasize in the process those elements of modernization that will most likely depress fertility—such as education, urbanization, geographical and class mobility, multi-family dwellings, commercial recreation, and conspicuous consumption. An industrial revolution is so enormous, however, and is instrumental to so many ends, that its feasibility and character are likely to be determined (as is true of birth control too) on grounds other than population alone. The benefits of industrialization are, in fact, among the things *for which* we wish to reduce the rate of population growth. In other words, rapid industrialization has the advantage that it will probably be adopted as an official policy regardless of its connection with population. The only question is whether or not the elements associated most closely with declining fertility will be emphasized. Some of them, such as education, almost certainly will be. But others, such as commercial recreation and class mobility, which are contrary to rural Indian traditions, will probably not be emphasized but will simply arise automatically.

The main disadvantages of quick industrialization as compared to a direct birth control policy (pretending for the moment that one is a substitute for the other) are twofold: first, it is more difficult, and second it is slower. Although economic change seems more acceptable than birth control measures because it interferes less with the mores, the truth is that any policy that rapidly industrialized Pakistan and India would be a far greater shock to the basic social institutions than would any policy that attacked fertility directly. Fast industrialization would sweep both the *ryot* and the *zamindar* from their moorings, transforming them into workers in a collectivized, mechanized agriculture utterly foreign to their habits. The Indian and Pakistani peasants would not undergo this transformation willingly; resisting, they would have to be forced to it. Judged by events in Russia, the cost of this transformation and of the resistance to it would be tremendous in loss of human lives, loss of livestock, and loss of food production. At the same time the existing industrial and commercial system of India and Pakistan would have to be completely overhauled and subjected to strong controls. Production schedules, prices, profits, wages, supply of raw materials, location of industries, flow of capital, and mobility of labor—all would have to be minutely planned and rigidly administered by a central government. [40] The powerful businessmen of the two countries would not necessarily submit willingly to this extreme governmental control. And yet how otherwise could a retarded agricultural region be industrialized rapidly? The Russian example shows that fast industrialization is possible, but it also shows that the cost is heavy. Since the present generation is reared in the customs and institutions that now exist, since it has vested interests (real or fancied) in things as they are, it will not voluntarily approve and bear the costs of a sudden industrial revolution. Its resistance consequently adds to the inherent costs of the economic transformation. Furthermore, its resistance (i.e. the re-

[38] A. P. Pillay, "A Birth Control Educative Tour," *Marriage Hygiene,* First Series, Vol. 4 (August, 1937), p. 49.
[39] Chand, *op. cit.,* p. 343.

[40] Bimal C. Ghose, *Planning for India, op. cit.,* especially pp. 63, 67, 72.

sistance of the people) means that to succeed, the government must become a dictatorship. Many people both outside and inside of the Indian area would rather see a slower pace of industrialization than a dictatorship established.

When, therefore, it is said that rapid industrialization is an easier policy to follow than a policy of direct birth control promotion, all that is meant is that the *statement of the policy* is easier. It cannot mean that the *execution* of the policy is easier. The people will willingly admit that industrial advances are needed; they will not so readily admit that fertility curbs are needed. In the execution of the policy, however, a program of forced industrialization would violate far more taboos and arouse more resistance than would the dissemination of birth control education and propaganda. This fact suggests that a good bit of the talk about rapid industrialization in India and Pakistan is just talk. It sounds good and elicits a favorable reaction. But whether enough official action will be taken to speed the industrial process beyond what its pace would be under ordinary business control is a moot question. If the process is not speeded up, then any announced policy of acceleration will turn out to be a failure.

The economic planners of India, e.g. those who made the famous Bombay plan which calls for a tripling of the national income and a doubling of the per capita income in 15 years, have not faced the true costs.[41] To put down in black and white all the changes, conflicts, privations, and issues involved in rapid industrialization would immediately inform people that not only an economic but a political, social, and religious revolution is in prospect. Except by a handful of Communists, the proposals would be rejected out of hand. So the planners, in order to have their plans even considered, must perforce play down the realistic means and emphasize the goal. Since the goal—a higher standard of living by means of industrial growth—is quite acceptable, it draws popular support for the plan. But when the means become known in detail, they will meet stiff opposition. In Russia the peasantry as a whole, the majority of the population, admittedly opposed collectivization.[42] Only a dictatorship could have forced through such a program.

This does not mean that the costs of forced industrialization will exceed the ultimate gains, but simply that the living generation, reared in the past, is the one that contemplates the proposals. It is this generation that will bear the greatest burdens and reap the fewest benefits. It is this generation that carries an institutional structure in many ways inimical to industrialization. In order for this generation to be willingly seduced, the extent to which the plans call for sacrifice, for social and religious change, and for subjection to political authority must be minimized. In the same way, of course, the advocates of birth control can talk about the advantages of proper child spacing, but straightway the means (contraception) becomes obvious and opposition is aroused.

In addition to its difficulty of execution, a second disadvantage of forced industrialization as a population policy is

its slowness. Even granting that industrialization can be greatly accelerated, the time required would nevertheless permit a huge interim growth in numbers. The death rate would for some time continue to fall faster than the birth rate.[43] If the achievement of a Western-type demographic balance were to take 80 years, the interim population growth would be enormous. The same rate of increase as Europe experienced from 1850 to 1933 (a rate smaller than that of India during the last 20 years) would give India and Pakistan in the year 2024 a combined population of 750 million and an average density of 482 per square mile. How fast the modernization process can be speeded up depends on the role of India and Pakistan in the world economy, on the ruthlessness with which industrialization is pushed, and on the absence of chronic internal strife; but it seems hard to believe that it can be done rapidly enough to avoid an enormous growth. Should industrialization be relied on as the sole means of reducing fertility, it could not be successful in time to achieve a marked rise in the standard of living. One can argue, of course, that if India and Pakistan become industrialized, this will automatically raise the standard of living; but it is equally true that the rise will be far below what it would have been had the fertility been lowered at an earlier time. For this reason it seems unwise to rely on rapid industrialization as a substitute for a strong birth control policy, just as it would be unwise to do the opposite.

IDEAL POLICY VS. PROBABLE EVENTS

The conclusion emerges that ideally, in order to maximize real income, the population policy of Pakistan and India would include at least three measures—a program of strategic emigration, a sustained and vigorous birth control campaign, and a scheme for rapid industrialization—because no one of these complex measures can substitute for the others or promise the maximum effect if pursued alone. Emigration would be encouraged with a view to losing as little as possible in terms of skills and capital and gaining as much as possible in terms of remittances. Birth control would be diffused with the help of films, radio, ambulatory clinics, and free services and materials; aided by research on both the techniques of contraception and the methods of mass persuasion; and linked clearly to the public health and child welfare movements. Industrialization would be pushed by central planning and control, by forced capital formation (through rationing and taxation), by intensive training programs, by sweeping agricultural reforms, and by subsidies to heavy industry. The skillful and vigorous pursuit of such a broad policy would probably shorten the rapid growth phase that normally accompanies the industrial revolution. If so, it would mean that control had been deliberately extended to fertility as well as to mortality, that the demographic transition had been achieved quickly by planning. It would mean, as far as demographic factors go, a higher standard of living and a more abundant life for future generations.

But there is little likelihood that such a comprehensive population policy will be adopted. The two governments must pursue other goals in addition to a high standard of living. They are limited as to the means they may use for reaching

---

[41] Ghose, *op. cit.*, p. 63, says: "The essential weakness of the Bombay Plan is the yawning gap between its far-reaching objectives and the means and machinery proposed to reach them." P. A. Wadia and K. T. Merchant, *Our Economic Problem* (Bombay: New Book, 1946), p. 561, maintain that the Bombay Plan fails to recognize that democracy and economic planning are irreconcilable under capitalism. The authors therefore praise the "People's Plan" of the Radical Democratic Party (by M. N. Roy) as being socialistic but claim that it too is too optimistic with reference to means.

[42] Ghose, *op. cit.*, pp. 69–73.

[43] It must be recalled that some elements of modernization—e.g. the remarriage of widows, improvement of maternal health, reduction of sterility—will favor high fertility in India and Pakistan.

any particular goal. They find that family behavior is too intertwined with religion and the mores to be manipulated in a purely instrumental way.

The one measure that has the best chance of being pushed is rapid industrialization, but not for demographic reasons. Both Pakistan and the Indian Union will probably try hard to improve their economies without encouraging lower fertility or greater emigration. They will doubtless attempt some reforms on the agricultural side but will place their greatest emphasis on industrial development. It seems likely that they will eventually succeed in industrializing, but because the obstacles are so great (including excessive population) they may not succeed until they have established totalitarian regimes, acquired almost completely planned economies, and experienced sharp temporary rises in mortality. On the other hand they may not succeed in increasing the pace at all beyond what ordinary business evolution would yield. After the economic revolution has been accomplished, the conditions of life for the individual should, as in Europe, North America, Australia, and Japan, be of such a type as to give a powerful personal incentive for limiting births. The birth rate should then drop and a modern demographic balance be achieved. The population will probably be much larger then than it would have been if a full-scale population policy had been carried out in the first place. How great the number will actually be is difficult to say, but it can hardly be double the present figure. How long the process of modernization will take is also hard to say, but it should not take more than a century.

Thus the effect of a full population policy would be not to prevent perpetual population growth (such growth is impossible anyway) but to balance the demographic books at an earlier time. In this way the total number to be cared for would be less and the living standard higher. We have seen that not all industrial peoples enjoy the same real income. The contrast between Japan and Europe, between Europe and America, suggests that the real income in industrial countries is strongly influenced by the point at which demographic growth is stabil-

ized with reference to resources. Even if the whole world becomes industrial, the countries with excessive numbers will still be penalized. Therefore, if India and Pakistan should achieve and hasten industrialization while controlling their population, the resulting level of living would be substantially higher than otherwise.

In short, if we look candidly at the probable future, we must admit that the demographic situation in Pakistan and India will get worse before it gets better. Also, it will get better later than it would if the two governments successfully carried through a comprehensive population policy. The main stumbling block to attempting such a comprehensive policy is birth control; yet if the benefits of civilization are to come increasingly to the people of this region, the birth rate must be brought down. The current discrepancy between the birth and the death rate, which is causing the rapid population growth, is in a sense artificial. The demographic account will have to be balanced sometime. Over any extended period it is impossible to control deaths and not control births. Eventually the birth rate must drop or the death rate rise. Strife, famine, and epidemic disease are an ever-present threat in India, capable of sending the mortality rate higher than ever before, precisely because the population is larger. In order to avoid a catastrophic rise in mortality, the birth rate must eventually fall. With a high density of population in relation to developed resources and with the virtual impossibility of solving the problem quickly by sheer economic measures or by emigration, the two countries must necessarily incorporate planned parenthood as an essential element in any program that actually raises the standard of living to the maximum possible and gives them the greatest national strength. The fact that they will probably not do this does not detract from its advisability. Their unwillingness to do it will not necessarily result in perpetual poverty for their citizens or in absolute catastrophes. But it will result in greater poverty than would otherwise be the case and in greater danger of catastrophes. It is exactly this sort of comparative loss that all policy, including population policy, is designed to avoid.

APPENDICES

Appendices

APPENDIX A

ESTIMATING THE POPULATION OF INDIA DURING THE PERIOD OF CENSUS TAKING

GIVEN seven decennial censuses of India, the first three with an officially stated improvement in method and the first five with a successive increase in territory covered, our problem is to estimate the actual population of India's whole area at each census date. This will give us a set of figures that are comparable as to territory and method, and hence a more accurate notion of India's population history.

The first step is to compute the percentage increase in the population each decade. The only adjustment necessary to accomplish this is to eliminate from the census at the end of each decade any people who are attributable either to improvement of technique or the addition of territory during that decade. This makes the census at the beginning of the decade comparable with the census at the end of the decade, and the resulting increase is a true measure of population growth. The decade increases, in percentage terms, are given in the text.

The next step is more complicated. Whereas the first step gives us the approximate percentage increase in each decade, it does not give us the actual population of India, because the territory covered in one decade may be quite different from that covered in another decade. Consequently, it is necessary to estimate the actual population of the whole Indian territory at each census date. The decade growth rates computed in Step No. 1 can be used for this purpose. It is possible, in short, to follow each increment of population due to new territory or method back to the number of people at each census that must have given rise to it. If 1.89 million were added in 1911, then we assume this 1.89 million are the result of the rate of population growth we found in Step 1 for the 1901–11 decade. This means that they were only 1.68 million in 1901, and this number we add to the 1901 census. Applying the 1891–1901 rate of growth to this same group, we find they were 1.67 million in 1891, and this number we add to the 1891 census; and so on back. By doing this for each increment of people due to new territory, we add six groups to the 1871 census, five to the 1881 census, four to the 1891 census, and so on until we add only one for the 1921 census.

The computations are given in Table 87. At the bottom of the table the estimated increments are gathered together to make the total number added to each census.

This method really amounts to assuming that all territory not covered by a given census but covered by a subsequent one grew in population during any decade at the same rate as the territory actually covered by the census at the beginning of

TABLE 87

Computation of Population Added by New Territory and Better Methods, India and Burma, 1871–1931

Date of Later Census	Population Due to New Methods and Territory [1] (1)	Rest at End of Decade as Per Cent of That at Start of Decade (2)	Estimated Number not Counted (3)	Date at Beginning of Decade
1881	45,139,081	1.013	44,559,803	1871
1891	9,213,902	1.095	8,414,522	1881
			8,306,537	1871
1901	2,872,077	1.015	2,829,633	1891
			2,584,140	1881
			2,550,977	1871
1911	1,793,365	1.065	1,683,911	1901
			1,659,026	1891
			1,515,092	1881
			1,495,649	1871
1921	86,633	1.012	85,606	1911
			80,381	1901
			79,193	1891
			72,322	1881
			71,394	1871
1931	35,058	1.106	31,698	1921
			31,322	1911
			29,410	1901
			28,975	1891
			26,461	1881
			26,121	1871

TOTAL THAT MUST BE ADDED			
1872	57,010,481	1901	1,793,702
1881	12,612,537	1911	116,928
1891	4,596,827	1921	31,698

[1] *Census of India*, 1921, Vol. 1, Part 1, p. 7; and 1931, Vol. 1, Part 1, p. 5. Improvement in methods was supposedly made only in the 1881, 1891, and 1901 censuses, the numbers allegedly added by this factor being 11,823,251, 3,405,791, and 192,657 respectively.

that decade. It is not a strictly true assumption, but it seems to be the best that can be made.

The computations necessarily include Burma, because Burma was covered in every census through 1931 and because it was the scene of territorial additions. Our third step therefore requires that Burma be taken out, but a difficulty is created by the fact that territorial changes in Burma, often great, are not precisely known because of the indefiniteness of her boundaries in early years. As a consequence, the estimates of her population, as of the territory of 1931, are hazardous. Our method was first to subtract the foreign born population from the census returns, since nearly all these were Indian— i.e. Hindus and Muslims.[1] Then the rest of the population in 1931 was assumed to have grown during the three previous decades at the same rate as the Buddhists (i.e. natives) in three districts having no territorial change.[2] This automatically gave population estimates for 1921, 1911, and 1901 on the basis of the 1931 territory. But three earlier dates were still unaccounted for. We simply assumed that the native population increased 10 per cent in each of the three decades from

[1] Census returns for Burma from *Census of India,* 1921, Vol. 1, Part 2, p. 6; 1931, Vol. 1, Part 2, p. 6; and *Population Index,* Vol. 8 (July, 1942), p. 236. Foreign born from the Burma volume of the census reports in each year of the Indian census.
[2] *Census of India,* 1931, Vol. 11 (Burma), Part 1, p. 13.

1871 to 1901—not a wild assumption in view of Burma's freedom from the famines and epidemics that afflicted India. Finally, we added the foreign born back again to our estimated figures for natives, to get a total population for Burma for the census years from 1871 through 1921. When the 1931 and 1941 census figures were added to the list, the following history of population in Burma was the result:

1872	8,007,000
1881	9,129,000
1891	9,778,000
1901	10,866,000
1911	12,288,000
1921	13,295,000
1931	14,667,000
1941	16,824,000

These figures could now be subtracted from the results obtained in Table 87 for India-plus-Burma, leaving the remainders as presented in Table 7 of the text in Chapter 4.

Even if the rough estimates are not exact with reference to Burma, the error will not greatly affect the much larger estimates for India. We are not acquainted with any other estimates for the previous populations of Burma on the basis of the 1931 territory.

APPENDIX B

ESTIMATING THE MORTALITY FROM THE INFLUENZA EPIDEMIC OF 1918–19

THE influenza epidemic took a tremendous toll of life in India. The usual estimates, however, seem to underestimate the influence of the disease, because they are based on the inadequate registration statistics. Sir John Megaw, a former Commissioner of Health, says that the epidemic killed about 10 million people.[1] A report of the Commissioner for 1936 gives the number at between 12 and 14 millions.[2] It can be shown that the mortality was, in all probability, substantially higher than this.

Our method is to use the *corrected* death rates—corrected by methods described in Chapter 5—to get an estimate of the amount by which the 1918–19 death rate deviates from average. The "average" or "normal" death rate is taken to be that prevailing in the years 1913–17 and 1920–24. The population to which the death rate applies is built up from the 1911 census figure by the corrected vital statistics. The difference between the expected and the actual deaths during 1918–19, determined by the corrected rates, is taken to be the measure of the influenza mortality. The following are the calculations:

1918

Reported Rates
(1) 1913–17, 1920–24 average = 28.94
(2) 1918 = 63.06
(3) Deviation: (2) ÷ (1) = 218%

Corrected Rates
(4) 1913–17, 1920–24 average = 40.87
(5) 1918: (3) × (4) = 89.10

Total Loss of Life
(6) Est. Pop. (322 million) × .0891 = 28,690,200 (actual)

(7) Est. Pop. × .04087 = 13,160,140 (expected)

(8) Actual—Estimated: (6)—(7) = 15,530,060 (est. loss)

(9) 15,530,060 ÷ 322 million = 4.8% (per cent loss)

1919

Reported Rates
(10) 1919 = 35.83
(11) Deviation: (10) ÷ (1) = 124%

Corrected Rates
(12) 1919: (11) × (4) = 50.68

Total Loss of Life
(13) Est. Pop. (309 million) × .05068 = 15,660,120 (actual)

(14) Est. Pop. × .04087 = 12,628,830 (expected)

(15) Actual—Estimated: (13)—(14) = 3,031,290 (loss)

(16) 3,031,290 ÷ 309 million = 0.98% (per cent loss)

1918 + 1919

Grand Total Loss of Life Due to Influenza Epidemic
(17) 15.5 million + 3.0 million = 18.5 million.

It thus appears that the total loss was in the neighborhood of 20 million lives, or about double the usual estimates.

CRITICISM OF METHOD

It might seem that the method is most open to question because of the method of correcting the death rates. The correction is made by assuming that the ratio between the total estimated deaths for the decade and the total registered deaths for the same decade holds for each single year in the decade. Thus the influenza mortality is incorporated into the corrections throughout the whole decade. But, logically considered, this seems to offer no obstacle, because the basis for calculating the influence of the epidemic still remains the *differential* between the epidemic years and the surrounding years. All that the correction does is step up the absolute, not the proportional, size of this differential.

The disruption to the registration services during an epidemic period may in fact make unrealistic the assumption that the differential in reported rates measures the true proportional differential. If, for example, one assumes that the efficiency of death registration decreased 20 per cent during the two epidemic years, the total number of deaths attributable to the epidemic would be 31 rather than 19 million. Our estimate would therefore appear to be conservative rather than radical.

A CHECK ON THE METHOD

The procedure described above can be checked by a rough technique that does not rely on vital statistics at all but depends entirely on the censuses. The average per cent growth of the population of India in 1901–10 and 1921–30 can be contrasted with that in 1911–20. The difference may be assumed to represent the influence of the influenza epidemic, because the 1911–20 decade as a whole had no other outstanding catastrophe. We find that the average growth of the population during the 1901–10 and 1921–30 decades was 8.35 per cent per decade. Applying this to the 1911 population, we get an expected growth of 25.3 million during the 1911–20 decade. Actually the population grew by only 2.7 million. The difference is 22.6, which, if attributed to influenza, gives us an estimate that is higher than the figure of 19 million deaths arrived at above. All told, we feel that an estimate of around 20 million is as satisfactory as any that can be made with existing data.

[1] "Public Health. The Great Diseases of India," in E. A. H. Blunt (ed.), *Social Service in India* (London: His Majesty's Stationery Office, 1939), p. 230.

[2] Public Health Commissioner with the Government of India, *Annual Report,* 1936 (Delhi: Manager of Publications, 1938), p. 18.

TWO UNOFFICIAL INDIAN LIFE TABLES

IN WHAT follows, the methods and results of constructing two unofficial life tables for India, one covering the decade 1911–21 and the other the decade 1931–41, are described. Although mostly similar problems were encountered in both tables, the two will be considered separately.

THE 1911–21 LIFE TABLE

The 1911–21 Life Table was constructed by using the population of the whole of India, as reported by the censuses at the beginning and end of the decade. No adjustment was necessary for changes of territory, because these were insignificant. More significant was emigration from India during this period. Still, because of World War I and the increasing tendency of Indians abroad to return home, our estimate of the total net emigration from India during the decade comes to less than a million. (See Chapter 13.) This is small enough to be ignored. We could therefore simply take the size of the population at the beginning and end of the decade as given. The only modification came from the necessity of smoothing the age distribution.

AGE SMOOTHING

Since we intended to construct the table by differencing two consecutive censuses, the age distributions had to be smoothed. As the age distributions stood, the same cohort that was deficiently reported at the first census could be overreported at the second census ten years later, or vice versa. This would yield, for the given cohort, a heavy underestimation or overestimation of the number of deaths.[1] To avoid this, we had to improve the age distributions as our first step. Before a smoothing formula could be applied, certain rough rectifications had to be made. One of these concerned the underenumeration of children aged 0–4, another the underenumeration of young persons aged 15–25, and a third the allocation of persons over 70 to specific ages.

Children 0–4 are obviously underenumerated in the Indian census. In order to increase their number, we took the registered births during each of the five years preceding the census, increased these births on the basis of the figure for underregistration obtained by the reverse survival method for the entire decade, and then, using survival rates from an appropriate life table, graduated each cohort until the census year was reached. Adding the estimated number of children who should have been enumerated, we obtained a new figure for the group age 0–4 in the census. The estimate was not high enough, because the correction of registered births is simply based on the entire age-group 0–9 instead of 0–4. Our estimate really reflects the difference between enumeration at ages 0–4 and at ages 5–9, the latter being used to correct the former. Nevertheless, some correction is better than no correction at all, and it was felt that a smoothing formula would do the rest.

The Indian age distributions show, as do those in many

other countries, a pronounced trough at ages 15–25, and a peak at ages 25–35. As Fig. 52 makes clear, the variation is such that a smoothing formula would not do justice to it. There is a strong suggestion that the trough at ages 15–25 is due

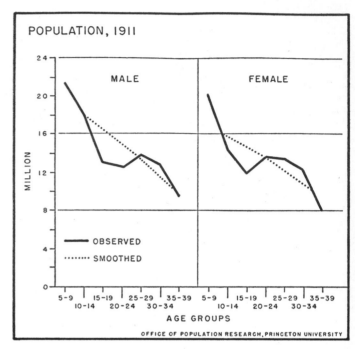

FIGURE 52. Freehand Smoothing of the Indian Age Distribution by Sex, 1911.

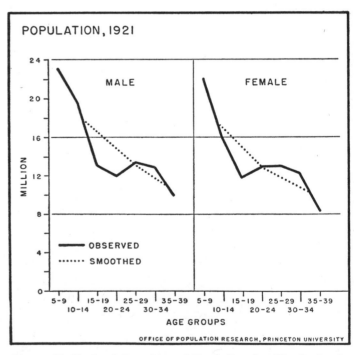

FIGURE 53. Freehand Smoothing of the Indian Age Distribution by Sex, 1921.

---

[1] The Indian age distributions happen to be among the world's worst. They show an average overloading on digits ending in "0" and "5" higher than that of any Latin American country, for example.

partly to underenumeration and partly to the erroneous recording of persons of these ages as older than they actually
are. In any case, the only procedure seemed to be to change
this part of the age curve by arbitrary freehand smoothing.
Figs. 52 and 53 illustrate how it was done for males and females.

As published in the 1911 and 1921 census volumes, the age
distributions end with the category "70-plus." In order to distribute the "70-plus" people in the specific five-year age
groups, we assumed that the percentages were the same as
those exhibited by Chile in 1930.

By these two corrections the population of 1911 was increased by 5.0 per cent for males and by 1.8 per cent for
females; and that of 1921 was increased by 5.8 per cent for
males and 2.4 per cent for females. It was thought better to
increase the 1921 population by a greater amount, because
this would help compensate for any influence that emigration
might have. The total amount added to the 1911 population
by the two procedures was 10.4 million, and to the 1921 population, 12.6 million.

With these corrections taken care of, the 1911 and 1921 age
distributions could be smoothed by formula. The following
formula was used: [2]

$$\int_{a=i}^{a=i+1} y \, dx = \frac{y_0 \, (a-x)^{1+\lambda}}{1+\lambda} \qquad (1)$$

This formula gave the area under the curve based on the midpoint of each age interval, but for the life table the population
at the beginning of each interval was needed. Consequently,
in the following equation,

$$y = y_0 \, (a-x)^\lambda \qquad (2)$$

the values already derived above for the constants were substituted, giving the desired figure for the beginning rather
than the midpoint of the interval. To get figures for single
ages, the values for y determined by equation (2) were each
divided by 5. This gave us the data necessary for differencing
the two censuses.

DIFFERENCING THE TWO AGE DISTRIBUTIONS

The life table mortality rates were obtained by the following formula:

$$10q_x = \frac{P_x^{1911} - P_{x+10}^{1921}}{P_x^{1911}}$$

where P is the population of x age. After the q_x values were obtained in this way for ages 0–9, 10–19, 20–29, etc., the rest of
the life table values were computed correspondingly in the ab-
breviated 10-year form.

AGES UNDER 10

It is not simply the total survival from age 0 to age 10 that
is desired, but the survival through still shorter intervals of
childhood. This problem has been the Achilles heel of Indian

life tables in the past. Those made prior to 1931 apparently
took their survival rates for ages under 10 from the experience
of the Proclaimed Clans from 1876 to 1891.[3] This was a group
for whom a careful account of male ages and male deaths was
kept, but its representativeness for the whole of India, particularly after 1900, is open to serious question. The 1921–31
values for ages under 10, with the exception of age 0, were
obtained automatically by the method adopted for that life
table, which was to average the age distributions of the two
censuses, then employ the difference between one age and the
next, modified by the survival rate of the ten-year cohort, as
the q_x value.[4] For age 0, however, a Makeham smoothing
formula adopted by George Hardy in previous life tables was
used. This formula, formerly applied to the Proclaimed Clans
data for ages under 13, was in this case applied to the Burmese
data, the l_0 being simply an extrapolation.[5]

In our case, a simpler approach was chosen. Assuming that
the change in childhood mortality as found in the registration
statistics represented a real trend (apart from the completeness of reporting), we obtained the difference in average mortality at ages 0, 1–4, and 5–9 as between the 1901–11 and
the 1911–21 decades. The percentage decrease was then applied to the q_x's from the 1901–11 table in order to get the
q_x's for the 1911–21 table. This method assumes the accuracy
of the 1901–11 life table, as well as the trend-accuracy of the
registration statistics. To check the method, we estimated the
"q_x's" from a series of regression lines in which the "q_x's"
under ten were plotted against $_{30}q_{10}$, the points being taken
from a large number of different life tables. This method
yielded higher estimates. The final figures used were averages
of the results obtained by the two methods.

THE RESULTS

Table 88 gives the 1911–21 life table values for males and
females. It reflects, as mentioned in the text, one of the highest
decade mortality rates on record. Is there any fundamental
error connected with it? Possibly the 1921 enumeration was
poorer than the 1911 enumeration, but if so, there is no indication of it. It is commonly believed that, in fact, the 1921
enumeration was better than the 1931 enumeration. Possibly
our techniques are bad, but the same techniques applied to the
1931–41 data yield, as we shall see, the lowest mortality values
yet found for India. In our opinion, therefore, our results are
what they are primarily because, for the first time, we have
measured the influence of mortality during a decade when
conditions were very bad in India. The values given in the
1911–21 table reflect the ravages of the 1918–19 influenza
epidemic. These values may be in error by as much as 5 or 10
per cent, but such a range of error would not alter the basic
conditions the life table represents.

THE 1931–41 LIFE TABLE

The other life table was constructed by the same methods,
but some of the conditions were different. In the first place,
the 1931 census officials smoothed the age distribution somewhat before publishing it. The actual returns were first
grouped, from age 4 upwards, into alternate groups of three
and seven. Thus the years 4, 5, and 6 formed the first group,
and the years 7–13 the next group. This placed the year end-

[2] A modification of Pearson-type IX, employed by Clyde V. Kiser
in constructing a life table for Egypt. See his article, "The Demographic
Position of Egypt" in *Demographic Studies of Selected Areas of Rapid
Growth* (New York: Milbank Memorial Fund, 1944), pp. 97–122. See
also M. R. El-Shanwany, "The First National Life Tables for Egypt,"
L'Egypte contemporaine, No. 162 (March, 1936), pp. 209–69. See also
W. Palin Elderton, *Frequency Curves and Correlation* (3rd ed.; Cam-
bridge: Cambridge University Press, 1938), Chapters 4–6.

[3] *Census of India*, 1931, Vol. I, Part 1, p. 151.
[4] *ibid.*, pp. 142–52.
[5] *ibid.*, pp. 151–52.

TABLE 88

Life Tables for Males and Females, India, 1911–21

Age x to x + n	Survivors to Exact Age x l_x	Probability of Dying in Age Interval nq_x	Population Living in Age Interval L_x	Total Years of Life Remaining to Survivors at Age x T_x	Average Years of Life Remaining to Survivors at Age x $\overset{\circ}{e}_x$
MALES					
0	100,000	.3015	78,171	1,942,048	19.42
1–4	69,850	.2631	229,297	1,863,877	26.68
5–9	51,472	.0888	244,596	1,634,580	31.76
10–19	46,902	.1910	424,072	1,389,984	29.64
20–29	37,943	.2313	334,880	965,912	25.46
30–39	29,167	.2733	250,958	631,032	21.64
40–49	21,196	.3276	176,226	380,074	17.93
50–59	14,252	.4018	112,897	203,848	14.30
60–69	8,526	.5319	61,120	90,951	10.67
70–79	3,991	.6955	24,725	29,831	7.47
80–89	1,215	.9967	5,089	5,106	4.20
90–plus	4	1.0000	17	17	4.25
FEMALES					
0	100,000	.2793	79,779	2,091,034	20.91
1–4	72,070	.2272	243,677	2,011,255	27.91
5–9	55,696	.0772	266,474	1,767,578	31.74
10–19	51,396	.2035	461,044	1,501,104	29.21
20–29	40,937	.2373	359,952	1,040,060	25.41
30–39	31,223	.2785	267,701	680,108	21.78
40–49	22,527	.3302	186,890	412,407	18.31
50–59	15,089	.3983	119,568	225,517	14.95
60–69	9,079	.4937	67,092	105,949	11.67
70–79	4,596	.6407	30,013	38,857	8.45
80–89	1,652	.8901	8,090	8,844	5.35
90–plus	181	1.0000	754	754	4.17

ing in "5" in the center of a group of three ages and the year ending in "0" in the center of a group of seven ages. These groups were then re-distributed into 5-year groups by a process of combining their halves. Thus the group 10–14 was formed by combining half the group 7–13 with half the group 14–16. The ages below 5, however, were treated differently. They "were formed by splitting up group 4–6 into six parts, two of which went to compose the group 5–10, three of which remained to represent the group 4–5, and one of which went to supplement half the number of those whose age to the nearest birthday was returned as three years to make the group 3–4. The group 0–1 was composed of those whose age was returned as *nil* plus half those whose nearest birthday was given as one year." [6]

While this procedure may have given a five-year age distribution that was closer to reality than would otherwise have been the case, it nevertheless made the 1931 distribution strictly non-comparable with either the 1921 or the 1941 age distribution. No way was left open by which the statistical analyst could get back to the original returns—either in 5-year groups or in single ages. [7]

[6] *ibid.*, Vol. 1, Part 1, p. 83.

[7] This situation illustrates the wrong role for a census bureau to take. The function of such a bureau is to present the data as completely as possible. No bureau can foresee all the purposes for which analysis

Fortunately, the 1931 census reports do contain three sample distributions on the basis of single year returns, one for the Punjab, another for Chingleput (Madras), and the third for Madras City. They contain, all told, 400,000 individuals, of which 300,000 are in the Punjab and 50,000 in each of the other two areas—a very small and unrepresentative number, but still indispensable. [8] With the aid of these we were

may be used. If subsequent investigators lack full data they cannot get the ultimate and necessary meaning out of them. It seems desirable for every census to publish a single-year age distribution—if not for the provinces, at least for the whole country. With such an age distribution the census itself may be adequately evaluated in comparison to others, fundamental relationships between age groups may be worked out, under-registration of births and deaths may be studied, and each research worker can use his own smoothing formula. To publish only a 5-year grouping or the smoothed figures is to put the data in a strait-jacket from which it is hard to rescue them.

What the bureau says it did with the ages under 5 and what it actually did are apparently different. By experimenting with sample distributions, and by using the suggested technique, we could not achieve the same results; instead, we got the proportions at ages under 5 far beyond the amount that the census people got. Some other technique must have been used. We do not know what it was, but we can work out empirically the results it gave and thus adjust the ages under 5 in the 1941 age distribution.

[8] The samples are found in *Census of India,* 1931, Vol. 17 (Punjab), Part 1, p. 148; Vol. 14 (Madras), Part 1, p. 127.

able to readjust the 1941 figures below age 10 in order to conform with the adjustment made in the 1931 figures.

As for the ages above 9, there was one saving fact—the life table aimed to get survival rates for ten-year age groups only. The method of readjusting the 1931 age figures did not shift many individuals from one ten-year group to another, but mainly affected simply the five-year groups. Therefore, the 1931 and 1941 age distributions could be smoothed above age 9 as they stood.

AREA AND POPULATION COVERED

The trouble in 1941 was of a different sort. In the first place, the summary volume for the 1941 census contains no age distribution; consequently, the distribution must be computed from the provincial volumes. In the second place, because of economies necessitated by the war, some of the provincial reports omit an age distribution altogether and others contain only a sample distribution.[9] It was necessary, first, to ascer-

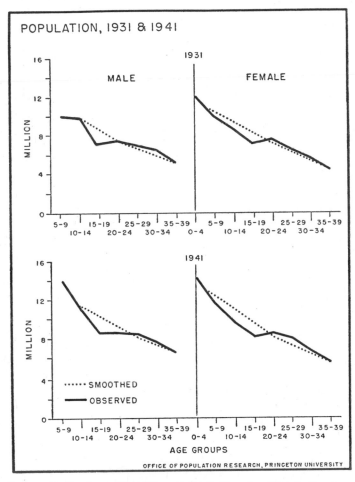

FIGURE 54. Freehand Smoothing of the Indian Age Distribution by Sex, 1931 and 1941.

[9] Those political units which, at the time the life table was made, contained an age distribution for the whole population were only four, as follows:

Ajmer-Merwara	Mysore
Jammu and Kashmir	Rajputana

Those which contained a sample (usually one-fiftieth) were eleven, as follows:

Assam	Delhi
Baroda	N.W. Frontier Province
Baluchistan	Orissa
Bengal	Punjab
Bihar	Sind
Bombay	

TABLE 89

1931 Area and Population Used in Constructing 1931–1941 Life Table

	Total Area	Life Table Area	Total Population	Life Table Population
PROVINCES				
All Provinces	862,679	*45.3%*	256,859,787	*51.5%*
Those in Life Table		390,674		132,234,356
Ajmer-Merwara		2,368		525,989
Bengal		77,521		50,114,002
Bihar		69,348 [a]		32,371,434
Bombay & Sind		123,599		21,803,388
Delhi		573		636,346
N.W.F. Province		13,518		1,176,691
Orissa		4,547		2,025,754
Punjab		99,200		23,580,852
STATES & AGENCIES				
All States & Ags.	712,508	*36.0%*	81,310,845	*30.6%*
Those in Life Table		256,499		24,845,600
Baroda		8,164		2,443,007
Bengal States		5,434		973,336
Jammu & Kashmir		84,516		3,646,243
Mysore		29,326		6,557,302
Rajputana		129,059		11,225,712
GRAND TOTAL, INDIA	1,575,187	*41.1%*	338,170,632	*46.5%*
GRAND TOTAL, TABLE		647,173		157,079,956

[a] In the case of Bihar, the territory is larger than that given in the 1931 census. The reason is that in this, as in all other cases, the territory of 1931 was adjusted so as to correspond to that of 1941. In 1941 Bihar included Chota Nagpur, but in 1931 it did not. So the figure given here represents the combined total for Bihar and Chota Nagpur in 1931. In some other cases, notably Ajmer-Merwara, N. W. Frontier Prov., and Orissa, the territory used was smaller than the total in the census. Data taken from various census volumes.

tain whether or not the samples were representative, and second, to raise them to the full population of the area sampled. Two provinces, Assam and Baluchistan, were omitted because of sampling errors, but the rest passed muster.[10] In all, at the time the life table was made, usable age distributions for nine provinces were available. Our 1931–41 life table therefore properly applies only to these areas. As Table 89 shows, they embrace 41 per cent of the area and 46 per cent of the population of India proper.

Again, as with the 1911–21 material, the age distributions had to be first smoothed by hand before they were smoothed by formula. Figure 54 shows what was done.

The "q_x's" for ages 0, 1–4, and 5–9 were obtained as in the case of the 1911–21 life table.

THE RESULTS

The life table values for 1931–41 are given in Table 90. The expectation of life at birth—32.1 for males and 31.4 for females—is considerably higher than it was in 1921–31. It is 19 per cent higher among males and 18 per cent higher among

[10] Assam's age sample is drawn from various groups, such as "tea garden laborers," "Muslims of North Sylhet subdivision," and "Hindus of all thanas of Gauhati subdivision except Gauhati." Since the proportions of these groups in the total population of the province could not be ascertained, it proved impossible to use these figures. In addition, Baluchistan's sample was drawn only from the rural population, and in 1931 a considerable part of its population was estimated and hence not returned as to age. These two provinces were consequently omitted.

females. This difference does not necessarily mean that mortality in India improved that much in one decade, although other evidence indicates that it did decline somewhat. It seems probable that the 1921–31 life table was too severe. The intrinsic rate of growth during the 1921–31 decade, calculated on the basis of this life table, was 20 per cent lower than the rate of growth actually observed in the population. Since the stable and the actual age structure were practically identical, this suggests that the 1921–31 life table was too severe. It is also possible that the 1931–41 life table made by us does not represent a fair sample of the population, because the provinces that published age distributions may have had a better mortality record than those that did not. A certain amount of error, other than a sampling error, may also be involved in our life table. There is little reason to believe, however, that our own table errs heavily on the optimistic side, because the omission of the migration factor tends toward an overstatement of mortality. Our view is that about two-thirds of the improvement in mortality suggested by these two life tables is a real improvement. This conclusion is reached by comparing the decline in the estimated crude death rate with the changes in the life tables.

TABLE 90

Abridged Life Table for India, 1931–1941

Age	Number Entering Each Age	Probability of Dying	Number Living at Each Age	Total Years Remaining to Survivors	Average Years of Life Remaining to Survivors
x to $x + n$	l_x	$_nq_x$	L_x	T_x	$\overset{\circ}{e}_x$
MALES					
0	100,000	.2175	84,253	3,208,851	32.09
1–4	78,250	.1730	276,080	3,124,598	39.93
5–9	64,713	.0495	314,613	2,848,518	44.02
10–19	61,509	.0958	586,198	2,533,905	41.20
20–29	55,617	.1182	523,969	1,947,707	35.02
30–39	49,043	.1504	454,298	1,423,738	29.03
40–49	41,667	.1986	376,055	969,440	23.27
50–59	33,392	.2751	288,548	593,385	17.77
60–69	24,206	.4071	192,489	304,837	12.59
70–79	14,351	.6620	92,135	112,348	7.83
80–89	4,851	1.0000	20,213	20,213	4.17
FEMALES					
0	100,000	.2039	85,238	3,137,193	31.37
1–4	79,610	.1655	282,480	3,051,955	38.34
5–9	66,435	.0452	323,783	2,769,475	41.69
10–19	63,432	.1197	596,802	2,445,692	38.56
20–29	55,839	.1456	518,117	1,848,890	33.11
30–39	47,709	.1799	434,428	1,330,773	27.89
40–49	39,126	.2271	346,853	896,345	22.91
50–59	30,240	.2948	257,469	549,492	18.17
60–69	21,326	.3976	169,850	292,023	13.69
70–79	12,846	.5658	90,026	122,173	9.51
80–89	5,578	.8526	28,722	32,147	5.76
90–99 [a]	822	1.0000	3,425	3,425	4.17

[a] The fact that the female table runs ten years farther than the male table is due to the fact that the smoothing formula used gave a negative quantity beyond age 90 for the males but not for the females.

APPENDIX D

TECHNIQUE OF ESTIMATING INTERCENSAL POPULATIONS UNDER REGISTRATION

THE PROBLEM

Until after the 1931 Census, the Public Health Commission with the Government of India published, in its Annual Report, birth and death rates based on the population at the *beginning of the decade,* making no allowance for the interim growth of population. This unfortunately caused a fictitious rise in the rates during the decade, especially in those decades when the population of the country was growing rapidly. A further difficulty grew out of the fact that the area under registration did not always remain fixed, and consequently the population under registration, though given by the previous census, varied from one year to the next in many areas. We had, therefore, to find some means of estimating not only a smooth trend of the population under registration, but also of taking account of the variations in area covered.

THE SOLUTION

To solve the problem, the following steps were pursued: (1) We took an average of the population under registration in the given Province for the entire decade. (2) Using this average as the starting point, and taking as the final point the population under registration at the end of the decade (given by the next census), we computed the annual geometric growth rate for the decennium. (3) Then, for each year, we took the difference between the officially given population and the average, and according to the algebraic sign, added it to or subtracted it from the population given by the geometric growth rate. This gave us the final estimate of the population under registration in that year. The census in India is usually taken in March, and we did not undertake to move the population up to the middle of the year.[1]

EXAMPLE

In 1913 the population under registration for all of British India was officially reported as 228,467,512. The average population under registration for the decade, however, was 228,675,197, and the geometric growth rate gave 229,403,099 as the population for 1913. Therefore, subtracting the officially reported population from the average, we had 207,685 left over—this being the amount by which the official population of 1913 failed to reach the average for the decade. Subtracting

[1] Fortunately the proportion of the population not under registration in British India and in particular provinces is not great, and therefore the variations on this score are not extremely important. Table 91 gives the proportions.

this from the geometric figure, we had 229,195,414 as the estimated population under registration for that year. It should be noted that, since the average was taken as the starting point for computing the geometric growth rate, the geometric figure for the initial year (1911 in the decade under consideration) and the average figure were identical; consequently, when the difference between the officially reported figure and the average was added to the geometric figure, we had simply the population officially reported as under registration for this year in the first place.

TABLE 91

Population of India and the Provinces under Registration, 1931[a]

Political Area	Percentage of Population under Registration[1]
India, Total (1911)	75.5
(1921)	75.4
(1931)	75.0
India, British	97.86
Madras	96.7
Bombay (inc. Aden)	99.4
Bengal	99.6
United Provinces	100.0
Punjab	99.5
Bihar & Orissa	100.0
Central Provinces & Berar	100.0
Assam	91.9
N. W. Frontier Prov.	97.3
Ajmer-Merwara	100.0
Coorg	100.0
Delhi	100.0

[a] This table deals only with the population under registration in the *British territory.* Some of the States have registration systems and specify the population under registration, but since they are not regularly reported in the statistics by the Government of India, they are omitted here. When we speak of the official statistics of India with reference to births and deaths, it is the British area that is meant, unless otherwise indicated.

[1] The data are derived from the *Statistical Abstract for British India,* 1911–12 to 1920–21, p. 377; 1919–20 to 1928–29, p. 409; 1922–23 to 1931–32, p. 499. The populations for all India on which the calculations are based came from *Census of India,* 1931, Vol. 1, Part 2, p. 6.

APPENDIX E

ESTIMATION OF BIRTHS IN INDIA

I. Using Census and Vital Statistics

One way to estimate births in India is to compare the census returns for children with the registered births. Each single-year age group in the census can be followed back, on the basis of the *deaths registered by age,* to the births that must have occurred in order to make the census figures possible. The estimated births can then be matched with the actually recorded births to form a notion of the extent of underregistration.

The procedure suffers from two handicaps. In the first place, children are likely to be underenumerated in the census. This can be partially remedied by smoothing.[1] In the second place, deaths as well as births are underregistered. When too few deaths are used to estimate the births that must have given rise to the census cohorts, the estimate is below the mark. One way of overcoming this difficulty, at least partially, is to make successive approximations. After a first estimate of births has been made, it can be assumed that deaths are equally underregistered. The deaths can be increased accordingly, and a new estimate of births prepared. The process can be repeated a third time, if desired.

In the present study this successive approximation procedure was carried out for males and females separately, but it was used mainly as a check on results obtained by other methods.

II. Using Census and Life Table Data

Instead of using registered deaths to move from the census cohorts to the births from which they must have sprung, it is possible to use the life table. Starting with the children 0–9 in the census, one gets by this procedure the total estimated births for the decade. Comparing these with the births registered during the decade, one gets some notion of the average underregistration. Since different childhood cohorts are unequally enumerated in the census, it is not wise to estimate births for any particular year by this method. But the average decennial underregistration can be used to correct the registered births for each particular year, and thus the corrected birth rate will have the fluctuations that the registered birth rate has. Since Indian life tables are not made on the basis of vital statistics, the estimate of births prepared in this way is independent of the one prepared by the method stated above.

The rate by which a cohort is traced back for a particular year is given by,

$$\frac{L_{x-1}}{L_x}$$

Thus in order to find how many people age 3 were living exactly one year prior to the census, the population age 4 in the census is multiplied by the appropriate rate, as follows:

$$\frac{L_3}{L_4} \times C_4 = C_3$$

[1] See Appendix C for a discussion of the 1931 age distribution.

where C stands for a cohort of a given age. When a cohort has been brought back to age 1 by this procedure, the appropriate rate is given by,

$$\frac{l_o}{L_o}, \text{ or } \frac{100,000}{L_o}$$

The procedure probably gives too low an estimate of underregistration, because of the underenumeration of children in the census, but it is the best technique available. It gives higher estimates of underregistration than the previously described method, but in most cases the difference is not more than 10 per cent (Table 92). It should be noted that the Indian life tables cover an entire decade and are thus suitable

Table 92

Estimated Birth Rates Obtained by Two Methods, Selected Provinces and States: 1926–1930 [a]

Province or State	Reverse Survival 1926–30	Successive Approximation 1926–30
British India	45.19	41.29
Ajmer-Merwara	46.31	
Baroda	44.67	
Bombay	44.46	41.75
Cent. Provinces & B.	45.83	47.29
Coorg	32.93	33.78
Hyderabad	50.40	
Madras	41.93	38.71
Mysore	40.70	
Punjab	47.11	42.76
Travancore	50.84	
United Prov.	46.32	40.66

[a] For various reasons, such as lack of data or laboriousness of the calculations, rates were not computed for all areas according to the methods of successive approximations and comparison with census natural increase.

for tracing back the cohorts at ages 0–9 in the census, but that they represent only an average experience. Since different cohorts cover varying lengths of the decade, application of average mortality to all alike will cause some error if mortality changed markedly during the decade.

In areas of pre-partition India nominally under registration, the percentage of births registered was certainly, as mentioned in the text, less than 75 per cent. Probably it is much less than that, but this is the figure found by our procedure. Necessarily the adequacy of registration varies greatly from district to district and from province to province. Table 93 gives for the years 1926–30 the percentage of registration for the British provinces and for those states that reported births during the period. The states show up more poorly than the

TABLE 93

Per Cent of Total Births Registered, 1926–1930

Province or State	Per cent Registration
BRITISH INDIA	74.7
Ajmer-Merwara	64.5
Assam	54.4
Bengal	58.4
Bihar & Orissa	77.7
Bombay	77.2
Central Provinces & B.	92.9
Coorg	64.2
Delhi	87.0
Madras	83.9
N. W. Frontier Prov.	57.0
United Provinces	74.6

STATES	
Baroda	56.1
Hyderabad	16.9
Cochin	27.5
Travancore	38.2
Mysore	45.4

British provinces. Only one state (Baroda) stood ahead of the lowest province (Assam). Such variations in the degree of registration necessarily put us on guard against using reported rates for comparison of different areas.

What is greatly needed in India and Pakistan is the selection of certain districts, typical of wider areas, for an intensive study of demographic phenomena. In such districts a strenuous effort could be made to secure complete registration of all births as well as other vital phenomena.

APPENDIX F

METHOD OF COMPUTING REPRODUCTION RATES

The Indian census, since it comes in the early part of the year, forms roughly the midpoint in a two-year span. For this reason we used, in computing reproduction rates, the average number of births registered during the two years surrounding each census, correcting these births for underregistration and for application to all India rather than British India.

Next we took, without smoothing, the census age distribution of all women between 15 and 49, in five-year intervals. To these we applied the age specific fertility rates of Chile in 1930–31, thus getting, by summation, the expected births if these rates had applied. An adjustment factor, obtained by comparing these expected births with those actually estimated for India (as described above) and by applying the sex ratio to get only female births, was then applied to the Chilean fertility to get the Gross Reproduction Rate for India.

Finally, we took the female population aged 15–49 from an appropriate Indian life table, multiplied each five-year cohort by the Chilean age-specific rate, summed, divided by the radix of the life-table, applied the adjustment factor, and thus obtained the Net Reproduction Rate.

The method is somewhat rough, but any errors introduced by the method are probably less than those contributed by the original data themselves. To check the influence of using Chilean data as a basis for distributing Indian fertility by age, we used a sample study of age specific fertility done in Cochin.[1] The rates for 1930–31 turned out to be 2.93 (GRR) and 1.26 (NRR), as compared with 2.99 and 1.25 using the Chilean schedule. This conforms to the finding of Glass that the kind of substitute distribution of births according to age of mother does not make a great deal of difference in the final rates obtained.[2]

[1] D. Ghosh and Rama Varma, "A Study in Indian Fertility," *Eugenics Review,* Vol. 31 (July, 1939), pp. 115–19.

[2] D. V. Glass, *Population Policies and Movements in Europe* (Oxford: Clarendon, 1940), pp. 387–99.

APPENDIX G

LOGISTIC PROJECTIONS FOR INDIA

IN FITTING a logistic curve to India's population growth, we took as our data the corrected population figures adjusted to the 1941 area—the same corrected figures as are given in Chapter 4. To get a curve that gave a good fit we found it necessary to assume a lower limit that is quite high, 245 million. This is, in our opinion, higher than reality, but it may be that the modern cycle of growth really started at some figure not much lower than that. As an upper limit we found 700 million to be satisfactory.

The formula of the curve fitted in this way is

$$Y - 2.45 = \frac{4.55}{1 + 3.3278e^{-.04322t}}$$

The goodness of fit can be judged from the following comparison with the population figures used.

Date	Given Population (millions)	Estimated Population (millions)	Deviation from Given (per cent)
1871	255	255	——
1881	257	260	1.17
1891	282	268	—4.96
1901	285	280	—1.75
1911	303	296	—2.31
1921	306	319	4.25
1931	338	350	3.55
1941	389	389	——

The chart in Fig. 55 shows the course of population growth according to this curve as extrapolated. This chart also shows

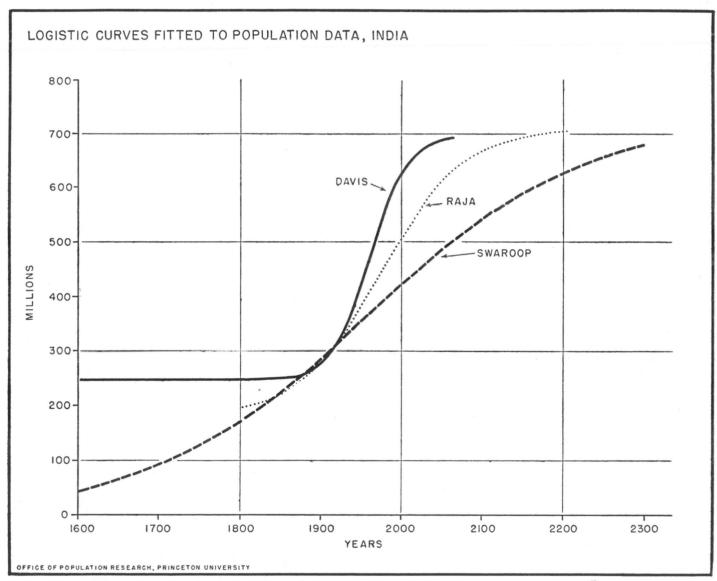

LOGISTIC CURVES FITTED TO POPULATION DATA, INDIA

DAVIS

RAJA

SWAROOP

MILLIONS

YEARS

FIGURE 55. Three Logistic Curves Fitted to Indian Population Data: (1) Davis, (2) Raja, (3) Swaroop and Lal.

the projections of two other investigators, Raja and Swaroop.[1] It will be seen that our curve has a much steeper slope at the point of inflection than do either of the others. This is doubtless due in part to the fact that we had the 1941 figure and they did not, and in part to the fact that, as necessitated by our use of more thoroughly corrected population figures, we took a higher figure for our bottom limit.

It is a commentary on the use of the logistic curve for purposes of prediction in a country such as India that no great success has been attained in the past. Both Swaroop and Raja came below the 1941 population, the first by 12.1 per cent, the second by 5.8 per cent. If they had simply extrapolated the 1921–31 rate of increase they would have missed it by less than 4 per cent. In Bengal, Griffiths and Porter missed the 1941 population by some 12 per cent, whereas a straight-line projection from the previous decade would have missed it by only 9.1 per cent. Of course, if the 1911 to 1921 experience had been used to estimate the population of 1931, a serious error would have been made; but no demographer would exercise such bad judgment, and, be it noted, no logistic curve fitted to 1871–1921 data would have done much better.

---

[1] Satya Swaroop and R. B. Lal, "Logistic Law of Growth and Structure of Indian Population," *Population*, Vol. 2 (August, 1938), pp. 100–21; K.C.K.E. Raja, "A Forecast of Population in India at the Census of 1941," *Indian Journal of Medical Research,* Vol. 24 (April, 1937), pp. 1183–91. In both cases the populations used were those for the 1872 territory. To compare their figures with ours, therefore, as is done in Fig. 55, we took the average ratio of their curve to ours for the period covered by the empirical data and raised their curve throughout by the same per cent.

APPENDIX H

THE DEFINITION OF "URBAN" AND OTHER CATEGORIES

For purposes of the Indian census a "village" is not necessarily a village in the ordinary sense, but a revenue district, or *mauza*. It includes all the hamlets or parts of hamlets located within the district boundaries, but it may be uninhabited. "Uninhabited villages are not included in the census statistics, though they are entered in the preliminary census records and inspected at the final enumeration in case any one should have taken up residence therein by the final census night."[1] In some areas, as in the hills of Assam, the census village is actually a residential unit and corresponds to the usual notion of a village, but in other areas, such as other parts of Assam itself, the census "village" has no relation to residential aggregations. It may be merely a survey area or a financial district. In parts where the village is not defined as the revenue unit but rather as an area of settlement, it becomes difficult to determine whether a collection of houses is sufficiently important to be called a separate village or should be regarded as merely an extension (*para*) of a larger collection of houses.[2] In view of the varying and frequently artificial nature of the "village," statistical measures—such as the average village density or the growth in the number of villages—are largely meaningless.[3]

The next higher unit, the "town," is supposed to be the first "urban" unit, but has a multiple and somewhat confusing definition. First, it includes all municipalities—i.e. places that have acquired a municipal form of government under provincial law. (Some States apparently have no municipalities.) Second, it includes all civil lines not included in municipal limits, and all cantonments. Third, it includes all places of *5,000 or more* persons which the provincial census superintendent—on the basis of character, density, and economic and historical importance—believes to be urban. Finally, it includes places *under* 5,000 which the census superintendent also considers urban. Obviously the division between "village" and "town" does not depend solely on the size of the population. A great deal is left to the discretion of the census authorities, with the result that in some provinces or states, and in some censuses, the definition is looser than in others. In 1931 Mysore reported a higher urbanization than Madras, but 66 of its 108 towns had a population of less than 5,000; if such towns be omitted from the urban population, the relative

position of the two areas with respect to urbanization is reversed. The percentage of the urban population found in places of 5,000 and less has varied from census to census, but not enough to make the total urban figure meaningless, as the following shows:

	Per Cent of Total Urban Population
1881	6.7
1891	6.2
1901	6.6
1911	6.9
1921	7.3
1931	5.7
1941	3.8

In Pakistan or the Union of India the distinction between a large village and a small town is often meaningless, because the mode of life does not differ, both being primarily agricultural rather than industrial.[4] Yet the line has to be drawn somewhere, and the population criterion is probably the most definite and consistent of all. For this reason, wherever possible, we have tried to classify places by size and to deal with trends in the urban population as a matter of places over 5,000, omitting those that are under this figure.[5]

The definition of a "city," as distinct from a "town," is also treacherous, first because the standard size of 100,000 or better is not observed, and second because there is the usual question of how much of the surrounding area should be included. In India the inclusion or exclusion of the adjacent cantonments, notified areas, etc., has always caused trouble. If such places are omitted, one does not get a true impression of the number of inhabitants concentrated together; if they are included, the population changes fortuitously from one census to another. Fortunately, the tables are published with the urban places divided into six classes according to the size of the population, and we are usually told whether or not a given table includes adjacent cantonments. In temporal and regional comparisons a certain amount of error is inevitable, but for many purposes the degree of error is not crucial. The statistics may be used with considerable confidence so long as the definitions are kept in mind.

---

[1] *Census of India,* 1931, Vol. 18 (United Provinces), Part 1, p. 121.

[2] *ibid.,* Vol. 3 (Assam), Part 1, p. 39.

[3] *ibid.,* Vol. 14 (Madras), Part 1, pp. 53–54.

[4] *ibid.,* Vol. 1, Part 1, p. 45.

[5] The census authorities have apparently come around to the same point of view. cf. *ibid.,* 1941, Vol. 1, p. 26.

APPENDIX I

REPRESENTATIVENESS OF THE CITIES FOR WHICH DATA ON CHARACTERISTICS COULD BE OBTAINED

FROM time to time in this monograph it has proved necessary to analyze the characteristics of the urban population. In many cases, however, this could not be done, because the characteristics were not given in the census for the urban and rural populations separately. The nearest approximation consisted of certain towns and cities for which the data happened to be given. Analyzing the data for these places, one can get not only some inkling of urban phenomena in India, but also can differentiate these cities and towns and discover certain relationships between their characteristics.

The only catch is that the places for which the data are obtainable include only a part of all the towns and cities in prepartition India. The question then arises as to whether or not the sample adequately represents the total number of urban centers. Since the sample varies somewhat according to which characteristic is under consideration—whether age, literacy, or occupation—the answer is presumably different for each one; but on the whole if, for the Census Commissioner, a town or city seemed worthy of detailed statistics in one respect, it usually seemed equally worthy in other respects. Hence in general the urban sample was roughly the same, and its representativeness practically identical, for several outstanding characteristics. For this reason the following discussion does not attempt to evaluate the sample with respect to each characteristic separately.

Naturally, the larger the city the more likely it is to be represented in the sample. The sample is therefore biased with reference to size, as Table 94 indicates. In fact, since the provinces were required to furnish data on certain characteristics in city populations (i.e. those with more than 100,000 inhabitants), practically all cities, strictly defined, are found in the sample. But below the 100,000 level, the representation drops off, until for towns of 10,000 to 20,000 it amounts to only two per cent, and for those having 5,000 to 10,000 it amounts to almost nothing.

It follows that, when characteristics are analyzed by size of city, the sample gives much safer results for places above 50,000 than for those below. Of course, even a very small sample of the lesser towns would be adequate if it were drawn at random. There is every reason to believe, however, that the sample of towns below 100,000 is not drawn at random. Rather, it would seem that the census gave its main attention to those towns that were *important*—i.e. which for one reason or another stood out in the economic and political life of the Province. This being true, it would seem safe to deduce that on the whole the most modern of the smaller places were likely to be chosen for detailed statistics. This would serve to understate the differentiation between the small and the large cities, and to overstate the difference between the small cities and the rural area.

The influence of this bias can, in all probability, be seen in each case in which the sample was used. In the occupational

TABLE 94

Sample of 87 Cities Used in Occupational Tables, as Percentage of Total Urban Population by Size Class, 1931 [1]

Size Class	Sample Cities as Per Cent of all Cities in Size Class
Cities 500,000 plus	100.0
Cities 100,000–500,000	96.4
Cities 50,000–100,000	58.8
Cities 20,000–50,000	9.0
Cities 10,000–20,000	2.0
Cities 5,000–10,000	0.4
Cities less than 5,000	1.5
Total	*33.3*
Cities less than 50,000	3.8
Cities 10,000 to 50,000	5.6

[1] Calculated from relevant tables of the various provincial volumes, *Census of India,* 1931.

distribution, it was found, for instance, that the cities below 50,000 had a greater percentage of workers in Public Administration and in Public Force than did any other class of cities. This is probably because the cities in this class for which occupational data have been published are important from a political point of view, being minor capitals in many cases. Also, it was found in the sample that the sex ratio of cities less than 50,000 is higher than that for cities 50,000 to 100,000, but for all cities under 50,000 this is not true.[1] Whether or not the bias influences the literacy figures by size of city is impossible to determine, but we may take it for granted that it does, though not sufficiently to overcome the differentiation by size of city.

In view of the biased character of the sample, its characteristics cannot be taken as absolutely representative of the cities in the smaller size classes, any more than it can be taken as representative of the total urban population. But since the net effect of the bias is usually to underrate the differentials rather than to exaggerate them, the differentials that are found in the sample may be taken as minimum statements of tendencies that really exist in the urban population. Viewed in this light, they give us a great deal of needed demographic information.

[1] The ratio is usually higher for towns under 5,000 than for those 5,000 to 10,000 or 10,000 to 20,000, but this is again the result of a selective factor. Only certain places with less than 5,000 inhabitants are dignified with the status of being a town. This is at the discretion of the Provincial Census Commissioner, and requires distinctly urban characteristics on the part of the place so dignified. Therefore, because of the basis of the selection, the places called "towns" in the "under-5,000" class, are more urban in some ways than the places with between 5,000 and 20,000.

APPENDIX J

ESTIMATES OF RELIGIOUS DISTRIBUTION FOR 1941

IN ATTEMPTING to adjust the figures given for those of "Tribal Origin" in 1941 so as to get a figure for those practicing a Tribal religion, some sort of estimate of the latter had to be made. The safest thing seemed to be to assume that, in the general population, the *proportion* of those practicing a Tribal religion in 1941 would be approximately the same as in 1931. The rationale of this was the belief that the Tribal religionists are probably diminishing in percentage terms at an accelerated pace, but that, because of political tampering, there were too few of them reported in 1931. Thus, by assuming that the Tribal religionists increased as fast as the rest of the population, but starting from a base (the 1931 figure) that was probably too low, we arrived at a figure for 1941 which may be somewhere near the truth.

This procedure gave us 8,791,354 Tribal religionists in 1941, instead of the 25,441,489 persons of Tribal origin as enumerated. This left a difference of 16,650,135 to be distributed to the other religions. The question was how it could be done.

As a first approximation an investigation was made of the census volumes for individual provinces, many of which give information on the religious affiliation of the aboriginals. In this way 6,689,842 Hindus, 958,354 Christians, 57,116 Muslims, and 225,548 Buddhists—a total of 7,930,860—were discovered under the Tribal heading. Unfortunately, however, this total did not equal the surplus of 16,650,135 which we had previously estimated. Since most of these were known to be Hindu and Christian, we assumed that our corrections from the provincial volumes were correct for Muslims and Buddhists, and set about discovering another way to distribute the surplus between Hindus and Christians.

It was assumed that between 1931 and 1941 the Christians grew at a rate 75 per cent as high as the rate at which they grew between 1921 and 1931. This was a rate faster than the general population, but still not quite so fast as the rather phenomenal growth of the prior period. The assumption yielded a total of 7,427,243 Christians instead of the 6,316,549 as reported in the census, and the difference (1,110,694) was subtracted from the Tribal surplus that remained after the Buddhist and Muslim corrections, as mentioned above, had been taken away. The remainder of the surplus (15,256,777, of which 6,689,842, be it remembered, had already been found to be Hindu) were given to the Hindus. This gave the latter a total population in India of 270,187,283, instead of the 254,930,506 as returned by the Census.

Putting the calculations in account form, they run as follows:

Tribals, as enumerated	25,441,489
Tribals, as assumed	8,791,354
Surplus	16,650,135

Tribals found to be Muslim	57,116
Tribals found to be Buddhist	225,548
Total	282,664
Surplus remaining	16,367,471

Christians, as assumed	7,427,243
Christians, as enumerated	6,316,549
Difference	1,110,694
Surplus remaining	15,256,777

Hindus, as enumerated	254,930,506
Hindus, as corrected	270,187,283

As a check upon the results, the Hindus were allowed to grow between 1931 and 1941 at the same rate as they did between 1921 and 1931. This gave them 263,321,790 adherents in 1941. Again, they were allowed to grow as fast as the general population did during 1931–1941. This gave them 274,489,406. We thus had two new estimates of the Hindu population. It can be seen that our estimate falls between them.

Low	263,321,790
Medium	270,187,283
High	274,489,406

The low estimate is probably too low, because the population of India (and hence in all probability the Hindus) grew faster in 1931–41 than it did in 1921–31. The high estimate is probably too high, because the Hindu population has never in census history grown as fast as the general population. The fact that our estimate falls between the two extremes, therefore, argues well for it.

Of course, the accuracy of these estimates is at best rough. They very probably overestimate slightly the number of Hindus and underestimate slightly the number of Christians and Muslims. But better figures will be hard to produce until the next census is taken. In a sense it does little harm to exaggerate the number of aborigines who are Hindu, not only because Hinduism is found to some extent in every primitive tribe but also because the drift of the aborigines, barring some major catastrophe, is in the direction of that religion rather than any other. Hence the error, though a distortion at the present time, tends to represent a future reality.

Wherever we have given totals and percentages in the various religions, these corrected figures for 1941 have been used. But of course the same cannot be done for the religious groups when their characteristics are discussed. In such cases the number originally enumerated must be used. Actually most of our discussion of characteristics by religion relates to the year 1931 rather than to 1941, so that little embarrassment is introduced by this statistical inconsistency.

Bibliography

The list below does not cover all literature touching upon the population of India and Pakistan, nor does it merely list the works cited in the present volume. It is intended, rather, to provide a working bibliography on the subject for future investigators, and above all to show the topical variety and geographical spread of publications (especially in India) on the subject. The items are listed under subject headings that are alphabetic in order.

AGRICULTURE AND LAND TENURE

BOOKS AND PAMPHLETS

Baden-Powell, B. H., *Land Revenue in British India* (Oxford: Clarendon, 1894).

Baden-Powell, B. H., *Land Systems of British India* (Calcutta: Office of the Superintendent of Government Printing, 1882).

Chatterjee, U. N. (ed.), *Developing Village India: Studies in Village Problems* (New Delhi: Imperial Council of Agricultural Research, 1946).

Darling, M. L., *The Punjab Peasant in Prosperity and Debt* (London: Oxford University Press, 1925).

Gangulee, Birendranath, *Trends of Agriculture and Population in the Ganges Valley* (London: Methuen, 1938).

Garratt, G. T., *An Indian Commentary* (New York: J. Cape, 1928).

Glover, Sir Harold, *Soil Erosion*, Oxford Pamphlets on Indian Affairs, No. 23 (London and Bombay: Oxford University Press, 1944).

Gupta, Mahendra N., *Land System of Bengal* (Calcutta: University of Calcutta, 1940).

Higginbottom, Sam, *India's Agricultural Problems* (New York: Institute of Pacific Relations, Eighth Conference, 1942).

Higginbottom, Sam, *The Gospel and the Plow* (New York: Macmillan, 1921).

Mukerjee, Radhakamal, *Fields and Farmers in Oudh* (Madras: Longmans, 1929).

Mukhtyar, G. C., *Life and Labour in a South Gujarat Village* (Calcutta: Longmans, 1930).

Ramaswamy, T. N., *Economic Stabilisation of Indian Agriculture* (Benares: Nand Kishore, 1946).

Singh, Tarlok, *Poverty and Social Change: A Study in the Economic Reorganisation of Indian Rural Society* (London and Bombay: Longmans, 1945).

Wilcox, Earley V., *Acres and People: The Eternal Problems of China and India* (New York: Orange Judd, 1947).

ARTICLES

Indian Journal of Agricultural Economics, Vol. 3 (April, 1948), pp. 74–105. (This issue has several articles on population pressure and agriculture in various regions of India.)

Mukerjee, B. N., "A Study of the Effect of Irrigation on the Pressure of Population in the United Provinces," *Calcutta Geographical Review*, Vol. 5 (March, 1943), pp. 18–21.

Mukherjee, Ramkrishna, "Economic Structure of Rural Bengal: A Survey of Six Villages," *American Sociological Review*, Vol. 13 (December, 1948), pp. 660–72.

Rahman, Shafiqur, "Can Bengal Support such a Large Agricultural Population?" *Indian Journal of Economics*, Vol. 27 (July, 1946), pp. 53–63.

CASTE COMPOSITION

BOOKS AND PAMPHLETS

Blunt, Sir E. A. H., *The Caste System of Northern India* (London: Oxford University Press, 1931).

Desai, Mahadev, *The Epic of Travancore* (Ahmedabad: Navajivan Karyalaya, 1937).

Ghurye, G. S., *Caste and Race in India* (London: Paul, Trench, Trübner, 1932).

Ghurye, G. S., *The Aborigines—"So-called"—and Their Future*, Gokhale Institute of Politics and Economics, Publication No. 11 (Poona: Oriental Watchman Publishing House, 1943).

Hutton, J. H., *Caste in India* (Cambridge: Cambridge University Press, 1946).

Ibbetson, Sir Denzil, *Panjab Castes* (Lahore: Superintendent, Government Printing, Punjab, 1916).

Nehru, S. S., *Caste and Credit in the Rural Area* (London: Longmans, 1932).

Noble, Margaret E. (The Sister Nivedita), *The Web of Indian Life* (2nd ed., new printing; Bombay: Longmans, 1918).

O'Malley, L. S. S., *Indian Caste Customs* (Cambridge: Cambridge University Press, 1932).

Russell, Robert V., *Tribes and Castes of the Central Provinces of India* (London: Macmillan, 1916).

Singh, Mohinder, *The Depressed Classes* (Bombay: Hind Kitabs, 1947).

Stark, Herbert Alick, *Hostages to India, or the Life-Story of the Anglo-Indian Race* (Calcutta: Star Printing Works, 1936).

Wiser, Charlotte V. and Wm. H., *Behind Mud Walls* (New York: Richard R. Smith, 1930).

ECONOMICS, INDUSTRY, AND OCCUPATION

BOOKS AND PAMPHLETS

Anstey, Vera, *The Economic Development of India* (London: Longmans, 1929).

Balakrishna, R., *Industrial Development of Mysore* (Bangalore City: Bangalore Press, 1940).

Banerjea, Pramathanath, *A Study of Indian Economics* (5th ed.; London: Macmillan, 1940).

Buchanan, Daniel H., *The Development of Capitalistic Enterprise in India* (New York: Macmillan, 1934).

Committee for India and Pakistan, *American Economic Relations with India and Pakistan* (New York: National Foreign Trade Council, 1948, mimeographed).

Das, Nabagopal, *Unemployment, Full Employment and India* (Bombay: Hind Kitabs, 1946).

Divatia, M. V., and H. M. Trivedi, *Industrial Capital in India (1938–39)* (Bombay: Tripathi, 1947).

Dutt, Romesh, *The Economic History of India in the Victorian Age* (2nd ed.; London: Paul, Trench, Trübner, 1906).

Gadgil, D. R., *Poona: A Socio-Economic Survey*, Part 1, *Economic*, Gokhale Institute of Politics and Economics, Publication No. 12 (Poona: Gokhale Institute of Politics and Economics, 1945).

Ghate, B. G., *Changes in the Occupational Distribution of the Population*, Studies in Indian Economics Issued by the Office of the Economic Adviser to the Government of India, Second Series, Aspects of Indian Social Economics, No. 1 (New Delhi: Government of India Press, 1940).

Ghose, Bimal C., *Planning for India* (Calcutta: Oxford University Press, 1945).

Ghosh, D., *Pressure of Population and Economic Efficiency in India* (New Delhi: Indian Council of World Affairs, 1946).

International Labour Office, *Wartime Labour Conditions and Reconstruction Planning in India* (Montreal, 1946).

Jathar, G. B., and S. G. Beri, *Indian Economics* (5th ed.; London: Oxford University Press, 1937).

Lokanathan, P. S., *Industrialization*, Oxford Pamphlets on Indian Affairs, No. 10 (3rd ed.; Bombay: Oxford University Press, 1946).

Matthai, John, *Tariffs and Industry*, Oxford Pamphlets on Indian Affairs, No. 20 (London: Oxford University Press, 1944).

Mukerjee, Radhakamal, and H. L. Dey (eds.), *Economic Problems of Modern India*, 2 vols. (London: Macmillan, 1941).

Nath, Pran, *A Study in the Economic Condition of Ancient India* (London: Royal Asiatic Society, 1929).

Papers on Indian States Development (London: East and West, no date).

Pillai, P. Padmanabha, *Economic Conditions in India* (New York: Dutton, 1925; London: Routledge, 1925).

Preparatory Asiatic Regional Conference, *The Economic Background of Social Policy Including Problems of Industrialisation* (New Delhi: International Labour Office, 1947).

Rao, B. Shiva, *The Industrial Worker in India* (London: Allen & Unwin, 1939).

Read, Margaret, *The Indian Peasant Uprooted* (London: Longmans, 1931).

Shah, K. T., and K. J. Khambata, *Wealth and Taxable Capacity of India* (London: P. S. King, 1924; Bombay: D. B. Taraporevala Sons, 1924).

Sharma, Tulsi Ram, *Location of Industries in India* (Bombay: Hind Kitabs, 1946).

Thakurdas, Sir Purshotamdas, and others, *A Plan of Economic Development for India* (London: Hunt, Barnard, 1944).

Tiwari, Ramswarup D., *Railways in Modern India* (Bombay: New Book, 1941).

Vakil, C. N., and S. K. Muranjan, *Currency and Prices in India* (Bombay: Vaibhav Press, 1927).

Venkatasubbiah, A., *The Structural Basis of Indian Economy* (London: Allen & Unwin, 1920).

Wadia, P. A., and K. T. Merchant, *Our Economic Problem* (Bombay: New Book, 1946).

EDUCATIONAL COMPOSITION

BOOKS AND PAMPHLETS

Ali Khan, Nowabzada Liaquat, *Muslim Educational Problems*, Pakistan Literature Series No. 7 (Lahore: 1945).

Bureau of Education, *Education in India* (Delhi: Manager of Publications). Annual Report.

Chatterji, Suniti K., *Languages and the Linguistic Problem*, Oxford Pamphlets on Indian Affairs, No. 11 (London and Bombay: Oxford University Press, 1943).

Hartog, Sir Philip, *Some Aspects of Indian Education Past and Present*, University of London Institute of Education, Studies and Reports, No. 7 (London: Oxford University Press, 1939).

Johnston, Rev. James, *Abstract and Analysis of the Report of the Indian Education Commission 1882–83* (London: Hamilton, Adams, 1884).

Johnston, Rev. James, *Our Educational Policy in India* (Edinburgh: John Maclaren, 1880).

Laubach, Frank C., *Toward a Literate World* (New York: World Literacy Committee of the Foreign Missions Conference of North America, 1938).

Noronha, George E., *Backgrounds in the Education of Indian Girls* (Washington, D.C.: Catholic University, 1939).

Olcott, Mason, *Better Village Schools* (3rd ed.; Calcutta: Y.M.C.A. Publishing House, 1937).

Parulekar, R. V., *Literacy in India* (London: Macmillan, 1939).

Wardha Conference, Committee, *Education Reconstruction* (Bombay: Vora, 1938). Articles by Gandhi and reports of the conference.

ARTICLES

Muzundar, Haridas T., "Contemporary Educational Policies in India," *The Social Frontier*, Vol. 5 (December, 1938), pp. 77–81.

FAMILY COMPOSITION AND MARITAL STATUS

BOOKS AND PAMPHLETS

Altekar, A. S., *The Position of Women in Hindu Civilisation* (Benares: Benares Hindu University Press, 1938).

Hauswirth, Frieda (Mrs. Sarangadhar Das), *Purdah: The Status of Indian Women* (New York: Vanguard, 1932).

Jones, V. R., and L. Bevan, *Woman in Islam* (Lucknow: Lucknow Publishing House, 1941).

Menon, Lakshmi N., *The Position of Women,* Oxford Pamphlets on Indian Affairs, No. 2 (Bombay and London: Oxford University Press, 1944).

Thomas, P., *Women and Marriage in India* (London: Allen & Unwin, 1939).

Thompson, Edward, *Suttee* (London: Allen & Unwin, 1928).

FERTILITY

BOOKS AND PAMPHLETS

Jain, S. P., *Relationship between Fertility and Economic and Social Status in the Punjab* (Lahore: Punjab Board of Economic Inquiry, Publication No. 64, 1939).

Sovani, N. V. et al., *The Social Survey of Kolhapur City: Part I—Population and Fertility* (Gokhale Institute of Politics and Economics, Publication No. 18, 1948).

ARTICLES

Das, Rajani Kanta, "Differential Fertility in India," *Congrès International de la Population, 1937,* Vol. 3 (Paris: Hermann, 1938), pp. 100–14.

Drysdale, C. V., "Birth Control in India: Mrs. How-Martyn on Her Tour," *Marriage Hygiene,* Vol. 3 (February, 1937), pp. 241–42.

Drysdale, C. V., "Mrs. Margaret Sanger in India," *Marriage Hygiene,* First Series, Vol. 2 (May, 1936), pp. 461–64.

Drysdale, C. V., "The Indian Population Problem," *Marriage Hygiene,* Second Series, Vol. 1 (November, 1947), pp. 98–100.

Ghosh, D., and Rama Varma, "A Study in Indian Fertility," *The Eugenics Review,* Vol. 31 (July, 1939), pp. 115–19.

Mathew, N. T., "Factors Influencing the Relative Proportion at Birth of the Two Sexes," *Sankhyā, The Indian Journal of Statistics,* Vol. 8 (October, 1947), pp. 277–81.

Pillay, A. P., "A Birth Control Educative Tour," *Marriage Hygiene,* Vol. 4 (August, 1937), pp. 48–50.

Rao, G. Raghava, "Fertility of the Andhra Females: A Study," *Marriage Hygiene,* Vol. 4 (August, 1937), pp. 34–35.

Sarker, S. S., "The Frequency of Multiple Births in India," *Transactions of the Bose Research Institute,* Vol. 16, Nos. 1–9 (1944–1946).

Young, Ruth, "Some Aspects of Birth Control in India," *Marriage Hygiene,* Vol. 2 (August, 1935), pp. 37–42.

FOOD AND NUTRITION

BOOKS AND PAMPHLETS

Aykroyd, Wallace R., *The Nutritive Value of Indian Foods and the Planning of Satisfactory Diets* (Simla: Government of India Press, 1939).

Brown, Michael, *India Need Not Starve* (London: Longmans, 1944).

Gangulee, N., *Health and Nutrition in India* (London: Faber, 1939).

McCarrison, Robert, *Problem of Nutrition in India* (National Abstracts and Reviews, Aberdeen, Vol. 2, 1932).

Mukerjee, Radhakamal, *Food Planning for 400 Millions* (London: Macmillan, 1938).

Mukerjee, Radhakamal, *Races, Lands, and Food* (New York: Dryden Press, 1946).

Singh, Baljit, *Population and Food Planning in India* (Bombay: Hind Kitabs, 1947).

ARTICLES

Aykroyd, W. R., "Malnutrition and the Rice Problem" in *Proceedings of the Fourth International Congresses on Tropical Medicine and Malaria,* Vol. 2.

Aykroyd, W. R., and B. G. Krishnan, "Diet Surveys in South Indian Villages," *Indian Journal of Medical Research,* Vol. 24 (January, 1937), pp. 667–725.

Bhattacharyya, S., "World War II and the Consumption Pattern of the Calcutta Middle Class," *Sankhyā, The Indian Journal of Statistics,* Vol. 8 (March, 1947), pp. 197–200.

Grajdanzev, Andrew J., "Food Crisis in India," *Far Eastern Survey,* Vol. 13 (January 12, 1944), pp. 2–7.

Hill, A. V., "Health, Food and Population in India—The Emergency of the Next 25 Years," *International Affairs,* Vol. 21 (January, 1945), pp. 40–52.

Hodgson, R. E., "General Problems of Human Nutrition in the Tropics in Relation to Animal Husbandry" in *Proceedings of the Fourth International Congresses on Tropical Medicine and Malaria,* Vol. 2.

Radhakrishna Rao, M. V., "Some Common Deficiency Diseases in India" in *Proceedings of the Fourth International Congresses on Tropical Medicine and Malaria,* Vol. 2.

Verma, O. P., C. K. Dilwali, and A. M. Thomson, "A Feeding Experiment on Indian Army Pioneer Recruits, with Special Reference to the Relative Value of Meat and Milk in Rations," *Indian Journal of Medical Research,* Vol. 35 (April, 1947).

GEOGRAPHY: ECONOMIC AND POLITICAL

BOOKS AND PAMPHLETS

Bartholomew, John (ed.), *Thacker's Reduced Survey Map of India* (6th ed.; Calcutta: Thacker, Spink, 1925).

Buckingham, M., *Tableau pittoresque de l'Inde* (2nd ed.; Paris: Chez Poulton-de-l'Épée, 1835).

De Montmorency, Sir Geoffrey, *The Indian States and Indian Federation* (Cambridge: Cambridge University Press, 1942).

Hörhager, Herbert, *Die Volkstumsgrundlagen der Indischen Nordwestgrenzprovinz,* Indien-Arbeiten, Hrsg. von Ludwig Alsdorf, Band 1 (Heidelberg: K. Vowinckel, 1943).

Joppen, Charles, *Historical Atlas of India* (London: Longmans, 1934).

Lyde, Lionel W., *The Continent of Asia* (London: Macmillan, 1938).

Morrison, Cameron, *A New Geography of The Indian Empire and Ceylon* (London: Nelson, 1926).

Pal, Dharm, *The North-West Frontier,* 1843–1947 (Bombay: National Information & Publications, 1947).

Stamp, Dudley L., *Asia* (2nd ed.; New York: Dutton, 1938).

MIGRATION: INTERNAL AND INTERNATIONAL

BOOKS AND PAMPHLETS

Akhtar, Sardar M., *Emigrant Labour for Assam Tea Gardens* (Lahore: Author, 1939).

Baxter, James, *Report on Indian Immigration* (Rangoon: Superintendent, Govt. Printing and Stationery, 1941).

Chandrasekhar, Sripati, *Indian Emigration to America* (New Delhi: Indian Council of World Affairs; London: Oxford University Press, 1945).

Committee on Emigration from India to the Crown Colonies

and Protectorates, *Minutes of Evidence,* Sessional Papers, Cmd. 5193 (London: His Majesty's Stationery Office, 1910).

Committee on Emigration from India to the Crown Colonies and Protectorates, *Report,* Sessional Papers, Cmd. 5192 (London: His Majesty's Stationery Office, 1910).

Dennery, Étienne, *Foules D'Asie* (Paris: Armand Colin, 1930).

Dev, Dharam Yash, *Our Countrymen Abroad* (Allahabad: J. B. Kripalani, All Indian Congress Committee, 1940).

Ferenczi, Imre, *International Migrations,* Vol. 1, *Statistics* (New York: National Bureau of Economic Research, 1929).

Gandhi, M. K., *Satyagraha in South Africa* (Triplicane, Madras: S. Ganesan, 1928).

International Labour Office, Studies and Reports Series O, Number 3, *Migration Laws and Treaties,* Vol. 1, *Emigration Laws and Regulations* (Geneva: International Labour Office [League of Nations], 1928).

Majumdar, Ramesh C., *Hindu Colonies in the Far East* (Calcutta: General Printers & Publishers, 1944).

Mukerjee, Radhakamal, *Migrant Asia* (Rome: Tipografia I Failli, 1936).

Olivier, [Lord], *The Anatomy of African Misery* (London: Wolf, 1927).

Rafi, Mirza M., *The Problem of Indian Settlers in Burma* (New Delhi: Indian Institute of International Affairs, 1946).

Sundaram, Lanka, *India in World Politics* (Delhi: Sultan Chand, 1944).

Sundaram, Lanka, *International Aspects of Indian Emigration* (London: East and West, 1930).

Willcox, Walter F. (ed.), *International Migrations,* Vol. 2, *Interpretations* (New York: National Bureau of Economic Research, 1931).

ARTICLES

Andrews, C. F., "India's Emigration Problem," *Foreign Affairs,* Vol. 8 (April, 1930), pp. 430–41.

Beatty, Willard W., "The Goal of Indian Assimilation," *Canadian Journal of Economics and Political Science,* Vol. 12 (August, 1946), pp. 395–404.

Chandrasekhar, S., "Les transferts de populations entre l'Hindoustan et le Pakistan," *Population,* Vol. 3 (October-December, 1948), pp. 683–90.

Choudree, Ashwin, "The Indian Problem in South Africa," *Asiatic Review,* Vol. 42 (July, 1946), pp. 201–11.

Hasan, K. Sarwar, "Indian Interests in the Pacific," *Journal of the Indian Institute of International Affairs,* Vol. 2 (October, 1946), pp. 9–21.

Kondapi, C., "Indians Overseas: A Survey of Developments in 1947," *India Quarterly,* Vol. 4 (March, 1948), pp. 60–77. (Surveys and articles on Indians overseas are a regular feature of the *Quarterly.*)

International Labour Office, "Rehabilitation of Displaced Persons in India," *International Labour Review,* Vol. 58 (August, 1948), pp. 187–98.

Kondapi, C., "Indians Overseas: The Position in Trinidad," *India Quarterly,* Vol. 4 (July-September, 1948), pp. 265–73.

Kondapi, C., "Indians Overseas: Their Position in Mauritius," *India Quarterly,* Vol. 3 (July-September, 1947), pp. 287–95.

Rao, M. V. S., "A Statistical Study of Labour in the Assam Tea Plantation," *Sankhyā, The Indian Journal of Statistics,* Vol. 7 (July, 1946), pp. 445–48.

Rao, P. Kodanda, "Indians Overseas: The Position in Malaya," *India Quarterly,* Vol. 2 (1946), pp. 150–62.

Srivastava, K. N., "The Problem of Refugees," *Indian Geographical Journal,* Vol. 23 (January-March, 1948), pp. 22–29.

Sundaram, Lanka, "The International Aspects of Indian Emigration," *The Asiatic Review,* Vol. 26 (October, 1930), pp. 741–48; Vol. 27 (January, 1931), pp. 113–21; (April, 1931), pp. 287–96; (July, 1931), pp. 588–98.

MORTALITY: CAUSES OF DEATH AND PUBLIC HEALTH

BOOKS AND PAMPHLETS

Blair, Charles, *Indian Famines* (Edinburgh: Blackwood, 1874).

Bradfield, Ernest W., *An Indian Medical Review, 1938* (Delhi: Manager of Publications, Government of India Press, 1938).

Calcutta School of Tropical Medicine and Hygiene, *Annual Report.*

Famine Inquiry Commission, *Final Report* (Madras: Government Press, 1945).

Famine Inquiry Commission, *Report on Bengal* (Madras: Government Press, 1943).

Hardy, G. F., *Memorandum on the Age Tables and Rates of Mortality of the Indian Census of 1901* (Calcutta: Superintendent of Government Printing, 1905).

Health Commissioner for Government of India, *Annual Report* (Issued under Public Health Commissioner, Sanitary Commissioner, or Commissioner of Health).

Health Survey and Development Committee, *Report* (Delhi: Manager of Publications, 1946), 4 Vols.

League of Nations, *Epidemiological Report of the Health Section of the Secretariat,* No. 177 (January-March, 1935), pp. 1–40.

Macdonald, George, *Report on the Control of Malaria in Industrial Labour Forces in India* (Calcutta: Ross Institute of Tropical Hygiene, India Branch, 1947).

Malaria Institute of India, *Records of the Malaria Surveys of India,* Vols. 1–7, October, 1929–December, 1937, published for Indian Research Fund Association (Calcutta: Thacker, Spink, 1929–37).

Pandit, S., *Summary of the Findings of Investigation into the Causes of Maternal Mortality in India,* Indian Research Fund Association Special Report, No. 17 (Kanpur: Job Press, 1948).

Ross Institute of Tropical Hygiene, India Branch, *Report of the Committee of Control,* 1946 (Calcutta: Royal Exchange).

Sanitary Commissioner with the Government of India, *Annual Report* (Calcutta: Superintendent, Government Printing, India). Serial publication.

Simmons, James S., et al., *Global Epidemiology, A Geography of Disease and Sanitation,* Vol. 1, Part 1, "India and the Far East" (Philadelphia: Lippincott, 1944).

ARTICLES

Angell, Sir Norman, "The Indian Famine," *Far Eastern Survey,* Vol. 13 (January 12, 1944), pp. 7–10.

De, J. C., "Social Security and National Health Service for

India," *Calcutta Medical Journal,* Vol. 42 (1945), pp. 271–74.

French, J. C., "Man-Made Famine," *The National Review,* Vol. 121 (December, 1943), pp. 428–31.

Gill, C. A., "Epidemics," *Encyclopaedia of the Social Sciences,* Vol. 5 (New York: Macmillan, 1931), pp. 569–72.

Greig, Major E. D. W., "Epidemic Dropsy in Calcutta," *Scientific Memoirs* by Officers of the Medical and Sanitary Departments of the Government of India, New Series, No. 49 (Calcutta: Superintendent Government Printing, 1912).

Hocking, Wm. Ernest, "Famine over Bengal," *Asia and the Americas,* Vol. 44 (February, 1944), pp. 74–5.

Lal, R. B., "Statistical Inquiry into the Epidemiology of Cholera in Bengal," *Indian Journal of Medical Research,* Vol. 29, pp. 425ff, 441ff.

Mahalanobis, P. C., et al., "A Sample Survey of After-Effects of the Bengal Famine of 1943," *Sankhyā, The Indian Journal of Statistics,* Vol. 7 (July, 1946), pp. 337–400.

Mahalanobis, P. C., "The Bengal Famine: The Background and the Basic Facts," *Asiatic Review,* Vol. 42 (October, 1946), pp. 310–18.

McCarrison, Lieut. Colonel R., "Beri-beri Columbarum," *Indian Medical Research Memoirs,* No. 10 (Calcutta: Indian Research Fund Association, March, 1928).

Megaw, John, "The Health of India," *Indian Journal of Pediatrics,* Vol. 13 (July, 1946), pp. 100–10.

Mhaskar, K. S., "Report of the Ankylostomiasis Inquiry in Madras," *Indian Medical Research Memoirs,* No. 1 (Calcutta: Indian Research Fund Association, October, 1924).

Morris, J. N., "Health of Four Hundred Millions," *The Lancet,* Vol. 248 (June 16, 1945), pp. 743–48.

Mukerjee, Karunamoy, "The Famine of 1943 and the Nature of Land Transfer in a Village in Bengal," *Modern Review,* Vol. 81 (April, 1947), pp. 309–12.

Mukerjee, Ram K., "Effect of the Food Crisis of 1943 on the Rural Population of Noahali, Bengal," *Science and Culture,* Vol. 10 (November and December, 1944), pp. 185–91, 231–38.

Orkney, Jean M., "The influence of Feeding on Infant Mortality," *Indian Medical Gazette,* Vol. 81 (1946), pp. 150–54.

Rogers, Sir Leonard, "The Incidence and Spread of Cholera in India; Forecasting and Control of Epidemics," *Indian Medical Research Memoirs,* No. 9 (Calcutta: Indian Research Fund Association, March, 1928).

Shortt, H. E., "Reports of the Kala-Azar Commission, India, No. II, 1926–1930," *Indian Medical Research Memoirs,* Supplementary Series No. 25 (Calcutta: Indian Research Fund Association, August, 1932).

"Tuberculosis in India," *The Lancet,* Vol. 236 (January 28, 1939), p. 219.

Ukil, A. C., "The Epidemiology and Pathology of Tuberculosis in India," *Indian Journal of Medical Research,* Vol. 17 (January, 1930), pp. 821–66.

Vaidyanathan, L. S., "Mortality of Indian Assured Lives," *Journal of the Institute of Actuaries,* Vol. 70 (1939), pp. 15–59.

Waters, H. S., "Neonatal Deaths and Stillbirths in Bombay," *Indian Medical Gazette,* Vol. 81 (August, 1946), pp. 301–05.

Yacob, M., and S. Swaroop, "Longevity and Old Age in the Punjab," *British Medical Journal,* Vol. 2 (September 29, 1945).

PAKISTAN AND PARTITION

BOOKS AND PAMPHLETS

Durrani, F. K. Khan, *The Meaning of Pakistan* (Lahore: Shaikh Muhammad Ashraf, 1944).

Hamza, El, *Pakistan: A Nation* (3rd ed.; Lahore: Shaikh Muhammad Ashraf, 1944).

Jones, George E., *Tumult in India* (New York: Dodd, Mead, 1948).

Pithawalla, Manekji B., *An Introduction to Pakistan: Its Resources and Potentialities* (Karachi: 1948).

Qureshi, Anwar Iqbal, *Economic Basis of Pakistan,* Pakistan Literature Series No. 12 (Lahore: Ashraf, 1947).

ARTICLES

Brown, W. Norman, "India's Pakistan Issue," *Proceedings of the American Philosophical Society,* Vol. 91 (April 5, 1947), pp. 162–80.

Spate, Oskar H. K., "The Boundary Award in the Punjab," *Asiatic Review,* Vol. 44 (January, 1948), pp. 1–15.

Spate, O. H. K., "The Partition of India and the Prospects of Pakistan," *Geographical Review,* Vol. 38 (January, 1948), pp. 5–30.

Waugh, Arthur, "India and Pakistan: The Economic Effects of Partition," *Asiatic Review,* Vol. 44 (April, 1948), pp. 121–27.

POPULATION ESTIMATES

ARTICLES

Krishnamurthy, T., and R. S. Krishnamurthy, "An Estimate of the Population of India for 1941," *Sankhyā, The Indian Journal of Statistics,* Vol. 5 (August, 1941), pp. 279–83.

Raja, K. C. K. E., "A Forecast of Population in India at the Census of 1941," *Indian Journal of Medical Research,* Vol. 24 (April, 1937), pp. 1183–91.

Raja, K. C. K. E., "Probable Trend of Population Growth in India," *Indian Journal of Medical Research,* Vol. 23 (July, 1935), p. 205.

Swaroop, Satya, and R. B. Lal, "Logistic Law of Growth and Structure of Indian Population," *Population,* Vol. 2 (August, 1938), pp. 100–21.

POPULATION, GENERAL AND MISCELLANEOUS

BOOKS AND PAMPHLETS

Chand, Gyan, *India's Teeming Millions* (London: Allen & Unwin, 1939).

Chand, Gyan, *The Problem of Population in India* (Bombay: Oxford University Pamphlets on India, 1944).

Chandrasekhar, S., *India's Population: Fact and Policy* (New York: John Day, 1946).

Department of Education, Health and Lands, *Report of the Population Data Committee* (Simla: Government of India Press, 1945).

Ghurye, G. S. (ed.), *Indian Population Problems* (Bombay: Report and Proceedings of the Second All-India Population and Family Hygiene Conference, 1939).

Karve, D. G., *Poverty and Population in India* (Bombay: Oxford University Press, 1936).

Narain, Brij, *The Curve of Population* (Lahore: Ripon Press, 1942).

Narain, Brij, *The Population of India* (Lahore: Rama Krishna and Sons, 1925).

National Planning Committee, *Population: Report of the Sub-Committee*, National Planning Committee Series, No. 6 (Bombay: Vora, 1947).

Penrose, E. F., *Population Theories and Their Application* (Stanford: Food Research Institute, 1934).

Ranadive, B. T., *The Population Problem in India* (Bombay: Longmans, 1936).

Sovani, N. V., *The Population Problem in India: A Regional Approach*, Gokhale Institute of Politics and Economics, Publication No. 8 (Poona: Gokhale Institute of Politics and Economics, 1942).

Thompson, Warren S., *Population and Peace in the Pacific* (Chicago: University of Chicago Press, 1946).

Wattal, P. K., *The Population Problem in India* (Bombay: Bennett, Coleman, 1934).

ARTICLES

Agarwala, Amar Nath, "Population of India and Its Future Trend," *Indian Journal of Economics*, Vol. 27 (April, 1947), pp. 389–400.

Chandrasekhar, S., "The Population Problems of India and Pakistan," *Eugenics Review*, Vol. 41 (July, 1949), pp. 70–80.

Davis, Kingsley, "Demographic Fact and Policy in India," *Milbank Memorial Fund Quarterly*, Vol. 22 (July, 1944), pp. 256–78.

Fischer, John, "India's Insoluble Hunger," *Harper's Magazine*, Vol. 190 (April, 1945), pp. 438–45.

Geddes, Arthur, "Half a Century of Population Trends in India: A Regional Study of Net Change and Variability, 1881–1931," *Geographical Journal*, Vol. 98 (November-December, 1941), pp. 228–53.

Geddes, Arthur, "The Social and Psychological Significance of Variability in Population Change; with Examples from India," *Human Relations*, Vol. 1 (1947), pp. 181–205.

Ghate, B. G., "A Study of the Population Movement in India," *Indian Journal of Economics*, Vol. 19, Part III (January, 1939), pp. 389–404.

Hoffman, Lawrence A., "India: Main Population Concentrations," *Geographical Journal*, Vol. III (January-March, 1948), pp. 89–100.

Meile, Pierre, "La Population de l'Inde," *Population*, Vol. 3 (January-March, 1948) pp. 127–46.

Notestein, Frank W., "Problems of Policy in Relation to Areas of Heavy Population Pressure." *Demographic Studies of Selected Areas of Rapid Growth* (New York: Milbank Memorial Fund, 1944), pp. 138–58.

Russell, A. J. H., and K. C. K. E. Raja, "The Population Problem in India," *Indian Journal of Medical Research*, Vol. 23 (October, 1935), pp. 545–68.

Singh, R. L., "The Trend of the Growth of Population in the United Provinces," National Geographical Society of India, *Bulletin* No. 3 (1947), pp. 17–29.

RELIGIOUS COMPOSITION

BOOKS AND PAMPHLETS

Archer, J. C., *The Sikhs* (Princeton: Princeton University Press, 1946).

Farquhar, J. N., *Modern Religious Movements in India* (New York: Macmillan, 1915).

Griswold, H. De Witt, *Insights into Modern Hinduism* (New York: Holt, 1934).

Pithawalla, Manekji B., and Beheram S. H. J. Rustomji, *Population Trends of Parsi Settlements on the West Coast of India* (Karachi: 1945), reprinted from *Journal of the University of Bombay*, Vol. 13 (January, 1945).

Sen, Dhirendranath, *The Problem of Minorities* (Calcutta: University of Calcutta, 1940).

Smith, Wilfred Cantwell, *Modern Islam in India: A Social Analysis* (London: Gollancz, 1946).

ARTICLES

Datta, Jatindra Mohan, "Proportion of Muhammadans in India through Centuries," *Modern Review* (Calcutta), Vol. 83 (January, 1948), pp. 31–4.

Mahalanobis, P. C., "Distribution of Muslims in the Population of India, 1941," *Sankhyā, The Indian Journal of Statistics*, Vol. 7 (July, 1946), pp. 429–34.

Schacht, Joseph, "Islam," *Encyclopaedia of the Social Sciences*, Vol. 8 (New York: Macmillan, 1932), pp. 333–43.

Sekar, C. Chandra, "Some Aspects of Parsi Demography," *Human Biology*, Vol. 20 (May, 1948), pp. 47–89.

SOCIAL AND HISTORICAL DESCRIPTION

BOOKS AND PAMPHLETS

Blunt, Sir E. A. H. (ed.), *Social Service in India* (London: His Majesty's Stationery Office, 1938).

Brailsford, Henry Noel, *Subject India* (New York: John Day, 1943).

Brayne, F. L., *Socrates in an Indian Village* (London: Oxford University Press, 1929).

Coupland, R., *The Indian Problem* (New York: Oxford University Press, 1944).

Cumming, Sir John (ed.), *Modern India* (London: Oxford University Press, 1931).

Cumming, Sir John (ed.), *Political India 1832–1932* (London: Humphrey Milford, 1932).

Dubois, Abbé, *Hindu Manners, Customs and Ceremonies*, trans. and ed. by Henry K. Beauchamp (3rd ed.; Oxford: Clarendon, 1924).

Emerson, Gertrude, *Voiceless India* (New York: Doubleday, Doran, 1930).

Holderness, Sir T. W., *Peoples and Problems of India* (New York: Holt, 1912).

Indian Statutory Commission, 3 vols. *Recommendations*, Sessional Papers, Cmd. 3568, 3569, 3572 (London: His Majesty's Stationery Office, 1930).

Mitchell, Kate L., *India without Fable* (New York: Knopf, 1942).

Mitra, S. M., *Anglo-Indian Studies* (New York, Bombay, and Calcutta: Longmans, 1913).

Moreland, W. H., *India at the Death of Akbar* (London: Macmillan, 1920).

Moreland, W. H., and Atul Chandra Chatterjee, *A Short History of India* (London: Longmans, 1936).

Moreland, W. H., and P. Geyl (Translators), *Jahangir's India: The "Remonstrantie" of Francisco Pelsaert* (Cambridge: Heffer & Sons, 1925).

Nanavati, Sir Manilal B., and C. N. Vakil (eds.), *India Speak-*

ing, Annals of the American Academy of Political and Social Science, Vol. 233 (May, 1944).

O'Malley, L. S. S. (ed.), *Modern India and the West* (London: Oxford University Press, 1941).

Parkin, Raleigh, *India Today* (Vancouver: Longmans, 1946).

Raman, T. A., *Report on India* (New York: Oxford University Press, 1943).

Schuster, Sir George, and Guy Wint, *India and Democracy* (London: Macmillan, 1941).

ARTICLES

Mukherjee, Ramkrishna, "The Economic Structure and Social Life in Six Villages of Bengal," *American Sociological Review*, Vol. 14 (June, 1949), pp. 415–25.

STATISTICAL SOURCES

BOOKS AND PAMPHLETS

Agricultural Adviser to the Government of India, *Review of Agricultural Operations in India* (Calcutta: Superintendent Government Printing, India). Serial publication.

Bombay, Director of Public Health, *Annual Report, 1947* (Bombay: Government Central Press, 1947).

Census of India. (The censuses of India are described in the text. Generally the central office, originally in Calcutta but more recently in Delhi, has published a summary volume in two parts, one being analysis and the other tables. Each province and major state has published its own volume, also in two parts.)

Census of India, *1941 Census Figures in Present Lay-out; Estimates for 1948,* Paper No. 2 (1949).

Commercial Intelligence Dept., *Review of the Trade of India* (London: His Majesty's Stationery Office). Serial publication.

Das, Dial, *Vital Statistics of the Punjab, 1901–1940* (Lahore: The Board of Economic Inquiry, 1943).

Department of Commercial Intelligence and Statistics, *Agricultural Statistics of India 1938–39,* Vol. 2 (Calcutta: Government of India Press, 1946).

Department of Commercial Intelligence and Statistics, *Statistical Abstract for British India* (London: His Majesty's Stationery Office). Serial publication.

Edge, P. Granville, *Vital Statistics and Public Health Work in the Tropics* (London: Baillière, Tindall & Cox, 1944).

General Report on the Census of India, 1891, Sessional Papers, Cmd. 7181 (London: Her Majesty's Stationery Office, 1893).

General Report of the Census of India, 1901, Sessional Papers, Cmd. 2047 (London: His Majesty's Stationery Office, 1904).

General Report of the Census of India, 1911, Sessional Papers, Cmd. 7377 (London: His Majesty's Stationery Office, 1914).

Great Britain Parliamentary Papers, *Statistical Tables Relating to the Colonial and Other Possessions of the United Kingdom,* Part 13, 1867 (London: Her Majesty's Stationery Office, 1869).

Hodson, T. C., *India. Census Ethnography, 1901–1931* (Delhi: Manager of Publication, Government of India Press, 1937).

Hunter, Sir W. W. (ed.), *The Imperial Gazetteer of India,* Vol. 1, *Abar-Benares* (London: Trübner, 1881).

Jammu and Kashmir, *A Hand Book of the Jammu and Kashmir State* (Jammu: Ranbir Government Press, 1944).

Lacey, W. G., *Some Aspects of the Census Operation of 1931 in Bihar and Orissa* (Patna: Patna University Press, 1933).

M'Culloch, J. R. M., *A Dictionary, Practical, Theoretical, and Historical, of Commerce and Commercial Navigation,* Vol. 1 (2nd ed.; London: Longman, Rees, Orme, Brown, Green, and Longman, 1835). American ed., 1845.

Memorandum on the Census of British India of 1871–72, Sessional Papers, Cmd. 1349 (London: Her Majesty's Stationery Office, 1875).

Ministry of Commerce, Government of India, *Monthly Abstract of Statistics,* Vol. 1, No. 1 (October, 1948).

Mysore, *The List of Villages in the Mysore State* (Bangalore: 1943).

Office of the Economic Adviser, *Statistical Summary of the Social and Economic Trends in India* (Delhi: Government of India Press, 1945).

Playfair, Wm., *The Statistical Breviary* (London: J. Wallis et al., 1801).

Statistical Abstract for the Several Colonial and Other Possessions of the United Kingdom, 1854–1868, Sessional Papers, Cmd. 146 (London: Her Majesty's Stationery Office, 1870).

Subramaniam, S., *Statistical Summary of the Social and Economic Trends in India, 1918–39* (Washington, D.C.: Government of India Information Services, 1945).

Subramaniam, S., *Guide to Current Official Statistics,* Office of the Economic Adviser (3rd ed.; Delhi: Manager of Publications, 1945).

The Indian Yearbook (various publishers for different years).

Webb, A. W. T., *These Ten Years: A Short Account of the 1941 Census Operations in Rajputana and Ajmer-Merwara* (Bombay: British India Press, 1942).

West Bengal, Provincial Statistical Bureau, *Statistical Abstract, West Bengal, 1947* (Calcutta: 1948).

ARTICLES

Chandra Sekar, C., and W. Edwards Deming, "On a Method of Estimating Birth and Death Rates and the Extent of Registration," *Journal of the American Statistical Association,* Vol. 44 (March, 1949), pp. 101–15.

Shirras, G. F., "The Census of India," *Geographical Review,* Vol. 25 (January, 1935), pp. 434–48.

Author Index

Subject Index